The Source and Significance of COINCIDENCES

The Source and Significance of COINCIDENCES

a hard look at the astonishing evidence

SHARON HEWITT RAWLETTE, PhD

2019

ISBN: 978-1-7339957-0-2

Portions of Chapter 1 were previously published in Sharon Hewitt Rawlette, "Coincidence or Psi? The Epistemic Import of Spontaneous Cases of Purported Psi Identified Post-Verification," *Journal of Scientific Exploration* 33, no. 1 (March 2019): 9-42.

The author gratefully acknowledges permission to reprint from the following works.
Material excerpted from ***The After Death Chronicles*** © 2017 by Annie Mattingley, used with permission from Hampton Roads Publishing c/o Red Wheel Weiser, LLC Newburyport, MA www.redwheelweiser.com./Material excerpted from ***Afterlife Encounters*** © 2005 by Dianne Arcangel, used with permission from Hampton Roads Publishing c/o Red Wheel Weiser, LLC Newburyport, MA www.redwheelweiser.com./*Angel Letters* by Sophy Burnham. Published by Ballantine Books, 1991. Used by permission./*The Buddha in Hell and Other Alarms: Distressing Near-Death Experiences in Perspective* by Nancy Evans Bush. Published in 2016. Used by permission of the author./ "Children with Life-between-Life Memories" by Ohkado Masayuki and Ikegawa Akira. Published in *Journal of Scientific Exploration* 28, No. 3 (2014): 477-90. Used by permission of the authors./From *Cosmic Cradle: Spiritual Dimensions of Life before Birth* by Elizabeth M. Carman and Neil J. Carman, published by North Atlantic Books, copyright © 2013 by Elizabeth M. Carman and Neil J. Carman. Reprinted by permission of North Atlantic Books./*Dreamer: 20 Years of Psychic Dreams and How They Changed My Life* by Andrew Paquette. Published in 2011 by O-Books, an imprint of John Hunt Publishing Ltd. www.johnhuntpublishing.com/6th-books/. Used by permission of the author and publisher./Excerpts [pp. 33, 36, 43, 64, 86, 88-9, 97-8, 101, 127, 146, 158-9, 163, 171, 175, 178-9, 181-2] from GOD AND THE AFTERLIFE by JEFFREY LONG, M.D. with PAUL PERRY, Copyright © 2016 by Jeffrey Long. Reprinted by permission of HarperCollins Publishers./All quotations from the Hebrew and Christian scriptures are taken from the HOLY BIBLE, NEW INTERNATIONAL VERSION®. Copyright ©1973, 1978, 1984 by International Bible Society. Used by permission of Zondervan Publishing House. All rights reserved./Material excerpted from ***Into the Light*** © 2007 by John Lerma, used with permission from Red Wheel Weiser, LLC Newburyport, MA www.redwheelweiser.com./Material excerpted from ***Lucid Dreaming: Gateway to the Inner Self*** © 2009 by Robert Waggoner, used with permission from Red Wheel Weiser, LLC Newburyport, MA www.redwheelweiser.com./Material excerpted from ***Meant to Be*** © 2000 by Joyce & Barry Vissell, used with permission from Red Wheel Weiser, LLC Newburyport, MA www.redwheelweiser.com./"The Rarity of Unambiguous Symbols in Dreams: A Case Study" by Andrew Paquette. Published in *Journal of Scientific Exploration* 30, no. 2 (2016): 199-216. Used by permission of the author./Excerpts [pp. 119-25, 130, 136, 142-3, 148, 155-7, 161-75, 194, 206-7: 690 words] from RETURN FROM HEAVEN by CAROL BOWMAN. Copyright © 2001 by Carol Bowman and Steve Bowman. Reprinted by permission of HarperCollins Publishers./*Stories of the Unborn Soul: The Mystery and Delight of Pre-Birth Communication* by Elisabeth Hallett. Published in 2002. Used by permission of the author./Excerpts from SURVIVING DEATH: A JOURNALIST INVESTIGATES EVIDENCE FOR AN AFTERLIFE by Leslie Kean, copyright © 2017 by Leslie Kean. Used by permission of Crown Archetype, an imprint of Random House, a division of Penguin Random House LLC. All rights reserved./Material excerpted from ***Synchronicity: The Art of Coincidence, Choice, and Unlocking Your Mind*** © 2012 by Kirby Surprise, used with permission from Red Wheel Weiser, LLC Newburyport, MA www.redwheelweiser.com./Review of *Telephone Calls from The Dead: A Revised Look at the Phenomenon Thirty Years On*, by Callum E. Cooper. Written by Erlendur Haraldsson. Published in *Journal of Scientific Exploration* 27, no. 2 (2013): 352-3. Used by permission of the author./*Third Eye Open: Unmasking Your True Awareness* by Susan Reintjes. Published by Third Eye Publishing, 2003. Used by permission of the publisher.

Douter de tout ou tout croire, ce sont deux solutions également commodes, qui l'une et l'autre nous dispensent de réfléchir.[*]

– Henri Poincaré, *La Science et l'Hypothèse*

[*] Doubting everything and believing everything are two equally convenient solutions, both of which save us from having to reflect.

CONTENTS

PART ONE
SOURCES

PART TWO
SIGNIFICANCE

CONTENTS
with section headings

PART TWO
SIGNIFICANCE

Introduction

Most of us have experienced a few thought-provoking coincidences in our lives, occasions on which it seemed like the world around us was responding to our thoughts or concerns in a way it had no business doing, at least not according to the laws recognized by current science. Many coincidences are easy to explain away as the conjuring tricks of selective attention and a pattern-seeking brain. But, for some of us, there has eventually come an experience so inexplicable by the ruling scientific paradigm that we couldn't help but accept that there is much more to this world than science has yet been able to understand.

On a crisp fall day in 2015, I was enjoying a weekend getaway with some old college friends in the mountains of central Pennsylvania. During the several weeks leading up to this event, my mind had been preoccupied with another old friend of mine, someone I had fallen out of touch with years before. This friend lived in France—a country where I myself had once resided and to which I was still strongly attached—and both France and my French friend were at the forefront of my mind during that weekend in Pennsylvania.

On Saturday afternoon, one of my college friends and I drove around searching for a supermarket where we could buy provisions for our evening meal. When a casual drive down several nearby roads didn't turn up anything, my friend pulled out her smartphone and asked it to locate the nearest grocery store. Then, because she was behind the wheel, she handed her phone to me. When I took it from her, it was displaying a list of grocery stores in our immediate vicinity, close to Johnstown, Pennsylvania. Then I tapped "MAP," in order to figure out which of them would be most convenient to us. The map took several seconds to load, but when it finally appeared, the stores it displayed were all labeled "E. Leclerc"—the name of a French supermarket chain—and each one was associated with the name of a French town, one of which I vaguely remembered from my time in France: Carhaix.

The appearance of these French grocery stores on my friend's phone was so bizarre that I didn't know what to do in the moment except shake my head and tell my friend, "Your phone thinks we're in France." I'd never had a GPS suddenly locate me in a completely different place, and for this phone to settle on the very country—across the Atlantic Ocean—that had been for weeks so present in my thoughts was simply astonishing, all the more so because my friend assured me she had never used her phone to look up anything in France. In fact, this event was such an unexpected but precise reflection of my current thoughts that I felt there had to be even more to it than this. When I got home a few days later, I Googled the whereabouts of my French friend on the day of this incident and discovered that, on that very day, he had been attending an event less than two miles from the center of Carhaix.

How on earth did a cell phone come to show me, not grocery stores in my own location in Pennsylvania, but grocery stores at the location of the person who was uppermost in my mind? I know smartphone technology is improving by leaps and bounds, but as far as I'm aware, mind reading isn't yet a standard feature! And the story doesn't end there. This startling incident eventually led me to get back in touch with my friend and find out about a momentous change that had happened in his life between the time of the GPS incident and our contact. This event, in turn, changed the course of my own life in a very positive direction, healing an old wound and giving me immense peace and joy.

The ability of such strange "coincidences" to guide us to healthier, more emotionally complete lives has been written about for many years—most famously by Swiss psychiatrist Carl Jung, who in the mid-1900s coined the term 'synchronicity' to describe a psychologically meaningful coincidence.[1] One of my favorite more recent works on the topic is Dr. M. Scott Peck's 1978 bestseller *The Road Less Traveled*.[2] Like Jung, Peck is a psychiatrist, and though his main interest in that book is to develop an understanding of psychological health and growth, he can't avoid discussing the topic of coincidences, because they have been so much in evidence in his therapeutic practice, as ways in which the universe has lent his patients' therapy a helping hand.

---

[1] C. G. Jung, *Synchronicity: An Acausal Connecting Principle*, trans. R. F. C. Hull (Princeton, NJ: Princeton University Press, 1960, 2010).
[2] M. Scott Peck, *The Road Less Traveled: A New Psychology of Love, Traditional Values and Spiritual Growth* (New York: Simon & Schuster, 1978).

The public awareness of coincidences as aids to personal growth has grown to such an extent that today it is *de rigueur* for self-help authors to suggest that coincidences be taken as signs that you are on the right path, going with the flow of the universe toward your best life. For instance, life coach Martha Beck writes in *Finding Your Own North Star* that synchronicities are "one of the best tools for finding jobs, friends, romantic partners, ideas, and just a general reassurance that life is on your side."[3] Creativity coach Julia Cameron urges readers of *The Vein of Gold* to align themselves with "a flow of what might be called luck, coincidence, or good orderly direction." When we do this, she says, "[w]e tend to be in the right place at the right time, encountering not only support, but also opportunity."[4] Coincidences also form the primary subject matter of Dr. Deepak Chopra's *The Spontaneous Fulfillment of Desire: Harnessing the Infinite Power of Coincidence*,[5] along with many other works.

But it's not only the self-help literature that urges attention to coincidences. Anthropologist Dr. Michael Harner advises in his classic *The Way of the Shaman* to "watch for the frequency of positive synchronicities as a kind of homing beacon analogous to a radio directional signal to indicate that the right procedures and methods are being employed."[6] Psychiatrist Dr. Stanislav Grof writes in an autobiographical work, "The occurrence of such favorable synchronicities is so extraordinary and pervasive that [my wife] Christina and I learned to use it as a compass for our activities, as an important criterion that we were 'on the right track'."[7] And writer and literary agent William Gladstone notes, in his foreword to psychologist Dr. Gary E. Schwartz's *Super Synchronicity*, "The universe is always trying to tell us what to do, where to go, and how to behave. We just have to listen."[8]

If you've picked up this book, it's probably because you yourself have experienced a striking coincidence or two, perhaps one that guided you at a major turning point of your life (or maybe even guided you to this book!). You should know, first of all, that you are not alone. Research suggests that

---

[3] Martha Beck, *Finding Your Own North Star: Claiming the Life You Were Meant to Live* (New York: Three Rivers Press, 2001), 234.
[4] Julia Cameron, *The Vein of Gold: A Journey to Your Creative Heart* (New York: Tarcher/Putnam, 1996), 20.
[5] Deepak Chopra, *The Spontaneous Fulfillment of Desire: Harnessing the Infinite Power of Coincidence* (New York: Three Rivers Press, 2003).
[6] Michael Harner, *The Way of the Shaman: A Guide to Power and Healing* (New York: Bantam, 1980, 1982), 114.
[7] Stanislav Grof, *When the Impossible Happens: Adventures in Non-Ordinary Realities* (Boulder, CO: Sounds True, 2006), 66.
[8] William Gladstone, foreword to *Super Synchronicity: Where Science and Spirit Meet*, by Gary E. Schwartz (Vancouver, BC: Param Media, 2017), xix.

one-third of people notice coincidences "with some frequency."[9] A survey conducted in Germany in 2000 revealed that 36.5% of the survey sample had had "certain things happen suddenly in such an amazing way that it was impossible for them to believe in pure chance any longer."[10] And an American survey published in 1989 found that 27% of sampled undergraduate students had experienced specifically "life-changing" coincidences.[11]

However, if you've been paying attention to coincidences for very long, you've likely also encountered some baffling experiences. Perhaps it seemed like coincidences were confirming that you ought to do something, but when you did it, things went badly for you. Or perhaps you thought coincidences were telling you something that turned out not to be true. Or perhaps you simply experienced a series of events that were so out of the ordinary that you felt they *must* have meaning and yet you could never make heads or tails of them.

The truth is that the phenomenon of coincidences is much subtler and more complicated than many of the books written on the topic would lead one to believe. One of Grof's experiences makes an excellent example. Interestingly, he tells this story in the same book in which he makes the statement quoted above, about synchronicities guiding his life in a favorable direction.

Grof was single at the time of this experience, looking for someone with whom to spend his life, and some friends of his told him excitedly that they had met someone who would be a perfect match for him. Unfortunately, this woman—Joan—lived in Miami, and Grof lived in Baltimore. However, one day he was getting ready to go to Dallas for a conference and thought perhaps he could stop by Miami on the way and meet her. Having gotten her number from his friends, he gave her a call. She proceeded to tell him that, unfortunately, she wouldn't be in Miami then—she'd be away in Dallas, getting ready for a conference.

---

[9] Bernard D. Beitman, "Coincidence Studies," *Psychiatric Annals* 41, no. 12 (December 2011): 561. Beitman cites Stephanie Coleman, Bernard D. Beitman, and Elif Celebi, "Weird Coincidences Commonly Occur," *Psychiatric Annals* 39, no. 5 (2009): 265-70; George Costin, Kristina Dzara, and David Scott Resch, "Synchronicity: Coincidence Detection and Meaningful Life Events," 41, no. 12 (2011): 572-5; and Sheryl Attig, Gary E. Schwartz, Aurelio José Figueredo, W. Jake Jacobs, and K. C. Bryson, "Coincidences, Intuition, and Spirituality," *Psychiatric Annals* 41, no. 12 (2011).

[10] Ina Schmied-Knittel and Michael T. Schetsche, "Everyday Miracles: Results of a Representative Survey in Germany," *European Journal of Parapsychology* 20.1 (2005): 3-21, pp. 11-12.

[11] M. B. Meyer, "Role of personality and cognitive variables in the reporting of experienced meaningful coincidences or 'synchronicity,'" PhD diss. (Saybrook Institute, 1989).

It turned out that, not only were the two of them going to the same conference, but they had booked rooms in the same hotel, one directly above the other. When Grof arrived in Dallas, the conference was already in session, so he tried to guess which lecture Joan might be in. He slipped into a darkened room where a film was playing and took the first empty seat. As he watched the film, his attention was repeatedly drawn to a woman sitting in the row in front of him, a few seats to the left. "I actually started seeing something like a light aura around her head," he writes. "After a while, she started turning her head in my direction, which was very unusual because she had to do it at a fairly large angle for our eyes to meet. This went on for quite a while and, by the time the movie ended, both of us felt so much certainty, that we simply went over to each other and confirmed our suspicions by introducing ourselves."[12] Coincidences continued to follow this couple, and they were soon married, in a ceremony that was itself graced by some rather auspicious signs from the universe.

Sadly, their marriage didn't last long. They divorced shortly afterward. Grof writes at the end of his account,

> I learned not to trust unconditionally the seductive power of such experiences and the enchantment and ego inflation that they engender. The ecstatic feelings associated with the emergence of archetypal forces do not guarantee a positive outcome. It is essential to refrain from acting out while we are under their spell and not to make any important decisions until we have again both feet on the ground.[13]

The moral of this story and of others you'll meet in this book—especially in Chapter 19, "Interpreting Coincidences"—is that there are no easy answers when it comes to coincidences. Coincidences are not a way to avoid decision making in our lives. They aren't a way to avoid having to think about the nature of life and what is worth pursuing. They are a door into a new way of perceiving, yes. But we must be actively engaged in that perceiving and not follow coincidences blindly, disregarding everything else we know about the world.

Coincidences even have the potential to be dangerous if one is not equipped to handle them. At the Parapsychological Consultancy in Freiburg, Germany, clinical psychologist Dr. Walter von Lucadou sees patients who come to him because they're "drowning" in their coincidence experiences.[14] The world seems to be talking to them so frequently and forcefully that they

---

[12] Grof, *When the Impossible*, 18.

[13] Grof, *When the Impossible*, 26.

[14] See the Parapsychological Consultancy's website (in German) at https://www.parapsychologische-beratungsstelle.de/. For an English summary of its work, see Walter von Lucadou's profile on the Parapsychological Association website: https://www.parapsych.org/users/wlucadou/profile.aspx.

have trouble sorting out what's real and what's just their perception. American psychologist Dr. Kirby Surprise sees patients in similar predicaments. He gives the example of a man he calls "B," who said his problems began when he was meditating to music on the radio and started to notice that the DJ's choice of songs followed the pattern of his thoughts. He came to the conclusion that someone or something was reading his mind and trying to communicate with him through these coincidences. Soon, says Surprise, the messages started to turn "paranoid and grandiose."

> A personal mythology around government conspiracies and secret technologies developed, along with delusions of why he was chosen. The SEs [synchronistic events] expanded from radios to TVs, to other people. SEs eventually included anything he paid attention to. Stories of messages from gods and demons came and went. His work and friendships drifted away as he chased more cosmic promises. He was eventually hospitalized.[15]

We should note, though, that B did have a psychotic episode even before he encountered this overwhelming series of coincidences. So perhaps B was not quite accurate when he said his problems *began* with his music meditation.

In any event, this is an extreme case. Most people who experience coincidences are not in danger of being declared mentally ill. According to sociologist Dr. Andrew Greeley, not only do surveys show that two-thirds of American adults admit to having had some sort of psychic experience,[16] but "[p]eople who've tasted the paranormal, whether they accept it intellectually or not, are anything but religious nuts or psychiatric cases. They are, for the most part, ordinary Americans, somewhat above the norm in education and intelligence and somewhat less than average in religious involvement."[17] And, as we saw above, approximately one-third of people notice coincidences "with some frequency." So, experiencing multiple coincidences is fairly common and is not, all by itself, an indication that a person will soon find themselves in psychiatric care.

However, most people who've had strong coincidence experiences will probably identify with the *fear* of going crazy. There is something about the experience of a particularly striking coincidence that disturbs the most basic conceptual apparatus of the modern mind, and it's not uncommon to feel in the wake of such an experience that you've lost your points of reference. You're not alone if you feel like you may be going a wee bit off your rocker

---

[15] Kirby Surprise, *Synchronicity: The Art of Coincidence, Choice, and Unlocking Your Mind* (Pompton Plains, NJ: New Page Books, 2012), 68.
[16] Andrew Greeley, "Mysticism Goes Mainstream," *American Health* 6, no. 1 (January-February 1987): 47-49.
[17] Andrew Greeley, "The 'Impossible': It's Happening," *Noetic Sciences Review* no. 2 (Spring 1987): 8.

trying to figure out what the heck is going on. While most people are able to deal with these experiences without being hospitalized, it's important to recognize just how much of a challenge these experiences present to our usual, mechanistic way of viewing the world, and how mentally stressful this can be. Writer Robert Moss reminds us that "[t]he difference between the mystic and the madman...is that the mystic can swim in waters where the madman drowns."[18] If you feel that you would benefit from talking about your experiences with a professional, you shouldn't hesitate to do so. But even those who don't seek professional help should keep in mind that coincidences are not always unmitigated blessings, and dealing with them wisely and in a healthy manner requires a fair amount of patience and mental effort.

French-Canadian psychologist Joachim Soulières points out in his book *Les coïncidences* that people who have been overwhelmed by coincidence experiences are easy prey for cults, because these groups may be the only communities they can find that give them a way to understand their experiences.[19] Certainly, if society at large doesn't give someone the tools to deal with these experiences, that person can hardly be faulted for looking for a group of people and a belief system that do. All of us want to understand what's happening to us. All of us want to make sense of the world around us, and we'll use the means that are available.

Many people, of course, will find a way to understand their coincidence experiences within the religious traditions with which they already identify. If they are Jews, Muslims, or Christians, for example, they may attribute their coincidences to the intervention of God or angels. And being raised with some conception of the world that goes beyond the physical and the mechanistic may offer an advantage in processing the experience of coincidences. At the same time, others may avoid contemplating the possibility of anything supernatural because they fear that, if there is a higher consciousness behind coincidences, it must resemble a not-so-positive image of God they learned in Sunday school. Others may fear believing in such a higher consciousness because they fear being wrong and possibly being ridiculed—or, even worse, emotionally and spiritually devastated if they later realize they put their faith in a chimera. I have known all of these fears, and I hope that this book will reassure those who are currently experiencing them.

We all need to be aware that we have a natural tendency to put our coincidence experiences into the metaphysical box most familiar to us. For some of us, that will be the box of "random occurrences." For others, it will be a religious concept, such as divine providence. We all need to remember

---

[18] Robert Moss, *The Boy Who Died and Came Back: Adventures of a Dream Archaeologist in the Multiverse* (Novato, CA: New World Library, 2014), 71.
[19] Joachim Soulières, *Les coïncidences* (Paris: Dervy, 2012), 81-82.

that the mere fact that something seemingly supernatural has happened to us does not guarantee that the first explanation we find for it is the correct one. While some people's experiences do fit neatly within their existing belief systems, many other people's experiences don't fit into any traditional scientific or religious understanding of the world, and not only can this lead to confusion, disappointment, and/or frustration for those people, but it should make all of us more thoughtful about the way we determine what's behind our own coincidences. Is it possible there's more to the world than what any of us has previously imagined? The coincidence stories in this book should challenge all of us to widen our perspective and open our minds to new possibilities.

My hope is that this book will serve two complementary purposes. I hope that it will serve, first of all, as an encounter with mystery, rattling whatever firmly established ideas you have about the nature of reality and the nature of your own coincidence experiences. At the same time, I hope that this book will also act as a guide—or at the least as a congenial companion—as you seek to establish a new, wider worldview that encompasses the highly variable nature of these enigmatic occurrences.

This book is the fruit of my own prolonged efforts to wrestle with the mysterious nature of coincidences, and with the relationship of mind to the material world. It systematizes the knowledge I've worked hard to obtain over my eight years of carefully studying the subject, both firsthand and through reading accounts of the experiences of others. Since my focus is on interpreting events that happen in the course of daily life, this book is necessarily filled with what are sometimes disparagingly referred to as "anecdotes." But these are not anecdotes in the sense of funny stories told around the table at a dinner party, stories which may or may not be true. These are stories of actual, real-life experiences, some of them my very own.

I have tried in compiling accounts gleaned from other published sources to stick as much as possible to two types of sources: firsthand accounts and accounts narrated by researchers who personally investigated the truth of the details they report. However, I also include a smattering of secondhand reports, and so I would like to say a few words about their reliability. While many people assume that accounts of unusual phenomena will get more and more outlandish the more they are retold by people other than the eyewitnesses—and certainly this does happen in some cases—at least some people who have carefully investigated the retelling of unusual stories find that the inverse is often true. For instance, American parapsychologist Dr. Walter Franklin Prince wrote in 1931,

> The too general assumption is that a second-hand story, if it distorts any details, is bound to do so by their improvement, their exaggeration, in the direction of supernormality. But long experience in testing such matters shows that an authentic incident of this character is much more

> often than not improved after one has found the original percipient or a witness who was actually present. The second-hand narrator is very apt to have forgotten, or at least to have omitted, some of the chief evidential details.[20]

And, in 1956, Dr. Hornell Hart and his co-investigators carefully rated the evidentiality of both firsthand and secondhand accounts of the same events and found that, in all three cases they studied, the firsthand account merited a higher rating.[21]

This is one of the reasons that I have sought out firsthand accounts whenever possible—because they are generally more detailed and thus are more likely to contain specifically evidential details. Unfortunately, space and copyright considerations prevent me from quoting in this book many of the firsthand accounts I have in my library. I am instead forced to summarize most of them, simplifying them and thus leaving them open to skeptical explanations that the detailed original account of the case would have shown to be incorrect. To compensate for this, I have provided as much data on my sources as I can so that you are able to investigate further those cases that you find to be of particular interest and to read the accounts of the experiencers in their own words.

You will note as well that I generally take people's firsthand accounts of what they've experienced at face value. Are some of them inaccurate? Quite possibly. Some of them may include details distorted by faulty memory, and a few of them could turn out to be outright fabrications. But the arguments I make in this book don't depend on any one source. They depend on the sheer accumulation of story after story all pointing to the existence of some little-understood force that is shaping events in the material world. The aggregate credibility of the accounts reported here vastly exceeds that of the eye-witness testimony that would be required to establish a verdict in a court of law. I realize that we are dealing here with overturning firmly held scientific beliefs, not with establishing the identity of a criminal, but it is scientists themselves who have insisted that one of the most important features of a scientific theory is its falsifiability.[22] If this evidence isn't enough to demonstrate the inadequacy of the reigning scientific paradigm, then that paradigm is not being treated as a scientific theory but as plain, old-fashioned dogma.

---

[20] Walter Franklin Prince, *Human Experiences, Being a Report on the Results of a Questionnaire and a Discussion of Them* (Boston, MA: Boston Society for Psychical Research, 1931), 109-10.

[21] Hornell Hart, "Six Theories about Apparitions," *Proceedings of the Society for Psychical Research* 50, part 185 (May 1956): 153-239, pp. 169-70.

[22] For the most famous example, see Karl Popper, *The Logic of Scientific Discovery* (London: Hutchinson & Co., 1959).

You will discover that, at some points in this book, and particularly in the chapter on after-death communication, I quote statements made by mediums and other psychics. Please understand that I *do not take such statements as generally reliable*, the way I do firsthand accounts of coincidences. I certainly do not automatically trust a source because it appears to be paranormal. If anything, the purportedly paranormal source of a piece of information will make me more doubtful of its truth, such sources being notoriously variable in their accuracy. For this reason, nothing that I say in this book will depend on the credibility of messages obtained through mediumship or any other psychic method. However, while I am justifiably wary of statements made by mediums, I am willing to consider the truth of what certain mediums say, especially when it can illuminate the source or meaning of other phenomena. Instead of just taking the medium's word for it, however, we should consider what they say as a tool to open our minds to new possibilities and help us imagine other ways of looking at what's going on. We can then test these ideas against our own experience and the experiences of others to see whether they hold up. Discernment and critical thinking are absolutely crucial in approaching the topic of psychic experiences. To paraphrase French mathematician and physicist Henri Poincaré, doubting everything and believing everything are both lazy ways out.[23] And that is why I remain open but resolutely cautious about paranormal sources of information. I will discuss the reliability of mediumship in more detail in Chapter 4, "The Deceased."

Because figuring out whom to believe and to what degree is so important in the field of psychic experiences—a field into which coincidences inevitably draw us—I want to allow you, the reader, to appreciate the wide variety of sources from which I've collected coincidence accounts as well as make it easy for you to investigate these sources more fully if you wish. To this end, I have adopted footnotes in this book, rather than the more widely employed endnotes. I think it's important that, whenever you find yourself curious about the provenance of a particular story, you can find the answer at a glance, without having to flip to the back of the book and search for the page containing the relevant information. Additionally, you will find at the end of this book a complete bibliography, listing all of my source materials in a single location.

Now I've assumed so far that you, the reader, have a pretty good idea of what I mean when I refer to "coincidences." However, different people mean slightly different things by this term, so some clarification is in order. Some people, for example, refer to all paranormal experiences as "coincidences." However, the more experience a person has of the paranormal, the more clearly certain phenomena distinguish themselves as

---

[23] Henri Poincaré, *La Science et l'Hypothèse* (Paris: Flammarion, 1902).

having specific sorts of paranormal causes. For instance, some people appear to routinely receive verifiable telepathic messages from other living persons, while others seem to routinely receive verifiable messages from spirits no longer connected to human bodies. I am not going to call these sorts of experiences "coincidences." I don't mean to imply that the source and function of these other phenomena are established beyond doubt, or that they aren't worthy of careful study. Rather, I'm purposely narrowing my use of the term because I want to focus in this book on a phenomenon that is likely puzzling *even to those who accept the reality of mediumship, telepathy, and/or other more easily classifiable paranormal phenomena.* Although I'll repeatedly bring elements of these other paranormal phenomena to bear on the explanation of coincidences—and many coincidences may turn out to be best explained in terms of these other phenomena, or vice versa—it is nevertheless the more mysterious phenomenon of coincidences that is my primary subject matter.

Many of the cases I'm interested in involve physical events that appear to reflect the contents of people's minds. The idea is that something seems to be happening that is outside the "normal" mind-to-mind sorts of communication that feature in telepathy and after-death communication, as well as outside blatant cases of psychokinesis—where someone announces their intention to mentally bend a spoon, for example, and the spoon proceeds to bend. In the coincidence cases I am interested in studying, the physical world appears to be involved in an unexpected and particularly enigmatic way in conveying personal meaning.

Many researchers of this phenomenon call it by the name 'synchronicity'. As I mentioned previously, this term was introduced by Jung to refer to *meaningful* coincidences, and in particular to *deeply* meaningful coincidences. As Jungian counselor Robert H. Hopcke says, "Ordinary coincidences may delight or amuse; synchronistic events resonate deeply and throughout time."[24] However, while I understand the desire of Jung and Hopcke to differentiate this particularly meaningful class of coincidence, I want to note at the outset that I am not limiting my own study to those clearly meaningful coincidences. I am just as interested in events that happen without any obviously profound meaning and yet seem too improbable to be the mere products of chance. For this reason, I do not generally employ the Jungian term 'synchronicity'. Instead, I prefer to stick to the more general term 'coincidence'.

I hope it's also clear that when I use the term 'coincidence', I don't mean to imply that the event I'm referring to is a mere product of chance. The term is often used in this way, as when we call something "*just* a coincidence" or "a *mere* coincidence." What we mean in that case is that two things just

---

[24] Robert H. Hopcke, *There Are No Accidents in Love and Relationships: Meaningful Coincidences and the Stories of Our Families* (Asheville, NC: Chiron Publications, 2018), 31.

happened to coincide, with no further explanation possible. However, things may also coincide because of a causal (or other explanatory) connection that exists between them, and in this book, I will use the term 'coincidence' in a way that leaves open the question of whether or not there exists such a non-random connection in any particular case.

Nevertheless, one of the first questions that many people coming to this book are going to have—certainly one of the first questions *I* had in exploring this subject—is whether all seemingly paranormal coincidences might in fact be just very rare chance events. Granted, these events are highly unlikely, but even highly unlikely events are going to happen eventually in a world of seven billion people, right? This is a very important and poorly understood statistical issue, and for that reason, I devote the first chapter of this book to taking a hard look at it. In that chapter, I summarize some of my original research on this subject and provide a method for estimating just how much evidence any particular coincidence gives us for believing that it had a paranormal cause of some kind. Some of you may discover after reading this chapter that what you thought were important coincidences aren't really that surprising after all. Others will likely discover that your experiences are very good evidence for some kind of paranormal process. And we'll examine one coincidence that is clearly much too improbable to be explained by chance.

Once we've established in Chapter 1 a method for showing that there are at least *some* coincidences out there that are too improbable to be the products of chance, we can begin looking at what might actually be behind them. The next several chapters will be devoted to examining possible non-chance explanations for these coincidences. In Chapters 2 and 3, we'll look at two of the most common sources to which people attribute coincidences: God and angels. We'll see how each of these explanations appears to be a good explanation for certain sorts of cases but falls short in explaining others. Chapter 4 will then discuss the evidence that coincidences can be a way for deceased loved ones (or, at times, not-so-loved ones) to communicate with us, and Chapter 5 will discuss the evidence that coincidences can be communications from children who have yet to be born.

In Chapter 6, we'll take a look at an often-overlooked source for coincidences: the precognitive and psychokinetic powers of the experiencer's own mind. Sometimes a coincidence can best be explained by one's own ability to unconsciously see the future—for example, when one has a dream that later comes true. But I'll also provide examples of cases in which a person's thoughts and feelings appear to change the physical world around them, showing that psychokinesis (PK) is a source of coincidences that must always be considered. As part of this discussion, we'll delve into the subject of the unconscious and the propensity for repressed feelings to manifest as coincidences. We'll also discuss the notion of a "higher self": a source of inner wisdom that could produce the coincidences we encounter.

In Chapter 7, we'll consider the fact that our physical environment can be altered, not only by our *own* thoughts and feelings (conscious or unconscious), but by the thoughts and feelings of *other* living people. I will provide evidence that suggests that other living people can, at times, send us messages through the coincidences we experience. Then, in Chapter 8, we'll explore the unsettling idea that coincidences may sometimes be caused by entities with malevolent intentions, whether these be other living persons, the deceased, or perhaps something even more powerful, such as demons.

Chapter 9 will take a significantly different and less personal tack, discussing the possibility that coincidences may be the result of a natural law, one according to which similar things tend to happen together. We'll discuss the possibility that such a law, if coherent, could explain the striking but seemingly "meaningless" coincidences we sometimes encounter.

In the final chapter of Part I, Chapter 10, we will discuss some of the difficulties encountered in attempting to distinguish among the many possible sources of coincidences. In fact, we will discuss the idea that these sources may not be distinguishable even in principle. We will examine evidence that our individual human minds are actually parts of a larger consciousness—perhaps the "mind of the universe"—which communicates with us through the medium of coincidences.

In Part II of this book, we'll shift away from explicitly discussing the sources of coincidences to discussing their effects. Most of the chapters in Part II will focus on specific kinds of positive effects coincidences seem to have: for instance, confirming decisions, providing protection, locating important information, giving material help, bringing together two people who love each other (or who will), keeping us on the path of our destiny, and promoting our spiritual growth.

In the last chapter of the book, we'll look at coincidences whose significance is particularly difficult to understand. We will specifically discuss dream interpretation as a useful analogy to coincidence interpretation, and I will point out that, while this book provides some ways of classifying and analyzing the source and significance of coincidences, analysis is not the primary mode by which we should approach coincidences. Much more important than analyzing our experiences is *experiencing them fully and intuitively*. Analysis is primarily useful *after* one has conducted a more intuitive exploration of their meaning.

As will become apparent throughout this book, we are swimming in a sea of consciousness, and ultimately our mental life is not separable from the physical world around us, nor from the mental lives of others. Coincidences point, above all, to this fundamental interconnectedness. They allow us a glimpse of a level of order to our world that is probably too complex for us to understand but that compels us to try, or at least to gaze in awe. Our normal, everyday experience makes us believe we are separate beings, each of us isolated within the shell of our own body and mind, but coincidences show us that this is an illusion. At a deep level, we are all connected, and nothing we think or feel goes unheeded by the universe.

But you don't have to take my word for it. Let's have a look at the evidence.

Part I:

Sources

Chapter 1
Chance

Some readers will be coming to this book because, although part of you feels that your coincidence experiences are significant, the rational, scientific part of you remains deeply skeptical. You know that things aren't always what they seem. You know that the human mind and heart play tricks. And so you want a rigorously objective method for determining whether your experiences are just the products of chance or if they truly point to some heretofore unrecognized feature of the world.

The stakes are high. That's what makes exploration of this topic so nerve-racking. The stakes are our fundamental picture of how reality works. Is the physical world just physical? Just a maelstrom of elementary particles swirling in the cosmic night? Is tomorrow just the mechanical result of whatever states these particles happen to be in today, combined with natural physical laws? Is each of us ultimately at the mercy of a universe that is indifferent to our innermost thoughts and aspirations? Or is there more to it than that? Does the universe sometimes hear the silent cry of our hearts and respond in unexpectedly direct fashion? Is there, in fact, a method to the madness of the universe—an order that exceeds the limits of our comprehension and that every now and then lets us know by subtle signs that it has our best interest at heart?

Some of us so long for the second picture to be correct that we are deeply suspicious of our ability to evaluate the situation objectively. Of course, others among us take more psychological comfort from the former, mechanistic picture of the universe, and that, too, could impair our ability to be objective when evaluating the significance of coincidences. No matter our predisposition, it seems that what we need is a rigorous, unbiased method of determining whether or not our coincidence experiences are evidence for an unrecognized aspect of reality. That is what I aim to provide in this chapter.

Mathematicians and philosophers have been writing dismissively about coincidences for thousands of years. For instance, the ancient Roman philosopher Cicero wrote the following.

> By applying conjecture to the countless delusions of drunk or crazy men we may sometimes deduce what appears to be a real prophecy; for who, if he shoots at a mark all day long, will not occasionally hit it? We sleep every night and there is scarcely ever a night when we do not dream; then do we wonder that our dreams come true sometimes?[1]

In 1814, French mathematician Pierre-Simon Laplace wrote briefly about coincidences in his *Essai philosophique sur les probabilités*, remarking that not enough attention was paid to how many noncoincidences there were.[2] And English logician John Venn—inventor of the Venn diagram—wrote in 1876 in *The Logic of Chance*, "There can be no doubt that, however unlikely an event may be, if we (loosely speaking) vary the circumstances sufficiently, or if, in other words, we keep on trying long enough, we shall meet with such an event at last."[3]

More recently, in 2004, physicist Freeman Dyson described the thoughts of 20th-century mathematician J. E. Littlewood on the relative banality of "miracles." According to Dyson, Littlewood proved that, "in the course of any normal person's life, miracles happen at a rate of roughly one per month."[4] Littlewood's idea was that, if a miracle is an event with a probability of occurrence of only one in a million, and each of us has events happening to us about once per second for eight hours every day, then about a million events happen to each of us each month—making it likely that at least one of these will be a "one-in-a-million" event![5]

---

[1] Cicero, *De Divinatione*, Loeb Classical Library, trans. W. A. Falconer (Cambridge, MA: Harvard University Press, 1938), book II, section 121, p. 507. Accessible online at http://penelope.uchicago.edu/Thayer/E/Roman/Texts/Cicero/de_Divinatione/2*.html.

[2] Pierre-Simon Laplace, *Essai philosophique sur les probabilités* (Paris, 1814).

[3] John Venn, *The Logic of Chance: An Essay on the Foundations and Province of the Theory of Probability, with Especial Reference to Its Logical Bearings and Its Application to Moral and Social Science*, 2nd ed. (London: Macmillan, 1876), 379.

[4] Freeman Dyson, "One in a Million," review of *Debunked! ESP, Telekinesis, and Other Pseudoscience*, by Georges Charpak and Henri Broch, translated from the French by Bart K. Holland (Johns Hopkins University Press, 2004), in *The New York Review of Books* (25 March 2004). Also available reprinted in Freeman Dyson, *The Scientist as Rebel* (New York: New York Review of Books, 2006), 321-32.

[5] Much has been made of "Littlewood's Law" in online forums, but while certain web sources cite *Littlewood's Miscellany* as the source for Littlewood's Law, it does

Littlewood's "Law of Miracles" is often referenced by those who are skeptical of the significance of coincidences,[6] but none of them, as far as I can tell, has yet attempted to determine whether the figure of one in a million bears any useful relationship to the probability of the striking coincidences that people actually experience. The fact that skeptics employ that particular figure and then proceed to behave as though the matter is settled implies that they think it *does* bear some useful relationship to actual experiences, but they don't actually calculate the odds of any of the real-life coincidences that lead people to believe in the influence of some hidden intelligence.

In this chapter, my goal is to significantly refine Littlewood's statistical method and show you how you can use it to determine the likelihood of the coincidences you actually experience and thus whether they happen more often than would be expected by chance. The method I show you here, which I call the "time-slice" method, is summarized from an academic paper I published in the *Journal of Scientific Exploration* in March 2019.[7] Interested readers are encouraged to refer to that paper for more detail. On the other hand, readers who aren't particularly bothered by the question of whether the significance of their coincidences can be mathematically justified may just want to skip this chapter and get right to the discussion of paranormal sources for coincidences starting in Chapter 2.

The Time-Slice Method for Calculating the Likelihood of Coincidences

Let me begin my explanation of the time-slice method with a hypothetical case. Imagine that you've recently been thinking about your old friend Debbie and wondering if you should call her. One afternoon, you're

---

not appear there. The closest Littlewood gets to anything resembling Dyson's description is when he makes the statement, "I sometimes ask the question: what is the most remarkable coincidence you have experienced, and is it, for *the* most remarkable one, remarkable? (With a lifetime to choose from, $10^6 : 1$ is a mere trifle.)" [J. E. Littlewood, *Littlewood's Miscellany*, ed. Béla Bollobás, rev. ed. (Cambridge, UK: Cambridge University Press, 1986), 104.] When I asked Dyson in 2017 about his source, he said that he thinks he remembers hearing Littlewood state his "Law" while Dyson was a student at Cambridge but is unaware whether Littlewood ever put it into print. As best I can tell, the only print source for Littlewood's Law is Dyson's article.

[6] See, for instance, Persi Diaconis and Frederick Mosteller, "Methods for Studying Coincidences," *Journal of the American Statistical Association* 84, no. 408 (1989): 853-61, p. 859.

[7] Sharon Hewitt Rawlette, "Coincidence or Psi? The Epistemic Import of Spontaneous Cases of Purported Psi Identified Post-Verification," *Journal of Scientific Exploration* 33, no. 1 (March 2019): 9-42.

playing a board game that involves rolling dice seven at a time, and you notice that one of your rolls produces Debbie's phone number: 225-4631. Immediately, you want to know what the odds are that this is just a fluke (and not a sign from God, for example).

To determine this, the first thing you need to figure out is exactly what you're trying to find the odds of. You might think that, since there are 279,936 possible outcomes each time you roll seven dice, the relevant odds here are 1 in 279,936. But things are a bit more complicated than that. For one thing, *any* combination of numbers on the dice would have had those very same odds. The reason that the combination 2254631 stands out to you is that it is *personally significant* to you. That is, it's a combination that corresponds in a meaningful way with your current state of mind (your thoughts, memories, desires, etc.). It is that meaningful correspondence between your state of mind and your observation of an external event that you want to find the odds of. You want to know how likely it is that, just by chance, you would roll such a personally significant combination.[8]

In order to do that, however, you have to consider more than just the odds of rolling Debbie's phone number in that moment. You also have to consider, for example, the odds of rolling some *other* number just as personally significant as that one. Consider the possibility that, instead of Debbie's phone number, you might have rolled your *own* phone number. Or that of a dear deceased relative. You might have rolled the first seven digits of your social security number. Or the first four digits of the roll might have corresponded to the address of a home you're considering purchasing. Once the roll has occurred, it's easy to forget all the other ways it might have been at least as personally significant, but to get an accurate idea of the relevant probability, it's essential to do a thorough job of exploring the personally significant alternatives.

---

[8] For those who are philosophically inclined, let me offer the following definition of "personal significance." An event E's personal significance for a subject S is the degree of correspondence between E and S's mental state, where our measure of this correspondence gives greater weight to more salient mental states—for instance, mental states of higher emotion or more enduring character—and to larger and/or more enduring external events. A definition of "correspondence" between a subject's mental state and an external event could be fleshed out using the notion of Kolmogorov complexity, according to which the complexity of a state is the size of its shortest description. If we notate the complexity of X as *C*(X), we could then define the correspondence between a mental state and an external event as:

$$\frac{C(\text{mental state}) + C(\text{external event})}{C(\text{mental state} + \text{external event})}$$

Now let's say that, once you consider your mental state at the time of rolling the dice and its relationship to all the possible dice combinations, it becomes clear that there was one other combination besides the actual one that would have been at least as personally significant for you. This means that the chance odds of obtaining on that particular roll a number at least this personally significant to you were 2 in 279,936—which simplifies to 1 in 139,968.

But we're not done. Imagine that you've been playing this board game for a little while. You've made several previous rolls, and none of those turned up Debbie's phone number or your other personally significant number. Let's say you'd already rolled the dice nine times before Debbie's phone number came up. That means you made 10 rolls total. The odds of one of those 10 rolls being as personally significant to you as Debbie's phone number are about 1 in 13,997. So not quite as surprising.

But why should we stop with this particular episode of playing this board game? Let's say that this is actually the 20th time you've played it in your life. And let's say, to keep the math simple, that each time you've played it, you've rolled the dice 10 times. The odds that you would, at some time, have seen the dice in this game turn up one of the two numbers that would be most personally significant to you are now only 1 in 700.

But we can't stop there, either. The fact of the matter is that, even when you weren't playing this game, there were times when you could have run across one of these significant numbers in other settings. For instance, you might have been driving down the highway when you saw a billboard urging you to call a personal injury lawyer who happened to have Debbie's phone number, just with a different area code. Or an online purchase you made might have had an order number that included the digits of her phone number. Or the mileage on your car's odometer (if you include the tenths' place) might have matched her number.

The fact is that you are constantly surrounded by opportunities to observe—by chance—numbers that are personally significant to you. And it's not just numbers, either. You might hear Debbie's unusual last name come up in the evening news. Or you might pass on the sidewalk someone who looks uncannily similar to her. And let's not forget that Debbie is not the only person or matter on your mind. There are many, many ways that the events you randomly observe could happen to correspond to your thoughts, memories, or desires. What we really need to know, in order to determine whether your rolling of Debbie's phone number is statistically surprising, is how many opportunities you've had throughout your entire life for the events you observe to randomly match your state of mind in a way that is as improbable as this individual roll of the dice.

Such a calculation may sound impossible, but there is a way to vastly simplify it by taking a cue from Littlewood's Law and focusing on a small slice of time. What we need to do is figure out approximately how much time your attention was occupied by observing the seven dice that produced Debbie's phone number. Let's say that observing those seven dice took your full attention for one second. That is, there's no way that, within that second, you could have observed any other coincidences *in addition to* the roll of the dice. Let's also say that, in this hypothetical case, the probability of your getting distracted from observing the dice is so low that it's not worth factoring in. (When we look at real-life examples, we'll deal with the question of distractions in more detail.) This means that the overall probability of your observing anything in this one second that is as personally significant to you as what you did observe is 1 in 139,968 (because we're assuming that one other of the 279,936 possible rolls would have been at least as personally significant). This in turn means that you ought to expect such personally significant events to occur by chance on average once every 139,968 seconds, or about once every 39 hours.[9] Which means that chance does do a pretty good job of explaining a coincidence like this—unless, of course, things like this are happening to you more often than every 39 hours or so.

Now that you have the basic idea of the method, it's time to apply it to some real-world coincidences and discuss their implications.

Example 1: Matching Descending Doubles

Let's begin with a real-world die-rolling example reported by Dr. Andrew Paquette. Paquette has written multiple peer-reviewed articles about spontaneous psychic phenomena as well as a book called *Dreamer: 20 Years of Psychic Dreams and How They Changed My Life*. In that book, he recounts an experience that occurred one night when he and his wife, Kitty, were playing backgammon. Paquette got a strange feeling that led him to announce that they were about to roll matching descending doubles, starting with sixes and going down to ones. Kitty then proceeded to roll and got two sixes. Then Paquette rolled and got two sixes. On the next round, they both rolled double fives. Then came double fours, double threes, and double twos. "At this point," says Paquette, "the staggering mathematical improbability of what I'd just seen hit me like a wave. I lost confidence and predicted we would not get the double ones. Kitty then rolled a pair of non-matching numbers."[10]

Before Paquette lost confidence, he and his wife had already produced a sequence of 20 rolls that precisely matched the prediction he made. As

---

[9] Despite what Littlewood may have said, we should count the hours we spend sleeping, since a coincidental event may wake us up—or even come to us as we sleep, in the form of a dream.

[10] Andrew Paquette, *Dreamer: 20 Years of Psychic Dreams and How They Changed My Life* (Winchester, UK: O-Books, 2011), 23-24.

Paquette notes in his book, the odds of rolling any particular 20-number sequence on a fair, six-sided die are 1 in 3,656,158,440,062,976. Approximately 1 in 3.7 quadrillion. Now, among these 3.7 quadrillion possible rolls, how many would have been at least as personally significant to Paquette as the one that actually occurred? I think we can make a very strong case that the actual roll sequence was at that time the *most* personally significant to Paquette of all 3.7 quadrillion possible sequences. This is not because none of the other possible sequences would have been significant to him at all. But, just moments before rolling this sequence, he experienced a strong conviction that he and his wife would roll the sequence of matching descending doubles that was actually produced (minus a coda of four 1s that they didn't manage to roll). This strong feeling, along with Paquette's subsequent announcement of his prediction to his wife, are enough in my view to make that particular 20-roll sequence the single most personally significant to him in that moment.

Now we need to determine how long Paquette's full attention would be required to observe the outcomes of all the rolls in this sequence. Note that we shouldn't count the amount of time between the observations of each of these rolls, when Paquette and his wife may have been preparing to roll, or perhaps discussing their astonishment at the rolls so far produced. All that we should count is the minimum amount of time required for Paquette to *actually observe* the outcomes of all 20 rolls in the sequence, without any extra time for him to notice any other information that could possibly contain coincidences. If it seems that observing 20 die rolls in 5 seconds, say, would leave Paquette with additional attention with which to observe other simultaneous happenings, then we need to reduce this span of time until we are reasonably certain that it is the minimum time necessary for Paquette to observe the rolls of the 20 dice. To be very conservative (in the direction of underestimating the significance of Paquette's coincidence), let's estimate this minimum at 2 seconds. I don't think anyone but the most highly trained die observer could consciously observe the outcomes of more than 10 rolls per second.

Now we need to consider the possibility of distracting events: events that would cause Paquette *not* to observe the outcomes of the rolls in the particular 2 seconds in which he did observe them but instead to observe some other information during that time. In some cases (and we'll see one of these in a moment), distracting events are going to be particularly important, because of the high probability that those distracting events could furnish coincidences just as personally significant as the coincidence that was actually observed. However, in Paquette's case, his prediction spoken to his wife shows that his state of mind is clearly focused on one very particular sequence of die rolls. It's hard to see how any remotely probable distracting event could correspond as closely to his mental state at this time as the actual

20-roll sequence he witnessed. Which means that, if we factor in the probability of any distracting event, it's actually going to *lower* the probability of Paquette's experiencing his die-rolling coincidence, making it appear even more statistically surprising. Thus, if we were to choose to simply ignore all possibly distracting events in this case, we would actually be erring on the side of a *conservative* estimate of the evidence that this event provides for some kind of paranormal process.

In fact, in Paquette's case, it does seem like it's appropriate to ignore possibly distracting events. In an email to me on October 30, 2017, Paquette elaborated a bit on the context of his experience. He wrote,

> at the time of the matching descending doubles incident, we lived deep in farm country outside Putney, Vermont. The nearest neighbor was half a mile away, but couldn't be seen or heard from the house we rented. Also, although we had a TV, we didn't have cable, so we only used it for VHS tapes, which we never played while doing something else in the dining room, like playing backgammon. We also didn't have a radio.

On a night spent deep in farm country with no near neighbors and no TV or radio on, there would be very few possibilities for distractions. I think we can safely ignore that possibility—with the knowledge that, if we are erring at all in doing so, it is on the side of making Paquette's coincidence seem less striking than it really is.

So now, if we take 2 seconds as the amount of time it would take Paquette to observe the die rolls in question and we know that that particular sequence of rolls had a chance of occurring of just 1 in 3.7 quadrillion, that means that Paquette's coincidence is the sort of thing that we should only expect to observe about once every 7.4 quadrillion seconds, or once every 234 million years. Clearly, we're looking at a "coincidence" that's a great deal more significant than the hypothetical one in which you rolled Debbie's phone number.

But is it statistically significant enough to justify Paquette in believing that something paranormal is going on, something beyond the bounds of currently recognized science? After all, since there are about 80 years in the average lifespan (in the developed world), a coincidence of this strength should be expected to happen by chance to approximately 1 in 3 million people sometime in the course of their life. Paquette might think to himself, "Well, in a world of 7 billion people, something this wild was bound to happen to over 2,000 of us just by chance, so it doesn't actually imply anything about the existence of the paranormal."

However, this common line of reasoning is incorrect. The number of other people in the world is only relevant to the significance of this experience if we have information about *how many of those other people have had similar experiences*. If Paquette doesn't know how many of the other 7 billion people on earth have experienced something this improbably significant, then the fact that there merely *are* 7 billion people on earth is irrelevant to his calculations.[11] Instead, he's going to have to think carefully about the number of people for whom he does have such information. How many people does he know who would have told him if they'd had a similarly significant experience? (We're going to assume, conservatively, that no one *has* told him about a similar experience of their own.) One way he could estimate this number would be to consider how many people he's told about *his* experience. That's probably about how many people he knows who would have told him about theirs. Say he's told 1,000 people in person about this experience, and that 50,000 other people have learned about it through his book and the internet. We'll assume (again conservatively) that any one of these people who'd had an equally significant coincidence happen to them would have contacted him about it. That gives us a total of 51,000 people whom he could expect to have heard from if they'd had an experience as astounding as his. Clearly, we are nowhere near 3 million. And, in fact, if the average age of the folks whose experiences Paquette is acquainted with is only 40 years old, he would actually need reliable knowledge that *6 million people* had not had a similarly improbable personally significant experience to counterbalance the evidence for a paranormal cause constituted by this single experience of his. In conclusion, Paquette's experience of matching descending doubles gives him *extremely strong reason* to believe that something besides chance produced this event.

Example 2: The Scarab under the Mat

Let's now try applying the method to a slightly more complicated coincidence, this time one taken from my own life.

One afternoon I was sitting on my front porch reading a book full of absorbing accounts of coincidences: Paul Davids' *An Atheist in Heaven*.[12] This got me thinking about all the meaningful coincidences I'd encountered in my own life and about the larger pattern they seemed to form. As I was

---

[11] If you require convincing of this, consider the fact that, if this restriction on the relevance of other observers didn't exist, then one could reduce the strength of any evidence for any hypothesis whatsoever to next to nothing merely by citing the existence of enough intelligent extraterrestrial beings, saying something like, "After all, in a universe of 700 trillion quadrillion intelligent beings, someone on some planet was bound to get these experimental results just by chance." But we quite rightly don't take the strength of our ordinary scientific evidence to depend on how much intelligent extraterrestrial life exists.

[12] Paul Davids and Gary E. Schwartz with John Allison, *An Atheist in Heaven: The Ultimate Evidence for Life after Death?* (Reno, NV: Yellow Hat, 2016).

contemplating this, a phrase came into my head—"It's bigger than you know"—and I understood this phrase to be referring to the pattern behind my coincidences. At this point, I stood up and began to walk inside the house. When my bare foot hit the welcome mat that sits just outside the door, I felt a lump in it, and I immediately thought to myself that I needed to look under the mat. I had the feeling that whatever was causing this lump could be a coincidence related to what I'd just been thinking about. So, I lifted the mat and discovered that the object underneath was a giant scarab beetle, more than an inch long and about three-quarters of an inch wide. This was quite a surprise, since I'd never encountered such a beetle, and I had lived 25 of my 35 years of life within a 30-mile radius of that location in Virginia and spent a fair amount of that time outdoors. In fact, I was so surprised and fascinated by this scarab beetle that it took a moment or two for the full significance of the coincidence to sink in. In the Western world, the one symbol that is most closely associated with the idea of a meaningful coincidence is a scarab, due to a famous coincidence related by Carl Jung. While doing a psychotherapy session for a woman who was telling him her dream about a scarab necklace, Jung heard a tapping at his office window and discovered that it was a scarab beetle bumping against the glass. He promptly scooped it up and showed it to his patient, saying, "Here is your scarab!" He used this coincidence as a prime illustration of the phenomenon of meaningful coincidences he dubbed "synchronicity,"[13] and this story has been mentioned in almost every essay or book about coincidences written since.[14]

It was startling to realize that I had found at that moment an object so intimately connected to the idea of coincidences. But, what was more, the scarab I found under my welcome mat was quite large—much bigger than any beetle I'd ever seen before in the wild. Its size seemed to echo the phrase I'd heard in my head just a minute or two earlier: "It's bigger than you know." Overall, the subjective feeling produced by this coincidence was that it confirmed, in an artful and highly improbable manner, the conclusion I had just come to about the pattern of coincidences in my life.

Let's now attempt to determine the statistical significance of this coincidence. First, we need to determine the minimum time required for me to observe both the lump in the mat and then the scarab underneath. Again,

---

[13] C. G. Jung, *Synchronicity: An Acausal Connecting Principle*, trans. R. F. C. Hull (Princeton, NJ: Princeton University Press, 1960, 2010), 22; and C. G. Jung, "On Synchronicity," in Jung, *Synchronicity*, 109-10.

[14] Images of scarabs also frequently appear in connection with the topic of meaningful coincidences. See, for example, the cover of F. David Peat, *Synchronicity: The Marriage of Matter and Psyche* (Pari, Italy: Pari Publishing, 2014) and the title image of John Blake, "The Other Side: Where do coincidences come from?" *CNN* (2015), http://www.cnn.com/2015/12/29/us/odd-coincidences-synchronicity-the-other-side/ (accessed 28 January 2017).

we don't want to count the time in between these two components of the observation, time during which I was turning around and bending down to lift the mat. We only want to count the time necessary for the observation itself. Let's estimate my minimum observation time for the lump and the scarab combined as one second. That is, it would take me at least one second to process all the relevant tactile and visual information and come to a conclusion about what I was observing.

Now we need to think about the other possible observations I could have made during this second. Let's focus first on all the other things I could have found under the mat. What percentage would have been at least as personally significant to me in that moment? The first thing that springs to my mind as being possibly *more* significant is a *golden* scarab. In Jung's anecdote, the scarab dreamed of by the woman was a golden one, not a glossy black one like I found. And Jung says that the scarab that tapped at his window was of the species *Cetonia aurata*, which sports a metallic green color with hints of gold, while mine was a *Xyloryctes jamaicensis*. Both are species of the family Scarabaeidae, but where I live, another member of this family is much more common and resembles more closely the color of Jung's *Cetonia aurata*: the Japanese beetle, *Popillia japonica*. Japanese beetles are a common garden pest in Virginia, and they are much smaller than *Xyloryctes jamaicensis*, being at most half an inch long. I would not have been surprised at all if I'd found one of them under my front mat or if one had flown up to me while I was going into the house. I probably would have been so unsurprised that I would have paid it no further heed and never would have thought to make any connection to Jung's scarab. In fact, I didn't even know until doing research for this paragraph that Japanese beetles were technically scarabs—probably since they look so unlike the ones featured in the 1999 film *The Mummy*! That is to say that, in my mind, with its particular pattern of references, the common Japanese beetle was not nearly as closely connected to the concept of *scarab* and thus to the concept of *coincidence* as was the giant black scarab that I actually found. For this reason, among all the insects and other small creatures that I have already had occasion to observe in the climate where I live (or in any other outdoor area I've explored), I don't believe there is any so closely corresponding to my state of my mind at that time as the large, black scarab beetle I indeed found.

But what about non-living things that I might have found under the mat or been otherwise confronted with during the second it took me to feel the lump under the mat and look underneath? I can think of only a few that would have borne a closer relationship to the concept of meaningful coincidence. For instance, I could have found a copy of Jung's book *Synchronicity* that someone had randomly left beside my door, or a note with Jung's name scrawled on it, or perhaps a photograph of him. Or I might have heard a neighbor yell out, "It's not a coincidence!" Or perhaps heard a plane fly overhead and turned to see that it had produced the phrase "Bigger than you know" in sky writing.

On the other hand, we should also consider that I might have observed something that, instead of evoking meaningful coincidences in general, would have borne a relationship to the particular patterns of coincidences I'd been contemplating in my life, coincidences with a couple of overarching personal themes. I can come up with a few ideas for items I could have found under that mat that would have borne as strong a relationship to those personal themes as the scarab bore to the idea of meaningful coincidence, but the likelihood of my finding them under the mat at my front door, or somehow otherwise being confronted with them at the moment that I was stepping on the mat or bending to look under it, seems much smaller than the probability of my finding the scarab. After all, the only manmade objects I've ever found under my doormat are keys and handwritten notes, none of which (to my disappointment) has ever been on the topic of synchronicity or the deep personal themes of my life.

Now comes the hardest part: estimating the relevant probabilities. We need to estimate how probable it was that I would observe in this second either this giant scarab or something else at least as personally significant to me. One of the things we need to decide in order to do this is what elements of the situation we are going to hold constant. In Paquette's die-rolling case, we held constant the fact that he was in a house in the country with no TV or radio on and that he was rolling dice. While, in his case, the setting may have influenced the probability of distracting events, we could safely assume it had no effect on the probability of his rolling any particular combination. The situation is a bit different in the case of the scarab, however, because the setting in which I find myself could vastly influence my chances of seeing a scarab. For instance, if I were indoors, my chances of seeing a scarab would be lower than they were outdoors. Time of day could also be a factor, as well as proximity to my front porch light. In fact, if we hold constant the fact that the scarab was already under my doormat and that I was stepping on that particular portion of the mat, then the likelihood that I would shortly be observing a scarab are quite high. How do we decide what factors we ought to hold constant in our assessment of the probability of this event?

As I explain in detail in my academic paper on the subject, it is essential that any features of the situation that correspond to my mental state *because of a normal causal relationship between them* have to be held constant. For instance, if I knew that scarabs were attracted to front porch lights and that knowledge led me to decide to sit near the front porch light to read about coincidences, then I would have to hold that part of the situation constant.

In fact, my decision to read this book on my front porch was not due to any such knowledge. And it might have been that, if some paranormal process indeed led me to encounter this scarab, it brought this about by subtly prompting me to read my book outside on this front porch on this particular day. It may also have previously influenced this scarab to come to this particular light and to burrow under this particular mat before expiring. If we're interested in testing the hypothesis that some paranormal process could have produced the coincidence in this way, then we can't hold constant the factors we believe it might have influenced, because the probability of those events is part of what we want to estimate. On the other hand, we should hold constant the factors that we don't think would have been paranormally influenced (if any paranormal influence in fact exists).[15]

In deciding how widely to "cast my net" for paranormal causation, I am here going to hold constant the fact that I was at home at the time (I'm not worrying about whether paranormal causation may have influenced my being

---

[15] Note that the choice of constants is an issue for research science in general, where the ability of research results to confirm a hypothesis depends on the size and type of effect the hypothesis posits. We run one kind of experiment (and one kind of statistical analysis) if we expect an effect of size x on variables Y and Z, and another possibly quite different experiment if we expect an effect of size $20x$ on variables K and L. Both of these experiments might be investigating paranormal phenomena, let's say, but if they are based on different hypotheses about how paranormal phenomena would work, they are going to look for different things and so possibly come to what look like opposing conclusions about the existence and/or strength of such phenomena. But there may in fact be no such opposition if the hypothesis confirmed in one case is not exactly the same as the one disconfirmed in the other, which it won't be if the experimental procedures imply different assumptions about the type and size of effect expected. The two experiments are simply testing slightly different things.

And this is true in our *post facto* experiments related to coincidences as well. In effect, what we are doing in using the method I'm describing in this chapter is designing the parameters of a research study. Instead of deciding what parameters we will hold constant before we run trials, we are taking the actual history of the world as possible data and deciding, by our choice of constants, which events in the history of the world count as trials in the experiment. A coincidence that looks pretty improbable given one set of constants can look pretty probable on another. A skeptic might want to say that the constants that make an event look more probable are the "right" ones, but they are no more objectively right than the constants that produce a result far from chance. *Both* conclusions are true. The same event can deviate far from chance expectation when we hold certain circumstances constant while at the same time be much closer to chance expectation when we hold *other* circumstances constant. This doesn't mean that "it's all relative," and that there's no deciding the question of paranormal influence. It means that the evidence in this case is strong for paranormal influence on certain factors of the situation and weak for paranormal influence on other factors. In reality, we're getting very specific information. Our choice of constants in evaluating coincidences allows us to ask very specific questions about very specific types of paranormal influence.

at home), but I am not going to hold constant the fact that I was outdoors, nor the fact that it was daytime. That is, I am going to allow the possibilities for potential observations to range over anything that might happen when I'm at home, outdoors or in, day or night.

At the time of this coincidence, I had lived 35 years of life with only one sighting of such a large scarab. Now, it's true that sightings of these beetles could be more or less common than my own experience would lead me to believe. A survey entomologist in my state has told me that he considers *Xyloryctes jamaicensis* a rare species and says the average person is not likely to encounter it. I conducted an informal survey of my own, showing five members of my family a picture of a *Xyloryctes jamaicensis* and asking whether they'd ever seen one. Two of them said they'd never seen one, two said they'd seen one in their life, and the fifth—my husband—said he probably sees them once or twice a year, but generally on blacktop surfaces and not around our home. Given all this additional information, I think my own experience of seeing one *Xyloryctes jamaicensis* in 35 years is pretty representative.

Now, I would estimate that over the course of those 35 years I have been "at home" (in one of my successive places of residence—I'm keeping constant that I'm not in public and my surroundings are largely populated by things chosen by me) about 22 hours out of every day. Over 35 years, that comes to about 1.01 billion seconds. Based on the fact that I have only seen one large scarab in this time, we could estimate the probability that I would observe a large scarab in the particular second that I did as on the order of 1 in 1.01 billion.

With that calculation out of the way, we now have the issue of adding in the probability of my observing some *other* coincidence at least as personally significant as this scarab. How many such random occurrences of coincidence-themed events can I recall experiencing around my home, at any time in my life? Of course, on most occasions such events wouldn't have stuck out to me as strongly as this scarab did (because most times I haven't been thinking so hard about coincidences just prior to experiencing them), so my memory is apt to underestimate the frequency with which such events have occurred. But I'm going to take a stab at a number. Remember that we're looking for not just any random mention of a coincidence by someone in my company, but one that has a connection to *meaningful* coincidences. Also recall that, besides bearing a relationship to meaningful coincidences, the scarab, in being so large, corresponded to my thought "It's bigger than you know." To rival the giant scarab in personal significance, an alternative event would similarly have to have some additional element of correspondence with my mental state.

I am going to estimate the number of times I have ever experienced, at home, an event not provoked by my interest in coincidences but just as closely related to "meaningful coincidences that are bigger than you know" as perhaps 4 in my entire life. If we add this to the probability of observing a giant scarab, we end up with an estimate of the overall odds of my experiencing anything in this second at least as personally significant as what I did experience as 5 in 1.01 billion, or 1 in 202 million. This is thus the sort of coincidence I should expect to encounter by chance once every 202 million seconds, or every 6.4 years or so. Clearly, this is not nearly as big a coincidence as Paquette's, but it's not tiny either. And if I'm encountering things like this *more* often than once every 6 years, then there's reason to think that, on at least some of these occasions, I'm experiencing the result of a non-random influence of some kind.

Example 3: Grandfather's Radio

The final coincidence we'll examine in this chapter is one reported by a well-known skeptic of paranormal phenomena: Dr. Michael Shermer, founding publisher of *Skeptic* magazine and a long-time columnist in *Scientific American*. In 2014, Shermer wrote in *Scientific American* about a striking coincidence that happened to him, a coincidence so strong that he says it "rocked me back on my heels and shook my skepticism to its core." It happened at his home on his wedding day in 2014.

On this day, Shermer's fiancée, Jennifer Graf, was longingly thinking of her family and friends, far away in her home country of Germany. She was especially missing her grandfather, who had been like a father to her but had died when she was a teen. She'd recently had some of her things shipped to the new home she shared with Shermer, and these included her grandfather's old 1978 Philips transistor radio, precious to her even though it hadn't worked in years. When it arrived, Shermer tried to bring it back to life, putting in new batteries and checking the soldering. He says he also tried "percussive maintenance": banging it against something hard. No luck. The radio sat silent in a drawer in the bedroom.

Three months after these failed attempts to revive the radio, Shermer and Graf held their wedding ceremony in their home, with Graf wistfully thinking about how she wished her grandfather could have been there to give her away. After the ceremony, when Shermer and Graf went to the back of the house for a moment of privacy, they were surprised to hear music playing in the bedroom. They searched all over for the source, only to find that the tune—"a romantic love song"—was coming from Graf's grandfather's old radio, still lying in the drawer. "My grandfather is here with us," concluded Graf. "I'm not alone."

Shermer emphasizes that the timing of the radio's functioning was very precise. Graf and Shermer had been getting ready in the back of the house just before the ceremony, and there had been no music at that time. Later,

Shermer's daughter told them that she had noticed the music playing just as the ceremony was about to begin. So it had to have started not more than a few minutes before the wedding did. Furthermore, the radio continued to play through the wedding night and then ceased functioning the following day. Shermer writes in his article that it has "remained silent ever since."[16]

So let's analyze this case. Since Graf is the subject whose state of mind is most relevant here, we are going to discuss the coincidence from her point of view. On her wedding day, which is the day when a father normally plays the most significant ceremonious role he ever plays in the life of his daughter, Graf was missing the closest thing she had to a father: her deceased grandfather. And a series of three events corresponded to this state of mind in unlikely fashion: the autonomous turning on of her grandfather's radio within a few minutes of the start of the wedding ceremony, its playing a love song (rather than something less related to a wedding atmosphere), and its autonomous turning off at some point the following day.

First, we need to determine the minimum time necessary for Graf to observe all of these events. A couple of them were observed in distinct stages, so I've listed in the following table a total of five components in Graf's observation of the relevant events, along with an estimate of the minimum time required for each.

Observation	*Minimum Time*
Graf heard music.	1 second
Graf observed this music to be a "romantic love song" coming from her grandfather's transistor radio.	2 seconds
Graf heard Shermer's daughter say that she heard the music when the ceremony was about to start.	2 seconds
Graf remembered that no music had been playing in the room with the radio just a few minutes prior to the ceremony.	2 seconds
Graf observed that the radio was no longer working on the following day.	2 seconds
Total	9 seconds

[16] Michael Shermer, "Infrequencies," *Scientific American* (October 2014). This article is also available online under the title "Anomalous Events that Can Shake One's Skepticism to Its Core": https://www.scientificamerican.com/article/anomalous-events-that-can-shake-one-s-skepticism-to-the-core/ (accessed 16 January 2017).

Remember that we are not estimating the entire span of time over which these observations actually took place. For instance, it took Graf much longer than two seconds to search various possible sources for the music and conclude that it was coming from the radio. However, what we are trying to estimate is the minimum time required for this observation such that, had any other event come to her attention during this time, it would have prevented her from making one of the observations necessary to experiencing the coincidence. That is, we're trying to figure out just how much of Graf's total available attention was occupied by observation of this coincidence, and I think we'd be conservative in estimating that amount of attention to be equal to her full attention over the course of nine seconds.

Our next task is to decide which elements of Graf's situation we are going to hold constant when judging the relevant probabilities. We have to hold constant, of course, the "percussive maintenance" that Shermer did on the radio, as well as any other way he or Graf may have intentionally influenced it toward working before tucking it into the desk drawer. Beyond that, let's hold constant only the basic facts we know about the wedding—for instance, that it took place at their home—and not any more obscure facts, such as a possible solar flare that caused a lot of defunct electronic equipment to suddenly begin working again that day. (That is, we are going to allow that, if there *was* a solar flare that affected electronic equipment beginning at the time of the wedding, that was part of the coincidence to be measured.)

This minimal specification of constants should suffice for this case, so let's now turn to determining what the probability was that something would happen during these nine seconds that would be at least as personally significant to Graf as what actually happened. We'll begin by estimating the probability that, during these nine seconds, she would observe that her grandfather's radio had begun functioning so significantly close to the beginning of the wedding ceremony. I'm going to estimate that the radio's suddenly beginning to function would have been just as significant if it had happened anytime in the five minutes before the start of the wedding up to five minutes after it began. So what we want to know, for the moment, are the odds that the radio would have begun to function during that particular 10-minute stretch of time.

I've consulted a man who's been repairing antique radios for the last 20 years, and he tells me that transistor radios of this age are known for having intermittent connections due to their having been frequently dropped. He suggested that a change in temperature or humidity in the house on the day of the wedding, or perhaps vibrations due to the number of people in the house, could have caused the radio to suddenly begin working and then stop again a day later. Since the intermittent functioning of old transistor radios is a common phenomenon, let's make the conservative assumption that the radio was going to start working again *at some point.* We know that, after Shermer's "percussive maintenance" of the radio, it spent three months not working and then, without being touched or having its state intentionally fiddled with in any way, suddenly sprang to life, and then spent at least another three months (that is, up to the publication of Shermer's article) not working. However, focusing on this time period will likely severely underestimate the improbability of the event. That is, it's probably not true that defunct transistor radios spontaneously begin working, on average, every six months. Let's estimate that this happens more like once every 15 years for a given radio. If that's true, then the odds that this radio would have spontaneously begun functioning during the 10-minute period surrounding the start of Graf's wedding was 1 in 788,940.

To keep things as simple as we can, let's now assume that, given that the radio began working when it did, the odds that Graf would *observe* this during the particular 9-second period in which she did were 100%. (That is, we're going to hold constant the fact that Graf went to the back of the house at that time, where she was sure to hear the music playing.)

Now let's consider the additional coincidence that the radio was observed to have stopped working again the day after the wedding. What are the odds that it would have stopped working during this period rather than at any other time? Let's suppose that, once a radio has stopped working and then surprisingly begun working again, it's pretty probable that it will stop again within a short period of time. Let's say the probability of its stopping again within the first 24 hours is about 1 in 5. Multiplied by the probability of its being observed to start when it did, we now have a chance probability for this combination of events of 1 in 3.94 million.

And we still have one more element of the coincidence to add: the fact that the radio was playing a love song. If we knew how Shermer and Jennifer fiddled with the tuning of the radio before putting it in the drawer, we could get a better idea of the improbability of a love song's playing when the radio came on. After all, if they had made no effort to tune the radio to a local station, the fact that it got any clear reception at all would be quite improbable. But let's assume that one of them *did* set the tuner to the frequency of a local station. And let's say, for illustrative purposes, that 20% of air time on that station is dedicated to love songs. That now brings the chance probability for this coincidence to 1 in 19.7 million.

That might seem quite impressive, but remember that we haven't yet considered all of the alternative observations that Graf might have made during the nine seconds of attention it took her to observe this one and what proportion of them would have been at least as personally significant to her state of mind. Unfortunately for us, this determination is one that is almost impossible for someone other than the subject in question to make with any accuracy, because only that person has the necessary detailed knowledge of their internal, mental landscape.[17] Nevertheless, we can mention a few alternative observations that Graf might consider when making this determination. For instance, instead of hearing her grandfather's radio, she might have caught a glimpse through the window of a rare bird that was exactly the kind that her grandfather used to love spotting outside their home in Germany. Or one of Shermer's relatives may have unknowingly put on the stereo the song that Graf and her grandfather used to dance to when she was a child. Only Graf knows the range of symbols that she would strongly associate with her grandfather. The radio certainly would be high on the list, as its connection to him is unambiguous, but it is likely not the *only* such symbol. Let's say that the probability of observing some other coincidence at least as significantly related to her grandfather in the nine seconds it took to observe the radio coincidence is somewhere in the neighborhood of 1 in 19.7 million, the same probability we assigned to the coincidence that actually occurred. This estimate is pretty arbitrary, but it's hard to avoid arbitrariness given how little we know about Graf's total state of mind during the wedding. Combined with the radio-related probability we already came up with, this gives us an estimate of the probability of such a significant coincidence's being observed by Graf in those nine seconds as 2 in 19.7 million, or 1 in 9.86 million.

But Graf would also need to consider if there were other aspects of her mental state unrelated to her grandfather that had the same level of salience for her at the time of her wedding. Sure, she was thinking of her grandfather, but maybe she was also thinking about her mother, and maybe observing an event related to her mother would have felt just as significant. For illustrative purposes, let's assume she was missing her mother just as much as her grandfather. If the chance of a coincidence related to her mother was equal to the chance of a coincidence related to her grandfather—and that seems to me a reasonable assumption in the absence of any information about differences between the two—then the probability of her observing in those nine seconds a coincidence as personally significant as the one she did observe now goes up to 2 in 9.86 million, or 1 in 4.93 million. Multiplied by the 9 seconds it took her to make the observation, we arrive at an expected frequency of once every 44.4 million seconds, or once every 1.4 years. Granted, this is a very conservative estimate (conservative in its tendency to

[17] Skeptics of paranormal coincidences have observed that people's coincidences tend to appear more striking to them than to other people. See, for instance, Ruma Falk, "Judgment of Coincidences: Mine Versus Yours," *American Journal of Psychology* 102, no. 4 (Winter 1989): 477-93. However, this difference in strikingness is precisely what we should expect given that the person who experiences the coincidence is the only one who knows exactly what they were thinking or feeling at the time, and thus how closely the coincidental external event corresponded to their state of mind.

overestimate the frequency with which such things should happen by chance), and the language of Shermer's article conveys that he took the coincidence to be much more improbable than this. If we had more accurate knowledge of Graf's state of mind at the time of the coincidence and of the probabilities related to the electronics involved, we could calculate a more accurate figure.

Some Further Considerations

Now that I've explained how to calculate expected chance frequency, I want to make some further comments about what this expected frequency can and can't tell us. It *can* tell us how often we should expect by chance to encounter coincidences at or above that particular level of improbability. That is, it gives us a control statistic against which to compare our actual rate of observation, to determine whether it is above this baseline. The virtue of this approach is that it allows us to show that certain coincidences—like that recounted by Paquette—are *so* improbable that it is extremely unlikely that we would ever encounter them, even in thousands of lifetimes, purely by chance.[18]

However, this method does *not* show that coincidences occurring at, or even below, the baseline can't be evidence for something besides chance. Those coincidences could still be evidence for some non-chance influence if they are distributed over time in a way that is better explained by a non-chance hypothesis.

Consider, for instance, the commonly made observation that people experience stronger and more frequent coincidences during times of heightened emotion or stress. This is probably one of the primary reasons that coincidences have been of such interest to psychiatrists. Jung is the most famous example, but others include M. Scott Peck, Ian Stevenson, and, more recently, Bernard Beitman. Psychiatrists as well as parapsychologists (people who study paranormal psychology) have hypothesized that strong desire and need produce powerful psychic effects in the external world.[19]

---

[18] If the expected frequency of a coincidence as improbable as Paquette's is 1 in 3 million lifetimes, then the probability that such a coincidence would occur sometime in 1,000 randomly chosen lifetimes is 0.0333%. In 10,000 lifetimes, it is 0.333%. And in 100,000 lifetimes, it is 3.28%.

[19] See, for instance, Stephen E. Braude, *Immortal Remains: The Evidence for Life after Death* (Lanham, MD: Rowman & Littlefield, 2003), 13. Also, Ian Stevenson has noted that life events known to have particular psychological significance are unusually frequent in case reports of seemingly psychic phenomena. He writes, "Death has special importance in spontaneous case reports because it is obviously unique for each person, but a number of other events can qualify almost as well,

Now, many skeptics actually concede that people experience stronger and more frequent coincidences during periods of heightened psychological need, but they explain this non-random distribution as the result of people's being more attentive to coincidences during such times. There's no objective increase in the number of significant coincidences, they say, just an increase in the number people notice. However, the time-slice method for finding expected chance frequency allows us to control for potential observation bias. Armed with this method, we don't need to know how many coincidences people are ignoring when they are not in a state of heightened psychological need. We only need to estimate how much time a particular person or group spends in such a state and measure whether the coincidences experienced by them in that state exceed the expected chance frequency *for that period of time.*

Another characteristic that could justify our restricting our attention to particular time periods is the presence of a subjective feeling that something psychic or otherwise paranormal is about to happen. (By "paranormal," I mean something not accepted by the reigning scientific paradigm. So-called "paranormal" phenomena may actually be the norm.[20]) Jung mentioned this sort of feeling in his classic essay "On Synchronicity,"[21] and the coincidence literature affords abundant examples. Paquette's case is one, and my own feeling that whatever was under my doormat would be a coincidence is another.

In a related vein, Stevenson writes in a discussion on testing the precognitive properties of dreams that "the proper comparison to be made is not that between all dreams and all events, but that between dreams (or other experiences) thought by the subject to be significant (at the time they occurred) which are veridical and those which are not."[22] Dr. William Braud, too, proposes using a feeling that he calls "anomalous attention" to predict which words in a person's experience are likely to be repeated in the near future at a rate greater than chance.[23] An excellent example of this feeling's arising in the context of reading comes from a young philosophy student (also named William), whose account is included in Joachim Soulières' book *Les coïncidences.* William says he has experienced this phenomenon several times, but he provides a specific example in which he felt a "short-circuiting"

---

e.g., birthdays, births of a first son, or (for most people) the date of marriage" ["The Substantiality of Spontaneous Cases," *Proceedings of the Parapsychological Association* 5 (1971): 91-128, p. 114].

[20] See, for instance, James C. Carpenter, *First Sight: ESP and Parapsychology in Everyday Life* (Lanham, MD: Rowman & Littlefield, 2012).

[21] Jung, "On Synchronicity," 105-6.

[22] Stevenson, "The Substantiality of Spontaneous Cases," 113.

[23] William Braud, "Toward the Quantitative Assessment of 'Meaningful Coincidences'," *Parapsychological Review* 14, no. 4 (July-August 1983): 5-10.

sensation upon coming across the name of a certain German knight in a book by the philosopher Henri Bergson. Later that day, he was surprised to find himself reading an unconnected comic in which the main character had this same name.[24]

It does seem to make sense that, if psychic phenomena exist, their occurrence would be accompanied by a unique subjective feeling that alerts the person involved to pay attention. What is more, the occurrence of such feelings before the coincidental event is observed provides an opportunity for *predicting* psychically caused events, in much the way Paquette reports to have done. But, certainly, if we can see that the rate of coincidence occurrence during times where one has such feelings is above the baseline (even if only at a chance level overall), this, too, would provide evidence for a paranormal process in these cases. And this is, after all, the way any other phenomenon is studied: one focuses one's attention on the cases where one has reason to expect the phenomenon, and the evidence for its existence is dependent on how large the deviation from chance is *in those cases*, not on how large it would be if averaged over all cases, even those where we have no reason to expect the phenomenon.

Finally, I should mention that, even in cases where no special psychological or environmental factor can be detected, the mere statistical clustering of coincidences could nevertheless be significant. That is, coincidences could tend to happen in clusters more frequently than would be expected by chance. Dr. Gary E. Schwartz argues in his 2017 book *Super Synchronicity* that this is the case with the coincidences in his own life,[25] and this phenomenon has also been observed by Jack Kelleher, who writes in *An Atheist in Heaven* that his most striking coincidences tend to happen at the beginning of a cluster, after a long dry spell.[26]

In conclusion, there is a range of ways in which the rate of coincidence observation could deviate from the expected baseline so as to constitute evidence for a non-chance hypothesis, and there is the potential for much further research in this area.

Do Paranormal Claims Require Extraordinary Evidence?

Having presented all of this statistical information, I now want to issue a word of caution. While my hope is that the statistical method presented in this chapter will help prevent you from overlooking the significance of wildly

---

[24] Joachim Soulières, *Les coïncidences* (Paris: Dervy, 2012), 46-47.
[25] Gary E. Schwartz, *Super Synchronicity: Where Science and Spirit Meet* (Vancouver, BC: Param Media, 2017), Ch. 1.
[26] Jack Kelleher, "Jack and the Mir-ack-ulous," in Davids and Schwartz with Allison, 156-74, p. 169.

improbable coincidences as well as from putting too much stock in events that could very easily be the products of chance, I want to note the very real possibility that some people will be tempted to use this method to write off more of their "mid-grade" coincidences than they should.

Each person has their own preexisting belief in how likely it is that a psychic or otherwise paranormal event of some kind would happen to them. For instance, those who have already experienced a lot of clearly paranormal occurrences are going to think that the odds of experiencing another one are pretty good, and so even an event that is not terribly improbable on chance will make them seriously consider a paranormal source for it. Other people without much personal experience of these things may only embrace a paranormal hypothesis if they experience an event where the odds against its being mere chance are exceedingly high. These people may see this as a virtue in themselves, proving that they are not gullible or overly credulous. They may even justify this approach with an appeal to a phrase made famous by Carl Sagan: "Extraordinary claims require extraordinary evidence." However, it's important to understand that claims about paranormal processes only qualify as "extraordinary" if present evidence is strongly stacked against their existence. And this is not the case.

There is a widespread misconception that science has proven that paranormal phenomena cannot exist, or that they are at least incredibly unlikely to exist. However, in a 1982 survey of 339 council members and section committee members of the American Association for the Advancement of Science—the world's largest multidisciplinary scientific society—29% of respondents said that they considered extrasensory perception *either an established fact or a likely possibility*.[27] And that was 37 years ago, before much of the most convincing scientific research on psychic phenomena had been conducted.

Many people assume that, because so many standard scientific textbooks don't mention psychic phenomena—what scientists now refer to as "psi" (pronounced like "sigh")—science must have shown that they can't exist, or that there is no evidence of them. But that is not true. It *is* true that, for the past few hundred years, most scientific endeavor has been focused on working out laws to predict the behavior of relatively simple physical systems. It has been very successful in that endeavor, and more successful the simpler and more reliable the phenomena are. However, physics hasn't been able to predict individual human behavior with any success, and psychology and medical science are still far from having the precision of physics. Some—perhaps most—scientists assume that physics *can* account

---

[27] James McClenon, "A survey of elite scientists: Their attitudes towards ESP and parapsychology," *Journal of Parapsychology* 46 (1982): 127-52.

for everything that happens in the human body and mind and eventually will, but there is no proof of this. That's merely a belief that some scientists hold.

In actuality, the behavior of physical particles that is observed by physicists and chemists is not incompatible with the existence of psi. The fact that many scientists haven't found evidence for psi is not the same as saying that they've found evidence *against* it. The truth is that most of them haven't been looking for psi. They haven't been doing the sorts of experiments that would reveal its presence. You wouldn't believe someone who insisted that something wasn't there if you knew they hadn't bothered to look in the places where it was most likely to be found. But that is what mainstream science has done: ignored the conditions under which people claim to experience psychic phenomena.

Not all scientists have done this, however. If we want to know the actual evidence for psychic phenomena, it would make sense to listen to folks who've actually gone looking for it. Organized scientific investigation into psi began in the late 1800s, with the organization of the Society for Psychical Research in England, quickly followed by the American Society for Psychical Research. Active in these societies were some of the sharpest minds of their day, including physicist Lord Rayleigh, British Prime Minister Arthur Balfour, philosopher Henry Sidgwick, and psychologist William James. They brought scientific and philosophical rigor to a field of investigation that was only just coming into being. In the 1900s, psi research continued with Drs. J. B. and Louisa Rhine's ESP and telepathy research at Duke University, and then in the 1960s and 1970s, it exploded with research into dream telepathy, remote viewing, and children's memories of past lives. Today, several peer-reviewed journals are devoted to psi research.

What psi researchers have found is not at all what the mutism of conventional science textbooks would lead one to believe. Several meta-analyses of studies of psychic phenomena show statistically significant psychic effects. For instance, in 1987, psychologists Charles Honorton and Diane Ferrari analyzed 309 forced-choice[28] precognition experiments published in peer-reviewed journals over the preceding 52 years, experiments that collectively involved more than 50,000 people and nearly two million trials. The average effect was very small (0.020), but the odds that an effect that size would occur by chance across such an enormous sample they calculated to be 6.3×10^{-25}, or about 1 in 1,600,000,000,000,000,000,

[28] The term 'forced-choice' refers to an experimental set-up in which the outcomes that subjects are asked to predict are (randomly) selected from a fixed set of possibilities known to the subject at the time of the choice: for instance, from five different symbols printed on the backs of cards.

000,000.[29] A larger effect size (0.21) was found in a meta-analysis of 26 presentiment experiments between 1978 and 2010, and chance odds were calculated to be between 1 in 18,000,000 and 1 in 370,000,000,000, depending on whether it was assumed that the presentiment effect varied randomly between experiments.[30] Similarly, a 2017 meta-analysis of 52 dream-ESP studies between 1966 and 2016 found an effect size of 0.18 with chance odds of 1 in 3,700,000.[31] These meta-analyses and others, including several focused on psychokinesis, are all discussed in Dr. Etzel Cardeña's 2018 comprehensive review of the evidence regarding psi, which he affirms supports its existence.[32]

These controlled studies provide strong evidence that there is some level of psychic causality operating in the world—that it is not a mere illusion, a trick of the untrained mind. Nevertheless, the psychic effects observed in these controlled experiments, while comparable to those produced by more widely accepted psychological phenomena,[33] are rather small. If we are interested in evidence for large-scale psychic effects, that evidence is going to have to come largely from outside the laboratory. That spontaneous sort of evidence is the kind that fills the remainder of this book.

So here is what I want to get across about the method I've demonstrated in this chapter. All of this is just statistics—it's just about probabilities. This method can't tell you what the truth is in any particular case, only what's likely to be true, given what you know. You may be one of those people who will not embrace any paranormal explanation unless the explanation of chance is super-super-improbable. In fact, I imagine that any reader who has gotten all the way through this chapter probably has this tendency. And I want to close this chapter by pointing out that this tendency may not serve you well. It may cause you to be skeptical of the origin of genuinely paranormal events. As we will see in the next several chapters, those events may bring messages of great love and comfort, and being overly skeptical

---

[29] Charles Honorton and Diane Ferrari, "'Future telling': A meta-analysis of forced-choice precognition experiments, 1935-1987," *Journal of Parapsychology* 53 (1989): 281-308.

[30] Julia Mossbridge, Patrizio Tressoldi, and Jessica Utts, "Predictive physiological anticipation preceding seemingly unpredictable stimuli: a meta-analysis," *Frontiers in Psychology: Perception Science* 3 (October 2012).

[31] Lance Storm, Simon J. Sherwood, Chris A. Roe, Patrizio E. Tressoldi, Adam J. Rock, and Lorenzo Di Risio, "On the correspondence between dream content and target material under laboratory conditions: A meta-analysis of dream-ESP studies, 1966-2016," *International Journal of Dream Research* 10, no. 2 (2017): 120-40.

[32] Etzel Cardeña, "The Experimental Evidence for Parapsychological Phenomena: A Review," *American Psychologist* 73, no. 5 (2018): 663-77, p. 672.

[33] F. D. Richard, C. F. Bond, Jr., and J. J. Stokes-Zoota, "One Hundred Years of Social Psychology Quantitatively Described," *Review of General Psychology* 7, no. 4 (2003): 331-63.

may cause you to miss out on the full benefit of receiving those positive messages.

I want to give you the same words of caution that William Stillman issues in his book *Autism and the God Connection*: "it is healthy to be skeptical, but please don't overlook the obvious."[34] If you feel that a coincidence has great personal significance for you but you find that it's not highly improbable given the methods of this chapter, my bet is that the coincidence nevertheless *is* significant and that you should pay attention to it. Don't do anything stupid, of course. Don't bet your life savings on a race horse just because a coincidence seems to indicate it's going to win. As we'll discuss in the final chapter of this book, interpreting coincidences is not a straightforward business, and they can be misleading. But if you have an intuition or a deep conviction that a coincidence is significant, it probably is, and you should consider taking it seriously. Ponder it. Mull it over. Learn what it may have to teach you. Statistics are useful, but they aren't everything. Consider all the possible sources for your coincidence that are discussed in the coming chapters of this book and then use both your head and your heart to help you decide what to believe.

---

[34] William Stillman, *Autism and the God Connection: Redefining the Autistic Experience through Extraordinary Accounts of Spiritual Giftedness* (Naperville, IL: Sourcebooks, 2006), 146.

Chapter 2
God

We've all heard people in ancient times called superstitious because they attributed every unusual event to the action of a deity. But a belief in divine intervention isn't found only in ancient civilizations or the surviving remnants of indigenous cultures. A survey conducted in 2009 of people affiliated with the University of Missouri-Columbia found that "the most strongly endorsed explanations for coincidences were God and fate."[1] That is, more than 200 years after the advent of modern science, God and fate still rank higher among the college-educated than the naturalistic alternative of chance.

Perhaps the explanation for the prevalence of this point of view—both in ancient times and today—is not superstition but personal experience. For instance, Elizabeth Gilbert relates in her best-selling memoir *Eat Pray Love* how she and a friend wrote a petition to God asking that Gilbert's agonizing, months-long wait for her husband to sign their divorce papers would finally come to an end. Within hours of writing this petition, Gilbert says, she got the long-awaited call from her lawyer saying that it was done.[2] Perhaps Gilbert's experience is not unique. Perhaps many of the respondents to the survey at the University of Missouri-Columbia had also experienced such timely answers to their prayers.

Or perhaps some of them had more dramatic experiences, like the one a veteran shared with hospice physician Dr. Pamela M. Kircher. He told her

---

[1] Stephanie Coleman, Bernard Beitman, and Elif Celebi, "Weird Coincidences Commonly Occur," *Psychiatric Annals* 39, no. 5 (May 2009): 265-70, p. 269.
[2] Elizabeth Gilbert, *Eat Pray Love: One Woman's Search for Everything Across Italy, India and Indonesia* (New York: Viking, 2006), 30-34.

that, during the Korean War, he heard "a quiet Voice that 'told' him to remain in the tent in Korea as his group was leaving. Three times the voice said 'Not now,' and three times he hesitated. After the third time, he heard explosions outside the tent. He would have died if he had not followed the voice."[3]

A few survey respondents may even have experienced something as downright astonishing as what happened to Dr. Mary C. Neal's friends when they were trying to rescue her after a kayaking accident, but were unable to reach her across several feet of rapidly flowing water. One of them, Tom, suddenly felt as though something supernatural—even divine—was about to happen. In fact, they watched as a rock suddenly materialized in front of them, giving them a place to stand in order to reach Neal. After she was rescued and hurried out to get medical help, two of her rescuers returned to the accident site to attempt to retrieve her boat. They discovered that the rock they'd used in rescuing her had disappeared.[4]

Still other people may have encountered something not as seemingly supernatural as this but which nevertheless gave them convincing evidence for the involvement of an intelligence greater than their own. For instance, a woman named Ruby Washington reports that she was washing dishes when she heard "the voice of the Lord" tell her to call her daughter Michele. She protested that Michele was in class, but the voice was insistent, so she called her daughter and found her in her dorm room after all. When Washington asked if she was okay, Michele revealed that she thought she was pregnant.[5]

Experiences like these seem to need more of an explanation than mere chance, and we can hardly fault the woman in the last case for interpreting the voice that came to her as "the Lord's." In fact, she may very well have been correct. Then again, she may have heard an authoritative, otherworldly voice and concluded on that basis alone that it must be God, when it might have belonged to an angel, or to her own telepathically gifted unconscious.

We all tend to interpret unusual experiences in whatever way is least upsetting to our existing worldview. Those who believe in a personal, interactive God may immediately assume that coincidences or other unusual experiences have all been produced by that God. Those who believe that angels frequently intervene in human life may attribute them to angels. Others may be more inclined to belief in the action of saints, spirit guides,

---

[3] Pamela M. Kircher, *Love Is the Link: A Hospice Doctor Shares Her Experience of Near-Death and Dying*, 2nd ed. (Pagosa Springs, CO: Awakenings Press, 2013), 27.
[4] Mary C. Neal, *To Heaven and Back: A Doctor's Extraordinary Account of Her Death, Heaven, Angels, and Life Again* (Colorado Springs, CO: WaterBrook Press, 2011, 2012), 61, 78.
[5] Sarah Hinze, *We Lived in Heaven: Spiritual Accounts of Souls Coming to Earth* (Rexburg, ID: Spring Creek Book Company, 2006), 58.

dead relatives, fairies, or extraterrestrials.[6] Still others prefer to see coincidences as manifestations of the psychokinetic abilities of living human beings, or of a natural law according to which similar events tend to happen together.

The following chapters will look at these hypotheses and consider their relative merits in explaining various coincidences. The question I'll be asking is what *evidence* there is for these different explanations, both overall and with regard to specific cases. I will describe many cases where a specific entity does seem to be behind certain physical or mental effects, but it will also become clear that many coincidences do not provide enough information to confirm which of these sources is behind them. The goal of Part I of this book, therefore, is not to give you certainty about who or what is behind your own particular experiences. That may not be possible. But hopefully these chapters will help you understand the breadth of this phenomenon and open your mind to possibilities you've previously overlooked—possibilities that might shed new light on the meaning of your experience.

Is God Necessarily the Source of All Coincidences?

SQuire Rushnell is the author of a long line of books about coincidences, which he refers to as "Godwinks." Some of the coincidences Rushnell recounts are fascinating—definitely worth the read—but, at least in his first book, he doesn't spend much time analyzing what might be behind these events. He asks who coincidences have been planned or arranged by and replies, "Most people will answer, 'By God, that's who.'"[7]

I agree that there is a sense in which, if one believes that God is the author of everything that happens in the universe, God is necessarily the source of all coincidences. But then that doesn't tell us a great deal since, by this logic, God is also the author of the Holocaust. I think that those who believe coincidences are the work of God see them as somehow more *directly* God's work, and having a more obviously positive intent. They might say that any unusual occurrence that seems to have beneficent aims is attributable to God. And again, in a sense, this might be necessarily true. It might be that God is by definition behind all good things that happen in this world. And so, when we see no more immediate cause, as in another human being's helping us (being a conduit for God?), we attribute the action directly to the divine.

---

[6] On the topic of coincidences experienced in connection with possible extraterrestrial beings, I highly recommend Mike Clelland, *The Messengers: Owls, Synchronicity and the UFO Abductee* (Richard Dolan Press, 2015).

[7] SQuire Rushnell, *When God Winks: How the Power of Coincidence Guides Your Life* (New York: Atria, 2001), 161.

And yet it doesn't seem like we can rule out the possibility that there could be some invisible intermediaries: entities besides God who are able to read our thoughts and affect the physical world in such a way as to help us. Perhaps we could say that these other entities are acting on God's behalf or even as "part" of God, but it could nevertheless be very edifying—or at least interesting—to know more about who they are and how they work. We might also learn some very interesting things about the nature of the physical and non-physical worlds.

Furthermore, while it may not matter so much whether we distinguish between the work of God and that of angels or saints or our departed loved ones—since presumably all of these folks have similarly beneficent aims—a blanket attribution of all paranormal phenomena to God (or to Satan, for that matter) can be confusing or downright harmful in cases where the intent of the event is not understood and in which harm might come to an individual if the event is interpreted incorrectly.

Consider, for example, what Hindu monk Swami Krishnanand told parapsychological investigator Dr. Ian Stevenson about the Indian "sorcerers" with whom Krishnanand was acquainted. He said that their paranormal accomplishments attracted followers to them who regarded them as holy and worthy of veneration, but he noted that these performances were more likely a sign that these sorcerers were involved in perilous associations with evil spirits.[8]

Disagreements about the origins of paranormal acts go back at least to biblical times. Indeed, Jesus himself was accused of doing miracles by the power of evil spirits. In Matthew 12:24, the Jewish religious leaders known as Pharisees responded to an incident in which Jesus healed a blind and mute man by saying, "It is only by Beelzebub, the prince of demons, that this fellow drives out demons,"[9] and in John 8:48, Jesus was accused of being "demon-possessed." In the second century C. E. and afterward, we find Jewish rabbis as well as the Greek philosopher Celsus attributing Jesus's miracles to sorcery.[10]

I believe it is important not to oversimplify the question of who or what is at the root of paranormal phenomena. To respond to such events appropriately, a more careful and discerning view of the source of such events—including coincidences—is necessary.

---

[8] Ian Stevenson, "Are Poltergeists Living or Are They Dead?" *Journal of the American Society for Psychical Research* 66, no. 3 (July 1972): 233-52, p. 241.

[9] All quotations from the Christian and Hebrew scriptures are taken from the HOLY BIBLE, NEW INTERNATIONAL VERSION®.

[10] Craig S. Keener, *Miracles: The Credibility of the New Testament Accounts* (Grand Rapids, MI: Baker Academic, 2011), 25.

Similarities between Paranormal Experiences Inside and Outside of Christianity

In his 2014 book *Miracles*, Christian author Eric Metaxas relates many stories of miraculous events that have happened to him and to people he knows well. One of the goals of his book is to open the minds of Christians who believe that God exists but that miracles, though they may have happened during biblical times, no longer occur. While I identify with his aims and agree with him that extraordinary events still happen today, I do think it's problematic that Metaxas doesn't spend much time critically examining whether these events might be understood in some way other than as the direct work of the God of the Christian Bible.

Let me give an example. Metaxas recounts that a dear friend of his once lost a very important set of keys that included master keys to various buildings at her place of work. After spending an entire weekend unable to locate them, she was dropping her daughters off at their nanny's on Monday morning when she asked the nanny to please pray that she would find the keys. The nanny, as it happened, decided to pray with her right there in the driveway. When they had finished their prayer, Metaxas's friend turned to get back in her car when she *saw the keys*. They were sitting in the middle of her windshield, where they obviously could not have been just moments before.[11]

While Metaxas may think it obvious that God was the source of this coincidence, we will encounter in Chapter 4 three accounts of missing objects' "materializing" in which those involved had some reason to attribute this materialization to the spirits of deceased persons. We will also encounter in Chapter 6 accounts of living persons' apparently materializing objects. Parallels like these have led acclaimed author Michael Talbot to remark that "nearly all of the miracles performed by saints and wonderworkers of the world's great religions have also been duplicated by psychics,"[12] and these parallels are one of the reasons that we shouldn't assume that a particular coincidence could *only* have been produced directly by God.

Take as another example a profound healing reported in Metaxas's book, that of a woman with a severe nut allergy. When this woman approached Christian healer Paul Teske, he acted as he'd learned to do in

---

[11] Eric Metaxas, *Miracles: What They Are, Why They Happen, and How They Can Change Your Life* (New York: Dutton, Plume, 2014, 2015), 271. Another case of lost keys' mysteriously appearing on top of a car in response to prayer can be found in Joan Wester Anderson, *Where Miracles Happen: True Stories of Heavenly Encounters*, updated (Chicago: Loyola Press, 1994, 2009), 30-31.

[12] Michael Talbot, *The Holographic Universe: The Revolutionary Theory of Reality* (New York: Harper Perennial, 1991, 1992, 2011), 120.

these situations, by praying for God to tell him if there was anything besides her nut allergy that needed prayer. According to Metaxas,

> the words "broken heart" immediately came to him. So [Paul] quietly asked her: "Who broke your heart?"
>
> "My father," she replied, and burst into tears. Paul probed more deeply into the woman's relationship with her father and found that it was severely strained. He then walked her through a prayer to forgive her father and to "release him to God." Then Paul prayed, asking God to heal her heart. …
>
> Paul then asked God to allow the woman's nut allergy to be healed as evidence of the restoration of her healed relationship with her father.[13]

This woman who had previously made many visits to the emergency room after unintentional nut exposure proceeded that very evening to test her supposed healing by gingerly biting into a nut-laden candy bar. She had no allergic reaction whatsoever. Six months later, her migraine headaches also disappeared, and the year after her initial healing, she stopped wearing her MedicAlert bracelet, which had been her constant companion for the last 30 years.

Metaxas tells us that this woman announced to the attendees of the conference where she was healed that her healing was the work of Jesus. But is there good evidence that her healing involved Jesus? Or was that just her way of understanding a more universal phenomenon?

Compare that woman's healing to one experienced by David Chetlahe Paladin, a Navajo who spied for the United States during World War II. Paladin was captured by Nazis and tortured by having his feet nailed to the floor and being left to stand in that position for days. He was eventually sent to an extermination camp, and when the camp was liberated, he was found unconscious and remained in a coma for the next two and a half years. When he finally regained consciousness, he could no longer walk. He resigned himself to living out the rest of his life in a veterans' hospital, but when he went to say a final farewell to his people, they would have none of it. Caroline Myss, who spoke with Paladin personally, tells us that

> the elders approached David, yanked the braces off his legs, tied a rope around his waist, and threw him into deep water. "David, call your spirit back," they commanded. "Your spirit is no longer in your body. If you can't call your spirit back, we will let you go. No one can live without his spirit. Your spirit is your power."
>
> "Calling his spirit back," David told me, was the most difficult task he ever had to undertake. "It was more difficult than enduring having my feet nailed to the floor. I saw the faces of those Nazi soldiers. I lived

[13] Metaxas, 197.

> through all those months in the prison camp. I knew that I had to release my anger and hatred. I could barely keep myself from drowning, but I prayed to let the anger out of my body. That's all I prayed, and my prayers were answered."
>
> David recovered the full use of his legs and went on to become a shaman, a Christian minister, and a healer.[14]

Compare those two healings to yet another one, this one entirely secular. Sociologist Dr. William Bengston reports that he'd had chronic severe lower back pain for five years when one day a friend of his who had strong psychic talents, Bennett Mayrick, appeared to unconsciously take on the pain of one of Bengston's attacks. When the two men realized that Mayrick's pain was actually a psychic reflection of Bengston's, Bengston impulsively suggested that Mayrick heal them both. Healing was not something Mayrick had attempted before, but Bengston urged him to put his hand on Bengston's back and try it. Bengston reports,

> Ben put his left hand on the small of my back. Almost immediately it started to feel warm. Then hot. As the heat penetrated my spine, I felt my lower back grow numb in a four-inch radius, as if shot with Novocain. With Ben's hand still on my back, the numbness wore off from the outer edges in. When he removed his hand, the last spot of numbness disappeared. The entire experience lasted less than ten minutes.[15]

Bengston's pain was gone, and at the time he wrote this account, 35 years later, it had never returned. His friend went on to become a professional energy healer, and in time, Bengston also learned to heal through his hands.

As you can see, one behavior of Christian healers that strongly resembles that of secular psychics is their telepathic "tuning in" to the malady someone is facing. In the first story above, Paul Teske prayed for knowledge about the woman's condition, and words came to his mind that proved accurate. However, this sort of thing often happens without any prayer for information's being made beforehand. Pastor Bill Jackson reports that the words "carpal tunnel" came to his mind when a certain man walked past him. When he asked the man about this, he said that he was having surgery for his carpal tunnel next week. Jackson prayed for him, and he was healed, sparing him the need for surgery. The man converted to Christianity.[16]

---

[14] Caroline Myss, *Anatomy of the Spirit: The Seven Stages of Power and Healing* (New York: Three Rivers Press, 1996), 164-5.

[15] William Bengston with Sylvia Fraser, *The Energy Cure: Unraveling the Mystery of Hands-On Healing* (Boulder, CO: Sounds True, 2010), 31-32.

[16] Keener, 488, from a personal interview conducted Nov. 13, 2007 in Corona, California, but also reported in Bill Jackson, *The Quest for the Radical Middle: A History of the Vineyard* (Cape Town: Vineyard International, 1999), 131.

There is also a tradition in Christianity in which healers who are unable to travel to see a sick person face to face send some object that is then used to bless (and hopefully heal) the person. For instance, in one modern example of this practice, Latter-Day Saints Apostle Howard W. Hunter endeavored to facilitate the healing of Sarah and Brent Hinze's sick, dehydrated infant by holding in his hand a handkerchief and one of the girl's baby booties, which Brent then placed in her hospital crib.[17] This practice, too, has secular parallels. As incredible as it may sound, the same William Bengston who was healed of back pain in the account given above has subsequently cured various ailments through sending patients cotton that has been mentally "charged."[18]

Testing the Spirits

Now, Eric Metaxas is not unaware of the existence of beings besides God capable of exercising paranormal powers. In one of the cases he describes, Metaxas does consider that a departed loved one may have been involved—when a Catholic woman prayed for the intervention of her departed husband and appeared to receive a sign of his presence.[19] And, in a few cases, Metaxas considers that angels may have played a role—for instance, when a mysterious hand rescued a girl from drowning,[20] or when another girl was falling from a bridge and was suddenly caught and set down on the ground 10 feet away from where she'd gone over.[21] (We'll consider many more examples of both of these kinds of cases in the next two chapters of this book.) Besides departed loved ones and angels, Metaxas also recognizes that invisible beings with less beneficent intentions may sometimes intervene in our lives. He notes the existence of demons and says that Satan may masquerade as an angel, so we have to be careful to "test the spirits" that come to us and make sure that they are of God.[22]

I agree with Metaxas that we need to "test the spirits": to not accept something as good or enlightened just because it is paranormal. In the words of Christian academic Dr. Paul G. Hiebert, "power is not self-authenticating."[23] In fact, the need to "test the spirits" will become a frequent

---

[17] Sarah Hinze with Laura Lofgreen, *The Memory Catcher* (Provo, UT: Spring Creek Book Company, 2012), 64.
[18] Bengston with Fraser, 191-6.
[19] Metaxas, 294-303.
[20] Metaxas, 236.
[21] Metaxas, 244.
[22] Metaxas, 235.
[23] Paul G. Hiebert, *Anthropological Reflections on Missiological Issues* (Grand Rapids, MI: Baker, 1994), 239.

refrain of this book. Where I differ with Metaxas is with regard to *how* one tests the spirits.

Metaxas believes that the only reliable reference against which to test a paranormal experience is the Christian Bible and its portrayal of God's character.[24] However, Metaxas doesn't explain in *Miracles* how he knows he can trust the Bible, nor why he thinks it more authoritative than other religious texts, ancient or modern. I'm not going to enter here into a debate about biblical authenticity or inerrancy, but I do want to make one fundamental point that applies to any texts that anyone from any religious persuasion may take as authoritative. That point is this: each of us must ultimately make our own judgment about whether a particular text is a worthy guide to the nature of God and reality. Ultimately, we must each decide whether the stories and information related by a book ring true to our own experience and our own heart's knowledge. Here's a thought experiment to help make this point.

Imagine that someone presents you with a document showing that great supernatural acts were performed a few thousand years ago by a certain fellow we'll call Hejebobel. The authenticity of this document has been investigated by scholars and scientists, and everyone agrees that the document is authentic and that the testimony in it is reliable; it seems this fellow Hejebobel really did do these incredible, miraculous things. But let's further imagine that the acts performed by Hejebobel intentionally brought about the painful, gruesome deaths of many hundreds of innocent people. Hejebobel, in fact, appears to be a very cruel person, albeit very supernaturally gifted. Hejebobel, furthermore, claims that he is God incarnate and lays out a lot of rules that he says people ought to live by if they don't want to incur his wrath and end up like those people who died horrible deaths. Would you believe that this guy was actually God? Would you feel an ethical obligation to follow his rules?

I don't think many of us would. But the reason we wouldn't is *not* that this guy doesn't jibe with the biblical God. (In fact, he jibes more with the God of the Old Testament than a lot of people want to admit.) We wouldn't accept this guy as God because we do not agree with his ethical approach to the world. We don't feel he is *worthy* of being revered and obeyed as God. But this is our *hearts'* telling us what to believe. And after all the historical scholarship that's been done on the Bible, it is nevertheless *our hearts* that ultimately decide whether we will accept those writings as accurate portrayals of a God who is worthy of worship. The statement that the Bible is our ultimate standard is simply not true. We always have to make a judgment about whether to take what is written in the Bible (or any other book) as reflective of the highest ethical authority.

---

[24] Metaxas, 78-79.

I believe the same is true for any paranormal encounter we have. We should do our best to inform ourselves about the wide variety of paranormal experiences had by people all over the globe and all through history, but even with all that context, we ultimately have to decide on the meaning of our own experiences. We have to listen to our own hearts and heads. The Bible can help us, certainly, but even there, we are going on faith that the Bible is worthy of our using it in the way we do. And choosing whether to believe a particular experience is from God is more an ethical and spiritual choice than it is an empirical one.

Do Paranormal Experiences Prove the Rightness of a Specific Religion?

Let's now return to Metaxas's example of the keys' materializing on the windshield of his friend's car. I assume that part of the reason Metaxas didn't feel much doubt about the divine origin of this event is the fact that it happened as the immediate result of prayer. And I'm not going to say that Metaxas is *wrong* in concluding that God did this. He may very well be right. However, what I want to emphasize is this: we should not be misled about how much this event tells us about God or God's action in the world. Specifically, we need to see this event inside a much wider context. Astonishing events like the materialization of these car keys happen to people who pray *as well as to people who don't pray*. You will encounter in this book evidence of their happening not only to Christians of many different persuasions but also to Jews, Muslims, Hindus, and atheists. What we must be very careful not to do is conclude that, because a miracle has happened to a member of a specific religion, this validates the truth of their specific religious beliefs. Just because we pray and receive a miraculous answer to that prayer does not mean that our ideas about the being who responded to our request are accurate.

Consider another analogy. When you were a young child, you might have believed in Santa Claus. In fact, you might have even written Santa Claus letters asking that he would bring you specific toys on Christmas morning. And you might have taken the fact that you received the very toys you requested as reason to continue believing that Santa Claus was real. Of course, when you got older, you discovered that the gifts had actually been coming from Mom or Dad or some other human being who loved and cared for you.

Here's the thing. Our current ideas about God and the universe are very likely just as far from the ultimate truth as our childhood belief in Santa Claus was from the reality of our parents' buying presents for us. The God that we imagine when we pray may have very little to do with Whomever is really there. Nevertheless, just as parents happily respond to their children's requests to Santa, whatever benevolent being or beings exist in our universe may be happy to respond to the requests that we address to the entities that are largely figments of our imagination. After all, as far as knowledge of God and the universe is concerned, we are like naïve (if adorable) children. But, just as getting what you asked Santa for doesn't prove that Santa exists, having your request to a specific deity or spiritual being granted doesn't prove that that being exists or exists the way you imagine them. This is a point we must keep in mind throughout this book, especially when coincidences happen as the result of specific requests. These coincidences are often good evidence that *something* is going on, but they don't tell us precisely what that something is, and we must be careful not to jump to conclusions.

Let me illustrate the importance of this with an example from my own life. I grew up attending a Southern Baptist church, and I very strongly believed in the God I was taught about in my church, as well as in the idea of salvation through Jesus Christ. As a teenager, I was dedicated to reading my Bible, praying, and sharing my faith with my non-Christian friends. However, when I went away to college (at a Christian school), I began to learn more about other perspectives and for the first time became capable of perceiving the world from another point of view. I was shocked when atheism quickly came to seem more convincing to me than the evangelical Christian view of things I'd had until then. This was very distressing, as this new perspective alienated me from my parents, my friends, my boyfriend, my school, indeed the entire Christian community in which I'd lived my whole life. I didn't *want* to be an atheist, but I suddenly found myself unable to locate any clear evidence of God's existence. I prayed many desperate prayers for God to reveal himself to me and keep me from giving up on my faith, but I didn't get anything that seemed like a response. After about a year of this, I formally wrote out all of my doubts and tearfully pleaded with God one last time to do something—*anything*—to show me that he was there, so I wouldn't have to walk away from my faith and distance myself from so many people I loved. But nothing happened. So I became an atheist.

That's not the end of the story, however. Nine years later, I had fully adjusted to a new identity outside the church. It had not been easy learning to feel comfortable in the world outside Christianity, but I had done it. I had made a new life for myself. It was at that time that another crisis struck—the loss of the man I was about to marry. It was in the midst of the deep grief and confusion that followed this event that I suddenly began to receive the kinds of signs I had once so fruitlessly begged God to provide. Suddenly I was surrounded by events that convinced me that I was not alone with my suffering, that Someone was there and desirous of my knowing it.

As this new reassurance began to soak in, I started to wonder why, if Someone *was* there, they hadn't answered me nine years before when I'd been so desperate for some sign of God's existence. What I began to realize was that, if I had experienced these same signs during my college years, I would have immediately plunged back into the same religious life I had led up until then. I would have taken them as signs that the religion I'd grown up in was true and that my often guilt-driven adherence to it was appropriate. I can only surmise that that is not what that Someone wanted for me. Yes, they eventually wanted me to know that I was not alone in the universe, that someone was watching over me, but only once I had weaned myself from the limiting religious beliefs of my childhood and was able to greet paranormal happenings with a wider perspective as to their meaning.

Let me be absolutely clear that I do not intend to say in this chapter that God does not exist or that God is not at the root of many of the coincidences we experience. I only want readers to understand that the mere fact that they experience miraculous events in the context of a particular religion does not mean that that religion is infallible, or even that it's generally accurate. Extraordinary experiences happen to too many different people, from too many different walks of life, to be definitive proof of any particular religion's accuracy.

Some Christians are well aware of this fact and freely admit it. For instance, Mary Neal, the Christian surgeon who wrote about her near-death experience in *To Heaven and Back*, states in the introduction to her book, "Miracles appear to be universal and are reported by Catholics, Protestants, Muslims, and Hindus."[25] Indeed, the Pew Forum on Religion & Public Life found just that in its 2007 U.S. Religious Landscape Survey. Among many other questions, it asked Americans of various religious affiliations whether they had "ever experienced or witnessed a divine healing of an illness or injury." Below is the percentage of people who responded "Yes," broken down by religious affiliation.

Protestant	43%
Catholic	27%
Mormon	69%
Jehovah's Witness	7%
Orthodox	34%
Jewish	17%
Muslim	27%
Buddhist	22%
Hindu	30%
Unaffiliated	15%
All Americans	34%[26]

[25] Neal, xvii.

[26] The Pew Forum on Religion & Public Life, *U.S. Religious Landscape Survey: Religious Beliefs and Practices: Diverse and Politically Relevant* (Washington, DC: Pew

And that list is certainly not exhaustive of all those who have experienced miraculous healings. Sociologist Dr. James McClenon states in his book *Wondrous Events: Foundations of Religious Belief* that "people from all cultures relate stories of spontaneous, miraculous cures."[27] And Christian New Testament scholar Dr. Craig S. Keener, author of the two-volume work *Miracles*, provides more than half a page of tightly condensed references to "the massive number of modern non-Christian supernatural activity claims and beliefs around the world," including in the contexts of shamanism, sorcery, spirit mediumship, Hinduism, Native American traditions, Judaism, Muslim mysticism, Umbanda, Voodoo, Filipino spirit healing, meditation, North American folk healing, and Wicca.[28] As one little taste of the diversity of the accounts out there, consider this one related by Swiss New Testament scholar Eduard Schweizer. Schweizer writes,

> There was an Indian in Zürich some decades ago who had a dagger driven through his heart, a feat that he had demonstrated before in other places. My colleagues in the medical faculty controlled and x-rayed everything. There was not the slightest doubt that a miracle had happened; he should have been dead, but he did not follow suit and remained alive. The experiment was even repeated afterwards. Yet we did not believe in that man and he did not want to lead us to believe in his god.[29]

Despite the fact that paranormal experiences happen in all sorts of religious and non-religious contexts, such experiences do lead many people to religious conversions. For example, experiences of apparent miracles were an important element in the spread of both Buddhism and Christianity during

---

Research Center, June 2008). The Pew Forum's finding that 34% of Americans believe they have experienced or witnessed a divine healing concords with the finding of a 2015 survey commissioned by Lee Strobel and conducted by Barna Research, in which it was found that 38% of American adults believed they had personally witnessed a divine miracle. See Lee Strobel, *The Case for Miracles: A Journalist Investigates Evidence for the Supernatural* (Grand Rapids, MI: Zondervan, 2018), 30-31. And, in case you think these people are gullible because of their lack of medical training, consider the results of a 2004 survey of American physicians in which 55% of them said they "had seen treatment results in their patients that they would consider miraculous" ["Science or Miracle? Holiday Season Survey Reveal Physicians' Views of Faith, Prayer and Miracles," BusinessWire (December 20, 2004), https://www.businesswire.com/news/home/20041220005244/en/Science-Miracle-Holiday-Season-Survey-Reveals-Physicians].

[27] James McClenon, *Wondrous Events: Foundations of Religious Belief* (Philadelphia: University of Pennsylvania Press, 1994), 131.

[28] Keener, 242-3.

[29] Eduard Schweizer, *Jesus the Parable of God: What Do We Really Know about Jesus?,* Princeton Theological Monograph Series 37 (Allison Park, PA: Pickwick, 1994), 44.

medieval times,[30] and today, supernatural experiences are one of the biggest factors leading to Christian conversions outside the developed world.[31] I would say they appear to be pretty effective within the developed world as well, as evidenced by the fact that Metaxas's book contains an entire chapter on "Conversion Miracles."

Now, I don't think that those who convert to a religion because of paranormal experiences are necessarily wrong to do so. These experiences may usefully point individuals toward a faith community that will be beneficial to them, or in which they can be beneficial to others. But, again, I do not believe we can take such experiences as proof of the accuracy of a particular religious doctrine, any more than we can take the fact that the members of a particular religious congregation are kind and generous as proof that their theology is correct. Kindness and generosity are found in many different contexts—religious and non-religious—and the same is true for paranormal occurrences.

Visionary Experiences of a Variety of Religious Figures

It might be argued, however, that *certain* paranormal experiences do provide evidence for the truth of particular religious beliefs. Take, for instance, the experience of a man who was healed from chronic liver disease after seeing Jesus appear to him.[32] Or that of a five-year-old girl named Debbie who had a near-death experience (NDE) while suffering abuse in her home and encountered a being who was called by various names including "Messiah," "Rabboni," and "Savior" and who told her that she had to return to her earthly life because she needed to raise her children.[33] Tom Doyle's 2012 book *Dreams and Visions: Is Jesus Awakening the Muslim World?* recounts many experiences in which Muslims had dreams either of Jesus or of Christians that they would soon meet, and these dreams led to their

---

[30] McClenon, *Wondrous Events*, 151-67.

[31] Hwa Yung, "The Integrity of Mission in the Light of the Gospel: Bearing the Witness of the Spirit," *Mission Studies* 24 (2007): 169-88, pp. 173-5. In particular, some surveys show 90% of new Christians in China citing healing as a reason for converting. See Edmond Tang, "'Yellers' and Healers—Pentecostalism and the Study of Grassroots Christianity in China," in *Asian and Pentecostal: The Charismatic Face of Christianity in Asia*, eds. Allan Anderson and Edmond Tang, Regnum Studies in Mission, Asian Journal of Pentecostal Studies Series 3 (Oxford: Regnum; Baguio City, Philippines: APTS Press, 2005), 467-86, p. 481.

[32] R. Andrew Chesnut, *Born Again in Brazil: The Pentecostal Boom and the Pathogens of Poverty* (New Brunswick, NJ: Rutgers University Press, 1997), 81-82.

[33] Sarah and Brent Hinze, "Visions of Future Children in Near-Death Experience," presentation at IANDS 2012 Conference in Scottsdale, AZ, available at https://www.youtube.com/watch?v=kdSL-HCxl4o, 29:13-33:27.

conversion to Christianity.[34] Doesn't the appearance of Jesus or his followers in such contexts provide some evidence for the truth of Christianity?

Again, the difficulty with this line of reasoning is that Christians are not alone in experiencing extraordinary events that make direct reference to their religious beliefs. While some people have experienced apparitions, dreams, or NDEs portraying Jesus or Mary,[35] others have had similar experiences portraying Muhammad, or involving Islam in some other way. For instance, a woman who recently converted from Christianity to Islam writes on AboutIslam.net about how she saw in a dream the man who introduced her to Islam before she ever saw him in waking life.[36] On YouTube, we find the testimony of an English Protestant Christian who converted to Islam after having an "inspirational dream" of Muhammad with his hand on two white tablets, which the dreamer later determined were the Qur'an and the Sunna. He says about the dream, "It led me to respect the Prophet Muhammad as a prophet, because I wasn't sure about him before. I hadn't heard much about Islam. … I literally knew next to nothing about it." He understood from the dream that Muhammad was "legitimate before God as a prophet and someone sent by God."[37] In another testimony available on YouTube, we hear from a former Christian from Mexico who had been exploring Islam for a couple of years when a dream of Muhammad clinched his decision to convert.[38] And, in a similar story, American quadriplegic Robert Davila had been studying Islam for a while when he dreamt of a man he recognized as Muhammad. In the dream, Muhammad pointed at a crucifix that Davila kept as a reminder of a deceased friend and told him that Jesus was a man who ate food, drank water, and went to the bathroom just like other men and that he was only a prophet, not a God. He told Davila that he should follow God,

---

[34] Tom Doyle with Greg Webster, *Dreams and Visions: Is Jesus Awakening the Muslim World?* (Nashville, TN: Thomas Nelson, 2012).

[35] For a comprehensive list of reported Marian apparitions, see the website The Miracle Hunter: http://www.miraclehunter.com/marian_apparitions/index.html. According to this site, "[s]ome scholars estimate the total number of apparition claims throughout history to be approximately 2,500 (with about 500 of those coming in the 20th century alone)" (accessed August 2, 2018). See also Scott Sparrow, *Blessed Among Women: Encounters with Mary and Her Message* (New York: Harmony, 1996).

[36] About Islam, "Does Allah Speak to Us Through Dreams?", http://aboutislam.net/counseling/ask-the-counselor/self-issues-ask-about-counselor/does-allah-speak-to-us-through-dreams/ (accessed July 26, 2018).

[37] YouTube, "Christian sees Prophet Muhammad (p.b.u.h.) in Dream & Converts! Amazing Description of RasulAllah," https://www.youtube.com/watch?v=0wuFFX3M0oY (accessed July 26, 2018).

[38] YouTube, "I saw the Prophet Muhammad (ﷺ) in My Dream - Mexican Brother Umar," https://www.youtube.com/watch?v=vG8SPH7q5oc (accessed July 26, 2018).

not men. The dream, again, clinched this man's decision to convert to Islam.[39]

Some researchers who study visionary experiences (a category that includes waking apparitions, dreams, and NDEs, among other experiences) have suggested that many of the apparent differences between people's experiences can be explained by the personal or cultural interpretation that the experiencer gives to them. For instance, Drs. Karlis Osis and Erlendur Haraldsson have extensively studied apparitions that come to people when they are on their deathbeds. They remark, "If a patient sees a radiant man clad in white who induces in him an inexplicable experience of harmony and peace, he might *interpret* the apparition in various ways: as an angel, Jesus or God; or if he is a Hindu, Krishna, Shiva, or Deva."[40] However, their study concluded that the dying experience is essentially the same across cultures and religions.[41] Dr. Raymond Moody, one of the pioneers of NDE research in the 1970s, seconds this point of view in his more recent book *Glimpses of Eternity*, writing that people's religious beliefs don't generally affect the core content of an NDE or end-of-life vision. People of all different persuasions will see beings of light, for example, but the religious are more likely to identify these beings with a specific religious figure.[42]

Laboratory research into the process of telepathy also suggests that there may be a layer of interpretation added to visionary experiences by the experiencers' unconscious efforts to understand them and put them in a comprehensible context. For instance, in one dream telepathy experiment, an awake individual was attempting to telepathically insert the image of a Jewish rabbi into the dreams of a sleeping person. The dreamer instead reported dreaming of "Saint Paul" and "an Anglican minister or priest."[43]

But while mistakes in interpretation may account for some of the differences among people's visionary experiences, I'm not sure they can account for them all. For one thing, not all of the identifications made of religious figures in visionary experiences are based upon previous belief and/or expectation, as we saw in some of the conversion experiences recounted above. A few other examples of this phenomenon come from Christian physician Dr. John Lerma, who reports that one of his aged Jewish patients had visions of Mary Magdalene (about whom she knew very little,

---

[39] YouTube, "Bayyinah Dream 2014 Visit Robert Davila," https://www.youtube.com/watch?v=AWGXw9lpll4 (accessed July 26, 2018).

[40] Karlis Osis and Erlendur Haraldsson, *At the Hour of Death* (New York: Discus, 1977, 1979), 37.

[41] Osis and Haraldsson, *At the Hour of Death*, 94.

[42] Raymond Moody with Paul Perry, *Glimpses of Eternity: An Investigation into Shared Death Experiences* (London: Rider Books, 2010), 140-1.

[43] Montague Ullman and Stanley Krippner with Alan Vaughan, *Dream Telepathy: Experiments in Nocturnal ESP* (Baltimore, MD: Penguin, 1973, 1974), 112.

for obvious reasons),[44] and from NDE researcher Dr. Barbara R. Rommer, who reports two cases of Jews meeting Jesus on the other side. However, it should be noted that one of Rommer's Jewish subjects, even though he was raised in a conservative Jewish home, had primarily Italian Catholic friends growing up,[45] and the other Jewish subject was married to a Catholic.[46] So Christianity was still a prominent feature of their mental landscapes.

Another case of unexpected identification of a religious apparition comes from Osis and Haraldsson, who write in their book on deathbed visions that "benign otherworldly visitors also appeared to patients who had no afterlife or religious concerns. A sixty-two-year-old ex-Marine in New York City was dying from cancer of the prostate. He told his doctor that he was an atheist. To the doctor's surprise, the patient had a vision of Christ—which lasted a few minutes—appear in his room."[47]

This next case shows something that I take to be even more extraordinary: that the unexpected personages in visionary experiences aren't always religious figures, and that their identity can sometimes be corroborated by a third party. In March 1982, Georgia police officer Harold Welch was worried sick about his teenage son Tony, who'd run away from home a few weeks previously. Welch was sure his son had gone to Los Angeles, because of a desire he'd expressed to get into the movies. Two days before Welch was planning to fly out to LA and look for his son, he had a very real-seeming dream in which a man gave him detailed information about the precise house where Tony was located in LA—information that eventually proved true and led to Welch's tearful reunion with his son. Who was the man who supplied this vital information? Elvis Presley.

The events just recounted occurred about five years after Elvis Presley's death. Welch says he'd never had any strong feelings about Elvis one way or the other—and he'd never dreamt about him before—but of course everyone, especially at that time, knew what Elvis looked like. Welch says that the Elvis in his dream "looked just like he did in his pictures. In the dream he was about six-feet tall and he looked to be thirty years old."[48] If Welch had any emotional connection to Elvis, it was through his son, who was a big fan. When Welch found Tony in LA, Welch didn't tell him about being guided by Elvis in a dream. However, interestingly enough, Tony remarked to his father on the first night after their reunion, "Dad, it's the

---

[44] John Lerma, *Learning from the Light: Pre-Death Experiences, Prophecies, and Angelic Messages of Hope* (Franklin Lakes, NJ: New Page Books, 2009), 145.

[45] Barbara R. Rommer, *Blessing in Disguise: Another Side of the Near-Death Experience* (St. Paul, MN: Llewellyn, 2000), 103.

[46] Rommer, 103.

[47] Osis and Haraldsson, *At the Hour of Death*, 94.

[48] Raymond A. Moody, Jr., *Elvis After Life: Unusual Psychic Experiences Surrounding the Death of a Superstar* (Atlanta, GA: Peachtree Publishers, 1987), 87.

funniest thing. Two times since I've been out here I've had dreams about Elvis Presley. In both dreams he told me you would be coming to get me. He said he was worried about me. He said he would work it out."[49]

The fact that both Welch and his son had independent, coordinating dreams of Elvis makes it seem unlikely to me that they identified him as Elvis only because of a mistake in interpretation. What is more, in Chapter 4, we'll encounter many cases in which other (less famous) deceased persons provide paranormal assistance, and the consistency between those cases and this one inclines me to believe that the deceased Elvis actually had a hand in reuniting Welch with his son. Does that make Elvis divine? Although some Elvis fans may disagree, I don't think so. Chapter 4 will provide ample evidence that many other deceased persons are able to intervene in earthly affairs in very similar ways. If an extraordinary experience is to provide support for revering certain figures as divine, it can't just be because Jesus, Muhammad, or Elvis happens to appear or be mentioned in them.

Deep Conflicts in the Content of Visionary Experiences

When deciding what conclusions to draw from extraordinary experiences, we also need to consider the fact that some of the differences between these experiences go deeper than the mere identities of the persons involved. For instance, Davila heard Muhammad say in his dream that Jesus was a man who ate, drank, and eliminated just like other men and thus was only a prophet, not God. These comments seemed to constitute the core content of the dream, at least as Davila understood it, and they appear to be at odds with the contents of other people's experiences.

For instance, consider an experience had by a Muslim patient in a case reported by Lerma. While in Lerma's hospice facility, this Muslim patient had visions of "Jesus" and for a while insisted that he was just a prophet, as her religion taught. "I believe Jesus would have told me he was the Son of God after all the time we spent together," she told Lerma.[50] However, on the day of her death, she said that she saw Jesus wash her feet and tell her he was ready for her. "He said he is Jesus Christ, who died for our sins," she said. "He was crucified and died for us, Dr. Lerma. … He is standing in front of all of us now. He is all white, and the angels, my family, and other prophets are now singing to him. Oh my! He is God! The one God! My God!"[51]

The issue is not just that this hospice patient and Robert Davila had visionary experiences of different religious figures. It's that the content of these experiences seems to be directly contradictory, because they convey

---

[49] Moody, *Elvis After Life*, 90.
[50] Lerma, *Learning from the Light*, 212.
[51] Lerma, *Learning from the Light*, 217.

opposing messages about Jesus' divinity. This makes it harder to justify taking the content of either of these experiences at face value. Perhaps the contradiction between them can still be explained away as a misinterpretation and it could still be the case that both of these experiences are veridical at their core, but it would take some work to show how this could be true.

Psychiatrist Dr. Stanislav Grof has spent more than 50 years researching visionary experiences and, in particular, those that are elicited by psychedelic substances or special "holotropic" breathing techniques. He concludes that the experiences elicited in this way are a combination of (1) material that originates in the depths of the individual psyche and (2) material that is accessed paranormally, from "sources of information that are clearly far beyond the conventional reach of the individual."[52] The reading I have done gives me the strong impression that this is true of visionary experiences in general. Waking visions, meditative experiences, dreams, lucid dreams, drug-induced trips, out-of-body experiences, and NDEs all seem to combine elements derived from the psychology of the individual with elements derived from other sources in a paranormal manner. As we will see in later chapters of this book, this paranormal information can sometimes be verified empirically, but much of it cannot, including information that purports to establish or disestablish the divinity of particular religious figures. We must remember that the apparent paranormality of an information source is not a guarantee of its accuracy. Rather, it is a reminder that caution is in order.

This is true even with regard to near-death experiences. Some people think of NDEs as being something like objective tours of the afterlife and treat accounts of NDEs "as if they were videotaped, journalistic reporting of the highest factuality."[53] But the differences that exist among NDEs from different persons, cultures, and time periods show that matters are not quite so simple.[54] While I'm inclined to think that much veridical information comes to us through NDEs (see Chapter 4 for evidence in this regard), it also

---

[52] Stanislav Grof, "Psychology of the Future: Lessons from Modern Consciousness Research," http://www.stanislavgrof.com/wp-content/uploads/pdf/Psychology_of_the_Future_Stan_Grof_long.pdf (accessed October 8, 2018), 45.

[53] Nancy Evans Bush, *The Buddha in Hell and Other Alarms: Distressing Near-Death Experiences in Perspective* (2016), 171.

[54] For example, religious studies scholar Dr. Carol Zaleski writes in her book comparing medieval and modern near-death experiences, "[G]one are the bad deaths, harsh judgment scenes, purgatorial torments, and infernal terrors of medieval visions; by comparison, the modern otherworld is a congenial place, a democracy, a school for continuing education, and a garden of unearthly delights" [Carol Zaleski, *Otherworld Journeys: Accounts of Near-Death Experience in Medieval and Modern Times* (New York: Oxford University Press, 1987), 7]. Also compare modern American NDE accounts with both contemporary and historic Tibetan experiences. See Lee W. Bailey, "A 'Little Death': The Near-Death Experience and Tibetan *Delogs*," *Journal of Near-Death Studies* 19, no. 3 (Spring 2001): 139-59.

seems clear from these experiences that, wherever it is that these experiences are taking place, appearances in those realms are more malleable than in the physical world we live in as humans. For instance, beings in NDEs seem able to change the way they appear to each other according to what they most desire to project. For this reason, it must be understood that seeing (or hearing) should not equal believing when it comes to NDEs. We also need to understand that there may be many different realms within what is thought of as the "afterlife," and the beings encountered in these various realms may not all be equally knowledgeable or trustworthy. (For further discussion of this subject, see Chapter 8, "Ill-Meaning Entities.")

NDE researcher Nancy Evans Bush emphasizes in her thought-provoking book *The Buddha in Hell* that the imagery encountered in an NDE is often symbolic, like dream imagery, and that its elements spring from deep in the subconscious, where everything is open to interpretation.[55] She elaborates,

> Two things I believe are really important when trying to understand what any spiritual experience means: 1) Like dreams, visionary experiences carry their messages in symbol, not in the observable, fact-filled terms of everyday speech. Taking them as their literal representation is rarely accurate. 2) In much the same way, near-death experiences seem directed to universal elements of the human spirit and psychology generally; as experiences, they do not customarily carry doctrinal messages for specific religions, although we often interpret them afterwards in terms of the traditions we know.[56]

Nevertheless, Bush emphasizes that an NDE may include religious symbolism with which the experiencer was not previously familiar. She writes,

> I don't scoff at cross-cultural content, because my NDE included figures which I later learned were the Chinese Yin/Yang symbol. It was not until I discovered, years after the NDE, the significance of the Yin/Yang, that I could interpret the experience adequately as an intensely personal event. I now know that the presence of the symbol in my experience was not to say that Buddhism is right and Christianity wrong. It took a very long time for me to understand that neither the Yin/Yang nor the experience itself was delivering a teaching about religious doctrine but was functioning as a symbol of something else entirely—like an arrow pointing beyond itself.[57]

With those caveats in mind, I think there is still a lot we can learn from NDEs, as well as other visionary experiences, as long as we keep our

[55] Bush, *The Buddha in Hell*, 27.
[56] Bush, *The Buddha in Hell*, 12.
[57] Bush, *The Buddha in Hell*, 12-13.

discernment caps on. Near-death experiences in particular seem to offer tantalizing slivers of knowledge regarding the bigger spiritual picture and how it may or may not align with the creeds of various religions. Is it possible that, beneath the apparent differences between NDEs, there might be a common thread that allows us to piece together a consistent picture of ultimate spiritual reality? Perhaps what appear to be some obvious contradictions among them may not be contradictions at a deeper level of understanding, if we understand what the various "arrows" of these experiences are pointing to. After all, NDErs are generally trying to translate into words a body of experience and knowledge that didn't come to them in written form, and what one NDEr means by "God" or "Jesus" or "evil" or "sin" may be different from what another NDEr means. If we work to understand the variety of ways in which people use the same terminology, we may be able to discern a common truth to which they all allude.

Let me offer an example of one such apparent contradiction that seems resolvable. A woman named Kara, who had an NDE after being brutally attacked by a neighbor, was asked by Barbara Rommer what she had taken from the experience. Among other things, Kara said,

> All that stuff about sin and forgiveness and that He died for sins is hogwash. ... Since that happened, I don't judge people and everyone looks the same to me.[58]

On the face of it, what Kara says seems to contradict the statements of another NDEr, Betty J. Eadie, who says she learned in her near-death experience that

> there are many laws by which we are governed—spiritual laws, physical laws, and universal laws.... When we break one of these laws, going against that which is the natural order, we have sinned.[59]

Eadie also says,

> I understood that he [Jesus] was the Son of God, though he himself was also a God, and that he had chosen from before the creation of the world to be our Savior.[60]

Eadie appears to be affirming the traditional Christian views of sin and forgiveness through the saving power of Jesus' death on the cross, the same doctrines that Kara's NDE led her to reject. However, if one reads Eadie's

---

[58] Rommer, 190.

[59] Betty J. Eadie with Curtis Taylor, *Embraced by the Light* (Carson City, NV: Gold Leaf Press, 1992), 55.

[60] Eadie with Taylor, 44.

report of her NDE carefully, one sees that she never mentions being given knowledge about Jesus' taking the punishment for human sins. She describes "a cause and effect relationship to sin," in which "we reap the natural consequences of breaking the laws of life"[61] (a description that, interestingly, resembles the Hindu doctrine of karma). When she reviews the events of her life in the presence of Jesus, he actually tells her, "You're being too harsh on yourself."[62] She is helped to see that "forgiveness of self is where all forgiveness starts."[63] And the picture of Jesus' role as "Savior" that emerges from Eadie's NDE is this: "His mission was to come into the world to teach love."[64] Perhaps these nuances are what Kara was getting at in saying that all that stuff about sin and forgiveness and Jesus' dying for sins was hogwash. Not that sin doesn't exist or that Jesus doesn't play an important redemptive role in our world, but that the reality of these things is more nuanced than what a lot of churches teach.

Eadie also makes the interesting statement that Jesus was both the "Son of God" and "a God."[65] Is it possible that Jesus' connection to divinity is mysterious and subtle enough that it could be true to say both that Jesus is divine and that Jesus is not in every respect identical to God? Could there be a valid reason for some persons (such as Robert Davila) to experience visions in which Jesus' distinctness from God is emphasized and others (such as John Lerma's Muslim hospice patient) to have visions in which the emphasis is on his *identity* with God?

The contents of NDEs and other visionary experiences are prime examples of how essential it is, when exploring paranormal experiences, not to jump to the conclusion that their meaning fits perfectly within the bounds of any human belief system. As we'll see throughout this book, it is much more fruitful to take coincidences and other paranormal experiences as invitations to question one's preconceptions—invitations to open oneself to the greater mystery of who we are and what this world is that we're a part of.

---

[61] Eadie with Taylor, 56.
[62] Eadie with Taylor, 113.
[63] Eadie with Taylor, 116.
[64] Eadie with Taylor, 44.
[65] It should be noted that Eadie was a member of the Church of Jesus Christ of Latter-Day Saints at the time of her experience and apparently became at least somewhat more active in that church following her NDE. It's important to consider that LDS doctrine on the divinity of Jesus may have influenced her experience and/or her interpretation of it. On the other hand, parallels between her experience and LDS doctrine may also have been part of what later motivated her to become more active in that faith. See Massimo Introvigne, "Embraced by the Church? Betty Eadie, Near-Death Experiences, and Mormonism," *Dialogue: A Journal of Mormon Thought* 29, no. 3 (Fall 1996): 99-119.

Visionary Experiences that Address the Relationship between Religions

Let's now briefly explore some of the ways in which visionary experiences have appeared to address the relationships between different religions and theologies. Though we shouldn't take any of these experiences to be definitive answers on these matters, they are part of the larger context that needs to be considered when drawing conclusions about the implications of coincidence experiences.

Consider, for instance, this waking vision reported by a mother who was with her 15-year-old son as he died from complications of diabetes. She reports,

> I saw Christ swoop in and lift him out of his body—I really did. I saw my son leave his body and enter into this intense, bright light in which he and I were surrounded by scenes of his life, down to the smallest details. …
>
> The light that surrounded and illuminated his life was Christ—that much I know. But personally I didn't have the feeling that Christ cared whether anyone called him by that name or not, only that they know the love that was present and fills us all regardless of whether we realize it.[66]

Is it possible that this mother is right? That visions had by people of many different religions have a common origin and that the most important thing is that these people feel the love of the being that is at their source, regardless of what they call that being?

This idea has parallels in the teachings of Jesus recorded in the New Testament. When questioned about divergent religious practices, he said, "a time is coming and has now come when the true worshippers will worship the Father in spirit and truth, for they are the kind of worshipers the Father seeks. God is spirit, and his worshipers must worship in spirit and in truth."[67] Jesus frequently emphasized the importance of the heart versus appearances, calling the religious leaders of his day "white-washed tombs" and warning in a parable that it was difficult to weed out the wicked without accidentally weeding out some of the righteous as well.[68]

The idea of appearances' being less important than the heart is also mentioned by near-death experiencers. For instance, NDEr Teri R. says, "The most beautiful Being of White Light was there. I knew that he took on an image so that I could relate to and feel comfortable with him, but his true essence was Light and Love." The "image" he'd taken on was that of a

---

[66] Moody with Perry, *Glimpses of Eternity*, 93.
[67] John 4:23-24.
[68] Matthew 13:24-30.

bearded man with long gray hair.[69] Lucia, another NDEr, reports, "I was in front of this being, and I knew he was holy. I felt this was God appearing to me as I had always imagined him: an old man with a large beard. He had taken on this persona so that I wouldn't be afraid."[70] Still another NDEr writes, "I believe that a person's experience is unique to their mind-set and belief system. I didn't need to see God or Jesus or a human figure because I have always understood there could be a God that was a 'being' but not necessarily 'human.'"[71]

Of course, many people will ask, "But who is it *really* that gets perceived in visions as all these different religious figures?" I can't help feeling that asking this question misses the point—or, rather, misses the answer that has already been given: This being is Love. And Joy. And Peace. This being is what it is! As God supposedly told Moses out of the burning bush, "I AM WHO I AM."[72] Labels don't mean much when one has had such an awesome encounter. An NDEr named Natalie explains it this way:

> All That Is can be perceived simultaneously as a force and as a consciousness that exists within each individual consciousness and yet is separate from each consciousness or being. It might be called God, but the ideas of gods that we have are a pale and incomplete shadow of the All That Is that I perceived.[73]

Dr. G. Scott Sparrow, author of *I Am with You Always: True Stories of Encounters with Jesus*, reports the experience of a Catholic woman who was sitting in a hunting blind deep in the woods when she noticed that the sun above her had begun to "pulsate." She reports,

> I saw a face in the sun that resembled Christ. Being cautious, when I heard a voice speak to me, I asked, "Who are you?" The light vision pulsated and answered, "Some call me Buddha, some call me Christ." I said, "I don't know Buddha." And he answered, "Then I am Christ."[74]

Is it possible that Christ and Buddha have the same spiritual identity? Sparrow notes that, "like the Jesus we encounter in the Gospels, the Being who appears in these accounts seems more interested in *loving and healing* people than in answering age-old questions about his ultimate nature.

---

[69] Jeffrey Long with Paul Perry, *God and the Afterlife: The Ground-Breaking New Evidence for God and Near-Death Experience* (New York: HarperCollins, 2016), 64.
[70] Long with Perry, 86.
[71] Long with Perry, 86.
[72] Exodus 3:14.
[73] Long with Perry, 175.
[74] G. Scott Sparrow, *I Am with You Always: True Stories of Encounters with Jesus* (London: Pan Books, 1995, 1996), 88-89.

Perhaps it is because he knows we cannot grasp the truth with our minds, anyway."[75]

Near-death experiencer Howard Storm reports that he asked Jesus during his NDE whether the things written about Jesus in the Bible were true. Storm reports,

> He said that the stories in the Bible about Jesus are only a small sample of who he is and what he has done. All the books in the world couldn't contain what he has done. The stories about him in the Bible are sufficient for us to know him and what he represents. He is the revelation of the unknowable God. That is what he wants us to know. He has spoken to many people in many times, millions upon millions throughout time in our world, so that people would know the intimate, personal love of God.[76]

Physician Dr. Jeffrey Long recently did a study of the theological implications of all the NDEs shared with the Near-Death Experience Research Foundation (NDERF) between November 11, 2011 and November 7, 2014. Out of the 420 experience accounts that met the criteria for inclusion in his study, 46% were had by people who reported encountering during their NDE "specific information/awareness that God or a supreme being does (or does not) exist,"[77] and almost every one of those who encountered such information said that it answered the question of God's existence in the affirmative. Long points out that the percentage of NDErs who were aware of God or a supreme being is higher than that of those who reported experiencing a tunnel, meeting deceased loved ones, or having a life review. One of them wrote, "There is no doubt in my mind God was there.... I went from an uncertain belief in God to a certain belief."[78] Another researcher, Dr. Melvin Morse, writes that studying near-death experiences makes it practically impossible not to believe in the existence of some sort of divinity.[79]

But perhaps more interesting than the conviction of NDErs that God exists is what *kind* of God they describe: a being of profound and total love. For instance, a soldier who had an NDE in Vietnam says, "Ever since then, I know that God is. It's no longer a matter of faith or belief for me, but one of knowing because I have seen Him as He is. And He is loving,

---

[75] Sparrow, *I Am with You Always*, 4.
[76] Howard Storm, *My Descent into Death: A Second Chance at Life* (New York: Doubleday, 2005), 74-75.
[77] Long with Perry, 36-38.
[78] Long with Perry, 43.
[79] Melvin Morse with Paul Perry, *Parting Visions: Uses and Meanings of Pre-Death, Psychic, and Spiritual Experiences* (New York: Villard Books, 1994), 166.

compassionate, and forgiving—which I hadn't expected."[80] Betty Eadie reports that God/Jesus "is nothing like what I had thought. He is filled with love."[81] Romy, a Buddhist living in Israel, reports, "The light that I encountered felt supreme—unending, unconditional, immense love, a force that feels eternal, powerful, and creative at the same time. This satisfies my definition of 'God.'"[82] Consider, too, a description of the NDE had by a 27-year-old named Joan when she attempted to commit suicide:

> She recalled screaming as she went into her NDE, "God, please let me know You forgive me before I die." From a bright light came two big hands, and then a loving, gentle voice, which took away all of Joan's fear, said, "Lift up your hands. I forgive you. I forgive you. I'll give you a second chance." Joan said God was love, compassion, kindness, total acceptance, and joy, and that He had a sense of humor and made her laugh. At one point during her NDE, she said, "I was silly, Lord," and He laughed. When she held His hands, her pain left her.[83]

The fact that NDErs show such an overwhelming consistency in their descriptions of the loving, compassionate nature of God strongly indicates that their reports reflect an objective reality.

Some NDErs, however, have actually questioned beings on the other side about the rightness of various religions. Cynthia, who had an NDE at the age of 12, asked God whether only followers of one religion would get to heaven. She tells us, "He said everyone who believes and has faith, even those who don't think they do, will make it. It depends on what's in their hearts."[84] NDEr Howard Storm asked Jesus and the angels, "Which is the best religion?" and was told, "The religion that brings you closest to God."[85] Another NDEr, Jean, asked a spiritual being who was clearly superior to herself, "What is the right religion?" She says,

> The man told me: "They all are. Each religion is a pathway trying to reach the same place." … I was then told that people choose to be born into whichever religion or group that will help them achieve the lessons they are sent here to learn.[86]

---

[80] Long with Perry, 33.
[81] Eadie with Taylor, 43.
[82] Long with Perry, 127.
[83] William J. Serdahely, "Loving Help from the Other Side: A Mosaic of Some Near-Death, and Near-Death-Like, Experiences," *Journal of Near Death Studies* 10, no. 3 (Spring 1992): 171-182, p. 174.
[84] Long with Perry, 181.
[85] Storm, 73.
[86] Long with Perry, 181-82.

Betty Eadie is half Sioux but was raised in Catholic and Wesleyan Methodist schools, and she was told something very similar to this when she asked Jesus during her NDE why there were so many different churches and religions in the world. He replied that people are at different levels in their understanding of the truth and different religions fulfill different spiritual needs. Eadie affirms, "Very special people with important missions have been placed in all countries, in all religions, in every station of life, that they might touch others."[87]

I hope that I have conveyed in this chapter that coincidences and other possibly paranormal events do not, by themselves, constitute proof of the accuracy of any religion that may be associated with them. But I hope that it's also clear from the experiences so far recounted that the God portrayed in these experiences does not seem particularly worried that one know the absolute truth about the spiritual world. The spiritual beings one meets in NDEs seem generally unconcerned with what religion one belongs to or what religious beliefs one holds and much more interested in helping people give and receive love.

The Enigmatic Role of Jesus

While holding that fact in mind, I would nevertheless like to close this chapter by offering a few more examples of the enigmatic role that the figure of Jesus appears to play in paranormal phenomena. For instance, I continue to be intrigued by the way in which Jesus pops up in the paranormal experiences of people who appear to have no particular interest in his doing so.

Dr. Andrew Paquette is a writer, artist, and educator who has faithfully recorded the details of his dreams over many years and published them in the book *Dreamer: 20 Years of Psychic Dreams and How They Changed My Life*. One of the many fascinating aspects of his book is that he appears not just to have clear, detailed dreams about important future events but also to have dreams about performing various activities in a spiritual world that strongly resembles the one reported by near-death experiencers.[88] And, although Paquette professes to "dislike some major aspects of Christian doctrine," he has seen the person of Jesus appear more than once in a dream that turned out to match the content of Jewish and Christian scriptures unfamiliar to Paquette.

Furthermore, in November 2004, Paquette had a dream in which he was shown a horrific tsunami drowning enormous numbers of people and was

---

[87] Eadie with Taylor, 46.

[88] Another example of connection between dreams and near-death experiences comes from a case in which the friend of an NDEr had a dream corresponding to the NDE, at the same time as the NDE occurred. See Rommer, 83.

told by an angel that this disaster would be a sign of Jesus' imminent return. In fact, the angel showed him the tsunami three times and each time repeated the same message.[89] The following month, on December 26, 2004, the Indian Ocean tsunami claimed over 230,000 lives.

Seeing such a dream so strikingly fulfilled would likely send a lot of people straight to their nearest church. However, there is at least one aspect of Paquette's dreams that tells strongly *against* traditional Christian doctrine. Paquette notes that he has dreamed of both Jesus and God and that they are "so far from being the same, there is no comparison between the two." That is, his dreams lead him to the conclusion that, although Jesus is clearly an important figure, he is not identical with God. Nevertheless, because of the obvious fulfillment of the tsunami dream, Paquette has determined that he must "take Jesus seriously," even if he remains puzzled by the precise role that Jesus plays in the spiritual realms.[90]

My own research leads me to take much the same approach. I acknowledge, based on what I've seen, that Jesus may have special status in the spiritual world, but it is far from clear to me that his role lines up with everything in traditional Christian theology. Consider the fact that, for 2,000 years, Christians have been expecting the imminent bodily return of Jesus. It seems plausible that much of this expectation is the result of people having dreams like Paquette's. The book of Revelation, after all, describes itself as the record of a spiritual vision.[91]

Nancy Evans Bush, the NDE researcher mentioned earlier, suggests that one reason for the fact that prophecies of the return of Christ have occurred over and over down through the millennia and yet don't appear to have been fulfilled may be that their symbolic meaning has been misunderstood. "Consider the possibility," she writes, "that the non-arrival is because the prophecy is not about the world but about the self of the prophet doing the proclaiming."[92] That is, the "return" proclaimed in prophetic visions may have less to do with world events and more to do with a change taking place in the psyche of the prophet—for instance, the new space Jesus is taking up within that individual's heart. Jesus himself, when questioned by the Pharisees about when the kingdom of God would arrive, is quoted as saying, "The kingdom of God does not come with your careful observation, nor will people say, 'Here it is,' or 'There it is,' because the kingdom of God is within you."[93] I think it's definitely worth considering

---

[89] Andrew Paquette, *Dreamer: 20 Years of Psychic Dreams and How They Changed My Life* (Winchester, UK: O-Books, 2011), 248.
[90] Paquette, *Dreamer*, 261-2.
[91] Revelation 1:1-2, 10; 4:1-2.
[92] Bush, *The Buddha in Hell*, 79.
[93] Luke 17:20-21.

that Paquette's dreams of Jesus' return may be symbolic of a personal, rather than global, religious event.

I would also like to share a few somewhat humorous examples of how the Jesus encountered in NDEs can subvert traditional Christian expectations. I'm not quite sure what to make of these encounters, but it does seem important for anyone trying to draw religious conclusions from paranormal experiences to be aware of such odd, paradigm-defying experiences.

The first example comes from a young girl who said she saw Jesus in her NDE. When investigator Melvin Morse asked her what he looked like, she sketched a man in a red hat seated on a log. Morse says he resembled Santa Claus much more than the picture of the classic white-skinned, blond-haired Jesus that was hanging on the wall in her room. "Had her vision been one of wish fulfillment," says Morse, "my guess is that she would have seen the version of Jesus that hangs over her bed.[94] Unless, of course, what the girl wished for was a Jesus who was more like Santa Claus!

Jeanie Dicus, a second-generation atheist, was surprised to encounter Jesus in her NDE and told him, "I don't believe in you." He apparently smiled at her and "said the etheric equivalent of tough shit, here I am." After a little back and forth between them, he asked if she wanted to be reincarnated, and she complained that she'd only just died, couldn't she get a little break? Later in her NDE, she suddenly realized that "God was coming." "I came to know that I had needed a human-looking Christ to relate to so I wouldn't be scared," she says. "The Light came.... God was love and love was light, and it was warm and it permeated every molecule of me."[95]

Finally, consider the experience of a woman named Paige. Her NDE included a vision of Jesus and her recently deceased husband sitting together on a yellow brick wall some distance above her. Jesus was starting to reach down toward Paige, presumably to help her enter the afterlife, when Paige's husband pushed his hand away, saying that their daughter wouldn't be able to deal with losing both of her parents so close together. Jesus' reply? "You're probably right."[96] Not quite the definitive response one would expect from a deity!

Ultimately, I believe the identity of Jesus and his role in the spiritual world is a subject on which we must keep our minds open—as we must about so many of the topics discussed in this book. For now, we are going to move on to examining the role that angels might play in the production of coincidences. Later, in Chapter 10, we will return to the idea of coincidences'

---

[94] Morse with Perry, 19.

[95] P. M. H. Atwater, *Beyond the Light: What Isn't Being Said About Near-Death Experience* (New York: Birch Lane Press, 1994), 58-59.

[96] Rommer, 114.

being caused by God, once we have thoroughly discussed possible causes that are less powerful and less omniscient.

I hope that nothing in this chapter will have led you to believe that I am dismissing as irrelevant the hypothesis of God as the source of coincidences. I believe it is in fact highly relevant. But I think we can only truly appreciate *how* relevant it is by first looking at which coincidences can and cannot be explained by other, less clearly divine sources.

Chapter 3

Angels & Guides

Many religious traditions contain references to spiritual beings who are not equal to God but who nevertheless have powers greater than those of human beings. In Judaism, Christianity, and Islam, these beings are known as "angels" and figure primarily as divine messengers. The scriptures of these religions tell us that angels issued warnings to the ancient Hebrew prophets, announced to Mary the coming birth of Jesus, and revealed the words of the Qur'an to Muhammad. The Greek word for angel, ἄγγελος (aggelos), which is used in the Christian New Testament, means "messenger," as do the Hebrew and Arabic words for angel: מלאך (mal'akh) and ملاك (malāk). However, angels also perform other functions in these religions, including the heavenly worship of God and the protection of earthly places and people. And, in all three of these religious traditions, angels are known to appear not only in an intimidating, otherworldly form, but also in the guise of ordinary human beings.

Other religions, such as Hinduism, Buddhism, and shamanic traditions, also contain references to beings that could be likened to angels.[1] Although Hinduism is traditionally understood as a religion with many gods, the Devas of Hinduism could instead be understood as more akin to angels. The Sanskrit word देव (Devá) literally means "heavenly," "divine," or "shining," and while the Hindu treatment of these beings is very different from the treatment of angels in Judaism, Christianity, and Islam, it seems possible that

[1] Craig R. Lundahl, "Angels in Near-Death Experiences," *Journal of Near-Death Studies* 11, no. 1 (Fall 1992): 49-56, p. 50; and Holger Kalweit, *Dreamtime & Inner Space: The World of the Shaman*, trans. Werner Wünsche (Boston: Shambhala, 1988), Chs. 10 and 18.

belief in the existence of the Devas arose from experiences similar to those that provoked belief in the existence of angels. Similarly with the devas of Buddhism and the guides of shamanism.

If these ancient traditions were in fact based on personal experience, it raises an interesting question: whether anyone is still having these sorts of experiences today. And, as it happens, even in this scientific age, people still report experiences that they take as indicating the existence of powerful spiritual beings with beneficent intentions. In fact, a 1994 *Newsweek* article reported that 13% of Americans "have seen or sensed the presence of an angel" in the last year.[2] A 2007 survey conducted by Baylor University reported that 55% of respondents agreed with the statement, "I was protected from harm by a guardian angel."[3] And this is not just an American phenomenon. One of the best collections of angel encounter stories—*Meetings with Angels*—was written by Dutch physician Dr. H. C. Moolenburgh and contains accounts of experiences sent to him from all over the world.[4] Furthermore, many people who have had near-death experiences and other visionary encounters report meeting beings who appear to play a guiding or protective role in their lives.

In this chapter, we are going to examine accounts of the sorts of experiences that have led people to belief in angels or angel-like beings. If these experiences provide strong reason to believe that such powerful, beneficent beings exist, this will make it more plausible that these beings could be the source of some of the coincidences we experience. In fact, near the end of this chapter, we will explore some evidence that specifically links these beings to the production of coincidences.

Protection by an Unseen Force

The experience of being supernaturally protected by an unseen force is one common experience leading people to the belief that they have been in contact with an angel. Some of these examples of protection are quite dramatic. For instance, Joan Wester Anderson reports in her excellent collection of angel encounters *Where Angels Walk* the story of a woman who realized she was driving too fast through a snowy intersection and tapped the brake, only to find herself skidding straight for a pole. "Oh, angels, help me!" she cried out. Suddenly, something lifted up the car and turned it around,

---

[2] Barbara Kantrowitz and Patricia King, "In Search of the Sacred: America's Quest for Spiritual Meaning," *Newsweek* 124, no. 22 (November 28, 1994): 54.

[3] Rodney Stark, *What Americans Really Believe* (Waco, TX: Baylor University Press, 2008), 57.

[4] H. C. Moolenburgh, *Meetings with Angels*, trans. Tony Langham and Plym Peters (Saffron Walden, UK: C. W. Daniel, 1992).

and when it came back down, it was back on the correct side of the road, facing in the proper direction![5]

Another woman was stuck behind a coal truck on a tight two-lane road. She looked around it to see whether she could safely pass, and thinking the coast was clear, she moved into the left lane. Only then did she see a tractor-trailer headed directly toward her. The driver next to her tried to move over to make way for her, but there was just not enough space. Then, as she was preparing for the inevitable head-on collision, the tractor-trailer coming toward her simply disappeared. "There were five of us in the car," she says. "All of us saw the truck coming. None of us saw what happened to it."[6]

In another driving case, a man was trying to change lanes on a freeway when his steering locked up, preventing him from moving into the next lane. It was only after he'd started thinking about how he was going to get the car safely to a service station that he saw the small vehicle that had been riding in his blind spot. Strangely, as soon as the other car went past him, his steering wheel began behaving perfectly normally again, and it continued doing so for at least the next 18 months, after which time he passed the car on to new owners.[7]

An unseen force preventing a dangerous action also features in the next two stories, about women who might have otherwise severely injured—or even killed—their own children. In the first case, Emily Frank-Pogorzelski was attempting to cook dinner but kept almost tripping over her toddler, who was riding her toy horse underfoot. Exasperated, Frank-Pogorzelski was reaching down to shove the horse and her daughter far out of the way when

> [s]uddenly I felt my whole arm stop in midair, like some sort of invisible block. I didn't feel another hand or a grip, but actual paralysis, which extended from my shoulder all the way down the upper extremity.[8]

Confused about the source of this strange block, Frank-Pogorzelski looked up to see that the door to the cellar was open and, if she had pushed her daughter like she'd planned, the toddler would have ended up tumbling down the stairs onto the cellar's stone floor.

Mary Stebbins was prevented from sending her own tiny daughter to a similar fate. Having a frustrating day and believing that no one else was in the kitchen with her, Stebbins was about to slam the basement door, but she was prevented from doing so by what felt to her like "a mass of invisible matter." It was only then that she realized her two-year-old was out of sight

---

[5] Joan Wester Anderson, *Where Angels Walk: True Stories of Heavenly Visitors* (Carmel, NY: Guideposts, 1992), 43.
[6] Anderson, *Where Angels Walk*, 42.
[7] Anderson, *Where Angels Walk*, 45.
[8] Anderson, *Where Angels Walk*, 90.

behind the door and would have gotten thrown down the stairs had Stebbins not been restrained.[9]

In a slightly different mother-daughter case, Janet Dean watched in horror as her two-and-a-half-year-old daughter Debra jumped onto a wicker chair that then tipped over and sent the toddler falling out of a two-story window. Dean yelled out, "God, help!" and, at that moment, she saw her daughter's feet stop in mid-fall. The girl hung there for a brief moment, and then, "as if a camera had just been reversed," says Dean, "Debra came back through the window, feet first, and ended up standing on the chair."[10]

If you find yourself thinking this account sounds too crazy to be true, consider that the woman who reported it, Janet Dean, was likely well aware of how outlandish it sounded. People generally don't like to be ridiculed, and it takes a lot of courage for someone to relate such a strange experience—and to put their name on it. Generally, people who report such bizarre events have a great deal more to lose than to gain, and this should be taken into consideration before writing them off as liars or loonies.

Finally, here are a couple of cases of invisible sources of protection taken from Eric Metaxas's book *Miracles*. The women who reported these experiences are both personal friends of Metaxas.

In the first case, April Hernandez was about to drown when a strong hand took her arm and pulled her to safety. By the time she managed to open her eyes and look toward her rescuer, she found no one there. There were not even any footprints in the sand.[11]

In the other case, teenager Eva Meyer climbed a wooden fence that was blocking off a bridge under renovation. Only once she was over the top did she realize that the bridge was completely gone on the other side. She was left gripping the fence as her legs dangled over traffic passing below. Eventually, she could hold on no longer. She was falling through the air when an invisible force suddenly caught her. It carried her back up to the other side of the fence, setting her down 10 feet from the location where she'd gone over. Two of her friends witnessed the event, and it spooked the three of them so badly that they all screamed and ran.[12]

It might be argued that all of the experiences just described could just as easily be explained by direct divine intervention as by the action of angels. Why not conclude that it was *God* who righted the car of the woman who lost control in the intersection, or who carried Eva Meyer back over the fence

---

[9] Anderson, *Where Angels Walk*, 90-91.

[10] Joan Wester Anderson, *Where Miracles Happen: True Stories of Heavenly Encounters*, updated (Chicago: Loyola Press, 1994, 2009), 249-50.

[11] Eric Metaxas, *Miracles: What They Are, Why They Happen, and How They Can Change Your Life* (New York: Dutton, Plume, 2014, 2015), 236.

[12] Metaxas, 243-4.

and placed her on solid ground? Why do we need to appeal to the existence of angels?

In fact, I don't think we need to—yet. The foregoing experiences provide evidence for some form of protective paranormal entity, but they don't contain any aspects that would enable us to differentiate between the action of angels and the unmediated action of God. However, we have many more cases to examine, and some of these contain elements suggestive of an entity with a nature between that of a deity and that of a human being. Does that mean these entities couldn't be God in disguise? No. After all, Christianity explicitly teaches that God took on human form in the person of Jesus Christ, and it seems at least logically possible that God could appear in the form of what looks like an angel or a human being. As we learned in the last chapter, we have to be cautious at taking appearances at face value. But, at the same time, appearances do seem like *prima facie* evidence that the beings in some of these experiences have a measure of existence separate from that of God. And, as you'll see, some of them include elements that very closely match traditional conceptions of angels.

Voices

One sign of individual personality that we find in paranormal protection cases is the presence of a voice. Bernadine Jones, for example, reports that she was driving alone in her car and about to enter a curve on an unfamiliar street when a voice coming from within her car told her, "Slow down now!" This was long before in-car GPS or Siri. Luckily, Jones listened to this mysterious voice, because a moment later, a vehicle coming around the curve in the opposite direction crossed into her lane exactly where she would otherwise have been.[13]

In another case, Andrew Smith was walking along after hunting with his friend Joe when he noticed that Joe was cradling his gun on the wrong side, the muzzle pointing at Andrew's head. Before Andrew could ask him to change the position of the gun, he heard a voice in his mind say, "Andrew! Take two quick steps forward." He had only just done so when the gun fired right behind him.[14]

As we saw in the previous chapter, sometimes people take the voice they hear to be God's. For instance, a man named Ed Tuttle once felt the room fill with a powerful presence that he "knew" to be God and heard an audible voice say, "I've taken care of you for these eighteen years. I'm not

---

[13] Anderson, *Where Angels Walk*, 43.

[14] Anderson, *Where Angels Walk*, 175.

going to stop now."[15] But other people explicitly identify such voices with angels. For instance, an anesthesiologist reports that one day during rounds at his hospital, he "distinctly heard an angel" speak to him. He was in the hall making notes on a chart when the voice said, "Go into the next room to your left and see the man in there. He needs you." The doctor actually wrote this message down word for word before going on to do what it said. In the room indicated to him he found a man who was clearly close to death and who had a Do Not Resuscitate order. The patient told the doctor he was scared of dying and pleaded for his help. The angel then spoke again to the anesthesiologist and said, "Don't worry. You'll go across with him." The doctor reports that when he touched the patient's hand, they both "crossed into another dimension and into a passageway of some kind." The man was then surrounded by beings that seemed to the doctor like family members, and the man now appeared happy. When the doctor shifted his focus away from this scene, he suddenly found himself back in the hospital room, beside the patient's expired body.[16]

Other people don't identify the voice they hear with an angel *per se*, but they immediately know they've heard something unusual. The ancient Greek philosopher Socrates, for example, spoke of "the prophetic voice I have got so used to, my supernatural voice, [that] has always in the past been at my elbow, opposing me even in matters of little importance, if I was about to take a false step."[17]

The guiding voices so far mentioned could all plausibly have been inside the head of the person hearing them, but there are also cases where there seems to be a physical voice. In some cases, the voice is so like that of a living human being that those who hear it don't realize it was "otherworldly" until later. In a particularly intriguing case reported in great depth in *Where Angels Walk*, a small plane was attempting to land in dense fog in Asheville, North Carolina, when the air-traffic controller informed the pilot that (1) the air field was closed because of the fog, (2) it had no capability for instrument landing, and (3) he would need to return to Greenville to land. When the pilot protested that he was almost out of fuel and wouldn't be able to make it back to Greenville, there was a pause and then he heard the controller tell him to come in on an emergency landing.

Relying on maps, the pilot began a descent onto what he hoped was the runway. At the last minute, a voice said over the radio, "Pull it up!" He did so, and just then he saw through a gap in the fog that he wasn't over the runway but over a highway and had been about to slam into a bridge! Unsure how he was possibly going to be able to land now, he finally heard the air-

---

[15] Metaxas, 136.

[16] Raymond Moody with Paul Perry, *Glimpses of Eternity: An Investigation into Shared Death Experiences* (London: Rider Books, 2010), 159.

[17] Plato, *Apology*, 40a, trans. Tom Griffith.

traffic controller say, "If you will listen to me, I'll help you get down." In spite of the fact that he'd previously said the airport didn't have the necessary equipment to perform such a landing, the controller proceeded to guide the pilot step by step through the landing process. The pilot saw nothing but fog until the controller finally said, "You're right over the end of the runway. Set it down…now!" And indeed, there he was, able to drop right through the fog to a safe landing. Once he'd taxied to a stop, the pilot thanked the controller for possibly saving his life, but the controller said he had no idea what he was talking about. They'd lost contact with him after telling him to go back to Greenville and couldn't believe it when he suddenly appeared on the runway.[18]

We should note as well that there are many cases in which guiding voices are recognized as belonging to deceased persons. For example, one man heard his deceased mother's voice telling him to take another route to work and thus avoided a 10-car pile-up in the fog.[19] Another man heard his deceased son tell him, "Watch out, Dad!" as he approached a railroad track. The voice stopped him just in time to not get hit by a train.[20] And Joel Rothschild was saved from being hit by a huge truck when he sensed his deceased friend Albert saying, "Stop the car!", even though the light in the intersection was green.[21]

In another case similar to those where mothers felt supernaturally restrained from making movements that would have harmed their children, an alcoholic man repeatedly tried to beat his wife but felt his hand restrained each time. His child, who is now grown, reports that he saw someone holding his father's hand back, and that it was a man in a sea officer uniform. His mother explained afterward that this was a deceased friend of hers.[22]

Consider also the case of teenager Katie Allred, who was in a violent car accident that took the car over an embankment and into some woods, killing the driver. The entire car was mangled, except for an area about two feet wide directly around where Allred sat. As Allred's aunt said afterward, "it looked like someone had put their hands over her and sealed her from the wreck." When the car came to a stop in the woods, Allred felt someone or something lift her out of the vehicle. Disoriented, she was trying to figure out where to go when she saw a glowing apparition of her recently deceased

---

[18] Anderson, *Where Angels Walk*, 22-26.

[19] Pamela Kircher, *Love Is the Link: A Hospice Doctor Shares Her Experience of Near-Death and Dying*, 2nd ed. (Pagosa Springs, CO: Awakenings Press, 2013), 69.

[20] Kircher, 69.

[21] Joel Rothschild, *Signals: An Inspiring Story of Life after Life* (Novato, CA: New World Library, 2000), 108.

[22] Erlendur Haraldsson, *The Departed Among the Living: An Investigative Study of Afterlife Encounters* (Guildford, UK: White Crow Books, 2012), 162.

grandfather, pointing in a particular direction. She followed his indication and was able to reach the road and get help.[23]

The fact that unusual protection is in some cases identified with known individuals leaves open the possibility that, even in cases where it is not so identified, the one playing the protective role may be the spirit of someone who has passed on. In fact, some people and traditions refer to the spirits of the deceased as "angels." We will look at evidence for the intervention of spirits of the deceased in great depth in the next chapter. For now, we should just keep this possibility in mind as we continue to look for evidence for the intervention of spiritual beings who are something *other* than deceased human beings.

Disappearing Acts

We're now going to turn to some cases in which the manifestation involves more than a voice. In these cases, someone intervenes who appears to be a human being, and yet there is something about them that makes them seem not quite of this world. Often, it's the fact that this person seems to come from nowhere and disappears again into nothing.

The first case in this category happened to the son of Joan Wester Anderson. It's the experience that prompted her to begin researching angelic encounters. Anderson's son, Tim, was traveling home from college for Christmas, driving with his roommate across the Midwest on a night with a record windchill of -80°F, when his car's engine sputtered and stopped far from any sign of life. All the two young men could do was pray that they would somehow be rescued before they froze to death. Suddenly, they noticed the headlights of a vehicle just behind them and to the left, even though they hadn't seen anyone approaching. It was a tow truck, and the driver offered to hook up chains and pull them. When they'd been safely delivered to the home of a friend in Fort Wayne, Indiana, Tim was scrambling to borrow some money from his friend to pay the tow truck driver when his friend pointed out that there *was* no tow truck. Tim's car was alone at the curb, though no one had heard the driver unhooking the chains or driving away. Tim ran back outside, only to discover that there was only one set of tire tracks in the snow: those of his own car.[24]

In another disappearance case, a woman ran out of breath while swimming in the middle of a big lake but was too far from shore for her cries to be heard by those on the beach. She prayed for help and suddenly caught

---

[23] Dianne Arcangel, *Afterlife Encounters: Ordinary People, Extraordinary Experiences* (Charlottesville, VA: Hampton Roads, 2005), 21.
[24] Anderson, *Where Angels Walk*, 4-5.

sight of a boat floating near her. However, when she got to it, she discovered that it had no oars and appeared to be anchored in some way. So she continued to yell for help. A man then appeared swimming near her, even though she'd previously seen no one else swimming anywhere. He said he was a "safety inspector" and that one of his jobs was "saving lives in water." He said he'd stay with her the whole way back to shore and help her if she ran out of energy. When she was able to swim all the way back, she turned to point out her rescuer to her friends, but there was no one there. And the resort apparently didn't employ any lifeguards or "safety inspectors."[25]

Stephanie Boudreaux writes about driving along a bayou in Louisiana with her mother and being annoyed that the woman in the car in front of them kept braking and slowing down. Eventually, this woman was crawling along at a pitiful 25 miles per hour on the highway. Finally, she turned off, making a right turn onto a shell road. Boudreaux says, "I watched her for a moment, then looked back at the road. When I looked for her again, she was gone. She had disappeared really quickly for someone who was driving so slowly before." As Boudreaux and her mother drove on, they discovered an accident that had just occurred in a curve of the road: a tractor-trailer had collided with a car. It appeared that the slow driver in front of them had prevented them from getting caught up in this accident. Furthermore, it was after they had passed the accident scene that Boudreaux realized what road they had been on and that *there were not any shell roads on the right side of that road*, because on the right side was the bayou. "Yet we both saw her," writes Boudreaux. "She definitely turned right!"[26]

Raymond Herzing couldn't find anyone to care for his aging mother, who was a bit of a pill. He prayed to God for help, and "some time later," a delightful woman showed up at his mother's front door. She said that he should call her "Angel," that she could stay for a year or so to take care of his mother, and that they could settle up the bill for her services at some later date. When Raymond's mother died about a year later, "Angel" disappeared without a trace, never receiving a single dollar in payment for her year of work.[27]

Perhaps the strangest disappearance case I've come across is that of William N. Lindemann. Lindemann was a young outdoorsman who decided one cold February morning to go for a walk on a frozen lake several miles wide. While he was walking, a storm came up and turned into a blizzard so thick he lost his orientation, becoming snow blind. Afraid of freezing to death, he prayed for help to find his way. That's when he heard the foghorn of the rescue station he knew to be only blocks from where he lived. Meanwhile, a voice counseled him to be careful of the breakwater, then to

---

25 Anderson, *Where Angels Walk*, 39-41.

26 Sophy Burnham, *Angel Letters* (New York: Ballantine Books, 1991), 29-31.

27 Anderson, *Where Angels Walk*, 195-7.

stay to the right and climb the concrete wall when he came to it. Eventually, he saw the light of the rescue station and made his way to the door. Lindemann tells us what happened next:

> The next thing I felt was being half pulled and half carried inside. A man with dark hair and a beard was there with hot coffee brewing.
>
> After asking me what I was doing, he said he thought he had seen me or someone out on the lake coming in this direction. Thinking the foghorn might help, he set it off. "Good timing," I responded. When I asked him why he was there in the middle of winter, he said he was finishing some research. When I finished my coffee, I decided to go. We said good-bye, and I walked home.[28]

When Lindemann got home and recounted his story to his roommates, one of them said there was no way the rescue station had been open. But of course Lindemann knew it had been, because he could still taste the coffee in his mouth! However, he went back to the rescue station the following day, and he found it locked. In fact, "[t]he door was nearly buried in a drift, which showed no signs of anyone having traveled there." Lindemann says, "I dug through the drift to the door and read a sign: CLOSED FOR WINTER, with inclusive dates from fall to spring. I called the county sheriff's department and was told no one had access during the winter and no one had been there the day before. I called the university and was surprised to hear the same story."[29]

White (and Black) Clothing

In some cases of "angels in disguise," the person suspected of being an angel is specifically noted as being dressed in white. For example, 12-year-old Mark Durrance was bitten by a rattlesnake while roaming the fields around his house. The venom hit a main vein, and no one could understand how the boy had somehow managed to make it the more than 150 yards back to the house and up the 13 steps to get inside and get help. Even though his parents immediately rushed him to the hospital, he was in a coma by the time he got there. It was only days later, when he'd emerged from the coma and been taken off the respirator, that he was able to tell his parents what had happened: a "man in white" had carried him home. When asked what he looked like, the boy said, "I never saw his face, only from his shoulders down. But he had on a white robe and his arms were real strong." The boy also said

---

[28] Burnham, *Angel Letters*, 41.
[29] Burnham, *Angel Letters*, 42.

that the man told him that he was going to be very sick but not to worry. Once he'd carried the boy up the steps, he was gone.[30]

In this next case, the rescue is spiritual rather than physical, but white clothing again makes the rescuer stand out. An emergency room doctor in a bad part of San Francisco had seen so many terrible things that she had ceased believing in God. Then one day she went hiking in the Sierras, and the beauty of the setting was so great that she felt compelled to pray for faith. She got down on her knees and prayed, "Let me know that you exist. I must have a sign, or I will go crazy, I will lose my reason to live." A woman dressed completely in white came around a bend in the trail and paused in front of the doctor. She said her name, followed by the phrase, "Go with God," and then departed.[31]

But if white clothing is rather common in stories of angelic rescue, I know of at least one case in which a rescuer stood out because he was dressed all in black. Sophy Burnham relates in *A Book of Angels* how she once fell skiing and was hurtling toward a precipice when a lightning-fast skier zipped in front of her and halted her slide. Unlike all the other folks on the slope, who wore bright colors, her rescuer was garbed entirely in black. He didn't speak to her, and he seemed to disappear in paranormal fashion.[32]

Selective Visibility

In a couple of the stories we've seen so far, there is the suggestion that the person who provided help might not have been visible to everyone involved. In other stories, this selective visibility is made more obvious and lends support to the view that the helper is not a human being. Consider the following experience recounted by Eric Metaxas.

John Bechtel, Nancy DeMoss, and Scott Hall were attempting to travel back to Hong Kong after a trip to Changsha, China, 400 miles away. They needed to be back as soon as possible in order to depart for an upcoming trip to the Philippines. Unfortunately, their flight was delayed for two or three days. They went to the train station, but it was Chinese New Year, and there were no available tickets. They couldn't even manage to find anyone who would sell them a ticket for the handsome sum of 200 dollars, when the original cost was only nine. Nothing they did seemed to work.

Then, suddenly, a Chinese woman approached Bechtel and asked him in perfect English if there was anything she could help him with. When he

---

[30] Anderson, *Where Angels Walk*, 61-66.

[31] Melvin Morse with Paul Perry, *Parting Visions: Uses and Meanings of Pre-Death, Psychic, and Spiritual Experiences* (New York: Villard Books, 1994), 14.

[32] Sophy Burnham, *A Book of Angels: Reflections on Angels Past and Present and True Stories of How They Touch Our Lives* (New York: Ballantine Books, 1990), 233-7.

explained their predicament, she said, "Come with me." She led the group towards the VIP entrance, where they had previously had a not-so-pleasant encounter with the guards. This time, however, the guards saluted and let them pass. The group then followed their guide through a second door and onto the train platform. From there, she had them board the train, and she showed them to a private compartment, when all they'd been hoping for were regular seats.

Bechtel and his companions were busy stowing their luggage when Bechtel realized he needed to offer this kind woman a tip, but she was already gone. He raced off the train and approached the employee stationed at the door through which they'd come out onto the platform. "Can you tell me where the woman is with the hat who brought us through here?" Bechtel asked, but the employee assured him that no one with a hat had accompanied them when they came through the door. In fact, the employee said there had been no one with them at all. "There were four of us," Bechtel said. "No, there weren't," insisted the employee. "There were three of you." Bechtel checked at another door, but the woman there said she'd seen him go through the first one, and repeated that there had only been three people in his group, not four. When he went back to the first woman and asked why she'd let them on the train, she said, "Because I was supposed to." When he asked who'd told her this, she said, "I just knew I was supposed to."

The wonders continued during the train ride. Food was brought to their compartment, and when the men who brought it were asked why, they said there'd been a note in the kitchen that they were supposed to bring food to that compartment. Upon their arrival at their destination, the passengers were expected to show their ticket, as was customary in China, but they realized they didn't have one. Bechtel told the ticket man, "We don't have a ticket." "I know you don't," he replied. "Thank you very much. Carry on." And that was that.[33]

It would seem that Bechtel and his companions were aided on their journey by a being that appeared human to them but that didn't appear *at all* to others in their vicinity. In other cases, however, the being with selective visibility has more otherworldly features. For instance, a three-year-old boy running through his living room tripped and was about to fly into the corner of a table when his mother saw him suddenly stop in midair. "Within a few seconds," relates Joan Wester Anderson, "he stood straight up again and ran on." Though the mother herself couldn't see the responsible party, the next day during playtime, her son suddenly volunteered his own perception of the event: "I saw a beautiful lady. With wings. … She caught me yesterday so I didn't hit my head against the table."[34]

---

[33] Metaxas, 251-5.

[34] Anderson, *Where Angels Walk*, 93.

Anderson also describes a case in which a figure resembling an angel appeared on six consecutive days outside the door of a pediatric intensive care unit, always around the same time of 4:30pm and always staying about 10 or 20 minutes. The strange part about this figure was that it was only visible on the hospital's closed-circuit television monitor. Multiple nurses as well as a patient's mother saw the figure, who appeared completely white "with a kind of outline around him" and seemed to make the windowless hallway brighter than normal. Yet, when they would open the doors to the unit, no one could be seen standing outside. What is more, over the six days of the figure's appearance, one particular 14-year-old girl—Chelsea Banton—who had such serious, ongoing health issues that her parents had just taken her off life support, made a sudden, profound recovery. At the same time, a toddler with a skull fracture made a sudden recovery, and a boy diagnosed with cancer had his diagnosis revised to a blood infection and was released during the time of the figure's appearance.[35]

In an interesting twist, there are many cases involving protection in which the people protected don't see a thing but others see enough to be severely intimidated! For instance, Dr. Norman Vincent Peale preached a sermon that aroused the ire of a dangerous political boss, who threatened to kill the minister. Some of Peale's friends offered to accompany him home from the event, but he assured them the Lord would take care of him. He returned home unharmed but years later was summoned to the deathbed of this political boss, who confessed he had meant to kill him that night. "I was in the woods with a club," he told him. When Peale asked him why he didn't carry out his intentions, the fellow replied, "What do you mean—why didn't I? Who were those two big men with you?" Peale said there had been no one with him, but the fellow insisted he saw them.[36]

Where Angels Walk contains several similar stories of intimidating figures who are only selectively visible, but I'll describe just one more. This one happened to a family camping at Big Bear Lake in California. They were set upon by six motorcyclists who demanded money from them at gunpoint. However, their aggressors suddenly took fright and fled. When the family developed their pictures from their trip, they noticed that one of them showed a white being "standing watch" over them and their campfire. Was that what had frightened the bikers away?[37]

In these protection cases, it seems as though the spiritual helpers appear only to those who *need* to see them. In cases where their visibility plays no role, they may be entirely invisible to all parties, as in the cases described above under "Protection by an Unseen Force."

---

[35] Anderson, *Where Miracles Happen*, 193-9.
[36] Anderson, *Where Angels Walk*, 85.
[37] Anderson, *Where Angels Walk*, 52.

I should also mention that I've come across one case in which the helping entity is *partially* visible. When Cuban pastor Carlos Alamino fell asleep at the wheel, the car he was driving "drove off the road over an embankment and crashed into a streambed that had almost no water." He and his companion were surprised to find that they were not hurt in any way, and his companion had a startling explanation for this: "When we were falling, I saw two hands holding the car and placing us in the stream, saving us from getting hurt."[38]

Supernatural Light

Sometimes a person who experiences an amazing rescue sees an inexplicable light, as when Peggy Anderson's car spun on a patch of ice, heading toward the edge of a bridge and the frigid marsh below. A "warm glow" filled the car, giving her immense comfort and reassurance. Her car still went off the bridge and rolled down a 30-feet incline, but it all happened in an inexplicably gentle fashion. When the car stopped, the comforting light disappeared.[39]

Sometimes the light contains an otherworldly figure. A woman who was being held at gunpoint in her car and about to be raped recounts that the car was suddenly filled from inside by an exceptionally bright light. Inside the light appeared a man who seemed familiar to the woman—"like I had always known him," she says. Her attacker bolted from the car, and when he had left, the light and the supernatural visitor both disappeared.[40]

In another case, a three-year-old girl went outside to play, but her mother saw her almost immediately squat down near the back door. A few moments later, an enormous branch fell from a tree nearby. When the mother asked her daughter why she'd squatted by the door instead of going into the yard to play, the girl said, "Mommy, a good god told me to sit down and not go under the tree, and I did just what she told me to do." She described the "good god" as being extremely bright and having long golden hair and wings.[41]

---

[38] Carlos Alamino, *In the Footsteps of God's Call: A Cuban Pastor's Journey*, trans. Osmany Espinosa Hernández, ed. David Peck and Brian Stewart (2008), 44.
[39] Anderson, *Where Angels Walk*, 98.
[40] Morse with Perry, 82.
[41] Burnham, *Angel Letters*, 55-56.

Visions of Angels

I'd say that, taken together, the cases we've reviewed so far are *suggestive* of the existence of powerful, beneficent spiritual beings, but not conclusive. However, some of the best evidence for angel-like beings comes from contexts other than emergency situations, where the experiencers have the time and presence of mind to observe more carefully and receive more complex communications from the beings in question.

Detailed perceptions of angel-like beings are particularly common among people who are in the process of dying but are not dealing with any immediate physical threat. Of over 500 hospice patients interviewed by physician Dr. John Lerma, 90% reported seeing angels in their end-of-life visions.[42] Curiously, several of those featured in Lerma's book *Into the Light* report the angels as having feathers. And many give them names like those of angels in the Bible: Michael, Gabriel, etc. They say that some of the angels are bigger than others and that they have different functions.[43] Some of their end-of-life visions of angels were accompanied by odd physical phenomena such as the physical manifestation of feathers that subsequently shrank and disappeared. Lerma reports that, on one occasion, two such feather incidents happened on the same day, as if to confirm each other.[44]

Visions of angels have also been reported by people who are not near death. In a case collected by Dr. Melvin Morse, a woman who was seven months pregnant was resting one afternoon—but nevertheless fully awake—when she suddenly found herself floating out of her body and looking down at it below. Floating next to her, she saw a glowing female being who spoke about the body on the bed in the third person, saying, "You know, she can't keep the baby. It is going to die." The pregnant woman says that, as this being spoke, she had the feeling that her baby's death "was part of a greater purpose and plan."[45] The child was actually born alive, but it died of Sudden Infant Death Syndrome during its first year.

Near-death experiencer Howard Storm reports how he visited a church after his NDE and was overcome when he saw hundreds of bright, golden angels on the ceiling. He was so awed by the sight that, despite adverse reactions from those around him, he couldn't help falling down on the floor and praising God.[46]

---

[42] John Lerma, *Into the Light: Real Life Stories about Angelic Visits, Visions of the Afterlife, and Other Pre-Death Experiences* (Pompton Plains, NJ: New Page Books, 2007), 229.
[43] Lerma, *Into the Light*, 41.
[44] Lerma, *Into the Light*, 80-82.
[45] Morse with Perry, 55.
[46] Howard Storm, *My Descent into Death: A Second Chance at Life* (New York: Doubleday, 2005), 112.

Eric Metaxas reports that his friend Peter Martin has had at least three separate visions of angels inside churches. One of these occurred on the fourth Sunday of Advent (just before Christmas) and lasted for about 20 seconds. Martin said the angel was 30 feet high (this was in Saint Thomas's Church on Fifth Avenue in New York City) and stood about 30 feet away from him. Martin told Metaxas,

> It expanded my mind, because it looked like super HD. … It had huge wings and held a huge sword and wore a suit of armor, and the colors were just dazzling: golds and blues and reds. … It was just sort of looking over the whole congregation. This thing was huge.[47]

Others have also reported seeing angels of enormous size. Anna Loomis writes, "Once in my bedroom I looked up, thinking I heard my husband's step, and saw an angel. He was very, very tall, and his head was going through the ceiling, which wasn't there anymore."[48] The disappearance of the ceiling echoes other reports, for instance, that of 10-year-old Daisy Irene Dryden who described the occasions on which she saw angels while she was lying on her deathbed, saying, "I do not see them all the time; but when I do, the walls seem to go away, and I can see ever so far…."[49]

Pam Larson also reports seeing gigantic angels, one of whom had a sword. An American, she had been in Costa Rica for months, dealing with the seemingly unending red tape surrounding the adoption of her Costa Rican-born son. When it seemed like they were finally going to get to go home together to the States, the assistant U.S. consul told Larson she needed one other document: her final approval from U.S. Immigration. Larson had already filed for this months ago and had a copy at home in Michigan, but the official told her a copy would not be sufficient. She would have to obtain an original by refiling in Washington, a process that would take at least six weeks.

After hanging up from this phone conversation, Larson was desperately pacing and praying in the garage when she suddenly saw, standing outside, two beings so tall that only their bare feet and ankles were visible from where she was standing. "One was blond and holding a sword," she says. "I could see the tiny holes in the weave of his garment, the bottom of the rope belt that hung from his waist." One of the beings told her he was called "Michael" and said, "We're here to do battle for you."

After a time, the angels faded away, and Larson felt an irresistible desire to call the assistant consul back. When she did so, the woman immediately

---

[47] Metaxas, 239-40.

[48] Burnham, *Angel Letters*, 96.

[49] William Barrett, *Deathbed Visions: How the Dead Talk to the Dying* (Guildford, UK: White Crow Books, 1926, 2011), 53.

asked her if she had been praying. Just after they'd hung up from their previous conversation, a messenger had delivered a pouch that, at the very bottom, contained Larson's missing document. The assistant consul had wanted to call Larson back to tell her, but she'd been unable to find her number![50]

While angel-like beings often seem to appear in response to need, Dr. S. Ralph Harlow—a man with an AB from Harvard, an MA from Columbia, and a PhD from Hartford Theological Seminary—wrote an account for *Guideposts* magazine of a seemingly gratuitous angel sighting had by him and his wife, Marion, while they were walking through the spring woods. They heard voices in the distance, and as the voices came up behind them, Harlow and his wife realized that the voices were actually coming from *above* them as well. Ten feet above their heads passed a group of six "glorious beautiful creatures that glowed with spiritual beauty," of which at least two appeared decidedly feminine. The beings were involved in conversation with each other and did not appear to notice Harlow and his wife. And, though they were fairly close, the couple couldn't understand what they were saying. Harlow remarked that it was like trying to listen to a conversation "outside a house with all the windows and doors shut." They watched the beings pass overhead and then heard their voices fade as they got farther and farther away.[51]

Children's Angel Sightings

Children seem particularly adept at perceiving angels. Sometimes they report seeing angels around their dying relatives, even if no one else perceives them. For example, a terminally ill woman named Diane was living with her daughter Martha's family. One afternoon, Martha's four-year-old son Michael was playing in the basement when he called up the stairs to Martha, "Mommy? The angels are here." Martha started to go to him to find out what he was talking about when he called again: "Never mind, Mommy. They're here for Grandma." When she heard this, Martha ran to her mother's bedside and discovered that she had just passed away.[52]

Interestingly, our next case *also* involves a four-year-old named Michael, although this may be a pseudonym. Just after his little brother Jacob died, *this* four-year-old Michael made an odd movement, avoiding sitting in a seat next to his mother. When asked why he did this, he replied, "There is an angel sitting next to you, so I couldn't sit there. Don't you see him, Mom?"

---

[50] Anderson, *Where Miracles Happen*, 93-94.
[51] S. Ralph Harlow, "The Day We Saw the Angels," *Guideposts* (1970).
[52] Anderson, *Where Miracles Happen*, 83-84.

Afterward, he had a vision of his deceased brother in the hall, laughing and doing somersaults. "The angels," he said. "They're in the hall with Jacob, and they told me his body is just a shell. They told me to come and see for myself. They are right." Multiple times over the following year, Michael reported that Jacob had come to play with him and that the angels "fly him in and out."[53]

A similar example comes from Sir William Barrett's 1926 volume *Deathbed Visions*. He quotes a case reported by Stainton Moses:

> Miss H., the daughter of an English clergyman, was tending a dying child. His little brother, aged three to four years, was in a bed in the same room. As the former was dying, the little brother woke up, and, pointing to the ceiling with every expression of joy, said, "Mother, look at the beautiful ladies round my brother! How lovely they are, they want to take him." The child died at that moment.[54]

Finally, scientist Dr. John C. Lilly also reports meeting and talking with his guardian angel when he was a child. He told French journalist Pierre Jovanovic in an interview, "I called them Angels, but that's a reminiscence of my Catholic education. Today, the more exact term to use is 'Being from a dimension higher than ours'."[55]

Angels in Near-Death Experiences

Further evidence for the existence of powerful spiritual entities with positive intentions can be found in near-death experiences (NDEs), some of which feature beings that seem to match traditional ideas of angels. For instance, an NDEr named Veronica states, "I understood the major superior being of love to be God, [but there] were other loving beings with God—like his spiritually evolved helpers or companions."[56] Another experiencer, Nan, relates an experience reminiscent of the New Testament book of Revelation, reporting,

> As we got close to the light I saw tens of thousands of beings dressed in white gowns all facing the Light and singing music I had never heard the

---

[53] Lerma, *Into the Light*, 47-48.
[54] Barrett, 60.
[55] This is my translation from Jovanovic's report, which is in French. Pierre Jovanovic, *Enquête sur l'existence des anges gardiens* (Paris: Editions Filipacchi, J'ai Lu, 1993), 21.
[56] Jeffrey Long with Paul Perry, *God and the Afterlife: The Ground-Breaking New Evidence for God and Near-Death Experience* (New York: HarperCollins, 2016), 77.

> likes of before. They were in the service of The Light and apparently "singing" praises to The Light.[57]

A man who had an NDE while fighting in Vietnam says, "I thought I saw Michael, the Archangel. He had wings, and he was bigger than life! When he saw you, he saw your soul. It was electrifying to the soul. I think it was Michael who said: 'It may or may not be your time. Patience for a moment.'"[58] Another NDEr reports that a group of 12 beings including an angel named Michael showed the NDEr "things about myself." The NDEr noticed that Michael as well as two of the other beings had wings.[59]

While beings encountered in NDEs are often described as wearing white robes with sashes around the waist, this description of beings with wings is somewhat unusual. In fact, let's pause for a moment to consider the implications of the variety of descriptions given for the beings encountered in NDEs. For instance, many other NDErs simply describe seeing "beings of light." NDE researcher P. M. H. Atwater believes that NDErs see whatever form best matches their current level of spiritual knowledge and familiarity with the spiritual realms, noting that more traditionally angel-like features generally disappear once a person gets comfortable in the "otherworld" and that those who have extensive experience journeying into these realms "seldom, if ever, report angels as having feature or form."[60]

While I think there is something to what Atwater is saying, I also want to point out that we shouldn't assume, just because the appearance of spiritual beings appears to tailor itself somewhat to the person perceiving them, that all spiritual beings are identical under their appearances. NDEr Howard Storm says that his NDE gave him "wonderful insights into the beings we call angels," and he reports, "Angels are messengers of God. There are uncountable kinds of angels. Their number exceeds the stars."[61] We'll discuss some of these possible types of angels below, in the section labeled "The Roles of Angels and Guides."

While we're on the topic of the appearance of angels, however, I should mention the record of at least one child who has reported a deathbed vision and expressed surprise that the beings she encountered did not have wings, demonstrating that the appearance of the beings she saw was not based solely on expectation.[62] In the same vein, while encounters with "guardian angels"

---

[57] Long with Perry, 146.

[58] Barbara R. Rommer, *Blessing in Disguise: Another Side of the Near-Death Experience* (St. Paul, MN: Llewellyn, 2000), 111.

[59] Rommer, 182.

[60] P. M. H. Atwater, *Beyond the Light: What Isn't Being Said About Near-Death Experience* (New York: Birch Lane Press, 1994), 104.

[61] Storm, 135.

[62] Barrett, 52-53.

were reported by at least 50% of the children who had NDEs studied by Melvin Morse,[63] at least one of the children whose experiences were studied by Morse did not immediately identify the being he saw in his NDE as an angel. Instead, he described it as "a wizard dressed in white,"[64] which suggests that he did not see this being as dressed in white *because* he had already conceptualized it as an angel.

Pierre Jovanovic tells us that, in one-third of the cases he himself has reviewed, NDE "angels" actually identified *themselves* in some way, saying things such as "I'm the one who is always with you," "I'm your guardian," or "I'm the one who watches over you."[65] Dr. Raymond Moody writes in his classic book on NDEs, *Life after Life*,

> In a very few instances, people have come to believe that the beings they encountered were their "guardian spirits." One man was told by such a spirit that, "I have helped you through this stage of your existence, but now I am going to turn you over to others." A woman told me that as she was leaving her body she detected the presence of two other spiritual beings there, and that they identified themselves as her "spiritual helpers."[66]

In an NDE reported by P. E. Johnson, a spirit being—upon being asked his identity—said, "I am your guardian angel; I have been following you constantly while on earth."[67] And NDEr Betty J. Eadie reports meeting three beings who said that they, as well as others, had acted as her "guardian angels." Nevertheless, these three seemed to have a special status. She felt they were her special "ministering angels."[68]

And guardian angels are not just a Christian notion, either. An NDE related by the ancient Greek philosopher Plato includes a section in which the experiencer sees souls who are on their way to incarnate on earth, and each one is designated a "Guardian Spirit, to guide it through life."[69]

---

[63] Morse with Perry, 19.

[64] Morse with Perry, 166.

[65] In French, "*Je suis celui qui est toujours avec toi*," "*Je suis ton gardien*," and "*Je suis celui qui te surveille.*" Jovanovic, 126.

[66] Raymond A. Moody, Jr., *Life After Life*, 25th anniversary edition (New York: HarperOne, 1975, 2001), 48.

[67] P. E. Johnson, "A testimony," *Relief Society Magazine* 3, no. 8 (August 1920): 451. Quoted in Lundahl, "Angels in Near-Death Experiences": 55.

[68] Betty J. Eadie with Curtis Taylor, *Embraced by the Light* (Carson City, NV: Gold Leaf Press, 1992), 32.

[69] Plato, *The Republic*, 620d-e, trans. Desmond Lee, 2nd ed., revised (New York: Penguin, 1987).

Angels & Guides in Other Contexts

People have also had experiences of guiding individuals in other contexts, including dreams. Lucid dreams—those in which the dreamer is aware that they are dreaming—seem to be especially conducive to their appearance. Veteran lucid dreamer Robert Waggoner says that almost all experienced lucid dreamers encounter figures who tell them they are there in order to guide or help them in some way. What is more, unlike most other dream characters, these guides seem to *initiate* interaction with the dreamer.[70]

Dutch psychiatrist Dr. Frederik van Eeden, who coined the term 'lucid dream', mentions the following intriguing dream in which he did not personally meet his guide but did talk with a deceased relative who apparently had had some communication with a guide of sorts. He recounts,

> In May 1903 I dreamed that I was in a little provincial Dutch town and at once encountered my brother-in-law, who had died some time before. I was absolutely sure that it was he, and I knew that he was dead. He told me that he had much intercourse with my "controller," as he expressed it—my guiding spirit. I was glad, and our conversation was very cordial, more intimate than ever in common life. He told me that a financial catastrophe was impending for me. Somebody was going to rob me of a sum of 10,000 guilders. I said that I understood him, though after waking up I was utterly puzzled by it and could make nothing of it.[71]

In fact, Van Eeden subsequently lost 20 times the amount of money cited in his dream—money that, at the time of the dream, he had not yet had in his possession.

Non-lucid dreams may also occasionally serve as a medium for messages from one's spiritual guides or guardians. Psychiatrist Dr. Judith Orloff says that her new patients have many times been introduced to her by a dream where someone says to her something like, "So-and-so is going to contact you for an appointment." She says the relationships introduced in this way turn out to have a "meant-to-be quality."[72] Carl Jung repeatedly encountered in his dreams and waking fantasies a character he named

---

[70] Robert Waggoner, *Lucid Dreaming: Gateway to the Inner Self* (Needham, MA: Moment Point Press, 2009), 132-3.

[71] Frederik van Eeden, "A Study of Dreams," in *Altered States of Consciousness*, ed. Charles T. Tart (Garden City, NY: Anchor Books, 1969, 1972), 147-60, pp. 156-7. Reprinted from *Proceedings of the Society for Psychical Research* 26 (1913): 431-61. Also available online at http://www.lucidity.com/vanEeden.html.

[72] Judith Orloff, *Second Sight: An Intuitive Psychiatrist Tells Her Extraordinary Story and Shows You How to Tap Your Own Inner Wisdom*, rev. ed. (New York: Three Rivers Press, 2000), 230.

"Philemon," whom he was convinced was a force coming from outside himself and represented insight superior to his own.[73]

Experiences with psychedelic drugs are yet another context in which adults have reported seeing angel-like beings. You'll recall that scientist John Lilly reported talking with his guardian angel as a child. Later in life, Lilly encountered these same beings while on LSD and took to calling them the members of the ECCO: the Earth Coincidence Control Office.[74]

Another psychedelic angel experience comes from a Jewish woman whose Buddhist daughter gave her some LSD. When the mother took it, she met a being who identified itself as her angel. The angel showed this woman that it was very hard being her angel, and also gave the woman a glimpse of what she looked like from the angel's perspective—bound all over her body by an enormous number of rubber bands. The angel explained that the rubber bands were her fears. "You have so many fears," said the angel, "that you can never hear me trying to talk to you, to tell you that I've got everything under control." The angel suggested that she cut the rubber bands off, and that's just what she did during the LSD trip. After that experience, the woman says, she never felt afraid again, and she talks to her angel every day.[75]

Are These Beings Just in the Mind?

Do dreams or drug-induced visions of guides *prove* that such spiritual beings have an independent existence? No. And neither do NDEs. As discussed in the last chapter, we know that visionary experiences often contain characters that are due at least in part to the activity of our own unconscious minds, so certainly a dream or a vision of a voice or figure doesn't guarantee that there's a specific, real consciousness conveying the information, independent of God or our own unconscious. However, we'll see extensive evidence in later chapters that dreams *can* be vehicles for information coming from outside our minds—for instance, telepathic information—and so I don't think we should discount the possibility that some of the figures in NDEs, dreams, and drug-induced visions represent entities independent of us. It's striking, after all, that researchers in all of these areas report such similar encounters. Melvin Morse speaks for many when he says that, in all of the various types of paranormal visions he's encountered

---

[73] C. G. Jung, *Memories, Dreams, Reflections*, ed. Aniela Jaffé, trans. Richard and Clara Winston, rev. ed. (New York: Vintage Books, 1961, 1989), 183.
[74] Jovanovic, 180.
[75] Caroline Myss, *Anatomy of the Spirit: The Seven Stages of Power and Healing* (New York: Three Rivers Press, 1996), 171-2.

in his research, "the same images of light and of the beings that dwell within it appear again and again."[76]

The truth about these beings may, of course, lie somewhere in the middle of the spectrum that stretches from pure products of our imagination to wholly independent entities. Robert Moss reminds us of the ideas that the Neoplatonist philosopher Plotinus had along these lines:

> Plotinus...instructed that the life teacher, or "tutelary daimon," is a self on a level above the one where we are currently operating. Plotinus maintained that each of us is a "cosmos," with access to a vast spectrum of possible levels of consciousness and the power to choose the levels we inhabit. Whatever level we choose, a personality on the next level up becomes the life guardian or personal daimon.[77]

One large body of evidence particularly relevant to this topic consists of the experiences of Robert Monroe, the famous out-of-body traveler. In his first book, *Journeys Out of the Body*, Monroe reports that "[o]ne of the greatest enigmas of this whole affair [of out-of-body journeys] is that someone—or more than one—has been helping me from time to time in such experimentation."[78] In his two later books, he reports out-of-body experiences (OBEs) in which he conversed with these helpers, whom he calls INSPECS—short for "intelligent species."[79] He was awed by these beings at first. They glowed brightly, and he believed they were "what some people would interpret as a god, an angel, or at the very least some extraterrestrial."[80] However, his feeling of awe gave way to "a great feeling of warmth, of understanding, much on the order of old deep friendships, yet filled with intense respect, not the usual pattern of expected angels, if that is what THEY were."[81] He says that, when he wondered whether they were angels, the INSPECS offered to grow wings, but he asked them not to. Monroe ended up continuing to use the label INSPECS for them because he couldn't find another name that was as philosophically neutral.

The Monroe Institute that Monroe founded has facilitated OBEs for many other people, by using a special auditory technology called Hemi-Sync. It seemed to Monroe that these other people's encounters with intelligent beings were prompted by an affirmation made prior to beginning the OBE,

---

[76] Morse with Perry, 89.

[77] Robert Moss, *The Boy Who Died and Came Back: Adventures of a Dream Archaeologist in the Multiverse* (Novato, CA: New World Library, 2014), 196-7.

[78] Robert A. Monroe, *Journeys Out of the Body*, updated edition (Garden City, NY: Anchor/Doubleday, 1971, 1977), 127.

[79] Robert A. Monroe, *Far Journeys* (Garden City, NY: Doubleday, 1985, 1987), 93; and Robert A. Monroe, *Ultimate Journey* (New York: Harmony, 1994).

[80] Monroe, *Ultimate Journey*, 18-19.

[81] Monroe, *Far Journeys*, 97.

which asked for the aid of "those individuals whose wisdom, development, and experience are equal to or greater than my own."[82] One of Monroe's subjects reported that one of these beings told him that "he is kind of my overseer…somewhat responsible for my growth and development."[83] Another subject reported on a meeting with one of these beings, saying,

> I got the idea that the earth was sort of his assigned beat. I also got the idea that he and other entities are made available to us to help us maximize or get through our earth experience…to help us get as much out of it as possible. They are there like explainers or helpers and not particularly assigned to earth duty.[84]

The most intriguing aspect of the INSPECs is revealed in Monroe's final book, *Ultimate Journey*, where he reports discovering in a later OBE that his INSPEC friend was actually an *aspect of himself*—in fact, his future self come back in time to help him.[85] Monroe also had conversations with other beings who said they were aspects of himself, and they acknowledged intervening in his physical life from time to time, twice protecting him from drowning and once helping him avoid a car accident.[86]

Now, I don't think that we have to conclude from Monroe's experience that all angels and spirit guides are nothing but aspects of ourselves, future or otherwise. Even Monroe says that there are other intelligences out there helping us. But his experiences do suggest that it would be wise to keep in mind that the "angels" we experience may not be exactly what they seem to us at first glance. In fact, Monroe reports having OBEs in which he encountered human souls just after their bodily deaths and they jumped to the conclusion that he was a god of some kind.[87] This is a great example of why it's important not to jump to an interpretation of our experiences according to the categories most familiar to us, but instead open our minds to consider alternative interpretations, some of which may turn out to be more accurate.

If the possibility that angel-like beings may actually be aspects of ourselves intrigues you, know that we will spend more time discussing the idea of personal identity and the higher self at the end of Chapter 6, as well as in Chapter 10.

---

[82] Monroe, *Far Journeys*, 39.
[83] Monroe, *Far Journeys*, 42.
[84] Monroe, *Far Journeys*, 43.
[85] Monroe, *Ultimate Journey*, 197-8.
[86] Monroe, *Ultimate Journey*, 168-9.
[87] Monroe, *Ultimate Journey*, 113, 136-7. In other cases, it seems like Monroe purposely appeared to the just-dead as familiar figures: "father, mother, departed friend, even some 'heavenly being'" (180).

The Roles of Angels and Guides

Let's now turn to some other potential sources of information on the roles of the guiding and protecting beings that so many people have experienced. You may recall Dr. Andrew Paquette from the end of the last chapter, where we discussed his dreams of Jesus. These are only a small sample of Paquette's huge number of psychic dreams, the contents of which have often been subsequently verified in great detail. That is not to say that everything that he dreams must be true, only to indicate why I find it so intriguing that Paquette's dreams have led him to the belief that spiritual beings are frequently behind events in the waking world.

Paquette uses a backstage metaphor, suggesting that most people are entirely unaware of the immense amount of activity that goes on behind the scenes of earthly life, carried out by many different categories of spiritual beings.[88] Most importantly for our present purposes, Paquette distinguishes between helping spirits and angels, the former appearing more human and the latter appearing much more awe-inspiring and intimidating. Paquette writes, "Angels possess authority, power, and righteousness to an almost painful degree. … [T]hey are definitely a breed apart, regardless of any variety among them."[89]

Paquette's distinction between helping spirits and angels bears strong similarities to the one NDEr Betty Eadie draws between "guardian angels," who have spirits similar to those of human beings but have elected not to incarnate so as to watch over people on earth, and "Warring Angels," whose purpose is "to do battle for us against Satan and his angels." She describes the latter as "giant men, very muscularly built…dressed like warriors, in head dress and armor…[and with an] aura of confidence" that makes it clear you wouldn't want to mess with them.[90]

Another interesting distinction I've heard regarding angels comes from the mouth of a child. Julie M. relates that, as soon as her granddaughter Gabrielle could talk around the age of 30 months, she described having conversations with her old friends "the angels." And she often mentioned the fact that she missed having her wings. Once, she took a flying leap across the living room and looked surprised when she landed on the floor. She laughed and said, "I forgot, I don't have wings anymore." Gabrielle also apparently corrected her Sunday school teacher for incorrectly telling the story of Noah's ark. Gabrielle said she knew what had really happened because she'd *been* there. On another occasion, Julie called Gabrielle's baby

---

[88] Andrew Paquette, *Dreamer: 20 Years of Psychic Dreams and How They Changed My Life* (Winchester, UK: O-Books, 2011), 149.
[89] Paquette, *Dreamer*, 240.
[90] Eadie with Taylor, 90-91.

sister a "little angel," and Gabrielle corrected her, saying, "Nani, I was an angel before I came here, but Abigail is just a little soul. People cannot be angels, and angels can only be people when Jesus asks them to. Like me."[91]

One final source I want to mention regarding information on the roles played by angel-like beings are the post-NDE visionary experiences of Christian surgeon Dr. Mary C. Neal. Neal reports in her book *To Heaven and Back* that, as she was recovering from her NDE, she had more than one experience of sitting "in a beautiful, sun-drenched field"[92] conversing with someone she ultimately identifies as Jesus.[93] She says that, during one of these conversations, she was given the following information.

> In preparation for our journey to earth, we are able to make a basic outline for our life. This is not to imply that we, the humans, are entirely in charge of our life's design. It is more like God creates it, then we review it and discuss it with our "personal planning" angel. Within the algorithm are written branch points in our lives at which times we may exit, returning to God, or we may be redirected to a different task and goal.
>
> We may be directed to these branch points by our own conscious choice and by our circumstances, or we may be pushed along by angelic intervention.[94]

Neal then specifically states that angels "are the ones orchestrating the 'coincidences' that occur so commonly in our lives."[95]

If the idea of a life plan orchestrated by angels seems to you a bit far-fetched, know that there is quite a bit of independent evidence for this idea, some of which we will explore in Chapter 17, "Destiny." For now, I'll just mention that this idea also appears in Betty Eadie's NDE, where she learned that "in the pre-mortal world we knew about and even chose our missions in life."[96] Eadie also says she saw in her NDE that many of the things in her life that she thought she'd achieved on her own had been brought about with the help of guardian angels.[97]

---

[91] Elisabeth Hallett, *Stories of the Unborn Soul: The Mystery and Delight of Pre-Birth Communication* (San Jose: Writers Club Press, 2002), 216-7.
[92] Mary C. Neal, *To Heaven and Back: A Doctor's Extraordinary Account of Her Death, Heaven, Angels, and Life Again* (Colorado Springs, CO: WaterBrook Press, 2011, 2012), 106.
[93] Neal, 213. Part of the "Q & A with Dr. Neal" found at the back of the 2012 paperback edition of the book.
[94] Neal, 98.
[95] Neal, 99.
[96] Eadie with Taylor, 48.
[97] Eadie with Taylor, 115.

Experiences Linking Coincidences to Angel-Like Beings

Now that we have all this background regarding the experiences people have had of angel-like beings, it's finally time to look at a few experiences that specifically link angel-like beings to coincidences. I've collected four such cases, and three of them involve knowledge obtained in a near-death experience.

In the first case, a woman named Leonor Reyes was having a cancerous goiter removed while her husband was fighting in Vietnam. She had an NDE and was told that she could decide whether to go on living or not, as well as whether she wanted her husband to go on living or not. An angel took her to see her husband in the thick of battle, and as she watched him, she decided they would stay on earth, since it would be too hard on their parents otherwise. Joan Wester Anderson reports that "[a]t that very moment [Leonor] saw a hand, almost invisible, reach down and cup over a grenade that had landed right next to David." Later, when David returned from the war, Leonor asked him "if he was ever in a bunker on a hill with another soldier when a grenade fell next to him during combat." He said it had only happened once, and thank goodness that time the grenade was a dud![98] While this may have appeared to him as good luck, Leonor had clear reason to believe it was the result of the intentional action of a spiritual being.

Another NDEr's experience suggests that this type of intervention may be much more common than we realize. An NDEr interviewed by Dr. Barbara R. Rommer reports that he saw in his life review that an angel had *repeatedly* intervened to save his life. He says, "All those times in my life that I had gone right to the point of death…in stepped a guardian angel."[99]

Another of Rommer's NDErs, Kara, reports that she was taken to a room without walls that contained a giant telephone switchboard operated by three "ladies" who listened to people's prayers and then plugged in a line so that "the entity or angel, or whatever, goes down to the right place to work on that prayer."[100] Kara says that she was told by the entity guiding her in her NDE that she herself was needed at this switchboard, that they had a lot of work for her to do. Kara, however, protested that her family on earth needed her a lot, too, and so she was allowed to return to her earthly life.

Are there really switchboards on the other side? The idea may seem silly, but keep in mind that NDEs and other visionary experiences often feature visual representations that are designed to convey a spiritual reality. The

---

[98] Anderson, *Where Angels Walk*, 200-1.

[99] Rommer, 88.

[100] Rommer, 189.

switchboard this NDEr saw could be symbolic of a real spiritual network that allows beings who are in spirit to coordinate intervention in human lives.

Finally, here is a non-NDE experience linking angels to what might otherwise have been taken to be nothing more than a strange random occurrence. A patient who was dying in a hospital in India had a staircase to the second floor located in his room, and someone had placed a drinking glass on the steps. One day he exclaimed to those present, "See, the angels are coming down the stairs. The glass has fallen and broken." A nurse who witnessed the event explains that everyone then looked at the stairs and

> saw the glass break into a thousand pieces without any apparent cause. It did not fall; it simply exploded. The angels, of course, we did not see. A happy and peaceful expression came over the patient's face and the next moment he expired.[101]

Conclusion

I believe that, taken together, the experiences reported in this chapter provide strong evidence for the existence of benevolent spiritual beings who are capable of intervening in our lives. Nevertheless, I believe it's important to keep an open mind about exactly what sorts of beings these may be. We can't just take it for granted that, when an experiencer says something looked like an angel, it *was* an angel of the sort conceived by any particular religion.

As a final cautionary tale, consider an experience recounted to clinical psychologist Dr. David Ryback. A teenage girl dreamt of a young woman in a flowing white gown running towards her barefoot across a meadow. She looked like "an angel without wings." Three days later, the girl's vision came true, as just such a person came running toward the girl and her mother while they were out about town. The "angel without wings" asked them for shelter, a request they obliged. They later discovered that this woman was a patient who had "wandered away" from the local psychiatric hospital.[102]

Of course, just because the woman in the white gown was a mental patient doesn't mean she couldn't *also* be an angel. After all, the writer of the New Testament book of Hebrews advised the early Christians, "Do not forget to entertain strangers, for by so doing some people have entertained angels without knowing it."[103] And entertaining a stranger is exactly what this mother and daughter did.

---

[101] Karlis Osis and Erlendur Haraldsson, *At the Hour of Death* (New York: Discus, 1977, 1979), 42.

[102] David Ryback with Letitia Sweitzer, *Dreams That Come True: Their Psychic and Transforming Powers* (New York: Doubleday, 1988), 25-26.

[103] Hebrews 13:2.

Chapter 4

The Deceased

Many coincidences contain elements linking them to people who have passed away, and it's natural for those who experience them to conclude that the deceased actually produced them. Those who are grieving the loss of a loved one often long for some sort of communication reassuring them that their loved one lives on, and these coincidences frequently seem perfectly designed for this purpose—too perfectly for them to be the mere products of chance.

Consider, for example, an incident related by Janis Heaphy Durham in her book *The Hand on the Mirror*. In honor of her deceased husband Max, she and her son took a trip to Italy. The two of them spent one particularly enchanted afternoon in Portofino on the Italian Riviera and snapped a picture of themselves along the water. When they returned home to the States and Durham had the photo developed, she saw that there was a boat in the background, and on the side of the boat, perfectly positioned between Durham and her son, were written the three letters of her husband's name: MAX.[1] The photo is reprinted in Durham's book, and the placement of the name just between their bodies is really quite striking. Could Durham's deceased husband have somehow influenced events so as to produce this particular photograph, which so beautifully symbolizes his continuing presence with his family?

The link between the appearance of the word 'MAX' and the action of a deceased person may seem tenuous to some readers. It may seem more

[1] Janis Heaphy Durham, *The Hand on the Mirror: A True Story of Life Beyond Death* (New York: Grand Central, 2015), 56.

parsimonious to explain this coincidence as the result of either chance or Durham's unconscious behavior. Perhaps she unconsciously saw the name on the boat and positioned herself and her son in such a way as to make it part of the photograph?

I believe that, if we're going to make an accurate judgment about the best explanation for this and similar coincidences, it's very important that we view them within a larger context. Specifically, we need to view them within the context of a wealth of independent evidence pointing to the existence of life after death and to the ability of the deceased to communicate with living human beings. For this reason, the first third of this chapter will be devoted to presenting the evidence for life after death that comes to us from apparitions, deathbed visions, dreams, near-death experiences, shared death experiences, memories of death in past lives, and mediumship. Once this evidence has been laid out, we'll turn to the evidence that specifically connects the deceased to the production of coincidences.

The Prevalence of After-Death Communication (ADC)

Let me begin by saying a few words about the number of people who believe they've experienced after-death communication—or ADC, as it's often called. When Durham's experiences in the wake of her husband's death led her to investigate this phenomenon, she was surprised to discover how common it was. Durham writes,

> What I thought was extraordinary was, in fact, ordinary. Apparently, paranormal is normal. I just didn't know it. And there's a reason. People are afraid to admit what they have experienced. They're reluctant to speak publicly about what they've experienced for fear of being judged.[2]

Many other writers on this topic have made a similar observation. Joel Martin and Patricia Romanowski, authors of *Love Beyond Life*, note that most people they knew of who had received what appeared to be after-death communication "believed they were the only ones in the world to have ever had such an experience."[3]

People may indeed be reluctant to discuss such experiences, even with close friends and relatives. They may fear ridicule or simply not want the understandable skepticism of others to tarnish what they know in their hearts to be true. But whether people are reluctant to discuss them or not, these experiences happen quite frequently. A 1973 National Opinion Research

---

[2] Durham, 165.

[3] Joel Martin and Patricia Romanowski, *Love Beyond Life: The Healing Power of After-Death Communication* (New York: Harper, 1997), 3.

Center poll found that 27% of Americans felt they'd been in touch with someone who'd died. And, of those who'd had a spouse die, fully *half* reported contact with them after death.[4] Results were comparable in Britain. In a Welsh survey, 47% of persons interviewed reported seeing, hearing, and/or feeling their departed spouses (though only a quarter of these had ever confided the experience to anyone else),[5] and a survey of widows in London returned a figure of 46%.[6] In the 1990s, another survey found the percentage of apparent contact from deceased spouses to be 60%.[7]

Careful study of such experiences goes back over 100 years, when accounts of ADC were first systematically gathered by the Society for Psychical Research, founded in 1882 by a group of British notables, including philosopher and economist Henry Sidgwick, physicist Lord Rayleigh, and future Prime Minister Arthur Balfour. In more recent days, Bill and Judy Guggenheim have collected and published a large number of ADC accounts in their well-known book *Hello from Heaven!*[8] Other noteworthy collections include Martin and Romanowski's *Love Beyond Life*, Dianne Arcangel's *Afterlife Encounters*,[9] Sylvia Hart Wright's *When Spirits Come Calling*,[10] Annie Mattingley's *The After Death Chronicles*,[11] and Icelandic psychologist Dr. Erlendur Haraldsson's *The Departed Among the Living*.[12] A further useful resource is Jenny Streit-Horn's 2011 doctoral dissertation, in which she reviewed 35 research studies of ADC from as long ago as 1894 and as recently as 2006. These studies involved more than 50,000 people in all.[13]

---

[4] Andrew M. Greeley, *Sociology of the Paranormal: A Reconnaissance* (Beverly Hills, CA: Sage Publications, 1975). Information on this poll can also be found in Andrew M. Greeley, *Death and Beyond* (Chicago: Thomas More Association, 1976).
[5] W. Dewi Rees, "The Hallucinations of Widowhood," *British Medical Journal* 4 (Oct 2, 1971): 37-41.
[6] Peter Marris, *Widows and Their Families* (London: Routledge & Kegan Paul, 1958).
[7] Martin and Romanowski, 7.
[8] Bill Guggenheim and Judy Guggenheim, *Hello from Heaven!: A New Field of Research—After-Death Communication—Confirms That Life and Love Are Eternal* (New York: Bantam, 1995).
[9] Dianne Arcangel, *Afterlife Encounters: Ordinary People, Extraordinary Experiences* (Charlottesville, VA: Hampton Roads, 2005).
[10] Sylvia Hart Wright, *When Spirits Come Calling: The Open-Minded Skeptic's Guide to After-Death Contacts* (Nevada City, CA: Blue Dolphin Publishing, 2002).
[11] Annie Mattingley, *The After Death Chronicles: True Stories of Comfort, Guidance, and Wisdom from Beyond the Veil* (Charlottesville, VA: Hampton Roads, 2017).
[12] Erlendur Haraldsson, *The Departed Among the Living: An Investigative Study of Afterlife Encounters* (Guildford, UK: White Crow Books, 2012).
[13] Jenny Streit-Horn, "A systematic review of research on after-death communication (ADC)," PhD diss. (University of North Texas, 2011). A summary of her findings is available online in a two-page, nicely formatted PDF: http://www.coe.unt.edu/sites/default/files/22/129/ADC.pdf.

But accounts of ADC aren't just abundant. Some of them actually constitute strong evidence for the existence of life after death, as we are about to see.

Evidence for Life after Death: Apparitions of the Dead

It becomes apparent when reading the research on ADC that one of the most common ways for a deceased person to communicate is through an apparition, which may or may not be accompanied by telepathic or audible communication. Haraldsson reports in *The Departed Among the Living* that apparitions are in fact the single most common type of ADC, representing 67% of the cases he collected.[14]

Apparitions Occurring Before Knowledge of the Death

It can be tempting to explain away apparitions and other forms of ADC as hallucinations induced by wishful thinking, but several pieces of evidence count against this blanket explanation. One of them is the fact that sometimes the people who see an apparition are unaware that the person appearing to them is dead, or even that they were in any danger of dying. Haraldsson reports that, of the 449 cases of encounters with the dead that he collected, one out of every nine happened within 24 hours of the death, and in 86% of those cases, the person having the experience did not yet know that the death had occurred.[15]

Consider the experience of Colonel D. Pritchard, which he recounts in Ben Noakes's book *I Saw a Ghost.* He was at a cricket match talking to friends in the pavilion bar when he noticed the famous cricketeer Douglas Jardine standing about 15 feet away. Pritchard knew Jardine quite well, and what was more, he was "distinctive looking and impossible to mistake." The two men looked at each other and raised their glasses in acknowledgment. However, a couple of minutes later, when Pritchard went over to speak to Jardine, he couldn't find him. Then, just before the cricket match began, the announcement came over the loudspeaker that Douglas Jardine had passed away the previous day.[16]

The Guggenheims' book *Hello from Heaven!* has an entire chapter dedicated to ADC that happens before the recipient is aware of the death. Many of these apparitions happen at approximately the same time as the death and thus don't offer as much evidence for survival *beyond* death, since

[14] Haraldsson, *The Departed Among the Living*, 2.
[15] Haraldsson, *The Departed Among the Living*, 41.
[16] Ben Noakes, *I Saw a Ghost: Eye-Witness Accounts by the Famous of Supernatural Encounters* (London: Weidenfeld and Nicolson, 1986), 121.

they could be explained by telepathic communication occurring in the moments just before death occurs. However, this is not true of all the Guggenheims' cases. For instance, they quote the account of Clare, whose long-time friend and colleague Hugh suddenly appeared to her one Monday morning. She recounts,

> He pinched me to get my attention! I saw him! He stood there by my bed, wearing a white shirt with his sleeves rolled up. His mood and expression were really sad, as though he'd lost it all.
>
> Hugh said, "I'm sorry, Clare. I didn't make it." He added, "Good-bye," as if forever. Then he just vanished.[17]

When Clare's radio played the morning's news, she discovered that Hugh had died the day before, when his seaplane went down in the Columbia River and he drowned.

Another case of an apparition that happened after the person appearing had died but before the person perceiving the apparition had been informed of the death can be found in a 1956 article in the *Proceedings of the Society for Psychical Research* called "Six Theories of Apparitions." There we find the case of a British military captain deployed in India, Captain Wheatcroft, who appeared to his wife beside her bed in the moonlight. He appeared to be suffering and was trying to speak but no sound came out. After a minute or so, he vanished. This experience led his wife to suspect that he had been killed or badly wounded, but it wasn't until weeks later that she learned of evidence that her husband had died about 18 hours before the apparition occurred.[18]

Now, here is a uniquely rich case of the apparition of someone not known to have died. A woman named Debbi relates that she awoke one night to see, at the foot of her bed, the minister who had officiated at her wedding not long before. He told her that her father needed to speak to her. Her father had died when she was only two, but he, too, proceeded to appear at the foot of her bed. He said many reassuring things, but then he told Debbi something that he said it was very important for her to remember. "We have a very special child chosen for you," he said. "This child will change your life, and make you very proud." The next day, Debbi discovered that the minister who had appeared and introduced her deceased father had himself suddenly passed away the day before. A few years later, she gave birth to a daughter with Down syndrome and many health issues. When it looked like the baby

---

[17] Guggenheim and Guggenheim, 247.

[18] Hornell Hart, "Six Theories about Apparitions," *Proceedings of the Society for Psychical Research* 50, part 185 (May 1956): 153-239, p. 160.

might not survive, Debbi held onto her father's words, and she says now, "Everything he said has come true."[19]

Apparitions of the deceased are especially common when the person experiencing them is close to death. These "deathbed visions," as they are often called, usually occur in the last day of life,[20] and experiencers will often see deceased friends and relatives and sometimes carry on extended conversation with them. Numerous examples of deathbed visions as well as discussion of the phenomenon can be found in Sir William Barrett's *Deathbed Visions*,[21] Drs. Karlis Osis and Erlendur Haraldsson's *At the Hour of Death*, Dr. Melvin Morse's *Parting Visions*,[22] Martin and Romanowski's *Love Beyond Life*,[23] Drs. Kelly Bulkeley and Patricia Bulkley's *Dreaming Beyond Death*,[24] and Dr. John Lerma's two books *Into the Light*[25] and *Learning from the Light*.[26]

Once again, important evidence for the veracity of these visions comes from cases in which the vision is of a person the experiencer doesn't know to be dead. Take, for example, the deathbed vision of a 53-year-old man dying from lung cancer. His doctor, John Lerma, entered his hospice room to find him talking to an invisible conversation partner. "Mom, I'm not worthy to go with you," said the patient. "I'm too far gone. Just go without me." Lerma tried to comfort the man, who had started to cry. Lerma reminded him that his mom was in New Orleans, alive. "No," replied the man. "She said she died after Hurricane Katrina, and she's here to help me cross over." When Lerma checked later, he discovered that this man's mother had indeed just passed away, though no one at the hospice—including the patient—had yet been informed of this.[27]

In this next case, the apparition is of someone already known to be dead, but the evidential value comes from other information conveyed by the apparition: the fact that, unbeknownst to the experiencer, he himself is near death. A widower named Gary told researcher Dianne Arcangel that his

---

[19] William Stillman, *The Soul of Autism: Looking Beyond Labels to Unveil Spiritual Secrets of the Heart Savants* (Franklin Lakes, NJ: New Page Books, 2008), 123-4.

[20] Karlis Osis and Erlendur Haraldsson, *At the Hour of Death* (New York: Discus, 1977, 1979), 62.

[21] William Barrett, *Deathbed Visions: How the Dead Talk to the Dying* (Guildford, UK: White Crow Books, 1926, 2011).

[22] Melvin Morse with Paul Perry, *Parting Visions: Uses and Meanings of Pre-Death, Psychic, and Spiritual Experiences* (New York: Villard, 1994).

[23] Martin and Romanowski, 62-70.

[24] Kelly Bulkeley and Patricia Bulkley, *Dreaming Beyond Death: A Guide to Pre-Death Dreams and Visions* (Boston: Beacon Press, 2005), 91-92.

[25] John Lerma, *Into the Light: Real Life Stories about Angelic Visits, Visions of the Afterlife, and Other Pre-Death Experiences* (Pompton Plains, NJ: New Page Books, 2007).

[26] John Lerma, *Learning from the Light: Pre-Death Experiences, Prophecies, and Angelic Messages of Hope* (Franklin Lakes, NJ: New Page Books, 2009).

[27] Lerma, *Into the Light*, 161.

afterlife encounters were becoming quite frequent and vivid. He had also had one particularly puzzling encounter: "I was washing my car, getting it ready to trade in, when I saw my wife standing there as plain as day. She said, 'Don't bother. Just enjoy your family and friends because you'll be with me soon.'" Gary had no idea what to make of this, as his health was great and he was at long last enjoying life again. Nevertheless, only hours later, Arcangel received a phone call from Gary's employer informing her that he had just been killed in a "freak car crash."[28]

Here's another case of the same type, important because of the exceptionally young age of the child who sees the apparition. This case was reported by a Mrs. H. and printed in the *Religio-Philosophical Journal* of May 5, 1894. Mrs. H. writes,

> In 1883 I was the mother of two strong, healthy boys. The eldest was a bright boy of two years and seven months. The other a darling baby boy of eight months. August 6th, 1883, my baby died. Ray, my little son, was then in perfect health. Every day after baby's death (and I may safely say every hour in the day) he would say to me, "Mama, baby calls Ray." He would often leave his play and come running to me, saying, "Mamma, baby calls Ray all the time." Every night he would waken me out of my sleep and say, "Mamma, baby calls Ray all the time. He wants Ray to come where he is; you must not cry when Ray goes, Mamma; you must not cry, for baby wants Ray." One day I was sweeping the sitting room floor, and he came running as fast as he could run, through the dining room where stood the table with baby's high chair (which Ray now used) at the side. I never saw him so excited, and he grabbed my dress and pulled me to the dining room door, jerked it open, saying, "Oh, Mamma, Mamma, come quick; baby is sitting in his high chair." As soon as he opened the door and looked at the chair, he said, "Oh, Mamma, why didn't you hurry; now he's gone; he laughed at Ray when he passed the chair; oh, he laughed at Ray so nice. Ray is going with baby, but you must not cry, Mamma." Ray soon became very sick. Nursing and medicine were of no avail. He died Oct. 13th, 1883, two months and seven days after baby's death.[29]

Here's one more case in this genre, but in this one the apparition indicates the impending death of someone other than the perceiver. Lois Miller recounts that she'd gotten up to go to the bathroom during the night and that, when she lay back down to go to sleep, she suddenly saw her deceased mother at the foot of the bed, surrounded by light. "She was facing toward my father's bedroom," says Miller, "and she was motioning to him to come with her. My mother loved my father for taking care of her when she was bedridden for seven-and-a-half years. The message I received was one

---

[28] Arcangel, 110.

[29] Barrett, 39-40.

of inner peace—that the end here is a new beginning there."[30] Miller's father died unexpectedly two days later, while taking a nap in his recliner.

Apparitions with Multiple Percipients

More evidence that apparitions of the dead cannot all be explained as hallucinations comes from the fact that they are sometimes perceived by more than one person. Chapter 21 of the Guggenheims' book *Hello from Heaven!* contains several examples of such cases. While it's not impossible that a hallucination could be shared, a collective hallucination does seem much less likely than an individual one. And it seems particularly unlikely in cases where an apparition is perceived by multiple people who are in different physical locations and unaware of each other's experiences at the time they are happening.

For example, just hours after the death of a young patient of hers, hospice nurse Lizabeth Sumner had a vision of him "happy and animated, holding a man's hand." When she told the patient's mother about this at the boy's funeral, the mother burst into tears, saying, "That's exactly what my husband saw. Right after Jimmy died, my husband saw the same thing."[31]

Hospice physician John Lerma reports a case in which a mother and her two daughters all separately, in their own rooms, saw apparitions of their deceased father and grandparents on the same night. All of them described them similarly.[32] And, in Joyce and Barry Vissell's book *Meant to Be*, Myrna L. Smith gives a detailed, two-page account of the night between Christmas Eve and Christmas Day when her deceased husband appeared separately to her and to each of her two sons.[33]

In other cases, an apparition appears in only one place, but the presence of another witness or witnesses nevertheless provides support for the objectivity of the event. In *The Departed Among the Living*, Haraldsson states that, out of the 89 apparition cases he collected in which another person besides the primary percipient was in a position to have also been able to see the apparition, 41 of them did perceive it: that is, almost half.[34] And while some apparitions are only visible to some of the people in a room, several cases collected and discussed in Hornell Hart et al.'s essay "Six Theories

---

[30] Louis E. LaGrand, *Messages and Miracles: Extraordinary Experiences of the Bereaved* (St. Paul, MN: Llewellyn, 1999), 97.

[31] Morse with Perry, xii.

[32] John Lerma, *Learning from the Light: Pre-Death Experiences, Prophecies, and Angelic Messages of Hope* (Franklin Lakes, NJ: New Page Books, 2009), 157-8.

[33] Joyce Vissell and Barry Vissell, eds., *Meant to Be: Miraculous True Stories to Inspire a Lifetime of Love* (Berkeley, CA: Conari Press, 2000), 177-9.

[34] Haraldsson, *The Departed Among the Living*, 201.

about Apparitions" demonstrate that people who do see an apparition see it from varying angles, as though the appearing person were objectively there.[35]

This suggests that at least some apparitions are actually located in space (rather than merely in the mind) but that not all people are equally adept at perceiving whatever it is they are made of. In fact, while some people have never seen an apparition of the dead, others appear to perceive them frequently, even when these apparitions are of people with little to no connection to themselves. For instance, Haraldsson quotes the testimony of a man who says he frequently sees the deceased and cites as an example a time when he woke up in the night and saw his mother-in-law's stepfather standing by his wife's side of the bed.[36] In this case, it seems logical that the mother-in-law's stepfather was present out of concern for the wife, and the husband just happened to perceive him as a sort of bystander.

Consider, too, another piece of testimony in Haraldsson's book, from a man named Gisli Frimannsson. As a young man, he was staying at Hjorsey when one night he awoke to see "an elderly man from the district...standing on the middle of the floor." The apparition remained for a bit and then disappeared. The following evening, Frimannsson received word that this man had died. A couple months later, he spoke to the man's widow, and she told him that she'd had a dream immediately after her husband's death in which he'd said to her, "I have already been to Hjorsey, but no one was aware of me there except Gisli."[37]

The reactions of animals also lend support to the objective quality of apparitions. In yet another case collected by Haraldsson, sheep were refusing to enter a certain pen. "They just shied away," reports the experiencer, "so I went to find out what was wrong. And there he [Erik, who had died at age 16] stood in the doorway of the sheep shed."[38] Chapter 21 of *Hello from Heaven!* also contains several examples of apparitions apparently perceived by pets as well as by their owners.

The Physicality of Apparitions

The physical nature of (at least some) apparitions derives additional support from the fact that apparitions have also been known to appear in photographs, and not just back in the Victorian heyday of "spirit

---

[35] Hart, "Six Theories about Apparitions," 207-12.

[36] Haraldsson, *The Departed Among the Living*, 15-16.

[37] Haraldsson, *The Departed Among the Living*, 44. Frimannson's testimony can also be found in Hafsteinn Björnsson, *Sögur ur safni Hafsteins midils* (Reykjavik, Iceland: Skuggsja, 1972).

[38] Haraldsson, *The Departed Among the Living*, 207.

photography."[39] Consider, for instance, the experience of a woman Annie Mattingley calls "Celeste." Soon after the death of her husband, Celeste attended a séance at which his head was seen under her chair, as well as photographed there. But Celeste herself didn't know about this for years, as her friends considered it too frightening to reveal to her until much later.[40]

In another case, William Stillman was investigating the home of an autistic man who reported being bothered by ghosts, one of whom he said had a beard. In fact, two photographs taken of the autistic man also showed "the face of a bearded man…hovering in the air at floor level; when digitally enlarged on a television screen, its features were distinct."[41] A video was taken during Stillman's investigation of the home, and upon replay, a pan of the home's windows revealed a face in one of the windows that looked like a bearded man. "This was not a reflection;" writes Stillman, "when compared against the static reflection of tree limbs and leaves in the adjacent glass panel, the face image moved and shifted and even seemed to blink."[42,43]

It seems that apparitions can actually vary in their solidity. Some apparitions are described as being somewhat transparent, while others appear just as solid as the bodies of living people and indeed are sometimes mistaken for them. The fact that people sometimes see apparitions "fading" out lends support to this idea of gradations of solidity.[44] It could be that the more concrete an apparition is, the more people are able to perceive it, and the more susceptible it is to being captured by camera. One of Haraldsson's

---

[39] For a good overview of this heyday, see James Coates, *Photographing the Invisible* (Chicago: Advanced Thought Publishing Company, 1911). For a more extensive list of sources, see Jule Eisenbud, *The World of Ted Serios: "Thoughtographic" Studies of an Extraordinary Mind* (New York: William Morrow & Co., 1967), 246.

[40] Mattingley, 107-8.

[41] William Stillman, *Autism and the God Connection: Redefining the Autistic Experience through Extraordinary Accounts of Spiritual Giftedness* (Naperville, IL: Sourcebooks, 2006), 187.

[42] Stillman, *Autism and the God Connection*, 195-6.

[43] We should note that the appearance of something on a photograph or video does not, by itself, prove that it was present in a physical way. We will discuss in Chapter 6 the phenomenon of thoughtography, in which persons have been known to make images appear on photographic film that bear no resemblance to any physical objects in the vicinity. Something like this could account for some examples of "spirit" photography. However, it doesn't seem like the best explanation in Celeste's case, since in that case, the apparition of her late husband's head was both seen in the room with the naked eye *and* seen in photography to be at the same location. This correspondence points to a more physical manifestation.

[44] For example, Mattingley describes her own experience of seeing the apparition of an unknown woman in Victorian dress on a landing in her home. She writes, "We stared at one another for a timeless moment, and then slowly, rather like the Cheshire Cat, she faded away before my eyes" (103).

informants suggests the idea that apparitions may come in degrees, saying, "The boat was haunted to such a degree that both people who had the special gift to see the deceased, and those who had no such gift, could see it."[45] One nevertheless puzzling aspect of apparitions is that some of them have been seen to produce reflections in mirrors,[46] while I know of at least one case in which the percipient specifically stated that there was no reflection (although it is not clear that this latter apparition was of a deceased person, rather than of some other spiritual being).[47]

We should note as well that apparitions also seem in some cases to be capable of affecting physical objects in their vicinity, as if they were solid beings. For instance, even those who have only sensed a presence rather than seen an apparition have sometimes noted that there has been a depression in the bed cover as though someone were physically sitting there. In one case, a woman staying in a bed and breakfast observed little paw prints moving up the bed toward her and then heard a loud purring sound. She was later told by the owner of the B&B that it was probably one of her deceased cats who loved climbing on that bed.[48]

The ability of the deceased to act on physical objects takes especially surprising form in the following case. A woman was driving over some railroad tracks when she saw a train coming and froze. She then heard the voice of her deceased friend say, "Drive this car!" and felt a foot stomp on top of hers, pressing the gas pedal and moving her out of harm's way. The really odd part about it was that she discovered afterward that she had a big bruise on her foot.[49]

Bruises also feature in a second case reported to the Guggenheims. In that case, a woman "tripped and started to fall and later discovered bruises on her arms where her deceased husband's hands had caught her from behind."[50]

Finally, here is an example of an apparition that appears to have had all the visibility and solidity of a living human being. According to the percipient, "She held out her hand, grasped my fingers hard and said: 'Hello there.' ... I had seen spirits before, [but] I had never seen the like of this and never touched one, not one which seemed to be of flesh and blood."[51]

---

[45] Haraldsson, *The Departed Among the Living*, 73.
[46] Hart, "Six Theories about Apparitions," 208.
[47] William J. Serdahely, "Loving Help from the Other Side: A Mosaic of Some Near-Death, and Near-Death-Like, Experiences," *Journal of Near Death Studies* 10, no. 3 (Spring 1992): 171-82, p. 180.
[48] Julie Beischel, "Survival of Consciousness: Animal Discarnates," in *Investigating Mediums* (Tucson, AZ: Windbridge Institute, 2015), 37-56, p. 51.
[49] Guggenheim and Guggenheim, 298-99.
[50] Guggenheim and Guggenheim, 299.
[51] Haraldsson, *The Departed Among the Living*, 212.

Long and Complex Apparitional Experiences

As suggested by the cases so far cited, apparitions are generally quite brief, often amounting to little more than a prolonged look before the apparition disappears. In fact, in half of the accounts collected by Haraldsson, the experience lasted no more than a few seconds.[52] However, there do exist some cases of longer, more complex apparitions. And this is important, since, the longer and more complex the apparition, the harder it would be for a mere hallucination to sustain a perfect imitation of a deceased personality. Consider the experiences of these people:

- Shirley, whose husband Sol appeared to her and guided her through the huge amount of paperwork needed for her to receive the pension money he had earned,[53]
- Johann Kuld, whose wife came to him in their bedroom and, after explaining what she'd been doing in the time since her death, lay in bed with him stroking his cheek and whispering "beautiful things,"[54]
- a woman whose dead son sat every night on a stool in her kitchen keeping her company until she was ready to say good-bye to him,[55] and
- Darrell Smith, who picked up a hitchhiker who looked and talked exactly like his deceased father and who told him, "I'm visiting with my son. He needs me."[56]

Consider, too, a case reported by Morse in his book *Parting Visions.* A man was out fishing when he saw his brother-in-law coming down a path toward him. They spent several minutes talking to each other, and then his brother-in-law said he had to go and walked into the woods. Some minutes later, it occurred to the man that his brother-in-law couldn't have actually been there. When he got home, he learned that, while he'd been out fishing, his brother-in-law had been killed in a car accident. Furthermore, this appears not to have been the deceased man's only visit to his family. "He was a

---

[52] Haraldsson, *The Departed Among the Living*, 119.
[53] Martin and Romanowski, 61-62.
[54] Haraldsson, *The Departed Among the Living*, 113. Kuld's account can also be found in J. J. E. Kuld, *Í lífsins ólgusjó* (Reykjavik, Iceland: Ægisútgáfan, 1979).
[55] Judith Orloff, *Second Sight: An Intuitive Psychiatrist Tells Her Extraordinary Story and Shows You How to Tap Your Own Inner Wisdom*, rev. ed. (New York: Three Rivers Press, 2000), 168, 172.
[56] Sophy Burnham, *Angel Letters* (New York: Ballantine Books, 1991), 46-49.

carpenter by trade," says Morse, "and visits his wife's son frequently with helpful suggestions about woodworking projects."[57]

One rather humorous case of a long, complex apparition involves a hospital doctor who had released a patient named Mr. Parker so that Mr. Parker could spend the Christmas holidays with his family. A few days after Christmas, the doctor saw Mr. Parker standing in a hallway of the emergency room looking at a gurney where a cadaver lay under a sheet. When the doctor pulled back the sheet, he saw that the body was that of Mr. Parker himself! The doctor says that he could then hear Mr. Parker's voice in his head joyfully telling him not to worry. The doctor could also feel the presence of other people in spirit gathered around him. Then, all of a sudden, the apparition of Mr. Parker just disappeared.[58]

The most extended interaction with an apparition I've encountered comes from a case investigated by Loyd Auerbach and reported by him in journalist Leslie Kean's excellent book *Surviving Death*. In this case, a "ghost" not only separately appeared to four members of the same family but carried on extended conversations with their teenage son, Chris. The family had bought their house and some of its furnishings after the death of a woman who had lived there her entire life since birth. Her name was Lois, and she apparently appeared to Chris regularly, telling him the stories of the furniture in the house, as well as helping him with his homework and giving him advice about girls!

When Auerbach arrived at the house to investigate, Lois seemed to be present the entire time, though visible only to Chris. The family, along with Auerbach and "Lois," all sat down in the living room, and everyone proceeded to ask Lois questions about herself, the answers being conveyed by Chris. Auerbach recorded all of the information Chris provided and subsequently verified the accuracy of the details pertaining to her former life with a surviving relative. Auerbach says this experience was a turning point for him. He concluded—I think rightly—that it made much more sense to believe that the deceased Lois was actually there communicating to Chris than that Chris was some kind of super-psychic who only ever got information about this one dead woman and also somehow managed to occasionally make her visible to his family members.[59]

Another case that deserves mention is that of Haley, a six-year-old girl who was lost in the Ozark Mountain Wilderness for a few days. When she was finally found, she said she'd spent her time in the woods with another little girl named Elisha, who had a silver flashlight of which she was very

---

[57] Morse with Perry, 190.

[58] Raymond Moody with Paul Perry, *Glimpses of Eternity: An Investigation into Shared Death Experiences* (London: Rider Books, 2010), 30-31.

[59] Leslie Kean, *Surviving Death: A Journalist Investigates Evidence for an Afterlife* (New York: Crown Archetype, 2017), 253-61.

possessive. Subsequent research uncovered that, two decades previously, a little girl by the name of Elisha had been murdered and buried in those woods. The murdered girl's mother reported that Elisha used to sleep with a silver flashlight under the covers with her and would cry when the mother would try to take it away from her.[60]

Children seem to be particularly prone to extended interactions with the spirits of the deceased. As our final apparitional account, consider what Margaret's young daughter Samantha told her one evening as Margaret was carrying her to bed. Looking over her mother's shoulder, Samantha gaily asked, "Oh, who's there?" This question creeped Margaret out, since as far as she knew, no one else was in the house with them. But Samantha then said with a happy smile, "It's the lady." Margaret got the sudden feeling that the "lady" was actually her own deceased mother. But she didn't tell Samantha this. She just asked her for more information about this person, and Samantha said she was "the lady that sits on my bed and plays with me." A week or so later, Margaret and her husband asked Samantha again about the lady, and Samantha pointed to a picture sitting on top of their TV. "That's the lady," she said. "That's the lady that sits on my bed and plays with me." Samantha had never been told who the person in that picture was, but it was indeed Margaret's mother.[61]

Evidence for Life after Death: Dreams

Though somewhat different from apparitions, dreams of the deceased can also provide evidence for life after death. As we will continue to see in the following chapters of this book, the experiences we have while sleeping are not purely the products of our private imagination. Dreams also appear to put us into contact with psychic information of various kinds, and this seems to be especially true of dreams of the deceased. Many of those who have had this experience remember it as so much more vivid than an ordinary dream that they don't think it should be called a "dream" at all.

"I was asleep," says one such experiencer, "but I was not dreaming." This statement comes from a man named Bob, the ex-husband of author Annie Mattingley, who recounts in her book *The After Death Chronicles* Bob's experience with their deceased daughter, Randi. Bob says that he encountered his daughter in a place "beyond" dreaming and that leaving that place felt like the opposite of waking from a dream. The realm where they

---

[60] Haley's grandmother's account of the incident is quoted in both Russell Targ, *The Reality of ESP: A Physicist's Proof of Psychic Abilities* (Wheaton, IL: Quest Books, 2012), 184-7; and Russell Targ, *Do You See What I See?: Lasers and Love, ESP and the CIA, and the Meaning of Life* (Charlottesville, VA: Hampton Roads, 2010), 225-9.

[61] LaGrand, *Messages and Miracles*, 166-7.

met "was like being in the middle of eternity," he says. There, his daughter Randi appeared to be about the age of 20, much younger than when she'd died, and she was glowing with a light that was all around them as well. They didn't talk to each other, just held each other for the longest time.[62]

It seems to me, from my reading and personal experience, that sleep opens up the possibility not just of ordinary dreaming—which itself frequently contains psychically derived elements—but of experiencing a realm similar to or the same as that experienced by NDErs. That is to say, the "after"-life seems to be accessible to some people here and now, through the medium of sleep. Abundant examples of such otherworldly dreams can be found in Dr. Andrew Paquette's book *Dreamer*, mentioned in previous chapters,[63] and a similar state also seems to have been reached by Robert Monroe and others who have used his method for inducing out-of-body experiences.[64]

Dreams offer particularly strong evidence for life after death when they come to more than one person and/or are independently corroborated in some other way. For instance, Robert Waggoner and his niece both dreamt that Waggoner's recently deceased father "wanted them to get something out of the closet." It was Waggoner's impression that this thing was in a pocket of one of his father's suit coats, so he called his mother and had her check. Lo and behold, she found some valuable family pictures that might have otherwise been lost.[65]

In a case collected by Dianne Arcangel, two separate people had repeated dreams of a deceased person, and they both described the same unexpected setting in the dreams: a house with a picket fence and a yard with a sign that read, "At Peace with Jesus." They both saw the deceased standing on the sidewalk with the sign to his left. What was more, in at least one of their dreams, the deceased repeatedly asked the dreamer to tell his widow to look at a specific location in their house—"in the hall, at the dead end, just south of the bedroom to the right of the light socket"—because he'd left something inside the wall there. When this message was finally shared with his widow, she opened the wall in that location and discovered a stash of thousands of dollars.[66]

---

[62] Mattingley, 130.
[63] Andrew Paquette, *Dreamer: 20 Years of Psychic Dreams and How They Changed My Life* (Winchester, UK: O-Books, 2011).
[64] Robert A. Monroe, *Journeys Out of the Body*, updated edition (Garden City, NY: Anchor/Doubleday, 1971, 1977); Robert A. Monroe, *Far Journeys* (Garden City, NY: Doubleday, 1985, 1987), 93; and Robert A. Monroe, *Ultimate Journey* (New York: Harmony, 1994).
[65] Robert Waggoner, *Lucid Dreaming: Gateway to the Inner Self* (Needham, MA: Moment Point Press, 2009), 209.
[66] Arcangel, 77-80.

Tandem dreams are even stronger evidence for life after death when they demonstrate the evolution of the deceased's consciousness through time. In another case collected by Arcangel, the deceased demonstrates continuity of consciousness by the adoption of a new strategy in pursuit of his goal. A woman named Debra dreamed of her deceased stepfather who came to say good-bye, as well as to say that he hadn't wanted to die but had to. When she told her mother about the dream, her mother "became very pale, saying, 'I dreamed about him too, but I told him I was afraid. I said, 'Go tell Debbie.'"[67]

Adoption of a new strategy by the deceased is also in evidence in the following case collected by Dr. David Ryback and described in his book *Dreams That Come True.* A single mother and her two children (one of whom was Ryback's informant for this case) were all quite sick and needed to move to a warmer climate but didn't have the strength or the means. While many people would look to their extended family for help in such a situation, the mother was currently on the outs with her father. However, one night she had a dream that her deceased grandmother came to her door and told her, "Bill [the father] will help, if you just let him know. Call him." But the young woman held her ground, replying, "He'll have to make the first move. I won't." She woke up thinking how strange it was that her grandmother had called her father "Bill" instead of "Wilbur," the name she'd always used for him in life.

A couple days later, the young woman got a letter from her father, asking her to call. They patched up their relationship, and both the woman's father and mother ended up coming to help her move. While they were on the road to the new home, the young woman asked her mother whether her grandmother had ever used the name "Bill" for her father. She said yes, but added that the grandmother had only started using this name for him about three months before she died.

The young woman then decided to tell her mother about the dream. When she did, she discovered that, on the very same night that she had had her own dream, her father had *also* received a dream visitation from her grandmother. She'd told him it was urgent that he get in touch with his daughter and said that it was up to him to make the first move, because his daughter wouldn't do it. Apparently, he got up before dawn to write and mail the letter that his daughter soon received.[68]

The case just described bears strong parallels to one we looked at in Chapter 2, the one in which Elvis Presley appeared in a dream to Georgia police officer Harold Welch and gave him detailed information about the whereabouts of his runaway son. Recall that, when Welch found his son, he

---

[67] Arcangel, 51.

[68] David Ryback with Letitia Sweitzer, *Dreams That Come True: Their Psychic and Transforming Powers* (New York: Doubleday, 1988), 131-2.

didn't tell him anything about his dream of Elvis, but his son said to him, "Dad, it's the funniest thing. Two times since I've been out here I've had dreams about Elvis Presley. In both dreams he told me you would be coming to get me. He said he was worried about me. He said he would work it out."[69]

Evidence for Life after Death: Perception During NDEs

Additional evidence for life after death comes from people who have near-death experiences (NDEs). While their bodies are dead or near death, some NDErs report seeing or hearing things they could not have normally seen or heard even if their bodies had been fully functional.

Titus Rivas, Anny Dirven, and Rudolf H. Smit have collected a number of cases of verified paranormal perception during NDEs in their indispensable book *The* Self *Does Not Die.*[70] For instance, in a case originally reported by Lerma in *Into the Light*, an 82-year-old man had an NDE in which he floated out of his body in the hospital trauma room. From a position up above the goings-on there, he saw a quarter sitting on the right-hand corner of the eight-foot-high cardiac monitor, a quarter dating from the year 1985. After he was resuscitated, he asked Lerma to go and check whether the quarter was really there, so he could know whether his very affecting spiritual experience was real. Lerma took a ladder and climbed up to look, and there indeed was the 1985 quarter, just as the patient had seen it.[71]

In another case, originally reported by Drs. Kenneth Ring and Madelaine Lawrence in an important article titled "Further Evidence for Veridical Perception during Near-Death Experiences," a patient reported an NDE in which she was pulled upward through the floors of the hospital until she came up out of the roof. From there, she noticed a red shoe. A skeptical physician later went onto the roof to check and discovered the red shoe as described.[72]

Other NDErs have received verifications for their perceptions of things as diverse as their wife and daughter discussing taking cuttings from a unique tree in a hospital courtyard,[73] their grandmothers both suddenly taking up

---

[69] Raymond A. Moody, Jr., *Elvis After Life: Unusual Psychic Experiences Surrounding the Death of a Superstar* (Atlanta, GA: Peachtree Publishers, 1987), 90.

[70] Titus Rivas, Anny Dirven, and Rudolf H. Smit, *The* Self *Does Not Die: Verified Paranormal Phenomena from Near-Death Experiences* (Durham, NC: IANDS Publications, 2016).

[71] Lerma, *Into the Light*, 10-12.

[72] Kenneth Ring and Madelaine Lawrence, "Further Evidence for Veridical Perception during Near-Death Experiences," *Journal of Near-Death Studies* 11, no. 4 (1993): 223-9.

[73] Rivas, Dirven, and Smit, 45.

smoking,[74] and details of the amputation of a leg in a nearby operating theater.[75]

Of course, anyone familiar with the phenomenon of clairvoyance/remote viewing will know that you don't have to be dead or near dead to perceive things at a distance, in space or time.[76] For this reason, verified paranormal perceptions are not by themselves proof that our spirit can survive independently of the body. In some cases, however, it can be verified that these paranormal perceptions occurred *during cardiac arrest and in the absence of brain function.*

One example of this is the famous case of the man who saw his dentures being removed and put on a tray on the crash cart. This event happened while the patient was "ashen gray, with livor mortis (in which blue-black discoloration occurs where blood pools in the lowest areas of the corpse) and blue lips and nails. He exhibited no blood circulation … [and] had no heart rhythm."[77] As Rivas, Dirven, and Smit make clear, "[d]uring cardiac arrest, the brain activity of the cortex is shut down within an average of about 15 seconds to such an extent that, according to materialists, no complex conscious experiencing can occur after this point."[78] By the time the man who saw his dentures removed was brought into the hospital, he had been in cardiac arrest for a great deal longer than 15 seconds. He had been found "unconscious, stone cold, and apparently clinically dead out in a meadow…. In the ambulance, they tried to resuscitate him, but failed…." This explains his blue appearance when he arrived at the hospital, where his dentures were removed before the renewal of resuscitation efforts. Those resuscitation efforts then took over an hour to be effective enough for the patient to be transmitted to the ICU. And yet, about a week later, the patient spoke to the nurse who had removed his dentures and said that he had *seen* the nurse place them on the pull-out shelf of a cart with lots of bottles on it, which is exactly what the nurse had done.[79]

Rivas, Dirven, and Smit devote an entire chapter of their book *The* Self *Does Not Die* to verified cases of awareness and perception during cardiac arrest. And it is because of these cases that they conclude that consciousness survives death. In their words, "*the presence of personal consciousness during a cardiac arrest implies that humans can expect personal survival after irreversible death.*"[80] They

---

[74] Rivas, Dirven, and Smit, 44.
[75] Rivas, Dirven, and Smit, 59.
[76] Those unfamiliar with the phenomenon will find an excellent introduction in Russell Targ, *The Reality of ESP: A Physicist's Proof of Psychic Abilities* (Wheaton, IL: Quest Books, 2012).
[77] Rivas, Dirven, and Smit, 63.
[78] Rivas, Dirven, and Smit, 55.
[79] Rivas, Dirven, and Smit, 63-64.
[80] Rivas, Dirven, and Smit, 226.

do consider the skeptical hypothesis that perceptions like those of the dentures could be obtained after resuscitation, by using extrasensory perception to look into the past and see what happened while the NDEr was unconscious, but they see this hypothesis as ridiculously *ad hoc*. Indeed, I see no independent reason to believe in such a convoluted chain of events, unless it's that one wants to cling to the notion of brain-dependent consciousness at all costs. Furthermore, if time is no barrier to our capacities of extrasensory perception, this implies that our consciousness can transcend time, and in that case, it's not clear that the concept of death—of our being alive at one time and dead at another—is even coherent.

Evidence for Life after Death: Apparitions of NDErs

However, NDEs have even more evidence to offer for survival. There are cases in which, not only did an NDEr perceive things going on at some distance from their body, but someone *at that location* was aware of their presence as well. For example, *The* Self *Does Not Die* contains a case in which a man was awakened from sleep by the sound of his girlfriend calling his name. At the same moment, she was undergoing surgery because of an ectopic pregnancy. When she awoke afterward, she remembered seeing her boyfriend lying on his bed at home and calling out his name to him.[81]

In another case, the only sign of the NDEr's presence was the front door of his brother's house in Brumath, Alsace, repeatedly opening during the night. After the first time this happened, the door was locked. Nevertheless, the locked door proceeded to open all by itself, not once but twice. Finally, the door was bound with rope, and then it did not reopen. It was discovered later that the brother of the owner of the house had died on that date. In fact, when he had already appeared to be dead, he opened his eyes one final time and said, "I just went on a grand journey: I went to see my brother in Brumath."[82]

In addition, Rivas, Dirven, and Smit present four cases of verified *visual* perceptions of NDErs.[83] The case they report in the most detail comes from a professional presentation by Laurin Bellg.[84] In that case, a young man was so estranged from his dying mother that she refused to allow him into her hospital room. While he was hanging out in a bar near the hospital, he saw

[81] Rivas, Dirven, and Smit, 165-7.
[82] Rivas, Dirven, and Smit, 157-8. Originally reported in Camille Flammarion, *L'inconnu et les problèmes psychiques* (New York: Harper & Brothers, 1900).
[83] Rivas, Dirven, and Smit, 158-65.
[84] Laurin Bellg, *Patient NDEs in the ICU*, presentation at The Monroe Institute (TMI) Professional Seminar. Retrievable from https://www.youtube.com/watch?v=xdScjvc14xE starting at 31:08 in the video.

her walk into the bar. He was amazed to see her there, because he knew how sick she was. As he got up to go to her, some other people passed between them, and when they had gone by, she wasn't there anymore. Around the same time, the woman, whose body was actually lying in her hospital bed, woke up and told her daughter who was with her, "I had the strangest dream. I dreamed that I was in a bar and I saw my son sitting at a table crying, and he got up to start coming to me. And I got scared and I woke up."[85]

There are three other cases in *The* Self *Does Not Die* that contain apparitions of an NDEr who independently reported perceiving themselves as being at the location in question. The fact that the apparitions of these people *near* death are experienced in much the same way as apparitions of the deceased, and that these NDErs are able to report *their subjective experience of having been at the location in question*, makes it seem exceedingly plausible that apparitions of the deceased likewise represent the conscious presence of the persons who are seen to appear.

Evidence for Life after Death: Apparitions of Non-NDE Out-of-Body Experiencers

Further evidence in this vein is supplied by a study conducted by Dr. Hornell Hart and his collaborators, in which they compared apparitions of the deceased to apparitions of living people who were not near death but who were nevertheless having out-of-body experiences (OBEs). In these OBEs, living people experienced being in a place other than the one in which their body was located and reported having specific perceptions in that place. Independently, witnesses saw an apparition of them in that remote location and were able to verify the perceptions they reported.

If you are interested in the details of such cases, you can see Chapter 7, where I describe a few of them in the section "Remote Psychokinesis." For now, I'll simply note the conclusions reached by Hart and his co-researchers. After they compared the rates of incidence of 23 basic traits in living-person apparitions to their rates of incidence in apparitions of the deceased, Hart et al. concluded that all of their evidence pointed to these two types of apparitions' being the same phenomenon. "Assuming that consciousness is dependent on the living physical brain," say Hart et al., "a sharp alteration should be evident in the character and behaviour of apparitions when the death point…is passed. But *no such alteration is evident in the data*—except such as might be expected from the alterations of purpose which death would produce in the appearer."[86] This evidence thus supports the conclusion that

---

[85] Rivas, Dirven, and Smit, 162-5.
[86] Hart, "Six Theories," 235.

apparitions of the dead are caused by the presence of a conscious, willing subject, just like apparitions of OBErs are.

Further bolstering Hart's point, I've even come across one case in which a person reported experiencing apparitions of *the same person* both before and after death. When this experiencer was between the ages of 8 and 13, their mother was in the hospital. But, at important moments, they would see her by their bedside at home. The experiencer only notes one difference between these pre-death apparitions and those that continued to happen after his mother died. "It was always dark above and behind her when I saw her while she was alive," says this experiencer. "After she died…it was always brighter all around her."[87]

In sum, verified out-of-body experiences not only demonstrate that, during our lives, we have some measure of consciousness that is not limited to our bodies, but also support the view that that part of us continues to exist after the body's death.

Evidence for Life after Death: Shared Death Experiences

In our discussion of NDEs in this chapter, we've so far neglected to mention some of their most common elements: for instance, the experience of floating out of one's body, seeing a tunnel and/or a light, perceiving deceased loved ones, and undergoing a review of the events of one's life. Don't these experiences offer additional evidence for survival of death?

Perhaps, but only if there's evidence that these experiences are more than mere "hallucinations of a dying brain." And, in fact, there is. One source of such evidence comes from shared death experiences. In the typical shared death experience, someone who is present at the death of a loved one will actually perceive along with the person who has just died many of the elements that are commonly reported in NDEs. That is, the living person may float above their body, see a beautiful light, and perceive other deceased loved ones who've come to escort the newly dead. They may even participate in the life review of the person just deceased. It is as though the living person is, for a few moments, caught up into the same spiritual world experienced by the one crossing over into death. And yet the living person cannot be accused of being the victim of a "dying brain."

An excellent overview of the phenomenon of shared death experiences is provided by Dr. Raymond Moody in his book *Glimpses of Eternity*. Consider the following experience taken from that book, related by a woman named Dana, who was holding her beloved husband Johnny when he passed away. At that moment, she says, "he went right through my body," giving her a

---

[87] Haraldsson, *The Departed Among the Living*, 139.

strong electrical sensation. After that, she and Johnny were suddenly enveloped in a wraparound display of their lives. "Everything we ever did was there in that light," she says. She even saw some of the things Johnny had done with other girls before they were married, and from what she saw, she was later able to locate those specific girls in Johnny's high school yearbook! During the life review, Dana and Johnny were also greeted—embraced, actually—by a child they had once lost to miscarriage. "She was not a figure of a person exactly as you would see a human being," says Dana, "but more the outline or sweet, loving presence of a little girl." This encounter gave Dana tremendous peace in a difficult time.[88]

Shared death experiences appear to be more common than their lack of press would lead one to believe. In his lectures around the world, Moody has found that 5 to 10% of the members of his audiences have had such experiences, making them only slightly less common among his audience members than the near-death experiences he's best known for writing about.[89]

But, if the existence of shared death experiences isn't enough to be persuasive, consider that they have also been known to happen to *multiple living people simultaneously*. That is, multiple people present at a death have had the same extraordinary perceptions, making it even harder to explain them away as unreal. For instance, Moody's book contains the case of two brothers, two sisters, and a sister-in-law who were all present for their mother's death and perceived some of the same extraordinary phenomena. At first, it was just a bright, unearthly light that appeared in the room where they were all gathered around their dying mother. But just after the mother breathed her last, the family saw "vivid bright lights that seemed to gather around and shape up into…an entranceway." They then saw their mother come out of her body and go into the entrance that had formed. It was apparently a very joyful experience for all involved, and one of the sisters even heard "beautiful music," though the rest of them did not.[90]

In another multiply shared death experience, two sisters participated in their mother's life review and discovered through that experience that their mother had a crush on her widowed neighbor! One of the sisters says, "What we saw was so real that we thought we had died too. For months it was beyond belief until we finally accepted it."[91]

To close this section, let me offer one more example of a shared death experience, this one extraordinarily impactful in its simplicity. It happened to an eight-year-old boy who was playing in the kitchen while his grandmother cooked. All of a sudden, his grandmother just fell over. But while the boy

---

[88] Moody with Perry, *Glimpses of Eternity*, 10-12.
[89] Moody with Perry, *Glimpses of Eternity*, 51.
[90] Moody with Perry, *Glimpses of Eternity*, 13-14.
[91] Moody with Perry, *Glimpses of Eternity*, 15.

could see her body lying on the floor, he could also see another—much younger—version of her who was still standing up. Then a man of about the same age appeared beside her. "The two looked at me and waved," he says, "and when they did I felt a deep love. Then they turned away as a unit and disappeared by walking away together through the kitchen wall." The experiencer, who is now a retired professor of philosophy, adds that these two people were more real than anything else he's ever experienced in his life.[92]

In conclusion, the abundance of shared death experiences shows us that near-death experiences are not the isolated, crazy imaginings of a brain in the throes of death. The phenomena of NDEs are corroborated by the experiences of many healthy individuals, which is exactly what we would expect if the phenomena perceived by NDErs are indeed real, though usually invisible to most of us.

Evidence for Life after Death: Memories of Past Lives

Yet another source of evidence for life after death comes from children (and some adults) who remember having lived previous lives. The idea of reincarnation will probably seem ridiculous to some readers—it certainly did to me at one time. While I don't have space here to lay out all of the evidence for the reality of this phenomenon, I invite those who are skeptical to familiarize themselves with the vast scientific literature on this topic, particularly with the late Dr. Ian Stevenson's extremely thorough work investigating the accuracy of children's memories of past lives,[93] work that has been replicated and expanded by other researchers, including Dr. Satwant Pasricha,[94] Dr. Antonia Mills, Dr. Erlendur Haraldsson, Dr. Jürgen Keil,[95]

---

[92] Moody with Perry, *Glimpses of Eternity*, 169.
[93] See, among Stevenson's many works, Ian Stevenson, *Twenty Cases Suggestive of Reincarnation,* 2nd ed. revised and enlarged (Charlottesville, VA: University of Virginia Press, 1980). A less detailed introduction to his work, suitable for a general audience, is available in Ian Stevenson, *Children Who Remember Previous Lives: A Question of Reincarnation*, rev. ed. (Jefferson, NC: McFarland & Company, Inc., 2001). Another excellent introduction is a book written by journalist Tom Shroder, who accompanied Stevenson on a few of his final research trips: Tom Shroder, *Old Souls* (New York: Simon & Schuster, 1999).
[94] Satwant Pasricha, *Claims of Reincarnation: An Empirical Study of Cases in India* (New Delhi: Harman Publishing House, 1990).
[95] Antonia Mills, Erlendur Haraldsson, and H. H. Jürgen Keil, "Replication Studies of Cases Suggestive of Reincarnation by Three Independent Investigators," *Journal of the American Society for Psychical Research* 88 (1994): 207-19.

and Dr. Jim B. Tucker.[96] These researchers, along with others, have gone to great lengths to carefully investigate whether the memories children report about their previous personalities are true of actual deceased persons, and whether it can be relied upon that the children could not have learned about the details of these deceased persons' lives in any "normal" way. For many of these cases, from all over the world, reincarnation seems to be the best available explanation. And there are not just a few isolated examples of this. Back in 2001, the University of Virginia (where Stevenson was based) had already collected over 2,500 cases that investigation showed to be suggestive of reincarnation.[97]

Researchers have also shown that children who report memories of past lives tend to have higher-than-average intelligence, and their memories do not appear to be due to any form of psychopathology.[98] Also, Haraldsson's tests of Sri Lankan children who remember previous lives have led him to conclude that "children who make verified statements about a previous life are less suggestible than other children," as measured by the Gudjonsson Suggestibility Scale.[99]

What is more, these children's memories share important commonalities with near-death experiences. For one thing, multiple NDErs report learning about reincarnation during their NDEs. Dr. Mary Helen Hensley, for example, was the daughter of a Baptist minister and as a young person didn't even have reincarnation on her radar. Nevertheless, when she had an NDE at age 21, she not only saw a play-by-play review of her current life, but she suddenly remembered many lives she'd lived before. She says, "Of the many things that I can remember [from the NDE], there is one that I feel compelled to convey with certainty—I think it is important to state that reincarnation is a *fact*."[100]

---

[96] Jim B. Tucker, *Life Before Life: Children's Memories of Previous Lives* (New York: St. Martin's Griffin, 2008); and Jim B. Tucker, *Return to Life: Extraordinary Cases of Children Who Remember Past Lives*, reprint ed. (New York: St. Martin's Griffin, 2015).
[97] Stevenson, *Children Who Remember Previous Lives*, 261, note 2.
[98] Jim B. Tucker and F. Don Nidiffer, "Psychological Evaluation of American Children Who Report Memories of Previous Lives," *Journal of Scientific Exploration* 28, no. 4 (2014): 585-96.
[99] Erlendur Haraldsson, "A Psychological Comparison Between Ordinary Children and Those Who Claim Previous-Life Memories," *Journal of Scientific Exploration* 11, no. 3 (1997): 323-35, p. 331.
[100] Mary Helen Hensley, *Promised by Heaven: A Doctor's Return from the Afterlife to a Destiny of Love and Healing* (New York: Atria, 2015), 11. See also Barbara R. Rommer, *Blessing in Disguise: Another Side of the Near-Death Experience* (St. Paul, MN: Llewellyn, 2000), 6, 28-9, 160; and Cathleen C.'s NDE recounted online at https://www.nderf.org/Experiences/1cathleen_c_nde.html. NDEr Betty J. Eadie says in *Embraced by the Light* that she learned "we do not have repeated lives on this earth" (p. 93), but she clarifies on her website, "There is a form of reincarnation

But past-life memories and NDEs also corroborate each other in another way. Many children who remember having lived previous lives have vivid memories of their deaths in those lives, including memories of the kinds of experiences related by NDErs: of leaving their bodies, going through tunnels, and/or being escorted to the afterlife by spiritual beings. For instance, three-year-old Stephen Ramsay remembered being a soldier fighting in the jungle and dying when a plane "hurt [his] tummy," causing it to bleed. He described dying as "just [going] to sleep in the trees." When he woke up, his tummy felt all better, but he was still in the trees. Then, he says, "[a] lady came to see me. … She was a nice lady and she told me to follow her. She took my hand and took me with her."[101]

A young Brazilian girl named Silvia had an inexplicable knowledge of the Italian language as well as a fear of airplanes flying overhead, apparently linked to her memories of living in a place she called the "*capitolio*," where planes would drop bombs. When she was three years old, Silvia told her grandmother about a boy who was carrying a bomb that blew up and hurt her, her cousin, and her friend. "Then my friend and me, we went up and up," she said. Her grandmother asked if she meant up the stairs of the *capitolio*, but she said, "No, Grandma, we went up, high up there." When Grandma asked what happened after that, Silvia replied, "I don't know. Then I came here."[102]

Another Brazilian child, Kilden, announced to his mother when he was around the age of three that his name was actually "Alexandre" and he was "the priest." His mother had in fact been friends with a priest named Alexandre, and she had heard on the radio that he had died after being in a car accident. But Kilden now told her that it hadn't been a car accident. He said he'd been riding a motorcycle and was hit by a truck. When she checked the police report, she discovered that this was what had actually happened to her friend Alexandre. I relate those verified details to lend credibility to something else Kilden said, when he explained to his mother what happens after someone is in an accident. He said,

> The person who suffered the accident arrives and is put in a room full of instruments. The doctors connect them…. Then the equipment is connected to the chest and the head, and the doctors keep trying to save

---

but not as we understand it here. … [W]e do not come back to this earth for repeated lives until we get it 'right.' … There are those who do return to this world when it serves our Heavenly Father's purposes and they come back as teachers" (https://embracedbythelight.com/qa/ qa.htm).

[101] Mary Harrison and Peter Harrison, *The Children That Time Forgot* (1983, 1989, 2014), 70.

[102] Guy Lyon Playfair, *The Flying Cow: Exploring the Psychic World of Brazil* (Guildford, UK: White Crow Books, 2011), 162-3.

> the life of the person. At this point the person flies into a corner of the ceiling, watching the doctors' fight to save him. Then a big hole like a funnel appeared in the corner of the wall near me, trying to suck me....

At this point, his mother interrupted to ask who he was talking about, himself or someone else. Kilden said, "Well, I think it was me. I saw my body and the doctors trying to save me." Then, at his mother's prompting, he continued with his description, alternating between the third and first person:

> When he was sucked through the hole into the tunnel, he saw a strong light at the end, so strong that I turned my head to one side. The light was very bright, and the hole closed behind him, near the wall. At that moment the doctors saw the screen on their machine stop.[103]

Chase, the five-year-old son of author Carol Bowman, displayed sudden hysterical fear one July 4 after hearing the cannon-like booms of fireworks. A family friend, trying to help Chase get to the bottom of his fear, asked him to close his eyes and tell them what he saw when he heard the noises that scared him. Chase immediately gave a long, detailed description of himself as a soldier on a battlefield that appeared to be during the Civil War. A few years later, when Chase was eight years old, his memories of being a soldier were evoked again when he saw television coverage of the First Gulf War. "They'll never make me fight again!" he proclaimed to his mother. He told her that he kept thinking about his memories of war and wanted to try visualizing them again. So Bowman again encouraged Chase to relax, close his eyes, and go back to the scene where he was a soldier. He again saw a very detailed series of mental images, and this time, they ended in his death. "I'm hit!" said Chase. "I'm floating above the battlefield. I feel good that I'm done. I see the battle and smoke below. As I look down on the battlefield, everything is still and smoky—nothing is moving down there. I feel happy that I'm done. I get to go to a happier life. I float over my house. I see my wife and kids. I say good-bye to my family. They don't see me because I'm in spirit, but they know that I'm dead."[104]

It is especially important for the purposes of this book to note that children with memories of dying in a previous life do sometimes remember

---

[103] Hernani Guimarães Andrade, *Reborn for Love* (London: Roundtable, 2010), 130-1. This case is also described in great detail in Erlendur Haraldsson and James G. Matlock, *I Saw a Light and Came Here: Children's Experiences of Reincarnation* (Hove, UK: White Crow Books, 2016), 204-8.

[104] Carol Bowman, *Children's Past Lives: How Past Life Memories Affect Your Child* (New York: Bantam, 1997, 1998), 5-11, 19-24. Note that, although Bowman is trained as a hypnotherapist, hypnotic induction was not used to elicit these memories from her son. In both cases, he was only asked to relax, close his eyes, and describe what he saw.

interacting with people on earth after their deaths. The following case gives particularly good evidence for the veracity of after-death communication through a dream. In this case, a Burmese woman dreamt that her deceased husband told her that he had left some money (a 5-kyat note) wrapped in a white handkerchief inside a small box. She subsequently found the handkerchief and the money, which she said was less important to her than verifying that what he'd said in the dream was true. But she was to get even more verification than that. A Burmese boy was born who, around the age of three, began recalling a past life in which he was this woman's husband. He also recalled how, after his death as that person, he had appeared to his wife in a dream and told her he'd left 5 kyats wrapped in a white handkerchief and how to find it![105]

In another case, a child said that, after his death in a previous life, he'd hung out near his previous family's house and sometimes taken their food. The family confirmed that they'd had food inexplicably disappear during that time.[106] This case provides evidence for a deceased person's being responsible for some "poltergeist-like" actions, though in this case relatively benign ones.

Here is another case that provides similar evidence, though the action taken by the deceased in this case was potentially more dangerous. An Indian boy remembered residing in a bodhi tree in the 11 years between a previous life and his current one. The tree was outside his former family's house, and he remembered that, when he became annoyed one day at two women swinging in a swing that was attached to a branch of this tree, he caused the wooden seat of the swing they were sitting on to break. This event was remembered not only by the boy but also by the father of the boy's previous personality.[107]

Let's finish this section with a more benevolent after-death interaction, this one from Hertfordshire, England. From the time she was born, Mandy Seabrook looked very much like another of her mother's children, one who had died at the age of five months. In fact, when Mandy was two years old, she began recounting memories of having *been* this other child. In particular, she remembered the circumstances of her burial and a particular object she said she'd been buried with: a fluffy yellow ball. Her mother remembered the

---

[105] Titus Rivas, Elizabeth M. Carman, Neil J. Carman, and Anny Dirven, "Paranormal Aspects of Pre-Existence Memories in Young Children," *Journal of Near-Death Studies* 34, no. 2 (2015): 84-107, p. 98. Originally reported in Ian Stevenson, *Reincarnation and Biology: Contribution to the Etiology of Birthmarks and Birth Defects*, vol. 1 (Westport, CT/London, UK: Praeger, 1997), 255.

[106] Ian Stevenson, "Are Poltergeists Living or Are They Dead?" *Journal of the American Society for Psychical Research* 66, no. 3 (July 1972): 233-52, p. 237.

[107] Ian Stevenson, *Cases of the Reincarnation Type, Volume I: Ten Cases in India* (Charlottesville, VA: University Press of Virginia, 1975), 328-9.

yellow ball but didn't think it had been buried with her child. Nevertheless, an older sibling later confessed to having slipped the yellow ball under the body of the dead child, thus verifying Mandy's memory. When Mandy was six, she asked her mother, "Do you remember the night I died? There was a bright star shining in the sky." When her mother thought about it, she *did* remember an especially bright star "hovering over the garden." She'd mentioned it to someone at the time because it was both strangely bright and low. Mandy continued, "That was my star. It was my way of telling you that I would be back."[108]

Evidence for Life after Death: Mediumship

We now turn to one last potential source of evidence for the survival of bodily death: mediumship. In some ways, mediumship is just an extension of the types of after-death communication we've already explored. A medium is someone who is particularly adept at perceiving the presence of the dead and can act as a go-between for them and their loved ones. But not all of those who claim to be mediums are truly gifted in this way, and even those who are can find their ability to communicate with the other side frustratingly variable. Mediumship rarely, if ever, operates like a direct line to the afterlife, and the messages received in this manner are notoriously ambiguous as to their meaning and source.

Philosopher Dr. Stephen E. Braude writes in his book *Immortal Remains* that "the best cases [of mediumship] are difficult to interpret as unambiguous evidence of survival. Without exception, they present a frustrating mixture of (a) material suggesting survival, (b) material suggesting psi among the living, and (c) apparent rubbish."[109] A great demonstration of the frustrating nature of this material can be found in Deborah Blum's book *Ghost Hunters*,[110] which is an account of parapsychology at the turn of the 20th century, including the psychical research of the famous psychologist William James. Another fascinating source is the late Joe Fisher's *The Siren Call of Hungry Ghosts*, about apparent spirits/guides who produced quite a bit of false information and ended up harming the lives of several people involved with them.[111] (We'll discuss Fisher's book in some depth in Chapter 8.)

---

[108] Harrison and Harrison, 18.

[109] Stephen E. Braude, *Immortal Remains: The Evidence for Life after Death* (Lanham, MD: Rowman & Littlefield, 2003), 54.

[110] Deborah Blum, *Ghost Hunters: William James and the Search for Scientific Proof of Life After Death* (New York: Penguin, 2006).

[111] Joe Fisher, *The Siren Call of Hungry Ghosts: A Riveting Investigation into Channeling and Spirit Guides* (New York: Paraview Press, 2001).

Controlled, multiply blinded studies of mediums have shown that some mediums are able to receive information from a source outside their five senses,[112] but the possibility remains that this information is coming from telepathy or clairvoyance and not from a deceased person. The ambiguity of the source of mediumistic phenomena goes even for those engrossing cases in which mediums not only spout information from the dead but also take on their mannerisms, speak a foreign language known by the dead person but not by the medium, or exhibit some other ability or skill. One particularly impressive case is that of a chess match played between grandmaster Victor Korchnoi and, ostensibly, the deceased grandmaster Geza Maróczy manifesting through German medium Robert Rollans.[113] Dr. Vernon M. Neppe argues that Maróczy's post-mortem survival is the best explanation for Rollans' performance in the chess match,[114] but Braude argues that the medium may have been choosing his moves based on telepathic information received from his opponent (or ESP from some other source).[115]

Nevertheless, some mediumship cases seem impressive to me as evidence for life after death, particularly those that reflect the way an autonomous, still-living entity would behave: popping up unexpectedly and without any particular connection to the desires or wishes of those they appear to. One example of this is the case of the apparition of Lois that repeatedly appeared to the teenage boy Chris, described above. She was emotionally connected to the house in which he lived, but Chris doesn't appear to have had any pre-existing motivation to communicate with her.

A similar case is reported by Marcia Mitnick of Hudson, New York. She writes,

> Of the many messages I received "from beyond," three were particularly amazing and significant. I communicated with three spirits known as Willy, John, and Steve. Incredibly, I discovered their former identities six months later when I met my new boyfriend! They had been his best friends and they had all been killed in Vietnam.[116]

---

[112] See Gary E. Schwartz with William L. Simon, *The Afterlife Experiments: Breakthrough Scientific Evidence of Life after Death* (New York: Atria, 2002); and Julie Beischel, *Investigating Mediums* (Tucson, AZ: Windbridge Institute, 2015).
[113] Wolfgang Eisenbeiss and Deiter Hassler, "An Assessment of Ostensible Communications with a Deceased Grandmaster as Evidence of Survival," *Journal of the Society of Psychical Research* 70, no. 2 (April 2006): 65-97.
[114] Vernon M. Neppe, "A Detailed Analysis of an Important Chess Game: Revisiting 'Maróczy versus Korchnoi," *Journal of the Society for Psychical Research* 71, no. 3 (2007): 129-47.
[115] Stephen E. Braude, *Crimes of Reason: On Mind, Nature, and the Paranormal* (Lanham, MD: Rowman & Littlefield, 2014), 172.
[116] Sophy Burnham, *Angel Letters* (New York: Ballantine Books, 1991), 125.

When unsolicited visitors pop up in a mediumship setting, they are called "drop-in communicators." One particularly well-documented example of drop-in communication is a case investigated by Erlendur Haraldsson. Indridi Indridason was a famous Icelandic medium active in the early 20th century, and careful minutes were kept of many of his séances. In 1905, a personality began to speak through Indridason who was not recognized by any of the people in the séance room. He told them that he was a Danish manufacturer by the last name of Jensen and that he had just been in Copenhagen, Denmark, watching a factory fire that was quickly brought under control. A month later, news arrived in Iceland that a factory fire had indeed broken out that night in Copenhagen but was quickly brought under control.

That was no doubt remarkable enough to those who had witnessed Jensen's statements, but what is even more intriguing is that, almost 80 years later, Haraldsson discovered the minutes of several more séances to which Jensen had shown up. In one of these later séances, Jensen gave several very specific details about his life, including his given name (Emil), that he was a bachelor with no children, and that he had siblings, none of whom had yet died. There was no record that anyone had ever attempted to verify this information, but Haraldsson went to Copenhagen and discovered that, of all the businesspeople in Copenhagen in the late 1800s, there was only one manufacturer named Emil Jensen. This Emil Jensen had lived two doors down from the factory that had caught fire, was a bachelor at his time of death, had no children, and had only living siblings at his time of death.[117]

Here, it seems, is a case of a personality whose statements exactly match the facts about a once-living person, but a once-living person to whom no one in the séance room had any particular interest in speaking. And, in fact, his identity was not finally verified until over 100 years after his communications. While it's still *possible* that the information coming through the medium was due to the psychic abilities of living people, it's hard to see what living agent would have had a motive for Jensen to appear in this way. It starts to look much more plausible that the origin of these communications was the deceased Mr. Jensen himself.

Another notable drop-in case concerns a patient of psychiatrist Dr. Stanislav Grof. The patient, Richard, became a *de facto* medium during a therapy session that involved the use of the hallucinogen LSD. While under the influence of the drug, he felt the presence of many discarnate beings who were urgently trying to communicate telepathic messages to him. One of

---

[117] Erlendur Haraldsson, *Indridi Indridason: The Icelandic Physical Medium* (Hove, UK: White Crow Books, 2015), 29-46. Haraldsson also describes this case in his chapter "Possible Evidence of Survival," in *Surviving Death: A Journalist Investigates Evidence for an Afterlife* by Leslie Kean (New York: Crown Archetype, 2017), 294-304, pp. 294-300.

these messages was extremely detailed. The being identified himself as Ladislav and asked Richard to contact his parents and tell them that he was all right. The being not only gave the names of his parents and of the city in Moravia where they lived, but he also provided a telephone number. When Grof later dialed this number and asked to speak with Ladislav, the woman on the other end told him tearfully that her son Ladislav had passed away three weeks prior. The patient, Richard, had no previous connection to this family.[118]

ADC researcher Dr. Louis E. LaGrand also reports an evidential drop-in case in his book *Messages and Miracles*. He personally investigated this case in which a medium, who had just arrived at a birthday party, asked the host if they could step away from the party for a moment because, as the medium put it, "Someone is knocking on my head." The medium proceeded to produce a long message, on which the host took two pages of notes. While they were doing this, the host realized that the medium's words matched a client of hers who had died many months previously, leaving behind a wife and daughter. When she finally decided to reveal the medium's message to the man's daughter, the daughter identified it as a genuine communication from her father, because of one particular piece of information it included: the medium's message said that the deceased approved of his daughter's fiancé, and the daughter hadn't yet told anyone about their plans to marry.[119]

This next drop-in case is particularly interesting because of the way it connects to coincidences. It comes from University of Arizona mediumship researcher Dr. Gary E. Schwartz. Along with his wife, Schwartz experienced several coincidences related to the famous inventor Thomas Edison and wondered if the deceased Edison might actually be somehow involved in their creation. Schwartz and his wife visited a medium they knew, who turned out to be the great niece of Edison, and they related to her the series of Edison synchronicities that had occurred, but they didn't ask her for a reading. However, within the week, they got an unexpected phone call from a different medium, with whom they had not spoken in two months and who knew nothing about the Edison synchronicities. She was calling about another matter, but at the end of her call, she mentioned something that had happened to her the previous Sunday, around the time of the Schwartzes' meeting with the other medium. Schwartz says, "*a new historically famous scientist spontaneously showed up in her house claiming to be participating in on-going research with*

---

[118] Stanislav Grof, *When the Impossible Happens: Adventures in Non-Ordinary Realities* (Boulder, CO: Sounds True, 2006), 177-78.
[119] LaGrand, *Messages and Miracles*, 120.

us. She re insisted that [I] would find this hard to believe. She stated his name was Thomas Edison."[120]

In his studies of mediums, Schwartz reports encountering several phenomena that seem like non-negligible evidence for independent entities' interacting with mediums, at least some of the time. In addition to the phenomenon of drop-in communicators, consider the following.

- Some mediums experience those they are communicating with as occasionally correcting not only the medium but the sitter as well, if necessary.[121] (The "sitter" is the person who is attempting to connect with their loved one(s) through the medium.) For instance, in one case, medium Laurie Campbell spelled the sitter's relative's name correctly, but the sitter thought it was wrong until he checked it out.[122] This counts against an explanation of mediumship as nothing but a telepathic connection to the sitter.
- Sitters at times experience the feeling of a "presence,"[123] as do many people who report episodes of spontaneous after-death communication.
- The deceased often show up before the sitting officially begins (sometimes before the medium and the sitter are even in the same location, if they ever will be) and sometimes stay after.[124] And they are not always the people the sitter was expecting.[125] That is, readings do not always (or even generally) conform to the expectations of the living people involved.
- Personality comes through strongly in readings, even to the point that people who were dominating in life can still be dominating from the other side. Schwartz writes in *The Afterlife Experiments*, "when [the medium] was attempting to communicate with my father, my mother came in unannounced and more or less dominated the conversation, precisely as she had done in life."[126]

---

[120] Gary E. Schwartz, "Possible Causal Mechanisms in the Occurrence of Synchronicities: Testing the Spiritual Assistance Hypothesis," *Journal of Spirituality & Paranormal Studies* 34, no. 4 (October 2011): 182-209, p. 208.
[121] Schwartz with Simon, *The Afterlife Experiments*, 138.
[122] Schwartz with Simon, *The Afterlife Experiments*, 232.
[123] Schwartz with Simon, *The Afterlife Experiments*, 153.
[124] Schwartz with Simon, *The Afterlife Experiments*, 186-89.
[125] Schwartz with Simon, *The Afterlife Experiments*, 264. For one especially intriguing case of an unexpected visit, see Julie Beischel, *Among Mediums: A Scientist's Quest for Answers*, in *Investigating Mediums* (Tucson, AZ: Windbridge Institute, 2015), 59-172, p. 88-89, 99-100.
[126] Schwartz with Simon, *The Afterlife Experiments*, 196.

While these phenomena could theoretically be imitated through telepathy and clairvoyance—that is, living-agent psi—taken all together, it is hard not to see them as evidence that some mediums are doing exactly what they experience themselves as doing: talking to dead people. Schwartz discusses the possibility that mediums just get their information from memory traces in the universe. He writes,

> The research to date does not eliminate a possible memory retrieval process from the "vacuum" of space. However, careful analysis of the language used by the mediums, plus examples like [a woman's] deceased grandmother seemingly continuing to communicate during the reading for the subsequent sitting suggests that the 'information' is not static or "dead" like information stored on a hard drive or CD.[127]

Mediums themselves second this impression. According to Dr. Julie Beischel's research, they experience themselves as receiving information from "independent, volitional beings," which is unlike how they receive information when they're just doing psychic readings that don't involve the dead.[128]

Is it possible that mediums are fooling themselves into thinking that some of their psychic information comes from spirits of the deceased? Beischel points out that many mediums' experiences began when they were small children and had no particular motive to frame their experiences as communications with the dead.[129] Additionally, when Beischel tested mediums by sometimes asking them to do readings on deceased people and sometimes asking them to do readings on living people, without telling them which were which (and without the experimenter knowing, either), the mediums were in 83% of the cases able to accurately report the living or deceased nature of the person whose name they were given.[130]

Beischel concludes from her research conducted through 2015 that the data support psychic interaction with the dead, at least for certain mediums.[131] Schwartz comes to a similar conclusion. Towards the end of *The Afterlife Experiments*, he writes, "if we were to apply Occam's razor to the total set of data collected over the past hundred years...there is a straightforward hypothesis that is elegant in its simplicity. This is the simple hypothesis that consciousness continues after death."[132] And, although philosopher Stephen Braude is very skeptical about the potential to make any mediumship

---

[127] Schwartz with Simon, *The Afterlife Experiments*, 265.
[128] Beischel, *Among Mediums*, 140.
[129] Beischel, *Among Mediums*, 134-35.
[130] Beischel, *Among Mediums*, 139.
[131] Beischel, "Mental Mediumship Research at the Windbridge Institute," in *Investigating Mediums*, 7-14, p. 11.
[132] Schwartz with Simon, *The Afterlife Experiments*, 254.

evidence into proof of survival of death, he also makes the Argument from Crippling Complexity, pointing out that "the super-psi hypothesis suggests that ESP faces too many natural obstacles to be consistently successful, at least to the degree required by the best cases of mediumship."[133] He says that "what makes the best cases so impressive is both the amount of correct material and the *consistency* with which subjects provide it."[134]

I would add three final pieces of evidence for the survival hypothesis, two of which draw on correspondences between mediumship and end-of-life experiences. The first correspondence is with near-death experiences. Italian journalist Paola Giovetti reports on an NDEr who said that, during his NDE, a woman named Mara gave him the choice of whether or not to go back to his earthly life. It was later discovered that a spirit named Mara who had been communicating with some spiritists also told *them* about her encounter with this NDEr.[135] Similarly, in the first half of the 20th century, both Ernesto Bozzano and Emil Mattiesen reported cases in which mediums received communications that corresponded to the visions reported by dying persons.[136]

The final piece of evidence is the large number of cases—at least 80, says researcher Michael Nahm—in which *living* agents have appeared to transmit messages through mediums.[137] While it may at first seem as though the evidence that living agents can communicate through mediums would count against mediumship as evidence for life after death, it actually supports this hypothesis in much the same way that the verified apparitions of living out-of-body experiencers support the hypothesis that apparitions of the dead are not just hallucinations. Cases in which living people can independently verify having communicated through mediums show that mediumship is at least sometimes not the mere hallucination of a conversation. Sometimes it is an actual conversation with a living personality. And if living people can be shown to have accurately communicated through mediums, it becomes more plausible that the deceased could do so as well and that, when a medium

---

133 Braude, *Immortal Remains*, 90.

134 Braude, *Immortal Remains*, 91.

135 Paola Giovetti, "Visions of the dead, death-bed visions and near-death experiences in Italy," *Human Nature* 1 (1999): 38-41. For another such case, see Emil Mattiesen, *Das persönliche Überleben des Todes*, vol. 2 (Berlin: Walter de Gruyter, 1936-39), 236.

136 Ernesto Bozzano, *Le Visioni dei Morenti* (Verona: Salvatore Palminteri, 1947); and Emil Mattiesen, *Das persönliche Überleben des Todes* (Berlin: Walter de Gruyter, 1936-39).

137 Michael Nahm, "Reflections on the Context of Near-Death Experiences," *Journal of Scientific Exploration* 25, no. 3 (2011): 453-78, pp. 461-2; and Michael Nahm, "Letter to the Editor: On Mediumistic Communications by Living Agents," *Journal of the Society for Psychical Research* 74 (2010): 53-56.

has the perception of conversing with someone deceased, that perception is accurate.

Coincidences Confirmed by Mediums

Now that we've reviewed the strong evidence for survival of death, it's time to return to the subject of coincidences and, in particular, the question of whether deceased persons might sometimes be behind them. We have already seen a case in which a child's past-life memory confirmed the significance of a star that appeared in the sky after the death of her previous personality, as well as cases where children's past-life memories confirmed that the disappearance of food from a family's house and the breaking of a swing were due to their actions after death in a previous life. We also saw a case where an NDEr reported taking an out-of-body trip to see his brother, and his brother reported that the door to his house was repeatedly unlocked and opened by unseen means. I now want to look at some cases in which the link between a coincidence and a deceased person receives evidential confirmation from a medium.

One of the most spectacular examples I've come across is that of a widower named Jim. Months after the death of his wife, Jim was driving home from a family reunion when he saw two meteors falling towards the earth. He actually braced himself for the shock wave he expected to feel when they impacted, but it never came. The meteors were suddenly just *gone*. A few weeks later, Jim discovered that his daughter-in-law had had a reading with medium Laura Lynne Jackson just hours after the meteor episode. When Jim watched a video of the reading, he heard his daughter-in-law ask Jackson whether Jim's deceased wife had ever tried to contact him. "Oh, yes," replied Jackson. "She has tried and tried and tried. But every time she gets close he goes deeper and deeper into the darkness. She doesn't want to hurt him, but she keeps trying. She has tried everything. She says she has even tried meteors!"[138]

Jackson reports having been told multiple times by deceased persons that they were influencing events from "behind the veil," or at least trying. In another case, a couple with the names Fred and Susan got a reading from Jackson. Their deceased college-age son communicated through her that he'd encouraged Susan to wear a particular pair of earrings to the reading. Susan confirmed that she had indeed been wearing a different pair originally, but at the last minute something made her go back and get the ones she was

---

[138] Laura Lynne Jackson, *The Light Between Us: Stories from Heaven, Lessons for the Living* (New York: Spiegel & Grau, 2015), 150.

wearing.[139] Jackson also reported to this couple, "He is thanking you for coming to this grief retreat. He is saying he was trying to get you here, and then you almost didn't come. He was so happy that you decided to come. He doesn't want you to deal with your grief alone."[140] This case might not have produced a coincidence *per se*, but it's evidence that the dead do try to influence our thoughts and actions and might, in this way, produce coincidences in our lives.

There is also evidence that the dead attempt to communicate with us by influencing the behavior of wild animals. Consider the case of Heather Rist. She was walking to a reading with medium John Edward when she asked for a sign that her loved ones would be contacted. She reports, "At that moment a bird jumped onto a railing, looked at me curiously, hopped a couple of steps closer, and looked at me curiously again, cocking its head to the side."[141] While she wanted to believe this was the sign she'd asked for, she couldn't be sure. However, during the reading, Edward mentioned a yellow bird, and just then a bird popped into view outside the window. "Do you see this bird?" he asked. "Does it mean anything to you? He [the deceased] says he is doing this."[142]

For whatever reason, the deceased seem to show a tendency for communicating through animals that have wings—especially birds and butterflies. Perhaps they appreciate the symbolism of unfettered flight? Or of nearness to heaven? In any case, medium Daria Justyn offers us another example of medium confirmation of a coincidence received through a winged animal. Justyn once told a man that she was getting the image of a butterfly from his deceased mother. When he told his family about this later in the day, at that very moment, a butterfly came and landed on his leg.[143]

While I'm inclined to believe that coincidences produced through mental influence are the easiest for the deceased to produce, there is also evidence that the deceased sometimes affect (otherwise) inanimate objects. Often these are small, easily movable objects like coins. We'll see many cases of this in the rest of this chapter. But there are also medium-confirmed cases in which the objects affected aren't small *or* easy to move. For example, medium Carrie D. Cox relates the case of a woman who'd lost her eight-year-old son and was desperate for a particular form of validation that he was still with her. She kept telling Cox over the phone, "I need to know for myself." That's when the deceased little boy told Cox he'd left something for his

---

[139] Jackson, 196.
[140] Jackson, 198.
[141] Schwartz with Simon, *The Afterlife Experiments*, 141.
[142] Schwartz with Simon, *The Afterlife Experiments*, 142.
[143] Julie Beischel, ed., *From the Mouths of Mediums: Conversations with Windbridge Certified Research Mediums*, Vol. 1: Experiencing Communication, reprinted in Beischel, *Investigating Mediums*, 217-322, p. 287.

mother outside of her door. "She went right outside the door where he said it would be," says Cox, "and lying in the snow was the back of a lawn chair that had been bent into the shape of a heart with the eternity symbol at the top."[144]

In the final case I've collected of coincidence confirmation from a medium, the deceased appears to have affected an electrical system—another theme we will see repeated throughout this chapter. In this case, medium Robert Burke wrote an email to a woman named Elisa Medhus, who'd lost her son Erik to suicide. Burke told her that he'd been in contact with Erik and that Erik wanted to know "if the floors were warm enough for y'all there in the cabin." At the time, Medhus was staying in a cabin in Norway, and indeed, a few days before she received this email, the in-floor heating in their bathroom had randomly started malfunctioning, heating up so much that the family couldn't even walk across the floor. They had immediately thought of Erik as the culprit, days before Medhus received the confirming message from Burke. Medhus assures us that there's no way Burke could have found out about the floor malfunction in any non-psychic way.[145]

Let me conclude this section by suggesting that readers particularly interested in confirmation of coincidences by mediums should check out an article by Gary Schwartz in which he proposes a triple-blind experimental protocol for using mediums to test links between coincidences and deceased persons.[146]

Coincidences Confirmed by Dreams

We now turn to another source of evidence for connections between coincidences and the deceased: dreams. As we saw above, some dreams offer strong evidence for life after death, and, depending on the circumstances, dreams may also offer independent corroboration of the involvement of the deceased in the production of certain coincidences. Similarly, the coincidences may offer corroboration of the dreams.

Let's start with a fairly simple case and work our way up to the more complex ones. You'll recall my mentioning that the deceased often communicate using small objects like coins. Well, Cindy Lou Rowe started noticing pennies after the death of her husband Michael, but she didn't really start paying attention to them until it got to the point where she was finding

---

[144] Beischel, *From the Mouths of Mediums*, 294.

[145] Elisa Medhus, *My Son and the Afterlife: Conversations from the Other Side* (New York: Atria, 2013), 31.

[146] Gary E. Schwartz, "Possible Causal Mechanisms in the Occurrence of Synchronicities: Testing the Spiritual Assistance Hypothesis," *Journal of Spirituality & Paranormal Studies* 34, no. 4 (October 2011): 182-209.

8 to 12 pennies *every day*. She found this phenomenon very puzzling until she remembered that, about six months after her husband's death, she'd had a vivid dream in which she saw him with a penny embedded in his chest. He asked if he should try to remove it, but she told him to leave it, as it might be good luck. Reflecting on the meaning of this, she concluded that the penny was over his heart to symbolize the exchange of love.[147] It seems plausible that the pennies she was finding were meant as a reinforcement of this message.

While some might attempt to explain Rowe's abundant penny coincidences as created by her own psychokinetic abilities (a phenomenon we'll explore in depth in Chapter 6), it's harder to explain the next case in that way. In this case, Gordon Miller's deceased wife, Ruby, appeared to him in a dream two nights before he got remarried. First, Ruby seemed to bless him, and then she pointed to a journal, as if asking him to read it. Upon waking, he dug out an old dream journal of his in which he'd recorded two whole weeks of dreams in which Ruby had asked him to find a new mother for their daughter. In one of the dreams, a man had appeared, showing him a large table of jewelry and communicating that he wanted Gordon to meet the woman who'd made it. He had also told Gordon his name: Joseph. Upon rereading the dream, Gordon realized that this was the name of the deceased husband of his wife-to-be. And his wife-to-be was in fact a jewelry maker—they'd encountered each other at a fair where she was selling her products. Furthermore, the description Gordon had written of the man in the dream matched his wife-to-be's deceased husband.[148]

While it's true that Miller could possibly have gained information about his future wife and her deceased husband through precognition (another phenomenon we'll explore in Chapter 6) and then presented this information to himself as coming from his own deceased spouse, this explanation is much more convoluted than the one in which Miller's wife actually communicates with him in a dream—especially when we consider the fact that his wife appears to have returned just before his marriage with the express purpose of *pointing out* to him that the information she'd previously given him was accurate. This seems like exactly the sort of behavior we would expect from a deceased spouse who wanted her still-living husband to know that she blessed his upcoming remarriage, and I see no reason not to interpret it in this way.

JoAnne Zawitoski didn't see her deceased husband in a dream, but she did hear a dream voice ask her an important question regarding his continued existence. The voice asked her whether she would accept as a sign that her husband was alive and well the finding of two objects that she hadn't been

---

[147] Vissell and Vissell, 191.

[148] Vissell and Vissell, 170-6. I provide more details about this case in Chapter 16.

able to locate since his death: his class ring and his pocket PC. Zawitoski accepted this proposition, and within 72 hours, both objects turned up.[149] What was more, both of them were found by people other than herself, with the involvement of these third parties adding greatly to the evidential quality of the case.

Here are several more dream examples involving third parties.

About two weeks after the death of Terry's husband, Ronnie, Terry felt him kiss her. She also smelled flowers, even though the windows were closed and there was no perfume around. The next day, a friend who knew nothing about this experience revealed that she'd had a dream of Ronnie in which he said he was trying to help Terry stop crying. "We're trying," Ronnie said. "We put flowers in her hair, but she keeps crying."[150]

Elisa Medhus dreamt of her deceased son Erik telling her that he was going to be forever watching over his good friend Stacy, whom he had always adored. Erik asked his mother to give Stacy this message. When Medhus did so, she discovered that Stacy had just experienced a strong coincidence involving Erik. Stacy had asked him to help her get a job she wanted at a day care, but when she went for her first day of work, she was nervous about not knowing anyone. No sooner did she enter the center than a little boy grabbed her legs, proclaiming, "Hi, I'm Erik, and I love you with all of my heart!" Medhus says Stacy knew immediately that this was a message from *her* Erik.[151]

Surgeon Mary C. Neal, who had a near-death experience during a kayaking accident, recounts that the widow of one of her former patients—a member of the Church of Jesus Christ of Latter-Day Saints—reported to her that her deceased husband occasionally visited her and gave her guidance. One day, he came to her in her dreams and told her that Neal had had a serious accident. This woman knew nothing about Neal's recent life-threatening adventure, but she was nevertheless able to describe it in a way that only an eye-witness could have. She said that her deceased husband had asked God whether he could be among those sent to rescue Neal, and he was extremely happy and excited that this request had been granted.[152] Indeed, Neal's rescue from her accident did appear to involve supernatural aid, both physical and emotional. It does not seem at all surprising, after reading Neal's account of her rescue and near-death experience, that a deceased person would claim participation in the event. And his description of *asking* to

---

[149] Sophy Burnham, *The Art of Intuition: Cultivating Your Inner Wisdom* (New York: Jeremy P. Tarcher/Penguin, 2011), 187.

[150] Martin and Romanowski, 150.

[151] Medhus, 20.

[152] Mary C. Neal, *To Heaven and Back: A Doctor's Extraordinary Account of Her Death, Heaven, Angels, and Life Again* (Colorado Springs, CO: WaterBrook Press, 2011, 2012), 140-41.

participate in her rescue is a particularly intriguing glimpse into orchestrations on the other side.

Now for our most complex example of dream-coincidence corroboration. The coincidence in question happened to author and film director Paul Davids, a week after he spoke at a tribute for his late friend Forrest J Ackerman. Davids was alone in his house when he printed a 24-page document from his computer and looked over it briefly before tossing it on his bed, with the intention of reading it in more detail after he made a trip to the adjoining bathroom. When he emerged from the bathroom, however, he discovered that, in the time he had been gone, one line on the first page of the document had been blacked out with ink, which was still wet. This "ink obliteration," as Davids calls it, can be seen in a photograph included in his book *An Atheist in Heaven*.[153]

By going back to his computer and viewing the file he had printed, Davids was able to ascertain that the line that had been blacked out consisted of four words: "Spoke to Joe Amodei." Joe Amodei was a man Davids had only spoken to once, and if the blacking out of this phrase was supposed to be a message of some kind, it didn't make sense to him. He suspected, however, that Ackerman was somehow involved, so he subsequently called up a fellow who had long been an assistant of Ackerman's, in hopes of obtaining some examples of manuscripts Ackerman had edited and comparing them with the mysterious ink obliteration. When Davids was eventually able to do this comparison, he found strong similarities, and an example of Ackerman's editing style is included in Davids' book as evidence.[154] However, before Davids could ask Ackerman's assistant about procuring the samples, the assistant told Davids there was something he had to tell him.

A few days after the recent tribute to Ackerman, the assistant had had a "super-conscious" dream in which Ackerman visited him and discussed the tribute. The assistant told Davids, "I'm a skeptic, Paul, you know that, but it was as if Forry [Ackerman] really came and spoke to me."

It was at that moment that Davids realized the true meaning of the words that had been obliterated by the mysterious ink. Ackerman's assistant was named Joe Moe. Thus, the words "Spoke to Joe Amodei" came incredibly close to describing what Ackerman had actually done when he *spoke to Joe Moe*. In fact, punning and finding names within names had been two of Ackerman's favorite pastimes—obsessions, really. And what was more, Ackerman had promised Davids that, if it turned out there was life after death (which Ackerman was convinced there wasn't), he would "drop him a line" from the other side. The obliteration of this four-word line of

---

[153] Paul Davids and Gary E. Schwartz with John Allison, *An Atheist in Heaven: The Ultimate Evidence for Life after Death?* (Reno, NV: Yellow Hat Publishing, 2016), 42.
[154] Davids and Schwartz with Allison, 299.

Davids' document could easily be considered a pun on the idea of "dropping a line." Thus, this one little ink obliteration appeared to convey not only the veracity of Joe Moe's dream visitation from Ackerman but the survival of important aspects of Ackerman's personality.[155] Given this constellation of connections to Ackerman, it seems reasonable to conclude that his spirit was indeed behind the ink's appearance.

Coincidences Confirmed by Apparitions

Perhaps the most striking evidence that coincidences can be caused by the deceased comes from cases in which coincidences are accompanied by apparitions. One example comes from Dr. Mary Helen Hensley, a chiropractor and metaphysical healer who lives in Ireland. In the space of one day, she heard two mentions of a location in Ireland she'd never heard of before: Mount Argus. The next morning, her five-year-old daughter Jemma roused her from sleep to tell her she had something to show her. "Mr. Burke woke me up," she said, referring to a deceased previous resident of their home who had taken to appearing to Hensley's daughters. Jemma went on to explain that Mr. Burke had woken her up to give her a clue about how to fix a terrible cough she had, a cough so violent that it often led to vomiting. Jemma led her mother to some bricks in the stairwell of their home and pointed to the "clue" he'd shown her. Written on a brick were the words "Mount Argus."

Feeling an immediate need to know the significance of this place, Hensley called her secretary, one of the people who'd mentioned Mount Argus the day before. The secretary explained to her that Saint Charles of Mount Argus was a healer of ailments of the chest. The appropriateness of this made it seem that the dead fellow Mr. Burke really had intended to help Jemma in some way by giving her this clue, but Hensley wasn't sure what to do about it.

She didn't have to wait long to find out. The next day, the brother of a friend of Hensley's, a man she had only met a few times, brought her an unexpected gift, saying, "Something told me you could use this." It was a relic of Saint Charles of Mount Argus. Hensley put it under her daughter's pillow that night, and Jemma never had her awful coughing fits again.[156]

This case is interesting for several reasons, one of which is the indication of the benevolent, healing intentions of a resident "ghost." Another is the suggestion that the deceased agent may have orchestrated the coincidences

---

[155] Davids and Schwartz with Allison, 41-53. Scientific analysis of the ink obliteration can be found in Ch. 5 of the same book.

[156] Hensley, 261-8.

in which Hensley heard Mount Argus mentioned twice on the day before Mr. Burke's apparition directed Jemma to the brick with this place name inscribed on it. While the case is open to alternative interpretation, it does seem plausible that Mr. Burke was first trying to slip Hensley this healing suggestion in a very subtle manner and then resorted to being more direct. Afterward, when Hensley wasn't sure what to do with this information, Mr. Burke seems to have prompted an acquaintance to provide her with the final piece of the puzzle.

Another case of coincidences associated with an apparition comes from the experience of a woman named Emine Fougner. The episode began when, in the middle of the night, Fougner saw a motion-activated light in the hallway outside her bedroom turn on three times in 20 minutes, when there was apparently no one there. NDE researchers Rivas, Dirven, and Smit summarize what happened next:

> She lay back down and then suddenly felt someone tapping her foot. She looked up and, to her utter amazement, saw her [deceased] grandmother standing there. She said, "Grandma? Is it you?" Right after that, she thought, "You keep waking me up with the lights in the hallway; you should just turn the bathroom light on." The next thing she saw was the bathroom light turning on.[157]

Her grandmother went on to tell her that her sister, who was pregnant, had gone into labor early and that it was going to be very difficult but she would eventually be okay. A few hours later, Fougner discovered that her sister had indeed gone into the hospital that night. The next day, after the baby was successfully delivered via C-section, Fougner's sister suffered heavy bleeding and multiple cardiac arrests. Though she was resuscitated, her future health was uncertain.

The following night, Fougner's seven-year-old daughter complained to her that she couldn't get to sleep because her great-grandma was fooling with the lights. This further manifestation of Fougner's grandmother comforted Fougner and her family, and her sister appears to have made a full recovery.[158]

The strange behavior of electric lights is a phenomenon often associated with communications from the deceased. Several other examples can be found in Chapter 13 of the Guggenheims' book *Hello from Heaven!* Fougner's case is especially interesting in that it provides independent confirmation that the deceased do in fact have the ability to affect electric lights and that they do so at least somewhat intentionally. It also shows that the deceased are, at least in some cases, concerned about their loved ones who are still living, and

---

157 Rivas, Dirven, and Smit, 145.
158 Rivas, Dirven, and Smit, 145-8.

particularly about giving them comfort in difficult circumstances. If they have to flicker the lights in the middle of the night to do this, then they will!

Phantom Phone Calls

The topic of electrical effects brings us naturally to this next group of cases: phantom phone calls. I regard these cases as something between apparitions and coincidences. They demonstrate the ability of the deceased to interact with electronic devices—in this case, telephones—and the connection to the deceased is particularly convincing because of the manifestation of the deceased's voice. The Guggenheims' book *Hello from Heaven!* contains a full chapter dedicated to telephone-based after-death communication, and many more cases can be found in Callum E. Cooper's more recent book *Telephone Calls from the Dead.*[159] Rather than recount here those cases that have already been collected, I'll relate some examples I've gathered from other sources.

The first case concerns a Frenchwoman, Marie-Hélène Verdubal. Verdubal's husband traveled frequently for his job, and each time he got to a new destination, he would call her and say the same little phrase: "*Je suis arrivé, ma grenouille,*" which translates to "I've arrived, my frog"—"frog" being his pet name for her. Verdubal's husband ended up dying from leukemia, and just days after his death, she got a late-night phone call at her house. When she picked up, she heard the voice of her just-deceased husband repeat his habitual phrase: "*Je suis arrivé, ma grenouille.*"[160]

In another French case, medium Geneviève Delpech's husband, the famous singer Michel Delpech, passed away on January 2, 2016 at 9:30 in the evening. That very night, one of their children received a call that was identified as coming from Michel's cell phone. When the son picked up, a voice that sounded just like his father's said, "*Mon fils, je vais partir, mais tout ira bien*": "My son, I'm going to leave, but everything will be all right."[161]

While we're on the topic of deceased musicians, let me throw in the fact that, on the day following Janis Joplin's death, producer Paul Rothchild and friend Bobby Neuwirth both reportedly received phone calls from her. According to Joplin's biographer—her sister Dr. Laura Joplin—the voice on

---

[159] Callum E. Cooper, *Telephone Calls from The Dead: A Revised Look at the Phenomenon Thirty Years On* (Portsmouth, UK: Tricorn Books, 2012).

[160] Jean-Jacques Charbonier, *Les 7 bonnes raisons de croire à l'au-delà* (Paris: Guy Trédaniel, J'ai Lu, 2012), 152-3.

[161] Geneviève Delpech, *Te retrouver: L'amour plus fort que la mort* (Paris: Editions First, 2017), 104.

the phone said something like, "It's okay, man. This is a good place. I'm in good shape. Don't worry about a thing."[162]

Now, back to less famous individuals. A woman named Jeannie reports the following incident involving a former boyfriend, to whom she hadn't spoken in 10 years. She was in the hospital having an operation when her husband got a telephone call from someone whose name he didn't recognize. He told Jeannie about it and said the caller had identified himself as "Pocco." Well, this was the nickname of Jeannie's high school sweetheart, Gary. She tried to find Gary's number so as to call him back, but with no luck. Years later, she happened on a social security website where she entered Gary's name and up popped the date of his death: February 10, 1998. Jeannie says, "That was the same time as my surgery and the phone call."[163]

Elisa Medhus also reports a telephone contact with her deceased son Erik. One day when she had just begun focusing on mentally communicating with him, her home telephone rang. The caller's name displayed as "unavailable," so she let the answering machine pick up. "What I heard made my heart stop," she says. "Although there was some static, it was clearly Erik's voice: 'Hey, it's Erik. It's me, Erik.' Then the line disconnected." When Medhus tried to replay the message, the machine said there were no new messages—it hadn't recorded anything at all. When she called the number that had shown on the caller ID, she was told it was not in service.[164]

Another phantom phone call happened to the wife of Erlendur Haraldsson, whose parapsychology research has been referred to several times in this chapter. He reports,

> It was a call from a relative in Copenhagen who had recently died in his nineties, and whom both of us had visited on several occasions. He greeted her in his usual affectionate way and started to say something, but then his voice slowly faded away. There could be no mistake about his voice, my wife told me. His voice was so easy to recognize. I remember that for days after this incident my wife brought it up again and again. She was so deeply impressed by this extraordinary phone call.[165]

Next, we turn to a case reported by Lerma. A hospice patient of his named Mary Esther had just passed away, and the nurses were attempting to notify her son, but his phone line was continually busy. While Lerma was at the nurses' station asking for an update on their attempts, the phone rang. The caller ID said the call was coming from Mary Esther's room. The nurse

---

[162] Laura Joplin, *Love, Janis* (New York: Villard, 1992), 312.

[163] Arcangel, 31.

[164] Medhus, 32.

[165] Erlendur Haraldsson, review of *Telephone Calls from The Dead: A Revised Look at the Phenomenon Thirty Years On*, by Callum E. Cooper, *Journal of Scientific Exploration* 27, no. 2 (2013): 353.

answered and obviously heard something that dismayed her, because she passed the phone to Lerma. He reports hearing a lot of static and a faraway voice saying, "Tell my son I'm okay. Tell my son I'm okay." The nurse said it sounded just like Mary Esther. Of course, they rushed into her room to see who might have placed the phone call, but there was no one there besides her cold corpse. Thirty minutes or so later, Mary Esther's son arrived at the hospital. He reported that he, too, had gotten a phone call from his mother, at a time he now knew to have been after her death. She told him over and over, "I am okay. I love you. Don't worry about me. I'm okay."[166]

The manifestation of the deceased's voice, as well as some of their personality and mannerisms, is strong evidence for a causal connection with the deceased. Someone wanting to play devil's advocate could argue that the living person's memories, combined with their strong wish to hear from them, might be capable of psychokinetically manifesting a phone call. But in two of the cases just reviewed, phone calls came to more than one person from the same deceased personality at approximately the same time. What is the likelihood that two people's grief would manifest itself in exactly the same anomalous way with regard to the same deceased person? What is more, in the case reported by Dr. Lerma, both he and a nurse heard the voice of the deceased patient during the very same phone call, and there is no reason to think that they were particularly wishing for after-death contact with this person, whom they knew only in a professional capacity. Given that there is such good evidence for life after death, attributing this phone call to the deceased makes the most sense. And once it has been established that the deceased *can* produce such phone calls, we have increased reason to believe that deceased persons are behind phone calls in other cases as well.

Perhaps the most astonishing phantom phone call I've run across happened to Joe Dioca. My astonishment stems from the amount of knowledge and instrumental reasoning displayed by the deceased in this case. Dioca's wife died suddenly only six days after he'd had a heart procedure performed, before he'd even had a chance to go back for his follow-up appointment. A week and a half after her death, but still five days before his scheduled follow-up, he got a call from his doctor's office. The receptionist told him they were going to move his appointment up to the following morning. When he protested that he was already scheduled to come in in just five days, she told him that were moving it up because his wife had left them a voicemail the previous night saying he didn't look good and needed to be seen sooner. When he went to the doctor the following day, it was discovered that he was experiencing a "life-threatening arrhythmia" requiring immediate treatment. Though Dioca himself is the primary source for the details of this case, his daughter Angela confirms that there is no normal explanation for

[166] Lerma, *Into the Light*, 172-3.

the voicemail the doctor's office received. "The only people who even knew about his appointment were Carol, Sean, Dad, and myself," she says, "and we were all blown away, as was the poor girl at the doctor's office. They even tried to retrieve the message but it had been erased."[167]

Before leaving the topic of the telephone, we should note that there are also phantom phone calls in which no voice is heard but there is some other factor identifying the deceased as a probable cause. For instance, one day while a man named Ricardo Flores was discussing a friend of his who had recently passed away, he got a phone call that his caller ID identified as being from that friend. When he picked up, there was no one at the other end of the line. Before he'd had time to integrate this strange experience, his *other* cell phone began to ring. (He had one for work and one for personal use.) This phone *also* identified the caller as his deceased friend, and again there was no one on the line.[168]

I would like to have known the whereabouts of Flores' deceased friend's phone at the time of this incident and whether it was possible that a living person could have been attempting to make calls from it. While the lack of those details makes the case less evidential, it certainly doesn't mean that Flores' deceased friend wasn't behind the calls. The latter hypothesis is lent credibility by another, similar case in which the whereabouts of the deceased's phone *were* known. William Stillman reports, "[A] woman I personally knew…received a phone call from her departed son's cell phone, which was in the same room with her, resting atop his cremains on her bureau! Unfortunately, despite her pleas of 'hello, hello,' she heard only static."[169]

Finally, I don't want to neglect phone calls of a more "coincidental" variety, like one that Stillman reports happened to him. He writes,

> One January Sunday morning, I was thinking fondly of Evelyn, an elderly and dear friend of mine. We had exchanged Christmas greetings, and I wondered when I'd hear from her next. A short while later that morning, the phone rang. It was a wrong number, but the caller asked for "Evelyn." My Evelyn was the only Evelyn I knew. When I told the caller she had the wrong number, her voice so impressed me for its unusual warmth. She apologetically, caringly said, "Oh, I'm so very sorry." It stayed with me. By early evening, Evelyn's daughter called to tell me Evelyn had passed the previous Friday.[170]

---

[167] Arcangel, 37-38.

[168] Davids and Schwartz with Allison, 322-3.

[169] William Stillman, *The Secret Language of Spirit: Understanding Spirit Communication in Our Everyday Lives* (Wayne, NJ: New Page Books, 2018), 55.

[170] Stillman, *The Soul of Autism*, 188.

While it doesn't appear that this case is a manifestation of the voice of the deceased, it is a very suggestive coincidence, not least because of its excellent timing. Was the caller who was looking for someone else named Evelyn prompted by Evelyn's departed spirit to call Stillman by mistake? Perhaps. This case also bears interesting similarities to some telephone cases we'll discuss in Chapter 16, "Meetings & Reunions," where wrong numbers or misdirected calls led people to get in touch with people they would not otherwise have contacted or been able to contact. Perhaps the kind voice of this woman on the telephone was a way for the departed Evelyn to prepare Stillman for the news of her death and give him some measure of comfort.

Association by Request

We're now going to turn to coincidences where, as in the Evelyn phone call, the connection to the deceased is not as independently evidential. Nevertheless, these cases are *strongly suggestive* of having been produced by the deceased. And, in light of all the evidence we've already seen for the ability of the deceased to produce coincidences, as well as their apparent desire to do so, I believe we have good cumulative reason to believe that the deceased have played a role in the coincidences that fill the remainder of this chapter.

Let's begin with cases in which the association with the deceased is strengthened because of a request made by a living person to the deceased. As a first example, take the case of a 16-year-old girl named Lori who lost her best friend, Gary. She went to the cemetery to visit his grave but couldn't locate it. "Gary…where are you?" she asked him. Though there were no trees above her, a leaf came out of the blue and drifted down until it eventually landed some distance away. She went to retrieve it and discovered that it had come to rest directly on Gary's grave.[171]

Timing in these request cases is often crucial. A woman named Mary lost her husband, Tom, and at his funeral, she placed a pink carnation on his coffin. Some weeks later, she was walking on a snowy street feeling particularly sad when she said to Tom, "if only I could know that you were in God's arms!" Suddenly she saw a pink carnation in front of her on the sidewalk.[172]

Charlotte lost her college-age son Todd to a drunk driver on the afternoon of New Year's Eve. His body was so badly mangled that she had been advised not to view it, which she didn't. But she wasn't sure it had been the right decision. About six months after his death, she was still drowning

---

[171] Arcangel, 30.

[172] Joan Wester Anderson, *Where Miracles Happen: True Stories of Heavenly Encounters*, updated (Chicago: Loyola Press, 1994, 2009), 118.

in grief. One afternoon she was crying over her photo albums, repeating over and over the phrase, "If I could only see him one more time...." That's when she heard the mailman arrive. And there, in the mail that day—six months after Todd's death—was a manila envelope *from her son*. The postmark read December 31, the day of his death. Inside the envelope was a handwritten note and a bunch of pictures of him with the family on their last Christmas together, which he must have had developed at a one-hour photo place just before his accident. It had taken so long to be delivered because he hadn't put enough postage on it and then, when it was returned to his college address, it had been subsequently sent out by someone with the address written incorrectly. Thanks to all those "mishaps," it arrived at the moment his mother most needed it.[173]

After the death of her three-year-old son Ryan, Teresa Griffin asked him for a sign that he was near. The words "a white rose, with dew" entered her mind, but she dismissed them. Later the same day, she opened a magazine and found herself looking at a two-page spread featuring an enormous white rose, complete with dewdrops. Her husband didn't know anything about this, but still later on the very same day, he came in the front door and presented her with a white rose that he'd picked from a bush as he passed. It bore a single drop of dew.[174]

Journalist Leslie Kean experienced a strong coincidence after she asked for a sign from her deceased brother. The "Laura" she refers to in her account below is medium Laura Lynne Jackson. Kean writes,

> During my birthday reading with Laura, she had said that my brother was handing me a red balloon. We then agreed (all "three" of us) that a red balloon would be a concrete sign to be delivered by my brother from then on as a way for him to show his presence to me—a red balloon along with the continuing electrical effects. Laura told me I would see real red balloons within the next few days. I found that hard to believe, and I took this prediction with a large grain of salt. She also said I could ask for these signs when I needed them, and he would show himself to me by delivering them. I honestly thought at the time that this would be too miraculous—it was just a medium engaging in wishful thinking, and it could never happen.
>
> Well, I saw two red balloons within the next few days—one outside a bookstore in Concord, Massachusetts, and another in a Manhattan subway station. However, Valentine's Day was that same weekend, so I

---

[173] Robert H. Hopcke, *There Are No Accidents in Love and Relationships: Meaningful Coincidences and the Stories of Our Families* (Asheville, NC: Chiron Publications, 2018), 209-11.

[174] Anderson, *Where Miracles Happen*, 156-7.

> assume there were a lot of red balloons floating around, and this could easily have been a coincidence.
>
> Two weeks later I was alone at home one evening, thinking about my brother and feeling connected to him. I lit a candle for him, and asked him to move the flame, or to do something physical for me...to send me a sign of his presence. (This was the first such request since Laura had suggested I ask.) I kept focusing on this throughout the evening, but nothing happened. Without thinking too much about it, I went to bed. When I woke up the next morning, I could not believe what I saw. In the tree outside my third-story New York City window, stuck in the branches, were three red balloons and one black one, together in a bunch. I had never seen a balloon in that tree before, nor have I since. What are the chances of red balloons getting caught in the branches of the tree opposite my window at the same time that I asked for a communication—something physical—having established that this was our specific sign?[175]

Laura Lynne Jackson appears to have known what she was talking about. And reading her memoir, *The Light Between Us*, will give you an idea of where she got this knowledge. Remember the mother whose deceased son told her he'd persuaded her to wear a certain pair of earrings? That same mother told Jackson that, when she once got a blank voicemail on her phone, she told her son, "Scotty, if that's you, you have to do better than one blank message." Later that day, she received *95* blank messages.[176]

Jackson herself has also received a fair number of signs in response to requests for confirmation. She says that, in the beginning, she used to ask for monarch butterflies as signs, but then she decided to "kick it up a notch." She told the universe that, if it wanted to send her a message, it should send her an armadillo, an aardvark, or an anteater. When she had to put her dog to sleep, she and her family were waiting for the veterinarian to take a paw print of him as a keepsake, and while they were waiting, she suddenly noticed a poster of an anteater on the wall in front of her in the waiting room. Then she took her kids to the bathroom and discovered, as she waited for them, that right next to her at eye level was a ceramic statue of a white miniature Schnauzer, the same breed as her dog. The statue was sporting a pair of angel wings. Despite these signs, the next day Jackson wanted even more reassurance that her beloved pet was okay. As she was driving, she asked that he would let her hear the word "angel" as confirmation. She then turned on the radio, and the first words out of the mouth of the singer coming across the airwaves were, "...must have been an angel." Later the same day, she called the vet's office to settle up the bill and at the end of the conversation

---

[175] Kean, 233-4.
[176] Jackson, 200.

asked the woman who had taken care of things what her name was. It was Angel.[177]

Jackson has also had at least one experience where she has been the apparent means for the creation of a coincidence coming from the deceased. She was once preparing a baked brie for her extended family's Christmas celebration, and she tried to cut a snowflake from dough to decorate the top, but it ended up looking like a star of David. Then, for some reason, she felt like taking a long strip of dough and putting a circle around the star. Her brother, who was watching, was visibly perturbed by this turn of events. After a moment, he confessed that he had recently asked his own deceased dog, Boo Radley, to give him a sign that the other side was real. He had specifically told the dog that the sign had to come from Laura Lynne and that it had to be a star with a circle around it.[178]

Leslie Kean also reports on a series of after-death communications experienced by a man named Jeffrey Kane, who has a PhD in education in the area of epistemology of science. Kane lost his 21-year-old son Gabriel in a car accident in June 2003. That summer, while driving in a national park, Kane told his wife that he wished Gabriel could give them a sign to show he was around. They both immediately saw the car clock jump ahead an hour. They thought perhaps there was some other explanation for this event, but then, three days later, when they were again driving together, Kane told his wife that if the clock jumped *two* hours, that event wouldn't be able to be explained by a malfunctioning cell tower. It wasn't but a minute or two later that the clock changed by two hours.[179]

Kane also received what seemed like thoughts coming to him from his son. He was a very skeptical person, however, and wanted to know whether the thoughts were really from his son or were just something he was making up to cope with such a staggering loss. He told Leslie Kean, "I'd rather live my life in absolute desperation and misery as long as I'm living in truth, than to live with a sense of hope and meaning in a world where I'm simply deceived."[180] So he asked his son to tell him something that he could objectively validate, something he'd never be able to make up on his own. He got three words from Gabriel: "I am red." He tried for a few weeks to make sense of this statement and find some sort of validation for it, but to no avail. Finally, he told his wife that he'd concluded it had all been his imagination.

However, about an hour after he said this to his wife, a package was delivered to his house. I'll let Leslie Kean take over the telling at this point.

---

[177] Jackson, 253-5.
[178] Jackson, 256-7.
[179] Kean, 242.
[180] Kean, 244.

> [The package] contained a painting of an angelic figure. Jeff said it reminded him of Gabriel immediately, and he began to cry. Janet [his wife] exclaimed, "It's red!" and only then did he notice the color. The package came with a note from the mother of someone Janet knew through her teaching, who wrote that she had passed the painting in a store window and for some reason she bought it. Something compelled her to send it. She stated clearly that she didn't know why she did so. She said they could throw it out, put it in the bathroom, do whatever they wanted with it, and she hoped it didn't offend them. Jeff then discovered that with the painting was a card from the artist. It said that the magenta color of the robes was the nearest color in our spectrum to the light emitted by *those who have died in their youth;* it is the color of communication, of love, from the so-called dead to the living.[181]

On yet another occasion, Jeffrey Kane was angered by an ambiguous and worrisome message his wife had gotten from a medium purporting to speak for Gabriel. He angrily told Gabriel, "I want to talk to you. I don't want any more cryptic bullshit. … I will talk to you in my sleep." It was 10:30pm at the time, but he couldn't seem to fall asleep. At 10:45pm, the phone rang. It was a psychic friend of his that he hadn't talked to in some months. "I was on the phone with my mother just now," she said, "and I heard Gabriel yelling at me. He said, 'Hang up! My father needs to speak with me! Hang up and call him now!' He was so persistent, I had to get off and call you. What is going on?" Through his psychic friend's ability to tune into Gabriel, Kane was able to get the clarification and reassurance he needed.[182]

Now here are some more examples of apparent communication from the deceased in response to a request. Linguist Lisa Smartt reports the case of a woman named Renee who, in an imagined conversation in her mind, invited her deceased mother and brother to come to a special family dinner. Moments after everyone sat down, a crash was heard. Of over 30 photos hanging in the hall, the one that had fallen down was the only one of her brother, and it happened to include her mother as well. In 10 years, no other photo had ever fallen in that hallway.[183]

In a case reported by reincarnation researcher Carol Bowman, a woman named Sheri who had lost her fiancé begged him for a sign that he could hear her. He had given her a porcelain figurine of a couple sitting on a swing, and all of a sudden, the swing starting moving of its own accord—first slowly, then very fast—even though nothing else in the room was budging at all.[184]

---

[181] Kean, 243.

[182] Kean, 244.

[183] Lisa Smartt, *Words at the Threshold: What We Say as We're Nearing Death* (Novato, CA: New World Library, 2017), 159-60.

[184] Carol Bowman, *Return from Heaven: Beloved Relatives Reincarnated within Your Family* (New York: HarperCollins, 2001), 203.

Annie Mattingley writes about an experience had by her Mexican friend Flor, who for 10 years had been receiving visits from a white butterfly that she was convinced represented her deceased mother. When Flor mentioned the connection between white butterflies and her mother to her niece Sandra, Sandra was understandably skeptical. But then they were walking together through a park in Oaxaca when Flor pointed out a white butterfly. Flor insisted it was Sandra's grandmother, and Sandra insisted it was not. Finally, Sandra said, "Okay, if you are my grandma, you come right over here!" and pointed a couple inches in front of her chest. "As if yanked by a leash," says Mattingley, the butterfly instantly flew to her, leaving Sandra in tears.[185]

Another woman, a children's book author named Shelley E. Parker, experienced some strange events after the death of her fiancé. About 12 days after he died, she was in a particularly grief-stricken state. She kept repeating, "I love you, I love you," when suddenly her phone emitted three beeps. This was not a usual noise for her phone to make, and she hadn't gotten any messages or received any calls. After that first time, each time she said, "I love you," the phone would make the same noise. It took her some time to figure out the pattern, she says,

> as I'd have breaks from crying and then the emotion would well up again. By the time I realized what was happening, this had been going on for around 15 minutes. The phone only beeped when I said, 'I love you.' I started talking to the phone as it was lying on my bedside table. …
>
> This started to calm me down and after a while longer, I started to feel tired. I remember saying to the phone that I was getting sleepy now and that no doubt he was, too. I said, 'I love you' one more time. The phone bleeped three more times and then went silent. It never did this again….[186]

Parker also notes that, at another location, her fiancé appeared to make a book that she'd published and dedicated to him repeatedly fall off the shelf.[187]

The stories I've related so far may seem a bit strange, but things are only going to get weirder from here. You'll recall the deceased Forrest J Ackerman from the ink obliteration case described earlier. Ackerman was a great fan of "creepy, crawly things," and, in a bold move, his friend Sean Fernald asked Ackerman to give him a sign of his post-mortem presence by having a spider bite him. Fernald hadn't had a spider bite in 10 years, but a day or two later, he received *two* of them.[188] Though Fernald wasn't aware of it at the time he asked for his sign, Ackerman had once written a short story, "A Letter to an

---

[185] Mattingley, 7-8.

[186] Penny Sartori, *The Wisdom of Near-Death Experiences: How Brushes with Death Teach Us to Live* (London: Watkins, 2014), 106.

[187] Sartori, 107.

[188] Davids and Schwartz with Allison, 150-51.

Angel," that featured, according to Paul Davids, "the concept that a spider could serve as a messenger or even harbor the very soul of a human being."[189]

The Guggenheims include in *Hello from Heaven!* the case of a woman named Iris who was having a hard time in the wake of the death of her husband of 38 years. On one day in particular, she was having difficulty because he had always taken care of paying the taxes and now that he was gone, she had no idea where to find the local tax bill amongst all his papers and files, or even what it might look like. She was standing in his office crying and berating him for leaving her in this predicament when, suddenly, she was flabbergasted to see the thick, hardback appointment book on the desk open all by itself. And there, at the opened page, was the needed tax bill.[190]

Recovering lost items by way of physically moving them was something of a specialty of the deceased family members of the late French journalist Philippe Ragueneau. It began with his deceased son, Alain, who routinely helped him find missing items. When Ragueneau had had enough of looking and asked Alain for help, the objects would suddenly show up precisely where they had not been a moment ago.[191] When Ragueneau's wife, Catherine, passed away, she got in on the act as well, once bringing his checkbook all the way from Paris to Gordes, seven hours away in the south of France.[192]

Erlendur Haraldsson includes another case of the deceased's assisting with the recovery of a lost article in his book *The Departed Among the Living*, although in this case the experiencer did not explicitly ask the departed for help. The experiencer in this case reports that their grandmother had always been very organized and helpful at finding lost items. The day after her death, her grandchild was home alone and having trouble finding some scissors. "As I went into the bedroom to look for them," the grandchild reports, "I heard the scissors drop loudly right behind me. I turned around and saw them lying in the window in the hall I was passing through." The grandchild reports feeling their grandmother's presence at that moment. "It was so much like her to know where to find the scissors," they said.[193]

Let me include here one more case in which the deceased may have helped recover a lost object, even though in this one the direct appeal appears to have been made to God. Chris Tozzo's husband ordered a ring for her that was only delivered after his death. And then, almost immediately, one of the stones in the ring went missing. After three days of vain searching, Tozzo fell to her knees on the kitchen floor. "I reached for the dustpan and brush

---

[189] Davids and Schwartz with Allison, 151.

[190] Guggenheim and Guggenheim, 206.

[191] Philippe Ragueneau, *L'autre côté de la vie: Un message d'espoir et d'amour pour ceux qui ont perdu un proche* (Paris: Editions du Rocher, Pocket, 1995, 1997, 2001), 94.

[192] Ragueneau, 107-9.

[193] Haraldsson, *The Departed Among the Living*, 52.

and was making sweeping motions," she says, "and I said out loud, 'Please God, help me find it.' In the silence there was a tinkling of bells like wind chimes—and the stone fell through the air and landed in front of me."[194] She believes this was the work of her husband.

Association by a Sign Promised by the Deceased

Sometimes an association with the deceased is established not through an after-death request but because the deceased, before death, has indicated that they will give a sign from the beyond. The association is especially strong when the promised sign is very precise, as was the one promised by the father of French anesthesiologist Dr. Jean-Jacques Charbonier. Before his death, Charbonier's father said that, if there was an afterlife, he'd send a sign by stopping the hands of a certain clock. And, indeed, the hands of that clock did stop at the precise time of his death.[195]

Now, clocks' stopping at the time of a person's death is rather common, suggesting that this could be some sort of "automatic" phenomenon related to what physically or metaphysically happens at death, without implying survival. However, that alternative explanation is somewhat undermined by the fact that there are many cases in which clocks stop, not at the actual moment of death, but days or weeks later at precisely the same clock time. We'll look at one of these in the upcoming section "Association by Anniversary or Important Occasion." For now, let's look at a couple more cases in which the deceased promised a sign.

John Lerma's father told him that, after death, he would manifest his presence through electrical circuitry, birds, or butterflies. While that's not terribly specific, he does seem to have made good on his promise. For three nights in a row after his death, lights and a ceiling fan came on in anomalous fashion around the hour he died.[196] As for butterflies, a few months later, Lerma saw a monarch on the door handle of his car. "Almost immediately," he says,

> I thought about my dad's comment regarding butterflies, so I said, "Is that you, Dad?" It would not move, even when I grabbed the handle and opened the door. The magnificent butterfly flew to the front windshield and flew away after the car began to move. As I arrived at my next home visit and walked out of the car, another (or the same?) monarch landed on my right shoulder. It stayed on my shoulder even while walking.[197]

---

[194] LaGrand, *Messages and Miracles*, 266.
[195] Charbonier, 168-9.
[196] Lerma, *Learning from the Light*, 36.
[197] Lerma, *Learning from the Light*, 37.

Now, one difficulty with signs promised by the deceased, as well as with many other types of after-death coincidences, is that it is hard to rule out the possibility that they are produced by the psychokinetic abilities of the living people who experience them. (Again, for an in-depth discussion of psychokinesis, see Chapter 6.) However, there are cases when the sign has been received by someone who *didn't yet know what the sign was to be.* Here's a case from *Love Beyond Life* where it seems the deceased was making an effort to show that she was producing the effect and not the psychokinetic abilities of the living.

Before dying, Mary told her friend Christina that she would come back after death and bang on the fridge to get her attention. However, nothing happened for five years after her death. Then Christina had a dream of Mary and her husband enjoying a meal at a picnic table. She shared it with Mary's husband, and he said it sounded like a place where they actually did have lunch together outside his workplace. Then he shared something that had recently happened to him: he'd heard banging in his home and discovered it was coming from the fridge door. For some reason, he'd had the conviction at the time that it was Mary. He'd spoken to her, affirming that he understood it was her, and immediately the banging stopped. He had known nothing about Mary's promise to Christina to bang on the fridge.[198]

Interestingly, this case includes an element of Mary's husband sensing her presence and sensing that she was the origin of the banging on the fridge, and this intuition seems to have been verified by the fact that Mary told someone else, before she died, that she would manifest herself in precisely this way. Perhaps Mary's husband could have telepathically gained access to this information and then used psychokinesis to produce the banging, but it seems just as plausible to me that he actually did sense her presence.

Cases like this one indicate that a "sense" that a certain person is present or behind a particular coincidence may very well be accurate. Annie Mattingley, who has interviewed many recipients of after-death communication, reports particularly about electronic phenomena that "it is startling to see how instantly people can recognize who is causing these incidents to occur."[199] It may be hard for those who prefer hard evidence to accept the validity of these intuitions, but when one has had such feelings verified in various ways, one begins to take them more seriously. Certainly, no one should believe every stray thought that crosses their mind—we'll see some of the reasons why not in later chapters of this book. However, some people err not on the side of believing too much, but on the side of believing too little. These people might benefit from the encouragement that such

---

[198] Martin and Romanowski, 97-98.

[199] Mattingley, 13.

cases provide: the encouragement that their intuition may have more to teach them than they realize.

Association by Thought

Now we'll move on to coincidences that are associated with the deceased, not because of requests or promised signs, but because something striking happens precisely when a living person's thoughts are focused on the deceased. We saw one strong example of this in Chapter 1: the case of Jennifer Graf, whose grandfather's non-functioning radio suddenly began to play on her wedding day, when she was particularly missing his presence. Some other interesting examples come from Janis Heaphy Durham's book *The Hand on the Mirror*, which I mentioned in the opening paragraphs of this chapter.

For instance, one night, Durham went out to a restaurant where she and her deceased husband Max used to love to eat. When she got back home, she felt compelled to take one of his books from its place on the shelf, and when she did so, something fell out of it. It was a receipt from a dinner the two of them had shared at that very restaurant, two years ago to the day.[200]

On another occasion, Durham was about to leave Cambridge, Nebraska, after a weekend of memorial for her deceased mother. She was wondering if Max was around when she went for a nature walk and came upon "The Max Bridge," a picture of which appears in her book. Later that day, while driving out of town, she passed a sign that read "Besler Industries." Besler was Max's last name, and according to the White Pages, there are only 750 Beslers in the entire United States.[201]

In another case of association by thought of the deceased, Linda Russek had been making some attempts to contact her deceased father when she noticed that her Seiko digital watch, given to her by her father, wasn't keeping the correct time. The jeweler who was tasked with replacing its battery discovered that the watch was in fact running backward. Neither he nor any of the other jewelers contacted by Gary Schwartz in a follow-up investigation had ever heard of this happening.[202]

We've seen that the deceased seem to have a predilection for influencing the behavior of electrical equipment and of animals, but it may come as some surprise that plants also appear to be responsive to the influence of the departed. In a case reported in *Love Beyond Life*, a woman purchased an angel-wing begonia shortly after her mother's death, feeling that it reminded her of

---

[200] Durham, 49-50.

[201] Durham, 260-1.

[202] Schwartz with Simon, *The Afterlife Experiments*, 6.

her mother somehow. The plant bloomed once, but for 15 years after that, it didn't produce another flower. Then one day this woman came home from the doctor after suffering a miscarriage. She was thinking about how much she missed her mother when she saw that the angel-wing begonia was in bloom again, for only the second time in 15 years.[203]

I've actually found two other cases of the deceased's apparently affecting the blossoming of plants, and they both concern Mary C. Neal, author of *To Heaven and Back*. The first occurred just after the death of Neal's stepfather. He died rather suddenly, and just the morning before his death, Neal and her mother had been discussing and looking at an ornamental pear tree that the mother and stepfather had planted outside their house many years before, but which had never blossomed. The stepfather had been so frustrated with it that he had been planning to cut it down that spring and plant another in its place. However, the following morning—the morning *after* his death—Neal and her mother looked outside the window to see that, in the space of one day, the tree had suddenly burst into full bloom, where before there hadn't been even a hint of possibility on it. It bloomed for five years straight and then was suddenly struck by lightning. Neal interpreted this latter event as a sign to her mother that it was time for her to move on with her life.[204]

Neal's other bloom-related coincidence occurred after the death of her teenage son. Neal had been deeply impressed that the site where her son Willie was struck and killed by a car while roller skiing was a particularly beautiful spot in nature, covered in wild alpine roses. She'd never seen wild alpine roses before gazing on them in the field where he died. However, when she returned home after his death and attempted to select a site on the acreage around her home to plant a garden in his honor, she discovered to her amazement that the ground encircling a group of willow trees had become carpeted by the blossoms of wild alpine roses identical to those in Willie's field. Willie, she says, knew about the story of the pear tree, and she was sure it was he who had sent the roses.[205]

But let's get back to discussing coincidences that are associated with the deceased because of the way they coincide with the experiencers' thoughts of them. Funnily enough, I've collected two cases in this category that both involve the singer and actress Barbra Streisand. One happened to Streisand herself, and she was unwittingly instrumental in producing the other.

You may be familiar with Streisand's 1983 movie *Yentl*, which she made in part as a tribute to her deceased father. After finishing the script, she visited her father's grave and wished that he could know the film was made

---

[203] Martin and Romanowski, 81.
[204] Neal, 132-3, 181.
[205] Neal, 178-80.

in his honor. Then she looked to the gravestone next to him and saw that the name on it matched the name of her film's main character: Anshel.[206]

The other coincidence involves a New Year's Eve concert special Streisand once did, in which she sang a song from *Yentl* called "Papa, Can You Hear Me?" Before beginning to sing, she lit a candle in memory of fathers who had died, including her own. A woman named Irene was watching this at home and was reminded of how she always thought of her deceased father when she heard this song. She remarked to her sister Sally that she wished she could know that her father was aware of what was currently going on in their lives. Now, before Christmas that year, Irene had decided to string up Christmas lights on her house the way her father always used to do, sometimes with her help. For some reason, when she'd put up the lights this Christmas, they wouldn't work, no matter what bulbs she replaced or connections she checked. However, as soon as she made the above comment to her sister and Streisand sang the first notes of the song "Papa, Can You Hear Me?", Irene's Christmas lights suddenly came on. What was more, they instantly started blinking, when usually they would only do this after warming up for several minutes.[207]

Our final example in this section also occurred during the Christmas season and comes from medium Daria Justyn, who tells about her friend Nancy's experience of having her deceased father suddenly pop into her head as she was headed to an antique store to shop for Christmas presents. The coincidences began when Nancy entered the store and it was playing her father's favorite song. Then she spied a silver Christmas tree just like her mother always used to put up, and under it she found an ashtray engraved with her father's name, Joe, and his year of birth: '28.[208]

Association by Anniversary or Important Occasion

Often, people's thoughts turn to the deceased on an important family occasion or anniversary. Apparently, the deceased pay some attention to important events or anniversaries as well. As evidence, consider this dream of a deceased person that came on the anniversary of his death, a date of which the dreamer was unaware.

A woman dreamt of an uncle of hers who had died long before. Though she had only ever seen him in a coat and tie, in her dream, he was coming down the stairs of her house in his pajamas and a maroon-and-gray-plaid bathrobe. She asked if he'd like something to eat or drink, and he said he'd

---

[206] SQuire Rushnell, *When God Winks: How the Power of Coincidence Guides Your Life* (New York: Atria, 2001), 107-8.
[207] Martin and Romanowski, 101-2.
[208] Beischel, *From the Mouths of Mediums*, 291-2.

love to have a cream puff. She was able to locate one in her dream kitchen, and they visited while he ate it.

The day after this dream, the woman decided to call up her uncle's widow. She asked her if he'd owned a bathrobe like the one in her dream. Indeed, he had. Then she asked whether there was any dessert her uncle especially liked to eat. As you might guess, the answer was cream puffs. What was more, she was informed by her aunt that this dream had occurred exactly 20 years after her uncle's death, to the very day.[209]

This woman's dream provides a clear identification of the deceased person involved, and the anniversary date only acts as a further validation that something paranormal is going on. But let's now examine some coincidences that are identified as coming from the deceased based primarily on the date on which they occur.

Again, we can turn to Janis Heaphy Durham for some examples. The title of her book *The Hand on the Mirror* derives from the fact that, on the first anniversary of her husband Max's death, Durham found a man's handprint on her bathroom mirror. And it wasn't just an ephemeral, barely visible smudge. It was made of a white, powdery substance that stayed for days–and eventually had to be scrubbed off.[210] Durham was able to photograph the handprint, and she includes the photo in her book. Her book also describes the odd white smudges that appeared on the same mirror on the *second* anniversary of her husband's death,[211] as well as the larger handprint that appeared two days before the *third* anniversary date, with fingers that this time appeared strangely curved and elongated.[212,213] On yet another anniversary—the seventh anniversary of their wedding day—Durham's home alarm system was set off by motion in the hallway when no one was home.[214]

Medium Concetta Bertoldi tells the story of her friend whose father had passed away recently. Her sister's birthday came around, for the first time since the death, and the sister's son went out to the mailbox on her birthday and returned with a birthday card sent by her deceased father. It had been postmarked the year before (2015) but not delivered until the very day of her birthday 2016. Bertoldi uses this as an example of how you don't *need* a

---

[209] Ryback with Sweitzer, 128.
[210] Durham, 1-3.
[211] Durham, 73.
[212] Durham, 89.
[213] Note that these prints, because they had to be scrubbed off, are not explainable in the way some mysterious handprints have been explained by Allison Zumwalde, Kendall Ciriaco, and John Allison in "Strange Handprints in Strange Places," *Journal of Scientific Exploration* 30, no. 4 (2016): 509-23.
[214] Durham, 88.

medium to tell you that certain things are messages from your loved ones; it's crystal clear.[215]

William Stillman reports that, on October 28, 2002, he was thinking about his deceased grandfather. This didn't happen often, since Stillman didn't know his grandfather that well, but he thought of him then because his grandfather's birthday was approaching on October 31. Stillman had these thoughts while getting ready for a doctor's appointment. Then, when coming out of the doctor's appointment, he looked at his watch to verify the date for the check he was writing, and he saw that "[i]nexplicably, the date had somehow *jumped ahead* several days and [his] watch now showed October 31—Grampa's birthday!" Stillman says that the time still showed accurately and that only the date had shifted. A jeweler he consulted said he'd never heard of such a thing happening.[216]

Several pages ago, I promised another case of a clock's stopping, and I'm presenting it in this section because it's a variation on an anniversary, since the clock didn't stop when the person concerned died but rather when that same time came around again, and again. In this case, Denys Cope was worrying about her brother because he had just died and she'd been told he'd cried out as he was dying. That evening, an heirloom clock belonging to their family suddenly stopped at 11:10. Thinking it was probably just because the clock was so old, Cope reset it, but the next night it stopped again at precisely the same time. And then on a third night as well. Her brother hadn't died at that time, so she had trouble making any sense of the clock's behavior. Then she remembered. Fifteen years earlier, her *father* had died at 11:10pm. It became clear to her that her father was trying to let her know that her brother was safe with him. And, once she realized this, the clock went back to functioning normally.[217]

In another, more traditional anniversary case, a mother named Ziek was used to her autistic daughter Elena weaving her way through groups of people and picking out the ones with whom she could form a nonverbal connection. One time, Elena slipped her hand into the hand of an elderly stranger, and when Ziek approached, she saw that the man had tears forming in his eyes as he held Elena's hand. He asked what the girl's name was, and when he was told, his tears began falling in earnest. He told Ziek that it was the anniversary of his wife's death, and his wife's name had been Elena.[218]

---

[215] Interview with Concetta Bertoldi, reported in Jenniffer Weigel, *Psychics, Healers, and Mediums: A Journalist, a Road Trip, and Voices from the Other Side* (Charlottesville, VA: Hampton Roads, 2017), 111.

[216] Stillman, *Autism and the God Connection*, 179-80.

[217] Mattingley, 142.

[218] William Stillman, *Autism and the God Connection: Redefining the Autistic Experience through Extraordinary Accounts of Spiritual Giftedness* (Naperville, IL: Sourcebooks, 2006), 166-7.

This next case doesn't deal with a specific anniversary but rather with several special family occasions that no doubt made the family particularly mindful of the person who was missing from their midst. Grant was a pilot who died young in a plane crash. He was the deceased fiancé of Sheri, mentioned above in the case of the porcelain figurines that began anomalously swinging. At important moments in the life of the family of this deceased pilot—when they were scattering his ashes, when his brother was getting married, whenever the family gathered outdoors for an important occasion—the family would hear the sound of a single-engine plane, when no plane was in sight.[219]

Finally, let's look at another pair of coincidences that happened in connection with Forrest J Ackerman. Two filmmakers, Ian Johnston and Michael MacDonald, had made a documentary about Ackerman's life that was to be shown at a tribute for him. The day before the tribute, they went to visit Ackerman's crypt, and in a playful gesture, they knocked on it. Within the hour, they returned to their hostel where MacDonald went to post something on Facebook and was required to enter a CAPTCHA code. The CAPTCHA code that displayed read, "Ackerman000." The spelling was precisely that of the deceased's last name. While the two filmmakers were discussing what this might mean, Johnston asked the question, "Is he really dead?" At that moment, *Johnston's* computer—which was asleep with its screen off and not connected to the Internet—uttered the words, "Oh my God, no way!" They discovered after some searching on the Internet that there was an animated emoticon available online that said these words, but Johnston had no memory of ever having seen it or accessed it before.[220]

Association by Favorite Things

Sometimes a coincidence appears to be connected to the deceased because it involves something that was independently associated with them: for instance, a material object or a piece of music. As my first example in this category, let me share an experience of my own.

Seven years ago, my relationship with a Frenchman whom I had been engaged to marry was ending. I had just spent my last night at his family's home, where he and I had intended to live after our wedding and where we'd spent many happy occasions with his father and sister. His mother had died from cancer five years previously, just months before I met his family for the first time.

---

[219] Bowman, *Return from Heaven*, 202-3.
[220] Davids and Schwartz with Allison, 45-48.

Before dawn on my final morning in their family home, my ex-fiancé and I were packing our bags to go to Paris for a few final days together. I had just finished reading a book that had belonged to his mother: the first volume of Neale Donald Walsch's *Conversations with God* series. The previous evening, I'd gone to the local bookstore hoping to find the second and third volumes of this three-book series, but the store only had the third one. Even though I would have preferred to read them in order, I bought it. The next morning, as my ex and I were packing, it occurred to me that I ought to check the bookshelves in the house for the second volume. If it was there, I could read it during the days we would be in Paris, before I flew back to the States. So, I went to have a look at the shelves in the study, and on the long bookshelf that ran across the front of the desk, I found the volume I was looking for.

More important, however, is what I found *inside* of it. At the end of her life, my ex-fiancé's mother had listened on repeat to the song "Tout le bonheur du monde" by the ska and reggae band Sinsémilia. The title of the song means "All the happiness in the world." During the last month of his mother's life, the lyrics to this song had served as her last wishes for her children and as a way of saying good-bye to them. Inside her copy of Volume 2 of *Conversations avec Dieu*, I found the liner notes for that Sinsémilia album, folded open to the lyrics for that song.

This was a big deal for the family, since it was possible that, had I not opened that book, they never would have found the album liner notes, or not for a long while yet. But it also held enormous personal meaning for me. I had always wanted to meet my fiancé's mother, and for some reason, I had been sensing her presence for weeks before this event. When I found these words of farewell from her less than an hour before leaving her home for the last time, it felt as if she was telling me *au revoir*, as well as reassuring me that she had been keeping a watchful eye over my presence in her family and thanking me for all the love I had given her son over the previous four years. I also had the impression she was telling me that the *Conversations with God* books were a gift from her, that she had wanted me to have the companionship of these books that had been her companions, too, at the end of her life.

Let's look now at another case featuring favorite music. Laurie was helping to comfort a man who was dying and felt some fear related to this. She talked to this man, Bert, about what would await him on the other side and then asked him if, when he got there, he would send her a sign to let her know it was true. This would also be a help to her own mother, who was fearful of death. Bert agreed to this, and because he so loved the soundtrack from the film *Out of Africa* that Laurie had been playing for him, he told her he'd use this music in his sign. Laurie tells us what happened next:

> About two weeks after Bert died, my mother was visiting me. All of a sudden, in the early hours of the morning, I found myself standing in the upstairs hallway. Mother had come out of her bedroom too.
>
> We were staring at each other wondering, "What on earth is happening?" We suddenly realized that the stereo downstairs was turned on as loud as it could go! And the music from *Out of Africa* was playing! There was nobody else in the house who could have turned it on. And Mother had double-checked everything before bedtime.[221]

This next experience happened to Joel Martin, one of the authors of *Love Beyond Life*. Martin was friends with a priest who had recently died. Two weeks before his death, the priest had sung a moving rendition of the song "I Believe." Upon returning from the priest's funeral, Martin overshot the radio station he was seeking and heard "I Believe" playing on the radio. When it was over, just as the next song began, the signal faded to static. The next day, on another station, Martin heard the same song again. And then, later that day, on yet another station. Three times in 24 hours. About a week later, he asked the deceased priest to let him know if he could hear him. Martin switched on the radio, turned the dial, and the song was on yet again. This happened over and over through the years. When Joel Martin's coauthor, Patricia Romanowski, came to deliver to him the chapter of their book manuscript containing this account, at the instant she walked in, "I Believe" began playing.[222]

Now here's another musical coincidence that happened to a different Joel. Six months after his dear friend Albert died, Joel Rothschild was leaving the gym when he heard Bette Midler's song "Wind Beneath My Wings" playing. He wasn't a big fan of love ballads, or any pop music for that matter. However, what happened next succeeded in getting his attention. He recounts in his book *Signals*,

> When I got to my car [outside the gym], I'd left my radio on, tuned to 103.5 "Coast Radio," where callers were invited to dedicate songs to someone they loved. As I turned on the engine, I heard the announcer say, "Here it is, because he loves you –" and again, "Wind Beneath My Wings" began to play. Enough of that, I thought, as I reached for a cassette tape from a bunch I kept in the car. It was dark; I grabbed the first one I could reach and put it in the deck and, again, to my amazement, "Wind Beneath My Wings" came soaring out of the speakers. I pulled over to the side of the road and looked at the tape, and remembered I had put some of Albert's old compilation tapes in my car a few days before. This was one of them, cued right up to the same song.
>
> It seemed the universe was trying to force it on me, and I felt compelled to sit there and actually listen to it. I found it very touching.

---

[221] Guggenheim and Guggenheim, 201.
[222] Martin and Romanowski, 86.

> The lyrics spoke of deep love and friendship, and I couldn't help but wonder if, somehow, Albert had arranged this coincidence. For the first time since the night he died, I felt his presence as a warm glow.[223]

Rothschild recounts some other intriguing coincidences surrounding his deceased friend Albert that fit into our present category of association through favorite things. For instance, Albert's favorite quotation was the ancient Chinese saying "Meeting is the beginning of parting." After his death, Rothschild found an antique book that bore the title *The Meaning of Friendship*, and he discovered an old bookmark inside it, marking a page where a phrase had been underlined by a previous reader. That phrase was "Meeting is the beginning of parting."[224]

On another occasion, Rothschild's computer printer randomly printed an extra page with a tiny heart in one corner. A friend reminded him that Albert had drawn a tiny heart on his final note before dying. The random heart then popped up seven or eight more times in his print-outs, on two different computers and printers, but always in the corner and beyond the margins. Then, singer Cathy Bolton, assistant to author Neale Donald Walsch, read Rothschild's book manuscript and sent him a copy of her latest album—titled, oddly enough, *Wind Beneath My Wings*. Before she knew of Rothschild's story, she'd placed a little heart on the liner notes, exactly like the ones Rothschild's printer created. Also, a few days after she and Rothschild discussed the heart coincidences, she printed out a report for Walsch, and *her* printer printed an extra blank page with four little hearts.[225]

Now here's one more musical example of an association by favorite things. A Canadian boy named Alexandre died at 13 from a rare disease, but during his short life, he made it abundantly clear that his favorite piece of music—perhaps his favorite thing *ever*, since he said at 12 that it would be the one thing he would take with him to a desert island—was the second movement of Beethoven's Seventh Symphony. A few weeks before his death, this symphony was played by the symphony orchestra of Quebec, where he lived, and he attended the performance. After Alexandre's death, his father was driving home from work one day, and at the same time that he was passing in front of the cemetery where his son was buried, he heard a theater director on the radio describe a play he was preparing, in which a deaf man was going to receive an ear implant and his son was going to choose the first piece of music he would listen to. The director explained—while Alexandre's father was still passing the cemetery—that he had chosen for

---

[223] Joel Rothschild, *Signals: An Inspiring Story of Life after Life* (Novato, CA: New World Library, 2000), 92.
[224] Rothschild, 84-85, 96.
[225] Rothschild, 158.

this piece none other than the second movement of Beethoven's Seventh Symphony.[226]

Alexandre's case shows once again how important timing can be in corroborating a connection to the deceased. Here are two more examples of association by favorite things in which timing plays an important evidential role. The first is something that happened to Denise Sexton the night her 17-year-old brother died from a blood clot. She was staying with a friend at the time and felt an impulse to look at the bracelet she was wearing, a bracelet that had been intended for her brother. She saw that the clock read 11:42pm, and then she felt the bracelet break. She later discovered that her brother had died at 11:42pm that night.[227]

In the second case, Lori Taylor's father died of a sudden heart attack, and about three months later, she drove her mother to visit his grave for the first time. Now, it's important to know that Taylor's father had always been her "car advisor," and that he'd told her many times how much liked her current car, a Toyota Camry. She and her mother parked the Camry and had begun walking through the deserted cemetery towards the grave when Taylor heard an engine start behind them. With shock, she realized that it was *her car* that had restarted, even though she had fully turned it off and removed the key. "[A]nd I did not have a remote control starter," she adds. When she ran back to the car, she saw that it was indeed running with no key and the ignition turned off. She tried to cut the engine but could find nothing that would work. So she and her mother ended up just letting it run while they visited the grave and then returned home. When they reached the house, the engine turned off in completely normal fashion. Taylor confirms that that day in the cemetery was the only occasion on which this kind of thing has ever happened.[228]

Some cases in the category of favorite things are particularly surprising because they involve the appearance of a physical object that was not previously present. When he was around three years old, Doug Vitro told his mother that his deceased father had visited him and, because he was sorry not to be there for Christmas, gave him a Matchbox car, which Doug showed to his mother. It was a red Porsche. Little Doug had no way of knowing it, but this was Doug's father's dream car. His mother did check whether any neighborhood children might have given Doug this car, but no one knew anything about it. It appeared to have come from nowhere.[229]

---

[226] Jeff Vézina, *Necessary Chances: Synchronicity in the Encounters That Transform Us*, trans. Carl Anger (Pari, Italy: Pari Publishing, 2009), 76-78. Vézina retrieved the account from a book written by Alexandre's father, Robert Jasmin: *Le temps d'Alexandre* (Québec: Editions Papyrus, 1989).

[227] Burnham, *Angel Letters*, 95.

[228] Arcangel, 35-36.

[229] Martin and Romanowski, 142.

A former neighbor of psychic William Stillman was also involved in a case involving the mysterious appearance of an object. Stillman writes,

> Her father was a major league baseball player who was buried with a significant baseball ring on his hand. Later, on her mother's birthday, the ring arrived in the mail, addressed to her in a script not unlike her father's longhand. The postmark was indistinct, and neither the post office nor the funeral home had an explanation.[230]

A final case involving the unexplained appearance of objects concerns a deceased grandmother who loved sewing. Trish and Rob MacGregor, authors of the book *The Synchronicity Highway*, relate how, after Trish's college roommate, Linda, lost her grandmother, straight pins began showing up all over their apartment. Neither of them was into sewing, but "[t]hey found pins scattered on the living room rug, stuck in couch cushions, laying around on the kitchen table, in the windowsills." This phenomenon in the apartment began just days after Linda's mother had found a straight pin on top of Linda's grandmother's tombstone. Linda's mother also reported finding straight pins underlining passages in the Bible. When Linda and Trish went to visit her, she showed them the Bible, and they found many more straight pins during their visit: "on the kitchen floor, on the stairs, on top of the TV." The phenomenon continued for several months before calming down.[231]

Now, this next case is not so much about a favorite object as it is about an object that the deceased "owed" to the living, but the connection to the deceased individual is still very clear. This is also another case of coincidence confirmation by a medium. Jessie was a teenage girl who died of a sudden illness. Before she died, she went to a camp run by the state police, and her father, Joe, gave her money to bring him back a hat. She forgot about his request, however, and spent the money on something else. Then, at Jessie's funeral, a police officer unknown to Joe approached him holding a blue policeman's cap. "I got this hat for you," he said to Jessie's father, seemingly searching for the appropriate words. "I don't know why, I really don't. I just know I'm supposed to give it to you." When Jessie's parents later had a reading with medium Laura Lynne Jackson, Jackson told them, among other things, that Jessie was showing her a blue policeman's cap.[232]

---

230 Stillman, *The Secret Language of Spirit*, 54. An account of this event can also be found in William Stillman, *Autism and the God Connection: Redefining the Autistic Experience through Extraordinary Accounts of Spiritual Giftedness* (Naperville, IL: Sourcebooks, 2006), 106-7.

231 Trish MacGregor and Rob MacGregor, *The Synchronicity Highway: Exploring Coincidence, the Paranormal, & Alien Contact* (Hertford, NC: Crossroad Press, 2013), 116.

232 Jackson, 128.

I'll close this section with the story of a young man named Christian, who died in a car accident on the night of his high-school graduation. Christian had always had a passion for rainbows, as could be seen from the large number of rainbow decorations with which he'd filled his bedroom. And he often longingly expressed his desire to find the happiness he believed was waiting for him at the rainbow's end. Though he was buried on a clear blue day—hot and dry, as days are wont to be in Texas—at the end of his burial service, a rainbow appeared, ending directly above his grave. It was photographed and a print given to his family as a memento.[233]

Association by Physical Likeness

Let's now look at a few cases where the association with the deceased comes through a physical likeness of them. The first concerns a photograph jumping from place to place. Glenda lost her 19-year-old son, Randy, to drowning. About four months later, she noticed that a basket she had just moved now had a photograph lying on top of it that hadn't been there before. It was a photograph of her son—the only one she had of her son laughing—and she hadn't seen it in a long time. She put the picture by her bed. Strangely, a few days later, she found the photograph tucked into her wallet. She decided to leave it there, but, a few weeks after that, the picture appeared on her dressing table—and she verified that it was not in her wallet any longer. She felt that these events happened when she was particularly depressed, and that her son was endeavoring to reassure her.[234]

In another case, the likeness was a mannequin in a store window. Carolyn Schroth saw a mannequin that eerily resembled her deceased mother. The mannequin was positioned so that it appeared to be looking at a calendar, and Schroth saw that on the calendar were the words "Lunch with Tommy" and "Call Ray." Tommy was Carolyn's brother and Ray her father.[235]

Sometimes the likeness can appear by electronic means. While watching the movie *Belle*, Paul Davids mentioned to his wife that a quote in it would be great for a feature documentary they were making about Marilyn Monroe. Davids and his wife paused the movie, left the room for a snack break, and then came back to find that the screen was no longer showing the paused movie but instead displayed a still of Marilyn Monroe that they had previously stored on their DVR.[236]

---

[233] Arcangel, 10-11.
[234] Guggenheim and Guggenheim, 208-9.
[235] Rushnell, 109-10.
[236] Davids and Schwartz with Allison, 330.

Finally, I should mention the phenomenon called "doubling," in which one sees a living, physical person who uncannily resembles the departed. Annie Mattingley relates an occasion on which her daughter saw "a woman who looked so much like her deceased sister, she gasped and tears rose."[237] In Chapter 7, we'll encounter a case in which doubling alerted psychiatrist Judith Orloff to a personal crisis experienced by one of her patients. The confirmation Orloff received in that case suggests that doubling is not just a chance phenomenon but can sometimes carry important information about the person whose likeness we encounter.

Association by Series

Some coincidences are associated with a deceased person primarily because the odd event is one in a long line of strange events that are connected to the deceased in more obvious ways. For instance, we've already gone over several of the strange events that occurred after the death of Janis Heaphy Durham's husband Max. It seems likely that it's primarily because of these other, clearer coincidences that Durham also associated with him certain other events that happened in the house: for instance, a pulsating wall in the room where Max had spent last month of his life and loud knocks on the front door when no one was there.[238]

Another example comes from Paul Davids. You'll recall the ink obliteration he experienced in relation to his deceased friend Forrest J Ackerman, related in the section on coincidences confirmed by dreams. On another occasion, Davids had the following experience. He had printed a letter to mail and set it on his dining table while he went to get an envelope. When he came back, all that was sitting on the table was a blank piece of his corporate stationery without the letter printed on it. He was extremely confused but could only conclude that he must have unconsciously filed the letter somewhere and put this blank stationery on the table instead. So he went and printed the letter again. However, when he returned the dining room afterward, he found the original letter right there where it was supposed to be. And there was no blank stationery in sight. As Davids notes at the end of his account, "Prankish behavior with ink and documents was beginning to seem like Forry's 'signature.'"[239]

---

[237] Mattingley, 185.

[238] Durham, 43-44, 46.

[239] Davids and Schwartz with Allison, 95.

Other Associations with the Deceased

We come now to the many additional coincidence cases in which an association with a deceased person is clear but doesn't fit into any of the categories so far named.

For instance, here's a case in which the timing of the events just after the burial of the deceased seems significant, but there's another connection to the deceased as well: in this case, through an object that the deceased *disliked.* During his life, Leslie's husband Kevin avoided technology, including telephones, and the nature of the events she experienced seemed to confirm his dislike. The day after he was buried, Leslie noticed her cell phone hadn't received any calls all day. It turned out that the battery had run down, even though she'd plugged it in the previous night. She plugged it in to charge again, but the next day she once again found it unplugged and uncharged, even though there was no one else in the house who could have touched it. After she *taped* the charger to the phone and still found it detached the next morning, she asked her deceased husband if he was behind this. She felt him reply that she needed some "downtime." In consequence, she voluntarily spent the next two days without turning on her phone and ended up finding this quiet time very helpful. Annie Mattingley says she interviewed Leslie seven years after this event. Leslie still had the same phone, and she reported that it had never again spontaneously unplugged itself.[240]

The next case involves important timing as well as an object associated with the deceased because it was brought out specifically for the funeral and placed near the casket. Cheri Carlson's baby daughter died of Sudden Infant Death Syndrome. Carlson brought to the funeral a musical teddy bear she'd had since she was a child herself, even though it had stopped working when she was 15. She says, "I placed him below Samara's casket for the funeral, lit candles, and *the bear played*—not just a note or two… he kept on. It was the night before the funeral, I was there 'setting up' with a few friends. He played while we got things ready; he played while we 'sat;' he was still playing when we left."[241]

Sometimes the timing of a coincidence is so precise and strongly linked to the deceased that no further associating element is necessary. For instance, medium Sherrie Dillard reports that, at the exact time of her mother's death, 4:04am, Dillard's bedroom speaker phone turned on with a very loud dial tone.[242]

---

[240] Mattingley, 63-64.

[241] Elisabeth Hallett, *Soul Trek: Meeting Our Children on the Way to Birth* (Hamilton, MT: Light Hearts Publishing, 1995), 223.

[242] Sherrie Dillard, *You Are a Medium: Discover Your Natural Abilities to Communicate with the Other Side* (Woodbury, MN: Llewellyn Publications, 2013), 258.

In this next case, it's not so much the timing that's important as it is the way that the coincidence imitates the behavior of the deceased in life. An older woman whom Annie Mattingley calls "Lillian" lost her husband suddenly to an accident. On several occasions after his death, Lillian woke up in the middle of the night because the doorbell was ringing. While other people might be stymied by such an occurrence, Lillian immediately knew it was her husband. Back when they'd been married for about 30 years, they'd been trying to put some romance back into their marriage, and as part of this, her husband snuck out of the house one day and rang the doorbell, surprising her with a bouquet of flowers when she answered. Lillian knew this was exactly the reference her deceased husband was making. And if you think the doorbell ringing in the middle of the night after his death might have been a freak malfunction, consider that it not only happened on multiple occasions, but in multiple locations as well—also occurring when Lillian was staying at her daughter's home.[243]

This next case employs the name of the deceased to make the necessary association. A woman named Susan lost her 68-year-old father, Samuel. A few days after his funeral, she took a rose from his grave in Southern California and carried it back to her home to Massachusetts, where she stuck it in a random page of the family Bible for safe keeping. A few days later, she discovered that she had unwittingly placed the rose in the book of the Bible that matched her father's name: Samuel. And, when she looked closer, she saw that, where the rose was bent over on the page, the bottom of the bud pointed to a sentence reading, "Now Samuel died." She took this as her father telling her that "he had died and was...okay."[244]

The next case also makes a name-based association. When Caroline Flohr's daughter Sarah was three years old, she went through a six-month period when she insisted that everyone call her by a name she'd invented: "FlowerBlack." When Sarah was 16, she died in a car accident. About six months after her death, her mother had just turned off her computer and lay down on the floor with some of her other children and the dog when suddenly the computer's printer sprang to life. It produced a single sheet of paper with a single word printed on it: F L O W E R B L A C K.[245]

Our final three cases in the miscellaneous category come from Paul Davids' book *An Atheist in Heaven.* In the first one, Davids' wife came to spend a weekend at Big Bear Lake with her husband and his colleague Sean Fernald, the fellow who would later ask Forrest J Ackerman to give him a spider bite as a sign. Davids' wife brought along a bottle of wine randomly grabbed from the assortment of 50 or so bottles people had gifted them over

---

[243] Mattingley, 13.

[244] LaGrand, *Messages and Miracles*, 236.

[245] Caroline Flohr, *Heaven's Child: A Mother's Story of Tragedy and the Enduring Strength of Family* (2012), 6-8, 82-83.

the years. She'd originally meant to take it to another friend she visited *en route* to Big Bear Lake, but she'd forgotten it in the car. When Fernald saw her arrive with the bottle, however, he "went into shock." It was the precise Spanish wine that was the *only* wine he had served at his wedding a few years before—and the year of the bottle matched the year of the wedding. What was more, there had been fewer than 10 guests present at the event, of whom one was the deceased Forrest J Ackerman and another was the fellow Joe Moe, who had already been visited by Ackerman in the dream recounted earlier in this chapter.[246]

The last two cases both involve names. In one of them, the partner of critic and author Robert Egby had just finished watching Davids' movie on his after-death communications from Ackerman when she accidentally hit the GPS on her smartphone, and it came up with a street map showing "Ackerman Road," which was about 10 miles away from her actual location.[247] The other name coincidence occurred soon after Ray Bradbury's death, when Jack Kelleher posted a tribute to both him and Ackerman on Facebook, mentioning "Forry's lifelong friend, Ray Bradbury, who has just been reunited with him." Not more than 30 minutes later, Kelleher turned on *Wheel of Fortune* to find the host introducing the first pair of contestants (during "Family Week"). Their last names were Ackerman and Bradbury.[248]

Coincidences Confirmed by Independent Repetition

Having explored many of the associations that link coincidences to the deceased, I now want to mention some further, very strong evidence that coincidences with these types of association are indeed caused by the deceased, at least on some occasions. This evidence comes from cases in which multiple people experience the same or very similar coincidences linked to the same departed personality, even though these living individuals aren't aware of each other's coincidences until after they've occurred. In these cases, the similarity in the coincidences clearly points to a common cause. If they were produced merely by the people experiencing them, we would expect them to vary more idiosyncratically in their expression, as well as in their timing.

Consider:

- Parapsychologist Loyd Auerbach was one of three men to all anomalously smell cigar smoke at the same time and connect it to a

[246] Davids and Schwartz with Allison, 144-48.
[247] Davids and Schwartz with Allison, 291.
[248] Davids and Schwartz with Allison, 171-2.

recently deceased mutual friend: science-fiction writer Martin Caidin, who was a big smoker of cigars. These three men were all in different places when this happened. Auerbach was in his car, his friend Bob was flying in a Cessna three time zones away in New Jersey, and the third man was flying in a plane over Florida.[249]

- A few months after the death of her son Erik, Elisa Medhus was told by a medium that Erik was going to connect with her by giving her goose bumps localized on specific areas of her body. Medhus's training as a doctor made her skeptical. "[F]rom the medical perspective," she says, "'regional goose bumps' just don't happen." Nevertheless, sometime later, she felt her son's presence nearby, and she suggested to him that he might produce goose bumps on the right side of her head. The goose bumps then proceeded to appear. She gave Erik a couple of other specific locations in which to manifest them, and they manifested there as well. It was only later that she discovered that other members of her family had had similar goose bump experiences after her son's passing.[250]
- In the week following the death of her friend Maxence, Viviane and four of their mutual friends experienced impressive coincidences involving an old song Maxence had been obsessed with: "Ta Katie t'a quitté""("Your Katie Left You"). One of these involved a near-stranger looking Viviane in the eyes and singing this song to her. Another involved a group of street singers stopping under the window of Maxence's best friend and singing this song.[251]
- Two people connected to the deceased Forrest J Ackerman independently experienced papers scattering in a strange fashion, as though they'd been thrown by an invisible hand. One of them was Dr. John Allison, a forensic chemist who was investigating the ink obliteration experienced by Paul Davids. In fact, the papers that were scattered were printouts of a scan of the ink obliteration.[252] The other person to experience this strange scattering was Suzanne Rick, a singer and actress residing in Ackerman's old mansion. She says it happened to her on multiple occasions.[253]
- After his mother's death, Paul Davids and his sister often found pennies in strange places at important times. We're not talking here about pennies found on the sidewalk or in a dusty corner of a room but something more striking. For instance:

---

[249] Durham, 133-4.
[250] Medhus, 20-23.
[251] Joachim Soulières, *Les coïncidences* (Paris: Dervy, 2012), 51-57.
[252] Davids and Schwartz with Allison, 120-1.
[253] Davids and Schwartz with Allison, 132-3.

- a penny appearing on a bookshelf that just moments before had been carefully examined and seen to have no penny on it,
- a penny appearing on the carpet between two people who were sitting talking,
- moving a vase and finding a penny beneath it,
- a penny appearing on a carpet that had just been vacuumed and steam-cleaned, and
- Davids' returning from a restaurant restroom to find a penny sitting in his seat, though his companion had no knowledge of his previous penny experiences.

But it is this next instance of a strange penny appearance and its independent corroboration that make this an especially fitting case to crown this section of the chapter. On one occasion, Davids was at a conference, sitting in a hotel lobby talking to a friend. As they were talking, he noticed that, under the glass top of the coffee table to his immediate right, were three pennies. He later found out that his sister had recently left three pennies on top of their mother's grave.[254]

Now it's logically possible that a living person capable of strong psychokinesis might be able to create coincidences *for other people* as well as for themselves, meaning that multiple similar coincidences might all have a single cause in a living person, not the deceased. However, I am not aware of any cases that offer independent evidence that, in a case where a coincidence *seemed* to be connected to a deceased person, it was *actually* produced by an absent living individual. If readers know of any, I would be very interested in hearing about them. On the other hand, there are many cases of coincidences where independent evidence supports the idea of their being caused by the deceased. So, in cases like the ones just listed, I am especially inclined to believe that it is the deceased at work.

Coincidences Lacking Strong Association with the Deceased

While you still have in mind the cases of appearing pennies described above, I want to add to them another case of an appearing—and disappearing—coin, this one related by Elisa Medhus, who was just mentioned in connection with the localized goose bumps. Here is her coin story, which occurred in her daughter Michelle's car.

> When we parked the car in my garage, I took everything out of the side compartment: pen, index card, and receipts. Then, true to my

---

[254] Davids and Schwartz with Allison, 324-5.

> compulsive nature, I swept my fingers up and down the compartment to make sure I had everything. …
>
> When we got back into the car [just a little while later], I glanced at the supposedly empty side compartment and saw a shiny dime glaring back at me. Where did that come from? There was absolutely no dime there ten minutes earlier. My OCD fingertips can attest to that. I asked Michelle if she had, for some crazy reason, decided to go around to the passenger side and slip some sort of donation on my side, but no, of course she hadn't. She had a special coin carrier in her drink holder, to keep her spare change. She saw the dime, shrugged her shoulders, and said, "I'm getting that it's from Erik." Then, I plucked the dime between my thumb and index finger, and *poof*—it disappeared completely. Vanished. Dematerialized between my fingers. … [And] there was no crease, no fold, no hiding place into which the dime could have slunk.[255]

The link to the deceased in this case is made purely through Medhus's daughter's intuition. As we saw in the refrigerator case in the section on signs promised by the deceased, such intuitions can sometimes be independently confirmed, so we can't completely dismiss them. I've presented this case here not only because it is a fascinating case of the anomalous appearance and disappearance of an object, but because I want to talk about the real possibility that events may be caused by a deceased person even when there is no obvious association with the deceased. The fact that we cannot *prove* that certain events are caused by a deceased person does not mean that they weren't. Many—perhaps most—events that people suspect were caused by the deceased are not particularly evidential with regard to their origin. But, if the person experiencing them believes them to have been caused by the deceased, they may be right.

The following account details how a 35-year-old woman named Beth received a measure of independent confirmation for a feeling she had about her deceased father's presence. She says,

> A friend and I were watching a movie on TV when I sensed my father's presence in a very strong way. The kitchen light started to turn on and off and I got up to check the light. When I sat back on the couch, I could sense my Dad's presence even stronger. All of a sudden my friend jerked his foot back and said, "Ow, something just hit me on the foot." His foot was exactly where I felt my Dad was standing.[256]

Consider as well how many reports there are of strange sounds following a death. Many people report knocks on doors when no one is there, or even doors slamming when no one is around and there are no drafts present. Should these events be dismissed as imagined? I think people who

---

[255] Medhus, 33.

[256] LaGrand, *Messages and Miracles*, 39-40.

insist that such an event they experienced was caused by the deceased should be given the benefit of the doubt—because of cases where such things have happened and they *were* accompanied by strong confirmation from other sources, sometimes even from apparitions.

Take, for example, an apparition case reported in Haraldsson's *The Departed Among the Living*. The experiencer was taking a break from doing renovations on her house when someone knocked at her door. It was a neighbor who used to visit her frequently, but this was the first time he'd come since he'd been dead! They apparently communicated with each other telepathically, with her asking the neighbor why he was there, and him replying, "I've come to stay with you, Magga dear." When she told him she didn't have any space for him, given the state the place was currently in, he seemed miffed. "I will have to come back later then," he told her, and slammed the door as he departed.[257]

If apparitions have been known to slam doors, and apparitions are often only visible to certain individuals (as we saw earlier in this chapter), then shouldn't we consider the possibility that unseen manifestations of the deceased may at times be the origin of otherwise inexplicably slamming doors? Or of other anomalously moving objects or anomalous sounds?

Why Do the Deceased Use Coincidences?

We are now going to turn to another question that arises in connection with coincidences and the deceased. If, as we saw early on in this chapter, the dead can actually appear to people and give them verbal messages, either in waking life or in dreams, why would they instead resort to coincidences to send a message? Is there anything that sets apart those cases in which the deceased choose to manipulate objects or situations rather than produce apparitions or verbal messages?

There are two basic categories of response to this question, which are not always separable. First, there's the possibility that the choice of a coincidence over an apparition or some other mode of communication occurs because of differences existing on the deceased's end of things. For instance, it could be that coincidences are easier for the deceased to produce than apparitions. The other possibility is that the difference between these cases depends on something going on at the receiving end of the communication. For example, perhaps the would-be recipient is not very psychically sensitive and is simply unable to perceive an apparition of the dead. Of course, *both* of these possibilities might be true at times, as in a case where the recipient of the communication is limited in their ability to receive

---

[257] Haraldsson, *The Departed Among the Living*, 17.

communication and the deceased is also limited in their ability to send it, in a way that leaves few to no possibilities that work on both ends. This could explain why after-death communication doesn't happen to everyone, and sometimes doesn't happen to the people who most desire it.

So, is there evidence that after-death communication is not that easy to produce—that those sending the message must have some skill and that those receiving it must have some also? Martin and Romanowski discuss this question in *Love Beyond Life*.[258] They say that it's quite common in the after-death communications they've come across for the deceased to mention their failed attempts at communication. They also reference something that Anne Puryear's deceased 15-year-old son supposedly communicated to her telepathically. He apparently told her, "The souls here try very hard to reach the people they knew. But hundreds of souls simply never get through to anyone because those they are trying to reach don't know that it's really possible to talk to us in this dimension. It can be very frustrating."[259]

The Windbridge certified research mediums interviewed by Dr. Julie Beischel affirm that it takes work for the deceased to learn to communicate.[260] Carrie D. Cox writes, "The way in which I receive information is as much about the skill set of the discarnate as it is about me. …I am like an instrument that they can play based on their skill set. One discarnate may be able to play like Beethoven and another may only be able to play 'Chopsticks.'"[261]

Another source for information about the experience of those on the other side is a text message received by a client of French medium Geneviève Delpech. She and the receiver of this text had done a session of automatic writing to contact a deceased friend of his, who had been like a brother to him. (Automatic writing is a phenomenon wherein a person writes something without exerting intentional control over the message produced, in hopes that the deceased or some other entity will communicate through the words written.) On March 27, 2015, the day after this automatic writing session, Delpech's client received the following text message. It was identified as coming from Delpech's cell phone, even though she did not send it.

> L'écriture automatique nous demande des efforts d'énergie les messages envoyés sur vos téléphones nous demandent moins d'efforts car seules nos pensées suffisent à imprégner le message sur vos téléphones Vos téléphones ont déjà eux-mêmes une énergie dont nous nous servons pour

---

[258] Martin and Romanowski, 137-8, 144-5.
[259] Martin and Romanowski, 212.
[260] Julie Beischel, ed., *From the Mouths of Mediums: Conversations with Windbridge Certified Research Mediums*, Vol. 1: Experiencing Communication, reprinted in Beischel, *Investigating Mediums*, 217-322, p. 303.
[261] Beischel, *From the Mouths of Mediums*, 268.

> communiquer avec vous Frangin ne t'inquiète pas pour les tiens laisse les morts enterrer les morts et occupe toi des vivants n'oublie pas Frangin pureté et impureté sont personnelles, nul ne peut purifier autrui c'est une perle Rare en Ce Monde que d'avoir un cœur sans désirs – je t'aime[262]

Here is my translation:

> Automatic writing requires energetic effort from us the messages sent on your [plural] telephones require less effort because our thoughts alone are enough to put the message onto your telephones Your telephones themselves already have an energy that we use to communicate with you [plural] Bro don't worry for yours let the dead bury the dead and you take care of the living don't forget Bro purity and impurity are personal, nobody can purify another it's a Rare pearl in This World to have a heart without desires – I love you

If this text message is any indication (and of course we have no guarantee of its origin), all methods of communication are not of equal difficulty for those on the other side.

This possibility is also suggested by a particularly evidential communication received by psychic Matthew Manning. Manning had done some automatic writing in Arabic, a language he didn't know. When this writing was shown to a professor at the American University of Beirut, he found it to be a hodge-podge of Arabic words and an English name written in Arabic: George Laing. There was some reason to believe that this was a true communication from a deceased George Laing, but researchers were puzzled as to why the communication was so fragmented. Not telling Manning any of the translation, or even that their question was related to the Arabic writing he'd previously given them, they asked Manning to see if he could find out through automatic writing any information about a "George Laing." Manning's hand produced the following message, in English this time.

> George Laing asks me to tell you that he was murdered by a servant of the king's household and not many know because the police were no good and his body was buried on the slopes. He wants to know why he died when he was trying to help to build houses and develop the ports. He was hit on the head and died in the Kingdom of Saudi Arabia. Poor George, how is his building? Carry him through and hoist the flag. We are only simple because you are stupid and we have many barriers to cross. Monique Vanderhout.[263]

---

[262] Geneviève Delpech, *Le don d'ailleurs: Autobiographie d'une médium* (Paris: Pygmalion, J'ai Lu, 2015), 183-4.

[263] Matthew Manning, *The Link: Matthew Manning's Own Story of His Extraordinary Psychic Gifts* (New York: Holt, Rinehart and Winston, 1974, 1975), 124.

This message corresponded so perfectly to the Arabic fragments previously produced as well as to the secret questions of the researchers that the researchers had a hard time believing it was real. Manning's description of this episode is definitely worth reading to get a full sense of its evidentiality, but the element that is most relevant to the subject at hand is the last sentence of the English message: "We are only simple because you are stupid and we have many barriers to cross." If the spirit of a deceased person named Monique Vanderhout was indeed at the origin of this message, her tone indicates she may have been a bit insulted by the researchers' complaints regarding the fragmented nature of communications from the other side. Clearly, she would like them to appreciate the difficulty of such communication.

When Manning subsequently asked this Ms. Vanderhout about George Laing's date of death, he received this response in automatic writing:

> Here is poor Monique who was killed by her loving husband's bullets, to tell you that George Laing joined us in 1943. This is odd, why must you put us off with the radio. It makes it so difficult for us in a small space...Monique Vanderhout.[264]

Manning notes that he was indeed doing this writing in a small room where a radio was playing. While this information could obviously have been unconsciously slipped into the message by Manning himself, the suggestion that audio noise might interfere with psychic communication—either on the side of the deceased or on the side of the living—is interesting enough to warrant further investigation.

The apparent difficulty of communicating from the other side could explain why the deceased resort to so many *different* modes of communication. In fact, they have been known to resort to coincidences even when communicating with professional mediums. Medium Traci Bray reports that she sometimes leaves the television on during a phone reading and will at times be drawn to something it's displaying, which then turns out to be relevant to the reading. She says, "I have learned to trust that the weather, media, outdoor noise (such as sirens), dogs barking, often bring messages that slip right into the reading accurately."[265] If the deceased employ coincidences to communicate with professional psychics, we shouldn't wonder that they often make use of them when communicating with those of us who are more psychically "dense."

Switching to discussion of the receiving side now, we should mention that one factor that seems to make communication more difficult is grief. Mediums frequently tell us that spirits say they have trouble making their

---

[264] Manning, 126.

[265] Beischel, *From the Mouths of Mediums*, 258.

presence felt to a loved one who is deep in grief. Their grief seems to put up a psychic barrier that is all but impossible to break through. Situations like this could be one reason that the deceased would resort to manipulating physical matter. While it may require more energy or skill for the deceased, it requires less psychic receptivity from the living person.

Sometimes, it seems, even mediums need their deceased loved ones to resort to coincidences when they are deep in grief. Medium Carrie Cox lost three of her own children and furiously blamed God for her inability to communicate with them on the other side. Finally, she told God, "I refuse to do this work for you any longer if you will not let me talk to my own children." No sooner had she said this than a man walking by stopped and asked her, "Do you have three children on the other side?" When she said yes, he said, "You look too young to have three children on the other side. They are always with you."[266]

While grief may make us temporarily impervious to psychic communication, it seems some people may suffer from a general inability to receive psychic information. People may also be more or less capable of perceiving apparitions of the dead. Insensitivity to apparitions could exist even if they are a physical, rather than a telepathic, phenomenon. After all, a wine connoisseur and a wine neophyte can both take sips from the same bottle and have very different experiences. In the same way, two people could receive the same visual or auditory input and one could discern information in it that the other can't. Either way, lack of the proper psychic or physical sensitivity on the part of the living might be a reason for the deceased to resort to coincidences involving easily perceivable everyday objects.

On the other hand, even if the living person is psychically perceptive, a coincidence might be easier for them to process. Perhaps it would feel less invasive—and less upsetting to their worldview—than suddenly seeing Aunt Mildred materialize in front of their eyes.

In many cases, coincidences may simply be preludes to more direct (usually telepathic) communication. This seems to be true of the case described above of a deceased wife's banging on the fridge door. Once her husband realized who it was and spoke to her, the banging stopped. In another case reported by Martin and Romanoswki, about six months after his father's death, John Hay smelled cherry pipe tobacco smoke in his car, the kind his father smoked all the time. He asked his wife if she smelled anything out of the ordinary, and she said she smelled the same thing. He used this as a prompt to "tune in" meditatively, and a message came to him strongly: "Get in touch with your mother right away. Call your mother. She's having an emergency." It turned out that his mother was in the beginning

---

[266] Beischel, *From the Mouths of Mediums*, 315.

stages of a stroke and would have died if he hadn't immediately gotten help for her.[267]

Medium Julia Assante lost her brother Michael and reports that, after his death, she experienced "eleven days of the telephone ringing, the fax twittering, and the answering machine switching to record, among other phenomena." She notes, however, that "[i]t all stopped as soon as real communication began."[268] Assante suggests that physical phenomena are a way to get our attention. She writes that coincidences "represent contact of some sort, but a type that is one-sided and often frustrating for the dead. It's as though they make a phone call, and even though you hear ringing, you haven't figured out how to answer it."[269] Even when one sees an apparition in space, Assante suggests mentally converting it to an internal image, since apparitions rarely last very long and internalizing the communication can make it faster and more sustainable.[270]

Sometimes, however, coincidences seem to come *after* more explicit communication, especially if the previous communication has been dismissed as unreal. That is, coincidences can be very effective ways to get the attention of people who are skeptical of apparitions or of telepathic communications with the deceased. They may need something more objective to assure them it's not all in their head. For instance, *Hello from Heaven!* contains the case of a man whose wife woke up in the middle of the night to the sense that her deceased grandmother was sitting at the foot of her bed smiling at her. She roused her husband to look at the apparition, but he didn't see anything and called her "crazy." They then heard a noise in another room and got up to investigate, only to find out that every light in the house had come on, along with the living room stereo and the basement television. "My husband went around the outside of the house and found the front door light on as well," she says. "There was nothing that could be on that wasn't on. Everything was going – everything!"[271] She doesn't say whether her husband was subsequently convinced of her grandmother's presence, but I daresay this experience must have made some sort of impression!

Another case that demonstrates the confirmatory role of coincidences is part of the series of coincidences concerning the song "Ta Katie t'a quitté" that was mentioned earlier in the section "Coincidences Confirmed by Independent Repetition." A Frenchwoman named Viviane had had a telepathic/mediumistic encounter with her deceased friend Maxence the

---

[267] Martin and Romanowski, 92.

[268] Julia Assante, *The Last Frontier: Exploring the Afterlife and Transforming Our Fear of Death* (Novato, CA: New World Library, 2012), 286.

[269] Assante, 287.

[270] Assante, 291.

[271] Guggenheim and Guggenheim, 198.

week after his death, but she immediately discredited it in her mind. A few minutes later, her son's speech therapist, who was normally quite reserved, randomly looked her in the eye and sang the song "Ta Katie t'a quitté." Not only was it a song that Maxence had been obsessed with, but it described some major features of his life. This incident made Viviane take her previous communication seriously and follow the request she'd heard from Maxence's spirit that she talk to his wife. When she mentioned her experience to the wife, she burst into tears. She said that, just after learning of Maxence's death and while driving to see his body, *that* was the particular song that she hadn't been able to get out of her head.[272] Viviane comments that coincidences are more troubling precisely because they're more "objective."[273]

A desire to provide objective confirmation could also be behind the case of a deceased young boy who came to his mother in a dream and told her to use his savings to buy something from their jeweler friend. He said she'd know it when she saw it. Indeed she did, but the butterfly necklace cost $200, more than she thought he could possibly have saved. However, when she called the bank, they said that his account contained exactly $200.47.[274]

In *The Hand on the Mirror*, Janis Heaphy Durham asked Dr. Paul Wendland, an experimental physicist with a keen interest in non-physical reality, the following question. "If the spirit world or Max is trying to tell me something, why don't they communicate in a fashion that we can more easily understand and interpret? If they want our help, why aren't they more helpful?" Here is Dr. Wendland's thoughtful reply.

> A reason those in another reality don't communicate fully with us is that crossing over into our world requires great effort. But more important, if the spirits shared all the information they have, and we, as a result, knew all the consequences of our actions in this life before we took them, we would be deprived of the opportunity to grow from discovering those outcomes ourselves. If we knew all, we couldn't learn. And the point of each life is to learn and experience different attributes of what it means to be human. We are part of the learning of the whole universe. Each of our experiences contributes to the whole, so we need those experiences to be completely freely made.[275]

That is, sometimes spirits may not communicate because it is better for us to be more independent: to have to think on our own, draw our own conclusions, and choose our own actions.

In a similar vein, Margaret Wendt's deceased grandfather apparently told her through a trance medium that she needed to stop trying to contact

---

[272] Soulières, 51-55.
[273] Soulières, 57.
[274] Guggenheim and Guggenheim, 267-8.
[275] Durham, 109-10.

him for "every little thing," but that of course he would still be available to her whenever she had a strong need.[276] The authors of *Love Beyond Life* write that they "noticed that people who had a series of contacts also sensed or were told by their loved one that the communications would cease at some point in the future…when their 'work' would be done."[277] After-death communication, it seems, is not meant to happen every day but rather to be an exceptional experience that serves a very specific purpose in one's spiritual evolution. Perhaps it's also true that coincidences sometimes fit into this mission better than more explicit communication in the form of an apparition or audible voice.

Some Words of Caution

Before closing this chapter, I feel it's important to point out some other limitations that the deceased may have. There can be a misperception that, just because someone has crossed to the other side, they will know everything (including the future) and that they will be more loving and "spiritual" than they were in life.

One can see how these misconceptions could arise. As we've seen, there are many cases in which the deceased *do* know things that the living do not, and sometimes they attempt to pass on this information. Furthermore, many deceased persons do appear to have learned a great deal from the process of dying, perhaps due to having undergone a play-by-play review of their actions in the life they just left. Often, in after-death communications, the deceased will apologize for things they never indicated regretting while they were alive. And they will express love that they perhaps never did before. Annie Mattingley, author of *The After Death Chronicles*, writes,

> Crossing the veil may make us invisible (not always!), but it also frequently transforms us. An innate generosity and wisdom often arise. When we are no longer restricted to our finite physical bodies, we seem more able to see the full picture of each situation, as if the act of dying strips us of blinders and sets our priorities straight.[278]

However, it would be a mistake to think that people become perfect just because they've "crossed over." In addition to those who seem to have important realizations after death, there also appear to be what are frequently referred to as "earthbound spirits": deceased personalities who are still stuck in the emotional quagmires of their earthly life and have not moved on at all.

---

[276] Martin and Romanowski, 170.
[277] Martin and Romanowski, 18.
[278] Mattingley, xxxi.

We will discuss this phenomenon in detail in Chapter 8, "Ill-Meaning Entities," where we will also address a question that may be bothering some readers: whether *all* of the deceased go on to a pleasant afterlife. If you feel an urgent need to explore this topic, please go ahead and skip to Chapter 8, although you will probably find that, in order to understand everything you read there, you will need to return afterward to the intervening chapters, especially Chapter 6, "The Experiencer."

We will also address in Chapter 8 some potential dangers posed by the spirit realm and by undiscerning communication with unseen entities. While I don't wish to deter anyone from believing in the authenticity of the spontaneous messages that come to them from their deceased loved ones, I believe it's also important to state that the psychic/spiritual realms are not all light and happiness. The psychic/spiritual realms are at least as complex as the physical world—likely more so—and indiscriminate interaction with these realms by inexperienced persons has the potential to be deceptive and even harmful.

Caution can be necessary with coincidences as well. Even if it seems certain that a particular coincidence is caused by a spirit, this shouldn't be taken as automatic reason to trust it. The deceased are not uniformly trustworthy. As Saint Paul said, we must "test the spirits." If a coincidence seems to be conveying a message from the deceased, consider whether it is a deceased person whom you knew and trusted while they were alive. And, even if you're convinced that it is, don't leave your critical faculties at home and blindly accept whatever message you believe you've received. Ultimately, *you* are the one who must decide whether any guidance offered by a coincidence or any other kind of after-death communication is worthy of being followed.

Of course, you can rarely go wrong sending love and forgiveness to those you knew in life. In fact, there are indications that your love and forgiveness can help those on the other side. Medium Sherrie Dillard has written an intriguing book full of cases that illustrate this. According to Dillard, we often serve as "living examples of how to succeed at the sometimes difficult life lessons that we all are confronted with in the physical world."[279] "Through our personal choices, struggles, and actions," she writes, "those who have passed over are inspired, encouraged, helped, and healed."[280] Martin and Romanowski echo Dillard, mentioning that their research into after-death communication has shown them that those on the other side "also need us to help them, with our acceptance, love, and forgiveness. Just as their lives go on, so does their work...."[281]

---

[279] Dillard, 7.
[280] Dillard, 6.
[281] Martin and Romanowski, 176.

And, as we're about to see in the next chapter, some of their work may have to do with preparing the souls of those who are about to enter earthly life.

Chapter 5

The Yet-to-Be-Born

While after-death communication is quite frequently considered as an explanation for coincidences, there is another similar explanation that is much more rarely explored: pre-birth communication. As the name suggests, this kind of communication comes from children before they are born, and often before they are even conceived. In this chapter, we will examine the substantial evidence that a person's consciousness exists before the formation of their body, as well as evidence that this pre-birth consciousness is capable of communicating with its future family in various ways, including coincidences.

Memories of Heaven

Some of the evidence for pre-existence comes from near-death experiences (NDEs) in which people either recall a previous life in "heaven" from before their birth or meet people in heaven whom they feel they know from having been there before. For instance, Betty J. Eadie had an NDE during which she met several people whom she recognized as her close friends from before her life on earth.[1] Another woman, who had an NDE during a particularly difficult pregnancy, was shown a review of the events of her earthly life, including "the time I was brought from heaven to the earth

[1] Betty J. Eadie with Curtis Taylor, *Embraced by the Light* (Carson City, NV: Gold Leaf Press, 1992), 32, 73, 82.

by angels to a body."[2] And Dr. Mary C. Neal reports that, when she left her body during a kayak accident, she was met by 15 to 20 souls whom she had known "for an eternity."[3] She also describes her arrival in heaven as a return to her "eternal home." "We were returning to God," she says, "and we were all very excited."[4]

Other people remember a life before their birth without the help of a near-death experience. A friend of mine, Anna, is in her early 20s but still remembers being somewhere else before her birth and feeling the love and encouragement of a whole group of friendly beings gathered behind her. She also recalls a moment in which she felt she was "diverted to a different path," which she describes like moving on to the next step of some sort of natural progression. Anna connects this memory to something she said to her mother when she was a young child. Although Anna is Caucasian American, her mother confirmed to me that, when Anna was still a toddler, Anna told her something along the lines of, "You're lucky to have me, because God was going to send me to China."[5] While Anna doesn't now have any pre-birth memories specifically related to China, she does remember that, at the moment when she felt her pre-birth shift to a new path, she was in a place that was very orange and sky-like, perhaps with some clouds, and that she was alone with one particular being. She imagines that this is the being that, as a child, she described as "God." When the shift to the new path happened, Anna felt her attention shift to the right, and the orange color of her surroundings became much whiter and more vivid. She also remembers a feeling that she was going to be trying something new, and she could feel the excitement of many other beings regarding this new adventure, as well as their willingness to support her and not judge her if she made mistakes.

Some other adults retain even more detailed memories of a pre-birth existence. Much longer accounts can be found in Toni Maguire's book *Memories of the Light* and Roy Mills' *The Soul's Remembrance*.[6]

---

[2] Michele R. Sorensen and David R. Willmore, *The Journey Beyond Life*, Vol. 1 (Orem, UT: Family Affair Books, 1988), 90.

[3] Neal, 69.

[4] Neal, 72.

[5] Anna also showed an early preference for Asian dishware and decorative objects, which she began to collect as soon as she was old enough to purchase them for herself (at about the age of 10). She was often teased by her siblings about being "Asian." Also, when Anna was around 8, her mother introduced her to a woman that her mother told her came from Vietnam. Anna, however, told her mother, "You say she's from Vietnam, but she's Chinese." When Anna's mother told the woman this, the woman confirmed that she was in fact three-quarters Chinese and only one-quarter Vietnamese.

[6] Toni Maguire, *Memories of the Light: A Story of Spiritual Existence before Physical Birth* (Bloomington, IN: iUniverse, 2000, 2012); and Roy Mills, *The Soul's Remembrance: Earth Is Not Our Home* (Seattle, WA: Onjinjinkta Publishing, 1999).

While many people will likely find these stories far-fetched and difficult to believe, they are in fact corroborated by a large, independent body of evidence: the spontaneous reports of young children. As you're about to see, my friend Anna is not the only child to have talked to her mother about events before her birth. These statements of young children are often dismissed by parents as fantasy, but, in recent years, several researchers have taken pains to collect these statements and have discovered that they not only show a great deal of consistency but in some cases include verifiable pre-birth details. Let's look at some of them now.

Children Who Met the Dead Before Birth

Let's begin with some comments in which children (and a couple of adults) strongly suggest that they have come from the same place to which the dead go. Note that these comments offer additional evidence for life after death, as well as for life before birth. Consider:

- Sheryl Reyes-Cuevas's three-year-old daughter pointed at a picture of a brother she'd never met, who died at 14 months old. She said, "I know him from before I was born."[7]
- Amy Elisabeth Rattigan remembers that, when her sister was preschool age, she told their mother that she missed "playing with her other two sisters in heaven." Though the girl was too young to know about it in any usual way, their mother had had two miscarriages before she was born.[8]
- Paula Conroy's first daughter died at almost three years old. Eight years later, when another of her daughters was three years old, the second daughter saw a video of the first and exclaimed, "That's my sister Beth! I knew her in heaven before I was born."[9]
- Darlene's two-year-old granddaughter was looking out of the car at her great-grandmother one day when she said, "I'm so sad for her because she lost the one she loved and is so sad." In fact, her great-grandmother had lost her husband just months before the girl was born, but no one could figure out how the two-year-old could have known this. When

---

[7] Wayne W. Dyer and Dee Garnes, *Memories of Heaven: Children's Astounding Recollections of the Time Before They Came to Earth* (Carlsbad, CA: Hay House, 2015), 16.

[8] Dyer and Garnes, 14.

[9] Dyer and Garnes, 17.

they showed her a picture of the great-grandfather in question, she said, "Oh, I know him…I talked to him before I came here!"[10]

- Janis Monachina's daughter remembered her grandmother's deceased twin. She said, "Yes, I was swinging with her in the clouds before I came. We were picking out my family and wearing pretty white dresses."[11]
- When Michele Mira and her husband were showing their three-year-old son photos of his deceased grandfathers, he said about his father's father, "I know him—he's Poppy Henry. I saw him on my way to you."[12]
- Barb O'Rourke told her young daughter that she was sorry she never got to meet her grandmother, who had died. Her daughter, who was close to three years old, said, "Yes, I did." When asked what she meant, she replied, "I saw her in heaven with God."[13]
- A "voice" repeatedly told Rhonda Thompson that she was going to have two more children and referred to them as Grace and Noah. When she became pregnant soon after, she figured she'd be having twins, but in fact she just had one baby, a girl. She nevertheless gave this girl the middle name Grace. Nine months later, she conceived a little boy and gave him the middle name Noah. When the daughter was two years old, she told her mom she'd always been Grace and that that's what "everyone else" called her. "God calls me Grace," she said, "so do Grandma and Grandpa in heaven, and so does Noah." Noah was eight months old at the time.[14]
- Betty Clark Ruff was struggling to explain to her two-year-old son Alan the death of his great aunt and told him she'd gone back to God. Alan immediately asked, "Who took her?" Ruff wasn't quite sure how to reply but told him it had to have been a person she knew. Hearing that, Alan cheered up. "Oh, I know what it's like," he said. "Grandpa Clark brought me when I came to you. He'll probably take me back when I die." He was actually able to give a description of this grandfather, who had died a decade before his birth and of whom he'd never seen a photograph. He said that Grandpa Clark had helped get him ready for coming to earth. And he told at least two other members of the family about this experience on separate occasions.[15]

---

[10] Dyer and Garnes, 18.
[11] Dyer and Garnes, 26.
[12] Dyer and Garnes, 27.
[13] Dyer and Garnes, 29.
[14] Dyer and Garnes, 30.
[15] Sarah Hinze, *We Lived in Heaven: Spiritual Accounts of Souls Coming to Earth* (Rexburg, ID: Spring Creek Book Company, 2006), 28-29. Originally published in

- Lois P. reports that she'd been telling her three-year-old, Johnny, stories about his great-great-grandfather when he asked if she'd tell him instead about "Grandpa Robert." This was his great-grandfather, who had died before Lois was even married. When Lois asked Johnny how he knew about Grandpa Robert, he replied, "Well, Momma, he's the one who brought me to earth."[16]
- Amy Steinman's three-year-old niece mentioned her great-grandfather, whom she'd never met on earth. When her mother told her she'd never met him, just seen him in a picture, the girl said, "Yes, I have, Mommy. I was with him when he was sick, and he was with me before I came down." The great-grandfather had been sick for a long time before dying of a brain tumor.[17] It's interesting to consider that this young girl's spirit may have accompanied this man during his illness even though no one on earth would have recognized who she was, or that she would one day be part of their family. This suggests the possibility that we may be attended by spirits we will never recognize as people we know in this life.
- Pre-birth memories often fade as children grow up, but Monica, who is now an adult, still remembers sitting on the lap of a grandmother who died six years before she was born. She knew she was a "baby spirit," who had never been born yet. "I know my grandmother was telling me all about my life and some of the important decisions I was going to have to make. She was trying to give me some guidance to make my life a little easier."[18]
- Another adult, Kirk D. Gardner, remembers a great deal about the time before he was born. "I remembered Great-Grandpa Apollus from the life before earth life," he says. "Following his death, he returned home to the spiritual world where we enjoyed many wonderful times together before my departure to earth."[19]

NDE Perceptions of Future Children

Confirmation of the idea that the dead and the yet-to-be-born share a spiritual location is provided by near-death experiencers who, during their

---

Betty Clark Ruff, "My Toddler Taught Me About Preexistence and Death," *Instructor* (February 1963): 61.

[16] Hinze, *We Lived in Heaven*, 27.

[17] Dyer and Garnes, 21.

[18] Elisabeth Hallett, *Stories of the Unborn Soul: The Mystery and Delight of Pre-Birth Communication* (San Jose: Writers Club Press, 2002), 190.

[19] Hinze, *We Lived in Heaven*, 67-69.

NDEs, observe the spirits of future children, whether their own or someone else's. For instance, NDE researcher Paul Perry mentions cases in which NDErs have seen groups of souls waiting to be born. In one of them, a 15-year-old boy who was knocked unconscious underwater had an NDE in which he saw a bunch of other kids along with a "real big" man. "I couldn't see his face," the boy reported, "because he glowed so beautifully, but from his voice I could tell that he was real nice." The man told him to enjoy himself in that beautiful place with all those kids and that the boy would be returning before they would. When the boy asked what the man meant by this, he replied, "These are people who haven't been to earth yet."[20]

Betty Eadie, an NDEr mentioned a few pages ago, also reports having seen spirits making preparations to come to earth. She watched one "exceptionally brilliant and dynamic spirit." This spirit had decided to incarnate in a handicapped body, because of all the opportunities for growth it would give him and the spirits who would be his parents, spirits whom he apparently already knew quite well. With great anticipation of feeling their tremendous love, he chose to enter his new body as early as possible—at the time of its conception.[21]

Eadie also mentions recognizing that a daughter she adopted some years after her NDE was in fact one of the spirits she'd met during her NDE.[22] This is just one of several cases in which an NDEr has encountered a spirit whom they later met in human form. For example, Richard Philips had an NDE at the age of 14 in which he says he met not only some brothers and sisters who had died before his birth and of whom he had not previously been aware but also a *future* brother, who was born to his parents four years later.[23]

Another such account comes from an NDE that occurred over 100 years ago, around 1913. Not long before this experience, Bertha, who had already borne 13 children, had decided not to have any more. We join this account of her NDE after Bertha has already arrived in the spiritual world and been greeted by many of her friends who preceded her in death. The experience is recounted by Bertha's granddaughter, who writes,

> Bertha was taken into another room where there were many children. On the far side of the room she saw two little girls, whom she did not know. They were so beautiful she could not look away from them.
>
> "Do you want them?" the guide asked.

---

[20] Paul Perry, foreword to *We Lived in Heaven: Spiritual Accounts of Souls Coming to Earth* by Sarah Hinze (Rexburg, ID: Spring Creek Book Company, 2006), xiv-xv.
[21] Eadie with Taylor, 94-5.
[22] Eadie with Taylor, 145.
[23] Pierre Jovanovic, *Enquête sur l'existence des anges gardiens* (Paris: J'ai Lu, 1993), 99.

> "Yes. Oh, yes," she responded quickly. "Can I return to earth life and have them?"
>
> "Yes," said the escort. "That is the purpose of this visit, to let you see them. Now we must return." Bertha returned to her body.... After recovering from the illness, Bertha told Jonathan [her husband] she wanted more children.
>
> A year later, after moving to Oakly, Idaho, Bertha gave birth to a new little girl whom she named Alberta. Two years later she delivered another little girl, LaVirle. For the remainder of her life, Bertha insisted these were the two little girls she had seen in the large room.[24]

More recently, a five-year-old named Debbie had an NDE while suffering from domestic abuse. During her NDE, a being whom others in the NDE referred to by various names including "Messiah," "Rabboni," and "Savior" told her that she had to return to her earthly life because she needed to raise her children. Imagine being five years old and being told you had to return to life to raise your kids! Debbie was actually shown her future children during her NDE. "Messiah" brought in four beings, and she knew they were her four children. The oldest two were boys and the youngest two girls, and each had a distinctive look. They insisted they wanted her to be their mother. Otherwise, their plans would be frustrated. Debbie asked Messiah, "Is there no other way?" and he replied, "Not if you want to fulfill the commitments you made with your children and with others before you were born." So Debbie returned to her earthly life, and many years later, she indeed had four children, about whom she says, "These children are the spirits that I met when I was five years old."[25]

One highly detailed, first-person account of an NDE meeting with future children comes from Ranelle Wallace, who had an NDE after being involved in a plane crash. She was severely burned in the crash, and, to reach help, she had to make "a tortuous four-hour descent in blinding fog down the icy mountain." It was only once Wallace was safely in an ambulance that she surrendered consciousness and found herself in the spiritual realm. Her grandmother met her there and talked about the importance of motherhood. She also told her she would be going back to her body, even though it would be painful and disfigured. When Wallace protested, her grandmother drew her attention to a young man coming toward them. He was very surprised to see Wallace. "Why are *you* here?" he asked, and started crying. Wallace came to understand that he was crying because she was supposed to be on earth

---

[24] Craig R. Lundahl, "Near-Death Visions of Unborn Children: Indications of a Pre-Earth Life," *Journal of Near-Death Studies* 11, no. 2 (Winter 1992): 123-8, p. 125. Originally published in Lee Nelson, *Beyond the Veil*, Vol. 1 (Orem, UT: Cedar Fort, 1988), 37-39.

[25] Sarah and Brent Hinze, "Visions of Future Children in Near-Death Experience," 29:13-33:27.

to become his mother, and here she was, protesting her return. She says his name was Nathaniel, and he told her that he needed her as his mother on earth in order to accomplish his own mission. "I saw that I was to open doors for him, to help him, to encourage him," she says.[26]

Obviously, Wallace did return to her earthly life, and two or three years after her NDE, she gave birth…to a baby girl! Years went by after that, but eventually she became pregnant again. While she was in labor, she became aware of a tall man in a white suit standing to her right. She recognized his sad eyes. This time, he was sad because of all the pain she was enduring to bring him into the world. Wallace recounts,

> He opened his mouth and said, "Thank you, Mom," and a wave of love came into me that blew my spirit into a spin. I looked at him through tears and said, "Thank you." Then he was gone. And my heart was filled.[27]

When Wallace finally delivered the baby, it was indeed a boy, whom she named Nathaniel.

Another NDEr, Ned Dougherty, admits he was living purely for himself when he had his near-death experience. An angelic being whom he later identified as Mary, the mother of Jesus, showed him a group of toddlers playing in a garden. "I perceived that I should know these children, but I was confused," he recounts. After the children slowly disappeared, instilling in him a feeling of terrible loss, he realized who they were. They were children he could have fathered during his life, if only he hadn't made the women in his life get abortions. He'd been reflecting on this for a while when another little boy appeared in the garden. This boy was blue-eyed with blond hair, and Dougherty understood that he was to be his future son. Soon after that, Dougherty was sent back to his body. Seven years later, he finally became a father—to a blue-eyed, blond-haired boy.[28]

The last case I'm including in this section is not an NDE but rather an after-death communication that was also a pre-birth communication. Still, it provides an indication from yet another source that the dead and the yet-to-be-born are in a similar state, one in which they can interact with each other. In this case, a man named Roy Caldwell dreamt about a friend of his, Lee, who'd just been killed in Vietnam. In fact, Caldwell had three dreams of him, on three successive nights. In the third dream, he saw a little girl with Lee. "[Lee] picked her up," he says, "placed her on his knee, and began telling her

---

[26] Hinze, *We Lived in Heaven*, 110.

[27] Hinze, *We Lived in Heaven*, 112.

[28] Sarah Hinze with Laura Lofgreen, *The Memory Catcher* (Provo, UT: Spring Creek Book Company, 2012), 120-3. Ned Dougherty recounts his NDE in his book *Fast Lane to Heaven: Celestial Encounters That Changed My Life* (Charlottesville, VA: Hampton Roads, 2001).

about me, my wife, and our home." At that time, Caldwell's wife was just about to give birth, and when their daughter grew up a bit, Roy recognized her as the girl he had seen in his dream on the knee of his deceased friend.[29]

Pre-Birth Awareness of Earthly Events

Once we begin to take seriously the idea that children's consciousness exists prior to their birth on earth, it's natural to wonder if the yet-to-be-born might be aware of earthly events in the way that the dead at least sometimes are. In fact, children's comments support this.

In Ohkado Masayuki and Ikegawa Akira's 2014 investigation of 21 Japanese children with memories from a pre-birth existence, 15 of the children reported being able to see what was happening on earth before they were born.[30] In one of Ohkado and Ikegawa's cases, a child told her mother, "I saw you in a gorgeous white dress. You were holding a dog." In fact, the mother clearly recalled that, after getting married and while still wearing her wedding dress, she had returned to a room where her dog had been kept and held it.[31]

Other children have also reported memories of events that happened before their birth that were confirmed to be correct. Lola Brady Everett is now an adult, but she still remembers how, "[a]s a small child, I had a clear memory of watching my parents before birth: I was looking down at them from above as they sat in a park. Years later my mom and I were talking, and she mentioned their favorite spot in a park, which they had gone to as a young married couple. I asked her to take me there, and it was the exact spot from my memories."[32]

When he was four years old, James Leininger told his father, "When I found you and Mommy, I knew you would be good to me." When his father asked *where* he'd found them, James replied, "Hawaii. … It was not when we all went to Hawaii. It was just Mommy and you. … I found you at the big pink hotel. … I found you on the beach. You were eating dinner at night." James' parents did once stay at a pink hotel in Hawaii—five weeks before his conception. And, on their last night there, they had had a moonlit dinner on the beach.[33]

---

[29] Hinze, *We Lived in Heaven*, 46-48.

[30] Ohkado Masayuki and Ikegawa Akira, "Children with Life-between-Life Memories," *Journal of Scientific Exploration* 28, no. 3 (2014): 477-90, p. 482.

[31] Ohkado and Ikegawa, 483.

[32] Dyer and Garnes, 24.

[33] Bruce and Andrea Leininger with Ken Gross, *Soul Survivor: The Reincarnation of a World War II Fighter Pilot* (New York: Grand Central, 2009), 153-4.

In a case collected by Carol Bowman, author of *Return from Heaven*, a two-year-old remembered hovering over his mother before his birth and seeing her cut herself and then go to the hospital to have stitches. He even told her she'd been wearing a yellow dress, which she had been. And there's no way he could have seen that yellow dress after he was born, because she'd thrown it away after it got bloody.[34]

In another book by Bowman, Hilda Swiger relates the following story about her grandson Randy.

> A couple of years ago, when Randy was four, we all took him on his first trip to Epcot Center. We were headed into a restaurant, when suddenly Randy said to his daddy, "You're going the wrong way. You sit right there." Randy pointed to a particular table on the side. "That's where you sat before."
>
> Suddenly my son realized that Randy was right. They sat at that very table on their last visit to Epcot Center, soon after Randy was conceived. My son asked Randy, surprised, "How did you know that?"
>
> Randy's reply took us all aback. "Oh, I was following you and Mommy around that day when you came here before I was born."[35]

Elisabeth Hallett reports in *Stories of the Unborn Soul* the experience of a woman named Wendy, who pulled out her flute for the first time since long before her children were born. Her son Philip remarked that he remembered when she used to play it often. When she told him she hadn't played the flute since long before his birth, he told her that it was when she lived in the house that had a wood-stove room that had to be stepped down into. Indeed, she had played her flute in that room, three houses before the house in which he was born. When she told him he'd never been to that house, he replied, "No, Mom, I wasn't alive yet, I was in Spirit."[36]

Sarah Hinze was an adult when her mother began opening up about the life of Hinze's grandmother, who died before she was born. When Hinze heard about the abuse her grandmother had suffered, she suddenly remembered being present for the events her mother was describing. She says,

> Suddenly—in a flash—I saw myself as a spirit person dressed in white. I knew it was before I was born. I was standing in my grandmother's bedroom in front of an old grandfather clock. My heart felt of her pain and I offered what comfort I could. I believe I was acting

---

[34] Carol Bowman, *Return from Heaven: Beloved Relatives Reincarnated within Your Family* (New York: HarperCollins, 2001), 180.

[35] Carol Bowman, *Children's Past Lives: How Past Life Memories Affect Your Child* (New York: Bantam, 1997, 1998), 333-4.

[36] Hallett, *Stories of the Unborn Soul*, 257.

> in the role of her guardian angel, but in God's wisdom I was not allowed to intervene at that time.[37]

I've even found one case of a child who recalls observing their parents as far back as their parents' childhood. In one of Ohkado and Ikegawa's cases, a Japanese child drew her mother a picture of "a four-story building surrounded by mountains" and said to her, "This is where you lived. I saw you there." The mother had lived in a four-story building with a mountain view when she was a child.[38]

One grown woman had all her life had a vision of herself floating above her parents in a mountain cabin, feeling loving and excited. After discussing the vision with a counselor, she decided to mention it to her mother. She described the cabin in detail to her mother, and her mother gasped. It was the place where her mother and father had secretly made love the week before their wedding.[39]

That story may be a bit disturbing for some parents, but it's actually quite vague compared to the memories some other children have of their conception. One vivid case is reported by an older gentleman named Rennie, who had a career as an Air Force pilot and intelligence officer. He remembers that, when he was only seven, he mentioned to his mother that he recalled where he came from before he was born and the people he was with. He asked her, "Was I placed with you and Dad when you were in the front seat of a car?" She brushed him off, calling his suggestion "indecent." But the memories kept going through Rennie's mind, and in his mid-20s, he asked his parents about it again. Specifically, he asked them if he'd been conceived in the front seat of their 1917 Overland. They both blushed and were reluctant to talk about it, but when he told them the details of what he remembered—specifically, about how they had opened the car door and his mother had checked to be sure Rennie's sister was fast asleep in the back—they confirmed everything he said.[40]

A 45-year-old woman named Nan also has a verified memory of witnessing her conception. She reports,

> My daddy came home, and Mother was cooking lunch. Dad said, "Drop everything, and let's go into the bathroom." Mom said, "I have to put on a diaphragm." He replied, "No, it'll be okay this time." I can remember that. I thought, "Now is my chance. Here is my door."[41]

---

[37] Hinze with Lofgreen, *The Memory Catcher*, 126.
[38] Ohkado and Ikegawa, 483-4.
[39] Case reported to Rev. Linda Bedre, published in Hallett, *Stories of the Unborn Soul*, 32-33.
[40] Elizabeth M. Carman and Neil J. Carman, *Cosmic Cradle: Spiritual Dimensions of Life Before Birth*, rev. ed. (Berkeley, CA: North Atlantic Books, 2013), 66-68.
[41] Carman and Carman, 59.

Nan finally told her mother about this memory when she was an adult, and her mother was understandably disturbed but did confirm that she and Nan's father had had sex in the bathroom at lunchtime, and that that was the one time they didn't use a diaphragm.

Children also seem capable of remembering things that happened while they—or at least their future bodies—were in the womb. Interestingly, some of these memories are consistent with the child's awareness being bound by the senses of the developing fetus, while others show some ability of the child to "see" or otherwise perceive events occurring outside of the womb. Taken as a whole, the evidence seems to indicate that the child has a consciousness that is able to perceive the world before the formation of its body and that it continues to be able to use this wider mode of perception for some portion of the time that its body is developing in the womb, sometimes in alternation with a consciousness that is restricted to the senses physically available to the fetus.[42] Usually by the time of birth—at the latest, a few hours after birth—

---

[42] Developmental psychologist Jenny Wade discusses the dual nature of fetal-period memories in her article "Two Voices from the Womb: Evidence for Physically Transcendent and a Cellular Source of Fetal Consciousness," *Journal of Prenatal and Perinatal Psychology and Health* 13, no. 2 (Winter 1998): 123-47. For instance, she points out that hypnosis has allowed people to remember verifiable visual details of their own birth that a newborn baby's undeveloped visual apparatus is simply incapable of perceiving (p. 135).

Another intriguing source regarding dual consciousness in early physical life is Toni Maguire's book *Memories of the Light.* About her memories of being an infant, she writes, "When I looked at my arms, it was as if I had two on each side to focus my eyes on. I could see my spiritual arm moving and feel my physical arm moving in a completely different direction. They didn't know how to work together" (p. 10). She says on the following page, "I felt like two different living creatures within the same space. I recall lying around in a cloth diaper in the living room floor of my grandparents' house thinking about a choice I made as a spirit before conception to come to my mother's womb and all the work I needed to do while I was alive. ... I then thought, '*How am I going to get everything done when I can't even walk yet?*'" (p. 11).

Later in her book, Maguire describes an out-of-body experience she had as a child, saying, "If I tried I could still feel the thoughts of my body up on the hill. It was feeling relaxed and thinking separately to my spirit, but it was happy to stand there and feel this peaceful sensation. My body could see what was happening to my spirit, and the same could be said of my spirit toward my body. Although we existed separately we were also still connected to the other's environment for the moment and the thoughts of my physical mind were saying to me, 'Go. I feel safe'" (p. 46).

the child's consciousness becomes limited to that of the physical body, in the way most adults generally experience their consciousness to be limited.[43]

Perhaps because of this dual nature of fetal consciousness, those who remember events that occurred while they were in the womb demonstrate an intriguing mix of understanding and confusion surrounding the reasons for these events. For instance, as an older child or teen, Marilyn recalled a memory of hearing her parents arguing through dim shadows. She heard her father say, "Then, you'll have to get rid of it!" and felt a zing and a feeling of terror. After remembering this, Marilyn went to her mom and asked if she had ever discussed aborting her. Indeed, she had. Her mother's life had apparently been in danger due to the pregnancy.[44]

Caitlin McKnelly was 20 weeks pregnant when she developed a tear that caused a loss of all the amniotic fluid. Ten days or so later, the baby turned breech, and his butt actually plugged the hole and allowed the fluid to start accumulating again. "The position he assumed is called a single footling breech," says McKnelly, "where one leg is flexed and crossed in the usual breech position but the other one is stuck straight out." She never talked to her son about the circumstances of his gestation or birth, but at eight years old, he mentioned to his doctor remembering being inside his mother. Specifically, he recalled that "something happened and all of a sudden he couldn't move and he was being horribly squeezed. With a tremendous effort, he gathered all his energy and turned his body so that he could stick out his foot and push against the wall so he wouldn't be squeezed out of me, and so that he could use his body to plug off the place where the fluid was escaping."[45]

In this vein, a psychically gifted nurse-midwife has reported to pre-birth communication researcher Elisabeth Hallett that she occasionally receives telepathic communication from unborn babies who alert her to negative conditions in the mother's body or in her environment.[46]

A Christian Indian woman, Prashant, still has a memory at age 40 of seeing her parents before she was born. Some of the details she remembers are particularly intriguing. She says,

> I recall being high up in the clouds descending toward Earth, like Google Earth, where you zoom in and get closer and closer. I'm conscious that I don't have a body. I'm a point of consciousness descending on the Earth. I approached until I was one hundred feet above the ground. I noticed a

---

[43] Jenny Wade, "Physically Transcendent Awareness: A Comparison of the Phenomenology of Consciousness Before Birth and After Death," *Journal of Near-Death Studies* 16, no. 4 (Summer 1998): 249-75, p. 262.

[44] Hallett, *Stories of the Unborn Soul*, 149.

[45] Hallett, *Stories of the Unborn Soul*, 127-8.

[46] Hallett, *Stories of the Unborn Soul*, 55-56.

> market or bazaar. My attention was drawn to a happy couple holding hands and singing. The man was wearing a light blue sweater and blue jeans; the woman was dressed in a traditional Indian orange sari. I zoomed in closer and closer to the woman and entered her womb. While I entered my mother's womb and looked up toward her, I was not seeing the inside of her body as such; I saw her as if seeing someone from inside a swimming pool—like looking out through a fluid of sorts, but the fluid was not a liquid. Rather it was like a luminescent fluid.[47]

As a child, Prashant thought of this memory as a dream, but when she was 17, she told her parents about it, and they confirmed that, when Prashant's mother was four months pregnant with her, they had worn those precise clothes to the engagement ceremony of a friend. Furthermore, that day was the only day on which they had ever held hands and sung in public, and they were indeed at a market when they did so: the New Delhi South Extension market.

Our final story in this section is long, but full of verified details. An elementary school teacher named Nicole recounts that she was present at the birth of her friend's baby son Mich'l, just months before her friend suddenly died. Mich'l was raised by his grandparents, and years later, he was in Nicole's fourth grade class. "I have never told him that I was there for his birth," she says, "because I didn't want the other students to think that he had special treatment and I didn't want to upset him with thoughts of his mother. Perhaps his grandparents told him that I was there, but I'm not sure. He does know, however, that his mom and I were friends."

One day in class, Nicole asked her students to think about the earliest events they could remember from their lives. While other students talked about their memories of being three or four years old, Mich'l raised his hand to say he remembered watching people from the sky, as well as being in his mom's belly. Then he said the really shocking bit. He told Nicole that he'd been invisible before his birth and that he had been in her gray car with her while she drove to the hospital. He said she'd been listening to the song "Winter, Spring, Summer or Fall," which she immediately understood to be his way of describing James Taylor's "You've Got a Friend." She indeed had kept a cassette recording of this song in the gray car she'd owned at the time of his birth (but sold two years later). Mich'l also told Nicole he remembered her stopping at a gas station and asking for directions to the hospital, as well as the fact that the hospital parking lot was partly closed, so she had to park on a corner and run in. All of this was true.

According to Mich'l, his presence with Nicole during the time leading up to his birth had to do with the fact that he knew his "real mom" wasn't going to live very long. He said that, while she was in labor with him, he'd

---

[47] Carman and Carman, 115.

asked God if Nicole could be his mom instead. But he was told no. Nevertheless, he apparently kept begging Nicole to consent and continued to follow her even once she arrived at the hospital. He said he saw her leave the birthing area to make a call from a pay phone and then, in the waiting room, put on a sweater that someone else had left behind. "I hate to admit this," says Nicole, "but I did find a nice warm cardigan in that waiting room and I put it on because I was so cold. I've never done anything like that before...." Her putting on the sweater was the last thing Mich'l said he remembered, which makes sense given that Nicole recalls that he was born about 30 minutes after she used that telephone.

Later, Nicole talked to Mich'l privately, and he expressed surprise that she didn't have any memories of her own birth. Then he offered her some reassurance, saying, "My life did turn out OK; so don't worry about not being my mom."[48]

Nicole says that she wondered whether maybe Mich'l's mother had somehow communicated all of this information to him from the other side. However, given the number of cases in which children *have* reported holding conversations with spirits of the deceased, it seems likely to me that, if Mich'l had gotten this information from talking with his deceased mother, he would have reported it that way, instead of saying that he was just thinking back to his earliest memories.

Apparitions and Dreams of the Yet-to-Be-Born

So, we've seen evidence that at least some children perceive their parents or other individuals before birth, but is there any evidence that these pre-birth spirits can themselves be perceived? Again, the answer is yes.

These cases, too, can range from very simple to very complex. On the simpler end of the spectrum, there's the case of a woman named Miriam, who was pregnant but hadn't yet told her young son about the coming baby. Nevertheless, he said to his mother one day, "Mama, there's a baby girl in our house. Do you see her?"[49]

There's also the observation that three-year-old Mark made to his mother one night at bedtime. "There's a little boy in our yard," he said. "I was talking to him earlier." When his mother asked what the boy had said,

---

[48] Nicole E Friend Experience, Near-Death Experience Research Foundation website, https://www.nderf.org/Experiences/1nicola_e_friend_other.html (accessed January 28, 2018).

[49] Elisabeth Hallett, *Soul Trek: Meeting Our Children on the Way to Birth* (Hamilton, MT: Light Hearts Publishing, 1995), 39.

Mark replied, "He hasn't been born yet. He's waiting for his mommy and daddy to be ready. They live in one of these houses [nearby]."[50]

Sometimes apparitions of future children serve a helping function. Sarah Skidmore was abducted as a three-year-old. She escaped her captor and spent a few days in a grove of trees in the desert before she began walking and was discovered by a hunter who took her to safety. Sarah reported that, while she'd been lost, she'd seen a small child with her in the desert, a child who looked like her sister Heather but was surrounded by a bright light. This shining visitor stood by her smiling for the two days she had stayed by the trees. A year later, Sarah's younger sister Jessica was born. Her family reports that, when Jessica was almost three, Sarah had a moment when she suddenly stared at Jessica very hard and then exclaimed, "Mommy, it was Jessica in the desert. Her hair is the same as it was then. She is the same size now. … Jessica was my shining friend in the desert!"[51]

While apparitions of future children often appear in child-like form, sometimes they look significantly older. When Laura, daughter of pre-birth experience researcher Sarah Hinze, was 10 years old, she had a vision during family prayer time of a grown man with his hands placed on her father's shoulders. She realized as she looked at him that he was someone she had "known and loved…forever." At the time of Laura's vision, her mother was pregnant, and when that child was born and grew up, he had the same physical characteristics as the man she'd seen in her vision. "He was my brother Matthew," she confirms.[52]

Though all the cases I've so far cited have involved the perceptions of future children *by* children, adults also sometimes see the yet-to-be-born. Sometimes this will happen in dreams rather than in waking life. For instance, a woman who had decided not to have children because she was so excited about her career subsequently had a vivid dream of a toddler asking when she'd be ready for him. "I am Timothy, your son," he said. A year later, she had an unplanned pregnancy, and she says the boy looks "remarkably" like the boy in her dream.[53]

Similarly, David Brunner had "visits" from the spirits of a young boy and girl. He describes these visits as being mostly in his mind's eye, except for at least one occasion on which he saw them each "separately (three dimensional etheric-like)." Once, the boy appeared wearing torn jeans and a shirt while David was doing work around the house. He seemed to be about seven years old and repeated the words, "Need more love." David later

---

[50] Carman and Carman, 21.

[51] Hinze, *We Lived in Heaven*, 78-84; and Hinze with Lofgreen, *The Memory Catcher*, 115-16.

[52] Hinze, *We Lived in Heaven*, 6-7.

[53] Bowman, *Return from Heaven*, 200. Bowman retrieved this case from Elisabeth Hallett's website, www.light-hearts.com.

realized that the boy meant that he and his wife needed more love in their relationship. Later, David had a son who, at the age of seven, matched the appearance of the boy in the vision.[54]

Joan was assaulted by a stranger in her home. He eventually locked her in the bathroom while he trashed her house. While in the bathroom, Joan began to feel near her the invisible presence of a "kind young woman," whom she sensed was related to her by blood. Joan had the impression that this woman was there to take her to the other side if she was killed. However, Joan was not murdered, and when the intruder left, so did the presence she'd felt. Ten months later, Joan discovered she was pregnant. The first time she looked into her new daughter's eyes, she found herself whispering to her, "It was you." She had the feeling this little person had been "watching [her] for a long time."[55]

Mindy R. was trying to decide whether to take a permanent birth control measure when she saw a strange, curly-haired toddler in her home, wearing overalls and a white T-shirt. The child peeked around a corner, then went into the family room where it played on the floor for five minutes or so before disappearing. When the same thing happened again the following day, Mindy told her husband that this child must be waiting to come to them. She figured it was a boy, because of the way it was dressed. Several weeks later, she found out she was pregnant. But, when the child was born, it turned out to be a girl. Nevertheless, by the age of 18 months, Mindy's daughter was the spitting image of the strange little visitor she'd seen, a resemblance that became especially apparent to Mindy one day when the girl was dressed in overalls and a white T-shirt.[56]

Janette P. had a lot of trouble giving birth to her four daughters and had experienced continued ill health that could only be cured by a procedure that would make her incapable of having further children. This wasn't something she wanted, especially since she had once heard a message telling her, "When you have a son, his name will be Michael." But there came a point when she couldn't bear her health situation any longer. She decided she was going to call her doctor and schedule surgery. Her hand was on the phone when suddenly a redheaded boy appeared before her. She knew it was this Michael, and that the sadness in his eyes was asking her, "Why don't you want me?" She reached out to hug him, but she says he "disappeared right before my eyes."

The next morning, two of Janette's daughters were playing in separate rooms when one of them called to the other, "Karen, come quick and play with Michael." There were no boys in the house, and the girls didn't have any friends named Michael. But both Karen and Janette ran to see what was

---

[54] Hallett, *Stories of the Unborn Soul*, 20-21.
[55] Hinze with Lofgreen, *The Memory Catcher*, 102-3.
[56] Hinze, *We Lived in Heaven*, 12-14.

happening. When they arrived in the other room, they were told they'd come too late, that he'd left.

That night, little Karen woke up in the night upset. It turned out she had seen a boy in her room, and that he had eventually floated up through the ceiling. When asked if he'd told her his name, Karen replied, "Michael."

Months later, Janette conceived. The pregnancy was not easy, but when the baby arrived, he turned out to be a redheaded boy. And, at least at the age of 10, he was very firm with everyone that they should not call him "Mike," only "Michael."[57]

Though pre-birth communication resembles after-death communication in many ways—including the prevalence of apparitions and dreams—one advantage that pre-birth communication has over ADC is the potential for subsequent validation from the party who was previously in spirit. For instance, *Stories of the Unborn Soul* contains the report of a woman who remembers as a little girl having bedtime conversations with her future daughter, who would sit in a rocking chair in her room. The woman's own mother also remembers these conversations taking place. When the woman eventually had a daughter and she got old enough to talk, the daughter asked her mother if she remembered when the daughter used to come visit her at night. She even asked her mother about the current whereabouts of the green rocking chair.[58]

In another case, a young woman named Susan became pregnant at 17. She spoke to her unborn child saying it wasn't a good time and promising they would be together again. She then miscarried. Two years later, Susan's best friend had a baby girl, and the night she was born, Susan was awakened by a voice saying, "Mama, I'm coming back." When the friend's daughter was three, she sat on Susan's lap and asked, "Do you remember when I was in your tummy?" Susan told her she was mistaken, that she'd been in her mom's tummy. But the girl shook her head. "Not that first time," she said. She went on to explain that she had cried when she was in Susan's tummy because the "ones that brought me to you" told her she couldn't stay and pulled her back, saying it wasn't time.[59]

Children's Memories of Miscarriage and Abortion

It is not that unusual for children with pre-birth memories to remember miscarriages and abortions. For example, a six-year-old Japanese boy spontaneously told his mother, "I entered mom's belly twice, but died. But I

---

[57] Hinze, *We Lived in Heaven*, 88-95.

[58] Hallett, *Stories of the Unborn Soul*, 254.

[59] Gladys Taylor McGarey with Jess Stearn, *The Physician within You: Discovering the Power of Inner Healing* (Deerfield Beach, FL: Health Communications, 1997), 70.

looked for it again, and I was so happy that I was able to find it." No one had ever spoken to him about his mother's two miscarriages.[60]

Obstetrician Dr. Gladys McGarey reports on a four-year-old named Dorothy who told her mother about a past life she remembered in which she had a different mommy and spoke a different language. She added, "But that wasn't the last time. Last time when I was four inches long and in your tummy, Daddy wasn't ready to marry you yet, so I went away. But then, I came back."[61] The mother thought that no one but herself, her husband, and her doctor knew about the pregnancy that had occurred before their marriage and before her husband had been ready to be a father. Four months into that pregnancy, she had chosen to have an abortion.[62]

Another mother lost a baby at six and a half months gestation. The baby turned out to have some deformities: her thumbs were misplaced. The mother was so devastated to have lost the child that she begged the soul to come back to her again, and one month later she became pregnant. This child was born, and when the child became old enough to speak, she said to her mom one night before bed, "Do you remember when C (her name) was a little baby? She didn't want to come, because her hands were not right. But now, the hands are good !! Look !!" The mother says there's no way this child could have known about her deceased sister, let alone the specific deformity of her hands.[63]

In Susan's case, related at the end of the previous section, her friend's child remembered having been Susan's miscarried child. There are several other cases like this, of children remembering having previously been in the

---

[60] Ohkado Masayuki, "Same-Family Cases of the Reincarnation Type in Japan," *Journal of Scientific Exploration* 31, no. 4 (Winter 2017): 551-71, p. 561.
[61] Gladys T. McGarey, *Born to Live* (Scottsdale, AZ: Inkwell Productions, 2008), 54.
[62] Years later, the little girl who related this memory became pregnant herself at the age of 16. Her mother and father talked things over and meditated about the matter, coming to the conclusion that they could "accept and love the child into our family" in order to give their daughter an alternative to abortion if she chose, but their daughter chose to have an abortion instead. The story doesn't end there, however. The mother had had a tubal ligation two years previously, but a week after her daughter's decision to abort, the mother missed a period and had a significant dream: "I saw an infant being carried out to sea on the top of a wave. I ran after it into the surf scooped it up in arms and brought it onto the sand, the color blue was around." A week later, she had a positive pregnancy test, and she eventually gave birth to a baby boy. While there's no hard evidence here that this baby was the child her daughter aborted (and as far as I know, he doesn't have memories of being in his sister's womb), an improbable pregnancy accompanied by such a significant dream make it a possibility to seriously consider.
[63] Anonymous, "Dina's Story," *PreBirthExperience.com*, http://www.prebirthmemories.com/Dina's%20Story.htm (accessed January 28, 2018).

womb of a different mother. One little girl, for instance, remembered having originally picked her grandparents as her parents, to whom she would have been born as a son. She told her dad, "I was going to be *their* little boy before *you* came. But I decided not to and left." The father only found out about that miscarriage after checking with his older brother. Interestingly, the memory of the miscarriage seemed to cause his daughter to worry about how her grandparents would feel if she moved out of town. "They will think I died," she told her mom.[64]

Another young girl remembered having been her mother's twin in the womb. At three years old, Brittany left a message on her grandmother's answering machine asking her to come over because she and her mom had argued. When her grandmother arrived and asked what was going on, Brittany explained, "Mommy doesn't 'member when I was in your tummy." The mother related that she'd tried to explain that Brittany had grown in *her* body, not the grandmother's, but Brittany protested, "No, *before* that, when I was in Meemaw's tummy *with you*, Mommy. I couldn't stay because I didn't want to be a boy." Her meemaw had indeed miscarried her mother's twin at seven months.[65]

One case that caused even more familial strife was that of two brothers who remembered being in their aunt's tummy as twins. (She had indeed miscarried twins.) One of the brothers was mad for a long time about not being in that family instead, and at one point he berated his little brother, saying, "It's all your fault! I told you I wanted to get born really bad and you didn't want to! Tell me how you took me out of there!" At another point, his aunt asked why he didn't get born to her, but he wouldn't say. Later, he told his mom he couldn't say because they would have laughed at him. "[B]ecause they know it's not allowed. … Switching tummies. *I had to get permission for that.*"[66]

By far the most detailed miscarriage memory I've encountered is that of a young woman named Elizabeth. As soon as she was old enough to speak, she told her mother, "I was in your tummy twice. The first time, I washed away. The second time, I came out like a zipper." Her mother had never mentioned her previous miscarriage to her daughter. And Elizabeth was born by C-section—she came out "like a zipper."

At age 28, Elizabeth still remembered being miscarried. She said,

> Mom was taking a shower. She had her hands on her head shampooing her hair. The last thing I saw was her looking down at me; then I went down the drain. I did not feel pain. I remember the strong thump of hitting the shower floor, shaking everything within my core. I recall falling

---

[64] Bowman, *Return from Heaven*, 163-6.
[65] Bowman, *Return from Heaven*, 161-2.
[66] Bowman, *Return from Heaven*, 166-75.

> out of her body in slow motion and the emptiness and vastness. I felt exposed, no longer being in the womb, feeling unprotected. The drain was dark; it slowly started closing up, and at that point, I died. Everything stopped. I ceased to have awareness of that experience.[67]

Elizabeth's mother confirmed that she had indeed miscarried a pregnancy. When she was 12 weeks along, she'd felt something fall out of her while in the shower and heard a thud as a white glob two or three inches long hit the floor.

But Elizabeth remembered more than just being miscarried. At age seven, she pointed at a building and said she had been there. Her mother told her that had been her doctor's office—"when I was pregnant with you the first time," she said. At that point, Elizabeth went on to tell her mother that she remembered how she'd been a boy the first time and that her parents had had a fight. Both of these things were true. The fight had been over whether to circumcise the baby. "I chose to leave and come back as a girl," seven-year-old Elizabeth told her mother.[68]

As an adult, Elizabeth explained her pre-birth awareness of the situation in more detail. "This issue [of circumcision] threatened their marriage," she said, "and I needed them to stay together to fulfill what I came here to do. So I chose to leave." Elizabeth even explained why, as a toddler, she'd told her mother about her memories: "I did not want Mom to think the miscarriage was her fault. I needed to let her know that I had made the decision to leave and come back. I felt Mom's relief when I told her."[69]

While some children who remember miscarriage or abortion are unfazed by it, others feel the lingering effects of trauma. Elisabeth Hallett suggests these differences may be due to the particular manner in which the pregnancy ends, how the mother and unborn child have communicated prior to that time, and even what degree of integration the soul had so far achieved with the fetus.[70]

For instance, a woman referred to as "Susan" had the recurring feeling as a child that she'd been born into the wrong family, as well as a strong phobia that she was going to be abandoned. Her emotional issues were so debilitating that she eventually cried out to God for help in understanding what was going on. Soon afterward, she discovered two crucial pieces of information. The first was that her father, as a four-year-old, had been convinced he had a sister about to be born into his family, but she never came. The feeling had been so strong that, even as an adult, he never stopped wondering what had happened to her. The other piece of information,

---

[67] Carman and Carman, 40.

[68] Carman and Carman, 49.

[69] Carman and Carman, 40-41.

[70] Hallett, *Stories of the Unborn Soul*, 150.

gleaned from a separate source in the very same week, was that, when the father had been a small boy, unbeknownst to him, his mother had gotten pregnant and had an abortion.

Susan knew she was the sister her father had sensed, the sister who had been aborted. And, about a year later, Susan actually found herself with a memory from that time. She was on the other side watching her grandmother get the abortion and screaming at her to stop. After this memory, Susan actually felt some hatred toward her previously intended mother, for killing her and for the fear that that experience had left within her. However, she began to release those negative feelings over time and heal. When Susan later died, a brother who knew nothing about any of these events revealed that he'd had a dream of Susan in heaven with her grandmother. "They were standing together, both radiant," he said, "and Susan and Grandma looked astonishingly alike—like sisters."[71]

Obstetrician Gladys McGarey writes about encouraging expectant mothers to communicate with their babies, especially if they are contemplating abortion. In her practice, she discovered that communicating with the unborn child about the difficulties created by the pregnancy was sometimes followed by a miscarriage, before an abortion could even be performed. It should also be encouraging to parents who are facing a miscarriage or abortion that, as we've seen, some aborted or miscarried children appear to have come back as children of the same parents, though others appear to have come back to friends or relatives. I've even come across one case in which the child seems to have come back into the original mother's life as a foreign exchange student![72]

Reincarnation and Intermission Memories

Children's memories of being miscarried and reborn in a different womb raise the more general subject of reincarnation. Indeed, many cases in which children remembering interacting with their parents before birth are also cases in which they remember having lived previous lives, even ones in which they were born and grew to adulthood. As I noted in the last chapter, the idea of reincarnation will be familiar to some readers but probably seem beyond the pale to others. I would again suggest to those who are skeptical that they familiarize themselves with the late Dr. Ian Stevenson's extremely thorough work investigating the accuracy of children's memories of past lives,[73] as well as the work that has been done by other researchers of this

---

71 Hinze with Lofgreen, *The Memory Catcher*, 146-9.

72 Hallett, *Stories of the Unborn Soul*, 153.

73 See, among Stevenson's many works, Ian Stevenson, *Twenty Cases Suggestive of Reincarnation,* 2nd ed. revised and enlarged (Charlottesville, VA: University of

phenomenon. As previously pointed out, children who report memories of other lives have been shown to be, on average, more intelligent than the average child, and their memories do not appear to be due to any form of psychopathology.[74] Furthermore, according to two separate studies, memories of the period between death and rebirth are reported in about 20% of reincarnation-like cases,[75] though Ohkado and Ikegawa give reasons to think that they may actually be underreported in these cases.[76]

What is particularly interesting for our purposes in this chapter is that an analysis of Burmese reincarnation-like cases conducted by Poonam Sharma and Dr. Jim Tucker shows that intermission memories (memories of the time between death and rebirth) are significantly correlated with a higher number of verified statements about a previous life. Sharma and Tucker put it this way: "Since the children who report such memories tend to make more verified statements about the previous life they claim to remember than do other subjects, and tend to recall more names from that life, their reports of events from the intermission period seem to be part of a pattern of a stronger memory for items preceding their current lives."[77] That is, the fact that intermission memories correlate with verified statements about previous lives lends additional credibility to these intermission memories. Also, Ohkado and Ikegawa report about the Japanese cases they investigated that "there do not seem to be notable differences between the life-between-life memories of the four subjects with past-life memories and those of the remaining 17 subjects without such memories."[78]

Virginia Press, 1980). A less detailed introduction to his work, suitable for a general audience, is available in Ian Stevenson, *Children Who Remember Previous Lives: A Question of Reincarnation*, rev. ed. (Jefferson, NC: McFarland & Company, Inc., 2001). Another excellent introduction is a book written by journalist Tom Shroder, who accompanied Stevenson on a few of his final research trips: Tom Shroder, *Old Souls* (New York: Simon & Schuster, 1999).

[74] Jim B. Tucker and F. Don Nidiffer, "Psychological Evaluation of American Children Who Report Memories of Previous Lives," *Journal of Scientific Exploration* 28, no. 4 (2014): 585-96.

[75] James Matlock and Iris Giesler-Petersen, "Asian versus Western Intermission Memories: Universal Features and Cultural Variations," *Journal of Near-Death Studies* 35, no. 1 (2016): 3-29; and Poonam Sharma and Jim B. Tucker, "Cases of the Reincarnation Type with Memories from the Intermission Between Lives," *Journal of Near-Death Studies* 23, no. 2 (Winter 2004): 101-17, p. 102.

[76] Ohkado and Ikegawa, 485.

[77] Sharma and Tucker, 116.

[78] Ohkado and Ikegawa, 484. There did, however, seem to be significant differences between the Japanese life-between-life memories investigated by Ohkado and Ikegawa and the Burmese ones investigated by Sharma and Tucker. Notably, many of the Burmese subjects described spending much of their time between lives living in a tree. The Japanese children tended to report being in the

In Volume 1 of his enormous work *Reincarnation and Biology*, Stevenson recounts two particularly intriguing cases in which children remembered their previous earth personality, remembered hanging around after death at a particular earth location, and remembered finally following one of their future parents home.[79] One of these cases was confirmed by circumstances of the day that were remembered by both the child and the parent: taking a bus to an unusual town on a rainy day. The other case involved the discarnate throwing rocks.[80] This book of Stevenson's is difficult to get one's hands on, but you can also find these cases summarized in Carol Bowman's book *Return from Heaven: Beloved Relatives Reincarnated within Your Family*.[81]

Bowman herself has come across hundreds of American cases in which souls seem to have reincarnated within the same family,[82] and she reports on many of them in *Return from Heaven*. In one case, a young girl began holding conversations on her pink toy telephone with her deceased teenage stepbrother and then began telling her entourage, "Roger said he's coming back very soon." A baby was subsequently born to Roger's mother, then 43, and it became evident as the child grew that he knew things about Roger's life as well as recognized changes that had taken place in the house since Roger had lived there.[83]

Another account of pre-birth communication in a same-family reincarnation case comes from Elizabeth M. Carman and Neil J. Carman's book *Cosmic Cradle*. Stephana and her husband had been trying unsuccessfully for five years to conceive a child and were a few days away from beginning the process of adopting when her father suddenly perished in a house fire. Ten days after her father's death, while doing housework, Stephana felt his

---

sky, a cloud, or light. See Ohkado and Ikegawa, pp. 484-5, for discussion of the differences and possible explanation in terms of differing religious beliefs between the two countries. Stevenson writes that intermission memories "correspond closely either to the habits of the previous personalities or to expectations of what should happen after death based on the local religions or other cultural traditions" [Ian Stevenson, "Some Questions Related to Cases of the Reincarnation Type," *Journal of the American Society for Psychical Research* 68 (1974): 395-416, p. 412].

[79] Ian Stevenson, *Reincarnation and Biology: Contribution to the Etiology of Birthmarks and Birth Defects*, vol. 1 (Westport, CT/London, UK: Praeger, 1997), 181-97.

[80] Stevenson writes, "Persons in Burma claiming to remember experiences in a discarnate realm during the interval between a previous life and their birth sometimes say that they threw stones at living persons in order to harass them or sometimes 'just for fun.' … [L]iving persons in Burma have sometimes claimed that stones had landed on or near them during the period when the subjects who later remember these pranks say they had engaged in them" [Stevenson, *Reincarnation and Biology*, vol. 1, 183].

[81] Bowman, *Return from Heaven*, 149-50.

[82] Bowman, *Return from Heaven*, 129.

[83] Bowman, *Return from Heaven*, 193-4.

presence in the room and a message saying, "Okay, I am ready for a new body. It is time to make a body, please." Stephana and her husband conceived that very day, in an unusually spiritual act of sex. At age two, their son asked Stephana, "Do you remember when I was your Dad and I died in a fire?" "He said it very matter-of-factly, out of the blue," says Stephana, "and then went back to his toys. He was not obsessed with it, nor upset."[84]

Grant, who died in a plane crash as an adult and whose case was discussed in the previous chapter on after-death communication, appeared in a dream to his brother, saying, "I'm getting ready to come back down one of those lines again. I'll see you." Then, shortly before Grant's brother's wife, Cindy, conceived her son Mason, Grant appeared to her in a dream, saying, "I already know you. We'll be together soon." When Mason was born, he was obsessed with planes and plane crashes from a very young age and even had nightmares of being in a plane crash.[85]

This next account comes from a grandmother in Brazil, whose daughter was expecting a child and was a few weeks past her due date. The family was sitting together in the brightly lit living room when the grandmother suddenly saw her deceased sister, Clara, standing behind the chair in which her daughter's husband was sitting. Clara had been killed nine years previously, by a bomb blast in World War II. Clara's apparition turned to her sister (the grandmother) and said, "Don't worry about mother. Everything is going well. The baby is alive and will be born on September 11th. It will be of the female sex, and the girl is me, reincarnating as your grand-daughter." The baby was in fact born on September 11 and was a girl. In addition, she had two birthmarks on her head, in precisely the same places where a witness of Clara's death said she'd been wounded in the bomb blast that killed her.[86]

The last few cases I've described show that the same incident can be both an after-death and a pre-birth communication. Given the overlap between these categories, it shouldn't be surprising that after-death and pre-birth communication resemble each other as much as they do, making use of the same methods. In fact, just as we saw in the last chapter that dreams were the most common form of after-death communication, they are also the most common form of pre-birth communication.[87] In fact, announcing dreams are so common in cases of apparent reincarnation that Stevenson listed them as one of the five typical characteristics of such cases.[88]

Furthermore, as with after-death communications, those yet-to-be-born seem sometimes to communicate with a third party in order to emphasize to

---

[84] Carman and Carman, 116-7.

[85] Bowman, *Return from Heaven*, 205-10.

[86] Guy Lyon Playfair, *The Flying Cow: Exploring the Psychic World of Brazil* (Guildford, UK: White Crow Books, 2011), 165.

[87] Bowman, *Return from Heaven*, 190.

[88] Stevenson, *Children Who Remember Previous Lives*, 99-101.

the intended recipient of the message that the communication is real and not just in their imagination. We see an example of this in the following same-family reincarnation case.

A woman named Deb was pregnant by a man who wasn't her husband, and they had decided to have an abortion. However, one morning the baby's father went to work and found his best friend crying. He said he hadn't been able to sleep the previous night because "he kept hearing a baby crying." He felt there must be a child someplace who needed help.

Well, the couple decided to keep the baby, whom they named Katie, and when Katie got old enough to speak, she turned out to have memories of being Deb's abusive mother. "Remember when I was your mummy?" Katie asked. "They used to call me Blondie." This was a name Deb's mother had once been called, but no one had used it for a long time, and certainly not in front of Deb's children. Katie then proceeded to tell Deb, "I didn't like you very much when you were my little girl." When asked why not, she said, "Because you always used to yell at me, and push me into my room and lock the door." Indeed, this was what Deb had felt forced to do as a child when her mother got drunk.

What could possibly be the benefit of having your abusive mother return as your daughter? Deb says that Katie's arrival "forced [her] to get out of a bad and dangerous marriage" (to a man who was not Katie's father). Deb is convinced that "she had planned her return, and that the timing was critical." As evidence, Deb cites something else Katie once told her, when they were on their way to visit her dad at his job. "Is Uncle Tom going to be there?" Katie asked. Tom was the friend who'd heard the baby crying in his sleep and convinced Katie's parents not to get an abortion. When Deb told her that he would in fact be there, Katie confided to her in a whisper, "He saved my life once."[89]

Physical Effects Produced by the Yet-to-Be-Born

So far, we've explored pre-birth communication in the form of apparitions, dreams, and telepathic messages, but we now turn to cases in which the yet-to-be-born appear to be capable of physical interaction with the earthly environment.

One common reason for this interaction is physical protection of future family members. For instance, Celestia Jasper appears to have been rescued from a life-threatening situation by her unborn son. She and her husband were driving from Minnesota to Montana in the dead of winter when their car flipped and landed in the Stillwater River. Her husband made it to shore,

---

[89] Bowman, *Return from Heaven*, 119-25.

but Jaspers was having trouble getting away from the car and to the bank. Eventually, she resigned herself to dying. But then a strange thing happened. She heard a voice say, "But I haven't even been born yet," and something grabbed the collar of her jacket and pulled her to safety. She heard the same words again—"I'm not born yet"—while she and her husband were awaiting their eventual rescue in a nearby cabin. Three years later, Jasper's son Frank James was born. She says that on the very first night she was at home with him, she realized that it was he who had spoken to her the night the car landed in the river.[90] It's reasonable to wonder whether it was also he who grabbed her collar and pulled her out of the river.

In another case, an unborn child apparently attempted to rescue a family member but was unsuccessful. Teresa Griffin's three-year-old son Ryan died after being found in their family swimming pool. Her grief was compounded by the fact that no one knew how or why he had ended up in the pool, since he was afraid of water. Almost three years later, her son Michael, with whom she'd been six months pregnant at the time of Ryan's death, came to her asking to talk about his older brother, about whom he knew little else but that he was in heaven. Griffin was quite unprepared for what Michael proceeded to tell her. He said, "I tried to put Ryan's soul back in his body, Mom, but I couldn't. … He was running, and he fell and banged his head, and then he went, 'Glug…glug….' … Then the Light came down, like a flashlight." Griffin asked if the light had said anything, and he replied, "The Light said, 'I love you, Ryan.'" With that, Michael went back to playing.[91]

As it happened, Michael's account of his brother's death was corroborated by something Teresa remembered having heard after Ryan's funeral, from the parents of one of his playmates. Ryan's three-year-old friend claimed that Ryan had come to play with him (after his death) and that Ryan had told him he'd hit his head and fallen in the water.[92]

These stories of pre-birth rescue or attempted rescue are just one more way that the behavior of the yet-to-be-born parallels that of the deceased. Here's yet another: a case that suggests that unborn souls can at times behave like poltergeists. Isadora Paymer recounts that, when she was three months pregnant, she and her husband began hearing "wild thumping and bumping" in the walls of their house during the night. Somehow, Paymer immediately knew it was her unborn son and was able to convince her husband he didn't need to search the house for intruders. When her son got old enough to talk, she discovered he had memories of being inside her body. He said, "I swam around and drank water. It was red in there." She decided to ask him about the thumping in the house, and he replied that he'd made all that racket

---

[90] Hallett, *Soul Trek*, 180-1.

[91] Joan Wester Anderson, *Where Miracles Happen: True Stories of Heavenly Encounters*, updated (Chicago: Loyola Press, 1994, 2009), 157.

[92] Anderson, *Where Miracles Happen*, 158.

because "he was bored." "He was a very active, colicky baby," says Paymer, "and I think that this was just another way for him to exercise his overactive nervous system. I think people come and go for a while until they settle down in their new body."[93]

Elisabeth Hallett, author of *Stories of the Unborn Soul*, agrees that there are many similarities between pre-birth and after-death communication and points out the many methods that show up in both sorts of communication. She does note, however, that while the deceased seem to love affecting physical objects—especially those that use electricity—the yet-to-be-born rarely make themselves known in this way.[94] But she nevertheless provides one plausible example of this kind of activity coming from someone yet-to-be-born. Here it is.

Before Barbara W. was sure she was pregnant, she was trying not to get her hopes up and thought to herself that she probably wasn't pregnant after all. All of a sudden, her bedroom light started repeatedly dimming and brightening. She turned it off for a bit, but when she flipped the switch back on, the light behaved in the same strange way. "Shortly thereafter," she says, "I had a positive pregnancy test."[95]

Later during her pregnancy—in which she turned out to be carrying triplets—Barbara and her daughter Jessi observed some very odd behavior from a helium balloon featuring Winnie the Pooh. This balloon actually moved *around* another balloon in order to work its way down the hall towards a nursery that was also decorated with Pooh. The balloon, being filled with helium, was touching the ceiling, but when it got to the nursery door, it actually moved *down* a foot or so as if to enter the door. However, the door was closed. The balloon then moved to a different bedroom door. Again, it lowered itself from the ceiling in order to enter, and in doing so, it got its string stuck on some artwork that was attached to the door. "The balloon tried to tug free," reports Barbara, "but it was stuck. After a couple of tugs, three of the light bulbs in the chandelier over the kitchen table simultaneously blew out, with a popping sound!"[96]

While this may not be proof of communication from Barbara's unborn children, it seems clear that *something* unusual is going on here. This is no mere air current. And it is especially intriguing that the balloon's "frustration" appears to manifest in the blowing of three light bulbs simultaneously. It is hard to think of a natural phenomenon that could be the common cause of these coinciding events. In the absence of indication that there were any other spirits interested in communicating with Barbara and her daughter at

---

[93] Hallett, *Soul Trek*, 182-3.
[94] Hallett, *Stories of the Unborn Soul*, 48.
[95] Hallett, *Stories of the Unborn Soul*, 48.
[96] Hallett, *Stories of the Unborn Soul*, 48-49.

this time, I would say that her inference that it was her unborn child or children attempting some form of communication is not unwarranted.

Another intriguing glimpse of possible physical effects caused by the yet-to-be-born comes from pre-birth researcher Sarah Hinze, who might not describe herself this way but is something of a Mormon medium. Her book *The Memory Catcher* recounts many experiences she's had of perceiving and communicating with the spirits of the departed as well as of the yet-to-be-born.[97] On one occasion, after a reception in a bookstore honoring her newest book, *The Castaways*, which was about the spirits of children who have been aborted, she stepped outside into a courtyard where there were some large trees. Though it was a windless day, she noticed the trees bending back and forth. She was really puzzled by this strange, inexplicable movement until she suddenly saw that the trees were full of playing children, dressed in white. She realized that some of them were the spirits of aborted babies, but all of them were happy. The message came to her, "The unborn children are joyous that their future parents and loved ones will read stories of *The Castaways* and their hearts will be changed toward them." After blinking away some tears, she realized that the children were gone and the trees had become still.[98]

Evidence Linking Coincidences to the Yet-to-Be-Born

Both the balloon incident and Hinze's swinging branches seem like they might be cases where the spirits of yet-to-be-born children have either intentionally or inadvertently influenced the physical world, leaving signs of their presence. But is there any evidence that unborn souls intentionally use *coincidences* to communicate? There is.

Let's begin with the case of Japanese parents Inoue Fumiko and Inoue Shuichi. After they had their stillborn daughter Kazune, they began to notice that when they spoke of Kazune or wondered aloud about her, they would coincidentally hear the song that had been Fumiko's favorite song to listen to during her pregnancy: Schubert's "Ave Maria." This coincidence recurred often enough, and with precise enough timing, that they began to take the song as their deceased daughter's way of letting them know she was still around. Two years after their daughter's stillbirth, their son Takatoki was born. In fact, his due date was on the same date as the deceased daughter's stillbirth. But he was *actually* born two days later, on the date that was the due date of their daughter, as well as the day on which her body was cremated.[99] Ichikawa Kimie observes that coincidences related to death and birth dates

---

[97] For examples of classic mediumship experiences from her life, see Hinze with Lofgreen, *The Memory Catcher*, 74-75, 84-85, 113, 132-3, 145.
[98] Hinze with Lofgreen, *The Memory Catcher*, 168-9.
[99] Ohkado, "Same-Family Cases," 559-60.

are commonly experienced in childbirth,[100] and at least one of Carol Bowman's cases involves this type of coincidence. In the case related above of brothers who claimed to have previously been twins in their aunt's stomach, the older boy was due to be born on October 19, the same day as the aunt's twins had died.[101]

In addition to corresponding dates, another element of the Inoue case cited above—the coincidentally playing song—illustrates a frequent mode of pre-birth communication. In a different Japanese case, a girl who died at six years old from leukemia appeared to be reincarnated as a son of the same mother. Evidence for this claim includes the fact that, before she died, the young girl told her mother, seeming to be speaking about her afterlife, "mom, I will write a letter, saying: 'Are you OK? Aren't you lonely?'" Ten years later, the woman's four-and-a-half-year-old son told her he'd written her a letter. To her, his writing looked like nothing more than two lines on a paper, so she asked him what it said. He read it aloud to her: "Mom, are you OK? Aren't you lonely?"

But that's not the pre-birth coincidence. Before this son was born, but five years after his sister's death, the mother had a dream in which her favorite band, Mr. Children, was playing a song with a beautiful melody and beautiful words. A couple of days later, she turned on the television to find this very band singing a song she'd never heard before. There were associations between the title of the song and her deceased daughter, and some of the lyrics seemed particularly meaningful. The investigator of this case, Ohkado Masayuki, gives the lyrics' translation as: "Even if this is goodbye forever,/I can hear you breathing/I just know that in some other form, with that same smile/You'll come to see me again."[102] The woman found out 11 days later that she was pregnant with the boy who would eventually write her the letter her deceased daughter had promised.[103]

This next story is about communication from a child yet-to-be-born who appears to have remained unborn, at least to this mother. The child in question perished through abortion, but before the procedure, the mother, Jilly, heard her unborn daughter tell her that her name was Lily. A couple of weeks later, Jilly was about to attempt suicide when she heard a strange voice say, "Not yet…." That stopped her. She lay down and had a dream in which she met Lily, who told her she knew the abortion would happen, that "it was

---

[100] Ichikawa Kimie, *Inochi no Musubi—Ai wo Hagukumu Yutaka na Shussan* (Tokyo: Koyo Shobo, 2014). As I cannot read Japanese, I owe this understanding of Ichikawa to Ohkado, "Same-Family Cases," 567.

[101] Bowman, *Return from Heaven*, 168.

[102] Ohkado references a fan site from which she drew much of her translation: https://ijahlovesmrchildren.wordpress.com/2008/11/16/mr-children-hana-no-nioi-the-scent-of-flowers/.

[103] Ohkado, "Same-Family Cases," 554-7.

meant to be, and holds a purpose for your life." Alongside Lily in this dream was Jilly's maternal grandmother, who had died six years before.

Many months later, Jilly began to doubt that this dream was a real communication. She said, "Okay, if this is real, if you really are Lily, and I didn't imagine it all, give me some kind of sign—prove to me that I was not just going through some kind of grief psychosis!" The next day, a long line of "Lily" coincidences began.

- On Day 1, Jilly went to house-sit for a friend, who had six cats, one of whom was named Lily. She was the only cat who slept with Jilly, or even would interact at all with her. Also, in the friend's bathroom, there was a picture of a racehorse named "Taccarro Lily."
- On Day 2, Jilly went to her weekly therapy appointment and discovered the office had just hired a new receptionist named Lily. Back at her friend's house, she turned on the TV and saw a guest character appear on the show *Veronica's Closet.* The character's name was Lily.
- On Day 3, Jilly went outside to clean the litter box and had to search for the hose. She finally located it behind some big pots with tags identifying their contents as lilies.
- On Day 4, Jilly's boss told her she'd adopted a dog and decided to name her Lily.

Jilly experienced a total of six Lily coincidences in the four days following her request for confirmation.[104]

Although these are all the strongly evidential cases of coincidences caused by the yet-to-be-born I've so far been able to locate, I should point out that they are by no means the only *birth-related* coincidences I've collected. For example, in the last chapter of this book, I'm going to describe four highly symbolic birth-related coincidences. Though nothing in these coincidences themselves points to their having been caused specifically by the child who was on its way, that hypothesis is certainly not out of the realm of possibility, and further research on such cases could turn up more evidence in this regard.

Some Words of Caution

Before closing this chapter, I want to mention that Jilly's experience of the Lily coincidences described above serves as an example that communication from an unborn soul does not always mean that that child will be born to you. And even when an unborn soul insists that they *do* wish

[104] Hallett, *Stories of the Unborn Soul,* 157-62.

to be born to you, you shouldn't feel required to allow it, especially if the contact happens before conception, as many do. As Elisabeth Hallett counsels, "You may be experiencing the presence of a soul wishing to join you.... But there is no need to feel pressured or that you must make an instant decision. Relax, tune in to the presence you feel, have a conversation with it and express your doubts and questions. Your desires and your child's intentions are both important. If it isn't right for you to have a child, there are other options for a soul wanting to be born."[105] Hallett writes a few pages later, "Many pre-conception contacts are gentle and unassuming requests to join the family. They offer us a chance to welcome the child, postpone conception for a while, or firmly close the door."[106]

Keep in mind, too, that you may not always know the reasons behind the specific pre-birth experiences you have. A woman named Janet tells about experiencing "a year's worth of communication about having twins. It involved many dreams and synchronicities—so many amazing, inexplicable things that the only conclusion I could draw was that I was being prepared to have twin girls. This was confirmed over and over again." When she became pregnant, she kept having even more specific dreams about female twins, even though an early sonogram showed only one baby. Then, ten days before the next sonogram, she asked for a dream to prepare her, and she dreamt of a baby boy. She told the boy he was not what she expected, and he responded, "We didn't communicate very well at the start." The dream also mentioned the baby's weight—seven pounds—and that "they" thought he wouldn't make it. When the baby boy was born, he was exactly seven pounds, and a nurse was overheard to say, "He almost didn't make it." Still, Janet is convinced that the twin dreams and synchronicities meant something. "Because it all was too much, too specific, too unusual to be meaningless."[107] Let this be a cautionary tale, however, that even seemingly clear coincidences may turn out to have a meaning different than we expect.

Along these same lines is the touching story of Dakota. Even before she met Dakota's father, Kara L.C. Jones had visions of a soul asking if she would accept it. In dreams, she had further conversations with this soul, who gave its name as Dakota. She learned in these dreams whom Dakota had chosen as its father: a man that Kara had just begun seeing, named Hawk. After quite a bit of turmoil, Kara and Hawk decided to marry.

Before their wedding, Kara and Hawk went up Mount Rainier with some family members, and when they emerged from a trip to the restrooms, they discovered that someone had written the name "DAKOTA" in the snow. Everyone in their party denied having done it. Then, while out driving one day on their honeymoon, Kara and Hawk pulled off the road at a spot

---

[105] Hallett, *Stories of the Unborn Soul*, 72-73.
[106] Hallett, *Stories of the Unborn Soul*, 77.
[107] Hallett, *Stories of the Unborn Soul*, 169-70.

overlooking the ocean. They parked in front of a boulder covered in graffiti. Right in the middle of it had been spray-painted the word "DAKOTA." It was on their honeymoon that Kara got pregnant. Of course, they knew what they would name the baby.

However, in a sad turn of events, a week before his due date, the baby's heart stopped. Kara says that she and Hawk nevertheless felt Dakota's presence in the years after his death. She speculates that they weren't living truly "authentic" lives before Dakota came to them, and that his coming and going helped them to grow. She writes, "The word 'Dakota' is a Sioux word meaning friend or ally. I think Dakota came, lived, and died as our friend and ally."[108]

Clearly, coincidences and other types of paranormal experiences don't guarantee happy endings, or at least not the happy endings that we had in mind. It appears that very often the other side has aims that differ from ours. While we may desire a life without trouble or pain, the other side often allows trouble and pain to come to us as a catalyst for spiritual growth. We will look at this function of coincidences further in Chapter 8, "Ill-Meaning Entities," and Chapter 18, "Spiritual Growth." For now, we turn to exploring the ways in which we may sometimes be the causes of our own coincidences.

---

[108] Hallett, *Stories of the Unborn Soul*, 171-9.

Chapter 6

The Experiencer

Many people who experience coincidences assume that they must be caused by God, an angel, or a discarnate spirit because those are the only individuals they know to be capable of affecting the world in a paranormal way. However, in this chapter, we are going to discuss evidence for the paranormal abilities of living human beings. Though some people appear to have these abilities to a greater degree than others, there is abundant evidence that you don't have to be particularly psychic to be capable of producing some of your own coincidences.

Coincidences Explicable by ESP

Extrasensory perception, or ESP, is the first of two broad categories of paranormal ability we're going to discuss in this chapter.[1] ESP seems like the best explanation for certain kinds of coincidences. For example, it does an excellent job of explaining the common coincidence in which you are thinking about someone just before they call you on the telephone. Now, there are a couple of different ways in which ESP could explain this coincidence. On the one hand, extrasensory perception of the future—which goes by the technical name 'precognition'—could give you unconscious knowledge that you're about to speak to that person, and this fact could cause you to think about them now, perhaps as a sort of mental preparation. On

[1] While I use the term 'extrasensory perception' because of its familiarity to readers, parapsychologists now generally refer to this ability as "anomalous cognition."

the other hand, this coincidence could be explained by extrasensory perception of the thoughts of the other person, also known as telepathy. The telepathic case consists of two further alternatives: it could be that the thoughts of the person who's about to call you affect your own thoughts, or it could be that your thought of that person telepathically causes them to subsequently call you. Dr. Rupert Sheldrake has done extensive investigation into the phenomenon of thinking of someone just before they call, and you'll find a very readable summary of his "telephone telepathy" results in his book *The Sense of Being Stared At*.[2]

In the next chapter, "Other Living Agents," we'll discuss the phenomenon of telepathy in much greater depth and look at its wide-ranging implications for the interpretation of coincidences. In the present chapter, however, I'm going to focus primarily on the first type of ESP I mentioned—precognition—and look at the many other varieties of coincidence that our own precognitive abilities can help us to explain.

Thoughts Produced by Precognition

Author and psychic Alan Vaughan reports that coincidences that seem to indicate some kind of unconscious precognition happen to him almost daily.[3] For instance, on one occasion, he told his wife how, back when he was in college, he'd constructed the characters of Hannibal and an elephant for a parade. Later on the same day in which he was talking about this memory, he saw an article about an elephant being used in a movie about Hannibal.[4] Again on that very same day, he was reading a magazine when, for no particular reason, he thought of a cat named Fortran who belonged to an acquaintance. Later in the magazine, he came upon an article on computers where a programmer said, "I always speak Fortran at home."[5]

The explanation for these coincidences that seems most compelling to both Vaughan and myself is that Vaughan had unconscious awareness of the articles he would be reading later in the day, and this unconscious awareness caused him to think of the Hannibal parade characters and the cat named Fortran *before* he physically ran across the written references, in much the same way that we might think of someone right before they call.

Part of my reason for thinking that this kind of unconscious knowledge of the future is possible comes from research done by parapsychologist Dr. Daryl Bem and reported in his 2011 article "Feeling the future: Experimental

---

[2] Rupert Sheldrake, *The Sense of Being Stared At and Other Aspects of the Extended Mind* (New York: Crown Publishers, 2003), Ch. 6.
[3] Alan Vaughan, *Incredible Coincidence: The Baffling World of Synchronicity* (New York: J. B. Lippincott Company, 1979), 48.
[4] Vaughan, *Incredible Coincidence*, 49.
[5] Vaughan, *Incredible Coincidence*, 49.

evidence for anomalous retroactive influences on cognition and affect." In two of the nine experiments reported in that article, Bem tested subjects on their recall of a series of words. He discovered that subjects were more likely to remember words that a computer helped them to review. That may not seem so surprising, until one learns that the computer did the review exercises with the subjects *after* they had already taken the test.[6] That is, the subjects of the experiment were more likely to remember words that they were randomly reminded of *after* the test had occurred.

Vaughan cites as another example of a coincidence likely caused by unconscious awareness of the future something that happened to Dr. Jule Eisenbud. One day, Eisenbud told his sister-in-law about a baby who had once fallen eight or nine stories without getting hurt. His sister-in-law returned home to New York the next day to find the *New York Times* reporting that, the same day she'd heard the story from Eisenbud, a baby had fallen eight stories *on the very street on which she lived* and had been unhurt except for a "swollen lip."[7] Of course, in this case, the coincidence is caused by the precognition of someone besides the experiencer of the coincidence, but it nevertheless illustrates the kind of coincidence that precognition is capable of producing.

Let's look at a few more cases taken from other sources. The American writer Oliver Wendell Holmes, Sr., recounts that, over dinner one night, he was telling the story of an interesting English law case that he hadn't referred to in months, or perhaps years. Afterward, he left the room and found a letter that had just been delivered from an acquaintance in England. The sole purpose of the letter was to enclose a report of the precise story he'd just finished telling. Holmes had never spoken of this matter with the writer of the letter, and he says, "I know of no train of thought which led me to speak of [that law case] on that particular day."[8] For these reasons, I believe it's likely that unconscious anticipation of the arrival of the letter is what led Holmes to think of the case and speak about it on that evening.

Similarly, parapsychologist Dr. Charles Tart reported to journalist Brian Inglis that he found himself one morning saying the words "*coup d'état*" over and over for no apparent reason. The morning after that, he received a letter from a Mrs. Coudetat, though he had never before gotten mail from anyone by that name.[9]

---

[6] Daryl J. Bem, "Feeling the Future: Experimental Evidence for Anomalous Retroactive Influences on Cognition and Affect," *Journal of Personality and Social Psychology* 100, no. 3 (2011): 407-25.
[7] Vaughan, *Incredible Coincidence*, 49.
[8] Oliver Wendell Holmes, *Over the Teacups* (Cambridge, MA: Riverside Press, 1890-91), 14.
[9] Brian Inglis, *Coincidence: A Matter of Chance – or Synchronicity?* (London: Hutchinson, 1990), 173-4.

In another case published by Inglis, a woman named Mary Higgs was doing chores around the house one day before work when she found herself making a phone call in her head, telling her employer that her father had died and so she couldn't come to work. This seemed totally silly to her, since her father was in fine fettle. Nevertheless, two hours later, she found out that her father had died in an accident, and she found herself having to call her employer and say the very things she had earlier imagined.[10]

Psychiatrist Dr. Judith Orloff relates a case in which a friend of hers was vacationing in Colorado and browsing a used-book store when the thought of Orloff suddenly popped into his head. He was still thinking of various memories of their times together as he went to the science fiction section and pulled from the shelf a book that caught his eye: Madeleine L'Engle's *A Wrinkle in Time.* "When he opened to the title page," says Orloff,

> he was amazed to discover my name—Judi Orloff—handwritten and dated November 1961, when I was ten. As a child, I always made it a point to write my name in all my books in case they ever got lost. When after high school I moved out of my parents' home [in Los Angeles], I donated stacks of these old books to Goodwill. Somehow, twenty years later, one of them ended up in Boulder and my friend had come upon it.[11]

Orloff relates this story as an example of the way coincidences in her life often reflect the affectionate bonds she has with others. While I would say that her friend's thoughts of her in the bookstore were most likely caused by the fact that he was about to run across her name, precognition doesn't explain the entire coincidence in this case. There is also the fact that Orloff's friend encountered the book with her name in it, 1,000 miles from where Orloff had last seen it. Perhaps he unconsciously sensed the presence of an object that belonged to her and was drawn to that bookstore and that shelf as a result. If this is the case, it could very well be the emotional bond between them that made him sensitive to the presence of the book and thus produced the coincidence.

Precognition in Literature and Art

Precognition is likely also the explanation of some other coincidences involving books. Without any apparent awareness of what they were doing,

---

[10] Inglis, *Coincidence*, 117.

[11] Judith Orloff, *Second Sight: An Intuitive Psychiatrist Tells Her Extraordinary Story and Shows You How to Tap Your Own Inner Wisdom* (New York: Three Rivers Press, 1996, 2010), 259.

several authors through the years have written stories that bear an uncanny resemblance to later events.

For instance, it's fairly well known that, 14 years before the *Titanic* sank, Morgan Robertson wrote a novel called *The Wreck of the Titan*, about a supposedly "unsinkable" ship that set out on its maiden voyage in April (the same month as the actual *Titanic*), hit an iceberg in the North Atlantic, and sank, leading to many deaths because of an inadequate number of lifeboats.[12] However, the author himself didn't think he'd had any paranormal foreknowledge of the *Titanic* disaster. As an experienced seaman who wrote about the maritime world, he reportedly said, "I know what I'm writing about, that's all."[13]

Oddly, another oft-cited case is also about a shipwreck. Edgar Allan Poe's 1838 short story "The Narrative of Arthur Gordon Pym of Nantucket" is about four survivors of a shipwreck who are floating in an open boat and three of whom eat the fourth, whose name is Richard Parker. In 1884, a trial was held for three sailors who, shipwrecked and in an open boat, killed and ate a cabin boy named Richard Parker.[14]

Sometimes literary foreknowledge becomes apparent even before a work is published. Londoner Pearl Binder describes how she and a couple of friends were amusing themselves coming up with ideas for a satirical novel when they latched onto the idea of homeless refugees in Hyde Park, and in particular, one older, eastern European man whom they decided to name Horvath-Nadoly. A couple of days later, they read in the paper that the police had found a foreign fellow wandering at night in Hyde Park. Incredibly enough, he had the name Horvath-Nadoly. (Their novel was later published under the title *Ladies Only*.)[15]

Author Elizabeth Gilbert relates that she once spent a great deal of effort researching to write a novel that she described as being

> about this middle-aged spinster from Minnesota who's been quietly in love with her married boss for many years. He gets involved in a

---

[12] For further information on this and other apparent premonitions related to the sinking of the *Titanic*, see Ian Stevenson, "A Review and Analysis of Paranormal Experiences Connected with the Sinking of the *Titanic*," *Journal of the American Society for Psychical Research* 54, no. 4 (October 1960): 153-71; and Ian Stevenson, "Seven More Paranormal Experiences Associated with the Sinking of the *Titanic*," *Journal of the American Society for Psychical Research* 59 (1965): 211-25.

[13] Heba Hasan, "Author 'Predicts' *Titanic* Sinking, 14 Years Earlier," *Time* (April 14, 2012), http://newsfeed.time.com/2012/04/14/author-predicts-titanic-sinking-14-years-earlier/ (accessed November 10, 2018).

[14] John Beloff, "Psi Phenomena: Causal Versus Acausal Interpretation," *Journal of the Society for Psychical Research* 49 (September 1977): 573-82.

[15] Arthur Koestler, "The Mysterious Power of Chance," *The Sunday Times* of London (May 4, 1974).

> harebrained business scheme down in the Amazon jungle. A bunch of money and a person go missing, and my character gets sent down there to solve things, at which point her quiet life is completely turned into chaos. Also, it's a love story.[16]

However, events got in the way of Gilbert's completing this novel, and when she finally got back to thinking about it, she found she'd completely lost her inspiration. Some months later, she discovered that another accomplished writer with whom she'd recently become friends, Ann Patchett, was working on a novel that bore astonishing similarities to the one Gilbert had abandoned. It, too, was about a spinster from Minnesota who has long been in love with her married boss and gets sent to the Amazon to straighten out a business deal after a bunch of money and a person go missing. This manuscript became Patchett's best-selling novel *State of Wonder.* Gilbert understands this as a case of her idea moving on to someone more willing and able to devote the time to bring it to fruition, but it might also be understood as a telepathic transmission of the idea from one writer to another, especially as Gilbert discovered that Patchett got the idea for her own novel right around the time she and Gilbert met for the first time.[17]

Lest you think precognitive inspiration comes only to writers, I should cite the testimony of painter and sculptor Elizabeth Whiteley, who says that she and others have been known to depict the future in their art. For instance, she once moved into a new apartment only to recognize the view as a scene she'd painted a decade previously.[18]

Precognitive Dreams

We now turn to a more widespread kind of coincidence that precognition does a good job of explaining: the experience in which someone has a dream of something that later occurs. Let me begin this discussion by noting that there are times when a dream matches reality, not because some part of the dreamer is able to see that reality "out there in the future," but because (1) the dream is a natural consequence of normal, physical signs that the dreamer has perceived and that indicate what the future likely holds or (2) the dream and the future reality both spring from the dreamer's own thoughts and feelings (as in the case where you dream of something you wish would happen and then your desire causes you to take actions that

---

[16] Elizabeth Gilbert, *Big Magic: Creative Living Beyond Fear* (New York: Riverhead Books, 2015), 53.
[17] Gilbert, *Big Magic*, 55.
[18] Sophy Burnham, *The Art of Intuition: Cultivating Your Inner Wisdom* (New York: Jeremy P. Tarcher/Penguin, 2011), 13.

subsequently bring it about). However, there are many dreams of the future that neither of these mechanisms can satisfactorily explain.

For instance, a man named Jim T. recounts that his wife, Allison, had a terrible nightmare in which her four-year-old daughter was on a train track and, in attempting to get her to safety, Allison herself was run down by a train. Not more than two weeks later, Allison and her daughter were at a train station seeing off a friend. An object fell onto the tracks, and, in an effort to be helpful, the little girl went to pick it up. Allison saw a train coming and rushed to save her daughter, but they were both hit and killed. Jim was of course devastated, but, in his grief, he says he did take some comfort in the warning they'd had of this event. It "makes me feel close to Allison and Tessa," he says, "because something I don't understand forewarned her."[19]

Dreams seem to be the area in which it is easiest for most people to access their ESP.[20] Precognitive dreams—that is, accurate dreams of the future—are actually quite common. Clinical psychologist and dream researcher Dr. David Ryback estimates that at least 1 in 12 people, and probably closer to 1 in 3, has had a dream that corresponded so closely to unexpected future happenings that it could not be explained in a non-psychic fashion.[21]

Ryback has collected many striking examples of this phenomenon, including the account of Jim T. summarized above. In another of Ryback's cases, a teenage boy dreamt that a car hit an electrical pole at an intersection near his house, causing the pole to break off and fall on the car and starting a huge fire. In the dream, the male driver was killed and stretched out dead on the sidewalk, while a female passenger by the name of Cleo was hurt but alive. When the boy woke up, he told his family about the dream, and they all went down the street looking for the accident but found nothing. They went back to bed only to wake up an hour later and discover that an accident

---

[19] David Ryback with Letitia Sweitzer, *Dreams That Come True: Their Psychic and Transforming Powers* (New York: Doubleday, 1988), 2.

[20] In 1973, Montague Ullman, Stanley Krippner, and Alan Vaughan reported, "Of over 7000 spontaneous cases of ESP studied in the United States, nearly two-thirds of the cases were dreams, and a similar proportion holds true in one thousand cases examined in Germany. In a British study of 300 cases, 40 percent were dream experiences. A survey of school children in India showed that about half of their ESP experiences were dreams." Montague Ullman and Stanley Krippner with Alan Vaughan, *Dream Telepathy: Experiments in Nocturnal ESP* (Baltimore, MD: Penguin, 1973, 1974), 24-5. Ullman, Krippner, and Vaughan cite Ian Stevenson, "Telepathic Impressions: A Review and Report of Thirty-Five New Cases," *Proceedings of the American Society for Psychical Research* 29 (1970): 1-2; and Louisa E. Rhine, *Hidden Channels of the Mind* (New York: William Sloane, 1961).

[21] Ryback with Sweitzer, 6-7, 11-13. The 1-in-12 figure comes from a survey Ryback gave to college students. The 1-in-3 number comes from the informal research of his colleague Letitia Sweitzer, who sampled a wider population.

had just occurred exactly as the boy had dreamt it: broken pole, fire, a dead man stretched out on the sidewalk, and a survivor named Cleo.[22]

Here are my summaries of several other impressive examples reported to Ryback.

- A man dreamt that he was in a bank opening a checking account when the bank was robbed. Later that day, the subject was actually in a bank opening a checking account, and the bank was indeed robbed, by robbers who "took exactly the same positions as in his dream."[23]
- A woman dreamt of being in a car accident in a red Volkswagen that a blond girl was driving with her baby in the backseat. She dreamt of the particular intersection and circumstances of the crash. It was only two months after the dream that she met the blond girl with the baby and the red Volkswagen for the first time. They often drove places together, but during high-traffic hours, they kept away from the intersection that had been in the woman's dream. Then, one day, they forgot. They used that intersection, and they were hit just as in the dream.[24]
- A woman who had been away from her home for a long period of time dreamt that she floated back into it through a broken window and discovered it was a complete mess and that many items were missing. When she woke up, she listed to her husband the items she'd seen missing in the dream. Two weeks later, it was discovered that someone had indeed robbed her home, breaking the same window she'd seen broken in her dream and taking the very same items.[25]
- A woman dreamt that her ex-husband called to tell her that he'd gotten home from work early to find his current partner exiting the house with another man, both of them carrying suitcases. Within a week, her ex-husband called her to relate exactly this experience.[26]
- A young man dreamt of a nighttime car accident, remembering specifically that the car's windshield was smashed in and that everything was quiet except for the car's eight-track player, which was playing Black Sabbath's "Sabbath Bloody Sabbath." A while later, the young man who had had this dream was out driving late at night with some friends when they wrecked the car. The windshield was smashed, and the song "Sabbath Bloody Sabbath" was playing.[27]

---

[22] Ryback with Sweitzer, 19.
[23] Ryback with Sweitzer, 7.
[24] Ryback with Sweitzer, 8.
[25] Ryback with Sweitzer, 9.
[26] Ryback with Sweitzer, 20.
[27] Ryback with Sweitzer, 35-36.

- A woman named Dana frequently dreamt about problems her children were having in real life but were keeping secret from her. In one of her dreams, her nine-year-old daughter owed money she couldn't pay back; in real life, it turned out to be $7 of school lunch money. In another dream, Dana's teenage son was smoking in his room; in real life, he did turn out to have taken up smoking. In still another dream, Dana's college-age daughter was running naked across a field, pursued by a man, when she tripped and fell. In reality, the daughter turned out to be considering whether to become sexually active with her new boyfriend. (She ended up deciding not to.)[28]

Experienced lucid dreamer Robert Waggoner reports a dream in which he was being chased around his hometown by gangsters. "When I passed 17th and Plum, I drove behind the old Vickers gas station to hide," he says, "but became lucid [realized it was a dream] when I saw a large car wash there. In waking physical reality, there was no car wash there—at least at that time. Probably five years later, a car wash was built in the exact location as in my lucid dream."[29]

Waggoner had a similar experience in another lucid dream of his hometown. In that one, he was parked in the lot of the Methodist church when he realized that the lot was too big and that the spot where he was sitting in his car was in reality the site of a house. Some years later, however, he went by the church and discovered that that house had been torn down to allow for expansion of the parking lot, and the resulting parking area was exactly what he'd seen in his dream.[30]

Brian Inglis reports on a precognitive dream had by Bari Hooper on the morning of October 27, 1982, particularly impressive because of the extreme rarity of its subject matter. Hooper dreamt of a bird something like an albatross that had had its upper beak sawn off. In the dream, the bird got a visit from a bird keeper who fit it with an artificial beak. The next day, Hooper saw in *The Times* of London an article about a pelican who'd had his upper beak sawn off and was getting it replaced with a fiberglass prosthetic.[31]

Writer and editor Frederick Greenwood dreamt one night that, while he was making a business call, he leaned on a mantelpiece and felt his fingers rest on something cold, which turned out to be a severed woman's hand. The next day, while on a business call, he was shown into a room with a fireplace

---

[28] Ryback with Sweitzer, 60-62.

[29] Robert Waggoner, *Lucid Dreaming: Gateway to the Inner Self* (Needham, MA: Moment Point Press, 2009), 190.

[30] Waggoner, 191.

[31] Inglis, *Coincidence*, 72.

and happened to look at the mantel. There he saw a mummified hand with a feminine-looking ring on it.[32]

Dr. Andrew Paquette began keeping a dream diary because his partner thought he was having precognitive dreams and he wanted to prove her wrong. Instead, he ended up convinced she was right. He eventually turned his precognitive dreams into the subject of his fascinating book *Dreamer: 20 Years of Psychic Dreams and How They Changed My Life*,[33] as well as several peer-reviewed papers.[34] For those interested in precognitive dreams—and psychic and spiritual phenomena in general—I heartily recommend his book for additional striking examples of precognitive dreams, including some involving the September 11th World Trade Center attack. We'll talk more about these September 11th dreams in a moment.

Vaughan has also experienced many precognitive dreams and, like Paquette, takes a very analytical approach to them. He reports in his book *Incredible Coincidence* on a 10-year study he made of his dreams. He gives the following statistics.

> [O]ver 25 percent of 222 recorded dreams had some literal correspondence with future events. The average time between the dreams and events in sixty cases was 680 days, or one year and ten months. The dream that took the longest time span for fulfillment was one of the most detailed, containing both literal and symbolic elements. Three thousand and fifty-seven days before the event….[35]

Vaughan makes another interesting comment about the timing of precognitive dreams in his book *Patterns of Prophecy*. He notes that, while one might predict that precognitive dreams would be most accurate when the events they're anticipating are closer to the dream in time, he hasn't found that to be true of his own dreams. "Rather," he says,

---

[32] Frederick Greenwood, *Imagination in Dreams and Their Study* (London: John Lane, 1894), 197.

[33] Andrew Paquette, *Dreamer: 20 Years of Psychic Dreams and How They Changed My Life* (Winchester, UK: O Books, 2011).

[34] Andrew Paquette, "A New Approach to Veridicality in Dream Psi Studies," *Journal of Scientific Exploration* 26, no. 3 (2012): 589-610; Andrew Paquette, "NDE Implications from a Group of Spontaneous Long-Distance Veridical OBEs," *Journal of Scientific Exploration* 26, no. 4 (2012): 791-824; Andrew Paquette, "Can Death-Related Dreams Predict Future Deaths? Evidence from a Dream Journal Comprising Nearly 12,000 Dreams," *Journal of Scientific Exploration* 29, no. 3 (2015): 411-23; and Andrew Paquette, "The Rarity of Unambiguous Symbols in Dreams: A Case Study," *Journal of Scientific Exploration* 30, no. 2 (2016): 199-216.

[35] Vaughan, *Incredible Coincidence*, 190.

> the dream is usually triggered by some present event, and by association the dream describes the next encounter with a similar event—whether that be within days, weeks, months, or years. This relationship seems to indicate that the images of the unconscious are organized not temporally but symbolically.[36]

I believe Vaughan means that the present event that triggers precognition of a future event does so on the basis of the *symbolic* properties of the two events, not merely on how far in the future the precognized event may be.

In an article he wrote in *Parapsychology Review*, Vaughan gives an excellent example of this phenomenon. He was participating in a dream telepathy experiment in which he was supposed to dream about a particular picture he'd never seen. The dream that resulted contained enough elements of the target picture that someone else was able to pick that picture out of a line-up and match it to a description of his dream. Yet Vaughan himself wasn't shown the target picture until two years later. What was fascinating was that it turned out that the dream he'd had during the experiment not only incorporated elements from the target picture, but also incorporated events that happened to him *on the day on which the target picture was finally revealed to him*, even though these events were unrelated to the reveal itself and happened a few hours after it was over.[37]

The case just described gives us some insight into the process by which precognition (and possibly other psi processes) occurs. It appears as though some element of our present experience (in Vaughan's case, the dream telepathy experiment) causes the unconscious to jump forward in time to a moment of similar significance. The unconscious then takes a snapshot of that future moment. And, like physical snapshots, it takes in all sorts of elements that are present, regardless of their relevance to the matter at hand. Who hasn't taken a picture only to look at it later and realize that it captured something going on in the background that we weren't even aware was happening while we were taking the photo? Our unconscious precognitive processes seem to operate similarly. In searching the future for relevant events, they capture a particularly relevant moment in time, but the picture we get in our precognitive dream may contain stray elements that aren't directly related to the matter that set the process in motion. And often we can't tell which are the relevant elements until we experience the actual event with all its additional context.

Another excellent example of a precognitive "snapshot" comes from Waggoner. In a lucid dream, Waggoner encountered a hexagonal shaft of light that he somehow knew was precognitive information and that suddenly

---

[36] Vaughan, *Patterns of Prophecy* (New York: Hawthorn Books, 1973), 156.
[37] Alan Vaughan, "Spontaneous Cognitive Dreaming," *Parapsychology Review* 4, no. 5 (1973): 24.

slammed into his temple, causing him to experience four or five precognitive dreams in the space of what seemed like only microseconds. When he woke up, he tried to write the dreams down as fast as he could, but while recording the first three, he forgot the rest. Nevertheless, those three subsequently received strong confirmation. Some three months later, he says, "[o]n an ordinary day in the middle of the afternoon, all three dreams played out in the course of about twenty minutes." This involved seeing a "rarely seen acquaintance" (and having certain feelings related to the encounter), responding to "a business phone call from an unusual person as kids played in the background," and receiving information about a friend's wedding plans.[38] In this example, however, Waggoner doesn't seem to have identified any present event that triggered his unconscious to take this snapshot of the future. That doesn't mean one didn't exist, just that triggering events may not always be easy to identify.

While Vaughan has stated that distance in the future doesn't seem to affect the accuracy of his precognitive dreams, I want to point out that distance in time is not entirely irrelevant. For one thing, it seems to be generally true that, the more momentous an event, the earlier we begin to dream about it. Vaughan agrees with this, writing that "very emotional or important events can be precognized at very great intervals of time, while trivial events tend to arrive soon after the precognitive impression."[39]

Paquette, for instance, had a series of dreams about September 11, 2001 back in 1989 and 1990. It was only 11 years later, on August 25, 2001, that a coincidence alerted him to the fact that his dreams were about to be realized. He was visiting Legoland with his wife and daughter but was in an explicably terrible mood, accompanied by an atrocious headache liked he'd never known before. He was about to tell his wife he needed to go back to the car when he saw the Legoland tableau of New York City and immediately knew that his suffering was connected to the dreams he'd had about a disaster occurring there. The odd thing about the tableau was that the towers of the World Trade Center were nowhere to be found. They were the most defining element of Manhattan's skyline at the time, and for some reason (artistic precognition?) they hadn't been included. Paquette told his wife on the spot, "That dream I had in New York about the earthquake that wasn't an earthquake, it's going to happen soon." As soon as he made this realization, his headache and general bad mood disappeared. Seventeen days later, the World Trade Center towers collapsed.[40]

I suggest the rule of thumb that, if you have your first dream of some very momentous event and suspect that it might be precognitive, the more momentous the event, the longer you should expect it to take to be fulfilled.

---

[38] Waggoner, 203.

[39] Vaughan, *Patterns of Prophecy*, 109.

[40] Paquette, *Dreamer*, 214-5.

However, this isn't a fail-safe rule, as shown by some of Vaughan's experiences where he perceived relatively unimportant details of events several years in the future. More importantly, many dreams of the deaths of others or of crises in their lives come *at the exact moment* of these events. (We'll see many examples in the next chapter.) So we can't assume that a significant-seeming dream is precognitive; it might be giving us information about something happening *right now*, if the unconscious deems it important for us to receive this information in real time.

Furthermore, whether or not we've had any earlier dreams on a particular subject, the fact that we are shortly going to experience an event that will resonate with us emotionally or symbolically does sometimes seem to cause us to dream about it just ahead of the actual event. Jungian psychiatrist Dr. Marie-Louise von Franz relates the story of a woman who told her analyst about dreaming of three scary-looking tigers who were sitting before her. This woman apparently had a strong power complex and tended to "devour" other people, so her analyst tried to help her understand the dream as a reflection of her personality. Later that same day, however, this woman was out walking when she came upon a barn where, quite unexpectedly, a bunch of people had gathered to look at three tigers! There was a circus visiting, but, as von Franz puts it, "the highly improbable coincidence of the inner and outer tigers in this woman's life…inevitably struck her as 'more than mere chance' and somehow as 'meaningful.'"[41] I would say it's likely that the woman's unconscious presented her with a dream of her impending encounter with the tigers precisely because of their relevance to her personality and her therapeutic process.

As another example in this vein, let me describe one of my own dreams. This dream had several important elements, but one of the first was that I found myself walking into a big stone building that resembled a Romanesque church and that I knew was dedicated to Saint Francis. This was a very unusual dream for me, as I'm not Catholic and have no particular interest in saints (or at least I didn't before this dream!), and two other saints figured in this same dream, though not in the same building. I was also aware in the dream that the building with Saint Francis in it was "my place," identified with me in a way that the other saints were not. I puzzled for several days over the meaning of this dream and spoke to a friend about it.

Six days later, I was watching a movie in which I saw a structure that reminded me of the one in my dream, with similar stone arcades. I was exclaiming to myself that this was just like the building from my dream when I saw that there was a statue under the arcade in the movie. I wondered if it would be Saint Francis. As the camera got closer, I saw that it was. Not only

---

[41] Marie-Louise von Franz, "Time and Synchronicity in Analytical Psychology," in *The Voices of Time*, ed. J. T. Fraser (New York: Braziller, 1966), 223.

did I recognize Saint Francis's robe and the birds on his shoulder and in his hand, but the next thing I knew, a Franciscan monk was appearing in the movie and telling the main character, "Saint Francis was a great man."[42]

At the time, I took this "manifestation" of my dream as confirmation that my dream of Saint Francis was as important as I'd originally felt it to be. The problem was that I couldn't figure out the dream's meaning. And as time went on and the dream remained just as obscure, I began to wonder if it might just have been a case of rather random precognition. I dreamt about a movie I was about to see—so what?

One person who would scold me for such an attitude is Jungian counselor Robert H. Hopcke. In his 2018 book *There Are No Accidents in Love and Relationships*, he writes about his amazement at the way people casually dismiss psychic events in their lives as "just ESP," as though it were a purely mechanistic phenomenon with no connection to their own needs and desires.[43]

As a matter of fact, I think Hopcke makes an excellent point. Why should we assume that, once we've shown that a coincidence can be attributed to precognition, there is no more meaning to be found in it? If precognition is such a special capacity, that we generally only become aware of in rather rare situations, wouldn't it make sense to ask *why* our precognitive sense has notified us of *this particular event* rather than any of the millions of others we will encounter in the future? Is our ESP trying, like a psychic doorbell, to tell us that something important is knocking at the door of our mind?

To get back to my dream, if Saint Francis was not significant to my psyche in some way, why would my dream have precognitively picked up on the image of his statue? What reason would my unconscious have had to make me dream about it so clearly in advance? One thing I did discover about Saint Francis after having this dream was that he was named Francis after the country of France. And, as I mentioned in the introduction to this book, the country of France is very dear to my heart. Those who know me best might say it's one of the defining aspects of my identity.

While I'm not prepared to say that precognition *always* turns out to be personally significant, I will say that, two years later, something about that particular precognitive dream still makes me think that I don't know the whole story yet. Perhaps there is more to come. When we're exploring the meaning of coincidences, it often pays to explore the possible meanings of a coincidence more fully, while at the same time realizing that there may be an

---

[42] James Redfield, Barnet Bain, and Dan Gordon, *The Celestine Prophecy*, DVD, directed by Armand Mastroianni (Culver City, CA: Celestine Films, 2005).

[43] Robert H. Hopcke, *There Are No Accidents in Love and Relationships: Meaningful Coincidences and the Stories of Our Families* (Asheville, NC: Chiron Publications, 2018), 110.

element of randomness involved—or at least an element of mystery too deep for us to solve. The tension between meaning and randomness is one we will explore more fully in the final chapter of this book.

Precognitive Waking Perceptions

Now let's turn to some examples of the way in which detailed precognitive information sometimes comes to people in a waking vision rather than a dream. The clearest example I've encountered of this phenomenon comes from Vaughan's book *Incredible Coincidence*. There, we read the firsthand account of Professor Richard Szumski who, while raking leaves in his yard as a teenager, had the sudden experience of being somewhere else. He was holding a brick in front of another house, accompanied by a young girl and boy whom he knew were his children. The vision he had was exceptionally detailed, and 20 years later, it was entirely fulfilled, except for one discrepancy: there was a brick wall in the vision that couldn't be seen from where he was standing when the vision came true. He realized, however, that if he had lived in the house *next door*, everything would have been exactly as it was in his vision.[44]

These small differences between precognition and reality often happen, suggesting that, at least in some cases, it is not the actual future that produces the vision but a possible future. For instance, Paquette once had a vivid dream of being mugged and killed. When, in real life, the preliminary events of the dream began to occur as he'd foreseen them, he was able to act differently than he had in the dream. He was able to confuse his muggers and thus prevent them from forcing him into the alley where he'd experienced himself being killed.[45] Because of this difference, it couldn't have been the *actual* mugging that caused Paquette's dream, but only a *very possible* mugging.

Prof. Szumski says that it made him uncomfortable to think that all of his decisions over the course of 20 years had amounted to a difference of only 30 feet between one house and the next.[46] But, of course, who's to say that the vision would have come true at all if Szumski had chosen a radically different path in life? The fact that we see what is likely to happen in our life doesn't mean that we aren't able to choose differently. Of course, we're all familiar with the dramatic plotline in which the actions that a protagonist takes in order to avoid their announced fate ironically become the very actions that seal that same fate. The limitations of human knowledge make this a perennial possibility. And Paquette's mugging dream actually provides

---

[44] Vaughan, *Incredible Coincidence*, 192-4.
[45] Paquette, *Dreamer*, 6-11.
[46] Vaughan, *Incredible Coincidence*, 194.

us with a partial example of this, which we'll discuss in Chapter 19, "Interpreting Coincidences." Clearly, precognition is not a simple affair.

Another example of this complexity is the fact that sometimes precognitive visions aren't related to one's own future but instead the future of the place in which one happens to find oneself. The Earl Lloyd George of Dwyfor, for example, relates that his grandmother was once sitting by a lake near a friend's house when she suddenly felt "chilled and uncomfortable" and the sky seemed to go dark. At the same time, she saw a man in a long tweed coat walk by her and *into the lake*. He walked until he was out of sight under the water. Then the sky brightened again. The earl's grandmother told her friend's father about this experience directly afterward, and he wrote down the details. It was only a week later that the significance of what she'd seen became clear. A week after this experience of hers, a local man put weights in the pockets of his tweed coat and killed himself by walking into the lake at precisely the spot where she'd had her vision.[47]

This case is very similar to visions that other people have had *after* a death has occurred in a place. It provides evidence that replays (or previews) of an event can be produced by precognition or retrocognition and are not necessarily indicative of the presence of the deceased's spirit.

In another case of precognitive vision (and precognitive touch) related to a specific place, the 5th Marchioness of Bath was walking to the dining room at Longleat House one evening when she noticed that dust sheets had been hung over the archways of the staircase hall. She had to pull the flaps of the sheets back twice in order to go on her way. While she was in the staircase hall between the two dust sheets, "she had the feeling that there were a lot of people around her, not only on the floor of the hall, but up the staircase and there seemed to be a murmur of voices around her." After she had passed through both sheets and was some way down the hall, "she turned round and looked again. At that moment a housemaid came out of a door at the end of the passage and everything disappeared." This occurred in 1914. It wasn't until 1916 that a fire broke out at Longleat and its aftermath necessitated hanging dust sheets in just the place where Lady Bath had seen them two years before. At that time, wounded soldiers were also staying at the house (hence the feeling of a crowd), and they helped to put out the fire.[48]

Other persons have reported precognitive hearing of various types. For instance, author Jean Plaidy reports hearing the 1983 Harrods bombing in London 12 hours before it actually occurred. In fact, she looked at her clock in both instances and reports that she heard the explosion *precisely* 12 hours before its actual occurrence.[49]

---

[47] Ben Noakes, *I Saw a Ghost: Eye-Witness Accounts by the Famous of Supernatural Encounters* (London: Weidenfeld and Nicolson, 1986), 104.
[48] Noakes, 18-20.
[49] Noakes, 117.

In an even stranger case, Sheelagh Davenport reports having wondered one evening while preparing for bed about the health of British politician Aneurin Bevan. He had been in the news for a while due to illness but then seemed to have dropped off the media's radar. The morning after Davenport was wondering about him, she awoke to the sound of a radio announcer saying, "Mr. Aneurin Bevan has had a relapse, and his condition gives cause for grave anxiety." This was strange not just because of her rather random thought about Bevan the previous night but because *her radio was not actually turned on*. What was more, Aneurin Bevan did have a serious relapse that day, but it only occurred *after* Davenport had heard this unexplained voice.[50]

This next case is confusing as to how it should be categorized. In different ways, it resembles both a multi-sensory precognitive experience and the pre-birth contact experiences related in the last chapter. A patient of Dr. Gladys McGarey was feeling down because she was having trouble getting pregnant, and the tests she'd had performed were inconclusive about the cause of her infertility. One night, after getting some of these tests done, she was waiting for her husband in a restaurant and feeling the lowest of any time in her life. She was sitting near an "open wrought iron wall," on the other side of which were a couple of candy machines. All at once, she noticed a small child standing behind the iron bars of the wall. The child looked to be about two years old, but she couldn't tell from the haircut if it was a girl or a boy. The child spoke to her, and she recounts their conversation thus:

> Child: "You're in jail."
> Me: "No, I'm not—you are!"
> Child, looking around: "The whole world's in jail."
> Me: "Who's going to let us out?"
> Child, very matter-of-fact: "God will."
> Me: "Who's going to ask Him for the key?"
> Child, cocking his head to one side, thinking, then with a big joyful smile: "I'll ask God for the key to let you out."
>
> At that instant, it was like a million pounds had been lifted from my shoulders—I was stunned by the freedom! Then I realized that the child was gone. I rose and went to look for the child, figuring that such a tiny child who spoke so well would be easily noticed. I could not find him—even asked several people if they'd seen him. None had! Then I began wondering if I'd had a vision.[51]

Two months later, this woman conceived a son. When he was 28 months old, she was having lunch with him in the same restaurant where she'd had her apparent vision. When he dropped a toy through the wrought-iron bars and she went around to get it for him, he looked at her through the

---

[50] Noakes, 41-42.

[51] Gladys T. McGarey, *Born to Live* (Scottsdale, AZ: Inkwell Productions, 2008), 44.

bars and said, "Bless you, Mom." That was when she realized that it was *him* she'd seen, two months before his conception. "He's very tiny for his age," she says, "and speaks very, very well." She says he even had the same androgynous haircut.

Was this woman's vision of her unborn son a pre-birth communication from him or a precognition of an event that would happen later in time? Because of the many differences between the vision and the later event (despite their similarities) and because of the fact that the woman holds an actual conversation with the child in the vision, I'm inclined to think that this was a case of pre-birth communication, and that being in the same restaurant years later and seeing her son behind the same bars simply triggered the mother to recognize him as the child she'd previously communicated with. However, it's still strange that, when she had this moment of recognition, he should be the same age that he was in the vision and have the same haircut. It makes one begin to contemplate even stranger possibilities. For example, could this woman's unborn son have been communicating with her *from the future*? At the very end of this chapter, we'll consider a form of time travel communication experienced by Robert Moss. I don't think we can rule out something analogous in this case. Sometimes it seems that, the more one delves into paranormal topics, the *more* possible explanations there seem to be, not fewer!

Presentiment

Returning now to more conventional examples of precognition, we should note that sometimes people don't have a detailed dream or vision, they just have a presentiment: a feeling that turns out to be related to the future. Paquette's oppressive mood and headache related to the impending September 11 tragedy are one example. Another tragic example is that of a man named Frank Ragusa who gave away a stained-glass window that he said gave him the creeps. It was of a rather graphic Sacred Heart that was struck through with thorns, as well as spouting flames and dripping blood. It turned out that Ragusa later died, along with his wife and sister, by being stabbed through the heart.[52]

The phenomenon of presentiment has also been studied in the laboratory, though these studies tend to focus not on conscious feelings but on unconscious physical reactions. Laboratory experiments have shown that physiological functions such as heart rate, pupil dilation, skin conductance, brain activity, and blood oxygen levels correlate with a random stimulus a

---

[52] Vaughan, *Incredible Coincidence*, 185-6.

subject is about to receive, but before they have any normal means of knowing what it is.[53]

Action Unconsciously Motivated by Precognition

The existence of unconscious presentiment or precognition could explain why people sometimes find themselves acting in an unexpected way without any knowledge why and only later discover what purpose was served by their odd behavior. Consider the case of Clio Mitchell. She was living in Paris and on her way to the metro station when, for no apparent reason, she suddenly began running. She thus likely got on an earlier train than she would have otherwise. Afterward, she had to change lines, and when the new train arrived, she felt another strange impulse: to get into the car to her left rather than the one right in front of her. She followed this impulse, and at the very next station, a good friend of hers stepped into the car with her. This friend was just passing through Paris on his way from Italy to England, and they never would have seen each other but for Mitchell's odd last-minute adjustments to her trajectory.[54]

I've included this case in the chapter on coincidences caused by the experiencer, so clearly I think there's a possibility that Mitchell was unconsciously aware of her friend's presence on that train and of her ability to meet up with him if she slightly modified her behavior on a couple of occasions. But how likely is this hypothesis? Does it make sense to attribute not just this unconscious knowledge but also this unconscious calculation to her? Or should this case be classified as one in which some higher intelligence is at work? It does seem from other cases we've seen that angels or spirit guides like to organize events by subtly influencing people's behavior or thoughts, and so I think we have to allow that, given our existing knowledge, this is also a possible explanation for this case. Then again, these two explanations may not be entirely distinct, as we'll discuss below, in the sub-section "The Higher Self."

Here are a few more similarly ambiguous cases.

- On her way to the airport one morning, a woman told her sister that the person she most wanted to talk to at the moment was Robert Moss. Later that day, when she was waiting for a connecting flight, she saw Moss seated at the gate, waiting for the very same flight![55]

---

[53] Julia Mossbridge, Patrizio Tressoldi, and Jessica Utts, "Predictive physiological anticipation preceding seemingly unpredictable stimuli: a meta-analysis," *Frontiers in Psychology: Perception Science* 3 (October 2012).

[54] Inglis, *Coincidence*, 118.

[55] Robert Moss, *The Three "Only" Things: Tapping the Power of Dreams, Coincidence & Imagination* (Novato, CA: New World Library, 2007), 120.

- Alan Vaughan confused the time of his dentist's appointment and so ran into one of his favorite authors—*while* Vaughan happened to be carrying one of the author's books. Vaughan played the meeting off as intentional, telling the author, "I've been waiting for you. Will you please autograph this book."[56]
- A New York lawyer was going to Greenwich Village to meet some friends. He planned to change from the local to the express train at 14th Street but instead made the mistake of exiting the subway. Rather than pay to reenter, he decided to walk the six blocks to his destination. As he did so, he came upon his friends, who were headed to an appointment elsewhere. If he had taken the train as planned, he would have completely missed them.[57]

Evidence for Psychokinesis

So far in this chapter, we've discussed the paranormal ability of ESP, particularly in the form of precognition. But there's another paranormal ability that is very common, though it may at first be hard to believe. This is psychokinesis: the ability to affect external objects using nothing but the power of one's mind.[58] Psychokinesis (PK) is a good candidate for causing a fair number of coincidences. And this is especially so because, as we'll see, a person's desires and moods can cause PK without their being consciously aware of the connection.

Poltergeist Phenomena

An excellent example with which to begin is the "poltergeist" experiences of author Michael Talbot. In his book *Beyond the Quantum*, Talbot recounts how poltergeist-like activities began occurring at his home around the time he was six years old. The first manifestations of this activity were inexplicable showers of gravel on the roof of the Talbots' house, a dwelling

---

[56] Vaughan, *Incredible Coincidence*, 82.

[57] Rex G. Stanford, "An experimentally testable model for spontaneous psi events: I. Extrasensory events," *Journal of the American Society for Psychical Research* 68 (1974): 34-57.

[58] I should note that it's not clear that psychic ability can really be neatly divided into separate categories such as ESP and PK. Indeed, as this chapter and this book progress, we'll see more and more that all kinds of distinctions start to look arbitrary when we regard the world from the perspective of psi. Nevertheless, the distinction between ESP and PK is a rough-and-ready one that can help us organize the evidence for psychic phenomena, even if we later find it must be transcended for a more holistic perspective.

located out in the woods in a rural area of Michigan and not readily accessible to pranksters. While out walking one evening, Talbot and some friends even had gravel rain down directly on their heads, apparently out of nowhere.

Later, these strange activities moved to the interior of Talbot's home. The poltergeist "stomped and rattled," he reports. At times, it would actually hurl small stones or bits of smooth-edged glass at him. It also appears to have had "a marked fondness for throwing the vacuum cleaner around."[59] Talbot even remembers once opening the door to a room and seeing a lamp immediately come on by itself and a drinking glass fly out, breaking in the hallway beside him and his friend.[60]

When Talbot became a teenager, he began attempting to interact with the poltergeist. He recounts,

> Late one night when I was standing in the kitchen I said aloud, "Okay, why don't you do something to show me that you're here?" When I made the remark I happened to be facing an open kitchen window—since our house was in the middle of the woods, we did not draw the curtains at night. No sooner had I mouthed the words when something invisible instantly began to pound on the glass, rapidly and with such force that I could not understand why the glass did not break. Taken off guard by the unexpected response, I panicked and screamed for the pounding to stop, and just as quickly as it had started, it stopped.[61]

With time, Talbot became more accustomed to the behavior of this phenomenon, and he found he could often get it to reply to him, though not in any sophisticated fashion. He likened its level of intelligence to that of a dog or cat.[62] And he discovered something else remarkable about it, which was that its behavior appeared to be linked to his own emotional state. Once, when he was in a particularly negative state of mind, a needle materialized and flew into his leg. And, on more than one occasion, a dark mood of his was accompanied by gouges appearing in his flesh. "At first I felt a stinging sensation," he reports, "and then, as I watched, a small hole simply appeared in my skin." (He notes that these strange activities were regularly witnessed by his friends; they were not figments of his imagination.) But when Talbot was feeling more positively—which he says was more usual for him—the poltergeist would do sillier things, like "laying a handful of dried noodles on

---

[59] Michael Talbot, *Beyond the Quantum: How the Secrets of the New Physics Are Bridging the Chasm Between Science and Faith* (Toronto: Bantam Books, 1987, 1988), 7.

[60] Talbot, *Beyond the Quantum*, 8.

[61] Talbot, *Beyond the Quantum*, 8.

[62] Another prominent poltergeist experiencer, Matthew Manning, calls the intelligence behind the disturbances he experienced "childish." Matthew Manning, *The Link: Matthew Manning's Own Story of His Extraordinary Psychic Gifts* (New York: Holt, Rinehart and Winston, 1974, 1975), 46.

my chest while I slept or draping all of my clean socks on various houseplants in the house."[63]

There were other indications as well that the poltergeist was somehow connected to Talbot rather than to anyone else in his home or to the place itself. His bedroom was the location of preference for its activities, even though the poltergeist did also produce effects in other rooms of the house. And when it "targeted" someone, it was more often than not Talbot who was on the receiving end of its antics. Furthermore, it followed him to other locations in his adult life, making itself known at every place he lived until his mid-20s, when it disappeared.

This person-centered behavior is typical for poltergeists, as is its concentration of activity during the person's adolescence. As Talbot notes, these facts suggest that the poltergeist isn't actually a ghost but rather the product of the person's unconscious psychic abilities. Talbot suggests that whatever autonomous will the poltergeist displays stems from the same mechanisms that allow characters in our dreams to behave independently of our conscious will, even though they are ultimately creations of our own mind.[64]

To see the persuasiveness of this explanation, consider another "poltergeist" case, this one occurring in a lawyer's office in Bavaria, Germany. Two Munich physicists investigated the phenomenon with the aid of remote-control cameras, which filmed moving objects that "gave the impression of being under intelligent control and to have a tendency to evade investigation."[65] It appeared that the effects were caused by a secretary who had fallen in love with the lawyer and was frustrated at being so close to him and yet not in the way she wished. This conclusion was bolstered by the fact that, when she was persuaded to give up her job at the law office, the anomalous incidents in the office ceased, but further poltergeist-like experiences subsequently plagued her relationship with another man who was a passionate bowler. "[O]ut of the fourteen occasions when she went with him to the bowling alley, the electronic system controlling the pins broke down eight times."[66]

Carl Jung also experienced a phenomenon that displayed a clear link between his emotions and a poltergeist-like effect. Interestingly, it happened in the context of an argument with that other great name in depth

---

[63] Talbot, *Beyond the Quantum*, 9.
[64] Talbot, *Beyond the Quantum*, 10.
[65] Hans Bender, "Der Rosenheimer Spuk—ein Fall spontaner Psychokinese," *Zeitschrift fuer Parapsychologie und Grenzgebiete der Psychologie* XI, no. 2 (Bern and Munich: Francke Verlag, 1968): 113-31, as quoted in Alister Hardy, Robert Harvie, and Arthur Koestler, *The Challenge of Chance: A Mass Experiment in Telepathy and Its Unexpected Outcome* (New York: Random House, 1973), 198.
[66] Hardy, Harvie, and Koestler, 199.

psychology, Sigmund Freud. Jung was visiting Freud and asked him about his thoughts on ESP and the like. Here is Jung's description of the discussion:

> Because of his materialistic prejudice, [Freud] rejected this entire complex of questions as nonsensical, and did so in terms of so shallow a positivism that I had difficulty in checking the sharp retort on the tip of my tongue. It was some years before he recognized the seriousness of parapsychology and acknowledged the factuality of "occult" phenomena.
>
> While Freud was going on this way, I had a curious sensation. It was as if my diaphragm were made of iron and were becoming red-hot—a glowing vault. And at that moment there was such a loud report in the bookcase, which stood right next to us, that we both started up in alarm, fearing the thing was going to topple over on us. I said to Freud: "There, that is an example of a so-called catalytic exteriorization phenomenon."
>
> "Oh come," he exclaimed. "That is sheer bosh."
>
> "It is not," I replied. "You are mistaken, Herr Professor. And to prove my point I now predict that in a moment there will be another such loud report!" Sure enough, no sooner had I said the words than the same detonation went off in the bookcase.[67]

When effects like these closely correspond to the emotions of a specific living person, the term 'poltergeist', which literally means "racket-making ghost," can be misleading, implying as it does the action of an independent entity. Because of this, a new term for such phenomena was coined in 1958 by poltergeist investigators Drs. William G. Roll and J. Gaither Pratt, who referred to them as "recurrent spontaneous psychokinesis," or RSPK.[68] As we'll see later in this chapter (as well as in Chapter 8, "Ill-Meaning Entities"), it's not clear that psychokinesis adequately accounts for all poltergeist-like phenomena, but it does seem to be the best explanation for some cases, such as the three we've just considered.

Physical Mediumship

Poltergeist phenomena bear a strong resemblance to another phenomenon called "physical mediumship," in which a medium purportedly invokes the ability of a discarnate entity to move or materialize objects, often in the setting of a séance. As with poltergeists, many researchers of physical mediumship have concluded that, while some of the phenomena reported are genuinely psychic in nature, they are the result of the PK of the living persons involved, not the actions of discarnate entities. Parapsychologist Dr.

---

[67] C. G. Jung, *Memories, Dreams, Reflections*, ed. Aniela Jaffé, trans. Richard and Clara Winston, rev. ed. (New York: Vintage Books, 1961, 1989), 155.

[68] J. Gaither Pratt and William G. Roll, "The Seaford Disturbances," *Journal of Parapsychology* 22 (1958): 79-124.

Ian Stevenson has surmised that this explanation for physical mediumship became fashionable when psychics appeared on the public scene who were able to duplicate the phenomena produced by mediums but didn't claim to be helped by spirits.[69] Stevenson cites the example of Daniel Dunglas Home, whose astounding psychic feats during the 19th century were particularly well investigated and included effects such as remote playing of musical instruments as well as levitations of persons and even heavier objects like pianos.[70] However, it has by no means been proven that *none* of the phenomena produced during séances are attributable to the deceased or other discarnates. And, even today, there are physical mediums such as Kai Muegge and Stewart Alexander who claim that the phenomena in their séances are due to spirits of one kind or another.[71] My intent here is not to argue that none of these phenomena could be produced by discarnate entities but simply to point out that it seems possible that many of them—in particular, in cases like Home's where no reference is made to any discarnate agent—are actually the result of living-agent PK.

PK After-Effects of Near-Death Experiences

In a related vein, near-death experience researcher P. M. H. Atwater mentions that people who've had distressing NDEs (see Chapter 8 for some examples) commonly experience "hauntings" afterward. She provides an example from her own life, recounting how she had an NDE in which she perceived "a gigantic form, like two cyclones one above the other in an hourglass shape, spinning at tremendous speeds—the one on top was moving clockwise and the bottom one, counterclockwise. Where the two cyclones should have touched but didn't, there burst forth rays of the strangest light I have ever seen—piercing in its intensity." She says that, after she came back from her NDE, the cyclones began to manifest in the physical world. "I'd be speaking with my oldest daughter, Natalie," says Atwater, "when she'd disappear and in her place would be the cyclones. I'd be at the kitchen sink doing dishes, look up, and be taken aback by the sudden emergence of these massive shapes."

You might think Atwater was just experiencing a hallucination, but at least one of the experiences she had with the cyclones can't be explained in that fashion. After over a decade of these sorts of experiences, one day she

---

[69] Ian Stevenson, "Are Poltergeists Living or Are They Dead?" *Journal of the American Society for Psychical Research* 66, no. 3 (July 1972): 233-52, p. 234.

[70] An excellent account of Home's phenomena can be found in Stephen E. Braude, *The Limits of Influence: Psychokinesis and the Philosophy of Science* (New York: Routledge & Kegan Paul, 1986), 70-108.

[71] On Kai Muegge and Stewart Alexander, see Leslie Kean, *Surviving Death: A Journalist Investigates Evidence for an Afterlife* (New York: Crown Archetype, 2017).

was at her computer writing about her near-death experience and attempting to vividly remember the cyclones, when the image on her screen actually took on the shape she was remembering. The shape grew increasingly large until it actually *burst out* of the screen, causing the monitor to break and "flinging sparkly particles of radiation-type substance all over." Atwater says the explosion was accompanied by a terrible smell: "a kind of flat, acrid ozone odor." She later showed the exploded monitor to a computer tech, who said such a thing was impossible.

Atwater appears to have a pretty good idea of the meaning behind this event. She says she had spent the previous 13 years trying to avoid the possible significance of the cyclones until finally they would not let her ignore them anymore. "The cause of my haunting was not the cyclones," she says, "it was unexpressed fear." Her subsequent research has led her to conclude that all post-NDE "hauntings" are manifestations of the buried emotions of the experiencers, similar to the poltergeists discussed above.[72]

Another case of post-NDE PK worth mentioning is that of Cherylee Black, who began to show signs of recurrent spontaneous PK after she had a near-death experience at the age of 10. Unlike most NDErs—who, if they experience odd physical effects, generally experience them, like Atwater, in the context of malfunctioning electronics[73]—Black appears to have quickly developed the ability to move medium-sized objects. For instance, a schoolteacher "apparently slapped her for inattention, and a book was lifted by an unseen force and thrown across the room, hitting the teacher"—causing Black to appear like a real-life version of Roald Dahl's Matilda. What is especially intriguing about Black's case, in contrast to the others we've looked at so far, is that she subsequently found herself able to move objects with her mind *intentionally*, and this ability of hers has been explored in controlled laboratory conditions.[74]

Laboratory Tests of PK

If the idea that a human being can affect external objects using nothing but the power of their mind seems to you harder to believe than purely mental feats like precognition, you're not alone. Perhaps this is because those

---

[72] P. M. H. Atwater, *Beyond the Light: What Isn't Being Said About Near-Death Experience* (New York: Birch Lane Press, 1994), 42-43.
[73] For some particularly intriguing examples, see Debra Diamond, *Life After Near Death: Miraculous Stories of Healing and Transformation in the Extraordinary Lives of People with Newfound Powers* (Wayne, NJ: New Page Books, 2016), especially Chapters 3 and 13.
[74] Titus Rivas, Anny Dirven, and Rudolf H. Smit, *The* Self *Does Not Die: Verified Paranormal Phenomena from Near-Death Experiences* (Durham, NC: IANDS Publications, 2016), 192-5.

of us with a naïve conception of physics imagine that this sort of feat would require sending out some kind of "force rays" from our brains to affect objects in the material world. It's not clear, however, that anything like this is required. Danish physicist Dr. Richard Mattuck and American physicist Dr. Evan Harris Walker have proposed a theory according to which PK does not introduce energy or matter into a system but merely *information*, which can reorganize pre-existing noise. According to their theory, PK could get the energy to move a macroscopic object by reducing the ambient temperature by merely a fraction of a degree Celsius.[75]

But more important than any particular theory of how PK occurs is the strong evidence that it *does* occur. In addition to the spontaneous cases so far described, there is a great deal of laboratory evidence supporting the reality of psychokinesis.

For almost 30 years between 1979 and 2007, the Princeton Engineering Anomalies Research (PEAR) program studied psychokinesis under carefully controlled laboratory conditions and discovered that even normal, "non-psychic" individuals had the ability to psychically affect random physical processes of various sorts: for instance, the operation of microelectronic noise diode units and the fall of polystyrene balls in a "random mechanical cascade," which looked something like a giant pinball machine with no levers. PEAR's research is summarized in an excellent volume written by the program's primary investigators, Dr. Robert G. Jahn and Brenda J. Dunne.[76]

PK laboratory research goes far beyond the PEAR program, however. A 2006 meta-analysis in *Psychological Bulletin* examined 380 PK experiments and concluded that there was "a significant but very small overall effect size."[77] The authors of this meta-analysis believed this apparent effect was likely the result of many unsuccessful studies' having been conducted but left unpublished—a phenomenon known as the "File Drawer Effect"—saying that approximately 1544 such missing studies would be needed to erase the apparent psychokinetic effect. However, in response to this meta-analysis, a survey was conducted of researchers who had contributed to the literature on PK, and it was concluded that there were possibly 59 studies that had been left unpublished, some of which showed significant positive results as

---

[75] Richard D. Mattuck and Evan Harris Walker, "The Action of Consciousness on Matter: A Quantum Mechanical Theory of Psychokinesis," in *The Iceland Papers*, ed. Andrea Puharich (Amherst, WI: Essentia Research Association, 1979), 111-59, p. 134.

[76] Robert G. Jahn and Brenda J. Dunne, *Consciousness and the Source of Reality: The PEAR Odyssey* (Princeton, NJ: ICRL Press, 2011).

[77] Holger Bösch, Fiona Steinkamp, and Emil Boller, "Examining Psychokinesis: The Interaction of Human Intention with Random Number Generators—A Meta-Analysis," *Psychological Bulletin* 132, no.4 (2006): 497-523.

well.[78] But even had all these unpublished studies shown no effect, their number is nowhere near enough to erase the effect visible in the 380 studies that *were* published.

Laboratory research has also been conducted to test the PK abilities of animals. In research conducted by Dr. René Peoc'h, chicks imprinted on a randomly driven robot appeared to cause it to come near them more often than chance,[79] and light-deprived chicks appeared to cause a robot with a candle on it to do the same.[80] In an experiment conducted by Dr. Fernando Alvarez, zebra finches appeared able to influence a random event generator to make a picture of a video of a snake displayed in their cage become less visible.[81]

Dr. Helmut Schmidt tested some animals other than birds and found that a heat lamp hooked up to a random number generator stayed on more often when a cat was around. He also tested the ability of cockroaches to affect a random number generator that determined whether they would receive electric shocks. To Schmidt's surprise, it turned out that the cockroaches received shocks *more* often would be expected by chance. He chalked this up to the process's being psychokinetically affected by his own dislike for cockroaches.[82]

These studies of animal PK—the cockroach experiments included—are an excellent demonstration of the ubiquity of PK phenomena. They make it clear that the ability to affect matter with one's mind is not the sole province of a few divinely privileged individuals. At the same time, laboratory research has also confirmed the abilities of some subjects who are especially gifted at PK, as we already saw in the case of Cherylee Black. Other examples include a Chinese experiment in which a Mr. Xiao was able to psychically remove a

---

[78] Dean Radin, Roger Nelson, York Dobyns, and Joop Houtkooper, "Reexamining Psychokinesis: Comment on Bösch, Steinkamp, and Boller," *Psychological Bulletin* 132, no. 4 (2006): 529-32.

[79] René Peoc'h, "Chicken Imprinting and the Tychoscope: An Anpsi Experiment," *Journal of the Society for Psychical Research* 55 (1988): 1-9.

[80] René Peoc'h, "Psychokinetic Action of Young Chicks on the Path of an Illuminated Source," *Journal of Scientific Exploration* 9, no. 2 (1995): 223-9.

[81] Fernando Alvarez, "A PK Experiment with Zebra Finches and a Virtual Predator," *Journal of Scientific Exploration* 26, no. 2 (2012): 261-71.

[82] Helmut Schmidt, "PK Experiments with Animals as Subjects," *Journal of Parapsychology* 34, no. 4 (1970): 255-61. Parapsychologists call the apparent ability of experimenters to exert an effect on the outcomes of their experiments the "experimenter effect," and the hypothesis that they are able to do this in a specifically psi fashion is called the "experimenter psi hypothesis." An excellent overview of research in this area can be found in John Palmer and Brian Millar, "Experimenter Effects in Parapsychological Research," in *Parapsychology: A Handbook for the 21st Century*, eds. Etzel Cardeña, John Palmer, and David Marcusson-Clavertz (Jefferson, NC: McFarland & Co., 2015), 293-300.

folded paper from a capped bottle. This experiment is reported in detail in a 2010 issue of the *Journal of Scientific Exploration*.[83]

Metal Bending

There does seem to be one form of rather exotic PK that is experienced by a wide swathe of the population: metal bending. Experience of this phenomenon is so widespread that it has led to the popularization of "spoon-bending parties," in which participants report watching stout metal cutlery bend without application of the physical force that would normally be necessary.

First-person accounts of successful metal bending abound and are given by, among others, parapsychologist Dr. Dean Radin,[84] laser physicist Russell Targ,[85] life coach and memoirist Martha Beck,[86] author Michael Crichton,[87] and retired senior Army officer Dr. John B. Alexander.[88] A particularly amusing account is offered by Andrew Paquette, who was having an argument with his friend Richard about whether the famous psychic Uri Geller had been cheating when he appeared to bend keys. They were about to enter Richard's university laboratory when Paquette declared, "Just because you figured out a way to imitate the result, doesn't mean it can't be done!" He said this just after Richard had taken out his keys to open his laboratory door. Richard then went to put a key into the lock, but he gasped and dropped it. The key he had tried to use was bent at a 45-degree angle.[89]

More Exotic Examples of PK

Types of psychokinesis even more exotic than metal bending exist as well, though they are much rarer. For example, stigmata are wounds that spontaneously appear in some people's flesh in the areas thought to correspond to the wounds Jesus received on the cross. This phenomenon has been observed since the time of Saint Francis of Assisi in the 13th century

---

[83] Dong Shen, "Unexpected Behavior of Matter in Conjunction with Human Consciousness," *Journal of Scientific Exploration* 24, no. 1 (2010): 41-52.
[84] Dean Radin, *Supernormal: Science, Yoga, and the Evidence for Extraordinary Abilities* (New York: Deepak Chopra Books, 2013), 219-20.
[85] Russell Targ, *The Reality of ESP: A Physicist's Proof of Psychic Abilities* (Wheaton, IL: Quest Books, 2012), 165.
[86] Martha Beck, *Finding Your Own North Star: Claiming the Life You Were Meant to Live* (New York: Three Rivers Press, 2001), 61.
[87] Michael Crichton, *Travels* (New York: Vintage Books, 1988), 319.
[88] John B. Alexander, *Reality Denied: Firsthand Experiences with Things that Can't Happen—But Did* (San Antonio, TX: Anomalist Books, 2017), Ch. 10.
[89] Paquette, *Dreamer*, 131.

and continues today. Supporting the hypothesis that stigmata are caused by PK is the fact that the placement of the wounds appears to reflect the bearers' beliefs. Even though Jesus would have been crucified according to the Roman custom in which nails were placed through the wrists, stigmata nevertheless appear in the *hands* of those who bear them, a location at which nails would never have been able to hold the weight of a body on a cross.[90] What is more, the precise nature, size, shape, and location of stigmata vary from person to person[91]—not what one would expect if they were directly psychically influenced by the wounds of Jesus instead of by the *thoughts* about such wounds held by the individuals involved. Stigmata thus seem like good candidates for explanation by way of PK acting on the human body, rather than as miracles issuing directly from a divine source.

Another exotic bodily phenomenon is exhibited by a woman named Katie who has been investigated by psychiatrist Dr. Berthold E. Schwarz and philosopher Dr. Stephen E. Braude. Katie has a variety of well-attested psychic gifts, but the strangest of them is that she often spontaneously manifests thin sheets of a gold-colored metal on different locations of her skin, as well as sometimes on her clothing and on or in other nearby objects. This metallic foil, which repeated analyses have shown to be brass composed of approximately 80% copper and 20% zinc, has appeared under the direct gaze of witnesses and in strictly controlled conditions in which her body has been thoroughly searched and she has had no opportunity to subsequently acquire foil from any hidden location. Investigations have also ruled out the possibility that Katie is sweating the metal through her pores or applying it to her skin in the form of a liquid solution. Interestingly, in his account of his investigations given in his 2007 book *The Gold Leaf Lady*, Braude outlines some of his reasons for thinking that the appearance of the foil meets one or more psychological needs for Katie, who appears to have a very difficult home life. This would make the case consistent with many other cases of PK, in particular the poltergeist cases described above.[92]

Braude devotes another chapter of the same book to describing the "thoughtography" of a man named Ted Serios, who was capable of psychically producing images on Polaroid film, many of them pictures of recognizable architectural landmarks. Psychiatrist and parapsychologist Dr. Jule Eisenbud devoted years to the careful, controlled investigation of

---

[90] D. Scott Rogo, *Miracles: A Parascientific Inquiry into Wondrous Phenomena* (New York: Dial Press, 1982), 74.

[91] Herbert Thurston, *The Physical Phenomena of Mysticism* (Chicago: Henry Regnery Company, 1952), 120-9.

[92] Stephen E. Braude, *The Gold Leaf Lady and Other Parapsychological Investigations* (Chicago: The University of Chicago Press, 2007), 1-23.

Serios's abilities and produced an excellent book on the topic: *The World of Ted Serios.*[93]

While Serios is often maligned in the popular press as a fraud, these charges have never been substantiated, and those who have seriously investigated his work have found that this explanation for his images doesn't hold up. Serios was capable of producing his thoughtographs using film and cameras provided by others while not even touching the machine and sometimes at great remove from it. Granted, he often liked to work with a small tube of black paper that he would place in front of the camera. This sounds very suspicious, but the tube was constantly under examination by others and, in control photographs, produced nothing like Serios's startlingly recognizable images. What is more, Serios "often produced multiple images in one experimental session (e.g., as many as fifty separate images during a series of sixty to eighty trials, or ten to twenty images in a shorter series of trials)."[94] Given that his entire person was searched and continuously observed during the sessions, it is exceedingly hard to see how he could have not only concealed the materials needed to produce so many different images in a fraudulent fashion but managed to get each of them surreptitiously into and out of the little gizmo he placed in front of the camera. A professional conjuror, W. E. Cox, observed one of Serios's sessions and stated, "I say absolutely and unequivocally that no lens or microfilm could be hidden in a gismo barrel under these conditions." What is more, his written statement said, "No conjuring techniques are remotely conceivable under the conditions."[95]

Perhaps the most interesting feature of Serios's images is the way in which the recognizable structures that appear in them differ in minor ways from their real-life counterparts. For instance, Serios produced an image of Williams's Livery Stable in Central City, Colorado, which can be recognized by the shape and placement of the windows and doors, the molding, the exterior light, and even the lettering on the building. And yet, in Serios's image, the texture of the brick on the actual building seems to have morphed into something more like embedded stone. Additionally, a playbill for the Central City Opera House across the street can be clearly seen in his image, where in present reality there was at that location only the shadow of an old playbill. And—most strangely of all—the windows and doors appear to be bricked in in Serios's image, where research on the building showed no evidence of this having ever been the case.[96]

---

[93] Jule Eisenbud, *The World of Ted Serios: "Thoughtographic" Studies of an Extraordinary Mind* (New York: William Morrow & Co., 1967). A second, revised edition of this work appeared in 1989 from McFarland & Co.

[94] Braude, *Gold Leaf Lady*, 111.

[95] Eisenbud, *World of Ted Serios*, 110.

[96] Eisenbud, *World of Ted Serios*, 167-8.

Eisenbud suggests that some of the distortions present in Serios's photographs may be akin to the distortions experienced in dreams, a hypothesis that gains plausibility from the fact that Serios's images seem mainly to be produced by his unconscious—that is, without his conscious control. I would also note that there is an almost eerie, dream-like quality to Serios's images. More specific evidence, however, that Serios's mind is distorting the images comes from an image he produced of a hangar belonging to the Air Division of the Royal Canadian Mounted Police. Serios was not a very good speller (due perhaps to the fact that he had dropped out of school after the fifth grade), and this image seems to bear witness to that, as the word 'Canadian' on the side of the building is misspelled "Cainadain"—a fact pointed out by the RCMP, who positively identified the building.[97]

The number of hard examples of Serios's thoughtography that can be pored over again and again in their intricate detail make his case of great value to those who study the workings of psychokinesis. Indeed, Braude says that many consider it to be "not only the most impressive and best documented case of thoughtography, but one of the most impressive cases ever of psychokinesis generally."[98] Other examples of thoughtography worth investigating for those with an interest in the subject can be found in the work of Tomokichi Fukurai, a Japanese psychology professor who stumbled upon the phenomenon while doing more conventional parapsychological work with a clairvoyant.[99]

Implications of PK for Coincidences

The fact that humans (as well as animals) are capable of influencing the physical world by non-physical means has important implications for determining the sources of coincidences. Perhaps the most important lesson we should take from the evidence cited above is that PK can operate unconsciously. People can produce psychic effects without consciously intending to do so, and even without being aware that they *have* done so. For this reason, when we encounter a striking coincidence, we have to be careful to consider whether we may have been unconsciously involved in its production.

Recall the case mentioned in the Introduction to this book of a man who began seeing coincidences everywhere he went and interpreting them as messages related to vast conspiracies and/or divine or demonic entities who

---

[97] Eisenbud, *World of Ted Serios*, 207-8.
[98] Braude, *Gold Leaf Lady*, 108.
[99] T. Fukurai, *Clairvoyance and Thoughtography* (London: Rider & Co., 1931).

had chosen him as their special communication partner. What sets this man's counselor, Dr. Kirby Surprise, apart from many others in the mental health field is that he recognized that the coincidences his client was experiencing were not simply in his head. Some of these events would happen during their counseling sessions, right in front of Surprise, so he had to take them seriously. But, while the client would point to these occurrences as proof of his paranoid/grandiose beliefs, Surprise endeavored to show him that these events were simply *reflections* of his thoughts, not *proofs* of them.[100]

Surprise describes a case in which a client of his had the delusion that he was being followed by undercover government agents. The client claimed that people were watching him everywhere he went. In a counseling session, Surprise asked the client to come to a window that looked out over the street and show him where the people were who were watching him, expecting that the patient would see that no one was doing this. "At that moment," writes Surprise, "a car drove by with two men in it. Both stared directly at the window we were looking out of as the car slowly passed. 'You see!' my client exclaimed. 'There they are, right there!'"[101] Surprise concluded from this that this man was *actually causing other people to stare at him more often than chance*.[102] But, instead of realizing that he was the source of this behavior, the client took it as external proof that his paranoia was justified.

Surprise's book *Synchronicity* fills a very important gap in the coincidence literature, which all too often overlooks our power to create our own coincidences. As the previous few chapters have shown, I don't believe that people are always delusional when they connect their coincidence experiences to a source outside themselves, but Surprise's work shows that those with poor reality testing and a poor sense of the boundary between their own ego and the world around them may be especially susceptible to reading their coincidences as proof of something more grandiose than what actually underlies them. If you wrote yourself a note and held it up to a mirror, seeing the message reflected in the mirror would not prove that it was true. Those who are aware of their own ability to psychically affect the physical world in accordance with their desires and thoughts will be more likely to attribute coincidences to outside sources only when there is evidence that warrants doing so.

Surprise demonstrates a more careful approach to coincidences with the help of an intriguing example from his own life: something that happened to him on a day when he was preparing to do a presentation on coincidences

---

[100] Kirby Surprise, *Synchronicity: The Art of Coincidence, Choice, and Unlocking Your Mind* (Pompton Plains, NJ: New Page Books, 2012), 69.
[101] Surprise, 51.
[102] For one possible explanation of how the client might be producing this effect, see Rupert Sheldrake, *The Science of Being Stared At and Other Aspects of the Extended Mind* (New York: Crown, 2003).

and feeling uncertain about the value of his theory on the topic. In particular, he was debating whether he could really say that coincidences were reflections of our personal preoccupations. He was thinking about this as he crossed a parking lot and something in a puddle caught his eye. He writes,

> I looked down into the reflection of my own face, and saw beneath it, in the water, what looked like a gold credit card. I reached through the reflection of my face in the water and picked up the plastic card. I brushed water and bits of grime from the surface and read from the bold stylized letters printed across the top of the card "Kirby, Kirby and Kirby."[103]

Kirby is Surprise's first name, and the card was a business card for a law firm in which all the partners bore this name.

Many people would interpret this event as clear confirmation that Surprise was on the right track, that his theory about coincidences as reflections of self was accurate and worth sharing with the world. But notice that there's an element here of the Liar Paradox. In the Liar Paradox, a person says something like, "This statement is a lie." According to the rules of deductive logic, there's no way for this statement of theirs to be either true or false, since, if the statement is a lie, then it's *not* a lie; and if it's not a lie, then it *is* a lie. In the case of Surprise's coincidence, if the coincidence is speaking "truly," then the coincidence is saying *about itself* that it is just a reflection of Surprise's thoughts, with no special claim to truth.

Surprise acknowledges that he wanted this coincidence to be proof of his theory, but he also acknowledges that it isn't any such thing. "The mirror shows you what you look for," he says. "Once you understand this, you can look for, and create, almost any pattern you like."[104]

Now Surprise doesn't discount the fact that many coincidences *seem* to be coming from other sources. In fact, he thinks that's part of what we create when we create the coincidence. If we want to feel that we're communicating with God, then we'll create coincidences that seem like they're coming from God. He gives an example from his own life. When he was a young adult, he was feeling overwhelmed at being on his own for the first time. One evening he was listening to the radio and feeling sorry for himself when he playfully raised his hands to heaven and said, "Father, I'm tired of this. How about a break?" The next words out of the radio, he says, were the title lyrics of Kansas's song "Carry On My Wayward Son."[105]

While Surprise says he can't know for sure that no coincidences are produced by God or some other spiritual source, he says he's seen enough coincidences in his own and his clients' lives to realize that the way

---

[103] Surprise, 48.
[104] Surprise, 49.
[105] Surprise, 193.

coincidences present themselves is very person-specific, even specific to the current beliefs of the person. I agree that that evidence makes it harder to see any coincidences as valid reflections of a source of consciousness outside ourselves. And yet I believe that the arguments of the previous chapters and of the following ones are *also* valid. I believe there *is* evidence that coincidences can be more than mere reflections of our own minds. I believe we must do the very hard work of keeping both of these possibilities in mind. We must understand that the world does often change to reflect our thoughts, desires, and beliefs, and at the same time, we must be careful not to dismiss coincidence-based communication with other persons and beings as impossible.

After all, if *we* are capable of psychically affecting the physical world, then so are others. And unless we are solipsists, believing that no one in the world but ourselves exists, then we should also believe that others can communicate with us through their effects on the physical world we share. Furthermore, the previous four chapters of this book have shown many ways in which the experiences of different people corroborate each other, together giving us strong evidence that the deceased survive death, that children's spirits are conscious before their births, and that some form of spiritual beings exist who are more knowledgeable and powerful than ourselves. Given this evidence, it is rational to believe that these other beings can *also* communicate with us through their own psychokinetic effects on the physical world.

This leaves us with the difficult task of discerning which coincidences come from ourselves and which ones come from other sources. Interpreting coincidences correctly is a subtle, complicated art that is not unlike learning to discern the true thoughts and motives of other people, even when they're attempting to be misleading. In coincidences, the thoughts and desires of many different individuals—incarnate and otherwise—can be mixed together, turning coincidence interpretation into an incredibly complex form of psychology, where some of the parties are entirely invisible.

As Surprise has pointed out, one way to identify coincidences as coming from a particular source is their resonance with that person's beliefs, thoughts, and/or desires. If one particular person is the only one who would have an interest in producing this sort of coincidence, it makes sense to attribute it to them. And again, we must remember that the operation of psychic abilities is very often unconscious, so the fact that we are not *conscious* of causing coincidences doesn't mean that we are not doing it. As PK researchers Jahn and Dunne suggest, "the anomalous effects may be associated with some deeper level of consciousness, one perhaps more closely identified with the autonomic dimensions of the mind than with its cognitive ones."[106] There are, in fact, psi experiments that have been conducted specifically to see whether people can alter outcomes psychically in a way that's beneficial to them even though they don't know the experiment is psychic at all. Again, the idea is that we can see people's "psychic fingerprints" because of what we assume to be their interest in a particular case.[107]

I myself have had at least one experience in which it seemed plausible that my thoughts unconsciously produced a psychokinetic event. For several years before this event, I'd experienced many psychologically important coincidences involving the number 33, including finding a life-changing piece of information on page 33 of a particular book. After that incident, I was attentive to page 33 of each book I read. One evening, I was reading a book at the kitchen table while preparing dinner, and I was maybe on page 23 or 24. I remember explicitly thinking about what might appear on page 33 of this book, but I was very conscious of not having reached it yet. At that point, I had to get up and stir something on the stove, so I put my bookmark in the book and closed it. A minute later, when I reopened the book to the bookmark, it was on page 33. My husband was right next to me at the table. Stunned, I asked him if he had touched my bookmark while my back was turned. He said no and looked at me strangely, as if to ask why he'd ever do a thing like that. I was just trying to understand how this could have happened. Could I have somehow not paid enough attention to where I was putting my bookmark? But I can't remember ever marking a page wrong at any other time in my life—me, who reads at least two books a week! Even if I *had* accidentally put the bookmark in the wrong place, it was very surprising that the wrong place would happen to be page 33, unless I had somehow unconsciously influenced its placement.

The Nature and Purpose of Unconscious PK

If it still seems implausible that people would be exercising PK abilities unawares, consider that there are *many* abilities—perhaps *most* of our abilities—that we exercise without conscious awareness. For instance, when

---

[106] Jahn and Dunne, *Consciousness and the Source of Reality*, 173.

[107] See, for example, R. G. Stanford, R. Zenhausern, A. Taylor, and M. Dwyer, "Psychokinesis as psi-mediated instrumental response," *Journal of the American Society for Psychical Research* 69 (1975): 127-33; John Palmer, "Covert Psi in Computer Solitaire," *Journal of Parapsychology* 64 (2000): 195-211; David P. Luke, Chris A. Roe, and Jamie Davison, "Testing for Forced-Choice Precognition Using a Hidden Task: Two Replications," *The Journal of Parapsychology* 72 (2008): 133-54; and David Luke and Shelley Morin, "Exploration of the Validity and Utility of a Reward Contingency in a Non-Intentional, Forced-Choice Precognition Task," *Journal of the American Society for Psychical Research* 78 (January 2014): 207-18.

we walk across a room, our minds are analyzing a large volume of sensory data and deciding which messages to send through our nervous system to coordinate the movements of many different muscles—all without our having to give a thought to anything except our desire to get to the other side of the room. In fact, in many cases, we may not even give conscious thought to *that.* Our desire may simply be to investigate an object across the room, and our body gets us there without any further conscious effort.

In a discussion of the mechanisms of psychic functioning, Stephen Braude mentions the way in which subjects in conventional, non-psi-oriented biofeedback studies have managed impressive feats such as firing single muscle cells by doing nothing more than willing it to happen. "In fact," says Braude, "subjects often do best in biofeedback tasks when they don't actively try to achieve the desired result. Typically, they succeed under a condition of *passive volition* (in which they don't actively strive for a result) or after a *release of effort.*"[108] The effectiveness of releasing effort—even in cases where someone is consciously trying to use PK to affect an outcome—has been frequently noted by psi researchers and adepts, including Jahn and Dunne, the principal researchers of the Princeton Engineering Anomalies Research program. They go so far as to say that "[e]xcessive cognitive attention, especially of an analytical, tightly focused type, may actually inhibit the state of mind that is conducive to anomalous effects."[109] Apparently, the best way to produce PK is to form an intention to create a particular effect and then forget about it. It's when you stop trying so hard that the "magic" happens.

In his book *First Sight,* clinical psychologist Dr. James C. Carpenter presents a theory about the mechanism behind ESP and PK in which the unconscious nature of psychic functioning plays a central role. He emphasizes that PK that we have caused will not necessarily *feel* to us like something we've created.[110] It may feel foreign, even dangerous. Of course, this feeling won't be surprising to anyone familiar with depth psychology, which holds as a central tenet that there are many aspects of our psyche with which we are not well acquainted and that we may avoid precisely because they feel foreign and dangerous to us.

In that vein, let's consider some possible reasons we might have for wanting to affect the world in a way that seems to be independent of us, even if in truth it's not. Why would our unconscious countenance this kind of self-deception? Braude suggests in *Immortal Remains* that "covert" psi might

---

[108] Stephen E. Braude, *Immortal Remains: The Evidence for Life after Death* (Lanham, MD: Rowman & Littlefield, 2003), 11. Braude refers readers to J. Basmajian, "Control and Training of Individual Motor Units," *Science* 141 (1963): 440-1; and J. Basmajian, "Electromyography Comes of Age," *Science* 176 (1972): 603-9.

[109] Jahn and Dunne, *Consciousness and the Source of Reality*, 335.

[110] James C. Carpenter, *First Sight: ESP and Parapsychology in Everyday Life* (Lanham, MD: Rowman & Littlefield, 2012), 95-96.

sometimes best serve our personal interests. He points out that, while some Westerners are open to the idea of benevolent psychic activities like healing, the possibility of malevolent psychic activity "raises intimidating issues of responsibility" that most of us could conceivably prefer to avoid.[111] Our unconscious psychic influence on the world may be a way for us to steer events to our advantage without having to take responsibility for this behavior—which could be especially helpful when our desires are not of the socially acceptable variety.

This explanation accords with the frequent observation that PK often gives expression to emotions that people don't feel at liberty to express in a more direct fashion. As Carpenter points out, "The effects of PK upon extrabodily processes can only be discerned when unconscious intention is strong and unequivocal and the processes are sensed to be highly pertinent, but action is prevented."[112] That is, PK will only be obvious when someone has a very strong desire that they can't act on in a normal, non-psychic fashion—either due to physical incapacity or to psychological reasons, such as a respect for social norms. In some cases, the action that is prevented is the mere expression of a feeling, which for whatever reason the person's conscious mind deems inappropriate or undesirable.

An excellent example of this comes from the life of a woman named Jenny Saunders. In the book *Life Between Life*, Dr. Joel L. Whitton and Joe Fisher recount how, on the morning of Thursday, April 10, 1980, Saunders awoke alone in her apartment to find four or five deep red blotches splattered on her living room wall above her childhood doll house. She couldn't think of any way she could have inadvertently created these splotches, which looked disconcertingly like blood. When she returned from work that evening, she found that the morning's splotches were still there, though "dried in ragged drips," and new ones had appeared as well. More splotches appeared over the next few days. Three of Saunders' friends witnessed their appearance while Saunders was not even at home. For instance, Saunders' friend Michelle Ouellette observed the stains upon arriving at Saunders' house to take her out to a movie, and then, when they returned from the movie, Ouellette saw that more stains had appeared in the interim. The blotches began to cover an increasing portion of the living room wall and even appeared on the side of the television set. "Curiously," remark Whitton and Fisher, "[Saunders] had no desire to wipe away the marks which dominated her thoughts. ... Not that she was enjoying this expanding abstract mural. She continually fretted over why this was happening and what she could do about it. But indecision claimed her until she awoke one morning to find that a bloody trickle had appeared on the peaked roof of the

[111] Braude, *Immortal Remains*, 13-14.
[112] Carpenter, 97.

doll's house." She stayed at a friend's that night, and the next morning found a new apartment to move into. Her old landlord was left with the job of scrubbing off the stains and repainting.

After this, Saunders went to see Dr. Whitton for a consultation, because he was known to have expertise in the area of "spooky" phenomena. After many sessions, he was finally able to get to the root of the matter. The previous summer, Saunders had become pregnant and, "terrified of having a baby," had scheduled an abortion. As it turned out, when she went for the abortion, it was discovered that the baby had already been dead for three days. Strangely, the miscarriage had coincided with the sudden shriveling and death of one of Saunders' house plants, one which went by the common name of "baby's tears." But what was the connection with the blood stains on Saunders' wall? Whitton confirmed in Saunders' gynecological records that, had her baby survived, it would have been due on April 10—the very day that the first blood stains appeared on the wall above the doll house.[113]

The blood stains appeared to be a way for Saunders to express her buried feelings of guilt over rejecting her unborn child. This explains her reticence to remove the splotches, as they were her way of reminding herself of something important, if repressed. In fact, Saunders' guilt and grief over the loss of her pregnancy were just two of a vast number of negative feelings and experiences she kept locked away in the recesses of her mind. Whitton and Fisher remark that the blood stains were "a form of release that probably kept her sane." They state as well that Whitton has observed "many patients who...have precipitated drastic or spectacular events which led them to search out the origins of their difficulties." Projecting inner conflicts onto the external world where they are highly visible and difficult to ignore may be one way for our unconscious to draw our attention to them, possibly leading us to more conscious recognition of the conflicts and a gradual process of working through and resolving them.

Talbot remarks in *The Holographic Universe* that "the greater and more emotionally charged our beliefs, the greater the changes we can make in both our bodies and reality itself."[114] Emotion seems to be the energy that feeds psychokinetic phenomena, and more intense emotions produce more drastic changes in the physical world. Psychic policeman Pat Price, when interrogated about how he was able to achieve psychic access to a super-secret National Security Agency listening post, responded that "[t]he more intent you are on hiding something, the more it shines like a beacon in psychic space."[115] So it seems to be with emotions that we continually ignore. They don't go away, and when they build up enough energy, they can burst

---

[113] Joel L. Whitton and Joe Fisher, *Life Between Life: Scientific Explorations into the Void Separating One Incarnation from the Next* (New York: Warner Books, 1986), 171-9.
[114] Talbot, *Holographic Universe*, 138.
[115] Targ, *Reality of ESP*, 25.

unexpectedly onto the physical stage. PK-produced coincidences are a way for our emotions to take material form, a way for them to say, "Hey, I'm *real.* You can see and touch me. And I'm not going anywhere until you acknowledge my reality."

In addition to expressing unconscious feelings, self-created coincidences may also be capable of revealing unconscious thoughts about solutions to problems, or useful information we've unconsciously picked up about other people or our environment. For example, this may be the best way of explaining the GPS coincidence I recounted at the very beginning of this book. Recall that a smartphone I was using to locate grocery stores in Pennsylvania suddenly showed me a map of grocery stores in France, including one less than two miles from what I discovered a few days later to be the location of a dear friend of mine who was at that time much in my thoughts. When this incident occurred, I didn't think too much about the process that created it. It seemed clear to me that it indicated that my friend and I were still deeply connected, even after a few years of not being in contact. That in itself was immensely reassuring. I did wonder, though, especially after more coincidences related to this person began to pile up, whether he was trying to make some kind of mental contact with me. And, after a few weeks, I finally wrote to him and discovered that a dramatic, life-changing event had happened to him about 10 days after the GPS incident. It's not entirely clear to me the best way of classifying what happened with the GPS, but it seems at least plausible that it was a PK event produced by my unconscious, which was attempting to express the importance of my psychic bond with this person as well as my unconscious knowledge of his whereabouts and of important events about to unfold in his life. What is more, I may have unconsciously received telepathic information from this person, and it may have communicated itself to my conscious mind through this arresting coincidence.

Interestingly, the other ready example I have of a coincidence that seems to convey unconscious information also involves a GPS. Life coach Martha Beck tells about a time when she was in her car contemplating a state of deep oneness she'd previously experienced. Her GPS—which was turned off at the time—suddenly announced to her, "You have reached your destination."[116]

GPS devices seem to have a knack for representing our *spiritual* location as well as our physical one. After all, in my own GPS coincidence, the map ended up showing me, not the location where I was physically, but the location where I was *mentally*—in France, with my friend.

---

[116] Martha Beck, *Finding Your Way in a Wild New World: Reclaim Your True Nature to Create the Life You Want* (New York: Atria, 2012), 65.

I hope that these examples will make it clear that designating a coincidence as "self-created" is not writing it off as of little or no value. Rather, self-created coincidences can be a powerful avenue for communication from our unconscious. These communications can be very helpful—as my GPS incident was to me, ultimately promoting profound healing—especially if we are aware of their origin and that they can't always be taken at face value. Even the coincidences experienced by some of Kirby Surprise's patients, in which they were told that they were divine entities or victims of enormous conspiracies, could be viewed as expressing a desire to imbue their lives with more significance. Properly interpreted, perhaps with the help of a counselor like Surprise, these coincidences could lead to increased self-awareness and personal growth.

Coincidences Reflecting Conscious PK

But PK doesn't have to be limited to the expression of repressed feelings or unconscious knowledge. Some coincidences appear to be the result of PK that's directly fulfilling a conscious desire. In the examples given below, we can't entirely rule out the possible intervention of other agents, but, at the same time, there doesn't seem to be any particular reason to appeal to that hypothesis in these cases. These could very well be examples of coincidences created by the PK of the person experiencing them.

Writer Michael H. Brown was in high spirits one evening because of a series of striking coincidences he'd recently experienced. As he was driving home, he decided to wish for a particular song to come on the radio. (Note that this was 1975.) "I wished for the song 'The Boxer' by Simon and Garfunkel to come on," he says. It did. Encouraged by this unexpected success, Brown made a second request. And that one, too, was fulfilled.[117] When a person consciously sets their mind to producing coincidences in this fashion, and those coincidences then appear, it's hard not to see PK as the best explanation for them.

Another good example comes from Jenny Saunders, the woman who experienced the mysterious bloody splotches described in the last section. One evening, she was out on a date with a man who afterward insisted on coming back to her apartment "for a coffee," and then proceeded to importune her with his sexual advances. Whitton and Fisher recount,

> the thought flashed into her mind: "If only the time was much later, he would feel obliged to leave." As that thought took shape, all four clocks in the apartment, including Jenny's wristwatch, jumped ahead to show a time of 1:37 A.M. Her visitor promptly got up and left. Closing the door

---

[117] Vaughan, *Incredible Coincidence*, 144.

behind him, Jenny turned on the radio to establish the correct time. The 9:00 news was drawing to a close.[118]

You can perhaps see how someone who experienced such a coincidence might attribute it to God or to a guardian angel, perhaps even to a deceased relative watching over them. Another of the reasons *not* to do so in Saunders' case—besides the lack of any evidence identifying an unseen agent—is that Saunders had typical PK phenomena happen around her quite often. In addition to the bloody splotches already described, there is the case in which a friend called her and asked her to come visit, but Saunders, not wanting to go, started making excuses. When she hung up the phone, a lead crystal bud vase that this friend had given her suddenly "broke off at the stem, fell to the floor, and smashed to pieces,"[119] an unmistakable physical expression of Saunders' current feelings for the person who'd given it to her. When a person has a history of such blatant psychokinesis, PK has to be considered as a likely explanation for coincidences they encounter as well.

Psychic Matthew Manning also had a history of psychokinesis, which makes a PK explanation for the following experiences quite compelling. One day, he went to buy the Ringo Starr record "It Don't Come Easy" but couldn't find it in either of the two stores he visited. However, when he returned home, a brand-new copy of this record was sitting on his desk, and he was never able to figure out where it had come from. He was certain that no one else who shared that residence with him owned one.

Another time, Manning was collecting material for a bonfire, but the only things he could find in the yard were a few cardboard boxes. He went into the house to ask his mother what he could use, but she had no idea. When he went back out into the yard, next to the cardboard boxes he'd previously located, he found a stack of logs and other wood amounting to several hundred pounds, even though there was no one around, and certainly no one who could have brought in such a quantity of wood so quickly. On another occasion, Manning appears to have materialized a bottle of beer and an apple pie.[120] Dr. Whitton relates that he tested Manning's psychokinetic abilities in Toronto in 1974 with the help of Dr. A. R. George Owen,[121] and some details of these reports can be found in Manning's book *The Link*.

Let's conclude this section by examining an intriguing experience that happened to mountaineer Alan Burgess. He was climbing with his twin brother, Adrian, when one of Adrian's ropes got caught on a rock. When Adrian freed it, a chunk of the rock broke off, falling toward where Alan was

---

[118] Whitton and Fisher, 176.
[119] Whitton and Fisher, 176.
[120] Matthew Manning, *The Link: Matthew Manning's Own Story of His Extraordinary Psychic Gifts* (New York: Holt, Rinehart and Winston, 1974, 1975), 97-98.
[121] Whitton and Fisher, 178.

on belay below. Twenty feet above Alan, the rock hit the rock face and broke into smaller but still sizeable pieces. Alan saw a chunk of it coming at him and tried to flatten himself against the face of the mountain but knew it was still going to hit him on his helmet or his back. Yet it didn't. Instead, a moment later, he found the 12x8x8-inch rock sitting on top of his pack, which was next to him on the ledge. What was even more extraordinary was what his brother Adrian had witnessed from above. Adrian said that the rock looked like it was headed right at Alan when it suddenly stopped and floated to the right where it came to rest on his pack.

When Alan told people about this experience, many of them attributed his rescue to God or a guardian angel. Alan, however, believed that he himself was responsible for the effect. He had been practicing and teaching Ashtanga yoga for some years and told author Maria Coffey that "what happened was to do with my own energy." In fact, he believes that high-altitude climbers are often unconsciously practicing yogic breath control. "Anyone at high altitude, breathing concentratedly without oxygen, taps into a spiritual world," he said. "Maybe it was the gathering of all my hopes, fears, and whatever else was going around—I'll accept a guardian angel if that's what it was—so that for a millisecond something else played out."[122]

Interestingly, Alan and his twin brother appear to have a telepathic connection as well. There have been a couple of occasions on which Alan has had mountaineering accidents and been thought dead, but on both occasions, Adrian told people that he knew his brother was actually alive. And he turned out to be right.[123] In the next chapter, we'll look at further accounts of telepathic connections between twins, as well as other people.

Ambiguity of Source

Alan Burgess's falling rock case is a nice illustration of the ambiguity of many coincidences with regard to their source—a theme we are now going to discuss in some depth.

As further examples, take some of Paul Davids' experiences. You'll remember from Chapter 4 that Davids experienced a great many coincidences in the wake of the death of his friend Forrest J Ackerman. However, some of the experiences Davids relates in his book *An Atheist in Heaven* have nothing to do with Ackerman. One of the these is the Marilyn Monroe coincidence mentioned towards the end of Chapter 4, where an

---

[122] Maria Coffey, *Explorers of the Infinite: The Secret Spiritual Lives of Extreme Athletes—and What They Reveal about Near-Death Experiences, Psychic Communication, and Touching the Beyond* (New York: Jeremy P. Tarcher/Penguin, 2008), 238-40.

[123] Guy Lyon Playfair, *Twin Telepathy*, 3rd ed. rev. and enlarged (Guildford, UK: White Crow Books, 2012), 81-82.

image of Monroe anomalously appeared on his television screen after Davids had just been talking about the film he was making about her.

A very similar coincidence happened when Davids was editing footage of some testimony given by Sgt. Jack Clemmons regarding Monroe's death. Clemmons was "the first L.A. policeman to arrive officially at the scene" and the first person to say Marilyn's death was not suicide but murder. When Davids took a break from editing his footage and went into another room of his house, he suddenly found that the TV in that room had a picture of Clemmons on it as well. This image was from a show that was in the memory of a device hooked up to the television, but not only did Davids not think he'd left the TV on, but he knew for sure that he hadn't turned on the device that contained the memory of the show.[124] While Davids classifies this incident as a "nudge from Marilyn," I don't think we can entirely rule out the possibility that Davids' own PK created this coincidence (and perhaps the one with the image of Marilyn Monroe as well), especially because outside observers such as Jack Kelleher have called Davids a "lightning rod" for such coincidences.[125]

Another excellent example of ambiguity surrounding the source of a coincidence comes from Kirby Surprise. In fact, I find the following to be Surprise's most fascinating coincidence of all. One day, he was sitting in his car waiting for someone when he heard a radio ad for the movie *Carrie*. This got him thinking about what it would be like to be able to crush a house with the power of one's mind, the way Carrie does in the movie. He remembered, too, seeing a *National Enquirer* headline about a house that was supposedly tipped over by some psychic power. Seeing an old house across the street from him, Surprise started wondering what it would feel like to move a house like that one with his mind. While he was staring at this house, it started to shudder, and then it *actually rolled over* so that he was now looking at its roof. After a moment of panic and internal reality checking, he said to himself, "If I just did that, then I want to see the house crushed like in the movie." Sure enough, the house began to implode. Not long after, a huge yellow bulldozer crawled over the top of the house and began tearing apart what was left of it, in what was now obviously a planned demolition.[126]

This incident typifies what is so stunning and mystifying about the way coincidences can appear to respond directly to our thoughts without doing anything that blatantly defies the known laws of physics. The concordance of Surprise's thoughts and the demolition of the house is too exact to be random. The statistical method outlined in Chapter 1 can be used to confirm the huge odds against this coincidence's occurring by chance. So clearly there

---

[124] Paul Davids and Gary E. Schwartz with John Allison, *An Atheist in Heaven: The Ultimate Evidence for Life after Death?* (Reno, NV: Yellow Hat, 2016), 329.
[125] Davids and Schwartz with Allison, 164.
[126] Surprise, 13-14.

is *something* psychic going on here. But it is stunningly impressive the way that the psychic linkage occurs through a series of events that have normal, everyday physical causes. How is it that impressive concordances between our thoughts and the material world can happen *at the same time* that the material world seems to obey purely physical laws?

Determining the precise mechanism by which this coincidence was produced is difficult, if not impossible. This coincidence resembles in some ways the coincidences we explained by precognition earlier in this chapter, but in this case, it doesn't seem like unconscious precognition of the fact that he's about to see the house demolished can entirely explain Surprise's thought that this is something he would like to see, because his thought was directly provoked by the radio advertisement he'd just heard for the movie *Carrie*. Could it have been that the radio advertisement was itself caused by the fact that Surprise was about to see a house demolished in a *Carrie*-esque way? Perhaps. But what accounts for the fact that, the one time in Surprise's life when he is perfectly positioned to observe a house appear to implode of its own accord, it also happens to be during the presumably few-week span in which the movie *Carrie* is being advertised? These two events lined up perfectly, and then Surprise arrived right in the middle of them and made a wish precisely appropriate to the spectacle he was about to witness. Was Surprise's wish the catalyst for this event—sending PK ripples backwards in time to set up the demolition of the house? Or did some source outside of him set up the event ahead of time and then plant the wish in his mind? Could Surprise somehow have been influenced to be in the right place at the right time? Yet he says he was there on that day because he was waiting to pick up a friend. Was the *friend* somehow influenced to ask him to be there at that time and put him in position to hear the radio advertisement, form a corresponding wish, and then observe the coincidence?

I don't think we can decide this question with any degree of certainty. Ambiguous cases like this will form the heart of our discussion in Chapter 10, "The Universe," because of the way they suggest that agency may not ultimately be attributable to one party or another. For now, I would simply offer Surprise's bulldozer coincidence as a case in which the experiencer's own PK seems as good an explanation as any other that appeals to a unique agent, precisely because Surprise had in his mind the exact experience he wanted to have, and then he subsequently *did* have it.

I now want to turn to some ambiguous experiences had by Andrew Paquette. After his die-rolling incident described in Chapter 1, this next experience is probably his most mind-boggling in its sheer improbability.

Paquette is a professional artist, among other things, and in 1990 he was hired by *The Atlantic Monthly* to do an illustration. Unfortunately, just before the issue went to press, Paquette was notified that he'd made a significant error in specifying the darkness of one of the colors, which he attempted to rectify over the phone. However, after hanging up, he realized that the only way the issue could be adequately addressed would be for him to see the artwork in person. He knew that the issue in which the illustration was to appear was being shipped that afternoon from Boston to the printer in Wisconsin, and all he could think was that it somehow needed to get rerouted to him so that he could correct the problem. He paced his living room, telling his wife over and over that this was the only option. "It has to show up here tomorrow," he said.

Paquette was awakened the following morning by a delivery man from Airborne Express who had an unmarked package for him. Suspicious, Paquette asked him where the air bill was, but the man didn't know. He just said that his supervisor had told him to bring the box to this address. When Paquette opened it, he found "every article, every original photo, every original slide, and every piece of original illustration art" for the forthcoming issue of *The Atlantic Monthly*, including the illustration he'd so desperately wanted to get his hands on. He discovered that, in fact, he hadn't made an error in his original specification of the coloring; his handwriting had just been misread. However, if he hadn't gotten to look at the artwork, the "fix" he had made over the telephone would indeed have ruined the illustration. When Paquette notified his contact at the magazine that he was in possession of the box containing that month's issue, he asked her if she knew whether the entire content of an issue had ever been misdirected like this before. "Never," she said. "Not in eighty years of publishing."[127]

This is only one of many experiences had by Paquette that look a lot like classic cases of PK, and the hypothesis of PK is one that he himself seriously considers. Yet he confides that this hypothesis doesn't seem to fit all aspects of his experiences. In particular, it doesn't seem to match the way in which they present themselves to him. For instance, consider the example from Chapter 1 in which Paquette and his wife rolled matching descending doubles from six to two. Paquette observes, "An odd thing about this incident is that it literally felt like someone else had softly made a kind of mental offer to me: 'Say this, and it will happen.'" He also notes how carefully chosen the predicted event seemed to be. After all, the source of the prediction, whatever it was, could have predicted some other 24-roll sequence that would have been a lot harder for Paquette to remember than "matching descending doubles." There appeared to him to be something poetic about how concisely the sequence was able to be described, which also contributed to his conclusion that this experience was not a result of psychokinesis. "If anything," he says, "the dice were controlled by another agent, most probably the one that made the suggestion. The symmetry of the rolls, if nothing else, look[s] anything but natural and that indicates some

---

[127] Paquette, *Dreamer*, 133-6.

conscious control, but by whom is a mystery." Paquette mentions that he has only made a prediction of this kind on two other occasions. On those two occasions, the predictions likewise seemed to have been "dropped" into his head, and they came true in a similar way. Further details of those events can be found in his book.[128]

Paquette also reports a case of telephone telepathy about which he had similar feelings of external suggestion. Out of the blue one day, he had the thought that he should call an art director from Houghton/Mifflin Books, Sara Eisenman, and give her his new address. It had been almost two years since he'd last spoken with her. When she answered his call, he identified himself and stated that he was calling with his new phone number and address. Eisenman was so surprised that she dropped the phone. When she recovered from her shock, she explained to Paquette that she'd just been on the phone with another art director who'd called her to ask about Paquette's new phone number. She'd told the other woman that she didn't have it but that, if he happened to call, she'd let her know. "I was still holding the phone when you called!" Eisenman told Paquette. "I had literally just put it in the cradle to hang up, but still had my hand on it when it rang again and it was you!"

Paquette explains that he originally thought of this case as a simple case of telepathy. However, at some later point, he realized that this wasn't how the information presented itself to him. He says it was more like someone asked him a question. Although it wasn't in words exactly, it resembled the idea, "Why don't you call Sara Eisenman?" And when he hesitated, it insisted. "In retrospect," he says, "it felt very much as if the suggestion to call Sara did not come from Sara directly or from me casually picking up on her interest in me, but from a third party."[129]

Paquette is right to carefully record the phenomenology of his experiences, so that it can be studied and compared to that experienced by others. I think we have to take seriously Paquette's perception of his own experiences, and I don't want to minimize the importance of firsthand perceptions and intuitions, because, in many cases, they can be our most helpful clues. At the same time, the mere fact that these predictions/ suggestions *feel* like they're coming from outside Paquette is not proof that this is the case. We have to consider the possibility that they could be coming from his unconscious—an unconscious that has psychic foreknowledge of events about to unfold. After all, our unconscious is different enough from the conscious mind that it could make sense for us to experience it as "other" than ourselves, even if it's intimately linked to our personal emotions and

---

[128] Paquette, *Dreamer*, 24-26.
[129] Paquette, *Dreamer*, 27-28.

desires. We'll examine this possibility further in the sub-section "The Higher Self" below.

For now, let's look at another of Paquette's PK-ish experiences. In this case, Paquette and his wife were in the back room of an art gallery looking at a painting that the gallery director had placed on a shelf for them. The shelf had a lip on it, and the painting was leaning back about six inches—clearly stable. Kitty was standing about three feet in front of the painting, and Paquette about four, when he asked her if she liked it. She said she did, and he replied, "Then I think you should have it." Paquette says,

> I saw a blur to my right as Kitty gasped and then was suddenly holding the painting in her arms. Ethan [the gallery director] also gasped, possibly louder than Kitty. His first words were, "It looked like a ghost picked it up and dropped it on her!" Kitty said, "It just jumped on me! If I hadn't caught it, it would have fallen on the floor!"[130]

Paquette believes it's reasonable to conclude that there was a connection between his comment that his wife ought to have the painting and its movement, which occurred precisely as he finished speaking. He also notes that this incident, like others he's experienced, implies that someone is listening to him and reacting to his stated desires, though he points out that, at least in this case, the reaction appears a bit childish.

I would agree with Paquette that this incident doesn't have the elegance one might expect if it were the direct work of God, or even of an experienced angel or spirit guide. It appears somewhat prankish, not unlike the work of a poltergeist. Paquette has chosen to call the unknown intelligence behind such incidents a *servo spiritus*, or "watching spirit."[131] It's unclear whether he thinks this *servo spiritus* might be a part of his own unconscious, but I don't think the evidence will allow us to rule that out.

One final incident that deserves mention is one in which Paquette burned himself on the fuser roller of a photocopier. A painful blister began to swell on his hand, and neither ice nor cold water seemed to help. After a few minutes, Paquette said aloud, "If there is anything to this psychic healing business, then heal this wound now." He reports that, "[w]ithin twenty or thirty seconds, as I watched, the blister reduced in size until it was completely gone. It was like watching a movie in reverse."[132]

Paquette says that similar events continue to happen to him, all following the pattern in which he makes a request and it's granted. He acknowledges that this can seem a lot like answers to prayer, although he says he wasn't praying in the way that term is normally meant. But he suspects

---

130 Paquette, *Dreamer*, 141.

131 Paquette, *Dreamer*, 142.

132 Paquette, *Dreamer*, 144.

that "something more" is going on. What does he mean by "something more"? Perhaps he means a phenomenon that, presumably unlike God, is amenable to further study and an increase in our understanding of it. What seems relatively clear, I'd say, is that what's going on is not a mere mechanical force of nature, but it's also not as refined or omnipotent as a deity. Some intermediate form of semi-intelligent, semi-intentional action appears to exist, connected to our thoughts and desires but carrying some autonomy from them as well.

Poltergeist Phenomena, Take Two

Now that we're deep into the ambiguity of identifying the invisible agents of coincidences—as well as the agents of blatantly psychokinetic phenomena—I want to offer some refinement to our previous discussion of poltergeists. Although my primary aim in this chapter has been to show how capable we are of producing our own coincidences, I don't want anyone to leave this chapter thinking that I don't take seriously any other explanation for poltergeist phenomena (or coincidences).

After all, some writers do imply that poltergeist phenomena are *all* explicable in terms of the PK of a living agent. Not long before his death, renowned paranormal writer Colin Wilson confessed that he himself was once of this opinion. He writes, "I still wince when I recall assuring a girl...that the poltergeist who kept setting alight her clothes in a wardrobe was caused by her own unconscious mind."[133] Dr. James C. Carpenter, author of the First Sight theory of the mechanism behind ESP and PK, mentions witnessing "a poltergeist agent who is terrified of being hurt by flying objects and wishes them to stop at the same moment that something hits her in the head from behind,"[134] but, as happened with the young Colin Wilson, this doesn't appear to have made Carpenter doubt the psychokinetic origin of the incident. Perhaps Carpenter is right that this experiencer had some unconscious motive for producing the phenomena—I don't have enough details about the case in question to come to an informed opinion of my own—but I think it would be wise not to assume that she *must* have had some unconscious motive. That would be as counterproductive as telling all medical patients that their symptoms are "all in their head" and never considering that some other hypotheses might need to be explored. Does psychosomatic illness exist? Yes. Is all illness psychosomatic? Probably not. I believe the same goes for poltergeist phenomena created by living agent PK.

Against those who think that all poltergeist phenomena must be created by living persons, we can set Dr. Alan Gauld and Tony Cornell, whose

---

[133] Colin Wilson, introduction to *Twin Telepathy* by Playfair, xvi.

[134] Carpenter, 95.

extensive experience investigating poltergeist cases left them open to the idea that some physical phenomena were due to the influence of discarnate entities.[135] We can also mention esteemed parapsychologist Dr. Ian Stevenson, who was particularly inclined to accept the discarnate explanation for a certain class of cases: ones in which objects abruptly changed their motion in midair. Stevenson cites the example of an Indian woman, Radhika, who had a reputation as a sorceress and, in particular, for spiriting food out of others' houses and into her own. Hindu monk Swami Krishnanand reported to Ian Stevenson that he once had contact with Radhika and requested that she demonstrate her powers to him in exchange for a healing treatment she desired. They were standing outside his hut, and Krishnanand knew that some women were preparing puran puris in a neighboring house about 100 feet away, so he asked Radhika to bring him some of them. After she muttered some words, two puran puris flew over the six-foot wall surrounding Krishnanand's hut and then slowly descended to the ground before him. Krishnanand then asked her to do the same thing again while they were inside his hut, and the puran puris arrived as before, though this time they not only had to go over the wall but also through the low open door of the hut. Krishnanand then asked Radhika to make the puran puris levitate there in front of them. The bread began jumping around in the basket. Finally, Krishnanand requested that Radhika fill a vessel with milk from where a man was milking a cow some ways from them. The vessel filled instantly, and the man milking his cow appeared astonished that some of his milk had suddenly disappeared.[136]

Now Stevenson does not say in his analysis of this case that the displacement of these objects *must* be the work of a discarnate spirit rather than the psychic abilities of Radhika herself. Though Krishnanand says that Radhika always began her feats by muttering some words that appeared to be instructions to a spirit, these might have just been for dramatic effect.[137] However, Stevenson uses this case as an illustration of the sorts of cases that ought to be increasingly collected and compared in the interests of determining if noticeable differences might emerge between two broad categories: cases in which a human being seems to be psychically responsible and cases in which some discarnate entity seems to be. He presents a list of 13 dimensions along which he conjectures the two types of psychokinetic activity might differ and summarizes the contrast between them as something like the contrast between the movement produced by a tornado and that produced by a carefully designed and regulated pneumatic tube system.[138] He

[135] Alan Gauld and A. D. Cornell, *Poltergeists* (London: Routledge & Kegan Paul, 1979).
[136] Ian Stevenson, "Are Poltergeists Living or Are They Dead?", 242-3.
[137] Ian Stevenson, "Are Poltergeists Living or Are They Dead?", 247.
[138] Ian Stevenson, "Are Poltergeists Living or Are They Dead?", 249.

acknowledges that it's not impossible that human PK could act in such a careful, discriminating way but says it seems to him less probable.

In sum, there are several characteristics that appear in poltergeist activity—among others, malevolence, foreignness to any perceived motives of living persons involved, and the carefully discriminating way in which objects are moved—that give us reason to keep an open mind about what explains the activity in any particular case. I think that, just as we must keep our minds open to the possibility that we create our own coincidences, we must keep them open to the possibility that other minds may create them as well. In Chapter 8, we will examine evidence that distressing physical phenomena can indeed be created by other minds—living or dead—who wish us harm. With such a variety of explanations possible, we must be willing to examine the specific characteristics of each case before drawing any firm conclusions about its source.

The Higher Self

Before we leave the topic of self-produced coincidences, however, we also need to address the idea of the "higher self." We've discussed the possibility that we might unconsciously be the cause of some of our own coincidences, and it's important to note that, while in the Freudian tradition the unconscious has gotten a reputation for being inferior to the conscious mind, there is much evidence for an unconscious part of ourselves that is *more* intelligent and knowledgeable than our conscious mind. The New Age movement has popularized this notion as the "Higher Self," but the idea of a wiser portion of us residing in the unconscious is by no means new. See, for instance, the description of 19th-century psychologist and philosopher William James, who wrote that the individual "becomes conscious that this higher part [of the self] is conterminous and continuous with a MORE of the same quality, which is operative in the universe outside him, and which he can keep in working touch with, and in a fashion get on board of and save himself when all his lower being has gone to pieces in the wreck."[139]

One nice illustration of the multi-faceted nature of our consciousness comes from some hypnosis experiments conducted by Dr. Ernest Hilgard and discussed in his book *Divided Consciousness: Multiple Controls in Human Thought and Action.* When subjects were hypnotized not to feel the pain of putting their hand and forearm in ice water, for example, or hypnotized to be deaf, they reported not feeling pain and not hearing anything, respectively. However, Hilgard was able to ask questions of a "hidden observer" who *did* acknowledge feeling pain and hearing things. One of Hilgard's hypnotic

---

[139] William James, *The Varieties of Religious Experience*, in *Writings 1902-1920*, ed. Bruce Kuklick, The Library of America (New York: Literary Classics of the United States, 1987), 454.

subjects said, "The hidden observer was an extra, all-knowing part of me.... The hidden part knows the hypnotized part, but the hypnotized part does not know the hidden one."[140] Could it be that, in everyday waking life, we are actually something like Hilgard's hypnotic subjects—that we are only consciously aware of a certain portion of our overall perceptions and thoughts? Is it possible that, outside the bounds of the perceptions and thoughts we can readily access, there nevertheless lies a part of us that *is* aware of it all?

Robert Waggoner draws a parallel between Hilgard's hidden observer and a consciousness that Waggoner has observed lurking behind his lucid dreams. A lucid dream is one in which the dreamer realizes they're dreaming and so can interact with the dream world more intentionally. Waggoner discovered that asking questions within the lucid dream world often returned very unexpected results. For instance, he once asked a figure in a dream what that figure represented, and instead of the dream figure answering, a voice from somewhere above Waggoner boomed out, "The acquired characteristics!" Then, when asked for more detail, the voice said, "The acquired characteristics of the happy giver!"[141] Waggoner was able to provoke many interesting and sometimes highly enlightening experiences by engaging this consciousness behind the dream. It's his belief that this "inner observer" is not identical with any individual dream figure but is nevertheless present behind the scenes in all lucid dreams and only becomes apparent when addressed in some manner.[142]

The experiences of Hilgard's hypnosis subjects and of lucid dreamers like Waggoner have another parallel in the experiences of the Rt. Hon. Sir Auckland Geddes, who had multiple near-death experiences in the early to mid-1900s. In the first, he received metaphysical information from a source he called his "Mentor," though he confessed he didn't know what this source was. In a later NDE, he asked a question of his "Mentor," referring to him by this name, and he was told, "There is no 'Mentor.' You yourself created him as a device to explain your own understandings."[143] It seems possible, then, that some people may confuse their own higher understanding with an independent entity such as a spirit guide.

I have also heard this higher understanding referred to as "the Wise One": for example, by Armando Vettorazzo, a man who underwent regression therapy with Brazilian psychologist Renate Jost de Moraes. Vettorazzo says, "The Wise One is an imaginary figure that supposedly

---

[140] Ernest Hilgard, *Divided Consciousness: Multiple Controls in Human Thought and Action* (New York: John Wiley & Sons, 1977), 209-10.

[141] Waggoner, 52.

[142] Waggoner, 95.

[143] Playfair, 103.

knows the contents of the unconscious and acts as a device to facilitate access to it."[144]

In fact, some people's experiences suggest that access to the hidden, higher self might be available to us within our ordinary (non-dreaming, non-hypnotized) state of consciousness. Waggoner, for example, while still a pre-teen, had experiences of interacting with an "inner advisor" while in a waking state. "At certain times," he says,

> when I considered things deeply, an inner knowing appeared in my mind. It was such a natural thing, I assumed everyone experienced this. It was like having the services of a wise old man inside. For example, after a very simple incident that most anyone would ignore, the inner knowing would make an observation about life or suggest the prosaic incident as a living parable. The comments seemed intelligent, even remarkable. I began to sense that all around me life had meaning, if I only cared to look.[145]

I should also mention that some people have the distinct impression of interacting with their own future (and past) selves. Robert Moss is one of them. While Moss says that sometimes his past and future selves simply "sent each other mental texts"[146] (an experience that sounds like it might resemble Waggoner's experience of his "inner advisor"), Moss also remembers as a young, sickly boy enjoying the comforting bedside visits of someone he called the "Big Man," who was apparently invisible to others. Though his childhood self couldn't have known it at the time, this man bore a striking physical resemblance to Moss's future self, with a big pink face, abundant white hair, and "slightly hooded" blue-gray eyes. He let the young Moss know that he would make it through his long period of illness and inspired him to begin doing the things that would become his life's work.[147]

Because our future selves are generally more knowledgeable and experienced than our present selves, one can see how they could be mistaken for a metaphysically "higher" self, or even for a different person altogether. You may recall from Chapter 3 the out-of-body experiencer Robert Monroe, who interacted over a long period of time with a being he called an INSPEC, for "intelligent species." Much later, he discovered that his INSPEC friend was his future self come back to help him.[148] As noted in Chapter 3, Monroe also had conversations with other beings who said they were aspects of himself and acknowledged intervening in his physical life from time to time, twice

---

[144] Elisabeth Hallett, *Stories of the Unborn Soul: The Mystery and Delight of Pre-Birth Communication* (San Jose: Writers Club Press, 2002), 34.
[145] Waggoner, 5.
[146] Robert Moss, *The Boy Who Died and Came Back: Adventures of a Dream Archaeologist in the Multiverse* (Novato, CA: New World Library, 2014), 8.
[147] Moss, *The Boy Who Died*, 36-37.
[148] Robert A. Monroe, *Ultimate Journey* (New York: Harmony, 1994), 197-8.

protecting him from drowning and once helping him avoid a car accident.[149] It seems we might need to take seriously the idea that our future selves could cause some of the coincidences happening to us today.

The Boundaries of Personal Identity

As my final comment before closing this chapter, I want to point out that the boundaries of personal identity may not only be difficult to define but may not even exist. That is, there may be no objective dividing line between my unconscious and yours, or between the consciousness of my "higher self" and that of a spirit guide or even of God. Annie Mattingley, who reports having had extensive conversations with her deceased daughter, Randi, once told Randi that she was worried that their "conversation" was just her talking to herself. Randi replied to her, "It is. On the soul level you and I are seamless, as we all are, so this contact is from the 'I and I' as the Rastafarians say, the many I's where we are the one I."[150] Perhaps, in the end, we all shade into one another.

In Chapter 10, "The Universe," we will discuss at length the idea of collective consciousness. But before we can usefully embark on that discussion, we need to explore the more obvious ways in which other living people can contribute to the coincidences we experience.

---

[149] Monroe, *Ultimate Journey*, 168-9.

[150] Annie Mattingley, *The After Death Chronicles: True Stories of Comfort, Guidance, and Wisdom from the Beyond* (Charlottesville, VA: Hampton Roads, 2017), 52.

Chapter 7

Other Living Agents

In the previous chapter, we saw that we each have ESP and PK abilities that could allow us to create some of the coincidences we experience. What we haven't yet explicitly considered, however, is that the psychic abilities of *other* people could make them capable of creating coincidences for *us*. What if, like the deceased persons discussed in Chapter 4, people who are still alive could communicate messages to us through playing meaningful songs on the radio, flashing lights in our house, or sending butterflies to give us a nudge? In this chapter, we'll see evidential examples of all these phenomena and more.

However, we're going to start by looking at some more direct examples of telepathy, cases in which two minds manage to communicate without producing intermediate effects on the physical world. This discussion of direct telepathy will give us some important context regarding the situations in which people are most likely to resort to psychic communication with each other, as well as the strengths and weaknesses of this mode of communication. We'll see as well some cases in which direct telepathy can result in the production of coincidences: for instance, fortuitous meetings.

Let me start by stating quite matter-of-factly that telepathy exists. The wealth of scientific research that's been done on this topic over the last century and a half makes this abundantly clear. If you're interested in an overview of controlled scientific studies of telepathy, you'll find an excellent one in Chapter 10 of Dean Radin's 2013 book *Supernormal*[1] and another

[1] Dean Radin, *Supernormal: Science, Yoga, and the Evidence for Extraordinary Abilities* (New York: Deepak Chopra Books, 2013).

excellent compendium of systematic investigation of the phenomenon in Rupert Sheldrake's 2003 book *The Sense of Being Stared At.*[2] Here I am going to focus on presenting you with a variety of spontaneous cases of telepathy that should not only make the reality of the phenomenon overwhelmingly clear but also give you a feel for the diverse ways in which it manifests.

Telepathy in Dreams

As with other forms of ESP, we seem most receptive to telepathy within dreams. We probably all have at least one example of a time we dreamt something about someone else that then turned out to be true. Sometimes these telepathic dreams can be about ordinary, everyday events that don't seem particularly significant. The most memorable telepathic dreams, however, are those that relate to crises in people's lives and, in particular, death.

For example, Deborah K. of Pennsylvania was asleep in the hospital when she awoke with a start at 2:10am. She had been dreaming, and all she could remember of her dream was the sudden, violent impact at the end, in which it was like her head had gone through a plate-glass window and someone had thrown a bunch of red paint at her face. She had also heard an unidentifiable voice scream out her name just before she woke up. The next morning, Deborah's husband and son came to the hospital to tell her that her brother had died that night in a head-on car accident that had sent him through the windshield. He had been pronounced dead at 2:15 that morning.[3]

There are many other examples of people dreaming about the last moments of their loved ones' lives. Sometimes the dreams are very literal, as Deborah's was, and other times they are more symbolic, as in the case of a son who repeatedly dreamed of his father falling off a cliff until one night in his dream he saw his father hit the ground. On that morning, his father died unexpectedly.[4]

Another literal telepathic dream comes from a child who dreamed of being a rabbit. The child could feel the rabbit's fear and its strong legs pumping as it ran for its life past a white picket fence. The next morning, the child's father mentioned that there was a partially eaten rabbit by their

---

[2] Rupert Sheldrake, *The Sense of Being Stared At and Other Aspects of the Extended Mind* (New York: Crown Publishers, 2003).

[3] David Ryback with Letitia Sweitzer, *Dreams That Come True: Their Psychic and Transforming Powers* (New York: Doubleday, 1988), 46-47.

[4] Victor Mansfield, *Synchronicity, Science, and Soul-Making* (Chicago: Open Court, 1995), 204-6.

basement window. Directly in line with that window was a white picket fence.[5]

Consider, too, the case of a devout Catholic woman named Kate who, about a year after she got married, began to have worrisome dreams about a man named Joe whom she'd loved 20 years before and for whose spiritual life she had been praying every day for the past two decades. Over the course of some weeks, Kate's dreams of Joe got more frequent and distressing, until on June 28 she woke up shaking after a dream in which she saw him surrounded by medical personnel. A few days after that, on July 2, she had a "night vision" in which Joe came into her kitchen and told her that he'd died and had a Christian burial. He took her hand, and they went to a funeral parlor where he showed her "a bronze casket, velvet-lined, all tufted inside." Lying in it was a man "in a dark blue suit, white shirt, maroon, blue, and silver tie." Kate didn't recognize the man, but Joe told her it was himself. "*I really am dead*," he said, "but I couldn't go without letting you know your prayers were not in vain. And I wanted to tell you I love you very much." He kissed her, then "faded away."

The next morning, Kate called a mutual friend and discovered that Joe had been in a coma since May 6, the night of her very first dream. He'd died on June 28, the night when she'd had the particularly distressing dream of him surrounded by medical personnel, and his burial took place that morning. Kate later told Joe's sister about her vision of Joe in a casket, and his sister confirmed all the details she'd noticed, including the fact that Joe had been physically unrecognizable after the coma and autopsy.[6]

While Kate's final "vision" would fit more in the category of communication from the deceased, her earlier dreams of Joe happened while he was still alive in body, and they show the power of a strong relationship to produce telepathic communication even after a separation of many years. This case also shows an important continuity—as well as some contrast, perhaps—between telepathy from the living and from the dead.

Let's turn now to some less life-and-death examples of telepathy. Because of the careful attention given to dreams in the process of psychotherapy, therapists are well placed to witness their telepathic content. Freudian psychoanalyst Dr. Geraldine Pederson-Krag reported in her 1947 article "Telepathy and Repression" on the way many of her patients' dreams reflected unconscious knowledge of her own private life. For instance, a man she was treating told her about a dream in which he was a bit mad because he took his girlfriend out to dinner and she ate "about seven dollars' worth of food," while his meal cost only two dollars. As it happened, on the night of the patient's dream, Pederson-Krag had gone out to dinner with her

---

[5] Ryback with Sweitzer, 47-48.

[6] Ryback with Sweitzer, 78-79.

children and a male colleague. The colleague wanted to pay for everyone, but Pederson-Krag "insisted on paying my share which came to a little over six dollars and his was only two dollars. I disliked the situation because of certain implications...." Pederson-Krag observed that her patients' telepathic dreams seemed to occur when she herself was repressing an unpleasant emotion that matched something being repressed by the patient.[7]

Therapy patients also seem to dream about *each other's* lives, even when they've never met. For instance, psychiatrist Dr. Jule Eisenbud reports that a patient of his told him about a dream that associated sexual impotence with inedible, stolen corn. When Eisenbud described this dream to a different patient, the second patient "was able to break through a long-standing block by remembering a repressed episode that involved unedible [*sic*] stolen corn and her first husband's impotence."[8]

If people are so good at telepathy in their dreams, wouldn't it make sense if people sometimes had the *same dream*? In fact, mutual dreaming does exist, and I have collected several interesting cases of it. In his book *Twin Telepathy*, Guy Lyon Playfair relates the story of a pair of seven-year-old twin girls who often dreamed the same dreams. For instance, one morning, one of the girls described to their mother a dream where she got on a bus full of dead people but couldn't buy a ticket so she got off and went to the park where some boys chased her. A little while later, the other twin, who had not been in the room when the first girl described her dream, separately related to her mother a dream with the same series of events. The girls also told Playfair about a dream they'd both had in which an owl was in their room staring at them. He asked them if they always had the same dreams, and the girls immediately replied, in unison, "Yes!"[9]

We'll explore more cases of telepathy between twins later in this chapter, but right now let's look at some cases of mutual dreaming that involve people who don't have a biological relationship. For instance, an adult woman reported to Dr. David Ryback that her friend Linda sometimes has nightmares that interfere with her own dreams and lead to her waking up. She says she's able to identify the content as coming from Linda and wishes Linda had a phone so she could call her and wake her out of the dreams that are disturbing her own sleep![10]

---

[7] Geraldine Pederson-Krag, "Telepathy and Repression," *Psychoanalytic Quarterly* 16 (January 1947): 61-68.

[8] Montague Ullman and Stanley Krippner with Alan Vaughan, *Dream Telepathy: Experiments in Nocturnal ESP* (Baltimore, MD: Penguin, 1973), 40. Eisenbud's account can be found in Jule Eisenbud, *Psi and Psychoanalysis* (New York: Grune & Stratton, 1970).

[9] Guy Lyon Playfair, *Twin Telepathy*, 3rd ed. rev. and enlarged (Guildford, UK: White Crow Books, 2012), 41-42.

[10] Ryback with Sweitzer, 51.

Dream researcher Dr. Robert L. Van de Castle was conducting an informal experiment in dream telepathy by way of asking readers of the *Dream Network Bulletin* to send him their dreams from a particular night. He was trying to see whether anyone would have dreams matching a secret target photograph. While a woman named Claudia B. did have a dream with interesting similarities to the target, even more striking were the similarities between her dreams and the dreams Van de Castle himself had on that night. In particular, they both had dreams in which they found themselves on a boat cutting into a fish whose head turned into that of a person. As Van de Castle notes, "The odds against two complete strangers on the same night, geographically separated by 500 miles, dreaming of being on a boat cutting open a fish and having the face of the fish turn into a bloody man's face are astronomical…."[11]

As I've related in previous chapters, author Robert Waggoner has frequent lucid dreams—dreams in which he realizes he's dreaming. In one such dream, Waggoner saw his friend Moe and tried to help her realize that they were dreaming. As a last-ditch effort, he made a peace sign with his fingers and put it right in front of her face, telling her that she could use this sign to become aware of when she's in a dream. Four months later, Waggoner saw his friend Moe in waking life when they arranged to meet for lunch. She walked up and put a peace sign right in his face. When he asked her why she did this, she shrugged it off, saying she'd just felt like it.[12] Whether Moe was actually "present" in Waggoner's dream or not, the gesture he made in his own dream does seem to have been transmitted to her in some fashion.

Here's another case of Waggoner's in which both parties clearly remember their mutual dreams. During college, Waggoner dreamt that he went to the dorm suite of five young women who were his (non-romantic) friends and went into each of their rooms, successively making love to each one of them. The next morning, another resident of their dorm hailed Waggoner on campus and said she'd heard he'd been quite the Romeo the previous night. She'd heard that both Nadine and Sheila had dreamt he'd made love to them in their dorm rooms that night![13]

This next case shows the potential of mutual dreaming for clear telepathic communication over a long distance. The prolonged physical separation of the parties involved is also reminiscent of the case of Kate and Joe above. This similarity between the two cases suggests that long physical separation between two parties with a deep attachment to one another may be particularly conducive to telepathic communication.

---

[11] Robert L. Van de Castle, "Exogenous dream continuity: Exploring the matrix of entangled dreams," *International Journal of Dream Research* 5, no. 1 (2012): 9-16, p. 13.
[12] Robert Waggoner, *Lucid Dreaming: Gateway to the Inner Self* (Needham, MA: Moment Point Press, 2009), 182-3.
[13] Waggoner, 207-8.

In this case, Fariba Bogzaran was intentionally attempting to dream about visiting an old friend she hadn't seen in almost two decades, due to their now living in different countries. Here's her account of a dream that resulted from this intention.

> I am walking in my old neighborhood where I grew up. Suddenly I ask myself "how did I get here?" I do not remember taking a plane. At that point I become lucid. I continue walking and have a strong intention to see Yalda my old childhood friend. [This friend had moved, and Bogzaran had never been to her new house.] I find the street where she lives and walk towards her house. The color of the door is pale blue. I ring the bell and she opens the door. I am overjoyed to see her. We cry and hug each other with overwhelming emotion. Embracing her feels absolutely real. The intensity of the experience wakes me up.[14]

The next morning, Bogzaran wrote a letter to Yalda with a detailed description of this dream, including the location at which she'd found her friend's home. *On the very same day*, her friend also wrote *her* a letter, describing the same dream, with the same scene at the front door. It arrived a week later.

Our next case is not a mutual dream, because one of the parties is awake, but it demonstrates the interesting fact that telepathic communication is not always instantaneous. In fact, more than one researcher has noted the tendency of telepathic information to "wait around" until we are available to dream about it. At times, our minds may be so full of other matters that it takes us a few nights before our dreams are able to integrate the telepathic information.

In this case, the dreamer, Andrew Paquette, didn't realize that anything telepathic had happened until his friend Lisa asked him one day if he'd dreamt of her recently. She wouldn't say why she was asking. Since Paquette kept a detailed dream journal, he was able to go back and read out to her a summary of a dream he'd had a couple of weeks previously. The dream took place in a bright room with hard, shiny surfaces, into which a man brought a stainless-steel platter carrying a bloody mess of an animal (or possibly two animals) not more than 18 inches long. Through a pair of windows, Paquette saw two girls looking in, one of whom was Lisa, and she was crying. Another woman entered the room with a knife and proceeded to cut the animal's head off its body. Paquette wanted to comfort Lisa but woke up.

Paquette thought the dream was a typical nonsensical "junk" dream, but Lisa thought differently. She told him that, three nights before he had the dream, her cat was run over by a car, partially decapitating it. She took the cat to the vet who attempted surgery on it. Unfortunately, the vet accidentally

---

[14] Stanley Krippner, Fariba Bogzaran, and André Percia de Carvalho, *Extraordinary Dreams and How to Work with Them* (Albany: State University of New York Press, 2002), 91.

cut its head the rest of the way off, killing it. What was more, the night after her cat's death, Lisa had thought about Paquette, thinking he might be able to console her in some way. She called out to him in her head. And then she *saw* him. According to Lisa, he appeared in her room, telling her the cat would be okay and that this would be for the best. Two days later, Paquette dreamt of the cat's fatal surgery, and the dream ended with his feeling an urge to comfort his friend.[15]

Telepathy by Apparition

In the case just described, telepathic information came to Paquette through a dream, but telepathic information in the form of emotional comfort was communicated back to Lisa in the form of an apparition. This is not an isolated case. While the general public is best acquainted with apparitions as communications from the dead, apparitions of living persons are far from rare. They are one of the many parallels between psychic communication from the living and the dead that we'll discover throughout this chapter.

Let's look at some further examples of apparitions of the living. In a case collected by Playfair, a twin was awakened from sleep by the sound of his name being spoken, and he saw his twin brother sitting on a trunk in his room. As the wakened twin jumped out of bed to greet him, the apparition disappeared. It turned out his brother had been wounded at that very time.[16]

In another case, Sonia Colvin-Snell was in a coma in an intensive care unit in New Zealand when two young women with whom she had worked encountered her "double" while visiting Ayers Rock in Australia. This "double" was sitting drawing, as Colvin-Snell liked to do. When the two women called her name, the double responded and "looked, talked, and laughed just like you," they told her later.[17]

A young man referred to as "Hal" was in the hospital following emergency surgery for a burst brain embolism. In the middle of the night, he saw his room door open and his maternal grandmother enter the room. She was carrying a bunch of dinner plates and proceeded to set them about the room, making quite a racket. Then, without saying a thing to him, she left. The following morning, Hal got a call from his mother, who'd been staying in a hotel across the street. She said she'd been awake during the night with the strong feeling that her mother was there in the hotel, but when she

---

[15] Andrew Paquette, *Dreamer: 20 Years of Psychic Dreams and How They Changed My Life* (Winchester, UK: O Books, 2011), 70-72.
[16] Playfair, *Twin Telepathy*, 75.
[17] Brian Inglis, *Coincidence: A Matter of Chance – or Synchronicity?* (London: Hutchinson, 1990), 80-81.

opened the door, there was no one in the hall. Though this case strongly resembles the cases of communication from the dead we read about in Chapter 4, Hal's grandmother was very much alive. And, in the day following her apparition, Hal received a card from her in the mail. It featured a picture of an elderly woman peering around a slightly open door, with a caption that read, "Just checking in."[18]

Like Paquette's case recounted above, the next two cases are combinations of dreams and apparitions. The first comes from Wynona, of Florida. She dreamt about her racecar driver brother working on his car and forgetting to hook something back up when he was through. She tried to warn him about it in the dream, but he was already driving off in the car and couldn't hear her yelling. The next morning, her brother called her to say that he'd had a dream that night about her yelling something at him, but he didn't know what it was. Even more strangely, his wife had woken him up from this dream saying she'd just seen Wynona's face over the bed and knew something was wrong. The two of them had actually searched the house in the middle of the night to see if she was there. After Wynona conveyed to her brother the details of her own dream, he decided to go check his stock car and discovered that the brake pedal cable was broken, an issue that could very well have resulted in a major accident that day, had her dream not warned him.[19]

This next case is especially interesting. A nurse had a dream that she was in her hospital working when she saw a patient's call light on and went to answer it. She recognized the man from waking life, and when he said his bed needed changing, she agreed to take care of it. She found it odd, however, that taking the sheets from the shelf and putting them on the bed seemed to take an unusual amount of effort, like she was particularly weak for some reason. The patient also asked her for some pain medicine, but she didn't have the right keys in her pocket, so she told him to go to the nurses' station and ask for it. When the nurse woke up, she felt extremely tired, but she was amused at the memory of telling the patient to go to the nurses' station for his meds, as in reality he'd had both of his legs amputated.

The week following, the nurse found herself walking through the real-life unit where this patient was located when another nurse stopped her to inform her that the patient in question had lodged a complaint against her, saying she "had told him he had to go to the nurses' station for his pain medication after [she] had changed his bed."[20] Fortunately, our nurse was able to ask what night this had occurred and to truthfully say she had not been on duty then!

---

[18] Annie Mattingley, *The After Death Chronicles: True Stories of Comfort, Guidance, and Wisdom from the Beyond* (Charlottesville, VA: Hampton Roads, 2017), 99.
[19] Ryback with Sweitzer, 55.
[20] Ryback with Sweitzer, 49-50.

Finally, we have three separate apparitions by a single person, a Mr. S. H. B., all investigated by an independent researcher and recorded with testimonies from each of the witnesses. These cases are unique in that, before going to sleep, Mr. S. H. B. would set the intention of being present at a particular location at a particular hour of the coming night. On each of the three occasions, one or two people who were present at that distant location mentioned to him later, without prompting, that they had seen him there at the particular time he'd fixed in his mind. Here is Mr. S. H. B.'s account of one of these occasions.

> On Friday, December 1st, 1882, at 9:30 p.m., I went into a room alone and sat by the fireside, and endeavoured so strongly to fix my mind upon the interior of a house at Kew (viz., Clarence Road), in which resided Miss V. and her two sisters, that I seemed to be actually in the house. During this experiment I must have fallen into a mesmeric [hypnotic] sleep, for although I was conscious I could not move my limbs. I did not seem to have lost the power of moving them, but I could not make the effort to do so, and my hands, which lay loosely on my knees about 6 inches apart, felt involuntarily drawn together and seemed to meet, although I was conscious that they did not move.
>
> At 10 p.m. I regained my normal state by an effort of the will, and then took a pencil and wrote down on a sheet of note-paper the foregoing statements.
>
> When I went to bed on this same night, I determined that I would be in the front bedroom of the above-mentioned house at 12 p.m., and remain there until I had made my spiritual presence perceptible to the inmates of that room.[21]

Here now is the testimony of a Mrs. L. referring to that same night.

> On Friday, December 1st, 1882, I was on a visit to my sister [Miss V.], 21, Clarence Road, Kew, and about 9:30 p.m. I was going from my bedroom to get some water from the bathroom, when I distinctly saw Mr. S.B., whom I had only seen once before, about two years ago, walk before me past the bathroom, towards the bedroom at the end of the landing. About 11 o'clock we retired for the night, and about 12 o'clock I was still awake, and the door opened and Mr. S.B. came into the room and walked round to the bedside, and there stood with one foot on the ground and the other knee resting on a chair. He then took my hair into his hand, after which he took my hand in his, and looked very intently into the palm. 'Ah,' I said (speaking to him), 'you need not look at the

[21] Edmund Gurney, Frederic W. H. Myers, and Frank Podmore, *Phantasms of the Living* (London: Society for Psychical Research, Trübner and Co., 1886), 106 (Case 15).

> lines, for I never had any trouble.' I then awoke my sister, I was not nervous, but excited....[22]

Similarly detailed testimonies are recorded for each of the other two occasions on which Mr. S. H. B. "willed himself" to a distant location and was independently perceived as being there.

Unconscious Sending

Though it's quite interesting to know that some people can consciously create apparitions at a distance from themselves, intentionality is more the exception than the rule in telepathy. It is much more common for strong emotion or physical pain to press the "Send" button on our thoughts without our conscious awareness. Here are a few cases illustrating this phenomenon.

In the first, a twin who is an American academic woke up early one morning and cried out that her twin sister, 3,000 miles away, was in trouble. It turned out that a bomb had exploded outside her sister's apartment at the very time she woke up.[23]

Janice Stiehler awoke at 1:10 in the morning thinking she heard someone breaking a window to get into her home, but when she checked things out, she could find no evidence of any broken glass, nor of anyone lurking about. An hour later, she got a call from the police that her teenage son, who had been out at a baseball game, had been horsing around and accidentally put his arm through a store window. The police said the event had occurred at 1:15.[24]

Françoise Fulin recounts that, one night while her 25-year-old daughter was living abroad in Italy with her partner, Fulin had a waking vision of them in their apartment. The partner was lying on the couch crying while Fulin's daughter, strangely, was behind the window curtain. When Fulin called her daughter the next day and told her what she'd seen, her daughter was disturbed by the accuracy of her vision. She confessed that "she was going to break up with her boyfriend because he'd surprised her hiding in the curtain responding to a phone call from a man she'd fallen in love with and who was harassing her to leave her current partner!"[25]

In this next case, it's not clear who is the sender and who is the receiver, but neither party appears to have been intending the telepathic interaction.

---

[22] Gurney, Myers, and Podmore, 107 (Case 15).
[23] Playfair, *Twin Telepathy*, 53-54.
[24] Joan Wester Anderson, *Where Miracles Happen: True Stories of Heavenly Encounters*, updated (Chicago: Loyola Press, 1994, 2009), 2.
[25] My translation from Jean-Jacques Charbonier, *Les 7 bonnes raisons de croire à l'au-delà* (Paris: Guy Trédaniel, J'ai Lu, 2012), 133.

Tracy Barnes had a deeply intimate week-long love affair with a man, "David," who then returned to his home on a different continent. Sometime in the month or two after their brief affair, Barnes was on a long train trip when she started experiencing strong mental images of David. "I visualised his face with great clarity," she says. "Soon, my head began to ache with the intensity of the experience, and I began to feel nausea. ... I remember screaming his name into my cupped hands…in a bid to exorcise this 'pain' or 'pressure' of his presence."[26] Barnes wrote down the time of her experience. A week later, she received a letter from David relating how, at approximately the same time on the same day, he'd had a lovely vision of her smiling and bending over him, putting her hand on his forehead.[27]

Conscious Sending and Receiving of Specific Messages

Here now are a few cases where a specific message is both consciously sent and consciously received. In the first one, a teenage girl named Aily was walking down a lonely country road when she got scared by a strange car passing and repassing her. She began running and spoke to her twin sister in her mind, asking her to tell their dad to come quickly. Alison says it felt "almost as if Aily was standing there." "It was quite a scary feeling," she says. "It was accompanied by a feeling of real panic – like 'Get Dad! Get Dad!'" Thankfully, their father quickly went to Aily, and things ended well.[28]

Sometimes it can be difficult for a person who receives a telepathic message to distinguish it from hearing a normal, physical communication. This can lead to humorous consequences, as in this case reported by Dr. William Grierson. He says,

> My mother used to be ill a great deal. One time when she was sick in bed I went off on my bicycle to visit relatives forty miles away. When I got back, the house was dark and I could not find my mother. Alarmed, I went from room to room and out in the garden calling for her. She had got up and, though sick, had ridden her bicycle to the church, a couple of miles away, for Evensong. On her return, she reproached me for embarrassing her by making such a fool of myself calling for her outside the church. She repeated, word for word, my worried calls for her. "Fortunately, everyone was very polite and pretended not to hear you."[29]

Another account of a precise message that was both consciously sent and consciously received comes from Patricia Culver, wife of mountaineer

---

[26] Inglis, *Coincidence*, 83.
[27] Inglis, *Coincidence*, 84.
[28] Playfair, *Twin Telepathy*, 48-49.
[29] Sheldrake, *The Sense of Being Stared At*, 60.

Dan Culver. Her husband was out climbing and supposed to be home for dinner, but he never showed. By 9pm, she was panicking. When she tried to soothe herself by meditating, "[s]uddenly this whole wave of information came in from Dan. There was nothing audible, just a feeling that he was saying, 'I'm okay, I'll call you tomorrow.'" Indeed, when morning came, the phone rang. Dan said he'd had some trouble and had to bivouac for the night. "By the way," he said, "did you get my message?" Around 9:30pm the previous night, he'd mentally focused on Patricia with the intention of telling her he was fine and would call her in the morning.[30]

Extended Conversations

The foregoing cases suggest the possibility that two people might be able to send telepathic messages back and forth, enabling them to carry on an entire telepathic conversation. This sort of thing is often reported as happening during near-death experiences—when NDErs telepathically communicate with the various beings they meet on the other side—but there are a few examples of its happening between two living human beings, sometimes repeatedly over a long stretch of time. One case involves a dying woman named Yukiko who told two people at her bedside that her mom had been there recently and that they'd had "the best conversation." It was clear that her mother had not been there physically, as she was on a different continent at the time, but Yukiko related the conversation in detail, along with the time at which it had taken place. In a subsequent email, Yukiko's mother mentioned that she had been talking to Yukiko at that very time, and on the same subjects.[31]

In this next story, too, one of the communicators is near death. Tony Bullimore was sailing around the world in a solo race when a storm capsized his boat and trapped him in the cold water underneath for several days. Though most people gave him up for dead, his wife felt sure he wasn't gone. Author Maria Coffey recounts,

> Kneeling by her bed in the middle of the night, [Bullimore's wife] started to communicate with her husband. He told her the storm had been terrible, that the boat had rolled over, that he was inside the hull. He said he was warm enough, and that he had food and water. They talked until

[30] Maria Coffey, *Explorers of the Infinite: The Secret Spiritual Lives of Extreme Athletes—and What They Reveal About Near-Death Experiences, Psychic Communication, and Touching the Beyond* (New York: Jeremy P. Tarcher/Penguin, 2008), 174.
[31] Lisa Smartt, *Words at the Threshold: What We Say as We're Nearing Death* (Novato, CA: New World Library, 2017), 125-6.

> he said he was tired, and had to sleep for a while. She made him promise he'd wake up.
>
> The following day she talked to him again. "Oh Lal, I'm in a mess," he told her. "It's wet. The boat won't stop rolling. I'm cold."
>
> She told him to hang on, that a rescue boat was on the way. "You're a tough little man, Tony Bullimore," she encouraged him. "Don't you dare go and leave me behind. Don't you dare."[32]

On the day after that, he was having trouble staying conscious when he saw a detailed vision of his being rescued by an Australian ship. On the following day, the vision came true, exactly as he'd seen it.

Unconscious Reception

Let's now look at some cases where the telepathic "sender" is consciously transmitting a message but the receiver does not consciously receive it. Generally, in these cases, the only evidence that the receiver has gotten the message is the fact that they subsequently behave in accordance with it, almost as though they were under the influence of posthypnotic suggestion.

For instance, Andrew Paquette relates how he was going to the movie theater to meet his wife when he felt a strong impulse to back home and retrieve a forgotten item. When he got back to his apartment, he looked around trying to figure out what it was he'd forgotten but had no idea. He did, however, see his wife's spare pair of glasses sitting there, and even though he knew she didn't need them, he picked them up. "You heard me!" she told him, when he handed them to her at the theater. She'd forgotten her other glasses at work and decided to mentally "shout" to Paquette to bring her other pair from home. Unbeknownst to him, he'd done exactly as she'd requested.[33]

Colin Wilson writes about a similar experience, this time from the point of view of the sender. He had been in the hospital for a check-up and was finished about an hour earlier than anticipated, long before his wife was planning to pick him up. This being in the days before cell phones, he decided to try to alert his wife by telepathy. "This was at about five past midday," says Wilson. "Five minutes later, the sister came to tell me that my wife was on the telephone, asking when to come and fetch me. When she arrived, I asked her what had happened. She said that she had felt a sudden impulse to check with the hospital in case I might be ready earlier than expected. The telephone boxes had been occupied, so she went into a chemist's shop to

---

[32] Coffey, 175.

[33] Paquette, *Dreamer*, 45.

make a purchase; when she came out a few minutes later, a box was empty. This accounted for the five minute delay before she rang."[34]

Certain people, it seems, are particularly adept at exerting this telepathic influence over others, and certain subjects are more amenable to being influenced than others. Jenny Cockell writes in her book *Past Lives, Future Lives* about the discovery she made as a teenager that she could transmit mental requests to animals. Interestingly, she discovered that dogs would gladly carry out her requests without a second thought, while cats would start to do what she asked and then stop and look at her, as if in reproach. Cockell also tried this technique on a person, mentally requesting that they carry out a certain sequence of behaviors. She says,

> The experiment was highly successful in that the person followed exactly the sequence of actions and manner I had been concentrating on, but I immediately realised that it was a very wrong thing to do. After carrying out my mental suggestions to the letter, my unwitting victim looked very confused and upset. I felt guilty about this for years afterwards and later wrote to apologise: I never attempted anything of this kind again.[35]

Perhaps this kind of telepathy—where the recipient unconsciously behaves in accordance with a telepathically communicated message—could explain coincidences like the following. A man who was going to be traveling on a train south from Philadelphia thought about arranging to see a friend during his layover in Washington, DC. In the end, however, he didn't contact the friend or make any plans. This appeared fortunate, since it turned out that he was not able to depart as early as planned and wouldn't have time for a visit anyway. While approaching Baltimore (still en route for Washington), his train was almost full. However, at a stop in Baltimore, his seatmate happened to get off the train. Someone else then boarded and took his place. Who should it be but the friend our traveler had originally wanted to see in Washington![36]

If telepathy does in fact figure in the case just described, it's not clear exactly where it enters, or at how many points. For instance, did telepathy influence the friend to take this particular train? Or was he already going to take this train and so telepathy influenced our original traveler to leave later than planned so that he, too, would be on it? Did our traveler have precognitive knowledge that they were going to meet on the train, thus causing him to think about his friend before setting off? What about the coincidence of sitting in adjoining seats? Did telepathy influence the seatmate

---

[34] Ben Noakes, *I Saw a Ghost: Eye-Witness Accounts by the Famous of Supernatural Encounters* (London: Weidenfeld and Nicolson, 1986), 141.
[35] Jenny Cockell, *Past Lives, Future Lives* (New York: Fireside, 1996), 13.
[36] Vaughan, *Incredible Coincidence*, 77.

to get up and off at Baltimore, or did it choose some person who would be getting off at that stop anyway and influence them to sit there in order that the seat be vacated at the right moment for the friend to sit in it? Given our limited information about this case, it's not easy to tell. Nevertheless, there appear to be several points at which telepathy may have entered the causal chain that produced this coincidence.

Here's a case that seems a little more straightforward. A woman named Bonnie was retiring from the job that had provided her with the lovely cottage where she'd lived for the last 20 years. As she was packing up to move out, one of her colleagues asked her what one souvenir she would most like to take with her. Bonnie replied that it was unfortunately something she couldn't have: a painting that an artist had once done of her garden at its height. At the time, she'd begged the artist to let her buy the painting, but the woman had said she never sold her favorite pieces. Bonnie was still telling this story to her coworker when a woman came up the drive with a package. Though Bonnie didn't recognize her at first, she introduced herself as the artist who had painted Bonnie's garden 15 years previously. She said she'd woken up at four o'clock that morning knowing that she had to come deliver the painting to her that day.[37]

Assuming that the artist hadn't heard about Bonnie moving out of the cottage after all these years and decided for that reason to show up on her last day with the painting she'd always wanted, it seems that Bonnie's longing was telepathically transmitted to the artist. If Bonnie hadn't been thinking about the painting until that very morning when her friend asked her what souvenir she would most like to take with her, then her telepathic communication may have been transmitted into the past, so that the artist would already be on her way to her when Bonnie realized what it was she most desired.

This next case also involves the recovery of a painting to which someone had an emotional attachment. Susannah Ardmore was a friend of artist Stuart Scott Somerville and acquired many of his paintings. Two years after his death, she was at home one cold rainy evening when she felt the inexplicable urge to drive out to one of her favorite art galleries. There she was immediately drawn to a Somerville portrait that she afterward discovered had only just been brought into the gallery a half hour before. She purchased it and took it home. Sometime later, she was in the town where Somerville's family lived and impulsively decided to pay them a visit. She found his son John at home and invited him back to her own place to see her collection of his father's work. When John came, she showed him her recently acquired portrait and told him of the strange way she'd come to buy it. He appeared

---

[37] Robert Moss, *The Three "Only" Things: Tapping the Power of Dreams, Coincidence & Imagination* (Novato, CA: New World Library, 2007), 116-7.

deeply unsettled by her story and had to quickly take a seat. He explained that an elderly woman had written him asking whether he might know the whereabouts of a Somerville portrait she'd once sat for as a young girl. He'd looked everywhere but hadn't been able to find it. Now, finally, here it was in front of him, thanks to a series of coincidences in which telepathy likely had a hand.[38]

Let me close this section with a particularly complex case, one in which an annoying brother by the name of Kenny appears to have unconsciously created repeatedly helpful coincidences with the aid of telepathically derived information. Kenny's annoying behavior consisted in his tendency to call his brother Bob at times that Bob found inconvenient for conversation. On one particular morning, a call from Kenny made Bob late leaving for work, so he did what he often did when he didn't get out of the house early enough to beat the traffic: he took Bay Area Rapid Transit (BART) instead. On that particular day, it happened that there was a huge accident on the Bay Bridge that disrupted traffic for the entire day, and which Bob would have been stuck in the middle of had his brother's call not kept him from leaving at his normal time. Afterward, he realized that this sort of thing had already happened on two previous occasions. In one case, Bob was already running late and about to head to BART, but Kenny—apparently unaware that Bob was planning to take BART that day—randomly called to tell him how he'd seen on the news that someone had fallen on a BART track and all the trains were stopped. On another occasion, Kenny asked Bob to come over to his house before work to relight his water heater, and because of this, Bob got on the freeway at a different point than usual and avoided being stuck for an hour on his usual ramp.[39]

Oddly enough, Kenny has never been conscious of helping Bob in this way, and Bob has never told him the ironic helpfulness of his annoyingly timed phone calls. Nevertheless, it seems possible that Kenny is unconsciously acting on a desire to help his brother and is using unconscious telepathic information about his brother's life in order to do so.

Synchronized Thought and Behavior

In some instances where a telepathic connection isn't conscious on either end, the only evidence for its existence is two people's synchronized thoughts and/or behaviors. For instance, sisters Marylin Crabtree and Marjorie Hartley unknowingly got engaged at the same time, and despite

[38] Inglis, 120.
[39] Robert H. Hopcke, *There Are No Accidents in Love and Relationships: Meaningful Coincidences and the Stories of Our Families* (Asheville, NC: Chiron Publications, 2018), 113-7.

there being 88 jewelers in the central part of Manchester, England, they both turned up at the same time at the same jeweler to look for a ring.[40]

Susan Reintjes tells us about another synchronization coincidence that happened to her and her sister, who were born three years and three days apart. She writes,

> Several years ago, I gathered a variety of gifts to send to my sister—silver earrings, lace wrapping paper, a humorous notepad and a funny card. When wrapping her presents, I had difficulty choosing a box for the earrings. I finally selected an octagonal-shaped box. I wrapped the gifts, added the card and packaged them to mail. I deliberated for several days about whether to use UPS or the U.S. Postal Service. I finally decided on UPS and sent the package the day before her birthday. I hoped it would arrive on time.
>
> The next day, I received a package from my sister via UPS. It arrived at 3:00 on her birthday. I put the package aside to await my birthday and called to wish her a happy birthday. My package had just arrived at her house—at exactly 3:00. My delay in sending her gifts enabled the package to arrive simultaneously. She had just opened the card and presents. Without explaining why, she said I needed to open my card and presents right away.
>
> Upon opening the cards, we discovered we had sent each other the same birthday card. The synchronicity grew as I opened her gifts. She had sent me silver dangle earrings in an unusually shaped box, lace napkins, and a humorous notepad.[41]

Twins are particularly well known for exhibiting synchronized behavior. For instance, one mother of twins reports watching them make identical twitches in their sleep. "One would move a finger," she says, "I would turn to look at the other and he would move the same finger." For the space of 10 minutes, she says, all their movements of hands and feet were identical.[42]

Playfair, who collected the above account, has also collected several cases in which twins have written nearly identical exam papers, even though there was no non-psychic way in which they could have communicated to one another the information contained in them. In one of these cases, a pair of twin boys had written so many identical exam papers that their teacher insisted they take their next Latin exam in separate rooms. On the day of the exam, one of the twins was given the list of exam questions, but he refused to start working on his answers, saying he wasn't ready. This went on for some time until another teacher came in and said that the other twin, in the

---

[40] Playfair, *Twin Telepathy*, 58. Originally published in *Daily Mail* (March 14, 2003): 48.

[41] Susan Reintjes, *Third Eye Open: Unmasking Your True Awareness* (Third Eye Publishing, 2003), 110-1.

[42] Playfair, *Twin Telepathy*, 41.

other room, hadn't received his copy of the exam questions yet. When these were finally given to him, both of the boys started writing right away. They then took precisely the same amount of time to finish, and their papers—written simultaneously in two different rooms under close supervision—turned out to be identical. They contained all the same vocabulary, syntax, and grammar, as well as the same mistakes.[43]

Simulpathity

On other occasions, what is shared between two minds is not a thought or a behavior, but a sensation. These cases are sometimes called "telesomatic." When the sensations shared are distressing ones, psychiatrist and coincidence researcher Dr. Bernard Beitman calls them cases of "simulpathity." Consider the following.

- Alison, one of the twins mentioned in a previous case, once had sudden pain in her nose for no reason. It was so bad that she had to get out of bed and take a painkiller. It turned out that her twin Aily had been swimming when another swimmer rammed her, breaking her nose.[44]
- A woman woke at seven o'clock in the morning feeling like something had just struck her in the mouth. When her husband came in from his morning sail on the lake, he reported that, around seven, his boat's tiller had suddenly swung around and hit him on the mouth.[45]
- A man woke up in the night feeling he'd just been hit on the head. When he asked his brother the next day what he'd been doing at that time, he said he'd fallen on the stairs and banged his head.[46]
- Beitman himself was once choking on something lodged in his throat and then learned a few hours later that his father (who was on his deathbed) had been choking around the same time.[47]
- Carl Jung relates being startled awake in the middle of the night by pain in his head, as if he'd gotten hit in the forehead and then in the rear of his skull. He also had the feeling that someone had just come into his hotel room, yet he could see no one. The next day, he found out that a

[43] Playfair, *Twin Telepathy*, 17.
[44] Playfair, *Twin Telepathy*, 49.
[45] Sheldrake, *The Sense of Being Stared At*, 70.
[46] Playfair, *Twin Telepathy*, 20-21. Originally published in David Lorimer, "Distant Feelings," *Network* 71 (December 1999): 19.
[47] Bernard Beitman, "Coincidence Studies," *Psychiatric Annals* 41, no. 12 (December 2011): 561-71, p. 562.

patient of his had killed himself by shooting himself in the head, with the bullet ending up lodged at the rear of the skull.[48]

In the last chapter, I reported a woman's precognitive dream of being in a car accident in a red Volkswagen that a blond woman was driving. In the dream, there was blood on her face, and she felt pain in her back and on her right side. When the accident actually occurred, she discovered that the blood came from her nose slamming against the dash and the pain from a bruised kidney. What is more, her mother was traveling to Canada at the time of the accident and "suddenly began to have pains in her right side and back, and her sinuses hurt so her eyes began to swell." She also felt a strong impulse to call her daughter.[49]

Toni Maguire reports more than one episode of simulpathity occurring with her sister. On one occasion, Maguire told her husband that she felt she had skin cancer growing into a muscle of her leg and showed him the spot where she felt it. A week or so later, she found out a doctor had discovered a malignant skin cancer on precisely that spot on her sister's leg. Another time, Maguire told her husband she thought she had "a cyst the size of an orange" on her ovary. Within a week, her sister called and told her, "The doctor found a cyst the size of an orange on my ovary."[50]

Obstetrician Gladys McGarey reports on a case in which a military man was sent to Korea right after his marriage. When he arrived there, he began having terrible nausea. For around three months, he vomited every morning and felt ill for most of the rest of the day. Tests revealed nothing wrong with him, and during all this time, he was unable to contact his wife. When they were finally able to communicate, she told him that she was three months pregnant. The husband got treatment for morning sickness, and when his wife got through the first trimester of her pregnancy, he had no more issues.[51] I wonder if the simulpathity in this case stopped because the man was finally able to talk to his wife. His feeling her morning sickness may have been her way of sharing the pregnancy with him during those three months when they were unable to communicate in any other fashion.

This next account comes from a 19th-century mathematician, James M. Wilson. He writes,

> I was at Cambridge at the end of my second term, in full health, boating, football-playing and the like, and by no means subject to

---

[48] C. G. Jung, *Memories, Dreams, Reflections*, ed. Aniela Jaffé, trans. Richard and Clara Winston, rev. ed. (New York: Vintage Books, 1961, 1989), 137-8.

[49] Ryback with Sweitzer, 8-9.

[50] Toni Maguire, *Memories of the Light: A Story of Spiritual Existence before Physical Birth* (Bloomington, IN: iUniverse, 2000, 2012), 142.

[51] Gladys T. McGarey, *Born to Live* (Scottsdale, AZ: Inkwell Productions, 2008), 49.

> hallucinations or morbid fancies. One evening I felt extremely ill, trembling, with no apparent cause whatever; nor did it seem to me at the time to be a physical illness, a chill of any kind. I was frightened. I was totally unable to overcome it. I remember a sort of struggle with myself, resolving that I *would* go on with my mathematics, but it was in vain. I became convinced that I was dying.
>
> ...
>
> Towards 11, after some 3 hours of this, I got better, and went upstairs and got to bed, and after a time to sleep, and next morning was quite well.
>
> In the afternoon came a letter to say that my twin brother had died the evening before in Lincolnshire. I am quite clear of the fact that I never once thought of him, nor was his presence with me even dimly imagined. He had been long ill of consumption, but I had not heard of him for some days, and there was nothing to make me think that his death was near. It took me altogether by surprise.[52]

The case just related serves as an excellent example, not only of the fact that twins (especially identical ones) often feel what the other feels, but also that they don't always know when the feelings are their own and when they're related to their twin. Playfair writes, "It seems that the twin connection can be so close that there are times when twins cannot be sure which are their feelings and which are the other's."[53] Twins Gloria Vanderbilt and Thelma Furness's experience of this confusing connection led them to the view that they were in fact a "common entity."[54]

Playfair presents another case very similar to the mathematician's experience just quoted, which further illustrates the potentially confusing nature of telepathy. In this case, Loy Henderson thought he was dying of typhus and even had a vision of his twin brother in which he told his twin good-bye. Henderson did *not* have typhus, however, and he did not die. He was soon back to his regular activities, and it was only later that he learned that his twin brother had died of a dental infection at the time of his good-bye vision.[55] The good-bye had been appropriate, but not in the way he'd thought.

Sometimes the confusion between one's own feelings and those of one's twin can have tragic consequences. In one devastating case, a man named Remus Cozma got exceedingly angry with his wife and tried to strangle her but ended up stabbing her to death with a knife. At the same time, Remus's twin brother Romulus was out with his girlfriend, Monica,

---

[52] Gurney, Myers, and Podmore, 280 (Case 76).

[53] Playfair, *Twin Telepathy*, 77-78.

[54] Gloria Vanderbilt and Thelma Furness, *Double Exposure: A Twin Autobiography* (London: Frederick Muller, 1959).

[55] Playfair, *Twin Telepathy*, 77.

with whom he seemed to have a much calmer, happier relationship. Nevertheless, Romulus suddenly felt compelled by some invisible force to grab his own girlfriend around the throat, and he ended up strangling her to death. This seems to have happened slightly before his brother murdered his wife.[56]

Transmission of Injuries

You wouldn't think things with twins could get much weirder than what we've just seen, but they sometimes do, to the point that the line between telepathy and psychokinesis begins to get quite blurry. For instance, sometimes an injury that happens to one twin will have effects, not just on the *feelings* of the other twin, but on that twin's *body* as well. In one case, one twin got a hand smashed in a door, and the other twin got accompanying bruises.[57] (Interestingly, the bruises were on the opposite hand. Mirror imaging like this often happens with so-called "mirror" twins, those whose embryos split from each other later than others', causing them to display reverse asymmetric physical features.)

Identical twins Silvia and Marta Landa have known many episodes of somatic synchronization. Their mother would always give them the same medications, knowing that even if one of them wasn't ill yet, she soon would be. While their coming down with the same diseases at similar times could be explained by their having similar constitutions and being exposed to the same environments, other events that happened to them are less easily explicable. For instance, one of the girls burned her hand on an iron, and both of them developed blisters in the same place, even though the other girl was away at her grandparents' house at the time. On another occasion, one of the girls, who was inside the house at the time, complained that she couldn't move her foot. It turned out that, at that moment, the other girl was outside with her foot stuck in the seat belt of the car.

The Landa girls' repeated telepathic episodes were so intriguing that researchers conducted a videotaped test with the girls. The test was able to capture the following correlations between them while they were physically separated from one another.

- Both girls threw a puppet at the investigator, one after the other.
- While one girl had light shone in her eye, her sister kept blinking.
- While one girl was subjected to a knee-jerk test, the other's leg kept jerking so much that her father had to hold it down.

---

[56] Playfair, *Twin Telepathy*, 61.
[57] Playfair, *Twin Telepathy*, 143.

- When one girl smelled some strong perfume, the other shook her head and covered her nose.
- When the girls were independently asked to arrange colored discs in any order they wanted, their orders were 431256 and 342156 (i.e., identical except for the reversal of two adjacent pairs).[58]

Telepathy and Autonomic Responses

There are some laboratory experiments that could shed light on cases of unconscious telepathy and somatic synchronization. Several experiments performed on non-twin subjects have shown that the human body can produce autonomic responses to what's happening to someone else who is outside the range of our normal perception. For instance, one person's polygraph reading can be influenced by an electric shock given to a person in a different room.[59] But the initiating event doesn't have to be so violent. In another study, it was found that a person's skin conductance increased significantly when a second person to whom they were emotionally bonded viewed a remote video image of them.[60] Experiments have also shown that white blood cells collected from a person's saliva and then connected to a polygraph will clearly respond to important emotional events that subsequently befall the person, even if the cells are at a distance from the person of several yards to several miles.[61] It appears there may be some manner in which the cells of a body, or even the bodies of two different people, are "entangled" with one another and so respond as one to certain types of stimuli, even at a great distance. We'll explore this idea further in Chapter 9, "Natural Law," where we'll also discuss some cases that suggest that the mechanism at work stretches beyond purely biological systems. For example, we'll see some further twin cases in which twins don't just have similar feelings or bodily reactions but actually experience similar external events.

---

[58] Playfair, *Twin Telepathy*, 37-39.
[59] Charles Tart, "Physiological Correlates of Psi Cognition," *International Journal of Neuropsychiatry* 5, no. 4 (1962).
[60] Dean Radin, *Supernormal: Science, Yoga, and the Evidence for Extraordinary Abilities* (New York: Deepak Chopra Books, 2013), 210-4.
[61] Cleve Backster and Stephen G. White, "Biocommunications Capability: Human Donors and *In Vitro* Leukocytes," *International Journal of Biosocial Research* 7, no. 2 (1985): 132-46; and Cleve Backster, *Primary Perception: Biocommunication with Plants, Living Foods, and Human Cells* (Anza, CA: White Rose Millennium Press, 2003). For the account of a senior Army officer who subsequently participated in Backster's research, see John B. Alexander, *Reality Denied: Firsthand Experiences with Things that Can't Happen—But Did* (San Antonio, TX: Anomalist Books, 2017), 131-7.

Telepathy Induced by Hypnotism

For now, let's return to the more narrow topic of telepathy. I have a few more phenomena to mention in this regard. One of them is the ability of hypnotists to *induce* telepathy, and in particular the sharing of sensation exhibited by some of the twins mentioned above. For instance, I've come across at least one report of a hypnotist's causing his subject to taste items that the hypnotist had placed in his own mouth, unbeknownst to the subject. Some elements of vision, hearing, and nociception (perception of pain) have also apparently been conveyed in this manner.[62]

Psychologist Dr. Charles T. Tart has written about an experiment he conducted in mutual hypnosis, where he had two people hypnotize each other. The result was something like a mutual dream, where the two subjects experienced the same alternate reality. Granted, they were in the same room and able to communicate verbally during the hypnosis session, but there were many times when neither of them spoke for a while, and yet, when they were questioned, they said that they were nevertheless communicating with each other. They also discovered, after their multiple hypnosis sessions, that they had common memories of shared experiences that they had not indicated in any way verbally during the sessions, as shown by the hypnosis session transcripts.[63]

Yet something more than a mere shared dream was going on in Tart's experiment. At some points, the subjects reported a feeling of "merging" with one another. Tart writes, "This seemed like a partial fusion of identities, a partial loss of the distinction between I and Thou. This was felt to be good at the time, but later the Ss [subjects] perceived this as a threat to their individual autonomy."[64]

Tart points out the possible danger in this sudden, unexpected intimacy: it may be more than the subjects are psychologically prepared to handle. He mentions a similar case of two married couples who took LSD together. He says,

> each [person] experienced an intense merging of identities with the three others. Because of the sudden and unexpected intensity of these feelings the couples had a great deal of difficulty in their emotional relationships

---

[62] Anita Gregory, introduction to *Experiments in Mental Suggestion*, by L. L. Vasiliev, rev. ed. (Charlottesville, VA: Hampton Roads, 1976, 2002), xxxii-xxxiii. Gregory cites W. H. C. Tenhaeff, *Aussergewöhnliche Heilkräfte* (Olton: Walter, 1957), 104ff.
[63] Charles T. Tart, "Psychedelic Experiences Associated with a Novel Hypnotic Procedure, Mutual Hypnosis," in *Altered States of Consciousness*, ed. Charles T. Tart (Garden City, NY: Anchor Books, 1969, 1972), 312-3.
[64] Tart, "Psychedelic Experiences," 312.

> to each other for several months afterwards, all centered around feelings that they had seen too much of each other's real selves, more than their previous relationship had prepared them to handle comfortably.[65]

The Importance of an Emotional Bond

The connection Tart uncovered between telepathically shared experiences and emotional intimacy does not appear to be an aberration. In fact, it has often been noted that the direction of causation generally runs in the opposite direction, with a pre-existing emotional bond making subsequent telepathic communication more likely.

Early psi researchers Edmund Gurney, Frederic W. H. Myers, and Frank Podmore collected a large number of telepathy cases and categorized them according to the relationship that existed between the people concerned. Fifty-three percent of their cases occurred between family members (including husbands and wives), 32% occurred between friends, 11% between acquaintances, and 4% with strangers.[66] We should keep in mind, of course, that these figures may not be accurate representations of the *incidence* of telepathy but only of its discovery. We may in fact have frequent telepathic dreams of strangers' lives but never discover it precisely because they *are* strangers and we don't know enough about their lives to see that they reflect the events of our dreams.

Telepathy does sometimes occur without an apparent emotional bond, especially in the lives of those who are particularly psychically sensitive. As psychic Dr. Mary Helen Hensley puts it, being psychic is "like being tapped into the spiritual internet. And you're literally just downloading information about things that are happening across the planet that you actually can't do anything about."[67] Here's a clear example of this from Jenny Cockell. She has had many telepathic experiences involving people emotionally close to her, but one of her strongest such experiences involved people she didn't know at all. It happened while she was practicing the martial art of Aikido. She writes,

> I was halfway [through] a particular throw when I suddenly became very dizzy and had to sit down. I felt that I was in a ship, trapped in a small corridor with about four men. It looked rather like the interior of a submarine, which was intensified by a horrible feeling of claustrophobia.

---

[65] Tart, "Psychedelic Experiences," 314.
[66] Gurney, Myers, and Podmore, 723.
[67] Mary Helen Hensley, "The Egyptian Ferry Tragedy," YouTube.com, https://www.youtube.com/watch?v=XPEJf7gLsbI (accessed July 4, 2018), 0:33-0:44.

> The ship was on fire, and the doors at each end of the corridor were sealed to keep out both fire and water. There was no way out, and the men were trapped.
>
> For about fifteen minutes I was sharing the last moments of these people whom I didn't know, and they were terrified. The fear left me when I felt them die, but the shock remained with me for considerably longer. ... Next day we heard that HMS *Sheffield* had been sunk the previous evening.[68]

This was during the Falklands war between the United Kingdom and Argentina. The *Sheffield* was a British Royal Navy destroyer that was sunk by an Argentinian missile, causing the deaths of 20 people and injuring many others.

In his lucid dreams, Robert Waggoner sometimes interacts with other living people who are also dreaming, and it seems possible that these are sometimes people he has never met in waking life. For instance, he once had a dream in which he interacted with a female librarian who also seemed to know she was dreaming. She told him she was from Moldova and took him to her apartment. "Upon waking, I thought the meeting imaginary," he says,

> since the woman told me her town sat on the river across from the Ukraine—and I felt confident that Moldova did not share a border with Ukraine. [But I] was stunned to discover that Moldova bordered the Ukraine and shared a river. I even found the likely town of the librarian from her pronunciation.[69]

Telepathy Between People Who Will Meet in the Future

Sometimes there appears to be telepathy between two people who will meet in the future. All three cases of this that I have collected concern future romantic partners.

When Carolina Williamson met her partner, Benjamin, not only did he seem to be the spitting image of a man she had dreamed of as a teenager, but he told her that, a few years before they met, he used to have nightmares "that his future partner was committing to another man." It turned out that this was the same time that Williamson had been engaged to marry someone else.[70]

Another case comes from a letter sent to the Koestler Foundation by a "Mrs. A." When she was a child, Mrs. A had had a "vision of a boy in a sailor

---

[68] Cockell, *Past Lives, Future Lives*, 20.

[69] Waggoner, 223.

[70] Joyce Vissell and Barry Vissell, eds., *Meant to Be: Miraculous True Stories to Inspire a Lifetime of Love* (Berkeley, CA: Conari Press, 2000), 69.

suit, standing on a roof and holding a plant in his hand." He began repeatedly appearing to her around bedtime, and they became friends of a sort. Many years later, after she had been married for 15 years, she saw some old photographs of her husband as a child. "My heart stopped, and I felt physically ill," she recalls. "There in front of me was the little boy from my childhood." He was standing on a roof wearing a sailor suit, and a tomato plant stood beside him.[71]

Here is another case that includes some very convincing details. During the Cold War, a British man was on his way to vacation alone behind the Iron Curtain when he impulsively entered a lingerie shop and bought a couple of pairs of women's stockings, something he says was completely foreign to his habits. While on vacation, however, he had an "electric" meeting with a woman with whom he went on to have a relationship. It turned out that this woman, living as she did behind the Iron Curtain, had been trying to get precisely this kind of stocking, but with no luck. And here he happened to have purchased them on a whim just before meeting her, choosing not just her correct size but her favorite color as well.[72]

Could it be that emotional bonds can work backwards through time? Or is it that we sometimes already have an unconscious bond with certain people we are destined to meet? More on that in Chapter 17, "Destiny."

Communication Difficulties That Motivate Telepathy

We now turn from the topic of who is most likely to be able to receive a telepathic message to why such messages get sent in the first place. In many cases, it's relatively easy to figure out the sender's motivation. As we've seen, many such messages are transmitted when the sender is in grave physical danger or when they are dying or wounded. Such messages can also be used to send love or comfort to those with whom we cannot physically communicate because of physical distance and/or the inability to access modern telecommunications. But there are other people who suffer from more prolonged difficulties in communicating: for instance, people in comas or those with mental or physical handicaps of various kinds. We would expect telepathy to be very useful to people in these situations, and indeed we see evidence that they avail themselves of this tool.

William Stillman, a psychic medium who also has Asperger's syndrome, has written extensively about the psychic and spiritual gifts of autistic people.[73] These gifts are not always an unmitigated blessing to those around

[71] Inglis, *Coincidence*, 200.
[72] Inglis, *Coincidence*, 62.
[73] William Stillman, *Autism and the God Connection: Redefining the Autistic Experience through Extraordinary Accounts of Spiritual Giftedness* (Naperville, IL: Sourcebooks,

them. For instance, a mother named Theresa told Stillman about how her 10-year-old autistic son Andrew could hear her internal monologues and, in many cases, would act out the fears she was mentally expressing. "I would be at someone's home," she says, "and think in my mind, 'I hope he doesn't pull down the drapes.' No sooner could I finish my thought, and he would walk over to the drapes and begin to swing on them like Tarzan." Theresa also explains how Andrew's ability to hear what others are thinking causes him to be overwhelmed in crowds, and she has had to help him learn how to regulate the flow of this information.[74]

Autistic adult Devlyn Lighthawk downplays the specialness of her telepathic abilities, noting that "telepathy is just us talking, beyond words, you know,"[75] but the accuracy of the telepathic abilities of autistic people can sometimes be positively uncanny. The grandfather of an autistic child named Noah relates what happened when the inclusion specialist at Noah's school had just finished giving him a series of tests for mathematics and savant syndrome. She proceeded to ask him some questions about her own family, questions to which Noah could not be expected to know the answers by any ordinary means. And yet he was able to tell her what her sister-in-law's name was, when she'd gotten married, and who was having a birthday that particular day. When she asked Noah how he knew all this, he replied, "God tells me." "Does He tell you everything?" she asked. "Yes" was his reply.[76]

As Noah's response might be taken to suggest, autistic telepathy is not limited to telepathic connections with those in the same room. Autistic author Donna Williams relates some of her childhood telepathic experiences in her autobiography *Nobody Nowhere*, writing,

> At school strange things were happening. I would have daydreams in which I was watching children I knew. I would see them doing the trivialist of things: peeling potatoes over the sink, getting themselves a peanut butter sandwich before going to bed. Such daydreams were like films in which I'd see a sequence of everyday events which really didn't relate in any way to myself. I began to test the truth of these daydreams; approaching the friends I'd seen in them and asking them to give a step-by-step detailed picture of what they were doing at the time I had the daydream.

2006); William Stillman, *The Soul of Autism: Looking Beyond Labels to Unveil Spiritual Secrets of the Heart Savants* (Franklin Lakes, NJ: New Page Books, 2008); and William Stillman, *The Autism Prophecies: How an Evolution of Healers and Intuitives Is Influencing Our Spiritual Future* (Franklin Lakes, NJ: New Page Books, 2010).

[74] Stillman, *The Soul of Autism*, 89.

[75] Stillman, *Autism and the God Connection*, 22.

[76] Stillman, *The Soul of Autism*, 196.

> Amazingly, to the finest detail, I would find I had been right. This was nothing I had controlled, it simply came into my head, but it frightened me.[77]

In fact, Williams may have been receiving this information through clairvoyance rather than telepathy. Telepathic ability in autistic people, as with others, seems to be only one aspect of their psychic gifts, which may include sensitivity to the spirits of the deceased as well as precognition.[78] Stillman reports multiple instances in which autistic children were able to foresee specific future events: for instance, a fireworks accident and the 2000 Concorde crash.[79] One high-functioning and verbal autistic boy told his mother out of the blue that *her* mother was going to die in 88 days. He turned out to be wrong. She died only 85 days later.[80]

Psychiatrist Dr. Diane Hennacy Powell is currently conducting scientific research on the telepathic abilities of autistic children. One of her subjects is a nine-year-old savant who is able to produce correct answers when asked to multiply six-digit numbers by each other or to find cube roots of six-digit numbers. One of this girl's therapists noticed that, when the therapist made a mistake in stating the problem or in figuring it on the calculator or computer, the girl's answer would mirror the mistake. Another therapist independently began to get the feeling that the girl was reading her mind. So, even though the girl had never been exposed to the German language, the therapist asked her, "How do you say 'I love you' in German?" (The therapist knew the answer to this question.) The girl typed out the correct response: "Ich liebe dich."

Powell decided to investigate the case, setting up an experimental protocol that made it difficult for this girl to gain any visual information from the therapist interacting with her. A barrier was placed between them, and, as Powell explained in an interview with Skeptiko podcast host Alex Tsakiris, "We had cameras documenting the experimental space entirely. We had cameras in front of them, behind them, mounted on either side of the divider, so that we saw everything. It was capable of a frame-by-frame analysis and we had a total of five different camera views watching everything." The room also contained three separate microphones. While everything was being so carefully recorded, Powell fed the therapist papers with equations written on them—equations containing large numbers produced by a random number

---

[77] Donna Williams, *Nobody Nowhere: The Remarkable Autobiography of an Autistic Girl*, rev. ed. (London: Jessica Kingsley, 1992, 1999), 67-68.

[78] Stillman's books contain many examples of autistic people's perceptions of spirits and angels, most of them tremendously positive. In Chapter 8, I relate some of the more negative encounters autistic people have had with spirit entities.

[79] Stillman, *Autism and the God Connection*, 88-93.

[80] Stillman, *Autism and the God Connection*, 123-4.

generator. The therapist then asked the girl to produce not only the "solution" side of the equation, but each number on the "problem" side as well. Powell explains, "There was a period of about ten minutes of where...out of 162 random numbers...she only made 7 errors. And each one of those she corrected on the second try." Powell's work also captures some of the girl's very telling "mistakes." When the therapist mistook a cube root sign for division by three, the girl didn't carry out the operation of division that was verbally indicated to her. Instead, she gave the cube root as it was correctly listed on the paper given to the therapist.[81]

Although I don't know of any cases as evidentially impressive as those of the autistic people Powell is studying, telepathic abilities also seem to be present among people with Down syndrome. In her book *Finding Your Way in a Wild New World*, Martha Beck relates many fascinating stories of receiving telepathic communications from her son Adam, who has Down syndrome.[82] Another particularly intriguing case is that of Roberta, a 16-year-old girl with Down syndrome. After having surgery and being discharged from the hospital, Roberta repeatedly told people that she was going to the "recovery room." She'd been in that room of the hospital immediately after her surgery, but the adults around her reassured her that she didn't have to go back. Yet she persisted in saying that she was going there. When someone finally asked her why, she said, "I'm going to tell the people there that they are not going to die, that they are going to get well." It turned out, when a nurse checked on the situation, that several patients had reported dreaming of a girl telling them they were going to recover. Some even said the girl was Asian, which would make sense given the shape of Roberta's eyes. "This went on for over two years," reports the nurse. When it stopped happening, someone asked Roberta if she still visited the recovery room, and she said, "No, I'm not needed there anymore."[83]

Telepathy has also been identified among psychiatric patients, who seem to employ it just as they're losing their ability to access other modes of communication. Psychiatrist Dr. Montague Ullman reports experiencing many telepathic connections with his patients. About two particular patients with whom he experienced this phenomenon, he writes,

---

[81] Alex Tsakiris and Diane Hennacy Powell, "Autistic...and psychic. Research reveals psychic abilities among autistic savant children," *Skeptiko: Science at the Tipping Point* [podcast] (2014), http://www.skeptiko.com/257-diane-powell-telepathy-among-autistic-savant-children/. See as well Powell's website: http://dianehennacypowell.com/telepathy/.

[82] Martha Beck, *Finding Your Way in a Wild New World: Reclaim Your True Nature to Create the Life You Want* (New York: Atria, 2012).

[83] Testimony of a nurse reported in Gladys T. McGarey, *Born to Live* (Scottsdale, AZ: Inkwell Productions, 2008), 19.

> They were both at critical points in their efforts to maintain their relatedness to people—to me. They were characterized by a lack of emotional responsiveness and profound feelings of withdrawal, resignation, cynicism, and futility. These are characteristics of the schizoid stage, or state bordering on schizophrenia, which seems to encourage telepathic manifestations as ordinary communication is cut off.[84]

Ullman points out that patients appear to lose this telepathic connection when they move into full-blown schizophrenia. Though they may still claim to have telepathic powers, this is likely just a memory of previous veridical experiences. Ullman is also quick to reassure readers that having telepathic experiences does not mean one is about to become schizophrenic. "On the contrary," he says, "ESP tests have shown that those who do best at ESP tend to have healthy, integrated, and open personalities. The schizoid personality is able to manifest telepathic ability only under conditions of anxiety and withdrawal, as a last-ditch attempt at communication."[85]

In the early years of life, all children have difficulty communicating with those around them, so perhaps we shouldn't be surprised that children under eight show more telepathic ability than older children or adults, with a peak in telepathic ability at age three.[86] There are many stories of telepathy with babies, and even with those still in the womb. Transpersonal psychologist Hara Willow reports the following occurrence from when she was about 12 weeks pregnant.

> One night I had a dream and in it I saw the face of the most beautiful boy. He was around three or four years old, and somewhat resembled my mother and maternal grandfather. He spoke to me and said, 'Mum, there's two of us in here.' When I awoke, I remembered the dream as if it were a waking experience and just knew that it was a genuine conversation with the spirit of my, as yet, unborn child.[87]

When she went to the doctor a few days later, a scan confirmed that she was indeed having twins. When the boys were around three, Willow recognized one of them as the face she'd seen in her dream.

Sometimes, though, the difficulty in communicating comes at the end of life. As Mary Helen Hensley's father lay on his deathbed, she had a nightmare/vision that she was with him in ancient times as he was dying from an infected wound in his knee. He told her, in old Gaelic, to leave him

---

[84] Ullman and Krippner with Vaughan, 51.
[85] Ullman and Krippner with Vaughan, 52.
[86] Ernesto Spinelli, "Human Development and Paranormal Cognition," PhD diss. (University of Surrey, 1983). As referenced in Playfair, *Twin Telepathy*, 40.
[87] Penny Sartori, *The Wisdom of Near-Death Experiences: How Brushes with Death Teach Us to Live* (London: Watkins, 2014), 99.

alone as he died. The dream was punctuated by a strange physical event that happened in waking life. Her father had always been proud of a birthmark under his knee, which marked many of the male descendants of Scotland's well-known Rob Roy MacGregor. He'd had this birthmark for 85 years, and the family had very recently photographed it to preserve it for posterity. However, the day after Hensley's dream, Hensley's mother discovered that the birthmark had disappeared. Both Hensley and her mother understood that the message of these events was that Hensley needed to leave her father's deathbed, that her presence was preventing him from "making the transition home."[88]

Another group that has difficulty with verbal communication but is perhaps able to make up for it telepathically is animals. You can read Dr. Rupert Sheldrake's *Dogs That Know When Their Owners Are Coming Home* for copious examples of animal telepathy.[89] I'll just add here a couple of examples collected by Dr. J. B. Rhine and Sara R. Feather of animals who were able to find their owners psychically. One was a Persian cat, lost along the route of a 100-mile move, who showed up a year later at the family's new home.[90] The other was a pigeon who, when his owner went into a hospital over 100 miles away, a week later appeared at the window of his hospital room.[91] I should also mention that at least one parrot has been found to say aloud what his human companion is thinking, even under controlled experimental conditions.[92]

Remote Psychokinesis

Thus far in this chapter, we've discussed how people can transfer their thoughts and feelings to one another at a distance, and in the previous chapter we discussed how people can transfer their own thoughts and feelings to their immediate physical environment. The question arises whether we might be able to combine these two abilities and psychically affect the environment of another person when we are not bodily present.

We noted earlier in this chapter some cases of telepathic apparitions, but we didn't discuss whether these apparitions were actual *objects* in the physical environment of the percipient or just internal to the percipient's

---

[88] Mary Helen Hensley, *Promised by Heaven: A Doctor's Return from the Afterlife to a Destiny of Love and Healing* (New York: Atria, 2015), 295-7.
[89] Rupert Sheldrake, *Dogs That Know When Their Owners Are Coming Home: And Other Unexplained Powers of Animals* (New York: Crown, 1999).
[90] J. B. Rhine and Sara R. Feather, "The study of cases of 'psi trailing' in animals," *Journal of Parapsychology* 26, no. 1 (1962): 1-22, pp. 12-13.
[91] Rhine and Feather, 16-17.
[92] Sheldrake, *The Sense of Being Stared At*, 24-27.

mind. As it happens, many cases of apparitions of living persons seem best explained as some aspect of the person taking on physical form in a location remote from their usual physical body. Consider the following case from the 19th century, recounted by a Mr. S. R. Wilmot. In October 1863, Wilmot was sailing from Liverpool to New York when his ship ran into a severe storm. After eight days, the storm finally started calming down, and Wilmot was able to have a restful night of sleep, during which the following happened.

> Toward morning I dreamed that I saw my wife, whom I had left in the United States, come to the door of my state-room, clad in her nightdress. At the door she seemed to discover that I was not the only occupant of the room, hesitated a little, then advanced to my side, stooped down and kissed me, and after gently caressing me for a few moments, quietly withdrew.
>
> Upon waking I was surprised to see my fellow passenger, whose berth was above mine, but not directly over it—owing to the fact that our room was at the stern of the vessel—leaning upon his elbow, and looking fixedly at me. 'You're a pretty fellow,' said he at length, 'to have a lady come and visit you in this way.' I pressed him for an explanation, which he at first declined to give, but at length related what he had seen while wide awake, lying in his berth. It exactly corresponded with my dream.
>
> ...
>
> The day after landing I went by rail to Watertown, Conn., where my children and my wife had been for some time, visiting her parents. Almost her first question, when we were alone together, was, 'Did you receive a visit from me a week ago Tuesday?' ...
>
> My wife then told me that...[on] the same night when, as mentioned above, the storm had just begun to abate, she had lain awake for a long time thinking of me, and about four o'clock in the morning it seemed to her that she went out to seek me. Crossing the wide and stormy sea, she came at length to a low, black steamship, whose side she went up, and then descending into the cabin, passed through it to the stern until she came to my state-room. 'Tell me,' said she, 'do they ever have state-rooms like the one I saw, where the upper berth extends further back than the under one? A man was in the upper berth, looking right at me, and for a moment I was afraid to go in, but soon I went up to the side of your berth, bent down and kissed you, and embraced you, and then went away.'
>
> The description given by my wife of the steamship was correct in all particulars, though she had never seen it.[93]

In this case, the person who appears remotely actually has an experience of traveling across space to the remote location and is perceived not just by one person at that location but by a second person as well. Thus, she is not just

---

[93] E. M. Sidgwick, "On the Evidence for Clairvoyance," *Proceedings of the Society for Psychical Research* 7 (1891): 30-99, pp. 42-43.

something in the "mind's eye" of her husband but apparently an actual figure in the room who was able to be perceived from multiple angles performing the actions she remembered performing at that location. This is consistent with more recent reports of what is today called astral travel, astral projection, or—most commonly—an out-of-body experience (OBE).

The percentage of people who have had OBEs is surprisingly high, given how little press they receive. In the 1960s, parapsychologist Dr. Jule Eisenbud cited the figure of 25% of the general population. He wrote how striking it was that, even though most OBErs at that time hadn't heard of the phenomenon before they themselves experienced it, they nevertheless all agreed that it was an entirely different experience than dreaming.[94] Detailed accounts of repeated out-of-body experiences, including evidence for their veridicality, can be found in the writings of Robert A. Monroe,[95] Robert Waggoner,[96] and Graham Nicholls,[97] among others. In one particularly interesting experience of Monroe's, while he did not appear to anyone at the location he visited, he did communicate telepathically with someone at that location and then pinched her. When he discussed his visit with this person three days later, she showed him where she still had bruises in the precise place he remembered pinching her.[98]

Another case of apparently physical contact during an OBE comes from the 1886 classic *Phantasms of the Living*. The Rev. P. H. Newnham reported in that volume,

> In March, 1854, I was up at Oxford, keeping my last term, in lodgings. I was subject to violent neuralgic headaches, which always culminated in sleep. One evening, about 8 p.m., I had an unusually violent one; when it became unendurable, about 9 p.m., I went into my bedroom, and flung myself, without undressing, on the bed, and soon fell asleep.
>
> I then had a singularly clear and vivid dream, all the incidents of which are still as clear to my memory as ever. I dreamed that I was stopping with the family of the lady who subsequently became my wife. All the younger ones had gone to bed, and I stopped chatting to the father and mother, standing up by the fireplace. Presently I bade them goodnight, took my candle, and went off to bed. On arriving in the hall, I perceived that my *fiancée* had been detained downstairs, and was only

[94] Jule Eisenbud, *The World of Ted Serios: "Thoughtographic" Studies of an Extraordinary Mind* (New York: William Morrow & Company, 1967), 231-2.

[95] Monroe's first and most famous book on this topic is Robert A. Monroe, *Journeys Out of the Body*, updated ed. (Garden City, NY: Anchor Books, 1971, 1977). See also *Far Journeys* (New York: Broadway Books, 1985, 2001); and *Ultimate Journey* (New York: Broadway Books, 1994).

[96] Waggoner, Ch. 3.

[97] Graham Nicholls, *Avenues of the Human Spirit* (Winchester, UK: O-Books, 2011).

[98] Monroe, *Journeys Out of the Body*, 55-57.

> then near the top of the staircase. I rushed upstairs, overtook her on the top step, and passed my two arms round her waist, under her arms, from behind. Although I was carrying my candle in my left hand, this did not, in my dream, interfere with this gesture.
>
> On this I woke, and a clock in the house struck 10 almost immediately afterwards.
>
> So strong was the impression of the dream that I wrote a detailed account of it next morning to my *fiancée.*
>
> *Crossing my letter, not* in answer to it, I received a letter from the lady in question: "Were you thinking about me, very specially, last night, just about 10 o'clock? For, as I was going upstairs to bed, I distinctly heard your footsteps on the stairs, and felt you put your arms round my waist."
>
> The letters in question are now destroyed, but we verified the statement made therein some years later, when we read over our old letters, previous to their destruction, and we found that our personal recollections had not varied in the least degree therefrom. The above narratives may, therefore, be accepted as absolutely accurate.[99]

A very recent account of physical contact during an OBE comes from writer Jenniffer Weigel, who was returning home from a road trip on which she and her friend Lisa Dietlin had not only visited medium Echo Bodine but also gotten readings from her psychically gifted brother and sister. At one point on their return trip in the car, Weigel noticed that Dietlin kept looking into the backseat. Finally, Dietlin said, "There's someone behind us…in the backseat." Apparently, when she looked in the rearview mirror, she saw a "smiling face." Then Weigel felt a "squeeze" on her right shoulder. This was closely followed by Dietlin's feeling of something grabbing her left arm. It was then that Weigel suddenly remembered that Echo's brother, Michael Bodine, had some experience with astral traveling. So she texted him, asking, "Where are you right now?" His reply came immediately: "In your backseat."[100]

Other accounts of "traveling" consciousness were given in Chapter 4, "The Deceased." There, we saw examples of cases in which people having near-death experiences appeared to others, as well as a case where an NDEr was *heard* and another in which the NDEr appeared to affect physical objects at a distance from their body. Those who are interested in an extended philosophical discussion as to whether someone who is having an out-of-body experience is actually *located* at the place where they and others are perceiving them as being can refer to an article by Hornell Hart and his collaborators that I mentioned in that chapter. Hart et al. conclude that the evidence supports apparitions' generally being physical objects and point out,

---

[99] Gurney, Myers, and Podmore, 225-6 (Case 35).

[100] Jenniffer Weigel, *Psychics, Healers, and Mediums: A Journalist, a Road Trip, and Voices from the Other Side* (Charlottesville, VA: Hampton Roads, 2017), 81-82.

among other things, how frequently they are accompanied by physical effects such as the "overturning of furniture, the shattering of glass and crockery, the ringing of bells, the stopping of clocks, and the like."[101]

I would simply note that, if a person is perceived as being at a place and has veridical perceptions as of being at that place, what more do we mean by asking whether they are *really* there? That place is the location from which they draw their perceptions and where their physical likeness is seen and their actions felt. What more would it mean for them to "be" there than that? They seem to be as much "there" as any of us "are" at the places we perceive ourselves to be. In the end, consciousness is probably not an object that can be located *anywhere*, even when we are in our most ordinary state of mind. We only consider our consciousness to be "in" our bodies because that is the location from which our perceptions appear to be taken and from which we appear to be able to affect the physical world. But should those limitations be lifted, we would begin to see that our consciousness is not in fact limited by the physical location of our body and that we may perceive and be perceived at other locations as well, perhaps even at more than one location at a time.[102]

Of course, people may not always be able to immediately link effects in their environment to the person who later emerges as the likely cause. Consider this case from someone whom Brian Inglis calls "Mary Wall," and who seems to have made herself into something of a remote poltergeist. She writes that, at 11pm on July 30, 1985, she began to think angry thoughts about an ex-lover of hers. "For an hour," she says, "I thought vengeful thoughts about the 'swine' and imagined all his pictures falling off the walls of his room." A couple of weeks later, she had a conversation with the fellow in question, in which he told her about a recent occasion on which he'd been in his room talking with a friend when a wind gust suddenly threw open the door and blew his pictures off the bedroom walls. When she asked him when this had happened, he said it was on July 30 around midnight.[103]

In this next case, a living person seems to resort to communication by way of the same kinds of electrical effects so often connected to the deceased. As NDE researchers Rivas, Dirven, and Smit have written elsewhere, "We begin to see a continuum of telepathic communication between living people,

---

[101] Hornell Hart, "Six Theories about Apparitions," *Proceedings of the Society for Psychical Research* 50, part 185 (May 1956): 153-239, p. 215.
[102] As far as persons' being in two places at once, see the examples of Mother Yvonne-Aimée de Jésus in René Laurentin and P. Mahéo, *Bilocations de Mère Yvonne-Aimée de Malestroit* (Paris: Editions de Guibert, 1995) and of Sathya Sai Baba in Erlendur Haraldsson, *Modern Miracles: Sathya Sai Baba: The Story of a Modern Day Prophet* (Guildford, UK: White Crow Books, 1987, 2013), Ch. 27.
[103] Inglis, *Coincidence*, 95-96.

between those living and those near death, and between the living and the deceased."[104] I doubt you'll be able to miss the parallels in the case below!

Robert H. Hopcke's husband, Paul, had late-stage Alzheimer's and was moved to a nursing facility. In the months that followed, many strange things happened in their home. First, the doorbell began ringing when no one was at the door. Then, one night, while Hopcke was contemplating what to post on Facebook about Paul's most recent decline in health, "with a kind of audible pop, every overhead light in [the] house turned on simultaneously." Hopcke even checked in the bedroom, and that overhead light was on as well, even though the switch on the wall was still in the off position. Another time, the central heating system suddenly started blowing hot air through the house at 3am even though the control panel said it was still turned off. In the middle of the night on another occasion, Hopcke woke up to a bright light shining in his face. It was his living room lamp that had suddenly come on and was being reflected into his face by the white shower curtain in the nearby bathroom. At other times, the TV, the VCR, a battery-operated radio, and a CD player all turned on randomly. Finally, in the one episode that Hopcke describes occurring *outside* his house, he was sitting in his parked car, no key in the ignition, full of emotion about his dying husband, when, "all at once, suddenly, every light in the car flashed on at once for about three seconds—the headlights, every notification light on the dashboard, the overhead light, the brake lights, every light in the car—and they all stayed on just long enough for me to be sure that I wasn't imagining it and then, off they went."

Hopcke reports that, after Paul's death and burial, the incidents abruptly ceased. In the four years between his husband's death and his writing about these events, none of them ever occurred again. Hopcke reflects on the possible cause of these events and suggests that they may have been due to his husband's "spiritual life-energy" beginning to shake free of his body, allowing him to leave the nursing facility and manifest his presence at home, where he much preferred to be. Hopcke also concedes that the incidents may have been effects caused by his own heightened emotional state. What Hopcke knows for sure, however, is that, "during that difficult and long transition of [Paul's] between life and death, the one thing I did not feel was alone."[105]

Let's look at some more examples that, if they are in fact communications from a living person, are arriving by way of PK rather than direct telepathy. These next two cases, both collected by Lisa Smartt, involve dying persons and text messages. The first comes from Joanne Moylan Aubé,

---

[104] Titus Rivas, Anny Dirven, and Rudolf H. Smit, *The* Self *Does Not Die: Verified Paranormal Phenomena from Near-Death Experiences* (Durham, NC: IANDS Publications, 2016), 169.

[105] Hopcke, *There Are No Accidents in Love and Relationships*, 181-7.

whose father was dying in an assisted living facility several miles away when her phone beeped and she saw a text message on it, displayed as if she herself had written it. The message read, "Was leaving heavily might be just wind and downy might be ready to go bad that I like pneumonia now maybe get tired I'm down I'm going to be around anymore." She called her brother, who was with her father at the time, and her brother was just as stunned and puzzled by this message as she was. "My dad has never texted or understood iPhones or technology," says Aubé, "and was clearly not conscious in the sense that we know." Nevertheless, the message she received seemed like a very plausible reflection of his dying state of mind.[106]

In the other text-message case, the wife of a man named Ka Lok had endured multiple strokes. She told him that she wanted to go home and soon after that lost consciousness. That night, at midnight, Ka Lok received a text message from a taxicab company reading, "The driver we sent has indicated that they could not find you at 95 Plenty Road. If you still need a cab at this address, reply yes." The address in question was Ka Lok's work address, but he hadn't requested a taxi, that night or any other night, as he always drove to his office on Plenty Road. However, his wife had sometimes taken a taxi from her own workplace. Could the message have somehow been connected to her? Perhaps the coincidence of the taxicab's message was prompted by her strong desire to be taken home.[107]

This next case involves an actual telephone call, apparently coming from a living person but in a non-normal way. Dr. Jean-Jacques Charbonier is a French anesthesiologist and the author of several books on topics related to consciousness and the afterlife. He was doing a book signing after a talk one day when a woman approached him and mentioned the fact that Charbonier knew she'd just lost her husband. He confessed that he didn't actually know this, that he didn't even know who she was. She told him her name, Fifou, and the fact that she'd written Charbonier through his website, but he still didn't remember her. Strangely, Fifou went on to recount how he had actually *called her on the phone* the previous night. "You called me on my cell to tell me that you were giving a talk here, barely fifty kilometers from where I live, you don't remember?" He didn't. "But it was definitely you, Doctor," Fifou insisted, "you really did call me to let me know. I recognized your voice right away because I've heard you several times on TV and on the radio. … You were very brief, and it really surprised me, because you didn't even know who you had on the line when you said, 'I'm giving a talk tomorrow in Toulon,' then you immediately hung up." Afterwards, Charbonier understandably took a look through his email inbox. He did find the message

---

[106] Lisa Smartt, *Words at the Threshold: What We Say as We're Nearing Death* (Novato, CA: New World Library, 2017), 156-7.
[107] Smartt, 157.

from Fifou. However, she hadn't given her phone number, so it was not as if he could have called her and then simply forgotten about it.[108]

In the introduction to this book, I related an experience I had in which I was using the GPS on someone else's phone when it suddenly displayed for me a map, not of my own location, but of the location of a dear friend of mine on the other side of the Atlantic. In Chapter 6, I discussed how my own ESP and PK abilities may have contributed to the production of this coincidence, but I also mentioned the possibility that there was some telepathy involved, some sense in which my friend was sending me a message through this incident. In fact, although I couldn't prove it, I felt deeply that there *was* a telepathic element to this incident.

This feeling was heightened when, for weeks afterward, I experienced coincidence after coincidence bearing specific reference to this friend. One of these coincidences involved hearing on a television commercial a song that I'd only ever heard in the context of my relationship with this person; in fact, it was from the first concert I ever attended with him. Hearing a line or two from it on television now, many years later, I felt prompted to pull out the CD he'd given me after the concert and listen to that song in its entirety. I felt it might somehow reveal the mystery of the message my friend was trying to convey through these coincidences.

In fact, the lyrics of the song blew me away with how perfectly they reflected the history of our relationship, from the time of that first concert right up to the present. But it was the final phrase of the song that really grabbed me. In closing, the singer repeats over and over the line, "Take a look at me now."[109] Somehow, I knew this line was telling me that something momentous had happened in my friend's life, something he was proud of. I was so convinced of this that I immediately looked up his blog online, hoping to find out what this momentous event could be, but there were no recent posts. It was only a few weeks later, when the unrelenting coincidences led me to finally write to him, that I discovered that, *just 17 hours before I listened to that song*, his first child had been born.

Kirby Surprise has experienced a similar episode in which a series of song lyrics tuned him in to what seemed like an important telepathic message from a friend. Surprise was busy doing housework when he noticed that his kitchen radio was playing the song "Woodstock." He was struck by this, though he couldn't quite figure out why. A little while later, he heard the DJs joking about the fact that they both had the same first name: Bob. This reminded Surprise of his friend Bob, who happened to live in Woodstock. Surprise hadn't seen Bob recently and thought about contacting him. Bob

---

[108] Jean-Jacques Charbonier, *Les 7 bonnes raisons de croire à l'au-delà* (Paris: Guy Trédaniel, J'ai Lu, 2012), 164-6.
[109] Stereophonics, *Dakota*, written by Kelly Jones, recorded 2005, from *Live From Dakota*, V2 Music Limited VVR1038098, 2006, compact disc.

was still on Surprise's mind as he listened to the next group of songs, which included "Leaving on a Jet Plane," "Monday, Monday," "Copa Cabana," and "some song about one person wanting to see another," says Surprise. "I knew it sounded crazy," he admits, "but I got the impression that I should go see Bob, that he was leaving for some tropical location." Bob didn't have a phone, so Surprise drove over to his house the following day (which happened to be Monday) and discovered that Bob was preparing to leave that very day to move to Puerto Rico for a job. "The contract was for a year," says Surprise. "If I hadn't gone to see him when I did, chances are I wouldn't have seen him again."[110]

In this next case, we again have a coincidence that brings to mind an old friend before an important departure. In this case, however, no physical reunion was forthcoming. The story begins when the wife of theoretical physicist Dr. F. David Peat decided one day around Christmas to go through some boxes of old papers. "Amongst these papers she found a number of audio cassettes," reports Peat.

> They had been recorded by an old school friend, Stuart Ogilvie, and contained humorous imitations of our school teachers and friends. On New Year's Eve I decided to spend the evening listening to these tapes, which lasted for several hours. I was constantly laughing and glanced up at the Christmas card we had received from the Ogilvies. I remarked to my wife that it was amazing, but those tapes had brought him totally to life. The next morning when I switched on my computer there was an email from Stuart's son that informed me that Ogilvie had died in the night. The coincidence of the two events was staggering—the fact that the tapes had lain unheard for fifteen years and my remark that he had been brought alive on the night of his death.[111]

Note that this coincidence, if indeed caused by the dying Ogilvie, may have been accomplished through some form of direct telepathy—prompting Peat to listen to the audiocassettes on that particular night, and perhaps even prompting his wife, some days earlier, to unpack the box containing them. Nevertheless, the content of Ogilvie's message is received by Peat through an external medium, in this case an audiocassette player.

The cases I've presented so far might give the impression that telepathic coincidences always arrive in electronic form, but that's not the case. Here are a few non-electronic examples.

Psychiatrist Dr. Judith Orloff was driving up Sunset Boulevard when she thought she saw a patient of hers in the car next to her. It turned out it

---

[110] Kirby Surprise, *Synchronicity: The Art of Coincidence, Choice, and Unlocking Your Mind* (Pompton Plains, NJ: New Page Books, 2012), 232-3.

[111] F. David Peat, *Synchronicity: The Marriage of Matter and Psyche* (Pari, Italy: Pari Publishing, 2014), 7-8.

wasn't her patient, but the similarity was so striking that Orloff knew the event was meaningful. She tried to call the patient that evening but couldn't get ahold of her. The next day, she discovered that the woman had just been fired from a job she loved. It would certainly make sense if, in this vulnerable time, Orloff's patient had psychically reached out for her therapist's help.[112]

Sixteen-year-old Katya and her dear friend Barbara had matching necklaces that they wore. One night, Katya woke up to find her necklace choking her, and she took this to mean that something terrible had happened to Barbara. She later discovered that, at the very time she'd been woken up by the chain around her neck, Barbara had been in a bad accident in another state.[113]

In a similar case, a woman named Janette woke up in the middle of the night to the sound of a loud crash in her bathroom. She at first thought there must be an intruder in her home, but in fact no one was there. Nevertheless, she discovered upon entering the bathroom that all of her many bottles of perfume (she worked for Chanel) had fallen from their shelves and broken on the floor. Janette says that she knew at that moment that something had happened to her twin sister, Annette. Just moments later, she got a phone call from a hysterical Annette, who told her she had just been delivering a nighttime bank deposit for her employer when she was robbed at gunpoint.[114]

Speaking of sisters, Annie Mattingley reports the case of sisters Vivian and Lea who lived far away from each other but learned to send each other "love taps" through the aid of butterflies. "They'd call up and say, 'Thanks for the good morning,' compare notes: 'Yes, it was a small, yellow butterfly. Yes, it came at 10:30.' They felt quite sure of themselves regarding this form of communication," Mattingley says.[115]

Psychic Matthew Manning, who as a young man was known for the abundant "poltergeist" effects he created around himself, also reports that similar effects would happen at a distance from him when he was trying to get in touch with someone but having difficulty doing so by normal means. A mentor of his found that, when Manning would be trying to get ahold of her by phone without success, various objects in her home would move about paranormally. For instance, one time when he tried calling her and she

---

[112] Judith Orloff, *Second Sight: An Intuitive Psychiatrist Tells Her Extraordinary Story and Shows You How to Tap Your Own Inner Wisdom*, rev. ed. (New York: Three Rivers Press, 2000), 255.
[113] Sylvia Hart Wright, *When Spirits Come Calling: The Open-Minded Skeptic's Guide to After-Death Contacts* (Nevada City, CA: Blue Dolphin Publishing, 2002), 71.
[114] Trish MacGregor and Rob MacGregor, *The Synchronicity Highway: Exploring Coincidence, the Paranormal, & Alien Contact* (Hertford, NC: Crossroad Press, 2013), 119.
[115] Mattingley, 72.

was out, a relative of hers answered the phone. "You've been trying to get her before, haven't you?" he asked. "Last night a lamp fell over in her sitting room, and this morning a chair had been put against my door from the inside." Indeed, Manning had tried at both of those times to telephone his mentor, but without success.[116]

Distinguishing Sources

The coincidence cases just related provide some examples of the diverse ways in which PK coincidences can be identified as originating with particular people. As with after-death communication, sometimes an association will be established by way of the person's physical likeness, or a song or object that is strongly connected to them. Sometimes, coincidences will convey a brand of humor or personality that goes along with a particular individual. What is more, some of the cases we've looked at, both here and in the chapter on the deceased, suggest that the coincidences concerned came with a sort of mental "attachment" identifying who was behind them. That is, the physical coincidence was accompanied by a mental message directing the person's attention to the creator of the coincidence. Jenny Cockell has noticed a similar phenomenon in the psychic "signatures" that accompany her experiences of simulpathity. She says, "With some people whom I know well I am now able to recognise a 'signature', so that when I sense a feeling or emotion from outside myself it is usually—though not always—easier to interpret."[117]

My own GPS coincidence and the many coincidences following it gave me a strong conviction that they had something to do with what was going on with my friend in France. While I believe that all of us have at least some telepathic ability, some of us are not very good at tuning into it or at believing what it tells us. Physical coincidences can be a real boon to people like me, making us aware of our telepathic intuitions and helping us to take them seriously. But that doesn't mean that the coincidences have to stand alone. We can generally interpret them much better if we learn to be attentive to the intuition that accompanies them.

Of course, intuition isn't *proof* of a coincidence's source, but in the case of a coincidence that we suspect of being produced by another living person, we often have the advantage of being able to subsequently *ask* that person whether they were aware of trying to communicate with us. We can find strong evidence for the rightness of our intuition if we discover that the

---

[116] Matthew Manning, *The Link: Matthew Manning's Own Story of His Extraordinary Psychic Gifts* (New York: Holt, Rinehart and Winston, 1974, 1975), 120.
[117] Cockell, *Past Lives, Future Lives*, 20.

person in question had strong motivation for producing such a coincidence, or even was consciously attempting to do so. And that will bolster our future confidence in our intuitive perceptions.

Additionally, there may be aspects of the coincidences themselves that point to the PK abilities of particular agents. In the case of Matthew Manning related at the end of the last section, his mentor identified the happenings around her as coming from him because they resembled the kinds of PK he had produced on other occasions when he was physically present. Along those same lines, Dr. Robert G. Jahn and Brenda J. Dunne of the Princeton Engineering Anomalies Research (PEAR) laboratory have found that some individuals who are trying to anomalously influence the operation of random event generators (REGs) have their own psychic "signatures," constituted by the particular way they cause the REGs' operation to depart from chance over time. Jahn and Dunne found that these signatures followed individuals across the various devices they influenced, though they did vary depending on whether an experiment allowed the individuals to choose how/when they wanted to influence the device. Jahn and Dunne even suggest that "individual signatures and their dependence on such parameters might constitute some sort of complex and subtle psychic 'Rorschach' test that could reveal features of the operator's consciousness not addressed in other venues."[118]

However, even if it appears that the PK of different individuals can sometimes be identified by their particular style—similarly to the way we can identify different individuals by their handwriting—there are also indications in Jahn and Dunne's research that the PK of different individuals may not always be distinguishable, even in theory. That is, at the psychic level, people's influence on the physical world may not always be separable into individual streams. We will address this complex metaphysical topic in Chapter 10, "The Universe."

Thoughtforms

One final complicating factor that I want to mention here, however, is the evidence that, not only can the thoughts and feelings of people influence other minds and physical objects, but people's thoughts and feelings can actually *take on lives of their own.* Recall our discussion of poltergeist phenomena in the last chapter, where we reviewed cases of people's repressed thoughts and emotions that seemed to have developed some measure of independent intelligence, so that these "poltergeists" were even able to respond to simple questions put to them by the very people whose

---

[118] Robert G. Jahn and Brenda J. Dunne, *Consciousness and the Source of Reality: The PEAR Odyssey* (Princeton, NJ: ICRL Press, 2011), 66-70.

thoughts and feelings had created them. Localized PK phenomena produced by a living person's repressed thoughts and feelings are actually a subset of what are known as "thoughtforms." Thoughtforms are thoughts or emotions that take on some measure of independent existence, and experience shows that their continued existence does not necessarily require the presence of the person whose thoughts or emotions first created them.

For instance, you may be familiar with the practice of psychometry, where a psychically sensitive person can get information about a person by touching an object that was once in contact with that person, preferably over an extended period of time. Medium and scholar Dr. Julia Assante gives the following example.

> You may, for instance, sit down in a chair that was recently vacated by someone absorbed in sorrow and suddenly feel great sadness without knowing why. You've sat in that person's cheerless spin-off, an emotional fragment the core personality wants to separate from. I've noticed a tendency among the aged residing in nursing homes, especially those who have Alzheimer's and other forms of deregulated consciousness, to throw off fragments strong enough to get picked up by others as ghosts. As I understand them, ghosts are highly developed thought forms made and shed by the living at critical turning points. Their growth continues whether their creator is alive or dead.[119]

Thoughts and feelings can also attach to places, rather than specific objects. For instance, Mary Helen Hensley relates that, when she went on vacation to new places as a child, she would get spontaneous glimpses into the pasts of those places, often seeing "mind movies" of the events that had once taken place at the historical sites her parents loved to visit.[120]

The thoughtforms encountered by Hensley were likely psychic residues that were unintentionally left behind by previous occupants of these places, but thoughtforms can be intentionally created as well. Kirby Surprise dedicates a chapter of his book *Synchronicity* to describing the nature of thoughtforms—also called "tulpas" in Vajrayana and Tibetan Buddhism—and how he occasionally intentionally creates them just for fun. "You just picture what you want to build in your imagination," he says, "and hold that object in your attention for a while. If you assume it will stay coherent, thoughtforms seem to follow that intent and persist after you turn attention elsewhere."[121] Surprise decided to amuse himself by creating a friendly three-foot-tall dinosaur to "haunt" his den at home. He says he programmed it to greet visitors but that most people couldn't see it. However, one of his daughter's friends once went into that room to find something and emerged

---

[119] Assante, 301.
[120] Hensley, 26.
[121] Surprise, 174.

"rattled and upset." "She said there was a giant lizard in my room," says Surprise. "It jumped up and greeted her like a puppy dog. She said it was some kind of dinosaur."[122]

In another case, Surprise created an owl thoughtform for an acquaintance, as a follow-on to a shamanic journey in which the woman had met an owl as her spirit animal. Interestingly, the thoughtform created by Surprise appeared to manifest in coincidences. "As soon as she imagined she had the bird with her," he says, "we were suddenly shocked by being buzzed by a private aircraft flying low over the beach. We all thought this was strange, and joked that it was her owl saying hello."

A couple days after he got home from that trip, Surprise had a lucid dream in which the owl thoughtform flew into his apartment, all disheveled and missing parts. The phone woke him up. On the other end of the line was the lady he'd made the owl for. She was terrified by the enormous number of owl coincidences that had been following her for the past two days and wanted him to bring an end to it at once. "I assured her [the owl] had already returned," he says, "and wasn't going to bother her anymore." "I didn't see much of her in class after that," adds Surprise. "Shame. It's just a party trick. People take these things much too seriously."[123]

All of this evidence suggests that strong thoughts or emotions that others direct towards us may manifest in the form of coincidences in our own life and that sometimes these thoughts or emotions may interact with us in much the same way that an independently existing, intelligent being would. Unfortunately, not everyone's thoughtforms are as harmless as the "party tricks" created by Surprise. That brings us to the topic of the next chapter: coincidences created by those who mean us ill.

---

[122] Surprise, 178.

[123] Surprise, 176-7.

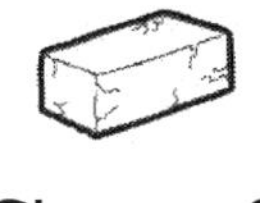

Chapter 8

Ill-Meaning Entities

Thus far, most of the coincidences we've examined appear to have been produced by sources that are benevolent, or at least benign. In this chapter, however, we are going to discuss the possibility that some coincidences may be produced by sources that mean to harm us. We'll begin by discussing malevolent psychokinesis (PK) originating with other living agents and then look at distressing coincidences caused by the spirits of the deceased. We'll discuss the evidence for earthbound spirits (and the related topics of hell and suicide) as well as the phenomenon of spirit possession. We'll also consider two other hypotheses for the origin of disturbing coincidence experiences: thoughtforms and demons. I'll conclude the chapter with a brief discussion of the nature of evil.

Malevolent Psychokinesis

We have seen in the last couple of chapters how we have the ability, on at least some occasions, to psychokinetically create coincidences for ourselves and others. Unfortunately, there is no reason to assume that these psychic powers will always be used for positive ends. Parapsychologist Dr. Jule Eisenbud, an advocate for recognizing the dark underbelly of psychic phenomena, points out that writers on the topic of coincidences (he mentions Carl Jung and Alan Vaughan) don't seem to consider the possibility of "negative" coincidences. "It is always someone running into someone he has just been thinking or talking about in a bar or an elevator," says Eisenbud, "never accidentally running over this person at an intersection, or learning that a friend has just perished in a fire not twenty feet from where one's car (of the same name, perhaps) had caught fire two days earlier."[1]

Alan Vaughan actually does provide some examples of negative-seeming coincidences in his book *Incredible Coincidence.* For instance, he gleaned from Arnold C. Brackman's book *The Search for the Gold of Tutankhamen* an account of some strange events linked to the treasures of Tutankhamen's tomb, and heralded by some as effects of the "Mummy's Curse." It appears that, in 1966, just after antiquities director Mohammed Ibrahim accepted that some objects from this tomb be transported to Paris for exhibition, his daughter was involved in a serious car accident. He then dreamed that, if he didn't block the removal of the tomb's contents from Egypt, he would meet a similar fate. Nevertheless, the French persuaded Ibrahim to go ahead with the exhibition. He was struck by a car and died two days later.[2] While Vaughan notes that the Mummy's Curse "has been debunked time and time again," since "[t]here were a number of deaths, but many more people who 'should' have died didn't,"[3] the case of Ibrahim is nevertheless rather striking, if indeed he did have the dream that's attributed to him.

But we don't need to rely on such sensational cases for evidence that psychic curses are capable of producing dramatically negative effects. Consider an experience had by medical anthropologist Dr. Alberto Villoldo early in his career, when he was still young and inexperienced. Believing that Voodoo curses couldn't work on people who didn't believe in their power, he bet a senior anthropologist in Haiti 100 dollars that a Voodoo priest couldn't affect him. The anthropologist took him to see a priest he'd done some work with. "You want believe?" asked the priest, laughing. They decided on a day when the priest would attempt to affect Villoldo, with the senior anthropologist requesting that the priest be careful not to hurt him. When the day arrived, Villoldo was back in the States dining with friends. He boasted to them that "that very evening the meanest Voodoo priest in Haiti was working on me, to no avail." Three days later, however, he got a headache that quickly became a migraine. By eight that evening, says Villoldo, "my gut had twisted into a knot, I was having intestinal spasms, and I was retching uncontrollably." At midnight, his anthropologist friend called from Haiti. He said the priest had had to delay his work until that day. The anthropologist had just gotten back from the ceremony and wanted to know if Villoldo felt any effects. Villoldo says, "I groaned into the phone and told

---

[1] Jule Eisenbud, "Seduction by Synchronicity," *Psychic* (October 1975). As quoted in Alan Vaughan, *Incredible Coincidence: The Baffling World of Synchronicity* (New York: J. B. Lippincott Company, 1979), 221.

[2] Arnold C. Brackman, *The Search for the Gold of Tutankhamen* (New York: Pocket Books, 1977), 221-2.

[3] Vaughan, *Incredible Coincidence*, 134.

him to go back to the Voodoo priest and ask him to undo whatever it was he had done. At that point, even death would have been a welcome relief."[4]

Consider as well some experiences recently written about by New Testament scholar Dr. Craig S. Keener. His Congolese brother-in-law, Dr. Jacques Emmanuel Moussounga, told him about a boy from his Sunday school who confessed to having made a pact with a man that he and two of his friends met on the street. This man drew blood from each of them and "promised that they would become powerful government ministers" as long as they kept quiet about the arrangement. Keener reports that it wasn't long after this that

> the oldest of the three boys dreamed that this older man and three others stabbed him; he awoke ill that morning and died in December. The day that the first boy died, the second boy had the same dream, then fell sick; he died in February. That day the third boy had the same dream and fell sick, and he was so afraid that in May he confessed this information. The Sunday school teachers who knew him, including Emmanuel [Keener's brother-in-law], fasted during the day for nine days, then came together to pray for the boy. Emmanuel felt the Spirit strongly as they prayed, and the boy was healed that night.[5]

Indigenous traditions around the world confirm that psychic powers—also known as "magic," "sorcery," or "witchcraft"—can be used for good or for ill. In addition to the account given above, Keener recounts an experience that happened directly to his brother-in-law Emmanuel, during a time when some practitioners of witchcraft were out to harm him. Emmanuel dreamt that a snake bit him in the heels, only to wake up and find that his heels had actual physical holes in them. Keener recounts,

> His legs gradually became immobilized as the poison spread up his legs, until he prayed with a person known for her prayerfulness; then he recovered. A PhD in chemistry from a French university, he noted that he never would have believed it had he not experienced it himself.[6]

Of course, the two incidents just related don't rule out all other possible explanations, such as that the boys and Emmanuel created these negative effects themselves, as a sort of self-fulfilling prophecy resulting from their fear. While I have to admit that this explanation is possibly true, it's also hard

---

[4] Alberto Villoldo, *Shaman, Healer, Sage: How to Heal Yourself and Others with the Energy Medicine of the Americas* (New York: Harmony, 2000), 4-5.
[5] Craig S. Keener, *Miracles: The Credibility of the New Testament Accounts* (Grand Rapids, MI: Baker Academic, 2011), 854. Keener notes that these events occurred in 2008 and that, as of 2010, the boy who had been healed remained well.
[6] Keener, 853.

to see what goal the victims would have had in producing such negative effects on their own bodies. Why would they have wanted to do this, even unconsciously? It's much easier to understand why someone *else* might have wished them harm. If we believe that other people's intentions can have psychic effects on our bodies—and the last chapter gave us strong evidence for this—then why should we reject the most obvious hypothesis in these cases: that these people were psychically harmed by the negative intentions of others?

An incident that seems even harder to explain as a self-fulfilling prophecy is one that happened to Keener himself. The events began on December 6, 2008, when Keener says he experienced "such an unusual and unnaturally dramatic spiritual assault I was literally not sure that I would survive the day." He did survive, however, and on the following day, he was out walking with his wife and son. They stopped under "a particular strong tree, about three stories tall," but his son advised they should walk a few steps away. As soon as they did so, the tree abruptly fell on the exact location where they had just been standing. Keener reports that the tree looked like it had been cut through, though presumably he and his family would have heard the operation of a saw had someone been deliberately cutting the tree as they stood there. Keener's wife's brother went for prayer and received a prophecy that Keener's family had been targeted by witchcraft and that, when the ill-intentioned spirit had had trouble attacking Keener's mind, it had "settled in a tree that was twisting about." The woman making this prophecy didn't understand this image of the tree until it was explained to her what had actually happened to Keener and his family.

Only a week after that incident, on December 15, another person prophesied about spirits' having attempted to kill Keener but being prevented from doing so by God. Keener states that, to his knowledge, he'd never before had someone prophesy about spirits attempting to kill him, or prophesy to him *anything* about spirits, for that matter. "[C]ertainly," he says, "no one had prophesied to me about a demon-afflicted tree."[7]

If we don't often experience such things in our Western, "scientific" culture, we have to consider the possibility that it may not be because they don't occur but because we are willfully ignoring them. Unwilling to consider the unsettling possibility of negative psychic effects (or even any psychic effects at all), we explain away the unfortunate things that happen to us as "bad luck." However, given what we've learned about psychokinesis, we can't rule out the possibility that our "bad luck" may at times be the direct result of human beings' or other entities' actively desiring, and psychically promoting, harmful coincidences in our lives.

---

[7] Keener, 854-5.

Earthbound Spirits

Some other striking examples of psychically inflicted harm can be found in Guy Lyon Playfair's book *The Flying Cow*, which is a detailed portrait of psychic phenomena in modern-day Brazil, including some hair-raising poltergeist encounters that feature several examples of paranormal spontaneous combustion.[8] Brazilian parapsychologist Hernani Guimarães Andrade, who has heavily researched poltergeist phenomena in Brazil, leans toward interpreting these events as the work of spirits—spirits whose help can be enlisted by living persons to serve their own nefarious ends. "To produce a successful poltergeist," says Andrade, "all you need is a group of bad spirits prepared to do your work for you, for a suitable reward, and a susceptible victim who is insufficiently spiritually developed to be able to resist."[9] Andrade points out that Brazil is full of centers for black magic where trade of this sort routinely takes place.

The idea of "bad spirits" is another concept that many readers may find completely foreign, but abundant evidence exists that all is not love and light on the other side of the veil. Consider a case investigated by Dr. Ian Stevenson of the University of Virginia. This case concerns the experiences of an Indian teenager, Sisir Kumar, in the early part of the 20th century. The events concerned were independently reported by two eye witnesses who agreed about the important details of the case.

About five years after his father's death, strange things began happening around Sisir. The first was that pieces of brick seemed to be paranormally thrown into an open window of his house. He and his friends heard the clatter from an adjoining room and, when they rushed in to investigate, saw the pieces of brick and the open window but no one outside who could have thrown them. The phenomena became more impressive as time went on. Bottles and other vessels started flying around the house or out of doors. Prepared food started disappearing from the kitchen and once was even knocked directly out of Sisir's hand. And the pieces of brick continued flying into the house, even when police were stationed outside to guard it.

Amidst all this, Sisir on several occasions had visions of his father "beckoning to him or seeming to warn him." One night, a bundle of herb roots appeared in Sisir's hand, and his father told him to attach the bundle to his arm with a copper band to protect him from a female spirit who meant him harm. When Sisir's family ignored the advice about the copper band and instead used thread or tape to attach the bundle, it was severed in seemingly

---

[8] Guy Lyon Playfair, *The Flying Cow: Exploring the Psychic World of Brazil* (Guildford, UK: White Crow Books, 2011), 179-221.

[9] Playfair, *The Flying Cow*, 204.

paranormal fashion, and some of the people present heard a female voice say, "I have taken it away. How now?" Sisir ran out of the room and found the herb bundle now under a bed. He reported that his father had taken it from the spirit and guided him to find it. The bundle was then reattached to his arm with an iron band, but that, too, was subsequently cut off in strange fashion. Only when a copper band was finally used did it remain undisturbed on Sisir's arm.[10]

These physical and auditory phenomena were supplemented by apparitions. In the early days of the phenomena, more than one person saw two hands approaching Sisir. His mother recognized them as the hands of Sisir's deceased father. There were also Sisir's multiple visions of his father apparently trying to warn him, in addition to the auditory communication Sisir received regarding the bundle of herb roots. In addition, Sisir and other witnesses perceived apparitions of a female. One of his aunts could see the apparition stooping to pick up bricks, and she warned others when they were about to be thrown. The others only saw the bricks themselves, flying through the air.

Sisir himself, just after the first instance in which the bundle of roots was cut from his arm, saw "a young woman in a red-bordered sari with the red circle of vermilion on her forehead…and dishevelled hair," who appeared to be the source of the female voice that said, "I have taken it away. How now?" Sisir also appeared to receive some communications from this female spirit while in a trance-like state. She apparently told Sisir, at some point after the first occasion of the root bundle's being cut, that she had been his wife in a previous life in which he had abandoned her. She had been searching for Sisir since their deaths and told him now, "I will take you away." She also gave Sisir an address that she claimed was where they'd previously lived together in Benares, but nothing could be verified, as the people currently living there had no information about its residents in decades past.

Stevenson concludes his account of this case by remarking that, over the course of the two months that all of this was going on, Sisir lost weight and seemed to be progressively under the thumb of the female spirit, as though she was hypnotizing him into doing her bidding. Apparently, Sisir's deceased father ultimately suggested taking Sisir to a nearby center of the goddess Bhadra Kali. When this was done and certain rituals were performed there, all of the phenomena stopped, and Sisir "had no further psychological disturbances up to the time of his death from tuberculosis nearly eighteen years later."[11]

---

[10] Stevenson notes that witnesses gave differing testimony about whether the first metal band was iron or copper. They agreed, however, that it had been cut in an apparently paranormal way.

[11] Ian Stevenson, "Are Poltergeists Living or Are They Dead?" *Journal of the American Society for Psychical Research* 66, no. 3 (July 1972): 233-52, pp. 235-40.

Sisir's case suggests that there exist spirits who, after the death of their bodies, remain pathologically attached to elements of their former life. The hypothesis of "earthbound spirits" gains support from many other sources as well, some of them highly unexpected. For instance, William Stillman relates in his book *Autism and the God Connection* that an autistic man named Josh was having severe trouble sleeping after moving to a new place: a house that was several decades old. When asked about the cause of his troubles, Josh said he was being bothered by "ghosts." He was even able to give some of the ghosts' names, and one of their ages. As Stillman reports,

> Samuel was twenty-one, and was the first to keep him up all night; Edward was a bearded man. Another was named Sarah. And a "woman" had taken up residence in the spare room across the hall. Josh indicated that, in all, there were five of them, and they were originating from the small cemetery that was adjacent to the property. (In my assessment of the house, I had never seen the graveyard, which was very small and hidden behind some trees.) Remarkably, when staff checked the names Josh had given them against the 1800s-era cemetery headstones, they *matched* even though Josh was always within the sight of his staff and had never been in the graveyard. Specifically, there was a Samuel who had died at age twenty-one.[12]

In fact, when Stillman himself went to inspect the cemetery, he found that the three names Josh had given—Edward, Sarah, and Samuel—were on three headstones right in a row.[13] Stillman prayed for Josh and asked the spirits to leave him alone, and another psychically sensitive person suggested to the spirits that they cross into the light. Stillman also told Josh that he could pray for protection from unwanted contact. After that, Josh was able to sleep well.

Another unexpected source for information about earthbound spirits is a four-year-old boy who told his father, "I remember when I was in heaven. I helped the dead guys." When asked for details, he continued, "Ya know, sometimes when people die they don't know they're dead, like when they die in car wrecks or real fast, they don't know they're dead. So we had to be there and wait until their soul left their body so we could help them get to heaven."[14]

Similarly, a "Mrs. Sch.," who has memories of dying in a previous life as well as of experiences in the afterlife before she was born into a new body,

---

[12] William Stillman, *Autism and the God Connection: Redefining the Autistic Experience through Extraordinary Accounts of Spiritual Giftedness* (Naperville, IL: Sourcebooks, 2006), 186.

[13] Stillman, *Autism and the God Connection*, 192.

[14] Carol Bowman, *Return from Heaven: Beloved Relatives Reincarnated within Your Family* (New York: HarperCollins, 2001), 136.

says about a particular period during her time on the other side, "I could help other people, such as people who had died too early and found it difficult to adjust to their new environment."[15]

Other people remember being earthbound spirits themselves. Just after moving with his family to a new town, two-year-old Alexander Dennison identified a nearby cemetery as where he had been "lying under the ground that time" after being "hurt in the war." He provided a fairly detailed description from the perspective of a spirit hanging around his buried body. "I was in the ground but I could still walk about and see the flowers," he said. He said he even went out onto the road next to the cemetery and tried to talk to some of the people who were there, but they wouldn't stop walking or listen to him, even when he shouted.[16]

The past-life memories of a Winnebago man are another demonstration of the confusion that can follow death, as well as the efforts some souls make to continue their earthly existence. The man recounts,

> Many years before my present existence, I lived on this earth. At that time, everyone seemed to be on the war path. I also was a warrior, a brave man. Once when I was on the war path, I was killed; it seemed to me, however as if I had merely stumbled. I rose and went right ahead until I reached my home.
>
> At home I found my wife and children, but they would not look at me. Then I spoke to my wife, but she seemed to be quite unaware of my presence. "What can be the matter," I thought to myself, "that they pay no attention to me and that they do not even answer when I speak to them?"
>
> All at once it occurred to me that I might in reality be dead. So I immediately started out for the place where I had presumably been killed. And sure enough, there I saw my body. Then I knew positively that I had been killed. I tried to return to the place where I lived as a human being, but for four years I was unsuccessful.[17]

This man's memories of his post-death state are similar to the experiences of some near-death experiencers who, while out of their bodies, try to communicate with people around them and don't understand why they aren't seen or heard. In fact, NDEr Jeanie Dicus says that during her NDE she was explicitly given a choice either to stay on earth where she could

---

[15] Dietrich Bauer, Max Hoffmeister, and Harmut Goerg, *Children Who Communicate Before They Are Born: Conversations with Unborn Souls,* trans. Pauline Wehrle (Forest Row, UK: Temple Lodge, 2005), 51-52.

[16] Mary Harrison and Peter Harrison, *The Children That Time Forgot* (1983, 1989, 2014), 83-85.

[17] Paul Radin, *The Winnebago Tribe* (Lincoln, NE: University of Nebraska Press, 1923, 1970), 222.

perceive what people were doing but not be able to interact with them or to be with God. She says she chose the latter.[18]

NDE researcher Dr. Raymond Moody relates in his book *Reflections on Life After Life* that several of the NDErs he interviewed reported perceiving "beings who seemed to be 'trapped' in an apparently most unfortunate state of existence." Moody describes three points of agreement among their various accounts:

> First, they state that these beings seemed to be, in effect, unable to surrender their attachments to the physical world. One man recounted that the spirits he saw apparently "couldn't progress on the other side because their God is still living here." That is, they seemed bound to some particular object, person, or habit. Secondly, all have remarked that these beings appeared "dulled," that their consciousness seemed somehow limited in contrast with that of others. Thirdly, they say it appeared that these "dulled spirits" were to be there only until they solved whatever problem or difficulty was keeping them in that perplexed state.[19]

Some of Moody's interviewees saw these beings try to communicate with living people. One man, for example,

> told how he saw an ordinary man walking, unaware, down the street while one of these dulled spirits hovered above him. He said he had the feeling that this spirit had been, while alive, the man's mother, and, still unable to give up her earthly role, was trying to tell her son what to do.[20]

In a later book, *Glimpses of Eternity*, Moody reports the experience of a child who appears to have helped one of these "bewildered spirits," as Moody calls them in *Reflections on Life After Life*. When she was seven years old, Linda Jacquin had an eye surgery after which she spent several days in the hospital with her eyes covered. While she was lying there recovering, she suddenly saw a light, out of which appeared one of her classmates from school, a boy named Jimmy. "Linda, I can't find my way home," he told her. "Can you walk me home?" She said that she could, and together, they walked "into the light until [they] got to his house." Young Linda only discovered afterward that Jimmy had been hit by a car and died on the very day of her surgery.[21]

---

[18] P. M. H. Atwater, *Beyond the Light: What Isn't Being Said About Near-Death Experience* (New York: Birch Lane Press, 1994), 59.
[19] Raymond A. Moody, Jr., *Reflections on Life After Life* (New York: Bantam, 1977), 18.
[20] Moody, *Reflections on Life After Life*, 21.
[21] Raymond Moody with Paul Perry, *Glimpses of Eternity: An Investigation into Shared Death Experiences* (London: Rider Books, 2010), 63.

It appears that, in many of the psychic dreams of Dr. Andrew Paquette, he is actually performing work in the spirit world. One of the jobs he has many times experienced doing is helping the spirits of persons who've died. Usually, he says, he helps them by taking a message to someone in their family, but he's also had several dreams in which his job is to help the spirits of the recently deceased understand that they're dead and encourage them to move on from their earthly life. Paquette describes in particular a dream he had about a man who had drowned in a river 15 years previously and still didn't understand what had happened to him. His spirit was still in the water, repeating over and over a strange pantomime of his death, never realizing the meaning of his ability to breathe underwater or the fact that no one could see him. Paquette did his best to help, but this spirit just couldn't take his attention off what had happened to him all those years ago. Paquette's best guess, from his own experiences of confusion in his dreams, was that this man's fear was holding him back from seeing the situation as it truly was.[22]

Veteran out-of-body experiencer Robert Monroe also describes experiencing an area close to Earth populated by spirits who don't realize they are dead. Monroe calls them the "Locked-Ins."[23] According to him, they would continue trying to live physical lives and communicate with physical people, but without success. Some, he says, were attached to particular physical sites that had been important to them in earthly life.[24]

Monroe gives a few brief descriptions of particular earthbound spirits in his book *Far Journeys*, but his major experiences in this vein came later and are reported in his last volume, *Ultimate Journey*. In one particularly memorable case, he encountered (during an out-of-body experience) a woman who was still living in her home years after her own death. This woman was lamenting that no one in the house paid any attention to her and that they'd taken all her pictures off the walls. After helping her realize she was dead and needed to move on, Monroe then remembered that he had met this spirit before. He'd been a renter in her house some months after her death, and he'd encountered her at that time—as a ghost![25]

The Monroe Institute, which Robert Monroe founded, actually facilitates out-of-body experiences through the use of a special auditory technology called Hemi-Sync. Furthermore, it offers a class called "Lifeline" in which OBErs help earthbound spirits move on to other areas of the afterlife. Medium James Van Praagh describes the class thus:

---

[22] Andrew Paquette, *Dreamer: 20 Years of Psychic Dreams and How They Changed My Life* (Winchester, UK: O-Books, 2011), 94.
[23] Robert A. Monroe, *Far Journeys* (Garden City, NY: Doubleday & Company, 1985, 1987), 239.
[24] Monroe, *Far Journeys*, 153.
[25] Robert A. Monroe, *Ultimate Journey* (New York: Harmony, 1994), 117-20.

> Human subjects are taught to not only travel outside of their physical bodies but also guide disincarnates that have exited physical existence and have not made the complete transition to the astral dimension. The theory works on the premise that some lost souls vibrate at such a slow rate that they're not able to "see" spirit helpers (who are vibrating much faster) who are there to chaperone them. It takes a human, having an OBE at a slower vibration, to help guide the trapped spirit to the light. It is also called soul rescue.[26]

Mediums frequently talk about trying to help earthbound spirits. Medium Echo Bodine has spoken in an interview about helping a whole group of souls of deceased teenagers who were hanging around a school go to the light. "Teenaged ghosts are very interesting because they all say the same thing," she says. "'Heaven is going to be boring.'" Instead of going to the light, they decide to hang around their old haunts, and eventually they start pulling pranks in order to let people know they're around.[27]

It's unclear what separates the earthbound spirits who are incapable of making themselves seen and felt from those who succeed in doing so. However, Sisir's case related above strongly suggests that earthbound spirits do sometimes succeed in affecting the physical world. Further evidence comes from another Indian case investigated by Stevenson, which you may remember from Chapter 4. In this case, an Indian boy remembered residing in a bodhi tree in the 11 years between a previous life and this one. The tree was outside his former family's home. He remembered that, at one time while he was "haunting" the tree, he became annoyed at two women who were swinging on a wooden seat attached to one of its branches, and in retaliation he caused the seat to break. What makes this case so evidential is that this boy was able to give enough information to identify the person he'd been in the life preceding this event, and the father of that deceased person *actually remembered the broken swing event happening outside his home.*

The broken swing case is also interesting in that it gives us another peek at the motivations behind the disturbing behaviors of earthbound spirits. While the boy's hijinks between incarnations certainly weren't benevolent in this case, he did seem to have some degree of conscience. He said he'd originally contemplated breaking the branch off the tree but was worried he'd kill the women.[28]

---

[26] James Van Praagh, *Adventures of the Soul: Journeys Through the Physical and Spiritual Dimensions* (Carlsbad, CA: Hay House, 2014), 40.

[27] Interview with Echo Bodine, reported in Jenniffer Weigel, *Psychics, Healers, and Mediums: A Journalist, a Road Trip, and Voices from the Other Side* (Charlottesville, VA: Hampton Roads, 2017), 43.

[28] Ian Stevenson, *Cases of the Reincarnation Type. Volume I: Ten Cases in India* (Charlottesville, VA: University Press of Virginia, 1975), 328-9.

In previous chapters, we met psychic Matthew Manning, who as an adolescent was afflicted with overwhelming poltergeist phenomena. While it's not entirely clear to what degree these phenomena were due to Manning's own psychokinetic abilities and to what degree they were caused by spirits somehow working through him, Manning eventually discovered that the most successful way to diminish the poltergeist phenomena around him was to engage in automatic writing, where he would put pen or pencil to paper and some force outside his own conscious will would move his hand to write messages. Many of these messages were written in languages and scripts unknown to him but were later translated by others. Some of them made little sense, but others clearly purported to be messages from deceased persons, who frequently signed their names and included dates. Matthew reports, "The messages mostly seemed to originate from people who had met an unpleasant end or from spirits who could not comprehend that they were no longer living on earth."[29] Manning's experiences suggest that some earthbound spirits may harness the PK abilities of living human beings in an effort to make themselves known. Once they've communicated their thoughts and feelings in writing, the physical disturbances stop.

Why would there be so many spirits who are "stuck" not realizing that they're dead and that they need to move on? Echo Bodine suggests that spirits who remain earthbound are generally young souls, that is, souls who haven't incarnated many times and aren't used to the process of returning to the afterlife. She says,

> I don't think I've ever seen someone die when it wasn't their time. But some of these ghosts are not accepting it. Most of the ghosts that I have met are really young souls. They aren't even aware that they have a life plan. [We'll look at evidence for the existence of life plans in Chapter 17, "Destiny."] The Elders make their life plan. So when they die, they don't say, "Oh, this was my life plan," they're like, "What do I do now?" So those are the guys who remain earthbound and become ghosts.[30]

Echo Bodine's brother, Michael Bodine, reports something slightly different. "The dead people I have a problem with," he says, "are suicides or drug overdoses. They're afraid to go to the other side because they're afraid they'll be judged or punished. Some of them don't even know they're dead."[31]

Clinical psychologist Dr. Edith Fiore also addresses the reasons that certain spirits remain earthbound. She draws most of her knowledge in this domain from hypnosis of her clients, some of whom remember while under

---

[29] Matthew Manning, *The Link: Matthew Manning's Own Story of His Extraordinary Psychic Gifts* (New York: Holt, Rinehart and Winston, 1974, 1975), 73.
[30] Interview with Echo Bodine, in Weigel, 45.
[31] Interview with Michael Bodine, reported in Weigel, 69.

hypnosis having once been earthbound spirits, and others of whom have earthbound spirits currently associated with them and able to speak through them while they are hypnotized. While I by no means accept uncritically the information produced by hypnosis, I have to say that Fiore's book *The Unquiet Dead* is the most cogent and detailed portrait of the phenomenon of earthbound spirits I've found, and I would be remiss not to mention it. Fiore writes that some spirits may remain tied to earth because there's something they still want to achieve here, such as revenge. However, she says that the most frequent causes for spirits' remaining earthbound are "ignorance, confusion, fear (especially of going to hell), obsessive attachments to living persons or places, or addictions to drugs, alcohol, smoking, food or sex."[32] Before we go any further, I'd like to address one of these items in particular: the fear of hell.

A Hellish Afterlife?

Those who have lost loved ones may be worried that the ones they have lost are not in the presence of God or the Light but rather are stuck in earthly limbo or—worse yet—hell. The bereaved may even experience some negative-seeming coincidences and wonder if these could be related to their loved ones' pain or anguish in the afterlife.

Right off the bat, let me offer reassurance that there is no good evidence in any of the literature I've read that not believing in God or Jesus condemns anyone to eternal separation from God after death. Near-death experiences and memories of the afterlife simply do not bear this out. Neither do end-of-life visions. In fact, many of them indicate exactly the opposite. For instance, Baptist pastor's kid Dr. Mary Helen Hensley reports that "the *last* person that my dad, a die-hard, disciplined Christian man, expected to see in 'the land beyond the river' was my grandfather." And yet, during the last months of his life, he had what he described as a vision of that land, and not only his mom but his dad was there as well. According to Hensley, who was present as he was witnessing this vision, he joyfully exclaimed, "I've had it wrong! I've had it wrong all along! Everybody is welcome here! ... *You can't mess this thing up!*"[33]

Christian hospice physician Dr. John Lerma recounts, "I've cared for a few atheists and they are usually highly intelligent, caring people, and they all see the angels at the end of their lives."[34] Apparently, he's often asked if

---

[32] Edith Fiore, *The Unquiet Dead: A Psychologist Treats Spirit Possession* (New York: Ballantine Books, 1987), 28.

[33] Mary Helen Hensley, *Promised by Heaven: A Doctor's Return from the Afterlife to a Destiny of Love and Healing* (New York: Atria, 2015), 294.

[34] Lerma, *Into the Light*, 188.

atheists have "horrific deaths," but he says their deaths are "easier…than most."[35]

Sarah Hinze reports that her father, who never believed in heaven and whom she'd never heard pray, had visions of heaven and his deceased loved ones just before his death.[36] Dr. Karlis Osis and Dr. Erlendur Haraldsson report that experiencers' level of religious involvement did not affect the content of the many deathbed visions they studied and that "[e]xperiences of great beauty and peace were also independent of the degree of patients' involvement in religion."[37] At the same time, Osis and Haraldsson do report that deeply religious experiencers had a higher likelihood of reacting to death with positive emotion.

All that said, distressing experiences of the afterlife do exist. There are, for example, some scary or otherwise uncomfortable near-death experiences and deathbed visions. However, these experiences are not correlated with a lack of belief in God or Jesus. If anything, they seem correlated with strong feelings of guilt, which can sometimes be exacerbated by belief in a judgmental God. For instance, Osis and Haraldsson studied 112 deathbed visions from the U.S. and India in which patients saw an environment other than the one in which they were physically located at the time. Only 10% of these were described as negative or threatening, and they found "only one case in all the American and Indian data where a patient saw 'Hell.'" This event occurred following a gall bladder operation. One of the patient's care providers described it thus:

> When she came to she said, "I thought I was dead, I was in hell." Her eyes were popping out of fear. "My God, I thought I was in hell." After I reassured her, she told about her experience in hell and said that the devil will take her. This was interspersed with descriptions of her sins and what people think about her. As fear increased, nurses had difficulty holding her down. She almost became psychotic and her mother had to be called in to quiet her. She had long standing guilt feelings, possibly stemming from marriage to a man who was 25 years older than her and an extramarital relationship which resulted in illegitimate children. Her sister's death from the same illness scared her. She believed that God was punishing her for her sins.[38]

Similarly to Osis and Haraldsson's study of deathbed visions, Jeffrey Long's study of NDEs found that only 3.6% of them were described as

---

[35] Lerma, *Into the Light*, 191.

[36] Sarah Hinze with Laura Lofgreen, *The Memory Catcher* (Provo, UT: Spring Creek Book Company, 2012), 127.

[37] Karlis Osis and Erlendur Haraldsson, *At the Hour of Death* (New York: Discus, 1977, 1979), 173.

[38] Osis and Haraldsson, *At the Hour of Death*, 167.

"frightening" (versus "wonderful" or "mixed") and only about 1% included experience of "landscapes, entities, or sensations that are unworldly, frightening, and suggestive of classical concepts of hell."[39] However, Long's research is based on experiences volunteered on the website of the Near-Death Experience Research Foundation, and people with distressing NDEs are likely more reluctant to volunteer them. NDE researcher Nancy Evans Bush has concluded from her more extensive review of the NDE literature that "[d]istressing NDEs are more common than has been thought, with a percentage possibly in the mid- to high teens."[40]

Are some NDErs really experiencing hell? To determine the correct answer to this question, we need to get a little more clarity about what we mean by "hell." If we mean a place of deep spiritual anguish, some subjects do seem to experience this. For instance, 12-year-old Denise Sexton reports that, when she was about nine, her aunt was murdered and several days later appeared to her in what she calls a "dream" but what sounds from her description more like a waking apparition. Sexton says, "[S]he told me that she had stayed in Purgatory for three days and to be as good as I could, for three days was a very long time and Purgatory was far worse than earth."[41] Note that this aunt does not talk about a place of eternal punishing torment but merely a temporary negative state. As we will see, there is other evidence that temporarily distressing death experiences can result from the state of the subject's psyche at the time of death.

Consider the experience of Howard Storm, recounted in his book *My Descent into Death.* While dying from a duodenal perforation, he found himself standing up beside the hospital bed where his body lay. Distant voices beckoned him to follow them, and as he did so, he found himself walking through a heavy fog. He began to ask the beings questions about what was going on, but they started shouting insults at him. Darkness descended, and the beings began shoving him, then biting him and tearing off pieces of his flesh. He finally lay down, exhausted and beaten, with his tormenters still circling around him.

---

[39] Jeffrey Long with Paul Perry, *God and the Afterlife: The Ground-Breaking New Evidence for God and Near-Death Experience* (New York: HarperCollins, 2016), 163.
[40] Nancy Evans Bush, "Distressing Western Near-Death Experiences: Finding a Way through the Abyss," in *The Handbook of Near-Death Experiences: Thirty Years of Investigation*, eds. Janice Miner Holden, Bruce Greyson, and Debbie James (Santa Barbara, CA: Praeger, 2009), 63-86, p. 81. For extended discussion of this topic, see Bruce Greyson and Nancy Evans Bush, "Distressing Near-Death Experiences," *Psychiatry* 55, no. 1 (February 1992): 95-110; Nancy Evans Bush, *Dancing Past the Dark: Distressing Near-Death Experiences* (2012); and Nancy Evans Bush, *The Buddha in Hell and Other Alarms: Distressing Near-Death Experiences in Perspective* (2016).
[41] Sophy Burnham, *Angel Letters* (New York: Ballantine Books, 1991), 93.

It was then that a voice coming from Storm's chest told him to pray. Storm initially resisted, as he didn't believe in God and felt prayer would be useless. But the voice twice repeated its admonition, and Storm eventually uttered a patchwork of the few religious phrases he could remember. This enraged the beings but also caused them to start backing away. Storm began speaking his prayer more strongly, and they finally left him entirely.

Storm was then alone in the darkness, where he lay contemplating his life for what seemed to him an eternity. He says that he'd always struggled with fear and anxiety surrounding death. He had tried to achieve fame, in the belief that this would give him some protection against the coming void, but he writes that "[t]he pit of despair I was now in gave me neither fame nor oblivion. I was stuck with myself, and it was frightening."[42]

Finally, Storm began hearing in his head a little boy—seemingly the child he had once been—singing the line "Jesus loves me…." It was the first ray of hope he'd felt, and it led him to yell pleadingly into the darkness, "Jesus, save me."

That is when he saw, far off in the distance, a pinpoint of light. It proceeded to get brighter and closer, and as it drew near to him, he realized it was not just light but a living being. Its light came into his body, healing him and filling him with joyous love. Storm identified this being as Jesus Christ.

Jesus picked Storm up and carried him far away to a place where he was able to see "the great light, center of all being, The One," as well as millions of lights flying around it.[43] Seven of these light beings joined Storm and Jesus for a review of his life, in which he saw how lovelessly he had behaved. Though the beings disapproved of many of his choices, they nevertheless conveyed their love toward him.[44]

Storm was allowed to ask many questions of Jesus and the "angels," as he called these particular beings of light. One question he posed to them was what happens after death. They told him many things, including how death can be confusing because one continues to be conscious of the world but without being able to interact with people or physical things in the same way. They also said that those who are ready to die and are looking forward to seeing their loved ones on the other side will make an easier transition. Then they told him, "After death, you will be receptive to God's love or you will not, depending on how you have lived your life." Storm paraphrases their message thus: "If we have loved God, loved the one that God has sent to us, loved our fellow person, and loved ourselves, we are drawn toward God. If

[42] Storm, 21.
[43] Storm, 27.
[44] Storm, 35.

we have not loved God, God's Son, our fellow person, or ourselves, we are repulsed by God's love."[45]

This might sound a lot like standard Christian evangelical teaching, but note that Storm also reports that Jesus and the angels told him that "[w]hether people claim they are Christians or not is not what is ultimately important. What is important is whether one loves as he loved."[46] When Storm asked Jesus and the angels which was the best religion, they answered, "The religion that brings you closest to God."[47]

It appears from Storm's account that Storm's selfish, unloving mindset during his life caused him, when he crossed into the afterlife, to be drawn to other spirits who had a similar attitude. Experiencing an environment ruled by that selfish mindset ultimately caused Storm to realize the true horror of his way of living and to turn toward love instead.

Dr. Barbara R. Rommer's in-depth interviews of patients (many of them her own) who've had distressing NDEs suggests the possibility that these experiences may be an important part of spiritual growth. In fact, she has found that frightening NDEs sometimes have even more positive effects than pleasant ones. A distressing experience, she says, tends to serve as a "spiritual wake-up call," guiding a person to reconsider the direction in which their choices have been taking them. She points out that we're all fallible people and all have something to gain by seeing the negative consequences of some of our past decisions. Her experience leads her to unequivocally reject the idea that only "mean" people have frightening NDEs.[48]

P. M. H. Atwater, who has probably studied more unpleasant NDEs than any other researcher, has a view of distressing NDEs very similar to Rommer's, emphasizing that people experience what they need to experience in order to further their personal growth.[49] Atwater concludes a book chapter on unpleasant NDEs with the observation that "hellish" NDEs are people's encounters with those parts of themselves that they have previously denied or avoided—encounters that carry a great potential for "healing and growth."[50]

As an example of this, consider an NDE reported to Dr. Melvin Morse. The experiencer was a violent teen criminal who almost died while trying to rob a store. On the other side, he encountered the faces of some of his deceased friends, who apparently had led similar lives of crime. They were

---

[45] Storm, 49-50.
[46] Storm, 67.
[47] Storm, 73.
[48] Barbara R. Rommer, *Blessing in Disguise: Another Side of the Near-Death Experience* (St. Paul, MN: Llewellyn, 2000), xx-xxii.
[49] P. M. H. Atwater, "Is There a Hell? Surprising Observations About the Near-Death Experience," *Journal of Near-Death Studies* 10, no. 3 (Spring 1992): 149-60.
[50] Atwater, *Beyond the Light*, 45.

"crying in pain that they said would never end." This bracing experience caused the teenage NDEr to realize the error of his ways and make some drastic changes in his life that led to his eventually becoming a minister.[51]

While the point here is the changed life of this teen gangster, let me add that, even if this man's deceased friends told him that their pain would never end, they are likely incorrect. Although it's understandable for someone in deep pain to feel that it will never end, evidence from a multitude of other sources indicates that the forces of love on the other side are always ready and willing to help those who are willing to accept that help. For example, consider another "hellish" NDE, this one reported by Cathleen C. on NDERF's website. When Cathleen realized she was dead, she also became aware that God was real but that she "wasn't with Him." She says she later learned that God was nevertheless with *her*, but at this point, she had no awareness of that. She was in a place where a "countless" number of souls were "weeping and wailing" in distress. "It was unbearable," she says. "I had to get out of that place. But how? I had no body and no voice. Then deep down in my spirit I screamed as hard as I could. I heard my own voice echoing on and on, 'God, help me!' Then a gigantic hand came down, moved under me, and lifted me out of that abyss."[52] Cathleen was lifted up away from the earth and taken to talk to someone she felt was God and who told her he loved her very much. They had a long conversation about the origin of evil and the role of free will in reincarnation.

The experience of rescue is quite common in "hellish" NDEs. Generally, as soon as a person asks for help in the afterlife, they are brought out of any spiritual suffering they may be experiencing and into the light and the presence of love. Long writes, "I have never read an NDE describing God casting the NDEr into an irredeemable hellish realm. … I personally believe that the poor souls in hell have the free will to both make good choices and return to the heavenly realms that seem to be our real homes."[53]

This view seems to be confirmed by experiences other than those collected by Long. Atwater says she has heard of entities in the NDE "tunnel" that were "disruptive and fearsome." She notes, however, that "their threats evaporated once the individual asserted him or herself, or called upon God for assistance."[54] For instance, a woman named Shandra attempted suicide and found herself in a dark place with only a single ray of light. She felt that this light was beckoning to her, telling her she could escape

---

[51] Morse with Perry, 173.

[52] Long with Perry, 158-9. All the NDE accounts that Long cites are accessible on NDERF's website. Cathleen C.'s account can be found at https://www.nderf.org/Experiences/1cathleen_c_nde.html.

[53] Long with Perry, 171.

[54] Atwater, *Beyond the Light*, 103.

from that place if she wished. "To me," she says, "hell is separation from God and we do that to ourselves."[55]

Consider, too, the testimony of one of Dr. Lerma's hospice patients, a 102-year-old woman named Grace Livingston who related that angels helped her manage her pain by taking her spirit out of her body to go traveling in the evenings. When Lerma asked her if they'd shown her heaven or hell, she replied that there was no hell like what people were generally taught, that there was only self-imposed separation from God, due to a person's feelings of guilt and inability to forgive themselves for their own choices.[56]

While we should be wary of blanket explanations, it does seem that at least some negative experiences of the other side stem from the person's own feelings of guilt or fear. Fiore reports about the earthbound spirits she's encountered in her therapy practice,

> Other entities confessed to being so ashamed of their former deeds that they didn't want to see their spirit loved ones. Often those who were brought up with a strong religious background were terrified of going to hell. These frightened spirits often desperately resisted the helpers who appeared at the time of their deaths.[57]

For instance, one spirit felt terribly guilty about having been a devil worshipper and wouldn't follow his Catholic mother into the afterlife because he thought she couldn't possibly forgive him.

Sylvia Hart Wright includes in her book *When Spirits Come Calling* the experience of a woman named Laura who had a disturbing dream about her husband not long after he committed suicide. "There was a grayish-brownish, a smog kind of mist," Laura says, "and it was like Dave's body parts were dismembered and he was calling to me in a panicked, distressed kind of voice saying, 'Laura, I'm stuck.' That really freaked me out because at the time I believed it was either heaven or hell. I didn't believe in any netherworld or purgatory or anything like that…." About a month later, Dave's sister told Laura she had been seeing waking apparitions of Dave three or four times a week in which he seemed to be serious and trying to tell her something. She told Laura she was worried he was "stuck."

Hearing that word again greatly disturbed Laura. She decided to consult a woman named Joene who had experience helping earthbound spirits. Joene was able to psychically connect with Dave and discovered that he "thought that where he had to go meant he was going to hell." She "had to make it clear to him that where he had to go was not hell but he had to deal with the

---

[55] Rommer, 48.
[56] John Lerma, *Learning from the Light: Pre-Death Experiences, Prophecies, and Angelic Messages of Hope* (Franklin Lakes, NJ: New Page Books, 2009), 144-45.
[57] Fiore, 30.

things that he did wrong in this life." Joene said, "What I did was I filled a hallway full of angels and love to draw him through so he'd know that this accounting he had to face would be done in an atmosphere of love and light and acceptance. Not hell." A month later, Laura asked Dave's sister if she'd seen him recently. She said she hadn't, and when Laura asked when was the last time he'd appeared, it was around the day Joene had done her work.[58]

Although some earthbound spirits apparently fear judgment for their misdeeds, when judgment is actually experienced in the afterlife, it is usually sensed to be coming from oneself, not others. Jean R. reports that, during her life review in her near-death experience, "I felt no disapproval—only my own reactions to it all. The feeling of unconditional love saturating me continued; I was judging myself—no one else was judging me."[59] Another NDEr, Terry Gilder, reports, "When I grew up as a Catholic, you were told that God will judge you. That isn't true. You are your judge. You are the hardest, most unsympathetic judge there is when you judge yourself."[60]

A man named John Simon reports on a series of dreams he had after the death of a friend. Only two weeks before his death, the friend had confessed to Simon his having committed "a terrible crime," a fact which may have some relevance to the content of Simon's subsequent dreams. In Simon's first dream of his friend, he did not see the friend but felt his presence and heard his voice say, "I'm in hell!" Simon was understandably quite disturbed. Six months later, Simon had another dream of his friend. In this one, the friend was smiling and standing beside a headstone. He told Simon, "Call my mother in Queens and tell her I love my headstone." Then he said, "I'm no longer in Hell. I'm going to school now!"

The next day, Simon did call his friend's mother and discovered that his friend's headstone had just been laid the day before. He drove to see it and found that it perfectly matched a sketch he'd made of the dream stone right after waking. This veridical information delivered by Simon's dream lends credibility to the statement his friend makes in the dream about no longer being in hell. And, though I don't have room to discuss it in this book, there is independent support for the idea of "schools" in the afterlife; that comment is not as strange as it may seem to those unfamiliar with the relevant literature.

About a year and a half later, Simon had one more dream of his friend. The friend confirmed that he was still going to school and then, in response to Simon's question about how he had managed to get out of hell, told him,

---

[58] Sylvia Hart Wright, *When Spirits Come Calling: The Open-Minded Skeptic's Guide to After-Death Contacts* (Nevada City, CA: Blue Dolphin Publishing, 2002), 78-80.
[59] Long with Perry, 101.
[60] Rommer, 165.

"I got out the moment I forgave myself!" The implication being that the only thing keeping him in hell was his own self-judgment.[61]

On a similar theme, consider the memories "Mrs. Sch." has of the period following her death in a previous life. She recounts,

> I can remember very well the period after my death in my last incarnation. I saw a great panorama of my last life as though I was looking at it from a raised position—a kind of huge picture in which my whole past life was spread out before me. I had to pull myself away from it and hold firmly in my awareness to what I should take with me from it; the essential thing was this retaining of something.
>
> After about three days—I still had an almost earthly feeling for time—this picture gradually disappeared, and I found this a very painful experience.
>
> Then it was as though I was being thrown into a dark space and I was alone with my faults. I was at the mercy of my own imperfections, as though I were drowning in them, and it was very painful. And to start with there seemed no end in sight. It lasted a long time—I do not know how long—until very gradually I felt easier.
>
> I now came together with a lot of other souls. There was a loving mingling with one another and then separating again, and it gave me great happiness to be with these people whom I particularly loved.[62]

Note that Mrs. Sch. at first felt that "there seemed no end in sight" to the painful darkness in which she was alone with her faults. Compare this feeling to what the deceased friends of the teenaged gangster told him during his NDE, that they were in a pain that would never end. And yet Mrs. Sch.'s pain *did* end, after she had sufficiently reviewed the actions of her past life.

These negative experiences that seem endless while they are occurring bear strong resemblance to a state described by scientist Dr. John C. Lilly, a veteran explorer of altered states of consciousness. In his autobiographical book *The Center of the Cyclone*, he describes a state of consciousness he calls "-3," in which a person experiences oneness with the universe but that universe is wholly negative and meaningless and one feels hopeless of ever escaping from it. He calls this state "the quintessence of evil" and says that it can be "an extremely high energy state lasting eternally, though by the planetside clock, one is there for only a few minutes."[63] Lilly describes in detail one of his own experiences of this -3 state, which he had while on LSD. He explains the experience as having an important positive purpose: to help

---

[61] Dianne Arcangel, *Afterlife Encounters: Ordinary People, Extraordinary Experiences* (Charlottesville, VA: Hampton Roads, 2005), 94-95.

[62] Bauer, Hoffmeister, and Goerg, 51.

[63] John C. Lilly, *The Center of the Cyclone: An Autobiography of Inner Space* (New York: Bantam: 1972), 160.

rid him of some of his limiting beliefs about a meaningless, mechanistic universe. "In order to get rid of these limiting beliefs," he writes, "I had to construct them into a completely rational whole with all of the negative emotion connected with them. ... This episode was what the Sufis call 'going to hell in order to realize heaven.'"[64] Lilly needed to experience the logical conclusion of his nihilistic beliefs about the universe in order to grasp the necessity of giving up those beliefs. And he realized, after the experience, that his angelic guides had been with him throughout.

The idea of a distressing NDE as a "dark night of the soul" that can serve as a spiritual initiation of sorts is one of the primary themes of an excellent and thought-provoking book published in 2016 by NDE researcher Nancy Evans Bush, who herself experienced a distressing NDE. She writes,

> Having worked my way through one, I know just how cataclysmic they can feel. But am I ready, after all these years, to say they point to a concept like a condemnatory hell? Not on your life. Or mine, either. The same universe, the same God, that has room for these profoundly traumatic events also brings the glorious and/or peaceful spiritual experiences, the ones people believe indicate heaven. ... Why should our spiritual landscape be different than that of the universe we inhabit? We are required to learn how to be with it all, in ways that make sense to us.[65]

While self-judgment is the only judgment reported by the overwhelming majority of NDErs, it should be mentioned that a few NDErs *have* reported experiencing external judgment, particularly during their life review. Rommer's book *Blessing in Disguise* contains a chapter devoted to discussion of this variety of NDE, singled out because of its relative rarity.[66] Rommer writes that external judgment usually occurred in cases "when suicide was either contemplated or attempted." Apparently, the experience of being judged by someone else helped these NDErs then judge themselves and change the path they were on.[67]

The topic of suicide surfaces frequently in discussions of earthbound spirits and distressing NDEs. Those who commit suicide seem to be especially prone to being earthbound, remaining stuck for a while in the emotions that caused their untimely death. Nevertheless, Fiore does note that she's encountered suicides where the soul "went immediately into the Light."[68] And medium Dave Campbell says, "I am often told that people who committed suicide are getting counseling, guidance, and healing much like

---

[64] Lilly, 94.
[65] Bush, *The Buddha in Hell*, 13-14.
[66] Rommer, Ch. 6.
[67] Rommer, 89.
[68] Fiore, 25.

they would if they were here."[69] Many other examples show that, whether the deceased committed suicide or not, if they do not experience the light or the love of God earlier, it is because they are ignoring it, not because it isn't there. Many earthbound spirits simply need to be reassured that the light is loving and that they are not going to be sent to hell if they enter it. Rescue always seems to be possible, as long as the spirit is willing.

Here's a case that illustrates how the distress of a deceased person may manifest itself in negatively charged encounters with living loved ones. It also shows the means of resolution found in this particular case. A woman named "Beverly" was receiving after-death contacts from her 39-year-old daughter, "Myrna," who died suddenly and without apparent explanation. Annie Mattingley reports,

> Soon Beverly began to experience Myrna's constant presence. There were occasional loving contacts, but most of the time her daughter seemed angry. Things fell off shelves for no reason. There were unexplained loud noises. A heavy chandelier swayed back and forth, especially as Beverly spoke about Myrna. …
>
> After eighteen months of this, as Beverly sat praying for Myrna with a person she called her "spiritual guru," this guru became aware of the presence of both Myrna and Mother Mary, who was there to escort Myrna across. Myrna, however, was not about to go easily; she had a proviso. ("My daughter was a very powerful woman," Beverly told me.) Myrna, with the guru's help, negotiated with Mother Mary. Myrna did not want the addiction issues she had inherited from her father to pass to her daughter. I won't go unless I can take that darkness with me, was her demand.
>
> Mother Mary told her, "This is not yours to do," but Myrna would not back down. Eventually it was Mother Mary who relented; Myrna's condition was met. Beverly was fully aware of the precise moment in which her daughter completed crossing over into death. … After that Beverly and her granddaughter received only benign and loving contacts.[70]

In another case, a seven-year-old girl was "troubled by sensations that her deceased aunt—who in life had been a highly disturbed person—was coming to her from time to time, urging her to act suicidally so she could join her aunt on the other side."[71] Fortunately, an experienced psychic counseled the girl to tell the aunt's spirit to leave her alone, and when she did, the spirit ceased bothering her.

---

[69] Julie Beischel, "Certified Mediums' Experiences with the Afterlife," in *Investigating Mediums* (Tucson, AZ: Windbridge Institute, 2015), 27-34, p. 28.
[70] Annie Mattingley, *The After Death Chronicles: True Stories of Comfort, Guidance, and Wisdom from Beyond the Veil* (Charlottesville, VA: Hampton Roads, 2017), 110-1.
[71] Wright, 63.

As we saw above, the deceased can sometimes be distressed by their life reviews. Here's an example of a case in which the distress provoked by such a review had effects on the living. It happens that this is another case of a living mother—in this case, Annie Mattingley herself—experiencing the influence of her deceased daughter. Mattingley's daughter Randi committed suicide and then, from the other side, began a long series of conversations with Mattingley. Mattingley reports that, throughout all of those experiences, she only had one "uncomfortable contact." Here is how she describes it.

> Four months after her death as I sat one evening watching a DVD, my stomach got queasy, and I suddenly felt a strange restlessness. The formerly engaging film lost its appeal. By its end I felt edgy and upset, as if I might be coming down with the flu. I went to bed quickly. Before my head had fully sunk into the pillow, I could feel Randi yanking at me. She came with so much commotion, I almost felt afraid. Her words tumbled over one another in a jumble. All I could understand was that she was being shown some aspect of her former life that she was not happy about. Very firmly I told her I was sure there were beings where she was who were much more capable of helping her than I was. I directed my daughter back to the land of the dead, and the moment she left, my stomach and mood settled.
>
> I slept well and dreamed of sleeping entwined in a woman's arms. In the morning Randi calmly made her usual visit as if the previous one had been no different than any other. I could not ignore it, though. I asked, "Can I do something to help?" She replied, Would you hold me please? We lay entwined on my bed as in my dream, while I smoothed her hair and kissed her forehead. We spoke about life's challenges and of her mistakes and regrets and of my own. It was a particularly intimate and satisfying contact, the only time I have ever felt as though she had physical substance.[72]

Fiore notes that it can sometimes be difficult to tell whether a deceased person who is communicating with you is still earthbound or has moved on into the light. She advises paying attention to the "feeling or tone" of the person's presence. When it's "positive, loving, and nonclinging," that's a good sign that the person has moved on. If it's "heavy, sad, anxious or angry," the soul is clearly still attached to the material plane.[73]

Some of the descriptions that I and other authors have used to describe earthbound spirits and the process of "moving on" into the afterlife may suggest that those spirits who have moved on are no longer present or accessible to those on earth, that they are "somewhere else." But, as Fiore indicates in the passage just quoted, we can still receive communications from our loved ones who have moved on in the afterlife, and in fact these

---

[72] Mattingley, 109-110.

[73] Fiore, 161.

are the most positive, uplifting communications we can get. There is no need to fear that, if your deceased ones are not earthbound any longer, you will be separated from them. The afterlife does not seem to be so much a different location as it is a different level of consciousness. Earthbound spirits remain trapped in the state of mind in which they died. When they go "into the light," they are reunited with their eternal soul. Their consciousness becomes much more expansive. They know more, they are capable of growth that was impossible while they were earthbound, and they are not limited by earthly emotions like fear. But they are still capable of communication with their loved ones on earth. They are not separated from us as much as they are *also* aware of a great deal else in the universe.

Possession

The primary focus of Fiore's book *The Unquiet Dead* is the phenomenon of spirit possession, and it is a natural topic to broach when discussing earthbound spirits, since those who choose not to go toward the light after death and remain earthbound may choose to "attach" themselves to living persons and exert some measure of control over them, thus producing a classic "possession" experience.

While many authors are reluctant to discuss the phenomenon of spirit possession, there are several authors who state that, though they were once skeptical of the phenomenon's existence, they eventually had an experience or set of experiences that convinced them of its reality, or at least made the hypothesis of spirit possession as plausible as any other. For instance, psychiatrist Dr. M. Scott Peck's book *People of the Lie* contains a chapter on possession and exorcism in which Peck relates the two cases that changed his own mind on the reality of the phenomenon.[74] He further elaborates on these cases in his much later book *Glimpses of the Devil.*[75]

Another example is Dr. John Lerma, who writes in *Learning from the Light* that, during his first 17 years as a doctor, he never considered that his seriously disturbed schizophrenic patients might be visited or possessed by malevolent spirits.[76] However, Lerma's experience of having one of his patients exorcised by a trained Catholic priest appears to have led him to the belief that possession is a rare but real phenomenon. Among other things, Lerma reports having caught on video:

---

[74] M. Scott Peck, *People of the Lie: The Hope for Healing Human Evil* (New York: Touchstone, 1983), 182-211.

[75] M. Scott Peck, *Glimpses of the Devil: A Psychiatrist's Personal Accounts of Possession, Exorcism, and Redemption* (New York: Free Press, 2009).

[76] Lerma, *Learning from the Light*, 77.

- "a blanket of darkness hovering over John [the patient] while he slept,"
- the patient's body levitating nearly two feet off the nearest surface,
- a box of tissues, a glass, and a pitcher flying off an end table that was at least six feet from any person in the room,
- and a "smoke-like entity...coming from the left corner of the room...and slowly mov[ing] toward John." Lerma says, "I could now see it enter John's body through the top of his head; simultaneously, John's body went into what appeared to be controlled seizures. Within minutes of this event, a dark essence left John's body from his head again, and John began to smile."[77]

I have myself come across enough evidence for the phenomenon of possession—from diverse enough sources, including one of my own dear friends—that I think it important to mention here, in case any readers are beset by experiences that could best be explained in this way. Readers in such a position are encouraged not to rely exclusively on my cursory treatment of this subject but to investigate the sources cited in this section for further information.

The most common type of possession appears to be possession by an earthbound spirit or spirits. While references to this type of experience can be found going back at least several hundred years—see, for instance, the *dybbuk* in Jewish mythology—contemporary accounts are not uncommon. The NDE literature includes a few accounts of NDErs who, while out of their bodies, attempted to enter the bodies of newborn infants.[78] One of these accounts is briefly described by Dr. Ian Stevenson in Tom Shroder's book *Old Souls*. Stevenson reports,

> A woman was unconscious and thought to be near death. When she revived, she said she had found herself in the presence of a woman who had just given birth and felt compelled to push herself into the baby's body. But just as she was doing it, she thought of her love for her family and pulled back.[79]

Other recently deceased souls appear to be successful in taking up residence in another person's body/mind. Medium Sherrie Dillard recounts the experience of one of her clients, Anna, who came to her saying she didn't feel quite right and was constantly tired for no apparent reason. In her

---

[77] Lerma, *Learning from the Light*, 91-96.
[78] See George B. Brownell, *Reincarnation*, 2nd ed. (Santa Barbara, CA: Aquarian Ministry, 1949), 15-17; Ian Stevenson, *Cases of the Reincarnation Type. Volume III: Twelve Cases in Lebanon and Turkey* (Charlottesville, VA: University Press of Virginia, 1980); and Tom Shroder, *Old Souls* (New York: Simon & Schuster, 1999), 92-93.
[79] Shroder, 92-93.

reading for this woman, Dillard saw a man with her who said he was waiting for Anna to tell him what to do. When Dillard asked him if he knew he was dead, he said he wasn't. Dillard asked her angels to send someone he knew and trusted "to help him cross over." Dillard felt his mother arrive, and felt him depart with her. Anna immediately felt better. However, less than a month later, she was back consulting Dillard again because she had started once more feeling tired and then woke up in the middle of the night feeling there was a man standing in the room staring at her. Dillard discovered that this was another confused spirit, and she asked for a helper to escort him to the light as well.

Dillard's discussion with Anna revealed that she had recently moved to a new office in her job as nurse supervisor at a hospital. Her office was directly above the hospital's morgue. Dillard thought it very probable that people who had just died were following their bodies to the morgue and then, sensing Anna's loving, comforting presence in the vicinity, attaching themselves to her. "Quite often," Dillard told Anna, "people who pass over who are confused or afraid of the afterlife are attracted to loving and strong people like you." Dillard taught Anna how to imagine white light protecting her and how to ask her angels to escort to the light any wandering souls who might approach her in the future.[80]

Dillard also relates the story of an elementary school boy who was having emotional problems and whom she discovered actually had a second spirit inside him, in addition to his own. The additional spirit was that of a baby girl who had died at birth in the same hospital where the boy was born, at roughly the same time. Lost, she had taken up residence in his body. The boy's mother confirmed that she had "heard rumors of a stillborn at the hospital when [she] was there." Again, Dillard called on the spirit world to help escort this lost soul into the light. In this case, however, the young boy had lived for so long with this other spirit in his body that he began to feel something important was missing and ended up asking the spirit to come back. His mother had to help him understand that, thought it might be difficult and sad at first, it was important for him to let the spirit stay in the spirit world, where she was supposed to be.[81]

Fiore has extensive experience with possessions caused by earthbound spirits, and she confirms that hospitals, graveyards, and any other places where many deaths have occurred are places where one is at greater risk for "picking up" unwelcome spirits. Furthermore, the weakened energy of patients in hospitals can make them especially vulnerable to possession, as can substance abuse.[82] Fiore says that a person's energetic aura is like a

---

[80] Sherrie Dillard, *You* Are *a Medium: Discover Your Natural Abilities to Communicate with the Other Side* (Woodbury, MN: Llewellyn Publications, 2013), 173-7.
[81] Dillard, 183-5.
[82] Fiore, 110-2.

spiritual immune system, but when it's not vibrating at a high enough frequency, parasitic entities can enter it.[83] (Those who think auras are just the imaginary creations of New Agers may be enlightened by author Michael Crichton's account of how he discovered their reality, contained in his memoir *Travels*.[84]) Fiore, like Dillard and others, advocates strengthening one's aura through the "White Light Technique."[85]

The idea that one can erect barriers to unwanted psychic interference is supported by the experiences of many mediums and other psychic individuals. One unusual confirmation of its reality comes from lucid dreamer Robert Waggoner. In one of his dreams, Waggoner attempted to do something he often did: go visit a friend. However, as he headed toward his friend on this occasion, Waggoner became aware of "a strange black zone that [he] intuitively knew was impenetrable." As he drew even closer, the dream "collapsed." When Waggoner mentioned this episode to his friend the next day, his friend told him that "he had intentionally determined not to be bothered by others in his dreaming that night."[86] (This is the sort of thing that starts to happen when you get a bunch of lucid dreamers together!)

However, even if there are measures that people can take against unwanted psychic intrusion, those who are naturally psychically sensitive appear to be particularly vulnerable to earthbound spirits' taking advantage of them. It is important for those with psychic gifts to understand that not everything on the other side is going to be helpful to them and that they are in special need of learning techniques for discernment and psychic protection. The memoir of French medium Sylvie Lorain-Berger, *Les messagers de l'au-delà*, is an enlightening description of her long struggle to free herself from emotionally monopolizing spirits, during which she often felt the same ambivalence experienced by the young boy who missed his possessor. Lorain-Berger felt loved and needed by the spirits who clustered around her, and the process of letting them go was not an easy one.[87]

William Stillman has found at least one possession-like case among autistic persons, a population that he has noted for its propensity to psychic sensitivity. In *The Soul of Autism*, Stillman relates the case of an autistic man named Vic who exhibited multiple personalities. Some of these personalities appeared to be coping mechanisms developed during his abusive childhood, but others of them had links to entities that were known to haunt two separate group homes in which he'd lived. Vic showed improvement when

---

[83] Fiore, 109.

[84] Michael Crichton, *Travels* (New York: Vintage Books, 1988), 322-34.

[85] Fiore, 138-40.

[86] Waggoner, 147.

[87] Sylvie Lorain-Berger, *Les messagers de l'au-delà* (Paris: Editions Exergue, 2006, 2008, 2014).

he was helped to develop stronger self-esteem, as well as the courage to tell the unwanted entities to leave.[88]

Another risk factor for possession is indiscriminate involvement with mediumship or occult practices. Stoker Hunt's book *Ouija: The Most Dangerous Game* describes many cases of lives upended by contacts made through Ouija boards.[89] In *Patterns of Prophecy*, psychic Alan Vaughan relates his own experience with a Ouija board and a voice that "got inside" his head. He says, "'She' seemed to be jealous that I was living while she was only a 'spirit'."[90]

Indeed, earthbound spirits appear to latch onto living people in the hope of living through them, reexperiencing the pleasures of earthly life and in particular the pleasures of food, drugs, and sex. Medium James Van Praagh recounts how his friend Laura once moved into a house in Los Angeles that made her uncomfortable from the very beginning. "I didn't want to stay in the house at all and would find all sorts of excuses to leave," she told him. "When I was out, I would want to stop in a grocery store for cigarettes, and you know, I don't smoke. But I had this overwhelming urge to buy cigarettes." She finally figured there was a ghost in her house, and when she consulted a psychic about it, the psychic confirmed that it still housed the spirits of two people who had died in it from a drug overdose. "She told me that the ghosts were the ones always sending me out for cigarettes."[91] Although this case suggests that we may be influenced by earthbound spirits without being possessed by them—perhaps "possession" is a kind of influence that comes in degrees—Fiore mentions addictions to food, drugs, or sex as warning signs of possession. She also includes in this list personality changes as well as sudden tiredness that doesn't appear to have any physical cause.[92] Many case studies suggest that earthbound spirits attempting to live through human beings siphon energy from them and cause them to feel unusually depleted.

I should also note that, although there are similarities between spirit possession and mediumship, these two phenomena do not appear to be identical, at least when mediumship is done correctly. Possession is a draining, involuntary phenomenon associated with less spiritually evolved entities. Fiore writes, "I never have conversed with a spiritually evolved possessing entity. Those must go automatically into the spirit world following their deaths."[93] However, the difference between earthbound spirits and

---

[88] William Stillman, *The Soul of Autism: Looking Beyond Labels to Unveil Spiritual Secrets of the Heart Savants* (Franklin Lakes, NJ: New Page Books, 2008), 132-50.
[89] Stoker Hunt, *Ouija: The Most Dangerous Game* (New York: Harper & Row, 1985).
[90] Alan Vaughan, *Patterns of Prophecy* (New York: Hawthorn, 1973), 2.
[91] James Van Praagh, *Ghosts Among Us: Uncovering the Truth About the Other Side* (New York: HarperOne, 2008), 54-55.
[92] Fiore, 119-21.
[93] Fiore, 154.

those communicating from their proper place in the afterlife may not be evident to an inexperienced psychic. Furthermore, it is important to be aware of the possibility that spirits may intentionally deceive us about their identity. Stillman writes,

> In my experience, it is of the utmost importance to protect oneself with prayer or meditation prior to engaging with spiritual allies. Where there is light, there is darkness. Destructive energies may manipulate and exploit the naïve or uninitiated. They do this by masquerading as something they are not, portending friendship, or making false promises. They may portray themselves as a departed grandma or even an angel. But because they are inauthentic, their masquerade will also be imperfect. The "angel" may give harmful instruction or "Grandma's" eye color will be all wrong. The most powerful way to hold them at bay is to illuminate the truth about one's own misgivings and shortcomings.
>
> To deflect and repel such destructive energies, always encapsulate yourself in a protective shield fashioned of glorious, golden light. Do this simply by visualizing it, from head to toe. Doing this in concert with prayer is a powerful combination.[94]

As you probably noted, Stillman's instructions are a variation of Fiore's White Light Technique. Fiore herself emphasizes how important training is in the areas of mediumship and channeling, noting that she had certain patients who engaged in these activities against her urging and were "constantly picking up new spirits," which she would then have to help them release. "From my conversations with *trained* mediums in Brazil and England," says Fiore, "I've learned that they too have had these experiences, much to their own discomfort and their families', until they brought their mediumship under control. Sometimes this involved intense training and help from other mediums for a few years."[95]

Dr. Alberto Villoldo, the medical anthropologist we met in the first section of this chapter, is now also a shaman trained in the Inkan tradition and is another advocate for adequate training among those attempting psychic work. In his book *Shaman, Healer, Sage: How to Heal Yourself and Others with the Energy Medicine of the Americas*, he emphasizes the importance of being guided in these efforts by an experienced practitioner, especially when it comes to attempting to identify and free earthbound spirits who are attached to living human beings, a subject he discusses in some depth.[96]

One of the services a more experienced medium can offer is help recognizing when a spirit is saying things that should or should not be

---

[94] William Stillman, *The Secret Language of Spirit: Understanding Spirit Communication in Our Everyday Lives* (Wayne, NJ: New Page Books, 2018), 45.
[95] Fiore, 117.
[96] Villoldo, 2-6, 39, 189-206.

believed. As a case in point, take an experience related by anthropologist Dr. Michael Harner in his classic book *The Way of the Shaman*. After drinking ayahuasca (a plant-based hallucinogenic brew), Harner encountered some dragon-like beings who said they were responsible for the origin of all life on earth, having come to this planet eons ago from outer space and created here various forms of life in order to disguise themselves. According to these reptilian beings, who appeared to Harner to reside at the bottom of his brain where it joined the spinal column, "[w]e humans were but the receptacles and servants of these creatures." When Harner shared with a local shaman the creatures' claims to be the "true masters of the world," the shaman was amused and said, "Oh, they're always saying that. But they are only the Masters of Outer Darkness." Harner says the shaman waved his hand toward the sky, and this gave Harner a chill, because he hadn't yet told the shaman that he had seen a vision of the creatures descending from outer space.[97]

The upshot seems to be that there was some truth to the story told to Harner by these dragon-like entities but that they were substantially exaggerating their power, a fact that only those with extensive experience and knowledge regarding these types of interactions could be expected to recognize.

The mentally ill seem to be particularly vulnerable to deception by ill-meaning entities. In the mid-20th century, clinical psychologist Dr. Wilson Van Dusen carefully interviewed mental patients about their hallucinations and found not only that they generally believed themselves to be communicating with other entities but that there were marked differences in the behavior of these entities, allowing their classification into higher and lower orders. The higher order of beings, which he estimated made up 20% or less of the total, seemed to have a consciousness superior to the everyday consciousness of the patients who interacted with them. They were generally "respectful of [the patient's] freedom, helpful, instructive, supportive, highly symbolic and religious." The lower order, on the other hand, appeared to be of much more limited intelligence and to use what intelligence they had to insult, threaten, deceive, and attack the patient. They appeared able to cause the patient pain and also, in some cases, to take over portions of the patient's body (for instance, an ear or an eye) or to speak through the patient's mouth, in a voice noticeably different from the patient's usual one. Unlike the higher order, who rarely employed verbal communication, the lower order talked incessantly inside the patient's head, demeaning the patient while bragging

[97] Michael Harner, *The Way of the Shaman: A Guide to Power and Healing* (New York: Bantam, 1980, 1982), 5-9.

about their own powers—powers which generally turned out to be much more limited than they led the patient to believe.[98]

In her book *Second Sight*, psychiatrist Dr. Judith Orloff offers an excellent example of the lower order of discarnate entities. She once saw as a patient a young man who had spent two years in a Turkish prison (many months of which he spent in solitary confinement) and who had emerged convinced that he had begun channeling the "Sun Spirits," who were sending him with a message to save the world. When he channeled the Sun Spirits in front of Orloff, however, "nothing about them felt authentic," she says. "When the voices came through him, they were often critical and cruel. … There was a psychotic flavor to it, a bizarre, condemning tone that rang false. The Sun Spirits seemed more a reflection of Steve's disowned feelings, mainly negative."[99]

Negative Thoughtforms

Orloff mentions that Steve's channeling may have simply been a reflection of his own repressed feelings, and this is a possibility that must generally be kept in mind. In fact, the connection between ill-meaning entities and the thoughts of living humans, past and present, is so frequent that at least one prominent medium, Dr. Julia Assante, actually denies that earthbound spirits exist, saying instead that there are only "thoughtforms." I have to say, however, that despite Assante's obvious knowledge in many areas, I believe this opinion of hers to be uninformed and incorrect. Assante writes,

> The earthbound-spirit hypothesis is not at all consistent with the findings of so many others who are either researching after-death communication or practicing it. In the thousands upon thousands of incidents collected, not one mention is made of encountering an earthbound spirit. Nor have any of us seen harm done to any living individual by the dead.[100]

As the examples given in this chapter illustrate, this is simply untrue.

---

[98] Wilson Van Dusen, "The Presence of Spirits in Madness: A Confirmation of Swedenborg in Recent Empirical Findings," *New Philosophy* 70 (1961). Accessible online at www.theisticpsychology.org/books/w.vandusen/presence_spirits.htm.
[99] Judith Orloff, *Second Sight: An Intuitive Psychiatrist Tells Her Extraordinary Story and Shows You How to Tap Your Own Inner Wisdom*, rev. ed. (New York: Three Rivers Press, 2000), 293-4.
[100] Julia Assante, *The Last Frontier: Exploring the Afterlife and Transforming Our Fear of Death* (Novato, CA: New World Library, 2012), 304.

As yet one more piece of evidence, here is an example of an incident that resembles the type of "haunting" that is often explained as a thoughtform lingering in a place where someone once had a traumatic experience. However, this incident shows clear signs of being intentionally produced by an intelligent consciousness.

In this case, a nurse who was once traumatically paralyzed by falling down some stairs appeared in a dream many years later to a woman who had no connection to her besides the fact that she happened to be sleeping in the place where the nurse's long-ago injury had occurred. What is so interesting is that the dream began with the nurse coming to the dreamer and specifically addressing her by name, telling her that she had something she wanted to show her. When the dreamer refused to let the nurse pull her out of bed, she was finally shown a "flash" of "the nurse falling down the stairs across from [her] dorm room and landing at the bottom of the stairs unconscious."[101] The dreamer later discovered that her dormitory had in fact once been a hospital, that a nurse had once fallen down the stairs there and become paralyzed, and that *that paralyzed nurse had died on the very night of the dream in question.* The timing of the dream, as well as the insistent behavior of the dream figure of the nurse, make it appear very likely that the spirit of the dying or recently deceased nurse did in fact come to this dreamer, and that the dream was not merely a thoughtform left behind by the trauma of the original injury.

This incident strongly resembles a type of dream that is frequently experienced by Andrew Paquette, where the spirit of a deceased person comes to him and shows him how their body died. Paquette says most of these dreams feature the spirits of people who died unexpectedly, that those who have had peaceful deaths don't generally remain earthbound and have their death weighing on their mind in this fashion. But what is especially relevant to our discussion here is that Paquette doesn't just dream of people's deaths; he dreams of the spirits of the deceased *intentionally displaying to him* their deaths. These spirits may be earthbound and not particularly enlightened about their current state, but they do appear to be conscious beings, capable of having desires and of intentionally interacting with whomever is sensitive enough to pick up on them.[102]

Nevertheless, I agree that some ghosts or possessing entities may be thoughtforms, not the spirits of deceased persons. For instance, this appears to have been the case with regard to an entity attached to Michael Crichton. In inner conversation with this entity, Crichton discovered that he had "made" this entity when he was four years old, in order to protect himself from his father, and that he had used it in the years since as emotional

---

[101] David Ryback with Letitia Sweitzer, *Dreams That Come True: Their Psychic and Transforming Powers* (New York: Doubleday, 1988), 127.
[102] Paquette, *Dreamer*, 98-99.

protection against other people. He describes in his memoir *Travels* how he became aware of this entity and ultimately asked it to depart.[103]

It seems that mediums, too, may sometimes be channeling thoughtforms rather than the spirits of the deceased, and these thoughtforms may not be attributable to any one individual but may rather be entities produced by the collective, unconscious influence of a group of people. For example, Polish philosopher and psychologist Dr. Julian Ochorowicz conducted investigations of the Italian physical medium Eusapia Palladino beginning in 1893 and participated in group séances in which Palladino produced manifestations of a personality who went by the name "John King." Ochorowicz concluded, however, that "John King" was not a separately existing individual—because his personal characteristics changed depending on who was present at the séance. For instance, Ochorowicz noted that "John King" spoke English in England, Italian in Italy, and some French and Polish when the medium was primarily surrounded by speakers of these languages. "When asked how he suddenly understood Polish," says Ochorowicz, "his answer was that, in the days when he lived on earth, he met some Poles during his wanderings in America. But a different explanation seems to be simpler—*our thoughts were reflected in Eusapia's mind*."[104]

Evil

Perhaps a collectively created thoughtform also explains another case I'm about to relate, although it's hard to escape the feeling that something more diabolical is at work here. In his memoir *The Siren Call of Hungry Ghosts*, journalist Joe Fisher recounts the harrowing experiences that grew out of his connection with a woman named Aviva who appeared to be channeling spirit guides. One of these guides, "Filipa," claimed to have been Fisher's lover in a previous incarnation in 18th-century Greece, a thought that appealed to Fisher, who apparently had had his share of romantic troubles.[105] From the start, this guide suggested that Fisher open himself up to more direct contact from her, contact that would offer him "direction" and "companionship." Fisher and other members of the group gathered around Aviva were only too open to such suggestions, and over time, the supposed guides began exhibiting possessive behavior toward members of the group, instigating

---

[103] Crichton, 335-44.

[104] Julian Ochorowicz, *Mediumistic Phenomena*, Part I, trans. Casimir Bernard and Zofia Weaver, ed. Zofia Weaver, *Journal of Scientific Exploration* 32, no. 1 (Spring 2018): 79-154, p. 127.

[105] Joe Fisher, *The Siren Call of Hungry Ghosts: A Riveting Investigation into Channeling and Spirit Guides* (New York: Paraview Press, 2001), 22.

interpersonal conflict among them, and generally abusing them psychologically.

An account given by one of the group members, Sandford, reads like the experience of someone caught up in a particularly vicious cult. Sandford told Fisher that his guide, Tuktu,

> would tell me that I was useless, that I couldn't make decisions, that I didn't stick up for myself and so forth. These derogatory remarks were made so that I would express anger, so that my "anger center" could be opened up. … They would scramble my thinking and feeling processes so that I wasn't able to function properly. And then they would be the ones to make me feel better. … The guides were out to create enormous dependency—and they succeeded.[106]

Sandford actually left his wife because of lies the guides told him about her, including repeated warnings that he would die if he stayed with her.[107] Fortunately, the couple was later reunited.

As for Fisher, he eventually went to Greece in an effort to confirm some of the things "Filipa" had told him about their supposed past life together. He went to the city of Alexandroupolis, which Filipa claimed to have visited during their 18th-century life, but he was shocked to discover that Alexandroupolis was a relatively young city that didn't become Greek until 1920, at which time it received the name "Alexandroupolis" to honor the 20th-century King Alexandros. Before then, it had gone by the Turkish name Dedeagats.[108] This, along with other inaccuracies Fisher unearthed on his travels, convinced him that the "guides" were not what they purported to be.

Sandford's conclusion was that Aviva's unconscious mind was colluding with duplicitous discarnate spirits. In an effort to form his own opinion about what was going on, Fisher had audio recordings of Aviva speaking as Filipa—sometimes in English and sometimes in Greek—analyzed by a Greek-born university professor who specialized in the study of modern Greek. The professor explained that Aviva's pronunciation at times indicated a Greek-born person, though at other times it sounded more like a person *learning* Greek. He also said that a remark she made about a difference in pronunciation between a dialect and formal Greek "could relate only to the years 1912-1920 when unofficial changes in Greek phonetics were institutionalized at the time of Thrace's incorporation with Greece following the Balkan Wars," and that her mention of the *drachma* was not appropriate

---

106 Fisher, 249.
107 Fisher, 246.
108 Fisher, 218.

to 18th-century Thrace, when the Turkish *kuruch* would have been used instead.[109]

As part of his extensive research into communication with discarnate beings, Fisher also spoke with Dr. Adam Crabtree, author of *Multiple Man: Explorations in Possession & Multiple Personality*. Crabtree told him he didn't believe any of the blanket explanations for the phenomenon, that is, "that the process of channeling is purely self-delusion or purely the individual's unconscious or purely what the entities, so-called, would have us believe."[110] Crabtree's feeling was that channeling generally involved discarnate entities but that, despite their ability to psychically access information, these entities were not truthful about their own identities. Fisher himself ultimately seems to have concluded that the guides he interacted with were earthbound spirits who lied in order to manipulate humans and also in order to avoid facing the fact that they were dead.

In an epilogue added to his book after its first publication in Canada and the UK, Fisher quotes at length the letter of a former spiritualist psychic who wrote to tell him that she felt his interpretation of the guides as errant earthbound spirits was "too kind." She expressed her view that mediums are not dealing with "lost souls" but with "masters of deception," who are incredibly intelligent and have seemingly unbounded psychic access to information they can use to deceive.[111] While Fisher doesn't follow this woman in all of her conclusions (and I would point out that the "guides" who speak through trance mediums often appear laughably limited in their knowledge[112]), Fisher does maintain, after all of his personal experience and abundant research, that "no highly evolved, spiritual being would ever speak through an incarnate human."[113] He concludes the 2001 American edition of his book with these three sentences:

> I am simply grateful to have survived my confrontation with the liars and deceivers of the spirit world. Only when the struggle was far advanced did I finally comprehend the meager state of my resources as well as the might and swiftness of the unseen enemy. Let this be a warning to all.[114]

---

[109] Fisher, 255.
[110] Fisher, 268.
[111] Fisher, 305.
[112] As just one example, take one of the early control spirits of Leonora Piper, a medium who was heavily investigated by parapsychologists at the turn of the 20th century. As noted by sociologist James McClenon, "Her early 'control' (a spirit who acted as a kind of master of ceremonies) claimed to be French but was unable to speak or comprehend that language. Often the information she gave was false." [James McClenon, *Wondrous Events: Foundations of Religious Belief* (Philadelphia: University of Pennsylvania Press, 1994), 193.]
[113] Fisher, 303.
[114] Fisher, 307.

Unfortunately, it is not clear that Fisher did in fact survive this confrontation. In 2001, the same year in which those words were published, he committed suicide by jumping from a cliff.[115]

I recommend that anyone who is convinced that no darkness lurks in the unseen realms—whether the realms of spirit or of the human psyche—read Fisher's book in its entirety. He looked very deeply into these matters, and his conclusions, as well as the testimony of his life and death, are sobering. I would also recommend reading Playfair's *The Flying Cow*, which, despite its playful title, contains a great deal of evidence for the reality of malevolent spiritual influence, taken primarily from poltergeist cases investigated by the Instituto Brasileiro de Pesquisas Psicobiofisicas (the Brazilian Institute for Psycho-Biophysical Research).

Indeed, I don't think we can rule out the possibility that there exist powerful paranormal entities with evil intentions—which, if we are inclined to a religious vocabulary, we might call "demons," or possibly even "Satan." Scott Peck describes most cases of possession in the literature as cases of possession "by minor demons." However, he describes the two cases he personally encountered as being "highly unusual in that both were cases of Satanic possession." "I know now Satan is real," he says. "I have met it." He grants that he can't transfer this certainty to readers who haven't had the same experience, but he does hope that "closed-minded readers will become more open-minded in relation to the reality of evil spirit."[116]

Having not had any personal encounters with what I would consider supernatural evil, I don't have much to contribute to the discussion, beyond recommending that readers consult the literature that is available on the topic. In particular, I suggest Peck's two books *People of the Lie* and *Glimpses of the Devil* and another book that Peck recommends: Malachi Martin's *Hostage to the Devil*.[117] Another account of possession that parallels those of Peck and Martin comes from healer Dean Kraft and is related in his book *A Touch of Hope*.[118] For contrast, I highly recommend also reading Edith Fiore's *The Unquiet Dead*, on possession by entities interpreted as earthbound spirits, as well as Adam Crabtree's *Multiple Man*, on the relationship between possession and multiple-personality disorder.

With regard to the objective existence of evil, the reports of near-death experiencers offer some intriguing suggestions. For instance, an NDEr who

---

[115] Loren Coleman, "The Sudden Death of Joe Fisher," *The Anomalist*, https://www.anomalist.com/milestones/fisher.html (accessed August 4, 2018).
[116] Peck, *People of the Lie*, 183-4.
[117] Malachi Martin, *Hostage to the Devil: The Possession and Exorcism of Five Contemporary Americans* (New York: Bantam Books, 1977).
[118] Dean Kraft with Rochelle Kraft, *A Touch of Hope: The Autobiography of a Laying-on-of-Hands Healer* (New York: G. P. Putnam's Sons, 1998), 63-68.

was raised Episcopalian reports communicating with an entity who said he was not God or Jesus but who nevertheless struck her as "good and all-knowing." She remembers asking this guide-like entity various questions, and one of the answers she got was very clear in her memory. "My upbringing had [led] me to believe that God was omnipotent," she says, "but the answer I got was that one can choose to be in the camp of good or in the camp of evil. Those two forces are constantly at balance with one another, with equal strength and power."[119] NDEr Betty J. Eadie reports being informed of something similar. She says that the universe contains positive and negative energies, both of which are necessary for "creation and growth," and both of which "God has absolute power over."[120]

The status of evil in our world is a matter of long theological debate. Much New Age philosophy promulgates the idea that evil has no objective existence in the spiritual realms, while traditional Christianity teaches that evil came into a good world through the free choice of God's creatures but will ultimately be conquered by God, who is purely good. Other views, such as Gnosticism and Manichaeism, view evil as more original to the world and as possibly just as powerful as good.

Most important, I would say, is one's own personal choice whether to align oneself with good or evil, as well as the maintenance of a discerning eye when evaluating the nature of one's personal experiences. While harm can likely result from denying the possibility of evil, we should also not be too quick to assume that apparently negative events are of evil origin. We must keep in mind that events that initially seem negative may in fact turn out to be positive (as well as vice versa). Even Joe Fisher cites the fact that his friend Sandford received some benefits from his traumatic experience with the "guides." Before beginning to attend the channeling sessions, Sandford and his wife had an uncommunicative and unhappy marriage. The guides ended up compounding an already difficult situation, but in the end, Sandford says, "[i]n some perverse way, the guides were our teachers. Without their intervention, Betty and I would probably still be locked in the same desperate nothingness that our marriage used to be."[121]

Of course, just because good can be made to come out of evil doesn't mean that the intent of the primary actors wasn't negative. Sandford would never have reaped the benefits of the guides' manipulations if he hadn't ultimately refused to heed their threats and acted on his own initiative. The credit for this happy result shouldn't go to the guides, but to Sandford, who stood up to them.

---

[119] Barbara R. Rommer, *Blessing in Disguise: Another Side of the Near-Death Experience* (St. Paul, MN: Llewellyn, 2000), 28.
[120] Betty J. Eadie with Curtis Taylor, *Embraced by the Light* (Carson City, NV: Gold Leaf Press, 1992), 57.
[121] Fisher, 251.

A strong enough personality, with perhaps some positive supernatural aid, can find the silver lining in almost any horror. As Scott Peck's experience as a psychiatrist has led him to observe, "The truth is that our finest moments are most likely to occur when we are feeling deeply uncomfortable, unhappy, or unfulfilled. For it is only in such moments, propelled by our discomfort, that we are likely to step out of our ruts and start searching for different ways or truer answers."[122] As we saw earlier in this chapter, those who have studied distressing near-death experiences have come to a similar conclusion: scary and unpleasant events can be what we need to propel us to the next stage of our spiritual growth.

Many Jungian psychoanalysts write optimistically about the growth potential of confrontation with our shadow side. For example, Robert A. Johnson writes in *Inner Work*,

> Characteristics that look immoral, barbaric, or embarrassing to us are the "negative" side of a valuable energy, a capacity we could make use of. You will never find anything in the unconscious that will not be useful and good when it is made conscious and brought to the right level.[123]

Dr. Victor Mansfield says in *Synchronicity, Science, and Soul-Making*, "The assimilation of the neglected member of a pair of opposites is at the center of individuation,"[124] and dreamworker Robert Moss puts the same point more colloquially: "if we are willing to face our night terrors, we may find a greater power that is seeking us."[125]

Indeed, there is some evidence that the symptoms of mental illness can actually be an avenue to improved mental health. John Lilly mentions meeting several people who had been through psychotic episodes and who "reported how beneficial this was to their subsequent life." Lilly suggests that psychotics are accessing altered states of consciousness similar to those that others have reached through meditation, sensory deprivation, or hallucinatory drugs. While our society is not set up to support people who remain in such states for prolonged periods, prolonged altered states of consciousness may be precisely what certain people need in order to heal.[126]

Nevertheless, Jung himself was never blasé about the dangers of confrontation with the darker side of the unconscious, which he knew

---

[122] As quoted in Caroline Myss, *Invisible Acts of Power: Personal Choices That Create Miracles* (New York: Free Press, 2004), 205.
[123] Robert A. Johnson, *Inner Work: Using Dreams and Active Imagination for Personal Growth* (New York: HarperOne, 1986), 71.
[124] Victor Mansfield, *Synchronicity, Science, and Soul-Making* (Chicago: Open Court, 1995), 65.
[125] Robert Moss, *The Boy Who Died and Came Back: Adventures of a Dream Archaeologist in the Multiverse* (Novato, CA: New World Library, 2014), 43.
[126] Lilly, 77-78.

intimately. As just one example, consider that, in the most chaotic and psychologically difficult period of his life, Jung had a dream after which a voice told him that he *had* to figure out the meaning of the dream, or else he'd have to shoot himself. He was frightened—not least because he knew there was a loaded gun in the drawer of his nightstand. Thankfully, the meaning of the dream soon came to Jung, and this tumultuous period in his life ended up producing his greatest work.[127] However, the experience of Joe Fisher shows that a positive outcome cannot always be assumed. In many cases, the danger appears to be real, and not every soul may be up to the extreme mental challenge of surmounting it.

That great psychologist and investigator of mediums William James cautioned,

> [R]eligious mysticism is only one half of mysticism. The other half has no accumulated traditions except those which the text-books on insanity supply. Open any one of these, and you will find abundant cases in which 'mystical ideas' are cited as characteristic symptoms of enfeebled or deluded states of mind. In delusional insanity, paranoia, as they sometimes call it, we may have a *diabolical* mysticism, a sort of religious mysticism turned upside down. The same sense of ineffable importance in the smallest events, the same texts and words coming with new meanings, the same voices and visions and leadings and missions, the same controlling by extraneous powers; only this time the emotion is pessimistic: instead of consolations we have desolations; the meanings are dreadful; and the powers are enemies to life. It is evident that from the point of view of their psychological mechanism, the classic mysticism and these lower mysticisms spring from the same mental level, from that great subliminal or transmarginal region of which science is beginning to admit the existence, but of which so little is really known. That region contains every kind of matter: 'seraph and snake' abide there side by side. To come from thence is no infallible credential. What comes must be sifted and tested, and run the gauntlet of confrontation with the total context of experience, just like what comes from the outer world of sense.[128]

I hope that you will take from this chapter an awareness of the need for discernment regarding the interpretation of coincidences and the trust one puts in them. Just like the voices studied by Van Dusen, coincidences can come in higher and lower forms. Should you encounter coincidences that lead you to think less of yourself or of others, know that you have the choice

---

[127] C. G. Jung, *Memories, Dreams, Reflections*, ed. Aniela Jaffé, trans. Richard and Clara Winston, rev. ed. (New York: Vintage Books, 1961, 1989), 180.

[128] William James, *The Varieties of Religious Experience*, in *Writings 1902-1920*, ed. Bruce Kuklick, The Library of America (New York: Literary Classics of the United States, 1987), 384.

to accept what they are implying or not. Should you feel trapped or threatened by your coincidence experiences, don't hesitate to seek out a trustworthy, open-minded person for advice. Having negative—even evil-seeming—experiences does not mean that you are a bad person, or even that you are ill. Some of the greatest human minds and souls have been at one time or another tormented by demons, whether literal or figurative ones. The mere act of confiding in another person about such experiences can sometimes relieve much of the burden they impose. At the very least, it is a helpful first step.

In the last chapter of this book, "Interpreting Coincidences," we will discuss in more depth how to puzzle out the meaning of obscure, or even disturbing, coincidences. In the meantime, let me leave you with the reminder that not everything that is scary is evil. While some thinkers undoubtedly underestimate the powers of darkness, even Scott Peck, who believes in the existence of demons, doesn't see them around every corner. He, too, knows that many of the things we fear in life are things that we would be better off embracing. "It is because our conscious self resists our unconscious wisdom that we become ill," he writes in *The Road Less Traveled.*[129] Many of the disconcerting feelings welling up from our unconscious are actually trying to heal us.

Recall from Chapter 6 the bloody stains that appeared on Jenny Saunders' wall. While some might see the paranormal appearance of blood and immediately think "evil," the stains in fact seemed to represent Saunders' guilt and grief over the loss of her unborn child. Feelings that we don't want to face can be terrifying, even when they don't manifest as bloody splotches on our living room wall. But choosing to acknowledge them can ultimately bring great healing. In the end, it's how we choose to respond to the distressing experiences of our lives that matters most.

---

[129] M. Scott Peck, *The Road Less Traveled: A New Psychology of Love, Traditional Values and Spiritual Growth* (New York: Simon & Schuster, 1978), 282.

Chapter 9

Natural Law

So far in this book, we've focused on coincidences that can be explained by appeal to the thoughts, feelings, or desires of a conscious being. What we haven't yet discussed are the many coincidences that are striking in their improbability but that don't seem to be connected to the motivations of any particular individual nor to have any obvious meaning for the people who experience them. Consider, for instance, a coincidence related by Drs. Allan Combs and Mark Holland in their book *Synchronicity*. One of the authors was driving across town when

> [h]e noticed that the car radio was playing an old popular song about "bad, bad, Leroy Brown," who among other things is said to be "meaner than a junkyard dog." The phrase stuck in his mind. He imagined that there must actually be such dogs living out their lives in junkyards, growing older and meaner by the day. These reflections were cut off abruptly as he switched stations. Instantly, he heard an advertisement for a local junkyard billing itself as the "home of the junkyard dog." He happened to look up and notice that he was passing a large junkyard. The sign read, "Home of the Junkyard Dog"![1]

That is, within the space of what was probably less than 60 seconds, the author heard two different radio stations mention "junkyard dog" and then found himself in front of the very junkyard advertised by the second station, complete with a sign bearing the same phrase.

---

[1] Allan Combs and Mark Holland, *Synchronicity: Through the Eyes of Science, Myth, and the Trickster*, 3rd ed. (New York: Marlowe & Company, 1996, 2001), 21.

Another author, Michael Talbot, describes a similar coincidence that happened to him. In a single day, he had three unconnected encounters with the name "Buffalo Bill."[2] While the timing of his encounters was not as tight as the ones in Combs and Holland's case, the phrase in question was once again a fairly unusual one.

After their improbability, the most striking thing about the coincidences just described is the triviality of their subject matter. "As incredible as this experience was," writes Talbot, "the only thing that seemed meaningful about it was its improbable nature."[3] The literature of coincidences is full of accounts like these: experiences of events that are unusual in their improbability but that don't seem to have any obvious significance. These sorts of coincidences are particularly apt to be dismissed (even by their experiencers) as demonstrations that, over enough people and enough time, even very odd events are likely to happen purely by chance. And that is certainly one explanation to consider. But there is another possibility. The prevalence of highly improbable but psychologically trivial coincidences suggests that there may exist some high-order regularities in nature according to which similar people, places, times, words, and events tend to arrange themselves in similar patterns. In this chapter, we are going to discuss the plausibility of this type of natural law and whether it could explain some of the coincidences we experience.

We'll begin by looking at some further examples of "gratuitous" coincidences that could be explained by such a natural law or laws. Note, however, that by including these examples in this chapter, I do not intend to say that all (or any) of them *should* be explained in this way. Some of them may be entirely the product of random forces—true coincidences—or they may turn out to be best explained by some of the other sources discussed in this book. However, through the course of this chapter, I hope that the enormous improbability of some of these cases, as well as their accumulation, will begin to show you why an explanation in terms of natural law has seemed persuasive to so many writers on the topic.

Thoughts and Their Objects

I'm going to organize my presentation of the coincidence examples in this chapter according to a few broad patterns. While these patterns may or may not reflect a deeper truth about the nature of the phenomenon underlying these cases—that is, they may or may not tell us something

---

[2] Michael Talbot, *The Holographic Universe: The Revolutionary Theory of Reality* (New York: Harper Perennial, 1991, 1992, 2011), 78.
[3] Talbot, *The Holographic Universe*, 78.

interesting about a potential natural law explaining their occurrence—they will at least give us a starting point for organizing our thoughts on the matter.

First, let's consider some cases that suggest a tendency of people, animals, and physical objects to show up when they are being thought about. One simple example is when you're thinking of someone and they call or stop by. As discussed in Chapter 6, this kind of coincidence can often be explained by your own ESP, where the idea is that you have unconscious psychic knowledge that you're about to run into someone or hear from them, and so you find yourself thinking of them just as they make their appearance. Such a coincidence could also be explained by the ESP of the other person, if your thought of them telepathically prompts them to contact you.

Telepathy might also explain cases like that of Adolf Portmann, who was about to tell a story concerning a praying mantis, in order to conclude a biology lecture he was giving in Italian Switzerland. Portmann had never before seen a praying mantis in Italian Switzerland, even though he spent time there every year, but just as he was getting ready to launch into his praying mantis anecdote, a praying mantis flew in the window, circled around his head, and alighted near a lamp, causing an enormous shadow of itself to appear on the wall behind him.[4]

We saw some evidence in Chapter 7 that animals are psychically suggestible, so perhaps this praying mantis was attracted to the room by Portmann's thoughts about the story he was about to tell. However, even if many cases of coincidences involving thoughts and their objects can be explained by ESP, there are also cases for which there are no neat psychic explanations because *both the thoughts and the presence of the objects of those thoughts have strong, independent explanations*, and yet these thoughts and objects manage to coincide in an uncanny manner.

Take, for instance, the case of Stephen Jenkins, who had just finished an exhaustive study of the biblical book of Zechariah, during which he had been particularly interested in Zechariah's reference to four horsemen with horses that were red, black, dapple, and white—horses that he noted reappeared as the Four Horsemen of the Apocalypse in the New Testament book of Revelation. On the evening of completing his study of Zechariah, Jenkins went out onto the balcony of the hotel room where he was staying and saw in the field below exactly four horses, in exactly the colors of red, black, dapple, and white. He even took a photograph of the horses the next day, because he didn't expect anyone to believe his story without it.

There was also a curious follow-up to this coincidence when, exactly 11 months later, Jenkins was on an outdoor excursion when he saw a small herd

---

[4] Gilles Quispel, "Gnosis and Psychology," in *The Gnostic Jung*, ed. Robert A. Segal (Princeton, NJ: Princeton University Press, 1992), 239-56, p. 247.

of Dartmoor ponies. Out ahead of the herd, by about 100 yards, were four ponies of the colors red, black, dapple, and white.[5]

If we focus on attempting to explain Jenkins' first horse sighting, we see that his thoughts about the four horses were caused by his long-term study of Zechariah, not by an unconscious precognition that he was about to see four such horses in real life. On the other hand, if we try to reverse the direction of explanation, there doesn't seem to be any simple way in which Jenkins' thoughts about the horses could have caused him to come across them at that particular time. The horses were presumably real horses that had been living in that paddock prior to the time of the coincidence. The most promising explanation in terms of individual psi would seem to be that Jenkins chose to stay at this hotel because he knew by unconscious ESP that these four horses could be seen from a room there. But even that explanation is fairly complex and not terribly convincing. This just doesn't seem like a case that is adequately explained by simple psychic influence in either direction.

Consider another case that presents the same problem. In this one, a Dr. James Durham was in between patients and decided to spend a few moments chatting with his new receptionist. Discovering she was from Prague, he asked her if she knew a beer hall he liked there, called the King of Brabant. In fact, she'd lived not far from it and had been a regular there. It was the only such place Durham and his receptionist discussed, and while they were still talking about it, the doorbell rang. The receptionist went to answer and came back pale-faced. "I don't know what's happening," she said, "it's the landlady of the King of Brabant." When Durham was in Prague, he had off-handedly told the landlady of the beer hall that, if she ever came to London, she should look him up.[6] But why should she appear at the door at that particular moment? Did Durham have unconscious precognitive information that she'd be showing up then, which led him to mention the beer hall to his new receptionist? Yet it seems like his mention of the King of Brabant followed naturally from his finding out that his receptionist was from Prague. If his thought of the beer hall wasn't precognitively prompted, then did it somehow have an effect backward in time, which prompted the King of Brabant's landlady to leave Prague and come to the UK at just the right time to show up at the particular moment when her beer hall was being discussed? Again, explanation of this coincidence in terms of psychic influence seems less than straightforward.

---

[5] Stephen Jenkins, *The Undiscovered Country* (Sudbury, UK: Neville Spearman, 1976), 108-9, as summarized in Roderick Main, *Revelations of Chance: Synchronicity as Spiritual Experience* (Albany, NY: State University of New York Press, 2007), 11-12.

[6] Alister Hardy, Robert Harvie, and Arthur Koestler, *The Challenge of Chance: A Mass Experiment in Telepathy and Its Unexpected Outcome* (New York: Random House, 1973), 205-6.

That's not to say that psychic processes can't be complex. According to the "magic wand hypothesis" of psychic influence, outlined by philosopher Dr. Stephen E. Braude (but not necessarily endorsed by him), complexity is no hurdle at all for psychic processes. On this view, says Braude, "even the most extensive or refined psi requires nothing more than an efficacious wish or desire, as if the subject simply waved a magic wand to achieve a desired effect."[7] This hypothesis gains some support from the fact that, in cases where it seems clear that people *do* manage to influence the world psychokinetically, they appear not to have to think through the steps of how they're going to do it. They just imagine their desired outcome, and somehow that outcome tends to happen. Given the psychological opacity of the underlying process, who can say how many psychic "steps" are being taken in such a case? And who can say how many steps make a psychic explanation for a coincidence unreasonable?

All we have to go on in determining the extent of our psychic capacities is evidence from cases where those capacities seem clearly to be the origin of the events in question. Are there cases where people have intentionally psychokinetically influenced the world in ways as complex as they would have to do to produce the coincidences just described?

This depends partly on what one means by 'complex'. Is it a *complex* task to make an accordion play without touching it, as Daniel Dunglas Home apparently did?[8] In some ways, it undoubtedly is. But it might not be complex in the same way as the creation of the above coincidences, which require the precise coordination of multiple actions of multiple agents.

The closest thing I can find to examples of equally complex coincidences that were likely caused by PK are two of the coincidences we examined in Chapter 6: the one in which Kirby Surprise wondered what it would be like to be able to make a house implode simply by willing it (and then found out) and the other in which Andrew Paquette willed that the materials for an entire issue of *The Atlantic Monthly* get delivered to his house instead of to the printer (and they did). I presented those cases as examples of the ambiguity that can surround the source of coincidences, even in cases where the experiencer intentionally willed the coincidence to occur. I concluded in that chapter that these cases were ones in which the experiencer's own PK seemed as good an explanation as any other that appealed to a unique source. And, while they are far from being *proof* that PK can produce such complex coincidences, they do give us some evidence that makes that hypothesis more likely than it might otherwise seem.

---

[7] Stephen E. Braude, *Immortal Remains: The Evidence for Life after Death* (Lanham, MD: Rowman & Littlefield, 2003), 11.

[8] On the well-attested feats of 19th-century medium Daniel Dunglas Home, see Stephen E. Braude, *The Limits of Influence: Psychokinesis and the Philosophy of Science* (New York: Routledge & Kegan Paul, 1986), 70-108.

However, there is a very important distinction between the Kirby and Paquette cases, on the one hand, and the four horses and the King of Brabant cases on the other. In the latter, there is not only no conscious intention on the part of the coincidence experiencers to create the coincidences, but there is not even any obvious compelling psychological reason for them to *want* to create these coincidences, even unconsciously. That is, it is not so much that it seems like they *couldn't* as that it seems like they *wouldn't*. These coincidences just don't seem like the sort of thing that any conscious being has a particular interest in creating. And that is why so many thinkers about coincidences have been drawn to the idea that there is some natural phenomenon that creates these gratuitous coincidences, quite apart from anyone's *willing* them to occur.

Images and Their Objects

With that distinction emphasized, let's turn now to a second type of gratuitous coincidence: that between a visual image and the object it portrays. While it's true that the presence of a human being in both of the cases described below means we can't rule out the possibility that it was actually this person's *thoughts about* the image or its object that produced the coincidence (because we don't yet understand the process by which any of these coincidences are produced), I believe it makes sense for now to note these cases as a category of potentially independent interest.

English writer J. B. Priestley describes an experience that happened to his wife, archeologist Jacquetta Hawkes. She had just received delivery of three large lithographs she'd purchased and leaned them against a chair in her bedroom to await the moment when she would hang them. The outermost lithograph, visible to the room, was of a grasshopper. "When Jacquetta got into bed that night," writes Priestley,

> she felt some sort of twittering movement going on, so she got out and pulled back the clothes. There was a grasshopper in the bed. No grasshopper had been seen in that room before, nor has been seen since. No grasshopper has ever been seen at any other time in this house.[9]

In another case, composer and conductor Arthur Butterworth was serving in the armed forces during World War II when he ordered a music book, to be delivered to his barracks. When it arrived, he unwrapped it, and a picture postcard fell out of its pages. "The picture might have been taken

---

[9] Letter dated February 7, 1972, as quoted in Alister Hardy, Robert Harvie, and Arthur Koestler, *The Challenge of Chance: A Mass Experiment in Telepathy and Its Unexpected Outcome* (New York: Random House, 1973), 201.

at that moment," he says, "...for it showed *exactly* the scene through the window I was then standing in front of."[10]

Location, Location, Location

Speaking of landscapes, several coincidences I've come across prominently feature physical locations. In Chapter 16, "Meetings & Reunions," we'll see cases where the same people seem repeatedly drawn to each other like magnets, but in the cases I'm about to relate, it appears to be a physical location itself that is doing the attracting, repeatedly drawing similar people or events.

For instance, writer Irving Kupcinet was staying at the Savoy Hotel in London when he found in a drawer in his room some things that belonged to a friend of his, Harlem Globetrotter Harry Hannin. Two days later, Hannin wrote to him from the Hotel Meurice in Paris saying he'd found a tie in a drawer in his hotel room with Kupcinet's name on it. Kupcinet had in fact recently stayed at *that* hotel as well.[11] How did these two friends end up staying in the same rooms of the same hotels in two different cities within two days of each other? (And why did they each leave behind a personal item that the other would recognize?)

On a related note, physician Dr. John Lerma has observed that people seem to be coincidentally drawn to certain rooms in his hospice facility, even though, as with most hotel guests, they have no control over the room to which they are assigned, and the staff doesn't know their history. Nevertheless, he says, "[p]eople who are in rooms next to each other often see the same visions, have some of the same experiences, and often die at the same time. It's also curious that sometimes people who have died in hospice have relatives who are assigned to the same room later on."[12]

This next case also suggests that a physical location may attract a particular type of experience, as well as specific people. Andrew Hudson was being driven along the M1 in England when the driver started to have trouble accelerating and had to pull over and call for assistance. Several months later, Hudson was again being driven along the M1 by a different person, but just after passing the spot where the previous incident had occurred, *this* car, too, had trouble accelerating, and the driver had to pull over and call for help. As

---

[10] Brian Inglis, *Coincidence: A Matter of Chance – or Synchronicity?* (London: Hutchinson, 1990), 19.

[11] Alan Vaughan, *Incredible Coincidence: The Baffling World of Synchronicity* (New York: J. B. Lippincott Company, 1979), 28. Originally published in Julia Green, "One in a Million," *Modern People* (October 27, 1974): 16.

[12] John Lerma, *Into the Light: Real Life Stories about Angelic Visits, Visions of the Afterlife, and Other Pre-Death Experiences* (Pompton Plains, NJ: New Page Books, 2007), 109.

if this weren't odd enough, as Hudson was standing by the side of the road waiting for help to arrive, he saw the car from the first incident several months before approaching, with that other driver at the wheel![13]

This case gives the humorous impression that the universe might have been trying to reconstitute the same event that had happened at that spot previously but gotten some of the actors' roles mixed up!

Situational Encores

In this next case, the physical location was not the same, but the circumstances that were repeated were very precise. A man named Alfred Smith saved the life of another man, Allen Falby, when Falby had a motorcycle accident and needed a tourniquet put on his leg. Five years later, Falby himself was at the scene of a car accident, and he in turn had to put a tourniquet on another man's leg in order to save his life. The really strange part of it was that the other man was Alfred Smith, who had saved his life five years before in exactly the same way![14]

Here's another excellent example of precise circumstances' seeming to summon the same actors. This is Carl Jung's summary of a case that's been cited by many writers down through the years. The "Monsieur Deschamps" in question is French poet Emile Deschamps.

> A certain M. Deschamps, when a boy in Orléans, was once given a piece of plum-pudding by a M. de Fortgibu. Ten years later he discovered another plum-pudding in a Paris restaurant, and asked if he could have a piece. It turned out, however, that the plum-pudding was already ordered—by M. de Fortgibu. Many years afterwards M. Deschamps was invited to partake of a plum-pudding as a special rarity. While he was eating it he remarked that the only thing lacking was M. de Fortgibu. At that moment the door opened and an old, old man in the last stages of disorientation walked in: M. de Fortgibu, who had got hold of the wrong address and burst in on the party by mistake.[15]

---

[13] Inglis, *Coincidence*, 27.

[14] Vaughan, *Incredible Coincidence*, 28-30. Originally published in Doug Storer, "Good Samaritan on Motorcycle Is Himself Saved by Man He Helped," *National Tattler* (November 10, 1974): 22.

[15] C. G. Jung, *Synchronicity: An Acausal Connecting Principle*, trans. R. F. C. Hull (Princeton, NJ: Princeton University Press, 1960, 2010), 15. Jung drew his account from Camille Flammarion, *L'Inconnu et les problèmes psychiques* (New York: Harper & Brothers, 1900). The original account was apparently given by Emile Deschamps in a memoir, but I have yet to track it down.

The Anniversary Effect

In addition to thoughts, images, places, and situations, there is another strange attractor in the world of coincidences: dates.

Now, some date coincidences can be explained by unconscious memory. Recall again the case from Chapter 6 of Jenny Saunders, who found red blotches splattered on her living room wall above her childhood doll house. While she couldn't make sense of these blotches herself, consultation with psychiatrist Dr. Joel Whitton uncovered that she had become pregnant the previous summer and, because she was "terrified of having a baby," had scheduled an abortion. But when she went for the abortion, it was discovered that the baby had already been dead for three days. Dr. Whitton confirmed in Saunders' gynecological records that, had her baby survived, it would have been due on April 10—the very day that the first stains appeared on the wall above the doll house.[16] It appears likely that Saunders was unconsciously aware of the importance of this date and selected it for expressing her feelings about her lost child, through "poltergeist" effects.

Another striking case involving an important date is recounted by shaman Dr. Alberto Villoldo. This is a more proper case of what is often called the "anniversary effect," but it is still one that could possibly be explained by unconscious memory combined with psychokinesis. A woman named Magda sought Villoldo's help for what she called her "terrible bad luck." He explains,

> She was a single mother when her only son, then seventeen years old, had been involved in a tragic automobile accident. Every year on the date of his death Magda would find herself in a life-threatening situation. One year her car was rear-ended while she was stopped at a traffic signal, and she had to be taken in for emergency surgery. The following year a case of indigestion sent her to the emergency room, where she was given an oral solution of barium for an exam. The doctors discovered that she was allergic to barium only when her heart stopped. This pattern continued for five consecutive years. Magda could not understand why she kept experiencing near-death trauma that occurred only on February 26.[17]

Despite Magda's confusion, it became clear to Villoldo in his consultation with her that she blamed herself for her son's death and that part of her wished that she had died instead of her son. This part of her seemed to be creating anniversary "coincidences" that expressed her desperate feelings of

---

[16] Joel L. Whitton and Joe Fisher, *Life Between Life: Scientific Explorations into the Void Separating One Incarnation from the Next* (New York: Warner Books, 1986), 171-8.

[17] Alberto Villoldo, *Shaman, Healer, Sage: How to Heal Yourself and Others with the Energy Medicine of the Americas* (New York: Harmony, 2000), 58-59.

guilt. Villoldo reports that, once he helped Magda to truly grieve her son's death and clear the "imprint" that this tragic event had left in her energy, "[s]he spent thc next February 26 in fine health."[18]

In my own life, I've experienced an example of the anniversary effect that shows that the memories involved don't always have to be negative ones. Several years ago, I was on a bus ride during which I suddenly found myself thinking about a man I'd once been briefly involved with. Though the memories were fond ones, I didn't consciously reflect on them very often, and it seemed strange to me that he should suddenly pop into my head in this way. I was all the more surprised when the bus then drove past two unrelated signs that each bore the first name of this man. It was only after seeing these two signs that I realized that day was the anniversary of the day we had met and begun our brief love affair.

Now, unconscious memory combined with psychokinesis might be able to explain the three examples of the anniversary effect I've just given, but there are many more examples that can't be explained in this way—at least not given the way we normally think of memory, as being directed toward the past. This is because many coincidences happen on the "pre-anniversaries" of important events, marking the important date before the event has even occurred.

Dreams in particular are famous for occurring on the pre-anniversaries of important events. For example, Cynthia Pearson once had a dream that her sister's building had a fire, and when her sister tried to make a phone call in the dream to find out what happened, the operator refused to connect her. This dream occurred one year to the day before the Los Angeles earthquake of January 17, 1994, when Pearson's sister's building was in fact so damaged that she was prevented from reentering it.[19]

A man named Edward Thornton dreamt of being in a room where a surgical operation was taking place and where a hymn was being sung just before it began. Exactly one year later, he had an operation to remove a brain tumor, and just at the beginning of the operation, a religious community with which he was affiliated began celebrating a High Mass for him.[20]

In my own life, I once had a dream that I was on a train that was taking me away from "the man I loved" (that was the only way he was identified in the dream) just as our baby was being born. Strangely, even though it was supposedly "our" baby in the dream, I was not giving birth. Rather, the birth

---

[18] Villoldo, 59.

[19] Cynthia Pearson, "Analysis and Arabesque: Observing 600 Dreams Using a Computer Database," presented to 14th Annual Conference of the Association for the Study of Dreams (Asheville, NC: June 20, 1997). Available at www.dreamjournalist.com/ncyndd.htm.

[20] Edward Thornton, *The Diary of a Mystic* (London: George Allen and Unwin, 1967), 126-32. As quoted and summarized in Main, 66 and 71.

was taking place off-stage, and the man I loved was notifying me of it by phone. I was scrambling hard to get off the train to go to him, but the train began moving with me in it. In the dream, I was both angry that I couldn't be there for this momentous event in our lives and awed with the knowledge that it had happened.

At the time I had this dream, I interpreted it as reflecting my feelings about my separation from my ex-fiancé, which had happened a few years previously. However, exactly a year *after* this dream, my ex and his new partner had a child, born on the same day of my dream a year before. When I realized this, I immediately knew that, while the dream was certainly about our separation, it was also about this very particular event that would follow in a year's time—an event for which I naturally wasn't present (just as in the dream) and that filled me with the same conflicting emotions of joy and sadness.

Sometimes, the fact that a dream is happening on a pre-anniversary is made explicit in the dream. For instance, Robert Waggoner reports a dream from June 16, 1973 in which he dreamt of "watching a moon cross the sky three times as a voice said that the event would occur in three years." "Then suddenly," he says, "I found myself in the midst of a ferocious riot with both blacks and whites. As I sought shelter, I noticed a Dutch-type windmill, similar to one in my hometown. Three years later, on June 16, 1976, the Soweto riots erupted in South Africa…."[21] (South Africa is a former Dutch colony in which some historic Dutch-type windmills can still be found.)

While the pre-anniversary dreams of the post-war German actress Christine Mylius were not as explicit about their timing as Waggoner's was, Mylius had so many of them that, when she went to review her dream diary, "[h]er first impulse in checking events [was] to review dreams of that same date years before." Here are some examples of her pre-anniversary dreams.

- She had a dream about swimming underwater with a baby whom she worried was staying under too long. Two years later to the day, she played a film role in which her infant fell off a boat and she jumped overboard to save the child but drowned.
- On Jan. 22, 1967, she dreamt that she and another woman had to play a "locomotive." That seemed strange. How exactly would one do that? But a year later, on Jan. 22, 1968, a friend of hers who was also an actress asked if she'd like a role in a new play she herself was acting in. The title of the play was *Locomotive.*
- On May 24, 1958, Mylius dreamt of being in a department store and shopping for something with a voucher of some kind. In the dream, she

---

[21] Robert Waggoner, *Lucid Dreaming: Gateway to the Inner Self* (Needham, MA: Moment Point Press, 2009), 283.

selects a beige wool jacket, but "the salesgirl slams down three too small for me…they don't fit and I must take them back to exchange again." In waking life, on May 25, 1959, a friend took Mylius to a department store to buy her a wool jacket as a present. The friend suggested she buy it in beige, which she did. At home, she discovered it was too small. She exchanged it but again got one too small. She then exchanged it a second time with the same result! Only after three jackets that were too small did she actually get one that was the correct size. What makes this case even stranger is that the dream of a year before appeared at the time to be triggered by the fact that, the day before the dream, Mylius's daughter had shown her a new beige jacket and Mylius had thought of buying one. Why should *that* event happen a year and two days before she would actually buy one? Perhaps the dream occurred because the thought of buying a beige jacket was so close to the anniversary of when she actually *would* buy one, and the dream was letting her in on the ordeal that the purchase would become. Or perhaps it's just a case of similar events happening at the same time of year, whether for "normal" reasons or for more obscure ones, like those we'll address in the section on astrology below.

- Finally, it's interesting to note that Mylius also once had a dream that *combined* elements of events that would happen to her one year later and five years later on the very same date.[22]

Some of those who've noticed the tendency of dreams and coincidences to extend both forward and backward in time from an important event have likened them to "ripples," like those that spread from the place where a stone is thrown into a pond. Paul Davids, for instance, writes that "some events that seem to be predictors of things that will come to pass may not be either coincidences or prophetic stand-alone incidents, but may resemble backward ripples or echoes from something that happens at some future time."[23] Dr. Kirby Surprise takes the analogy a step further, providing an example of a case in which a highly emotional argument with his girlfriend seemed to be preceded by discomfiting coincidences that increased in frequency and intensity up to the time of the argument itself and then continued after it with decreasing frequency and intensity. "The emotions of the argument," he writes, "were like ripples in time,"[24] and, just like the ripples in a pond, they got less powerful the farther they traveled from their source.

---

[22] Alan Vaughan, *Patterns of Prophecy* (New York: Hawthorn, 1973), 113-8.
[23] Paul Davids and Gary E. Schwartz with John Allison, *An Atheist in Heaven: The Ultimate Evidence for Life after Death?* (Reno, NV: Yellow Hat Publishing, 2016), 141.
[24] Kirby Surprise, *Synchronicity: The Art of Coincidence, Choice, and Unlocking Your Mind* (Pompton Plains, NJ: New Page Books, 2012), 227-8.

While neither of these authors draws an explicit connection between ripples and the anniversary effect, it is not difficult to see how this could be done. The ripples in a pond—which are in fact tiny waves—have wavelengths: the distance from the peak of one wave to the peak of the next. If coincidences and psychic dreams are the effect of psychic "ripples," those ripples could have wavelengths, and it might be that one common wavelength is the space of a year.

You might think that dates of the year are just a social construction and that it wouldn't make sense for there to be a natural law by which coincidences and psychic phenomena are highly likely to recur on the same date. However, the length of a solar year is first and foremost a natural phenomenon. When the same date comes around again each year, it means that the earth is in the same spatial relationship to the sun as it was on that date in previous years, which not only recreates the same patterns of light and darkness on the earth's surface but also creates similar patterns of gravitation and electromagnetism. This yearly rhythm—called the "circannual rhythm"—is programmed deeply into the human body and throughout the biological world.[25] Experiment at the University of Toronto has shown, for instance, that golden-mantled ground squirrels, when kept sheltered from the outside world at a constant 0°C and with 12 hours of light shone on them per day, will nevertheless hibernate in October and wake up in April.[26] If this rhythm has so deeply affected the biology of squirrels, to the point that they don't even need light or temperature cues to time their hibernation, should we be surprised if the circannual rhythm also shows up in coincidences?

Besides the circannual rhythm, another clear biorhythm is the circadian rhythm, based on the time it takes the earth to rotate once in relationship to the sun. Does this rhythm also emerge in coincidences? There's some evidence that it does. Geneviève Delpech recounts how, one evening at 10:14pm, her sister received on her cell phone a message containing the image of a fluorescent green cross. It was tagged as being from Delpech, but Delpech hadn't sent it. She didn't even have any idea how one would go about creating such an image, which took up the entire screen of her sister's phone. The significance of the mysterious cross became clear when, exactly 24 hours later—at 10:14pm the next night—the two women were notified of their father's death.[27]

---

[25] Lyall Watson, *Supernature: A Natural History of the Supernatural* (London: Coronet Books, 1973, 1974), 17-21.

[26] E. T. Pengelley and S. J. Asmundsen, "Annual Biological Clocks," *Scientific American* 224, no. 72 (1971). As summarized in Lyall Watson, 17.

[27] Geneviève Delpech, *Le don d'ailleurs: Autobiographie d'une médium* (Paris: Pygmalion, J'ai Lu, 2015), 158. Anomalous but meaningful messages apparently coming from

Recall as well the case from Chapter 4 in which Denys Cope realized, after her family's heirloom grandfather clock stopped on three successive nights at exactly 11:10pm, that this was the time at which her father had died 15 years earlier. Her brother had recently died as well, and she took the clock's strange behavior as confirmation that the two of them were together on the other side.[28]

Now it may be that coincidences frequently occur according to the circannual and circadian rhythms not because of any direct effect of the earth's relationship to the sun but rather because of the importance of these rhythms to *us*. Nothing that I've said here rules out the possibility that the timing of coincidences responds to whatever the human beings involved find significant. There are many other ways besides straightforward cosmic rhythms that the timing of an important dream or coincidence has been taken to be significant. For instance, Cynthia Pearson has noted that her dreams have, on a number of occasions, coincided "uncannily" with events that occur on the day she happens to enter the dream into her dream database, sometimes years after their occurrence. She gives this example:

> On June 19, 1996, I entered a dream from October 20, 1991, called "Snake Bites Henry's Puppy." Henry is my brother, and at the time of the dream, his daughter was dying of a brain tumor; the sad and awful symbolism of his puppy's being killed was obvious at the time. But on the day I entered it in the database, almost 5 years later, I had just finished a book Henry had lent me called *Salvation on Sand Mountain: Snake Handling and Redemption in Southern Appalachia*.[29]

Examples like this suggest that the connections a psychic event creates through time may depend to some extent on when we happen to think about that event, or about elements of related significance. It may be that our thought somehow "grounds" one leg of the psychic phenomenon in that particular moment. On the other hand, Pearson may have been psychically led to enter that dream on that day because of its relevance to the book she'd just been reading. Or it might be that she was led *both* to read that book *and* enter that dream at that time because of some sort of psychic/coincidence rhythm that had peaks at the time of her original dream as well as at the time she entered it. At this early stage in the systematic study of coincidences, I believe we have to remain open to all of these possibilities.

Delpech's phone have been a common occurrence for Delpech. See pp. 183-9 of *Le don d'ailleurs*.

[28] Annie Mattingley, *The After Death Chronicles: True Stories of Comfort, Guidance, and Wisdom from Beyond the Veil* (Charlottesville, VA: Hampton Roads, 2017), 142.

[29] Pearson, *op. cit.*

Patterns in Persons

Another category of evidence that suggests some sort of natural law as an explanation for certain coincidences comes from the repeating patterns that we find in the personal lives of people. Many of the most staggering coincidences in this vein come from the lives of identical twins. Many of the similarities in their lives can, of course, be attributed to their shared genetic make-up or to similarities in upbringing. But I find these explanations less than convincing when it comes to the following constellations of similarities.

For instance, in 1979, a pair of identical twins who had been separated a few weeks after birth were finally reunited after 39 years apart. Besides the fact that they had both been named "James" by their adoptive parents, James Lewis and James Springer discovered the following list of similarities between their "parallel" lives.

Both had married a girl called Linda, divorced her, *then* married a second time, to a woman called Betty
Lewis had named his first son James Alan, Springer had called his James Allan
Both had owned a dog as a boy, and named it Toy
Both men had worked part time as deputy-sheriff; both had been employed by McDonald's, the hamburger chain; both had been attendants in filling stations
Both spent their holidays at the same beach near St Petersburg in Florida (a stretch of sand only 300 yards long); both drove there and back in the same kind of car, a Chevrolet
Both bite their fingernails—right down until there is nothing left
Both drink Miller's Lite Beer
Both have white benches built around the trunk of a tree in the garden
Both have basement workshops and work in wood, building frames and furniture
Both chain-smoke Salems
Both put on 10 pounds when they were in their teens, for no apparent reason, and both took it off again later
Both enjoy stock-car racing and dislike baseball
Both have had vasectomies
Both enjoy doing the household chores at weekends
Both scatter love notes around the house

... Both grew up with an adopted brother called Larry; both had the same favourite subject at school, maths, and both hated spelling, and were not

> good at it; both have the same sleeping problems and use the same slang words.[30]

Although Lewis and Springer's story is one of the most impressive with regard to parallels in the lives of separated twins, many other startling similarities between separated twins were uncovered in a subsequent study conducted at the University of Minnesota by psychologist Thomas Bouchard. For example, British twins Terry Connolly and Margaret Richardson had been separated for 17 years when, unbeknownst to them, they married on the very same day less than an hour apart. Another set of British twins, Dorothy Lowe and Bridget Harrison, discovered upon reuniting that they had separately purchased identical diaries and written in them on the same days.[31]

We saw in our discussion of telepathy in Chapter 7 that some twins (as well as some non-twins) can feel each other's pain. We even saw some cases in which physical injuries in the form of bruises and blisters seemed to convey from one twin to the other. Here's another case of apparent bruise transfer, reported by Guy Lyon Playfair, author of the excellent book *Twin Telepathy*.

> In 1975, a hospital worker named Nita Hust felt sudden pains in her left leg, and found that bruises had appeared on the left side of her body. The matron saw some of them appear spontaneously. At about the same time, Nita's twin Nettie Porter was involved in a car crash four hundred miles away in which she bruised herself in exactly the same places.[32]

In another account recorded by Playfair, the transferred injury was much more severe. A young woman named Alice Lambe was sitting reading one afternoon when a huge blow coming from her left knocked her out of her chair. She yelled, "Something's happened to Dianne," and then passed out. Dianne was Alice's twin, and as it happened, Dianne was involved at the same time in a train wreck that broke two of her left ribs. The strangest bit of this case is that Alice's "borrowed" pain did not immediately disappear. She ended up having an x-ray, and it was discovered that her own ribs were fractured in the same places as her sister's.[33]

Playfair even reports a case in which a transfer of injury led to the death of the recipient. An Australian woman, Joyce Crominski, wrote to a magazine

---

[30] Peter Watson, *Twins: An Uncanny Relationship?* (Chicago: Contemporary Books, 1981), 10-11.
[31] Peter Watson, 12.
[32] Guy Lyon Playfair, *Twin Telepathy*, 3rd ed. rev. and enlarged (Guildford, UK: White Crow Books, 2012), 56.
[33] Playfair, *Twin Telepathy*, 55-56.

with the story of a tragedy that had befallen her sisters: twins named Helen and Peg. Peg was in a car accident that crushed her chest, and she died on the way to the hospital. Her twin, Helen, woke up screaming with great pain in her chest, and then she, too, died on her way to the hospital.[34]

These cases of injury sharing could be explained by some form of telepathy or remote psychokinesis, but unlike many cases of telepathy during crises, it doesn't seem like the connection in these cases serves the interests of either party. It seems rather as though a type of coordination is taking place between their bodies that has very little to do with what either of them might *desire* to have happen. It is as though their bodies are simply behaving as if they were a single organism.

Whether one adopts the telepathy/psychokinesis hypothesis or the single organism hypothesis, both explanations find themselves challenged by this next sort of coincidence: that of twins who experience *the same accidents* in close temporal proximity. Here are my brief summaries of several such cases reported by Playfair.

- One twin fell through a window. Three days later, the other twin fell through the same window and had to have the same number of stitches in the same place.[35]
- Liam & Aaron Lynch were admitted to the hospital with broken collar bones within half an hour of each other. One had been climbing a fence; the other tripped and fell while running.[36]
- John and Michael Atkins both broke their legs at exactly the same time—noon—on exactly the same day, while skiing at different locations.[37]
- One Finnish twin died crossing a road on his bike when he didn't see a truck coming. Two hours later, just a mile away on the same road, his twin crossed on his bike and was hit by a truck that came right after a car.[38]
- Romulus Cozma fell and broke his leg climbing, and around the same time, his twin brother Remus fell down the stairs at home and also broke the same leg.[39]
- Mirror twins Natalie and Zara Heywood both fell off bicycles within minutes of each other, cutting themselves on opposite legs. They also pulled muscles in opposite legs while swimming at almost the same

[34] Playfair, *Twin Telepathy*, 56.
[35] Playfair, *Twin Telepathy*, 59.
[36] Playfair, *Twin Telepathy*, 59.
[37] Playfair, *Twin Telepathy*, 59.
[38] Playfair, *Twin Telepathy*, 59-60.
[39] Playfair, *Twin Telepathy*, 61.

> time, and they broke opposite arms while roller skating within the same half hour.[40]

If we are going to use something like the single organism hypothesis to explain these cases, it appears that our concept of an "organism" is going to have to be significantly broadened, to include coordinated elements in the *environments* of these twins.

Peter Watson, who is skeptical of any paranormal twin connection,[41] suggests that these environmental parallels might somehow be explicable by genetics. He mentions various research studies that have revealed a tendency for twins to die at the same age, *even when death is accidental and not related to inheritable diseases.* "Scientists are asking," says Watson, "is there a genetic basis to accident-proneness?"[42]

It seems reasonable to me that there would be *some* genetic basis for accident-proneness, having to do perhaps with eye-hand coordination and other types of coordination between perception and response. It also seems reasonable that genetically identical twins would have bones and muscles that would be subject to developing the same types of weaknesses. Nevertheless, genetics seems woefully inadequate when it comes to explaining the precise timing of parallel accidents in the lives of twins.

Furthermore, people whose lives show improbable coincidences aren't always closely related genetically. We've all heard of doppelgangers, those people who look just like us somewhere else in the world. The wife of psychic Alan Vaughan, for example, discovered that she had a doppelganger who not only shared her face and personality but also the same first and last names: Diane Dudley.[43] I myself once met a man who reminded me strongly of my friend's husband, Paul, and moments later discovered that this new acquaintance was *also* named Paul.

While Juliet Capulet may have thought that a rose by any other name would smell as sweet, a 2017 article in *Journal of Personality and Social Psychology* describes eight experiments demonstrating that our names and our physical appearances are linked. In these experiments, "participants examining an unfamiliar face accurately select[ed] the person's true name from a list of several names, significantly above chance level." The effect remained even when socioeconomic cues were controlled for. On the other hand, the effect could also be generated when participants saw *nothing but a person's hairstyle*, implying that people may change how they wear their hair to reflect subtle social expectations associated with their names. It was also found that

---

[40] Playfair, *Twin Telepathy*, 87-88.
[41] Peter Watson, 136, 189.
[42] Peter Watson, 152.
[43] Vaughan, *Incredible Coincidence*, 59-60.

"socially using one's given name is necessary to generate the effect."[44] So perhaps many coincidences between names and appearances can be explained by subtle social cueing.

Could the same sorts of subtle cues be at work in prompting people with similar names to take up the same professions? When a Miss Barbara Brice who worked for the UK Admiralty received a telephone call from someone who had meant to contact a *different* Barbara Brice who also worked for the UK Admiralty—but apparently also had dark hair and was about her height—the first Barbara Brice decided to look up her doppelganger in the Admiralty's phone book. She discovered that, not only did their own names match, but they had colleagues with almost identical names: Cheshire and Chesher![45]

Even if social cues can explain that case, however, neither social cues nor genetics seem sufficient to explain the correspondences in the following three accounts which, among other things, include coincident birthdates.

French philosopher Michel Cazenave discovered by way of a misdelivered letter that there was another young man in France with his son's first and last name—Tristan Cazenave—and that this other young man was born not only on the same day and year as his son but within two minutes of him![46]

Two Wanda Marie Johnsons lived at the same time in Prince George's County, Maryland, and shared a birthday: June 15, 1953. As you might imagine, their identical names and birth dates, as well as similar social security numbers, caused them significant grief with credit card companies and the Department of Motor Vehicles. The two Wanda Marie Johnsons also shared other similarities such as that they both had two children and, at the time that the *Washington Post* wrote an article about them, both owned the same year and model of car.[47]

Finally, consider this rather astonishing case. Susan Reintjes recounts going to a party to which she'd planned to take her usual artichoke dip. However, at the last minute, she decided to make a fruit salad instead and ended up assembling it at the party location. When she set it out with all the other food, she saw another fruit salad sitting there with the very same fruits in it: watermelon, blueberries, and plums. She thought to herself that she'd like to meet whoever had brought it. She says,

---

[44] Yonat Zwebner, Anne-Laure Sellier, Nir Rosenfeld, Jacob Goldenberg, and Ruth Mayo, "We look like our names: The manifestation of name stereotypes in facial appearance," *Journal of Personality and Social Psychology* 112, no. 4 (2017): 527-54.
[45] Inglis, *Coincidence*, 21.
[46] Jeff Vézina, *Necessary Chances: Synchronicity in the Encounters That Transform Us*, trans. Carl Anger (Pari, Italy: Pari Publishing, 2009), 33.
[47] Vaughan, *Incredible Coincidence*, 202-4.

> Before eating, we gathered in a circle to meet one another. Our hostess suggested that we share our names and birth dates. Across from me sat a woman who introduced herself as Susan, born July 2. I spoke up and told her that my name was also Susan and that I was born on July 2. We proceeded to find out that we were born the same year and were both in the healing profession. Suddenly I knew that she had brought the twin fruit salad. She added that she planned to bring marinated artichoke hearts but had changed her mind at the last minute and brought the fruit salad instead.[48]

Astrology

The existence of patterns connecting our birth dates to our psychological make-up as well as to the pattern of the physical events of our lives is a foundational premise of the age-old practice of astrology. Astrology is much maligned in our "scientific" age, even though some of the great scientists of the past were actively involved in astrological observation and prediction—for instance, the Renaissance astronomers Tycho Brahe and Johannes Kepler[49]—and even though there is increasing scientific evidence that the positions of other astronomical bodies with respect to Earth do affect the overall course of life on our planet, as well as affecting individuals in ways that correlate with the arrangement of these bodies that existed at the time of their birth.

We've already discussed the way in which Earth's position with regard to the sun is the origin of fundamental biorhythms. However, there is also evidence that the positions of the other planets in our solar system indirectly affect what goes on on Earth, through their effects on the sun. While it's commonly known that solar storms can disrupt earthly radio communications and even power grids, it's less well known that these electromagnetic fluctuations affect our bodies. A 2017 article in the *International Journal of Environmental Research and Public Health* affirms that "solar and magnetic influences affect a wide range of human health and behavioral processes," particularly the body's cardiovascular and nervous systems. The article also describes new research suggesting that our nervous systems "can synchronize with the time-varying magnetic fields associated with geomagnetic field-line resonances and Schumann resonances." These

---

[48] Susan Reintjes, *Third Eye Open: Unmasking Your True Awareness* (Third Eye Publishing, 2003), 111.

[49] James Herschel Holden, *A History of Horoscopic Astrology: From the Babylonian Period to the Modern Age*, 2nd ed. (Tempe, AZ: American Federation of Astrologers, 1996, 2006), 170, 172-3.

phenomena, in turn, are largely determined by the influence of the sun and solar wind.[50]

But what does solar activity have to do with the positions of the planets? Well, it is widely recognized that sunspots and solar flares follow an 11-year cycle in activity. Though it is not generally agreed what is responsible for the length of this cycle, almost as soon as the 11-year sunspot cycle was discovered in 1843, speculation began about the possible role of the planets in creating it, and since that time, many correlations have been observed between this cycle and the relative positions of the planets around the sun.[51] It may not be mere coincidence that, also every 11 years, the planets Venus, Earth, and Jupiter all come into alignment with the sun, forming a straight line across the solar system. A 2016 article in the journal *Solar Physics* theorizes that the combined gravitational effect of these planets on the sun, though small, is enough to cause the oscillations in the sun's magnetic field that are responsible for the 11-year sunspot cycle.[52]

If this theory is correct, then there exists at least one mechanism by which the alignment of the planets indirectly affects human physiology, including the nervous system. It's not hard to see how changes in the human nervous system could then affect human behavior. Alterations in mood could affect the tendency to commit crimes, and differences in reaction times could lead to increases in traffic accidents. It is not a stretch to imagine that the positioning of planets in the solar system could be associated with global increases in civil unrest as well as world-wide periods of calm. And indeed, these are precisely the sorts of global trends that students of astrology have noticed correlating with planetary alignments. An excellent recent work on this topic is the book *Cosmos and Psyche*, written by philosopher and cultural historian Dr. Richard Tarnas.[53]

But if there is some reason to think that the cosmos exerts global effects on humanity, there are also indications that its precise effects may vary according to the individual. That shouldn't be surprising, given the variation

---

[50] Rollin McCraty, Mike Atkinson, Viktor Stolc, Adbullah A. Alabdulgader, Alfonsas Vainoras, and Minvydas Ragulskis, "Synchronization of Human Autonomous Nervous System Rhythms with Geomagnetic Activity in Human Subjects," *International Journal of Environmental Research and Public Health* 14, no. 7 (July 2017). Accessible online at https://www.ncbi.nlm.nih.gov/pmc/articles/PMC5551208/.

[51] G. A. J. Ferris, "Planetary Influences on Sunspots," *Journal of the British Astronomical Association* 79, no. 5 (1969): 385-8.

[52] F. Stefani, A. Giesecke, N. Weber, and T. Weier, "Synchronized Helicity Oscillations: A Link Between Planetary Tides and the Solar Cycle?" *Solar Physics* 291, no. 8 (October 2016): 2197-212.

[53] Richard Tarnas, *Cosmos and Psyche: Intimations of a New World View* (New York: Plume, 2006, May 2007).

in our individual physiologies. What will likely be more surprising to many readers is that at least some personal behavioral patterns appear to be correlated with the relative positions of the planets, sun, and moon at the time of a person's birth. For instance, French researcher Michel Gauquelin discovered many years ago that highly successful athletes were more likely than the general population to be born when the planet Mars had just risen over Earth's horizon or just after it had passed its highest point in the sky. He found the same correlation existing for military leaders, chief executives, and doctors. And though Gauquelin's discovery is commonly referred to as "the Mars effect," he actually discovered correlations related to other planets as well. He found Jupiter, in the same positions, to be linked to "success in politics, cinema, theater, and journalism." Saturn was linked to scientific accomplishment, and the moon was correlated with accomplishment in writing.[54] His work has understandably been the subject of controversy since its original publication in 1955, but his core findings have withstood scrutiny and been independently replicated.[55]

How could it be true that the positions of planets at the time of birth correlate with people's professions when they're grown? Biologist Dr. Lyall Watson has speculated that it's not that the alignment of the solar system at the time of birth affects one's biorhythms but rather that the biorhythms that people already have in utero make them responsive to certain alignments and more likely to be born when those alignments exist. He writes in his best-selling 1973 book *Supernature*,

> I do not believe that emanations from the planet Mars make a man "decisive, freedom-loving, and a pioneer." This is simplistic nonsense. But I do believe that there are complex patterns of cosmic forces that could predispose an individual to develop along these lines. The astrologers may be right in asserting that these conditions prevail when Mars is coming over the horizon, but even if that is true, the planet is merely a symptom of the over-all complexity. It is like the second hand on a watch, which provides a visible indication of the precise time but depends entirely on all the hidden springs and wheels that actually set the pace. I also disagree with the notion that birth is the critical moment. It seems far more reasonable to assume that cosmic forces are acting on everything all the time and that the moment of birth bears the same relation to the rest of life as the momentary position of Mars does to the rest of the cosmos. We know that the time of birth is related to lunar cycles, to solar rhythms, and to an inherited tendency to respond to these

---

[54] Michel Gauquelin, "Is There a Mars Effect?" *Journal of Scientific Exploration* 2 (1988): 29-51. Gauquelin originally published his discoveries in *L'influence des astres: Etude critique et expérimentale* (Paris: Le Dauphin, 1955).
[55] Suitbert Ertel and Kenneth Irving, *The Tenacious Mars Effect* (Somerset: Urania Trust, 1996).

> patterns in a certain way. It seems likely that birth, the early stages of fetal development, fertilization, and even intercourse are related in the same way, forming a continuum in which no one moment is intrinsically more important than another.[56]

Be that as it may, Watson himself cites a series of experiments performed on fruit flies that show them to have innate circadian rhythms that can be made to start at any desired time—if the eggs they hatch from are kept in total darkness and, after hatching, the larvae are exposed to a single flash of light. That flash sets the rhythm going and causes all of the flies to eventually emerge from their puparia at the very same moment. (By contrast, flies kept in total darkness throughout their entire process of development emerge randomly.)[57] In fact, this kind of triggering event—known technically as a "*zeitgeber*," or "time-giver"—is known to set circadian rhythms in all kinds of species, including humans. But if a single flash of light can determine the timing of a fruit fly's innate circadian rhythm, isn't it possible that an event as momentous as the separation of a human infant from its mother's body could determine the timing of innate rhythms in the infant's body, perhaps rhythms that, like the circadian ones, are patterned on the movements of celestial bodies?

The existence of rhythms synchronized with the moment of one's birth are an integral premise of traditional astrological prediction, and there are multiple ways in which practicing astrologers attempt to make predictions about the timing of important events in a person's life based on the positions of the planets, sun, and moon at the time of their birth. These methods include the use of transits, primary directions, and secondary directions. Having only a cursory knowledge of these methods, I will not attempt to describe them here. Instead, I will direct you to some evidence suggestive that astrological prediction, when done by someone eminently knowledgeable, can produce extraordinary results.

In the final chapter of his book *The Gold Leaf Lady*, philosopher Dr. Stephen E. Braude describes some of the predictive feats performed by his astrologist wife, Djurdjina (Gina for short). For six years, Gina used data on the birth dates and times of European and Chinese soccer players to counsel coaches on the most effective strategies they could employ at particular moments of particular games. Braude writes, "Most of Gina's astrological work was for two teams, and in both cases it seems her combination of psychological and astrological guidance enabled those teams to rise to the

---

[56] Lyall Watson, 75.
[57] C. S. Pittendrigh and V. G. Bruce, "Daily Rhythms as Coupled Oscillator Systems," *Photoperiodism and Related Phenomena in Plants and Animals* (Washington, DC: American Association for the Advancement of Science, 1959).

top of their respective leagues or divisions (from previous positions of overall mediocrity)."[58]

Braude describes as well how he and his wife decided to test her skill at determining the optimum time for gambling. Over a multi-day trip to Las Vegas, Gina used her astrological acumen to pinpoint, in the middle of one particular night, a 40-minute period that looked especially propitious. Indeed, that period was the only time they had any sustained wins at the slot machines.[59]

Braude also shares another story about his wife that illustrates just how precise her predictive power can be. Generally, astrologers need a person's time of birth in order to provide them with an accurate horoscope. However, Gina's extensive experience has taught her that, with enough additional information about the timing of important events in the person's life, as well as events in the lives of those who are close to them, one can actually *figure out* the time that a person must have been born. Gina actually did this for a friend of hers who didn't know her time of birth and told this friend the precise minute at which she must have been born, according to the other information she had. The friend later found her birth certificate, which displayed the exact time Gina had deduced.[60]

Though we have very little scientific understanding of why such predictions based on the arrangement of celestial bodies at the time of birth should be accurate, the evidence we have seen suggests that there are real, predictable patterns at work. Some of them may be complex effects of gravitational and electromagnetic interactions, and others may be due to some still undiscovered phenomenon that also explains the other strange, gratuitous coincidences noted in this chapter.

Like Attracts Like as a Mechanistic Natural Law

Some of the popular literature on coincidences suggests a fundamental natural law that could explain the occurrence of gratuitous coincidences, as well as a great deal else. These days, this law is often referred to as the "Law of Attraction," and its most basic formulation is "like attracts like," the idea being that similar things tend to happen together. One of the earliest dedicated investigators of coincidences, Austrian biologist Dr. Paul Kammerer, attempted to demonstrate that coincidences are due to such a natural, unifying principle. He wrote in his book *Das Gesetz der Serie*, published in 1919, "We thus arrive at the image of a world-mosaic or cosmic

---

[58] Stephen E. Braude, *The Gold Leaf Lady and Other Parapsychological Investigations* (Chicago: University of Chicago Press, 2007), 157.

[59] Braude, *The Gold Leaf Lady*, 165-6.

[60] Braude, *The Gold Leaf Lady*, 166.

kaleidoscope, which, in spite of constant shufflings and rearrangements, also takes care of bringing like and like together."[61]

We know that something like the principle of "like attracts like" operates in certain areas of the physical world. We know, for instance, that when one object is set to vibrating, other objects in the vicinity that have the same natural frequency will begin producing observable vibrations as well—a phenomenon known as resonance. Perhaps resonance is a more pervasive feature of the world than we've heretofore realized. Perhaps there are properties other than vibrational frequency that allow objects—or events or people—to be particularly affected by other objects that share those properties. Quantum physics, for instance, teaches us that elementary particles can become entangled with one another, so that a measurement made of one of them will always correlate with a measurement made of the other, even if they are separated by great distances. Just recently, scientists have succeeded in bringing this phenomenon of entanglement to the macroscopic level, entangling two objects almost large enough to be visible to the naked eye.[62]

Some readers may worry that a natural law modeled on resonance or entanglement could account for *all* coincidences, meaning that the coincidences they thought were intentionally produced messages from a departed loved one or a faraway friend are actually just the results of the operation of some impersonal law. The first thing to remember, however, is that even if some coincidences are the result of some "mindless" form of interaction between similar events or objects, that does not mean that they all are. Rather, psychic phenomena may actually make use of natural patterns of resonance as a vehicle for people—or spirits—to intentionally convey information. We have seen how people with an emotional bond tend to experience more telepathy with one another as well as produce more powerful psychokinetic effects. Psychics, too, have found that they are better able to read people who are similar to themselves. In a quaint but no less illuminating reference to early 1970s information technology, psychic Alan Vaughan compares people to old-fashioned computer cards, with "holes punched for each experience." When two people's cards are laid atop one another, he says, psychic "light" will shine through in the precise places where the holes of their experiences line up.[63]

---

[61] Paul Kammerer, *Das Gesetz der Serie*, (Stuttgart-Berlin: Deutsche Verlags-Anstalt, 1919), 165, as translated in Arthur Koestler, *The Roots of Coincidence: An Excursion into Parapsychology* (New York: Random House, 1972), 86.

[62] C. F. Ockeloen-Korppi, E. Damskägg, J.-M. Prikkalainen, M. Asjad, A. A. Clerk, F. Massel, M. J. Woolley, and M. A. Sillanpää, "Stabilized entanglement of massive mechanical oscillators," *Nature* 556 (2018): 478-82.

[63] Vaughan, *Patterns of Prophecy*, 96-97.

Vaughan suggests elsewhere in the same book that "synchronicity fundamentally could be considered the basic 'particle' of psi, including both ESP and PK."[64] Indeed, a better understanding of seemingly meaningless coincidences may actually help us to better understand how psychic phenomena work and how we can employ them more effectively. Seemingly meaningless coincidences may be the door that opens up our understanding of certain subtle natural resonances, permitting us to use them similarly to the way we've used the resonance produced by radio waves. Radio waves are a natural, impersonal phenomenon, but when we built transmitters and receivers for them—in the form of radios, televisions, and cell phones—we were suddenly able to use that natural phenomenon to transmit very personal information. Future scientific advances could enable us to harness the natural resonance that underlies gratuitous coincidences and use it to send personally meaningful messages. In fact, this may be what our loved ones in spirit—as well as some talented human psychics—are already doing.

On the other hand, there is no proof that any law in the universe actually operates "impersonally," that is, without some degree of awareness and intention behind it. Braude has written an essay called "The Synchronicity Confusion" in which he argues that similarity is not a relationship that can inherently exist between two objects or events. That is, he argues that it is not a relationship that can exist without reference to a mind who chooses which properties are relevant to the determination of similarity.

Braude's specific goal in his essay is to show that you can't get the kinds of humanly meaningful correlations between events that Jung calls "synchronicities" from a mindless natural law, because only a mind can provide the frame of reference according to which those events are seen as similar in meaning. I think Braude is right on this point, and I think Jung might have even welcomed his conclusion, since Jung seems to have understood the nonhuman world as nevertheless full of "mind" of some kind.[65] As Dr. Marie-Louise von Franz, Jung's most prominent student, wrote,

---

[64] Vaughan, *Patterns of Prophecy*, 153.

[65] In *Synchronicity*, Jung refers to "self-subsistent meaning" (pp. 86-87), but then he also says in a footnote on p. 86, "In view of the possibility that synchronicity is not only a psychophysical phenomenon but might also occur without the participation of the human psyche, I should like to point out that in this case we should have to speak not of *meaning* but of equivalence or conformity." This seems like the place where he comes closest to explicitly committing the error Braude attributes to him. And yet, in Jung's conclusion to that work, he says that synchronicity "ascribes to the moving body a certain psychoid property which, like space, time, and causality, forms a criterion of its behaviour. We must completely give up the idea of the psyche's being somehow connected with the brain, and remember instead the

> The most essential and certainly the most impressive thing about synchronistic occurrences…is the fact that in them the duality of soul and matter seems to be eliminated. They are therefore an *empirical indication* of an ultimate unity of all existence, which Jung, using the terminology of medieval natural philosophy, called the *Unus Mundus*.[66]

However, while Braude's explicit target in his essay is the idea of mind-independent synchronicity, he argues against this idea by employing a broader argument that there are no mind-independent relationships of similarity between *any* objects or events at all. While Braude may be right about this—it's a scintillating prospect—I suspect that his argument for this momentous conclusion is going to need to be more complex than the one he presents in "The Synchronicity Confusion."

For instance, it might be suggested as an argument against Braude that we could get some sort of mind-independent measure of similarity from the notion of Kolmogorov complexity, according to which the complexity of something is measured by the size of its shortest possible description. (Any readers uninterested in such technical details are invited to skip the rest of this paragraph!) As I mentioned in a footnote in Chapter 1, we can get a measurement of the similarity between two things, A and B, by comparing their Kolmogorov complexities in the following way, where $C(\mathrm{x})$ stands for the size of the shortest possible description of x.

$$\text{degree of similarity between A and B} = \frac{C(\mathrm{A}) + C(\mathrm{B})}{C(\mathrm{A} + \mathrm{B})}$$

However, we are then admittedly confronted with the question of whether there is a mind-independent fact of the matter about the length of the shortest possible description of any particular object or set of objects. Heisenberg's Uncertainty Principle suggests that we can't have a complete description of anything in the world, not even a single particle. The more precise our knowledge of one property of a particle—say, its velocity—the less precise our knowledge of another—in this case, its position. Furthermore, some quantum physicists are of the opinion that there is no fact of the matter about what's physically going on in the universe without the presence of a conscious observer, that is, without a mind of some kind interacting with the system.

'meaningful' or 'intelligent' behaviour of the lower organisms, which are without a brain" (89).

[66] Marie-Louise von Franz, *C. G. Jung: His Myth in Our Time*, trans. William H. Kennedy (London: Hodder and Stoughton, 1975), 247, as quoted in Mansfield, 229.

It seems to me that, if the kind of philosophical difficulty Braude raises in "The Synchronicity Confusion" is valid, it is valid for *any* natural law, even the laws of physics. It threatens the fundamental idea that objective reality could change over time in any way that is both law-like (based on similar causes producing similar effects) and mind-independent. It suggests, in fact, that *nothing* in this world occurs in a purely mechanistic fashion: that anything that is not random is determined by a mind of some kind. And perhaps that idea is not so far-fetched. After all, physicist Sir James Jeans wrote as long ago as 1930,

> Today there is a wide measure of agreement, which on the physical side of science approaches almost to unanimity, that the stream of knowledge is heading towards a non-mechanical reality; the universe begins to look more like a great thought than like a great machine. Mind no longer appears as an accidental intruder into the realm of matter; we are beginning to suspect that we ought rather to hail it as a creator and governor of the realm of matter....[67]

This might not even be a very surprising conclusion, given how ubiquitous we've seen psychic phenomena to be. Once we accept that these events really do happen, at a rate greater than chance, we have to begin to wonder whether, instead of aberrations, they are signs that the mechanistic paradigm is completely off-base. Most phenomena in the world may be amenable to being squeezed into the mechanistic mold, at least when we scrunch up our eyes so that we are blind to most of the world's detail, but these coincidences may very well be the indication that mechanics is *not* what is *ever* at work in this world, that in fact the world obeys very different laws, and that these laws are at the root of everything we see, not just the exceptional "coincidence" that points out the inadequacies of current scientific theory. For example, parapsychologist Dr. Rex G. Stanford has proposed that the normal, everyday connection between our conscious decisions and the motion of our bodies may in fact be psychically mediated.[68] And Braude writes,

> ...since the nonexperimental evidence for observable PK seems to demonstrate that PK does really occur in naturalistic settings outside the lab, then for all we know, everyday PK might blend smoothly and imperceptibly into ordinary surrounding events, and real-life PK might affect or cause events of a sort that we usually believe are independent of

---

[67] James Jeans, *The Mysterious Universe* (New York: The Macmillan Company, 1930, 1937), 137.

[68] Rex G. Stanford, "Toward reinterpreting psi events," *Journal of the American Society for Psychical Research* 72, no. 3 (1978): 197-214.

> PK (e.g., heart attacks, car crashes, good or bad "luck," ordinary decisions and volitions, and both healing and illness).[69]

If it's true that mind is behind all of the patterns of the natural world, then the seemingly "meaningless" and "random" coincidences we've looked at in this chapter may in fact be the effects of psychic processes as well. But the mind ordering these apparently gratuitous coincidences may be harder to discern. Perhaps that's because these coincidences are the compound result of the interests and intentions of many minds, or even the mind of the universe as a whole. It is to this intriguing subject that we now turn.

---

[69] Stephen E. Braude, *Crimes of Reason: On Mind, Nature, and the Paranormal* (Lanham, MD: Rowman & Littlefield, 2014), 184.

Chapter 10
The Universe

So far in our investigation, we have generally assumed that, while different coincidences may have different sources, each individual coincidence is ultimately attributable to one source or another. While we've seen that we *all* have more power to directly affect physical reality than is generally understood, we have generally assumed that, at least in principle, there is a difference between *God's* producing a coincidence, a *spirit's* producing it, *your* producing it, or some other source's producing it. But there are hints scattered throughout the literature on these topics that the matter may not be so simple.

This chapter is going to be the most philosophical and metaphysical of any in this book, as we explore the reasons to think that none of us is as separate from the rest of the world as we tend to imagine. We are going to explore evidence for profound interconnections among the minds of human beings as well as evidence that we are all parts of a much larger consciousness, one whose creative power stretches to the very limits of the universe.

Strange Combinatory Effects in PK

We're going to begin with a discussion of the strange ways in which psychokinetic effects appear to combine the influence of separate individuals. First, let's look at a couple of suggestive experiences reported by mediums. Medium Sherrie Dillard reports that a woman named Elise asked her during a reading, "Is my father working with me in any other way? Is he close?"

Dillard relates that, as if in reply, a strange orb-like light entered the room through a window. As it floated across the room, the computer suddenly turned on and began to print a bunch of lines, some in color, some in black. Afterward, Dillard returned to listening to the messages she was getting from the other side, and she reports,

> I was told that Elise and her father were both learning how to affect and influence matter through will and intent. Elise had a well-developed awareness of metaphysics and a strong spirit, and because of this, her father had been able to easily connect with her. They were both practicing and learning how to influence and affect physical matter through nonphysical means, and their efforts were positively affecting each [other]. Although Elise was not aware of it, they often developed their abilities together. It was like two people joining forces to carry a heavy box or push a cart up a hill, my guides told me. When we work in unison with others, we are able to accomplish more than we could do on our own.
>
> "Plus," they told me, "Elise's father was showing off a bit. Sending an orb of light into the room and turning on the computer was his way of making the session memorable."[1]

Here's another, older case in which the spirit of a deceased person apparently referenced psychokinetic cooperation with living humans. Back in the early 1900s, British physicist Sir Oliver Lodge attempted psychic communication with his deceased son who had been killed in World War I. Some of these communications took place through table tipping, a practice in vogue at the time. Lodge would sit with three other people—his wife, a medium, and one other sitter—around a small table. The table, supposedly manipulated by the son's spirit, would tilt three times for "yes" and once for "no." Or the alphabet would be recited, and tilts of the table would indicate which letter came next in the message being spelled out. At one point, Lodge asked whether his son could explain how he was able to make the table move. The table spelled out the message, "YOU ALL SUPPLY MAGNETISM GATHERED IN MEDIUM AND THAT GOES INTO TABLE AND WE MANIPULATE."[2] That is, the people gathered in the room supplied a power that was concentrated by the medium and then harnessed by those on the other side.

---

[1] Sherrie Dillard, *You Are a Medium: Discover Your Natural Abilities to Communicate with the Other Side* (Woodbury, MN: Llewellyn Publications, 2013), 131.

[2] Sylvia Hart Wright, *When Spirits Come Calling: The Open-Minded Skeptic's Guide to After-Death Contacts* (Nevada City, CA: Blue Dolphin Publishing, 2002), 115-6. This case was originally described in Oliver J. Lodge, *Raymond, or Life and Death, with Examples of the Evidence for Survival of Memory and Affection after Death*, 2nd ed. (London: Methuen & Co., 1916).

Such descriptions of people and spirits using their psychokinetic powers in concert may sound like a bunch of New Age hooey, but laboratory evidence indicates that there's some truth to the messages conveyed by Sherrie Dillard and by Lodge's table tipping. We saw in Chapter 7 that telepathy tends to occur between people with strong emotional bonds, and research at the Princeton Engineering Anomalies Research (PEAR) laboratory has shown that such bonds influence psychokinetic abilities as well, with strange theoretical consequences. PEAR researcher Brenda J. Dunne has shown that two people with a strong emotional bond can produce much stronger PK effects than either person alone. She reports that bonded pairs produce results almost *seven times as large* as either person working by themselves.[3] This multiplying effect implies that the source of the PK can't be neatly separated into "Agent A's" influence and "Agent B's" influence, because the whole is greater than the sum of its parts. This suggests that a search for the unique source of individual coincidences may be misguided and, in some cases at least, doomed to failure.[4] Dunne and her co-investigator Dr. Robert G. Jahn note that

> "intention," *per se*, may be only one factor stimulating the anomalies, and...the ability of an individual to establish a resonant bond with another participant, or with a machine, may be a factor of comparable, or even greater, consequence.[5]

As if that weren't interesting enough, anecdotal evidence suggests that the effects of bonded pairs may not always be positive. For example, writer Paul Auster notes that, though he has only ever had four flat tires in his life, which occurred in three different countries over a period of eight or nine years, the *very same person has been in the car with him each time.* And it happens that this person is someone with whom he has always felt "an edge of unease and conflict."[6] While the flat tires could have been psychokinetically caused by either Auster or his acquaintance, given the PEAR research just mentioned, it appears plausible that the flats were the product of their uncomfortable *relationship*.

---

[3] Brenda J. Dunne, "Co-Operator Experiments with an REG Device," Technical Note PEAR 91005, Princeton Engineering Anomalies Research, Princeton University, School of Engineering/Applied Science (Princeton, NJ: December 1991). For a summary, see Robert G. Jahn and Brenda J. Dunne, *Consciousness and the Source of Reality: The PEAR Odyssey* (Princeton, NJ: ICRL Press, 2011), 79.
[4] See also Jahn and Dunne, *Consciousness and the Source of Reality*, 111-2.
[5] Jahn and Dunne, *Consciousness and the Source of Reality*, 171. They also reference Robert G. Jahn and Brenda J. Dunne, "Sensors, Filters, and the Source of Reality," *Journal of Scientific Exploration* 18, no. 4 (2004): 547-70.
[6] Paul Auster, *The Red Notebook and Other Writings* (London: Faber and Faber, 1995), 28-29.

Also relevant to our discussion of the combinatory effects of PK is the research of the Global Consciousness Project. For over 15 years, researchers have monitored several dozen random number generators (RNGs) located all over the globe and discovered that, during important world events such as the 9/11 attacks, the output of these RNGs deviates from chance in a correlated, predictable way, suggesting that the emotions shared by people all over the world are combining to anomalously influence a physical process. It is interesting to note as well that correlation between the individual RNGs decreases with the distance between them, implying that the RNGs may be more influenced by the emotions of those nearby than the emotions of those farther away.[7]

Mind Melds

It can be mind-boggling to consider that coincidences (as well, perhaps, as many everyday events that we don't notice as being unusual) may be the psychokinetic effects of multiple sources and that their influence may not be neatly divisible. But we're about to go even farther down the rabbit hole. We are now going to consider evidence that *the sources themselves are not separate, distinguishable entities.*

We saw through our survey of telepathic experiences in Chapter 7 that the boundaries of a person's consciousness are not the rigid and impermeable barriers we often assume them to be. In fact, we saw that thoughts and feelings can be shared by people to such a degree that it is not easy for the individuals involved to tell where their own thoughts and feelings stop and those of the other person begin. You'll recall that the experiences of twins Gloria Vanderbilt and Thelma Furness led them to the view that they were a "common entity."[8] Some couples report a similar fusion during lovemaking. For instance, a woman going by the pseudonym "Gwen" reports, "we just lose our identities in each other.... Events lose their edges, so that we're nothing but lovemaking, and neither of us is doing it so much as we're a unified field of love manifesting."[9]

Some professional psychics also report a loss of awareness of personal identity when they are performing psychically. For instance, psychic Alan Vaughan writes, "I tended to lose my own sense of ego and merge my identity

---

[7] Roger D. Nelson, "Implicit Physical Psi: The Global Consciousness Project," in *Parapsychology: A Handbook for the 21st Century*, eds. Etzel Cardeña, John Palmer, and David Marcusson-Clavertz (Jefferson, NC: McFarland & Co., 2015), 282-92.

[8] Gloria Vanderbilt and Thelma Furness, *Double Exposure: A Twin Autobiography* (London: Frederick Muller, 1959).

[9] Jenny Wade, *Transcendent Sex: When Lovemaking Opens the Veil* (New York: Paraview/Pocket Books, 2004), 77.

with whomever I was trying to read."[10] Martha Beck emphasizes that telepathy and psychokinesis are facilitated by achieving oneness with the consciousness of the other entity involved, whether it's a person, an animal, or a metal fork one is attempting to psychically bend.[11]

While experience and training can help one anticipate and navigate the feelings of fusion that psychic exchange engenders, some people who have no guidance in this area can find themselves fatally confused. At least one tragic event has resulted from such a melding of feelings. Recall the young man who appeared to take the violent feelings of his twin brother for his own, leading him to murder his own girlfriend at approximately the same time his brother murdered his wife.[12]

The most prolonged demonstration of mutual telepathy that we've seen in this book is Dr. Charles T. Tart's experiment in mutual hypnosis, related in Chapter 7. Recall that Tart had two people hypnotize each other and that the result was a sort of engrossing mutual dream in which the two subjects had inner experiences of the same alternate reality. They were in the same room and able to communicate verbally during the hypnosis session, but on several occasions neither of them spoke for a while, and yet, when they were questioned, they said that they were nevertheless communicating with each other. They also discovered, after their multiple hypnosis sessions, that they had common memories of shared experiences that they had not indicated in any way verbally during the sessions, as shown by the hypnosis session transcripts.[13]

You may also recall that the subjects of this experiment reported a feeling of "merging" with one another at some points. Tart reports, "This seemed like a partial fusion of identities, a partial loss of the distinction between I and Thou. This was felt to be good at the time, but later the Ss [the subjects] perceived this as a threat to their individual autonomy."[14] Tart points out the possible danger in such sudden, unexpected intimacy, warning that it may be more than some people are psychologically prepared to handle. He writes about a different case, in which two married couples took LSD together,

---

[10] Alan Vaughan, *Patterns of Prophecy* (New York: Hawthorn, 1973), 81-82.
[11] Martha Beck, *Finding Your Way in a Wild New World: Reclaim Your True Nature to Create the Life You Want* (New York: Atria, 2012), 62.
[12] Guy Lyon Playfair, *Twin Telepathy*, 3rd ed. rev. and enlarged (Guildford, UK: White Crow Books, 2012), 61.
[13] Charles T. Tart, "Psychedelic Experiences Associated with a Novel Hypnotic Procedure, Mutual Hypnosis," in *Altered States of Consciousness*, ed. Charles T. Tart (Garden City, NY: Anchor Books, 1969, 1972), 312-3.
[14] Tart, "Psychedelic Experiences," 312.

> each [person] experienced an intense merging of identities with the three others. Because of the sudden and unexpected intensity of these feelings the couples had a great deal of difficulty in their emotional relationships to each other for several months afterwards, all centered around feelings that they had seen too much of each other's real selves, more than their previous relationship had prepared them to handle comfortably.[15]

The possibility that the sense of merging identities experienced by these couples under LSD may reflect a deeper metaphysical reality is suggested by a near-death experience had by scientist Dr. John C. Lilly. In Lilly's case, the "superior beings" he encountered warned him that he was not developmentally prepared to experience the underlying reality of his oneness with these beings. He recounts,

> As they move closer, I find less and less of me and more and more of them in my being. They stop at a critical distance and say to me that at this time I have developed only to the point where I can stand their presence at this particular distance. If they came any closer, they would overwhelm me, and I would lose myself as a cognitive entity, merging with them. They further say that I separated them into two, because that is my way of perceiving them, but that in reality they are one in the space in which I found myself. They say that I insist on still being an individual, forcing a projection onto them, as if they were two. They further communicate to me that if I go back to my body as I developed further, I eventually would perceive the oneness of them and of me, and of many others.[16]

Another NDE account, this one collected by Dr. Raymond Moody, also makes reference to a merging of identity. A ball of light took a hospital patient out of his body and led him to the hospital's recovery room, to show him where he would later find himself. The patient reports,

> Now, immediately, when I had joined him to take the trip to the recovery room and had become a spirit myself, in a way we had been fused into one. We were two separate ones, too, of course. Yet, he had full control of everything that was going on as far as I was concerned. And even if we were traveling through the walls and ceilings and so forth, well, it just seemed that we were in such close communion that nothing could have bothered me.[17]

---

[15] Tart, "Psychedelic Experiences," 314.

[16] John C. Lilly, *The Center of the Cyclone: An Autobiography of Inner Space* (New York: Bantam: 1972), 23-24.

[17] Raymond A. Moody, Jr., *Life After Life*, 25th anniversary edition (New York: HarperOne, 1975, 2001), 99.

Recall, too, Robert Monroe's discovery that some of the entities he'd been interacting with in his out-of-body experiences eventually identified themselves as aspects of himself and said that they were responsible for intervening in his life at various points—for instance, saving him from drowning on two occasions.[18]

Dreams as a Stage for the Mingling of Consciousness

One area in which many of us routinely experience a connection with other minds is in our dreams. We have seen throughout this book how our dreams, so often taken to be the creation of our individual unconscious minds, actually contain an impressive amount of psychic information about the thoughts and actions of others, be they living human beings, the spirits of the deceased, or other forms of consciousness altogether. The "unconscious" that is creating our dreams does not seem to be limited to our own mind in its choice of material, which is the reason that Carl Jung coined the term 'the collective unconscious'. The part of us that we normally think of as "our" unconscious appears in fact to be a doorway to the consciousness of the rest of the universe.

It might be useful to think of dreaming as a method of tapping into a psychic worldwide web. We could then think of an individual dream as the results returned by a psychic search engine, where the search terms are the dreamer's current desires and preoccupations. But we also need to acknowledge that dreams are composed with more intelligence and artistry than Google is currently capable of. The difficulty of drawing lines between conscious entities is made all the greater by the fact that our unconscious is not just a source of brute information but is capable of complex reasoning and problem solving, as evidenced both by the creative solutions we often glean from our dreams and the fact that, when it comes to complex decision making, conscious deliberation has been shown to be inferior to deliberation *without* conscious attention. Scientific experiment has shown that waiting to make a decision, but not consciously thinking about it, leads to better outcomes.[19]

What is more, the characters who figure in our dreams seem at times to be capable of various degrees of independent thought. Experienced lucid dreamer Robert Waggoner arranges dream characters on a spectrum according to the degree of knowledge, intentionality, and reasoning ability they exhibit. The simplest, least independent dream figures he calls "thought-forms." They are brief expressions of thoughts or emotions and are so

---

[18] Robert A. Monroe, *Ultimate Journey* (New York: Harmony, 1994), 168-9, 197-8.
[19] Ap Dijksterhuis, Maarten W. Bos, Loran F. Nordgren, and Rick B. van Baaren, "On Making the Right Choice: The Deliberation-Without-Attention Effect," *Science* 311 (March 2006): 1005-7.

functionally limited that they can't even give intelligible replies to questions posed to them. A little further along the spectrum are "aspect-forms," which represent more permanent issues or features of the dreamer. Waggoner writes, "Core aspect-forms may achieve considerable psychological complexity and function as the building blocks for greater ego awareness. I believe they may emerge intermittently into waking reality such as when we 'don't seem ourselves' or 'act out of character.'" Waggoner even suggests that core aspect-forms may form the basis for exteriorized personalities manifesting in multiple personality disorder or dissociative identity disorder. But the dream figures that exhibit the most complex behavior are those that represent our own "inner self" (with a seemingly deeper understanding of us than even our waking mind) and those that represent consciousness outside of us, such as other dreamers or the spirits of the deceased.[20] In addition, there is the wealth of knowledge and wisdom that is transmitted to us not by specific dream characters but by the way all the different threads of a dream are knitted together.

When these various levels of complexity are combined, a picture of dreams emerges in which a vast congregation of consciousness interacts. On the stage of our dreams, we see not only personifications of aspects of our own personality—perhaps ones with which we are not consciously familiar—but also the personalities of others and, it seems, some overarching consciousness that has greater insight than our waking selves.

But if our dreams are psychically collecting information and providing solutions based upon it without our being consciously involved in the collection or reasoning process, then how exactly do we know that it is *us* doing the collecting or reasoning at all? What exactly justifies us in laying claim to the unconscious as *our* unconscious, rather than a mind that lies outside—or within—us all?

And, furthermore, what if the commingling of consciousness that occurs in dreams is a reflection of a commingling that goes on all the time, a commingling that our attention to the vivid concerns of waking life generally drowns out? The occasional spontaneous intrusion of telepathy and precognition into waking life suggests that we may always be in psychic contact with the rest of the world at some level, and only when the signals get strong enough or important enough do we become consciously aware of them.

Coincidences, too, could then be understood as dream elements making their way into waking awareness. And just as the landscape of our dreams may not be attributable precisely to ourselves or to any of our dream

---

[20] Robert Waggoner, *Lucid Dreaming: Gateway to the Inner Self* (Needham, MA: Moment Point Press, 2009), 135.

characters, the coincidences that dot our waking landscape may not each be attributable to individual psychic sources either.

Is Human Consciousness Divisible?

I now want to turn to an intriguing idea suggested by the fact that some of our dream characters represent aspects of ourselves. Could it be that, just as we are each psychically connected to the consciousness of other human beings, our own consciousness is a web composed of many smaller units, each of which is itself conscious?

Spirit Consciousness and Body Consciousness

In 1927, Sir Auckland Geddes presented to the British Royal Society of Medicine an intriguing NDE case, of which an abridged, first-person account is found in G. N. M. Tyrrell's book *The Personality of Man*. The experiencer in this case seems to have been suffering a severe case of food poisoning. He recounts,

> [A]t no time did my consciousness appear to me to be in any way dimmed, but I suddenly realised that my consciousness was separating from another consciousness which was also me. These, for purposes of description, we could call the A- and B-consciousnesses, and throughout what follows the ego attached itself to the A-consciousness. The B-personality I recognised as belonging to the body, and as my physical condition grew worse and the heart was fibrillating rather than beating, I realised that the B-consciousness belonging to the body was beginning to show signs of being composite, that is built up of 'consciousness' from the head, the heart and the viscera. These components became more individual and the B-consciousness began to disintegrate, while the A-consciousness, which was now me, seemed to be altogether outside my body, which it could see. Gradually I realised that I could see, not only my body and the bed in which it was, but everything in the whole house and garden, and then I realised that I was seeing, not only 'things' at home but in London and Scotland, in fact wherever my attention was directed, it seemed to me; and the explanation which I received, from what source I do not know, but which I found myself calling to myself my mentor, was that I was free in a time-dimension of space, wherein 'now' was in some way equivalent to 'here' in the ordinary three-dimensional space of everyday life.[21]

---

[21] G. N. M. Tyrrell, *The Personality of Man: New Facts and Their Significance* (Melbourne: Penguin, 1947), 197-8.

The idea that what we normally think of as our single, unitary consciousness is in fact made up of parts that can be distinguished under certain conditions is not unique to this NDEr. A woman named Toni Maguire who had multiple out-of-body experiences as a child describes one in particular in which she was aware not only of the consciousness connected to her spirit but of a separate consciousness connected to her body as well. She writes,

> If I tried I could still feel the thoughts of my body up on the hill. It was feeling relaxed and thinking separately to my spirit, but it was happy to stand there and feel this peaceful sensation. My body could see what was happening to my spirit, and the same could be said of my spirit toward my body. Although we existed separately we were also still connected to the other's environment for the moment and the thoughts of my physical mind were saying to me, "Go. I feel safe."[22]

A similar experience came to a grown woman while she was making love. She says, "I was definitely in my body, *and* I was sort of floating.... It wasn't an out-of-body experience so much as it was as though there were a channel...connecting the physical body with me in it and this other sort of energetic being where I was so I could be in both places at once."[23]

The idea of two or more conscious entities linked to what we normally think of as a single person also finds support in the *Journal of Prenatal and Perinatal Psychology and Health*, in an article by developmental psychologist Dr. Jenny Wade titled "Two Voices from the Womb: Evidence for [a] Physically Transcendent and a Cellular Source of Fetal Consciousness." Wade argues there that veridical memories of prenatal life exhibit a complexity of thought and a degree of extrasensory knowledge that suggest the fetus has a non-physical source of consciousness that interacts with its physically-based source.[24]

As Wade also mentions, many veridical memories of prenatal life have been accessed by the use of hypnotic regression. That is, hypnotized subjects have remembered experiences from their prenatal life that were then confirmed by independent sources. While I have generally stayed away from presenting in this book material elicited by hypnosis—because it is not uniformly reliable—I would nevertheless be remiss not to mention here the striking way in which hypnotic regression has confirmed the dual consciousness experiences described by Toni Maguire and the NDEr quoted above.

---

[22] Toni Maguire, *Memories of the Light: A Story of Spiritual Existence before Physical Birth* (Bloomington, IN: iUniverse, 2000, 2012), 46.

[23] Wade, *Transcendent Sex*, 114.

[24] Jenny Wade, "Two Voices from the Womb: Evidence for Physically Transcendent and a Cellular Source of Fetal Consciousness," *Journal of Prenatal and Perinatal Psychology and Health* 13, no. 2 (Winter 1998): 123-47, p. 144.

It's common for those who are hypnotically regressed to before their birth to report remembering the joining of their spirit to the personality of their physical body, a process that appears to go more smoothly in some cases than in others. In fact, the account of one of Dr. Michael Newton's hypnosis clients is so fascinating—especially given our discussion of the phenomenon of possession in Chapter 8—that I am going to quote it here at length.

Under the influence of hypnosis, the client (S) appears to be speaking from the perspective of their spirit or soul, with all of the knowledge and memories that this entity is aware of during the time between its incarnations on earth. We join the transcript of this session just after Newton has asked S what it's like to enter a baby's mind. Here is S's reply.

> **S:** In the beginning I think of it as a betrothal. I entered my current body in the eighth month. I prefer to enter on the late side when the brain is larger so I have more to work with during the coupling. … I want to be able to talk with the child when there is more mutual awareness. … The child may say, "Who are you?" I answer, "A friend who has come to play and be a part of you." … This mind and my soul were created to be together. … I have joined with babies who welcomed me as if I were expected.
>
> **Dr. N:** There are souls who have had a different experience.
>
> **S:** Look, I know souls who are clumsy. They go in like bulls in a china shop with their over-eagerness to get started with an agenda. Too much frontal energy all at once sets up resistance.
>
> **Dr. N:** In your current lifetime, was the child at all anxious about your entry?
>
> **S:** No, they don't know enough yet to be anxious. I begin by caressing the brain. I am able to immediately project warm thoughts of love and companionship. Most of the babies just accept me as being part of themselves. A few hold back—like my current body.[25]

A bit later in the session, the subject says that the presence of a soul enhances a human personality, increasing its depth. And when Newton asks whether the work of merging the two beings is over at birth, the subject says no. "I talk to my body as a second entity up to the age of six," they say. "It is better not to force a full meld right away. We play games as two people for a while."[26] This timeline matches what Toni Maguire says about having had

---

[25] Michael Newton, *Destiny of Souls: New Case Studies of Life Between Lives* (Woodbury, MN: Llewellyn, 2000), 391-2.

[26] Newton, *Destiny of Souls*, 394.

her out-of-body experiences when she was between five and seven years old,[27] as well as Wade's assertion that research on children's memories of early life indicates that they generally have a greater ability to access their transcendent source of consciousness before around five years of age.[28]

Effects of Organ Transplants on Consciousness

Let's return now to the NDE case where the experiencer felt his bodily consciousness to be a composite that was disintegrating into components associated with his head, heart, and viscera. This idea of units even *within* the bodily consciousness—and, particularly, units associated with specific bodily organs—is also suggested by the literature surrounding the anomalous effects of organ transplants.

For example, heart-lung transplant recipient Claire Sylvia relates in her book *A Change of Heart* how her transplant led her to experience some surprising personality changes that she later discovered reflected her donor's personality: for instance, newfound tastes for beer, green peppers, and fast-food chicken nuggets as well as an incredibly high energy level and, strangely enough, difficulties with spelling. She even had an "unusually vivid" dream about a man whom she "inhaled" and whom she somehow knew was named "Tim L." It was only a year and a half later that a series of coincidences led her to the discovery that her donor was in fact named Tim Lamirande.[29]

Sylvia writes the following about some of the more difficult-to-describe feelings she experienced in the wake of her transplant.

> I noticed that I no longer felt lonely, even when I was by myself. On weekdays, when I was separated from [my daughter] and my friends, I didn't miss them much. Sometimes I had the feeling that somebody else was in there with me, that in some intangible way, my sense of "I" had

---

[27] Maguire, 44.

[28] Wade, "Two Voices," 143. Wade cites Jenny Wade, *Changes of Mind: A Holonomic Theory of the Evolution of Consciousness* (Albany, NY: State University of New York Press, 1996); David B. Chamberlain, *Babies Remember Birth: and Other Extraordinary Scientific Discoveries about the Mind and Personality of Your Newborn* (Los Angeles: Tarcher, 1988); Ian Stevenson, *Cases of the Reincarnation Type*, Vols. 1-3 (Charlottesville, VA: University Press of Virginia, 1975-80); and Ian Stevenson, *Children Who Remember Previous Lives: A Question of Reincarnation* (Charlottesville, VA: University Press of Virginia, 1987).

[29] Claire Sylvia with William Novak, *A Change of Heart* (Boston: Little, Brown & Company, 1997). Sylvia does not reveal her donor's real last name in her book, but it can be found in later news articles. See, for instance, Dennis Tatz, "Woman dies 21 years after heart-lung transplant that gave her a taste for beer," *The Patriot Ledger* (August 29, 2009), http://www.patriotledger.com/x866753736/Organ-transplant-recipient-dies.

> become a kind of "we." Although I couldn't always detect this extra presence, at times it almost felt as if a second soul were sharing my body.[30]

Claire Sylvia is not an isolated case. In her book, she relates the similar experiences of several other organ recipients who were part of her post-transplant support group. She writes, "[A]ll of us had some sense after the transplant that we were not alone. And each of us had at some point spontaneously experienced our new heart as an 'other' with whom some form of communication was taking place."[31] Other books written by organ recipients with strange experiences include *L'Intrus* by French philosopher Jean-Luc Nancy[32] and *De coeur inconnu* by French actress Charlotte Valandrey.[33] Valandrey describes very precise dreams of the car accident that took the life of her donor (who was unknown to her at the time) as well as a newfound taste for lemon meringue pie *sans* meringue, an odd preference she later came to find had been shared by her donor. In an even stranger twist, Valandrey actually fell in love with the widower of her donor, before she knew him to be such.

In addition to these book-length accounts, several scientific researchers have collected accounts of personality changes from large groups of organ recipients. In a study published in 1992, Viennese researchers interviewed 47 recipients of heart transplants, asking them if they felt the same way about themselves after the heart transplant or if they felt changed. Three of the 47 recipients (6%) said that they had experienced a distinct change due to their new hearts. One of the three even acted like the donor was living inside him, "growing older with him." When this man was asked how he was doing, he would reply, "WE are o.k." Seven of the remaining transplant recipients (15% of the total of 47) said their personality had changed but not because of the new heart. They said things like, "I've simply ordered my priorities differently, and have a new outlook on life." The remaining 37 recipients (79%) said that their personalities had not changed at all after the transplant. However, the researchers were surprised to find "massive defense and denial reactions" among this group. Out of the 37 who said their personalities hadn't changed at all, 29 answered abruptly and quickly changed the subject or ridiculed the question. Six others said they'd experienced no change at all but made jokes that indicated otherwise, and the final two in the group made

---

[30] Sylvia with Novak, 107.

[31] Sylvia with Novak, 136.

[32] Jean-Luc Nancy, *L'Intrus*, expanded (Paris: Galilée, 2000, 2010).

[33] Charlotte Valandrey with Jean Arcelin, *De coeur inconnu* (Paris: le cherche midi, 2011).

comments indicating that they'd previously asked other people's opinions about whether they were the same as before.[34]

A Canadian study published in 2014 analyzed video recordings of interviews with 25 heart transplant recipients in which they were asked questions such as "*Has having a new heart changed the way you think about your body? … Has having a heart transplant changed how you feel about yourself as a person? … Some people say you become a different person after you receive a heart transplant. What is your opinion?*" Analysis of the interviews revealed three major themes in the responses. The most common was the report of changes in feelings of identity or bodily integrity. The other two were feelings of "interconnectedness with the donor" and vivid ideas of what the donor was like. On the theme of interconnectedness with the donor, some of the reports were fairly negative, with recipients saying things like, "I felt I had an alien thing in me" or "For a while I felt as if there was an alien in my body…a foreign identity." Others were neutral to positive: for instance, "I feel as if another person's spirit is in me," or "I think one of the things I would say to [the donor's family] is…the person that you lost is still living through me."[35]

Some of the organ recipients in the aforementioned studies brought up specific changes in personality they felt were related to their transplant. In the Viennese study, a patient reported feeling that the person they'd gotten their heart from must have been a calm person, because they were feeling much calmer, and another reported loving to listen to loud music through earphones, something he didn't ever do before.[36] In the Canadian study, a woman said she was no longer interested in having sex with her husband and attributed this to having received a male heart.[37]

While neither of these studies systematically compared recipients' statements about perceived personality changes with independent information about their donors, another study published in 1999 in the journal *Integrative Medicine* focuses on this kind of comparison and presents 10 cases in which there are undeniable correlations between them. I provide

---

[34] B. Bunzel, B. Schmidl-Mohl, A. Grundböck, and G. Wollenek, "Does changing the heart mean changing personality? A retrospective inquiry on 47 heart transplant patients," *Quality of Life Research* 1 (1992): 251-6.

[35] Oliver E. Mauthner, Enza De Luca, Jennifer M. Poole, Susan E. Abbey, Margrit Shildrick, Mena Gewarges, and Heather J. Ross, "Heart transplants: Identity disruption, bodily integrity and interconnectedness," *Health* (2014), DOI: 10.1177/1363459314560067.

[36] Bunzel et al., 254.

[37] Mauthner et al., 9.

summaries of five of these cases below, but I heartily recommend reading the original article, which is composed largely of verbatim transcripts.[38]

- A 7-month-old boy named Carter received the heart of a 16-month-old boy, Jerry. Before Carter had ever met Jerry's father, he picked him out of a room full of people, running right up to him, climbing into his lap, and saying, "Daddy." When his mother asked him why he'd done that, "he said he didn't. He said Jerry did and he went with him." When Jerry's parents spent the night at Carter's home, Carter went into their bedroom and asked to sleep with them, cuddling between them the way Jerry used to do. He told them not to cry because Jerry said everything was okay. It is also interesting to note that Jerry had suffered from mild cerebral palsy predominantly on his left side, and after the transplant, Carter developed "stiffness and some shaking" on his left side as well.

- A 47-year-old white man received the heart of a 17-year-old black man. His wife reported that he had become more comfortable with his black friends, inviting them over to the house for the first time, for example. He himself said that one big change in him was that he now loved classical music, playing it all the time. "I know it's not my new heart," he said, "because a black guy from the hood wouldn't be into that." Unbeknownst to him, his donor was a violinist whose friends always made fun of the music he liked.

- A 47-year-old man received a heart from a 14-year-old female gymnast. The girl's mother reported that her daughter "had some trouble with food," sometimes skipping meals or purging. She also said her daughter "had this silly little giggle when she got embarrassed." The man who received her heart developed a tendency to giggle (his brother called it a "girl's laugh") that annoyed his wife to no end. He also found himself nauseated after eating, wondering if it would help if he threw up.

- A 9-year-old boy received the heart of a 3-year-old girl who had drowned in a backyard pool. The boy's mother reported he was now "deathly afraid of the water" even though he used to love it. The boy himself said of his donor, "I talk to her sometimes. I can feel her in there. She seems very sad. She is very afraid. I tell her it's okay, but

[38] Paul Pearsall, Gary E. R. Schwartz, and Linda G. S. Russek, "Changes in Heart Transplant Recipients that Parallel the Personalities of Their Donors," *Integrative Medicine* 2, nos. 2/3 (1999): 65-72.

she is very afraid. She says she wishes that parents wouldn't throw away their children. I don't know why she would say that." Apparently, the girl's parents had gotten a divorce and left her alone a lot. She drowned while the babysitter was on the telephone.

- A 5-year-old boy received a heart from a 3-year-old boy named Timmy who fell while trying to retrieve a Power Ranger toy that had fallen onto a window ledge. Without knowing Timmy's name, age, or manner of death, the recipient of his heart said, "I gave the boy a name. He's younger than me and I call him Timmy. He's just a little kid. He's a little brother like about half my age. He got hurt bad when he fell down. He likes Power Rangers a lot I think, just like I used to. I don't like them anymore though. I like Tim Allen on *Tool Time*, so I called him Tim. I wonder where my old heart went too. I sort of miss it. It was broken, but it took care of me for a while."

If you've read Chapter 8 of this book, you've probably been struck by similarities between some of these cases and the cases of apparent spirit possession related in that chapter. The question arises whether these transplant cases are evidence that consciousness and memory are diffused throughout the body or whether they are instead cases of people's souls' remaining earthbound and possessing the recipients of their donated organs. Given the resemblance to cases where spirit possessions occurred in hospital settings, it seems plausible to me that some, or even all, of these transplant cases could be explained in this way. Philosopher Dr. Stephen E. Braude points out, in favor of the possession hypothesis, that the cases in which the recipients' behavior and descriptions are most suggestive of possession are those in which the recipients are young, and presumably less influenced by society's ideas of what they ought or ought not to be capable of experiencing.[39]

If transplant personality effects are caused by spirit possession, however, it would seem that they ought to be treatable in the same way that other possession cases are—for instance, by asking the possessing spirit to leave and go to the light—leading to the disappearance of the personality effects and a reversion to the pre-transplant personality. I have so far been unable to locate any reports of cases like this, though Claire Sylvia does note in her book that the personality changes due to transplants tend to fade with time. This could possibly be because the possessing spirits finally move on after a while. On the other hand, it could be because the transplanted organ

---

[39] Stephen E. Braude, *Immortal Remains: The Evidence for Life after Death* (Lanham, MD: Rowman & Littlefield, 2003), 244.

adjusts to the rest of the body over time and loses some of its distinctive characteristics.

We should remember, too, that even if some transplant cases are cases of possession by an earthbound spirit, that doesn't mean that possession by a spirit is behind *all* of the noted effects. The reports of the NDEr, the OBEr, and the subject of hypnotic regression noted in the previous sub-section all indicate that there is a bodily consciousness separate from that of the person's spirit, and the NDEr specifically refers to consciousness related to the vital organs. Combined with the data from the transplant cases we've just seen, this testimony becomes even more compelling. I believe we must consider the idea that some measure of personality is intimately connected with the organs of the physical body and that this bodily consciousness may be transmitted to an organ recipient in a phenomenon distinct from possession by the donor's spirit.

Intelligence of Simple Organisms and Elementary Particles

Further evidence for the hypothesis of organ consciousness comes from research demonstrating the intelligence of simple organisms: for instance, slime molds. The slime mold *Physarum polycephalum* has been shown not only to remember and anticipate the rhythm of repeated shocks of dry air[40] but also to have spatial memory,[41] the ability to "find the minimum-length solution between two points in a labyrinth,"[42] and the ability to solve simple puzzles.[43] This suggests the possibility that the organs and even the individual cells of the human body may have their own memory and problem-solving abilities, as indeed neurons and immune-system cells are already widely acknowledged to have. We likely need to begin conceiving of our bodies not as single units with a single consciousness confined to the brain but as communities of trillions of organisms all learning and communicating and contributing to a joint consciousness.

---

[40] Tetsu Saigusa, Atsushi Tero, Toshiyuki Nakagaki, and Yoshiki Kuramoto, "Amoebae Anticipate Periodic Events," *Physical Review Letters* 100, no. 1 (January 2008), 018101. DOI: https://doi.org/10.1103/PhysRevLett.100.018101.
[41] Chris R. Reid, Tanya Latty, Audrey Dussutour, and Madeleine Beekman, "Slime mold uses externalized spatial 'memory' to navigate in complex environments," *Proceedings of the National Academy of Sciences* 109, no. 43 (October 2012): 17490-4.
[42] Toshiyuki Nakagaki, Hiroyasu Yamada, and Ágota Tóth, "Intelligence: Maze-solving by an Amoeboid Organism," *Nature* 407 (September 2000): 470.
[43] Toshiyuki Nakagaki, Ryo Kobayashi, Yasumasa Nishiura, and Tetsuo Ueda, "Obtaining Multiple Separate Food Sources: Behavioural Intelligence in the *Physarum* plasmodium," *Proceedings of the Royal Society B* 271, no. 1554 (November 2004). DOI: 10.1098/rspb.2004.2856.

You might wonder how our trillions of cells could communicate with each other well enough to form a joint consciousness. Of course, the cells in our body are already well known to communicate with each other chemically as well as through electrical signals. But there is some evidence that our cells communicate by psychic means as well. You may recall from Chapter 7 the experiments showing that white blood cells collected from a person's mouth and then monitored for changes in electrical potential respond to important emotional events that subsequently befall the person, even if the cells are at a distance from the individual of several yards to several miles.[44] In these experiments, the white blood cells that were isolated from the person's body were hooked up to a "lie detector," and they produced the same kinds of reactions that would be expected had they been attached to the body itself.[45]

I should also mention some evidence that consciousness and its attendant coordination of behavior may exist at scales even smaller than that of individual cells: the level of elementary particles. Physicist Dr. David Bohm discovered in the 1940s that particles in a plasma behave in an organized manner, more like parts of an organism than parts of a mechanistic system. The plasma is not only capable of regenerating itself but also surrounds and isolates impurities, somewhat like an oyster coats an intrusive grain of sand.[46] After his work with plasmas, Bohm later found electrons in metals also behaving in highly organized fashion, as if they all knew what the others were doing. Their behavior frequently left Bohm with the impression that the electron sea was "alive."[47] He told author Michael Talbot many years later, "The ability of form to be active is the most characteristic feature of mind, and we have something that is mindlike already with the electron."[48]

---

[44] Cleve Backster and Stephen G. White, "Biocommunications Capability: Human Donors and *In Vitro* Leukocytes," *International Journal of Biosocial Research* 7, no. 2 (1985): 132-46; and Cleve Backster, *Primary Perception: Biocommunication with Plants, Living Foods, and Human Cells* (Anza, CA: White Rose Millennium Press, 2003). For a first-person account from a senior Army officer who subsequently participated in Backster's research, see John B. Alexander, *Reality Denied: Firsthand Experiences with Things that Can't Happen—But Did* (San Antonio, TX: Anomalist Books, 2017), 131-7.

[45] Backster and White, 144.

[46] B. J. Hiley and F. David Peat, "General introduction: the development of David Bohm's ideas from the plasma to the implicate order," in *Quantum Implications: Essays in Honour of David Bohm*, eds. B. J. Hiley and F. David Peat (London: Routledge & Kegan Paul, 1987), 1-32, p. 3.

[47] John P. Briggs and F. David Peat, *Looking Glass Universe: The Emerging Science of Wholeness* (New York: Simon & Schuster, 1984), 96.

[48] Michael Talbot, *The Holographic Universe: The Revolutionary Theory of Reality* (New York: Harper Perennial, 1991, 1992, 2011), 50. Talbot cites private communication with Bohm, October 28, 1988.

Scaling Up Consciousness

While it might be hard to imagine what it would be like to be an electron, try thinking for a moment about what it would be like to be a cell in your body. You go about your business, taking in food from the bloodstream, storing energy, releasing it, reproducing by fission when the time seems right. You might think you and all the other cells in the body of which you're a part are solely individuals, who are often able to work together for common goals but sometimes are at odds with each other. Yet sometimes you get the feeling—perhaps because of certain patterns in the chemicals you're picking up in the bloodstream or maybe it's just a hunch you can't explain—that there might be some higher intelligence coordinating you and your buddies' actions, sending you signals about when it's time to store more energy, when it's time to release it, when it's time to reproduce. You probably won't be able to comprehend the nature of this intelligence—it's of such a different sort than anything you've ever encountered—but you might be able to recognize that the signals coming in to you aren't just random, and aren't just the sum of what all the other cells in the body are doing. You might suspect that there's a *mind* somewhere in this body, working to coordinate the body's actions for its own obscure purposes. Perhaps you'll never be able to attain proof of this intelligence, but you can certainly have a strong hunch that it's there, and you can learn to trust the messages it sends you as reliable indicators of future conditions and of the actions you need to take to thrive in those conditions.

Consider this analogy as a way of understanding the place of human beings in the larger universe. While our consciousness may be so complex that it seems like something of a "god" to that of our cells, each of us humans may in turn be just a tiny cell in the body of the earth. The earth in turn may be just a cell in the body of the galaxy, which itself may be a cell in the body of the universe. And there may be conscious, intelligent, purposive organization at each of these different scales in the universe, and many others besides. Furthermore, even if these higher levels of consciousness are too complex for us to understand, their knowledge and intentions may nevertheless influence us in the form of the uncannily intelligent "unconscious" that shows up in our dreams, our intuitions, our premonitions, our sudden inspirations, and the coincidences we experience.

Consider an experience that Robert Waggoner once had while relaxing in a creek in the Grand Canyon. He was feeling playful and decided to ask the canyon what it had to say to him. The immediate mental reply he got was, "Get out while you still can." Surprised by this, Waggoner checked to make sure that he wasn't doing any physical damage to the area where he was sitting and then asked his question a second time. He got the same reply, but with more urgency this time. This prompted Waggoner to tell his wife that they needed to go, that something wasn't right. And indeed, he soon spotted a huge storm cloud headed their way. He and his wife warned the other bathers and helped an elderly woman climb to a nearby trail before the rain let loose. Without the canyon's early warning, however, they all could very well have been caught in the ensuing flash flood.[49]

Indigenous people all over the world are known for their attentiveness to the natural world and their respect for the intelligence of its messages, which often come through a combination of physical signs and telepathic content. If we take seriously the possibility that there are forms of intelligent consciousness that far surpass our own, in both their knowledge and their wisdom, it is hard not to conclude that some of the coincidences we experience are the infiltration of that wider consciousness to our level of perception and understanding. As writer and theoretical physicist Dr. F. David Peat has put it, "It's almost as if something outside ourselves is trying to talk to us. It is as if we are coming into contact with the whole."[50]

The renowned medieval philosopher Thomas Aquinas compared such experiences to that of two servants who don't realize that they've received similar instructions from the same master. "When a master sends two servants to the same place," he wrote, "their meeting may seem to them a chance encounter. So a happening may seem haphazard or casual with respect to lower causes when it appears unintentional, but there is nothing fortuitous about such events with respect to a higher cause."[51]

Indeed, some people who have such meetings actually seem to *feel* the influence of some outside force directing them. A 41-year-old French telecommunications engineer named Nestor relates an experience in which he had a strong need to speak with a particular person: a psychotherapist whom he had consulted some years before and on whom he had something of a secret crush. Unfortunately for him, his therapist was very busy and couldn't fit him in for another month. Nestor felt that perhaps writing her a letter in the meantime would lift the weight he felt pressing on him, so he sat in a café for a couple of hours one day and wrote it. There was a post office nearby, but instead of going there and mailing the letter he'd just written, he decided to go in the opposite direction, towards the cathedral to pray. However, he found a funeral in progress there and so decided not to go in, to just continue walking towards downtown.

---

[49] Waggoner, 246-7.

[50] F. David Peat, *Synchronicity: The Marriage of Matter and Psyche* (Pari, Italy: Pari Publishing, 2014), 13.

[51] Thomas Aquinas, *Philosophical Texts*, sel. and trans. Thomas Gilby (London: Oxford University Press, 1952), 117-8 (from Opusc. XII, *Compendium Theologiae*, 137).

About a hundred feet farther on, he says, he felt a strange, intrusive shiver go down his back and all the way to his feet. He then felt a force pulling him toward the city port. "It was like someone was pulling me by my shirt at the level of my stomach," he says. This force took him through a deserted area to a square in front of a shopping mall, where it stopped him. He then felt a similarly exterior force move his eyes back and forth over the square. Suddenly, they fixed on a couple walking in his direction. One of the people called out his name before he even realized who she was: his psychotherapist!

The therapist and her boyfriend approached, and she and Nestor exchanged some brief small talk with one another. But the couple was in a hurry, so everyone soon went on their way, and Nestor didn't even think to give his therapist the letter he had in his pocket. A year later, he asked her about this incident, and she clearly remembered that she had actually been talking to her boyfriend *about Nestor* at the very moment he had appeared before them.[52]

Here we have yet another case where it is difficult to isolate the source of the events that transpired. The whole thing could theoretically be due to psychokinesis and telepathy originating in Nestor's strong need to connect with his therapist in some way (an intention that had been highly focused by his letter writing), but the fact that the therapist was talking about him at the moment they saw each other indicates that she might have had some involvement as well. And the physical force compelling Nestor toward the square where he would run into her seems, on the face of it, external to him. Why not consider the possibility that each of us is like a single neuron in a global brain, and that our minds work together to create a coordinating intelligence that far outstrips the abilities of any one of us?

In a coincidence account collected by Alan Vaughan, a woman named Lee Baxter tells how, after placing an order for several books, she found herself wishing she'd left one of them off the order and instead asked for two copies of another. Strangely, when her order arrived, this is precisely what had happened—by "mistake." The book she'd least wanted failed to arrive, and there were two copies of the book she'd wanted in duplicate. This experience led Baxter to wonder how many of the mistakes we make are not really mistakes.[53] Could some of our errors be the result of our unconscious responsiveness to the higher purposes of a coordinating intelligence?

Alan Vaughan talks about "psychic synchronization" between people and describes a synchronicity as "the resultant vector of the enmeshed consciousness of several individuals, each of whom contributes psychically

---

[52] Joachim Soulières, *Les coïncidences* (Paris: Dervy, 2012), 33-35.
[53] Alan Vaughan, *Incredible Coincidence: The Baffling World of Synchronicity* (New York: J. B. Lippincott Company, 1979), 113.

to the coincidence."[54] He says he first became aware of this phenomenon when he was writing about dream experiments for the book *Dream Telepathy*, which he co-authored with parapsychologists Montague Ullman and Stanley Krippner.[55] "By tracing the elements of the dreams and also how the experimenters' and subjects' needs were being met," says Vaughan, "I found that each person contributed to the total equation of the dreams, which finally reached equilibrium when everyone was getting what he or she wanted."[56]

The meshing of consciousness in the creation of shared dreams is interesting enough, but it appears that these dreams are just a simpler version of a process that goes on all the time in waking life, orchestrating the events of waking life so as to respond to the needs of all the parties involved. Some parapsychologists have assumed that, since none of us is aware of conducting this process of orchestration, it must take place in a mechanical, unconscious fashion, along the lines of a natural law, as we discussed in the last chapter. But it's also possible that this orchestration is a highly conscious, intelligent process carried out by a consciousness more complex than our own. And the thoughts and advice of this higher consciousness might be making themselves known to us through the dreams, intuitions, and coincidences that fill our lives.

Along these lines, Carl Jung tells us about a time when he was traveling in East Africa and an Englishman who had been in Africa for 40 years offered him this advice: "You know, mister, this here country is not man's country, it's God's country. So if anything should happen, just sit down and don't worry."[57] Jung understood this to mean that God's "inscrutable design" coordinated everything that went on there.[58]

But is there sufficient evidence for this higher consciousness and its high-level orchestration of our reality? Couldn't we just as well account for all the coincidences in our lives as the combined effects of human ESP and psychokinesis? No, I don't think so. I believe that the evidence laid out in Chapters 2-5 of this book makes clear that human beings are not the sole origin of all our paranormal and coincidental experiences. In those chapters, we explored a wide variety of evidence for the existence of various non-material beings, some of whom appear to have knowledge that far outstrips our own. Furthermore, some people have actually had a first-person glimpse of a more encompassing level of consciousness. A man whom Jenny Wade

---

[54] Vaughan, *Incredible Coincidence*, 211.
[55] Montague Ullman and Stanley Krippner with Alan Vaughan, *Dream Telepathy: Experiments in Nocturnal ESP* (Baltimore, MD: Penguin, 1973).
[56] Vaughan, *Incredible Coincidence*, 219.
[57] C. G. Jung, *Memories, Dreams, Reflections*, ed. Aniela Jaffé, trans. Richard and Clara Winston, rev. ed. (New York: Vintage Books, 1961, 1989), 256.
[58] Jung, *Memories, Dreams, Reflections*, 257.

calls "Jason" reports that during lovemaking he had a transcendent experience in which he suddenly experienced the world from many different points of view simultaneously. He was not only seeing the world from the perspective of his own body making love but also from the perspective of the ocean, the stars, the sky, the air, and the land. "I was all the facets of this prismatic sense," he says. "I was everywhere, and seeing everywhere all at once."[59]

But there is yet another form of evidence for a higher intelligence that we have not yet explored. Over the last century, scientists have discovered evidence for intelligence and intention at the most fundamental level of our universe. They have discovered that the physical constants of the universe—as well as the properties of events in the universe's early history—happen to be within the extremely narrow range that is necessary in order for life to exist.

For example, if the strong nuclear force had varied by 5% in either direction, life would not have been possible.[60] Or if the strength of gravity had varied by as little as a tenth of a duodecillionth (1/10,000,000,000, 000,000,000,000,000,000,000,000,000,000) of its actual value, life-sustaining stars like our sun could not exist.[61] Or if the strength of the Big Bang had varied by only one-novemdecillionth (1/1,000,000,000,000,000,000,000,000, 000,000,000,000,000,000,000,000,000,000,000,000) of its actual strength, the entire universe would have either collapsed back in on itself almost immediately or expanded too quickly for matter to aggregate into stars and thus support life. This degree of accuracy is akin to firing a bullet at a one-inch target on the other side of the observable universe, 20 billion light-years away, and hitting it.[62]

These astonishing facts are at the core of what is called the "Fine-Tuning Argument" for the universe's having been designed with the purpose

---

[59] Wade, *Transcendent Sex*, 112.

[60] John Leslie, "How to Draw Conclusions from a Fine-Tuned Cosmos," in *Physics, Philosophy and Theology: A Common Quest for Understanding*, eds. Robert Russell et al. (Vatican City State: Vatican Observatory Press, 1988), 297-312, pp. 4 and 35; and John Barrow and Frank Tipler, *The Anthropic Cosmological Principle* (Oxford: Oxford University Press, 1986), 322.

[61] Paul Davies, *Superforce: The Search for a Grand Unified Theory of Nature* (New York: Simon & Schuster, 1984), 242.

[62] I owe this analogy and the foregoing references to Robin Collins, "The Fine-Tuning Design Argument: A Scientific Argument for the Existence of God," in *Reason for the Hope Within*, ed. Michael J. Murray (Grand Rapids, MI: Eerdmans, 1998). Collins in turn gives credit for the bullet analogy to John Jefferson Davis, "The Design Argument, Cosmic 'Fine-Tuning,' and the Anthropic Principle," *International Journal for Philosophy of Religion* 22, no. 3 (1987): 139-50, p. 140.

of supporting life,[63] and we might think of them as the greatest coincidence of all. As you might expect, there are quite a few scientists who are uncomfortable with the idea of attributing these properties of the universe to a higher consciousness. One of their most popular responses to these well-accepted physical facts is to point out that, because there may be an enormous number of universes, all with different, randomly determined physical constants, it's no surprise that we're in the one with the constants necessary to support life, since that's the only one that's capable of producing us. However, in his paper "Fine-Tuning and Multiple Universes," MIT philosopher Dr. Roger White dissects the logic behind this argument and shows that, unless there is independent reason to believe that there *are* many universes, living in a universe finely tuned for the existence of life does not in itself give us reason to embrace that view.[64] The fine tuning of the universe remains a fact in strong need of some other form of explanation, such as the existence of a higher consciousness.

Perhaps the refusal of so many scientists to consider (at least publicly) that there might be a form of consciousness in the universe more advanced than our own stems in part from their knowledge of the way that religious belief has hampered scientific progress in the past—for instance, when the Catholic Church fought against a heliocentric view of the solar system because it made human beings less central to the cosmos. Ironically, scientists who refuse to consider the hypothesis of a higher consciousness may be committing an error very similar to that of the Renaissance-era Catholic Church. These scientists likely view humankind as the most advanced consciousness in existence (at least in our neck of the universe), and they are unwilling to consider the vast amounts of evidence that suggest this view is wrong. They take increasing pains to explain away the appearance of design in our universe as well as to explain away the recurring human experience of contact with various forms of higher consciousness, as described in Chapters 2-5. What is more, they fight to explain away highly meaningful coincidences as statistically insignificant events, even though these experiences are ubiquitous in human life and some of them are extraordinarily improbable on the basis of chance alone. It seems possible that these scientists do all of this because of their repugnance for the hypothesis that simply and elegantly accounts for this data: the hypothesis that there is an intelligence in the universe that vastly exceeds our own.

---

[63] For an overview of the Fine-Tuning Argument, see Robin Collins, "The Teleological Argument: An Exploration of the Fine-Tuning of the Universe," in *The Blackwell Companion to Natural Theology*, eds. William Lane Craig and J.P. Moreland (Oxford, UK: Wiley-Blackwell), 202-81.

[64] Roger White, "Fine-Tuning and Multiple Universes," *Noûs* 34, no. 2 (2000): 260-76.

Is God the Mind of the Universe?

In this chapter, we've looked at evidence suggesting that consciousness exists in very small, relatively simple units of life as well as at levels of complexity exceeding that of the human mind. We've also looked at evidence that these levels of consciousness are "nested," with our more complex form of consciousness containing some of the simpler forms as components. We saw, for instance, evidence that each human mind can to some extent be broken down into a component identifiable with an immaterial spirit as well as components connected to bodily organs. This pattern of nested units of consciousness suggests that human consciousness may in turn be a component of a more complex consciousness. And, indeed, we have seen extensive evidence that each of our minds is telepathically connected to those of others—that we are part of a greater network of consciousness, which often manifests to us as what we call our "unconscious" or even the "collective unconscious." Could this collective unconscious be what is responsible for the fine tuning of the universe? Could it possibly even deserve the name "God"?

Jung himself explicitly states that 'God' is a synonym for the unconscious.[65] He accepts that the more religious term can be useful because of its personal, "emotional" quality, but he also warns that talking this way can cause people to fall into the trap of thinking they know more about this entity than they really do. You'll recall that I pointed out in Chapter 2 that we can't jump from the evidence that there is a higher intelligence to the conclusion that it must be a deity of the sort espoused by a particular religion. It is one thing to know that there is some sort of higher intelligence in the universe and another thing to know what its characteristics are. In fact, it would be very surprising if we were able to grasp the precise nature of an intelligence greater than our own.

For this reason, I don't think we should go Jung's route and automatically equate our unconscious with God. There may, after all, be levels of consciousness not accessible to us through our "unconscious," perhaps because they are so vastly superior to ours that meaningful communication between us is all but impossible. Even if we knew that the consciousness of the entire universe was joined in one cosmic mind—whether we would call that our unconscious or not—I don't think we could automatically equate that enormous joint consciousness with God, not as long as there is the possibility of something's existing that is even greater than our universe.

---

[65] Jung, *Memories, Dreams, Reflections*, 336-7.

For instance, the Hindu Vedas and various yogic texts refer to the universe as a dream in God's mind. A physicist out-of-body experiencer who was exposed to something like this idea during an OBE says,

> I had the impression that…[j]ust as we can daydream and invent characters and situations, we are characters in a situation that was invented or dreamt, quite consciously dreamt by a more advanced sort of consciousness. The part that we have to play in this daydream is one of education, one of learning and bettering ourselves, striving to become more. Now, I'm not clear why this kind of overconsciousness or over-soul is having this daydream, but I have the feeling that it is for its own education. It learns as we learn.[66]

The analogy with a dream in the mind of God suggests that God may have a "real life" in a dimension that we dream characters can never know anything about. Furthermore, if God is to have fine-tuned the physical constants of the universe, God may have to exist independently from it. I believe these are all possibilities we have to keep our minds open to. The questions here are just too big for us to have any settled ideas about whether God is or is not identical with the collective consciousness of our universe.

Oneness with God

At the same time, I do want to mention some of the evidence that points to our being part of the mind of God and sharing God's essential characteristics in some very important ways. A large number of NDErs report experiencing that all of reality is one and that all of reality is one with God. For instance, one NDEr reports, "I realized that the 'I Am' was who I was and always had been and always would be. What bliss! I had a choice to rest in this truth and stay on the 'other side,' or I could continue to play the 'game' of being an imaginary person."[67]

NDE researcher Dr. Jeffrey Long says that the oneness with God expressed by NDErs surprised him, as this was quite different from what he'd been exposed to in his study of religion.[68] He provides many examples of their descriptions in his book *God and the Afterlife*. He found that NDErs repeatedly said things like:

---

[66] Robert A. Monroe, *Far Journeys* (Garden City, NY: Doubleday & Company, 1985, 1987), 51.
[67] Jeffrey Long with Paul Perry, *God and the Afterlife: The Ground-Breaking New Evidence for God and Near-Death Experience* (New York: HarperCollins, 2016), 16.
[68] Long with Perry, 89.

- "Each soul is part of the whole, or God."[69]
- "I...had this knowing that the essence or spark of the Highest is in everything—every mineral, vegetable, animal, and human."[70]
- "I had the awareness that a spiritual force exists that is all of us combined, not separate. If the word 'God' is used, then God is all of us."[71]

These comments suggest that the interconnectedness of the universe and the relationship of that universe to God is even more profound than the nested levels of consciousness we've previously discussed. There is a sense not of distinct pieces that *add up* to a whole but of pieces *each of which is identical* to the whole.

One of Robert Waggoner's particularly impactful dreams left him with a similar sense. After he woke from the dream, he says he knew that "[t]he awareness of the collective could be accessed in the awareness of the tiniest speck. … Behind each life, each object, each action, an awareness exists joined to all other life, objects, and actions."[72]

Historical Examples

The idea of profound unity in the world has a long philosophical history. I've already mentioned its presence in Hindu and yogic thought, but it appears repeatedly in the Western tradition as well. In ancient Greece, Hippocrates ascribed to the "sympathy of all things" and is said to have written the following.

> There is one common flow, one common breathing, all things are in sympathy. The whole organism and each one of its parts are working in conjunction for the same purpose…the great principle extends to the extremest part, and from the extremest part it returns to the great principle, to the one nature, being and not-being.[73]

The Neoplatonists, whose philosophy flourished from the third to the seventh centuries, were also proponents of holism, believing the entire

---

[69] Long with Perry, 89.
[70] Long with Perry, 179.
[71] Long with Perry, 178.
[72] Waggoner, 248.
[73] Hippocrates (ascribed to), *De alimento*, in *Hippocrates on Diet and Hygiene*, trans. John Precope (London: 1952), 174, as modified in a quotation in C. G. Jung, *Synchronicity: An Acausal Connecting Principle*, trans. R. F. C. Hull (Princeton, NJ: Princeton University Press, 1960, 2010), 74.

universe to emerge from a single principle of divine consciousness.[74] And interest in this idea was also very strong during the Renaissance, especially among perennial philosophers. In 1550, the Italian perennial philosopher Giovanni Pico della Mirandola wrote,

> Firstly there is the unity in things whereby each thing is at one with itself, consists of itself, and coheres with itself. Secondly there is the unity whereby one creature is united with the others and all parts of the world constitute one world. The third and most important (unity) is that whereby the whole universe is one with its Creator, as an army with its commander.[75]

Christians may also be reminded of the writings of Saint Paul, who repeatedly referred to the followers of Christ as the members of Christ's body, of which he was the head.[76]

Among European philosophers of the early modern period, Baruch Spinoza is the best-known proponent of holism. He argued in his posthumously published work *Ethics* that there can only be one substance to reality—God—though that substance has infinite attributes.[77] Another early modern philosopher, Gottfried Wilhelm Leibniz, believed in multiple substances but wrote that "every substance is like a complete world and like a mirror of God or of the whole universe, which each one expresses in its own way, somewhat as the same city is variously represented depending upon the different positions from which it is viewed."[78]

The Holographic Analogy

In the 20th century, theoretical physicist Dr. David Bohm became a prominent proponent of a holistic theory of the universe, which he described in his 1980 book *Wholeness and the Implicate Order*.[79] He points out in that book that the two major 20th-century revolutions in physics—relativity theory and quantum theory—are both characterized by "undivided wholeness." Relativity theory implies that "no coherent concept of an independently existent particle is possible, neither one in which the particle would be an

---

[74] Christian Wildberg, "Neoplatonism," *The Stanford Encyclopedia of Philosophy*, ed. Edward N. Zalta, Spring 2016 Edition, https://plato.stanford.edu/archives/spr2016/entries/neoplatonism/.

[75] Giovanni Pico della Mirandola, *Opera Omnia* (Basel: 1557), 40-41, as translated in Jung, *Synchronicity*, 75.

[76] See Romans 12:4-5, 1 Corinthians 12:12-27, and Ephesians 5:23, 29-32.

[77] Baruch Spinoza, *Ethics Demonstrated in Geometric Order* (1677).

[78] Gottfried Wilhelm Leibniz, *Discourse on Metaphysics* (1686), in *Philosophical Essays*, trans. Roger Ariew and Daniel Garber (Indianapolis: Hackett, 1989), 42.

[79] David Bohm, *Wholeness and the Implicate Order* (London: Routledge, 1980, 2002).

extended body, nor one in which it would be a dimensionless point."[80] This led Alfred Einstein to the view that the concept of particles should be regarded as secondary to the concept of fields, which can extend indefinitely into space and overlap one another. Quantum theory went even further in the direction of wholeness by demonstrating that entities like electrons show non-local, non-causal connections as well as appearing to behave in either a particle-like or wave-like manner "depending on the environmental context within which they exist and are subject to observation."[81] The upshot, says Bohm, is that "the entire universe has to be thought of as an unbroken whole."[82] Any element of the universe on which we choose to focus our attention exhibits properties that depend crucially on what's going on elsewhere.

Bohm likened this holistic aspect of reality—an aspect he said had largely been ignored by physicists[83]—to the holism of a hologram. A hologram is a two-dimensional interference pattern recorded on a piece of film that, when properly illuminated, creates a three-dimensional image. A hologram is holistic in that you can cut it into many pieces and each piece will be independently capable of recreating the entire three-dimensional image (though the quality of the image will decline as the pieces get smaller, as will the range of angles from which the image can be viewed). That is, unlike in conventional photography, where each part of the image is stored on a different part of the film, a hologram stores the entire image on *every* part of the film. Similarly, information contained at any particular location in our universe reflects the state of the universe as a whole.

We could actually describe this part of the holographic analogy using some more familiar physical processes. Think, for example, of all the cell phone conversations and television and radio programs currently being transmitted through the space in which your body is located. All of that information is already right there, moving through your body in electromagnetic waves, and to access it, all you need is a receiver that responds to the kind of waves you want to focus on. In fact, your body already has a built-in receiver for certain wavelengths of the electromagnetic spectrum: the wavelengths of visible light. Your eyes are able to provide you with an image of what's going on all around you, based on nothing but the patterns of the electromagnetic waves currently within your eyeballs. Look around the area where you are currently located. No matter where you stand within that area, you can obtain similar information about the surrounding environment, because similar information about that environment is located at every point within it. If you are standing outside at night, your eyes can

---

[80] Bohm, 220.
[81] Bohm, 222.
[82] Bohm, 222.
[83] Bohm, 18.

even discern information about stars many light-years away. Your eyes are able to detect information about many far-flung parts of the universe because that information is actually currently present within the tiny circumference of your eyeballs.

There's even more to Bohm's holographic model than this, however. A hologram is constructed by splitting a single laser beam into two parts, one of which is reflected off a three-dimensional object before the two beams are then brought back together and their interference pattern recorded on a piece of film. This record of the interference pattern is the hologram. When it in turn is illuminated, it produces a three-dimensional image of the original object. Bohm suggests that the everyday reality we see is like an interference pattern. If we look directly at a holographic interference pattern, it looks like a picture of many separate objects. We can tell that there are some repeating patterns within it, but the overall image appears incredibly complex, even chaotic. When illuminated with the right light, however, it reveals itself as the record of an object in a higher-dimensional space. Similarly, in our everyday view of reality, we see our world as filled with separate physical objects and events, and though we notice some recurring patterns, overall the world seems very complex, even chaotic. Bohm suggests that all the apparently separate objects and events in the universe are nevertheless reflections of a single object existing in a higher-dimensional space.[84]

If this is true, it could help to explain some of the gratuitous coincidences discussed in the last chapter. While a coincidence may seem like two oddly similar events from our perspective, perhaps those two events are actually a single event in the higher-dimensional space that created the hologram in which we live. Maybe we are just getting two slightly different "perspectives" on a single, higher-dimensional object.

The holographic model also offers us a way of thinking about the religious questions we considered above. If the universe is really like a hologram, then no matter what chunk of the universe you pick out, that chunk contains all the information about the higher-dimensional object that the universe is reflecting, an object that some of the NDErs cited above would likely refer to as "God." This would mean that, just like every other part of the universe, each of us is a miniature, four-dimensional reflection of a God whose full being stretches through many more dimensions.

If we follow the analogy even further, we reach the conclusion that our actions are God's actions, and God's actions are ours. We do not move independently, any more than a reflection in a mirror moves independently of the object casting it. According to this view, we are created in the image of God in a metaphysically radical way. God's choices are our choices which are the choices of the cells that comprise our bodies which are the choices of

---

[84] Bohm, 239-40.

the electrons and photons and other elementary particles that appear to fill our universe. We are not all separate organisms in a hierarchy. Instead, we are an indivisible whole. As Michael Talbot puts it in *The Holographic Universe*, "We cannot ask if the part is creating the whole, or the whole is creating the part because *the part is the whole*."[85]

The concrete scientific analogy of holography may actually shed some light on the age-old Christian paradox involving God's simultaneous immanence and transcendence. This paradox is usually discussed as it concerns the person of Jesus, said to be both completely human and completely divine. But Jesus and the authors of the New Testament spoke of Jesus' followers, too, as being "children of God," and of their having God resident within them in the form of the Holy Spirit as well as having God outside and beyond them. The hologram may be a useful analogy for understanding this relationship in our science-oriented culture. Again, each of us could be understood as a miniature, four-dimensional reflection of a God whose full being stretches through many more dimensions.

Christian psychiatrist Dr. M. Scott Peck does a nice job of summing up this analogy's spiritual implications. He writes,

> If you want to know the closest place to look for grace, it is within yourself. If you desire wisdom greater than your own, you can find it inside you. ...[T]he interface between God and man is at least in part the interface between our unconscious and our conscious. To put it plainly, our unconscious is God. God within us.[86]

I would only caution, as I did when Jung made a similar identification of the unconscious with God, that we shouldn't allow this identification to limit our conception of God. We shouldn't say, "Well, I know what the unconscious is, so I know what God is." The unconscious is precisely that of which we *are not conscious*, that which influences us and connects to us but which we cannot fully grasp. At the same time that it's important to note the ways in which God may be within us, it's also important to note that God is potentially a great deal more than anything we can currently fathom.

Conclusion

My hope is that this chapter leaves you stimulated, if a bit puzzled. In the earlier chapters of Part I, we saw many examples of coincidences that seemed capable of being straightforward effects of a particular source, but in

---

[85] Talbot, *The Holographic Universe*, 285.

[86] M. Scott Peck, *The Road Less Traveled: A New Psychology of Love, Traditional Values and Spiritual Growth* (New York: Simon & Schuster, 1978), 281.

this chapter, I've tried to focus on the possible origin of those coincidences whose source is less easy to pinpoint. And, as we've seen, the notion of sharp dividing lines between conscious beings—or any other aspects of reality, for that matter—dissolves the more deeply we investigate psychic phenomena. I hope you will leave Part I of this book in awe of all the potential sources for your coincidences, as well as the possibility that the entire universe may be working together to produce them.

Finally, remember that whatever language we use to describe the intelligent consciousness that pervades our universe, the evidence makes it clear that there *is* such an intelligence. It is clear that a force is at work throughout the universe that is greater than the limited conscious minds with which we routinely identify ourselves. This intelligence is both greater than we are and at the same time intimately connected with us. Both transcendent and immanent. Both within and without.

Part II:

Significance

Introduction to Part II

In Part I of this book, we focused primarily on coincidences that provide major clues as to their source. This focus may have given the impression that most coincidences provide such clues, but in fact the vast majority of coincidences provide very little indication of their origin. And this lack may well be intentional on the part of their creator or creators. It may be that, for most coincidences, their source is much less important than their *significance*.

In Part II, we are going to start by looking at an array of coincidences whose purpose and meaning are fairly easy to make out, usually much easier to make out than their origins. Rather than focusing on where these coincidences have come from, we will here be looking at what they *achieve*.

Psychiatrist M. Scott Peck has noted that watching the operation of coincidences in his psychiatric practice has given him the distinct impression that the obviously beneficial ones far outnumber those that cause harm.[1] And many others have noted through the years the tendency that coincidences have to bring about beneficial outcomes. That, of course, is why they are a favorite topic in self-help publications. And while we did see in Part I that some coincidences can have deleterious consequences, Part I has also given us a good idea of why so many coincidences nevertheless have beneficial effects—because so many of them are produced by persons or beings who have the *intention* of helping us, and that includes our own unconscious!

---

[1] M. Scott Peck, *The Road Less Traveled: A New Psychology of Love, Traditional Values and Spiritual Growth* (New York: Simon & Schuster, 1978), 256.

In Part II, we'll look at several distinct ways in which coincidences provide this help. Specifically, we'll look at coincidences that:

- revolutionize our perspective on the universe and our place in it,
- provide confirmation for important decisions,
- protect us from physical harm,
- help us find books or information,
- provide material help such as the location of lost items or the provision of new ones,
- enable us to meet important people in our lives or be reunited with them,
- direct us toward our personal destinies, and
- facilitate spiritual growth.

Once we've gotten a good look at all of these coincidences that have clear significance, we'll spend the last chapter of this book dealing with the hard cases: coincidences that puzzle or even mislead us. We will discuss the phenomenon of clarificatory coincidences, which can seem to be straightforward confirmations of what we ought to do but then turn out to have been tests of our decision-making capacity. One of the upshots of this discussion will be the importance of not jumping to conclusions about how a coincidence ought to be interpreted. We will discuss what we can learn about the process of coincidence interpretation from the vast literature on dream interpretation, as well as from the literature on precognition and clairvoyance. We will also discuss the potential dangers of paying too much attention to coincidences and look at the role psychic phenomena can play in mental illness, as well as in its resolution.

Chapter 11
A New Perspective on the Universe

Far and away, the most common effect of coincidences is to revolutionize the experiencer's conception of the universe and their place within it. A Frenchwoman named Viviane speaks for many when she says a series of coincidences "turned my life upside down and changed my vision of the world."[1] Coincidences can do this paradigm-shattering work in a number of ways. We'll examine three of them in this chapter.

You Are Not Alone

The most basic and ubiquitous realization that experiencers of coincidences tend to have is the realization that they are not alone. Even if we are surrounded by loving friends and family, we can often feel that no one really understands our innermost feelings. A well-timed coincidence lets us know that the world outside is in fact aware of and responsive to our inner struggles.

Let me give an example from my own life. Several years ago, I was in the midst of a heart-rending breakup with a man I had been engaged to marry. He was a spiritual person, and quite attentive to coincidences, and for some months prior to our breakup he felt he was surrounded by coincidences involving the number 33. At first, I was extremely skeptical that anything out of the ordinary was going on. I was an atheist—or at least an agnostic—and

---

[1] Joachim Soulières, *Les coïncidences* (Paris: Dervy, 2012), 57. My translation. The original French reads, "ont bouleversé ma vie et changé ma vision du monde...."

I saw no reason to believe he wasn't just seeing what he wanted to see. Nevertheless, as we were going through our extremely emotional long-distance breakup, I, too, began noticing what seemed like an inordinate number of 33s. Street signs, phone numbers, clocks…they all seemed to say 33 just a little too often to be explicable by chance. Still, I figured, it could all be explained by selective attention. I told myself that, in my emotional distress, I was just paying more attention to 33s as I tried to weave some semblance of meaning out of my personal chaos.

Then I got on a plane, to fly to see my ex-fiancé for the first time since he'd told me he wasn't going to be able to marry me. I didn't know what this meeting held in store. I'd been on an emotional rollercoaster for over a month at that point. I was sitting in my seat waiting for take-off from Reagan National Airport, feeling extremely sad and alone, when I looked out the window and saw a little yellow sign stuck in the grass beside the tarmac. The sign had nothing written on it but the number 33.

The plane taxied down the tarmac, and a few seconds later, we passed another small, yellow sign with nothing on it but the number 33. Then we passed another. And another. *So you don't believe in signs?* I thought to myself. *Even yellow ones that are two feet square?* I looked more closely and saw that, between the yellow signs, there were also large white numbers painted on the asphalt of the connecting taxiways: 33. Seeing all these glaring 33s one after another, I was overwhelmed by the distinct feeling that something—or someone—was telling me, "You are *not* alone."

I understood, of course, that 33 was the number of the runway. But even my deep-seated skepticism about coincidences couldn't prevent me from feeling that that runway number—and the sheer quantity of signs displaying it—was designed to get my attention. I didn't have the energy to analyze the feeling or calculate the probabilities involved. All I knew was that, as the plane accelerated down the runway, I was able to shut my eyes and relax for the first time in a long while.

A couple of hours later, I made a connection in Philadelphia and boarded my second flight. This time, I had a seat far from any windows, so I had no way of knowing if I was again on Runway 33. I felt the sadness creeping back over me, thinking again about what awaited me at the end of my journey. Specifically, I was thinking about how, when I got off my second flight, I would have to take a train to meet my ex. I pulled out my train ticket to check how much time I'd have to get from the plane to the train station, but what I noticed first was not the departure time. It was my seat assignment on the train: Seat 33.

However much my head wanted to say that this 33 was just a coincidence, my heart knew better. The tears coursing down my cheeks showed how keenly my heart felt the presence of *someone* who knew exactly what I'd been feeling these last several weeks, someone who knew exactly how deep my hurt and despair ran. I was convinced that that someone wanted me to *know* that they knew—wanted me to know that I was not alone.

That experience, which was actually my second experience of losing a man I was engaged to marry, makes me strongly identify with the family that experienced this next coincidence. The parent of a young woman who was also "jilted for the second time" was earnestly searching for some way to comfort their daughter when they "distinctly heard the words 'As the sun sets, it also rises.'" They then conveyed these words to their daughter. When the daughter ended up marrying a year later, she and her groom had their picture taken in front of the garden entrance of an old mansion. The location of the picture was chosen for the good light, but it was then discovered that carved in stone above the doorway where the couple stood was the phrase, "As the sun sets, it also rises."[2]

If it were me who experienced this coincidence, I would take it as powerful confirmation that someone was watching over the events of my family's life—that even in our darkest moments, we were not alone. Scanning books on coincidences makes it clear that this is a very common message that people glean from them. SQuire Rushnell says in *When God Winks*, "Little winks *do* mean something: that you're not alone, that there is a constant cosmic presence."[3] Robert H. Hopcke writes in *There Are No Accidents*, "When such events occur, we feel the story we are living more deeply, the story that says: you are not alone."[4] Robert Moss writes that "these signals alert us to the fact that we are not alone."[5] And French author Jean Moisset writes in *Enigmatiques coïncidences*, "The message of synchronicity contains a truth crucial for our little self lost in a gigantic universe of unimaginable dimensions, apparently more or less indifferent to our destiny. It's a message of hope, showing us that we are not alone...."[6]

Sometimes the message that we are not alone is very explicitly conveyed by a coincidence. For instance, Donna Leonard was having a difficult time

---

[2] Alister Hardy, Robert Harvie, and Arthur Koestler, *The Challenge of Chance: A Mass Experiment in Telepathy and Its Unexpected Outcome* (New York: Random House, 1973), 175-6.

[3] SQuire Rushnell, *When God Winks: How the Power of Coincidence Guides Your Life* (New York: Atria, 2001), 153.

[4] Robert H. Hopcke, *There Are No Accidents: Synchronicity and the Stories of Our Lives* (New York: Riverhead, 1997), 93.

[5] Robert Moss, *The Three "Only" Things: Tapping the Power of Dreams, Coincidence & Imagination* (Novato, CA: New World Library, 2007), 122.

[6] Jean Moisset, *Enigmatiques coïncidences: Loi des séries – Synchronicité* (St Vincent sur Jabron, France: Editions PRESENCE, 1993), 168. My translation. In the original French, it reads, "Le message de la synchronicité contient une vérité cruciale pour notre petite personne perdue dans un gigantesque univers aux dimensions inimaginables, apparemment plutôt indifférent à notre destinée. Il s'agit d'un message d'espoir, nous montrant que nous ne sommes pas isolés...."

dealing with the death of her husband, who had been in her life for 45 years. One night, she was lying in bed and felt a hand hold hers. "I could never describe the warmth that entered my entire body," she says. Some weeks later, she was sleeping in an unfamiliar room when the alarm clock went off at 12:30am. "I grabbed it in the dark trying to shut it off," she says. "[I]nstead I must have hit the radio button and a message said, 'Fear not, you will never be alone.'"[7]

Other times, this same message is implicit in a coincidence because of a request that's been made. For instance, one lonely woman was gazing at a magnolia tree and wishing for a sign that God was present with her. Though all the magnolia's buds were entirely closed, she suddenly saw one of them unfurl right before her eyes.[8]

As in that case, the message of an understanding presence is often taken as coming from the Divine, but sometimes it comes from a more personal source, when that is what's needed. A clear example is reported by Joel Rothschild, who was at the gym one day when he heard the spirit of a deceased person giving him a four-word message to deliver to another gym patron. When Rothschild finally got up the courage, he went over to the man in question and described the spirit he was perceiving. The man not only recognized who it was but knew exactly what the message was before Rothschild even told him. The night before, this other man had been asking the deceased over and over, "Can you hear me? Can you hear me?" The four words Rothschild had been asked to deliver to him were, "I can hear you."[9]

The Universe Is Full of Meaning and Design

Besides reassuring us that someone is listening and that we are not alone with our deepest fears and hurts, coincidences often convey the related message that there is a great deal more meaning and design in the universe than we've realized. It has been frequently noticed that coincidences jolt their experiencers out of their usual habits of thought, making them see the universe around them in a whole new light, usually a friendlier one. A frequent reaction to this mind-expanding effect of coincidences is a feeling of awe.

Moss recounts the following as an example of a coincidence that inspired such a feeling.

---

[7] Louis E. LaGrand, *Messages and Miracles: Extraordinary Experiences of the Bereaved* (St. Paul, MN: Llewellyn, 1999), 20.

[8] Joan Wester Anderson, *Where Miracles Happen: True Stories of Heavenly Encounters*, updated (Chicago: Loyola Press, 1994, 2009), 205.

[9] Joel Rothschild, *Signals: An Inspiring Story of Life after Life* (Novato, CA: New World Library, 2000), 114-5.

> I was standing in a very clean park—no litter to be seen—talking on my cell phone about how in the Middle Ages the Christ energy came to be identified with the stag. ... And I glanced down and right at my feet was a round piece of cardboard that might have been a coaster. It displayed a stag with immense antlers with the Calvary cross between them. ... I had that unmistakable sense of something reaching through the curtain of the obvious world to give me the message, *Right on.*[10]

It is moments like that one that make us blink hard and wonder whether we are dreaming. Is it possible that we could have seen or heard what we *think* we saw or heard? Could the universe really be capable of responding to us so directly and precisely? Moments like this don't make believers out of everyone—some people are not ready for such an immense change in worldview, and so they shove the memory of such moments to the backs of their minds—but I'd wager it's rare that anyone suddenly becomes a believer *without* experiencing some such unexpected encounter.

Out-of-body experiencer Graham Nicholls writes in *Avenues of the Human Spirit*,

> It is not through a philosophical change that spirituality truly grows, it is through direct contact with something greater than we could imagine before.
>
> Interconnectedness is an understanding that begins with something like a vision, OBE or even a traumatic experience, something outside our comprehension, something that pushes us to let go of our preconceptions.[11]

A few pages later, Nicholls points out that this something is "something beyond ourselves, yet somehow still at our core."[12] This is part of the great mystery contained in coincidences: that they seem both intimately related to us and "other" at the same time. We see what we thought was our subjective inner world written on the objective outer one. Our joys and sorrows, our convictions about value and meaning—we suddenly see them outside of ourselves, enacted by processes that we heretofore took to be entirely indifferent to our interests. By breaking down this barrier between the subjective and objective worlds, coincidences bridge one of the fundamental distinctions of Western thought, leaving us awed and mystified.

---

[10] Moss, *The Three "Only" Things*, 106.

[11] Graham Nicholls, *Avenues of the Human Spirit* (Winchester, UK: O-Books, 2011), 28.

[12] Nicholls, 31.

Psychic Connections Are Real

In a similar way, many coincidences appear designed with the particular goal of revealing to us our psychic connection to the rest of the world. An excellent example of this is the way in which I discovered the full extent of the GPS coincidence recounted in the introduction to this book. Recall that I was in the countryside of Pennsylvania, using someone else's smartphone to find nearby grocery stores, but the stores the phone displayed for me were actually in France, near the location of a friend of mine who had recently been much in my thoughts. At the time of my seeing this map on the phone, I didn't know the precise location of my French friend, and I also didn't know in what region of France the towns that I saw on the map were located. I recognized the name of the town Carhaix, but it was only when I got home and looked it up online that I discovered Carhaix was in Brittany, the region where my friend lived. However, once I'd discovered this, I knew that the coincidence was too strong for it not to "go all the way." If a GPS in Pennsylvania had decided to suddenly show me some towns in Brittany, I figured it *had* to be because the friend I had been thinking so much about was near those towns on that particular day. But how to know?

On impulse, I punched my friend's name into Google, followed by the date the coincidence had occurred. Lo and behold, my search returned a page from his blog, where he had recently announced that, on that date, he would be in the Breton town of Kergloff. By yet another search, I discovered that Kergloff was a tiny hamlet less than two miles from Carhaix.

Now here's the aspect of the coincidence that relates to our current discussion. In the five years my friend has had this blog, he has only posted his whereabouts for six days: that is, for only one day out of every 300 or so. So not only did the GPS produce this incredible coincidence of showing me the overseas location of the person uppermost in my mind at the time, but in an *additional* coincidence, this incident occurred on one of the few days when I was able to confirm my friend's location by independent means.[13] That is, a second coincidence occurred *in order to make me aware of the psychic significance of the first one.*

---

[13] I should mention that, once I saw the page of my friend's blog listing his coming appearances, I realized I had a vague memory of having looked at it at some previous time, probably a few months prior. So I might have maintained an unconscious memory of this list's existence, and possibly of the dates that appeared on it. And I possibly could have employed that memory in psychokinetically creating this coincidence at this particular time. However, I had no conscious memory of the name of the town of Kergloff, and I could think of no way in which I could have known of its location within Brittany before I searched for it online following the GPS incident.

Though this is the most impressive case of this phenomenon in my own life, this same sort of thing has happened to me on other occasions as well. I'll have a psychic impression of some sort—perhaps a strange dream—and then it will "just so happen" that someone volunteers information that makes it clear that my psychic impression corresponded to a reality unknown to me at the time.

Another excellent example of this phenomenon comes from Michael Talbot. He describes how, as a teenager, he had a vivid dream one night in which he seemed to be floating, first above his sleeping body and then out of the house over the surrounding landscape. He saw in the grass below him a book of short stories by Guy de Maupassant. The absurdity of such an incongruous element convinced him that this was indeed just a dream. However, the very next day he crossed paths with a neighbor of his who said she'd been recently walking near his house and feared she had lost a library book along her route. She asked if he happened to have seen a collection of short stories by Guy de Maupassant. Together, they walked to the spot where he had seen the book in his "dream," and they discovered that it was nestled in the grass just as he'd perceived it.[14]

Here now is another, even more staggering, example of this phenomenon. In his book *Super Synchronicity*, Dr. Gary E. Schwartz relates the story of a woman who had vague memories of having an out-of-body experience (OBE) while undergoing surgery. She had also been informed after her surgery that something upsetting had happened to one of the medical staff directly after the completion of the operation, but she wasn't told what it was.

A few weeks after the surgery, this woman happened to watch the (fictional) movie *Dragonfly*, in which children who've had near-death experiences come back bearing messages that the deceased want to send to the living. After watching this movie, she began to wonder if there was some connection between the upsetting experience had by one of the medical staff and her vague memories of an OBE. Had she perhaps visited the afterlife during her surgery, or been connected to it in some way?

When this woman subsequently questioned her surgeon, she was told the following story. Apparently, *while she was anesthetized during surgery*, she sat bolt upright and looked around at the medical staff. She focused on one of the five people in the room and said, "There is a woman here. Her name is Sarah. She has a message for you. She wants you to know that it is not your fault that she died." Then she collapsed back into unconsciousness.[15]

It turned out that the person to whom she spoke this message had been blaming himself for the death of his wife, Sarah, who had committed suicide.

---

[14] Michael Talbot, *Beyond the Quantum* (New York: Bantam, 1988), 83-84.

[15] Gary E. Schwartz, *Super Synchronicity: Where Science and Spirit Meet* (Vancouver, BC: Param Media, 2017), 80-81.

This man received an enormous gift in the operating room. Of course, he would have received this gift even if the patient who delivered it to him had never become aware of it. However, because this woman happened to see the movie *Dragonfly* a few weeks later, she was led to discover the amazing nature of what she'd done while under anesthesia and became cognizant of her profound psychic connection to others.

Yet another example of such a meta-coincidence comes from Eric Metaxas. Metaxas once had a dream about a family photograph being taken of his German relatives in Großstöbnitz, Germany. In the dream, he had the feeling that he was watching all this from a time before he'd ever visited that place. And, though he longed to be part of the photograph, he knew he couldn't, because he wasn't actually physically present.

Because Metaxas had the feeling that he was about five or six years old in the dream, he was able, upon waking, to date the dream's events to sometime between 1968 and 1970. He was so affected by what he'd experienced that he immediately called his mother to tell her about it, but she didn't pick up her phone. Thinking she must be at his aunt's house, Metaxas called his aunt, who told him his mother was on the road and wouldn't be reachable for at least another hour. Feeling that he just had to talk to someone about the dream, Metaxas decided to tell his aunt instead. After listening to his account, his aunt revealed to him that, just the day before, she and her husband had gotten an email from their relatives in Großstöbnitz with a photograph taken around the time Metaxas had narrowed down for his dream.[16] If Metaxas had been able to reach his mother that day, he might never have mentioned this dream to his aunt and never discovered its full psychic significance.

Let's now turn to a case reported by mathematician Dr. Warren Weaver. He writes,

> My next-door neighbour, Mr. George D. Bryson, was making a business trip some years ago from St. Louis to New York. Since this involved weekend travel and he was in no hurry, since he had never been in Louisville, Kentucky, since he was interested in seeing the town, and since his train went through Louisville, he asked the conductor, after he had boarded the train, whether he might have a stopover at Louisville.
>
> This was possible, and on arrival at Louisville he inquired at the station for the leading hotel. He accordingly went to the Brown Hotel and registered. And then, just as a lark, he stepped up to the mail desk and asked if there was any mail for him.
>
> The girl calmly handed him a letter addressed to "Mr. George D. Bryson, Room 307," that being the number of the room to which he had just been assigned.

---

[16] Eric Metaxas, *Miracles: What They Are, Why They Happen, and How They Can Change Your Life* (New York: Dutton, Plume, 2014, 2015), 259-61.

> It turned out that the preceding resident of Room 307 was another George D. Bryson, who was associated with an insurance company in Montreal but came originally from North Carolina. The two Mr. Brysons eventually met, so each could pinch the other to be sure he was real.[17]

Now, there could have been a clerical reason for the two Brysons' being assigned to the same room, but that doesn't explain why two people with exactly the same name (down to the middle initial!) would decide to stay at the same hotel, one right after the other. However, what I find most fascinating about this case is Bryson's decision to ask for his mail—"just as a lark"—since of course he'd only just arrived at the hotel, and no one else knew he would be there. Did his unconscious prompt him to do this so that he could enjoy the coincidence of being in the same room as another person with the same name? The event must have made an impression on him if he eventually made a point of meeting the other George D. Bryson.

In conclusion, some coincidences just seem designed to call attention to themselves and to the paranormal nature of our experiences. In some people's lives, this theme can be so strong as to lead them to say, with Paul Davids, "It has begun to feel that the substance of life is like a sort of simulation—a virtual reality show that has been twisting and shaping and molding itself to keep showing me that I am being led."[18] Indeed, many of the purposes for coincidences that we'll discuss in the next several chapters could have been achieved in ways that would have been less remarkable, that wouldn't have stood out as events that deviated from the normal operation of the world. For this reason, we must consider that part of the intent of many of these coincidences might be, not just to achieve protection or a meeting or to put a person in the path of their destiny, but also to let the people involved know that these things are being done purposefully, by some invisible intelligence.

---

[17] Warren Weaver, *Lady Luck and the Theory of Probability* (New York, 1963), 282-3. As quoted in Hardy, Harvie, and Koestler, 214-5.
[18] Paul Davids and Gary E. Schwartz with John Allison, *An Atheist in Heaven: The Ultimate Evidence for Life after Death?* (Reno, NV: Yellow Hat, 2016), 332.

Chapter 12
Confirmation

Coincidences are commonly taken as confirmation that a decision the experiencer has made or is considering making is the right one, especially when several coincidences arrive in a row, all pointing in the same direction. Of course, as we'll discuss in a later chapter, the mere fact that you experience a striking coincidence doesn't automatically mean you're doing the right thing. Sometimes coincidences that we thought were confirmations turn out instead to be tests, designed to clarify our thoughts and feelings. (See the section "Clarificatory Coincidences" in Chapter 19.) But it does seem that many times a coincidence comes with a strong inner conviction that it is indeed a confirmation. After the coincidence, there is no conflict in our heart, just certainty.

One excellent example of this sort of coincidence happened to me one day while I was driving and reflecting on a long-standing problem. After about a half hour of such reflection, I got stuck in stand-still traffic, and as I was sitting there, I finally formulated for myself what I needed to do about the issue at hand. "Maybe it's time to let go of this," I said to myself. I had only just put the solution in these terms when the vehicles in front of me moved slightly and revealed the license plate of a car a few spots ahead of me. It read, "LETGO."

What was more, two or three minutes later, I finally reached my exit, and as I pulled out of the traffic into the exit lane where I could at long last accelerate freely, I passed right behind the car with the LETGO license plate. My physical transition at that moment was an apt metaphor for the mental transition I was in the process of making: letting go of this major problem and breaking free of the traffic jam that my life had recently become. These coincidences perfectly mirrored what was in my heart, and I had no doubt that I was on the right path.

I received another confirmatory coincidence when I was on a first date with a man I'd recently met. We had both driven separately to a restaurant in a suburban outdoor mall (with me arriving about 10 minutes before he did), and after a nice dinner with lots of good conversation, we walked over to a nearby movie theater. The date was going quite well, but we barely knew each other, and I wasn't sure if I was willing to jump into this relationship with both feet. However, when we came out of the movie theater, late on a Wednesday night, the parking lot that had been full when we arrived was now basically empty except for two cars parked right next to each other, one of which was mine. "Is that your car?" I asked, about the other one. My date nodded. Discovering that we had "accidentally" parked next to each other in such a crowded lot was precisely the confirmation I needed in order to take the next step in that relationship. I ended up dating that man for nine months, and though we were not meant to be together for the rest of our lives, I do believe he was meant to come into my life—as a gentle, healing companion during what was for me a particularly difficult period.

One of my sisters has also experienced a coincidence that confirmed a decision at a particularly difficult turning point in her life. Here's her story in her own words.

> After a very difficult few weeks emotionally and after struggling hard with the decision to move from California back home to North Carolina without jobs lined up, my husband and I set out with our 15-month-old, our dog, and a small trailer with just the belongings we most wanted to keep. As we pulled out to start the 2,500-mile journey I put my husband's iPod on shuffle. The first song to play (out of the over 5,000 songs stored on it) was "Carolina in my Mind" by James Taylor. We both smiled, looked at each other and said "I can't believe that!" And then we just sang along. From the moment we decided to move I knew it was the right thing to do - despite it logically not making sense to leave behind a job that paid the bills. Hearing that song helped me celebrate the beauty of this move and the excitement and fear involved in this new adventure.

My sister notes that she already knew she and her husband were doing the right thing even before the coincidence arrived. This can often be the case with confirmatory coincidences. Sometimes they seem to happen not so much to reassure us as to let us know that the universe is joining us in celebrating an important step in our lives.

Let's look now at some confirmatory coincidences I've collected from other sources. Take the story of David, a young man who had felt emotionally distant from his family his whole life. His parents and two sisters seemed to mesh well in their personalities, and David always felt a bit like he was on the outside looking in. Once he moved out of the house, this emotional distance turned into estrangement. His parents only came to visit him twice at his home in California, and his sisters didn't come at all.

But then, when David was in his late 20s and living with his longtime boyfriend Harry, he heard from his sisters that they were coming to California on vacation and wanted to see him. So David and Harry planned a multi-course dinner for their visit, and on the big day, Harry decided they were going to go all out and serve Schramsberg champagne with dessert. There was a crisis, however, because they didn't own any champagne flutes. They almost got into an argument over it, with Harry wanting David to go out and find some and David refusing.

In the end, David's sisters arrived without any champagne flutes' having been found, and the dinner went wonderfully well. For the first time, David felt like he clicked with his siblings, and he appreciated how they knew him in a way no one else in his life could. When it was time for dessert, Harry started to say something about the Schramsberg and the champagne flute fiasco, but suddenly David's sisters announced they'd brought him a gift. They handed him a bag, and inside was a bottle of Schramsberg champagne and four flutes. For David, it was a sign that his sisters really did understand him, that they "were meeting *me* in *my* life," he says.[1]

A woman whom Dr. Jenny Wade calls "Leona" had suffered sexual abuse as a child, and the trauma of this experience haunted her in adulthood, to the point that it caused the end of a relationship with a man very dear to her. As part of her efforts to recover from this loss, Leona bought a special candle that she put on her home altar, telling herself that, when the candle burned down, she would be in a new place emotionally. Several years passed, and she was in a relationship that she found to be very sexually healing. The abuse she had suffered had made it difficult for her to experience orgasm, but one day she was making love with this new partner and climaxing in an incredibly expansive way when she started smelling smoke. "I turned to look at my altar," she says, "and that candle had burned all the way through! I mean *all* the way. *The entire bottom of my altar was on fire!*"[2] This event would have carried some symbolism had it happened with any candle at that precise moment, but for it to happen with the very candle that Leona had settled on to represent her moving to a new place in life made it particularly confirmatory.

As one might expect, many of the confirmatory coincidences I've found in the literature involve romantic relationships. Take, for instance, this

---

[1] Robert H. Hopcke, *There Are No Accidents in Love and Relationships: Meaningful Coincidences and the Stories of Our Families* (Asheville, NC: Chiron Publications, 2018), 134.

[2] Jenny Wade, *Transcendent Sex: When Lovemaking Opens the Veil* (New York: Paraview/Pocket Books, 2004), 52.

coincidence reported by Sarah Hinze. Hinze first heard Tchaikovsky's Piano Concerto No. 1 in her college music appreciation course and loved it so much that she purchased the record and played it over and over, trying to figure out why she was so drawn to it. A year or so later, she met the man she would marry. Not long after their meeting, she discovered that he played the piano, and she was stunned when she learned that his favorite piece was Tchaikovsky's Piano Concerto No. 1. What was more, as he played it for her, she had a memory of hearing that piece in heaven before her birth.[3] While it doesn't seem from her memoir that Hinze was in any particular doubt about her feelings for her future husband, this extra little wink from heaven surely didn't hurt.

Connie Van Dam's story is even more dramatic. She was raped one night while leaving her job as a second-grade teacher, and she became pregnant from the rape. Because she was at an age where she had given up hope of marrying or having children—even though she desperately loved children—she decided to keep the baby. This was a choice that her family had a hard time understanding, and so she decided to move to Holland and live there with her grandmother, who supported her decision to keep the child. While finishing her pregnancy in Holland, Van Dam met Willem, who was her grandmother's gardener. He had a very young daughter, and the three of them became quite close. Eventually, Van Dam asked Willem about the girl's mother, and he told her that she had been pregnant with their second child when she and the baby were killed in a car crash by a drunk driver. It turned out that the car crash had happened on the very same day as Van Dam's rape. That is, *Van Dam's baby was conceived on the same day that Willem's baby and wife perished.* Willem agreed with Van Dam's feeling that her baby was there to bring healing, and in Van Dam's last month of pregnancy, he proposed marriage to her. Five years later, Van Dam reports that their two daughters practically look like twins.[4]

Neither Sarah Hinze nor Connie Van Dam mentions having doubt about their respective relationships, but other couples have received confirmation precisely when they were in the midst of questioning their relationship. For instance, Christopher Hegarty and his girlfriend Marian cared a great deal for each other but were reluctant to marry. (He, at least, had been married before.) One evening, he was drawn to read a book on his shelf, *The Nature of Love*, which discussed the Lebanese-American poet Kahlil Gibran. Hegarty ended up calling Marian and reading to her some sections on marriage that seemed very appropriate to their situation. She was astonished, as she was holding the same book in her own hands, having just

---

[3] Sarah Hinze with Laura Lofgreen, *The Memory Catcher* (Provo, UT: Spring Creek Book Company, 2012), 31.

[4] Joyce Vissell and Barry Vissell, eds., *Meant to Be: Miraculous True Stories to Inspire a Lifetime of Love* (Berkeley, CA: Conari Press, 2000), 99-104.

finished underlining the same sections, which she intended to share with *him*. They had no idea that the other even knew the book existed. They took this as a sign that they should marry. Then, at their wedding, the minister read the passage from Kahlil Gibran's *The Prophet* that they had discussed that night. Hegarty and Marian each thought the other had asked the minister to do this, but in fact neither of them had ever even spoken to the minister before the day of the wedding.[5] It seemed like yet another confirmation that they were on the right track.

Robert Gitlin tells about a time when he was wondering about the future of his relationship with a woman named Karla. He couldn't decide if she was truly "the one" or not. Then one day, "almost as a direct response to these doubts," he says, he caught sight of a woman so gorgeous he was immediately flooded with the certainty that *this* was the woman he was supposed to be with. She was some distance away from him on the street, but he rapidly made his way toward her. He felt a little guilt when he remembered his relationship with Karla, but the desire he felt to meet this woman was simply overwhelming. As he approached her, he fantasized about shouting out, "We were made for each other!" That was when the woman suddenly turned around. The woman of his dreams…was Karla. After that, he had little doubt that they were indeed "made for each other."[6]

Another fellow, Simon Areeze, was having doubts about his relationship with a woman named Alice, possibly because he'd met her so soon after getting out of another relationship. One evening, Alice wanted to come over when Areeze had been looking forward to having the evening to himself. Over the phone, he told her rather harshly, "Listen, Alice, don't you think we're spending too much time with each other?!" She got angry that he couldn't just say he didn't want to see her that evening and hung up.

Feeling bad, Areeze impulsively turned on his computer and entered a singles chat room he hadn't visited in years. He felt a little guilty, but he came across a young woman named Connie who, like him, was feeling sad and lonely. Introducing himself as "Josh," he told her that he felt like loneliness was an invitation to understand oneself more fully. Connie thanked him for this beautiful insight and wished him well. Areeze logged off and spent the next half hour listening to his loneliness and coming to a better understanding of himself and of why he had reacted to Alice the way he did. After a bit, Areeze called Alice and apologized. She apologized, too, for trying to use him to take away her feelings of loneliness.

Then Alice said she needed to confess something. That evening, she'd gone online and gotten some very helpful advice from someone named Josh. Areeze and Alice quickly realized they'd stumbled upon *each other* in the chat

---

[5] Brian Inglis, *Coincidence: A Matter of Chance – or Synchronicity?* (London: Hutchinson, 1990), 141-2.

[6] Vissell and Vissell, 92-93.

room and unwittingly helped each other resolve their difficult feelings. They took this as an amazing sign: as Areeze put it, "a miracle with the power to dissolve doubt."[7]

Not all relationships are meant to endure for a lifetime, however. And sometimes coincidences confirm that separation is the right course. Judy Bishop was at a bridal shower in New York City when she got to thinking about how her own marriage wasn't doing too well. Getting into her car, she looked through a nearby window into an apartment and thought to herself, "That's where I should be." She went home and suggested to her husband that they move to the city, in an effort to put some spark back into their marriage. He refused, however, and they decided to separate. Bishop then decided to return to New York to look at apartments on her own. When her broker took her to see her first place, she discovered it was the exact apartment she had previously seen through the window, the one that had made her think, "That's where I should be."[8]

In other cases, relationships continue much longer—even beyond death—and coincidences happen to confirm that this enduring connection is real. An Australian man, Garry Roonan, lost his "sweetheart" in 1993, but six years after her death, he started to notice coincidences' happening when he was thinking about her. It might be her favorite song on the radio or her name written somewhere unexpected. Eventually, he began hearing communications from her in his mind, but he wasn't sure it was really her until he experienced a particularly confirmatory event. "One night I was bored," Garry says, "so I went downstairs. I picked up a book, opened it at random, and directly before me in big letters were the words *Garry, I love you.* I looked at the title and discovered the book was about spiritual communication."[9]

That case, along with this next one, shows that sometimes the meaning of coincidences can be literally spelled out for us. Six years after her son John's passing, Carol Poole received a very clear written message from him. To fully appreciate the significance of this message, it's important to know two things: first, that John had an interest in herbs, and second, that at the time of this experience, his mother was writing a book, *Shared Blessings*, in which she'd written that she never received afterlife messages in the form of butterflies or rainbows because they were too "subtle" for her to pick up on. Well, one day Poole was sitting in a used-book store reading through a volume that she ultimately decided not to buy. She put the book back on the shelf, and as she got up to leave, she saw "a bright yellow Post-it note…stuck

---

[7] Vissell and Vissell, 93-97.

[8] SQuire Rushnell, *When God Winks: How the Power of Coincidence Guides Your Life* (New York: Atria, 2001), 61-62.

[9] Dianne Arcangel, *Afterlife Encounters: Ordinary People, Extraordinary Experiences* (Charlottesville, VA: Hampton Roads, 2005), 123.

on the edge of the shelf in front of the herb books." She was certain it hadn't been there before and also that no one had come by who could have placed it there in the interim. Written on it was this message, in an adult's handwriting (though not that of her son):

> *Mother!*
> *I Love you!*
> *I'm thinking of you!*
> *Thanks for your* (a drawing of a heart appeared here) *notes* [10]

At the bottom was a sketch of a butterfly. Poole could hardly doubt this confirmation that her son still loved and cared for her from the beyond, and that she *could* indeed receive after-death messages involving butterflies!

Now let's take a look at a few confirmatory coincidences occurring in contexts other than personal relationships. This first one happened to Joseph Campbell, the famous mythologist, while he was in his Manhattan apartment doing research for the book *The Way of the Animal Powers*. It was while he was thinking about something Laurens van der Post had written about his childhood nanny being able to communicate with a praying mantis that Campbell suddenly felt compelled to get up and open one of the rarely used windows in his apartment. For some reason, he immediately looked to the right, and there was a praying mantis—climbing the side of the building 14 stories up. It apparently "turned its head toward him and gave him a meaningful look," confirming for him the truth of what van der Post had written.[11]

Irish actress Dearbhla Molloy has written about a time when she was returning to the stage and had been offered a job that was not as high-profile as she wanted. While wondering if she should accept it or wait for something better, she impulsively drove to visit the cottage of Ellen Terry, once Britain's leading Shakespearean actress. There, Molloy found herself "mesmerised" by a metallic green dress that was on display. An employee told her that Terry had worn this dress when playing Lady Macbeth. Molloy then went outside and spoke to Terry in her mind, asking her for help in figuring out whether she was still leading lady material. When Molloy returned home afterward, she had a message from her agent. Around the time she'd been asking for Terry's help, a theater company had called to offer her the role of Lady Macbeth. Dearbhla Molloy not only had not interviewed with the director of this production, but she'd never even met the director or worked anywhere in the city in question.[12]

---

[10] Arcangel, 141.
[11] Stanislav Grof, *When the Impossible Happens: Adventures in Non-Ordinary Realities* (Boulder, CO: Sounds True, 2006), 9.
[12] Inglis, 204-5.

William Stillman recounts an occasion on which he asked for a specific sign as confirmation that he was on the right track in his new professional endeavor of conducting environmental assessments of group homes for people with autism. Because the film *Wizard of Oz* had always been one of his greatest passions, while Stillman was on his way to the location of his first assessment, he thought to himself, "If I'm really supposed to be doing this, show me a *Wizard of Oz* sign." As he and his driver turned onto the country road where their destination was located, they passed a farm market "with a large scarecrow on its sign, his arms outstretched as if awaiting Dorothy's rescue."[13] Stillman has come to call such coincidences "alignments": "little guideposts to let us know we're doing precisely what we should be in the moment, all according to plan."[14]

Not unlike Stillman, cabinetmaker Tom Anderson felt overwhelmed by the new responsibilities engendered by his recent decision to go into business for himself. While driving to an appointment, he prayed for God to tell him what God wanted him to do. Just at that moment, he sped past a police car and realized he was going substantially over the limit. Predictably, the policeman pulled him over. Less predictably, the policeman, seeing the tools on his front seat, asked him what he did for a living. When he found out Anderson was a cabinetmaker, the policeman told him to drive more slowly in the future and then said that he himself had a second job as a general contractor. "I've got sixteen custom kitchens and fifteen bathrooms that all need cabinets right now," he said. "Think you'd be interested?"[15]

Theology professor Dr. Roger E. Olson relates how, when a doctor's visit led him to worry about a medical issue that might require surgery, a very old hymn started running through his mind, a hymn he hadn't heard since he was a child. The lyrics were ones of "comfort and assurance," and throughout the following week, the hymn wouldn't stop going through Olson's head. "I simply thought it was my own mind's way of handling the emotional distress I was experiencing," he says. However, when he went to church that Sunday, he opened the hymn book to the first hymn, #220. According to the worship folder, #220 was supposed to be "Crown Him with Many Crowns," but the hymn that appeared in the hymnal as #220 was not "Crown Him with Many Crowns." It was the hymn he'd been hearing in his head all week! Upon investigation, Olson discovered that the hymnal he'd grabbed from the pew rack in front of his seat wasn't like all the other

---

[13] William Stillman, *The Soul of Autism: Looking Beyond Labels to Unveil Spiritual Secrets of the Heart Savants* (Franklin Lakes, NJ: New Page Books, 2008), 189.
[14] William Stillman, *Autism and the God Connection: Redefining the Autistic Experience through Extraordinary Accounts of Spiritual Giftedness* (Naperville, IL: Sourcebooks, 2006), 97.
[15] Joan Wester Anderson, *Where Miracles Happen: True Stories of Heavenly Encounters*, updated (Chicago: Loyola Press, 1994, 2009), 24-25.

hymnals in the church. It had a different church's name embossed on the front cover. What was more, the church's regular hymnal didn't even contain a copy of the old hymn he'd been hearing. Olson had no explanation for how this other hymnal had gotten there, or why it happened to be right in front of his seat, but it did seem to serve as a strong confirmation of the reassuring message of that particular hymn.[16]

Dr. Mary C. Neal's stepfather was admitted to the hospital with pneumonia while her mother was staying with Neal on the other side of the country. Though Neal and her mother were assured by the doctor that Neal's stepfather was responding well to antibiotics, they debated about whether her mother should fly home to be with him. They were reflecting on this when suddenly a great grey owl—a species they'd never seen before—alighted on the nearby deck railing and began to stare at them in an uncanny manner. Over the course of the next few days, as the two women continued to debate whether Neal's mother should stay there with Neal or fly home to be with her husband, the owl continued to lurk around the house, actually giving them the impression of following them when they moved between rooms. When Neal finally resolved to send her mother home and was seeing her into a taxi, the owl staked out a post nearby and stared at her "insistently." Neal says she "could not ignore the intensity of its gaze and felt as though it would come and land directly on my head if I didn't immediately give it my full attention."[17] When she did so, she felt that the owl was telling her to accompany her mother on the trip.

Neal did go with her mother, and it was a good thing, because her stepfather's health went quickly downhill. In fact, he passed away within a few days, and Neal was well aware that, if he had died without her being there, she would have been devastated. It seems that, when we're waffling on an important matter, we sometimes need a confirmatory coincidence to literally stare us down until we do what it asks of us! Interestingly, when Neal returned home afterward, she saw the great grey owl once more, whereupon she thanked it for its guidance and then never saw it again.[18]

---

[16] Roger E. Olson, "Does God Still Speak…?", Roger E. Olson: My Evangelical Arminian Theological Musings (blog), Patheos, April 20, 2016, http://www.patheos.com/blogs/rogereolson/2016/04/does-god-still-speak/.

[17] Mary C. Neal, *To Heaven and Back: A Doctor's Extraordinary Account of Her Death, Heaven, Angels, and Life Again* (Colorado Springs, CO: WaterBrook Press, 2011, 2012), 130-1.

[18] Neal, 131-4.

Chapter 13
Protection

In the last chapter, we looked at coincidences that confirm we're on the right path, or that our intuition about what we ought to be doing differently is correct. But what about when we're headed towards danger and are blissfully unaware of it? A few of us may be treated to blatantly paranormal rescues like those recounted in the chapter "Angels & Guides," but others of us will likely be protected in more covert fashion, with the aid of one of the following subtle techniques.

Telepathic Nudges

Telepathic nudges can often lead people to perform actions without their knowing why, and these sorts of nudges can be employed in order to protect us. For instance, journalist Pierre Jovanovic was riding in a car along the 101 in California when he suddenly threw himself to his left. A second later, a bullet came through the windshield and hit exactly the spot where he'd just been a moment before. He couldn't figure out why it was that he had suddenly moved, but whoever or whatever was at the origin of his sudden movement, the saving consequence of it was clear enough.[1]

In November 1971, a despairing young architect threw himself in front of a train in the London Underground. Before the driver of the train even had time to put on the brakes, a passenger who had no knowledge of what had happened had already pulled the emergency handle. Because of the odd

[1] Pierre Jovanovic, *Enquête sur l'existence des anges gardiens* (Paris: J'ai Lu, 1993), 9.

impulse of this passenger (whom London Transport considered prosecuting for their unjustified pulling of the emergency handle), the train stopped just before it would have killed the man on the track. So close was the call that the train had to be jacked up in order to extricate him.[2]

Protective "Mistakes"

Sometimes protective nudges lead us to make what seem like mistakes. Only later does their purpose become clear. For example, a theater company was performing a scene that ended with a song during which the cast was to move about on stage according to a predetermined pattern. The leader of the song, however, accidentally sang the second verse an additional time, so the actors kept in their second-verse positions instead of moving to their places for the chorus. A huge light then fell in the middle of the stage—right where the actors would have been standing at that moment had the song been correctly performed.[3]

One Sunday morning, actor Sir Alec Guinness overslept, despite his using two alarm clocks. Furthermore, when he awoke, he for some reason misread the time and didn't realize just how long he had overslept. So he hurried a bit and then went about what he thought was his usual routine of going to 8am Mass—except he realized while he was at the cathedral that he was actually at the *9am* Mass. If Guinness had realized his error earlier, he might have skipped Mass in lieu of the next item in his usual routine, which was to catch the 9:50 Portsmouth train. However, it was fortunate that he was prevented from doing this, because when he arrived at the station to catch the 10:50 instead, he discovered that his usual train had been involved in an accident—an accident that affected the specific car in which he normally rode.[4]

But the protective error isn't always committed by the person who's being protected. In a case reported by psychiatrist Dr. Bernard Beitman, a woman was planning to let her abusive husband come back and live with her. She was about to pick him up at the airport when she got a phone call from a woman who'd dialed the wrong number. This woman started telling her how her own boyfriend was abusing her. The fear in her voice led the first woman to decide not to let her husband come back and live with her after

---

[2] Alister Hardy, Robert Harvie, and Arthur Koestler, *The Challenge of Chance: A Mass Experiment in Telepathy and Its Unexpected Outcome* (New York: Random House, 1973), 183.

[3] Arthur Koestler, "The Mysterious Power of Chance," *The Sunday Times* (London: May 4, 1974), as described in Alan Vaughan, *Incredible Coincidence: The Baffling World of Synchronicity* (New York: J. B. Lippincott Company, 1979), 45-46.

[4] Hardy, Harvie, and Koestler, 185-6.

all. Though we can't be sure what might have happened had she allowed her husband back, he had previously been driving drunk and wrecked the car with his children in it, so the consequences may have been quite dire.[5]

Diversions

In other cases, protection is achieved by diverting the attention of the person to be protected, thus drawing them away from the threat. Writer Frederick Forsyth was a journalist in the Nigerian civil war. Standing in a doorway one day and feeling like someone was watching him, he saw a wooden post fall over nearby and jerked his head to look at it. At that precise moment, a bullet whizzed past and buried itself in the doorjamb. If Forsyth hadn't turned to look at the falling post, the bullet would have gone through his head. He later examined the fallen post and saw that it appeared to have gone over because of termite damage. He noted that "one termite must have given the last nibble that separated the last strand of wood."[6]

In this next case, the diversion was more clearly paranormal, and that appears to be why it worked. One morning, Joe Dioca had placed three roses in a vase on his wife's grave before going to sit on a bench about 50 feet away. "Just as I sat down," he says, "I noticed one of the roses actually lifting up and out of the vase, so I jumped up and rushed to grab it before it hit the ground." In the instant he reached it, lightning struck behind him. It destroyed not only a tree but the bench where he'd been seated just seconds before. "The lightning was so close to me," says Dioca, "that it burned the right shoe off my foot! It was as if Ellie called me closer to escape the lightning strike."[7]

Silver Linings

Sometimes the protective technique employed is an apparently negative event that turns out to have a silver lining for us or someone else. A Hollywood director of photography whom Eric Metaxas identifies simply as "Mark" was severely depressed, to the point of being on the verge of suicide. A coworker of his contacted a man whom he thought might be able to help Mark—Dr. Larry Poland—but Poland's schedule was so busy that he didn't

---

[5] Bernard D. Beitman, "Coincidence Studies," *Psychiatric Annals* 41, no. 12 (December 2011): 561-71, p. 562.
[6] Ben Noakes, *I Saw a Ghost: Eye-Witness Accounts by the Famous of Supernatural Encounters* (London: Weidenfeld and Nicolson, 1986), 57.
[7] Dianne Arcangel, *Afterlife Encounters: Ordinary People, Extraordinary Experiences* (Charlottesville, VA: Hampton Roads, 2005), 112.

immediately have a chance to follow up. Then, one day, Poland's assistant was frustrated because so many people were cancelling their appointments with him at the last minute, including his breakfast appointment for the following morning. Poland was suddenly reminded of Mark and asked his assistant to dial Mark's number. Mark answered, and he somewhat reluctantly agreed to have breakfast with Poland the next day. Their meeting turned out to be life changing. Mark revealed that, when Poland had called him the day before, he'd been holding a razor, about to kill himself. He'd yelled out, "God, if you're there, help me!" That's when the phone rang.[8]

When we get annoyed at kinks in our schedule, it's good to remember that what's a minor inconvenience to us may be life-saving for someone else. You simply never know.

[8] Eric Metaxas, *Miracles: What They Are, Why They Happen, and How They Can Change Your Life* (New York: Dutton, Plume, 2014, 2015), 282-5.

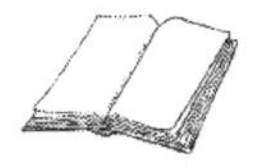

Chapter 14

Books & Information

Coincidences seem to be particularly adept at bringing people the information they need at the precise time they need it, especially in the form of books. In fact, this phenomenon is so prevalent that the great collector of coincidences Arthur Koestler gave it a name—the "library angel"—and said that "[t]his type of coincidence...is so frequent that one almost regards them as one's due."[1]

Helping Writers and Researchers Locate Sources

As one would imagine, the library angel is a particularly invaluable companion in the lives of writers and researchers. Koestler provides the following example from Dame Rebecca West, who was searching for information on a particular event that happened during the Nuremberg war crime trials. Unfortunately, she discovered that the library where this information was stored had multiple shelves full of abstracts of these trials, all catalogued in an infuriatingly arbitrary way. After spending hours searching among them to no avail, she resignedly expressed her despair to the assistant librarian and then took a volume from a shelf at random. When

---

[1] Alister Hardy, Robert Harvie, and Arthur Koestler, *The Challenge of Chance: A Mass Experiment in Telepathy and Its Unexpected Outcome* (New York: Random House, 1973), 172. Koestler appears to have derived this name from Count Xavier de Maistre's references to "*l'ange distributeur de pensées*": "the angel who distributes thoughts." See p. 174 of Hardy, Harvie, and Koestler.

she looked at the page to which she had haphazardly opened it, there was the very information she had been so fruitlessly seeking.[2]

Parapsychologist D. Scott Rogo has had the library angel repeatedly bring him information for writing his various books. Several examples can be found in his memoir *In Search of the Unknown*. In one of these, Rogo was writing about the spirit obsession/possession work of Dr. Titus Bull but had woefully inadequate source material. He decided one morning to start work on his chapter about Bull but found he just couldn't concentrate. He drove around somewhat aimlessly and ended up in MacArthur Park in Los Angeles, then recalled a bookstore across from the park. Although he remembered its having an abysmal selection, he decided to go there anyway. His memory was confirmed, but as he was going to leave, he saw a bunch of magazines in a mess on the floor. A partially exposed yellow cover reminded him of the old cover of the *Journal of the American Society for Psychical Research*, and when he unearthed it, he saw that it was in fact this journal and that there were several issues of it. Even more astonishing, inside them he found eight long reports on the work of Titus Bull, work Rogo hadn't known existed until that moment. He now had all the material he needed to finish his chapter.

The following week, Rogo found himself in need of material on Dr. Elwood Worcester. He knew that it was to be found in Worcester's book *Body, Mind and Spirit*, so he wrote away to the Parapsychology Foundation for a photocopy. The next day, he went to a bookstore he hadn't visited in months—again, because it had such a poor selection, compared to the others on Hollywood Boulevard that he frequented. When he entered, he went straight to the "psychical research" section, and the first book on which his eyes rested was Worcester's *Body, Mind and Spirit*, which was, interestingly, misplaced in the occult book section. Rogo says this could not have been a case of cryptomnesia (unconscious memory of something not consciously remembered) because he knew every relevant book in all those shops. He would never have forgotten it if he had ever seen it there.[3]

Another intriguing book coincidence comes from pediatrician and author Dr. Melvin Morse, who decided to "test" the meaning of a coincidence he encountered one day while he was browsing his favorite used-book store, where he frequently found old medical books to add to his collection. He and Dutch cardiologist Dr. Wolfgang von Lommel had recently been having a disagreement over whether coincidences were meaningful or not, and on this particular day, the only set of old medical books that were in the store were in Dutch, which was von Lommel's native language but incomprehensible to Morse. "I thought this was a funny coincidence," says Morse, "and then thought of my colleague's insistence

---

[2] Letter received October 6, 1972. Quoted in Hardy, Harvie, and Koestler, 173.

[3] D. Scott Rogo, *In Search of the Unknown* (New York: Taplinger, 1976), 183-6.

that there were no coincidences. So I purchased the books and sent them to him. My test was that if it was just a coincidence, then these books should have no meaning for Dr. von Lommel. But if he was correct, then these books would have some sort of special meaning for him, which in fact they did. He stated that these were a set of old medical texts that he had a particular interest in and had been looking for."[4]

Our last case in this section involves a prop: an important stone that was supposedly from Jesus' tomb and that French medium Geneviève Delpech had lost in a move from one residence to another. A few years later, after she had moved house a second time, Delpech's father died, and she began writing a book inspired by her father's life. She needed information about Vietnam and China back in the 1960s and went to her personal library to look at what she had, thinking maybe a book by the intrepid French traveler Alexandra David-Néel would be useful but believing that she and her husband didn't own any. However, when Delpech moved a painting on the bookshelf to see if any useful books might be hiding behind it, what should she find but the stone she'd lost four years and two moves ago, propped up against a book by David-Néel called *En Chine* (In China). Delpech opened the book, and on the left page it read, "La mort du père" (The death of the father) and on the right page it said, "Mon voyage en Chine" (My trip to China).[5] I would say that the reappearance of the stone in this case serves to emphasize the importance of the book lying behind it and likely indicates paranormal involvement on the part of Delpech's deceased father.

My Own Library Angel Experiences

Being an avid reader and researcher, I have myself had quite a few encounters with the library angel. In fact, my foray into the field of the paranormal began with just such an encounter. In a French bookstore, I came across a recent release called *Les miracles de l'esprit*: Miracles of the Mind.[6] It was a philosophical book about similarities between the way clairvoyants access information and the way we normally access our memories. I wasn't sure I wanted to buy it, because I wasn't really "into" that kind of stuff at the time. But I flipped it open nevertheless, and the first thing I saw was a passage that talked about a researcher who had done a serious study of stories of

---

[4] Melvin Morse with Paul Perry, *Parting Visions: Uses and Meanings of Pre-Death, Psychic, and Spiritual Experiences* (New York: Villard Books, 1994), 180-1.

[5] Geneviève Delpech, *Le don d'ailleurs: Autobiographie d'une médium* (Paris: Pygmalion, J'ai Lu, 2015), 139-41.

[6] Bertrand Méheust, *Les miracles de l'esprit: Qu'est-ce que les voyants peuvent nous apprendre?* (Paris: La Découverte, 2011).

supposed reincarnation, Dr. Ian Stevenson. (At the time, I had no idea who he was.) Stevenson said that a lot of children who reported details of having lived previous lives also bore birthmarks that corresponded to the places where their remembered personalities had been mortally wounded in their previous lives. I was sufficiently intrigued by this to plop into a nearby beanbag chair and turn to the previous page so I could read this discussion from the beginning. That's where I discovered that Ian Stevenson had worked at the University of Virginia, about two hours from where I grew up, and that he had passed away in 2007, a year that had particular significance for me. I continued reading and came upon a footnote. It was the first footnote I'd run across in this book, and it was numbered 33, a number that (as I explained in Chapter 11) was also significant for me. When I looked down to read footnote 33, I saw that it gave the name of a book by Stevenson: *20 cas suggérant le phénomène de reincarnation* (*Twenty Cases Suggestive of Reincarnation*).[7] It said that this book had been published in pocket edition by the publisher J'ai Lu, and it immediately occurred to me that the book would probably be on the shelves of the store where I was at the time. I raised my head to look directly in front of where I was sitting, and as soon as my eyes focused on the shelf in front of me, I saw that the book at which I happened to be staring was *precisely that book*: *20 cas suggérant le phénomène de réincarnation.* Needless to say, I bought both that book and *Les miracles de l'esprit*. And, over the following few weeks, it was those two books that definitively opened my worldview to the realities of psi and reincarnation, and ultimately led to the writing of the book you hold in your hands today.

Interestingly, I'm not the only one who's had a coincidence involving Ian Stevenson's *Twenty Cases Suggestive of Reincarnation*. A fellow named James Bolen had promised to lend his copy of that book to a friend, but he couldn't find it after moving to a new office. Alan Vaughan was enlisted to help him locate it, and they both eventually concluded it must be at the bottom of a huge unpacked box, whereupon they gave up the search. The next day, however, Vaughan found on his desk a brand-new edition of the book. The office assistant explained that it had arrived in the morning mail, straight from the publisher at the University of Virginia.[8] I wonder if the book turned out to be as transformative for Bolen's friend as it was for me.

Another of my library angel coincidences occurred while I was in the midst of writing a memoir and had the thought that I would like to read Elizabeth Gilbert's bestseller *Eat Pray Love*. This was in 2011, five years after the book's publication in 2006. Since I was at my parents' home, where one of my sisters was also living at the time, I went to her room and asked her

[7] Ian Stevenson, *20 cas suggérant le phénomène de réincarnation*, trans. Ariane de Lestrange (Paris: Editions Sand, J'ai Lu, 1974, 1985).

[8] Alan Vaughan, *Incredible Coincidence: The Baffling World of Synchronicity* (New York: J. B. Lippincott Company, 1979), 114-5.

whether she had a copy. She looked at me strangely. "I just bought it today," she said. It was still in the plastic bag on her floor, and she pulled it out and handed it to me.

In yet a third, even stranger, run-in with the library angel, I was trying to find a Christmas present for my French boyfriend. We almost always gave each other books as gifts. In fact, I had already found one book that holiday season that I thought would be perfect for him, but then I ended up reading it myself and loving it so much that I just had to ask him, before Christmas, whether he had ever read it. When he received my email asking him this question, a copy of the book was actually lying on the floor at his feet. He had bought it the previous summer, apparently when we were shopping together. Perhaps my unconscious remembered seeing it, and that's why I thought it'd be perfect for him. In any case, that's not the coincidence. That's just to explain why, four days before Christmas, I was again searching for a book to give him.

I finally found, in a secondhand store, a book that seemed even more perfect for him than the last one. Our interests were so similar, however, that I again couldn't resist reading it myself. In fact, just after purchasing it, I went to a nearby coffeeshop and basically read half the book over the next couple of hours, all the while exclaiming to myself, "This is perfect for him! He's going to love this!" I was also quite confident that this was not a book he had ever read before.

Well, my boyfriend was in France at the time, and I was in the States. The next morning, he sent me an email that included a picture of a book he'd just bought. The title was in French, and it took me a minute to realize that it was the French translation of the book *I* had just bought. When I asked him where he'd come across it, he told me that, that very morning, he had decided to go into the city to a little esoteric bookstore where he had never previously set foot, and that's where he'd seen and purchased it. That is to say, 12 hours after I was in the coffeeshop exclaiming to myself how perfect this book was for him, he went into an unfamiliar bookstore on the other side of the Atlantic and bought it. I should add that this book came out in 1996 in the US and in 1999 in France, so 14 and 11 years, respectively, before this coincidence occurred. And the book was *The Soul's Code* by psychologist James Hillman, who is deeply interested in synchronicities. I joked with my boyfriend that, because the postal service had recently been taking so long to deliver transatlantic packages, I'd decided to send him his Christmas present by telepathy.

Strangely enough, all three of these book-related coincidences happened to me within the space of two months. I believe what psychologists and psychiatrists say about coincidences' being especially common in periods of transition. That was probably the most transitional period of my life (so far), and these book coincidences helped pave the way for an exciting new stage of growth.

A more recent book-related coincidence happened to me when I was preparing to write *The Source and Significance of Coincidences* and wondering whether I should order Kirby Surprise's *Synchronicity* as part of my research. Part of me thought it could be very important, but another part of me wasn't sure, and I didn't want to waste my money. I'd been hesitating for a week, maybe two, when I was visiting some friends in New Hampshire and went out with them to eat in a restaurant/coffee shop that had a shelf or two of books on display for their patrons' browsing pleasure. Because I had been telling my friends about my coincidence book project during our visit, they understood my great delight in finding on the shelf across from our table not only a book titled *Synchronicity*, but the very book of this title that I'd been wondering about buying. It took only a quick glance at it for me to determine that I absolutely needed to purchase it, which I did immediately upon returning home.

Finding Books in Strange Locations

In the library angel coincidences we've looked at so far, the needed books have been found in fairly normal locations: primarily, the shelves of libraries and bookstores. However, important volumes can also show up in stranger places. For instance, English Lord Birdwood says he often profits from coincidences in his work. Once he left an important book in a London taxi, a book of which he was sure there was no other copy in the UK. Two weeks later and six miles away, he drove by some children who were playing with that very book. In their play, they threw it over a hedge. So Lord Birdwood stopped his car and picked it up![9]

Actor Anthony Hopkins wanted to study for his role in the 1974 film adaptation of George Feifer's novel *The Girl from Petrovka* but couldn't find a copy of the book in any of the London stores he visited. Then, while in an Underground station, he saw a copy of it that someone had apparently left behind on a bench, and he took it. When George Feifer later visited the set of the movie in Vienna, Hopkins told him about the strange coincidence that had brought the book to him, as well as about the odd red marks he'd found in various places in the book. Hopkins handed the book to Feifer and asked him, "Might that copy have some personal meaning for you?" As it happened, it had once belonged to Feifer. The red marks were changes he'd wanted to make for the Americanized edition, but it had been lost two years

---

[9] Brian Inglis, *Coincidence: A Matter of Chance – or Synchronicity?* (London: Hutchinson, 1990), 54-55.

previously when he'd lent it to a friend. Feifer had searched all over for it and even offered rewards for its recovery, but with no success. Now here it was, brought back to him through this extraordinary chain of events.[10]

In another case of a needed book showing up in a strange location, Dr. Lawrence LeShan had lunch with fellow psychologist Dr. Nina Ridenour, who have him a list of volumes he should read to improve his understanding of mysticism. He was particularly motivated to find Bing's *A Vision of Asia*, as Ridenour told him that it was crucial for understanding the difference between Eastern and Western mysticism. However, LeShan went to two different libraries that afternoon without finding it. He was hurrying home that evening when, on a whim, he took a strange detour. While he was waiting to cross a street, he happened to see a book lying on the ground. It was, of course, *A Vision of Asia*. In an odd footnote to this story, when LeShan told Ridenour the next morning that he had a funny story to tell her about Bing's *A Vision of Asia*, she said she had never heard of the book. And yet the reference was clearly written down in the notes he took while at lunch with her, and he distinctly remembered her comment on its being crucial to his understanding.[11]

The book in this next case was not in a particularly strange place—just a mailbox—but the manner in which French author Philippe Ragueneau was led to find it was decidedly strange. Another French author, physician Dr. Jean-Jacques Charbonier, recounts that, while reading Ragueneau's book about communications from his deceased wife,[12] Charbonier felt seized by the need to send Ragueneau one of his own books (and found his address in a coincidental way). Sometime after mailing the book, Charbonier got a letter from Ragueneau that recounted an interesting series of events. Ragueneau had been about to leave home to spend the summer on the Mediterranean Sea when he was at his local bakery and realized that he had somehow lost his house keys. His baker suddenly had it pop into her head that his keys were sitting at home on his mailbox, and, though she felt a bit silly, she told him this. When Ragueneau went home to check, he indeed found the keys where she'd said. Furthermore, sticking out of the mailbox was the package containing Charbonier's book. Ragueneau retrieved it and took it along with him on his trip, something he would not have done had he not been forced to return to his house to look for his lost keys. This became all the more significant when it turned out that, after leaving for the Mediterranean, Ragueneau never returned to his house again. He passed away not long after,

---

[10] Stephen E. Braude, *The Gold Leaf Lady and Other Parapsychological Investigations* (Chicago: University of Chicago Press, 2007), 133.

[11] Lawrence LeShan, letter, *International Journal of Parapsychology* 10, no. 2 (1968): 223-4. Quoted in Vaughan, *Incredible Coincidence*, 118-9.

[12] Philippe Ragueneau, *L'autre côté de la vie: Un message d'espoir et d'amour pour ceux qui ont perdu un proche* (Paris: Editions du Rocher, Pocket, 1995, 1997, 2001).

joining the spirit of his beloved wife, Catherine. And it was in fact Catherine that Ragueneau credited with feeding the location of his keys to the baker and alerting him to the presence of Charbonier's book in his mailbox, before he took his final voyage.[13]

Books That Pop Off Shelves

As if the last two cases weren't bizarre enough, there's a whole genre of book coincidences that involves books' physically popping off shelves when they are particularly relevant to the people who are present. For instance, astrophysicist Dr. Victor Mansfield describes in detail how Carl Jung's book *Aion* jumped off his shelf three different times, each time while the same people were in the room with him. Mansfield had never read the book, but after it flew off the shelf the third time—this time hitting his worktable, which was several feet away—he decided he should probably investigate its contents. He came to discover that this work of Jung's perfectly explained the psychological reality that was in the process of unfolding among the persons present on these three occasions.[14]

Perhaps unsurprisingly, books seem to pop off shelves particularly in connection with the deceased. For instance, Carl Langspecht was hoping for a sign after his mother died. While he was in a bookstore, the Guggenheims' book on after-death communication, *Hello from Heaven!*, popped off the shelf at him.[15] In another case, children's author Shelley E. Parker lost her partner of 24 years in a helicopter crash. She had published a book dedicated to him, and after his death, it began to repeatedly fall out of its place on his parents' bookshelf.[16]

A 50-year-old man named Allen died suddenly when an undiagnosed kidney tumor burst. His wife reports that, on the day of his funeral, she was far from the bedroom bookcase when one of his "offbeat" spiritual books fell rather forcefully from an upper shelf. On the page she opened it to were some words attributed to the character of Jesus: "Everyone is focused on the nature of my death, the violence and the blood." The Jesus in this book then went on to say, "it was a violent and shocking death but people forget that

---

[13] Jean-Jacques Charbonier, *Les 7 bonnes raisons de croire à l'au-delà* (Paris: Guy Trédaniel, J'ai Lu, 2012), 136-8.
[14] Victor Mansfield, *Synchronicity, Science, and Soul-Making* (Chicago: Open Court, 1995), 161-5.
[15] Paul Davids and Gary E. Schwartz with John Allison, *An Atheist in Heaven: The Ultimate Evidence for Life after Death?* (Reno, NV: Yellow Hat Publishing, 2016), 323.
[16] Penny Sartori, *The Wisdom of Near-Death Experiences: How Brushes with Death Teach Us to Live* (London: Watkins, 2014), 107.

for most of my life I was, as I am now, alive." Allen's wife felt these words were meant to remind her of Allen's ongoing life and presence.[17]

Another case of a popping book occurred 20 years after the death of the person who was apparently involved. Twenty years after her mother's death, Melissa was expressing her anger at her mother for leaving her alone. She was vehemently shouting and screaming. The next day, a book that was wedged into the bookshelf flew off—a book her mom used to read to her. An hour later, it happened again. So many strange things happened, in fact, that Melissa's husband got spooked. Melissa then told her mother that she'd gotten the message and these events needed to stop or her husband was going to move out of the house! The events ceased.[18]

Finally, medium Suzanne Giesemann reports an experience in a bookstore in which a book didn't jump off the shelf but rather appeared to move a half inch to the right and then back again. Twice. When Giesemann bought the book, she felt a voice prompting her to turn straight to the pictures. There she discovered drawings like those made by a deceased young man she'd been communicating with, along with a caption—"Pachamama"—that explained a word she'd had trouble understanding from him in one of her readings.[19] Giesemann understood the book's apparent motion as an illusion created by spirit, but if the deceased can make books fly off shelves, I don't see why they couldn't move one back and forth *on* the shelf!

Non-Book Sources of Information

To close this chapter, let me offer a few examples of coincidences that bring needed information in a form other than a book. In this first case, the information is provided even before the need for the information has had the chance to arise. Jean Burden was stuck in traffic driving home one evening when she let a truck merge in front of her and was drawn to the numbers on its license plate: 15644. For some reason, she slightly rearranged the numbers in her head to 61544 and then thought to herself that this was medium Eileen Garrett's unlisted home number. (This was back in the days when phone numbers had only five digits!) Since Burden usually called Garrett at her office number, she hadn't called this number in a long time. But when Burden returned home and was still opening the door, she heard

---

[17] Robert H. Hopcke, *There Are No Accidents in Love and Relationships: Meaningful Coincidences and the Stories of Our Families* (Asheville, NC: Chiron Publications, 2018), 196-7.

[18] Elisabeth Hallett, *Stories of the Unborn Soul: The Mystery and Delight of Pre-Birth Communication* (San Jose: Writers Club Press, 2002), 221-2.

[19] Suzanne Giesemann, *Wolf's Message* (2014), 60-65.

the phone ringing. It was a friend calling and frantically asking for Eileen Garrett's unlisted home number.[20]

Author John Campbell Bruce was researching his book *Escape from Alcatraz* and having trouble because the former warden of the prison wouldn't give him some information he wanted. Feeling at a dead end in his writing, Bruce decided to go a high school friend's retirement party. There he met a man who turned out to be the sole witness to the long-ago prison break Bruce was researching, a fact made even more astonishing by the fact that the fellow had only been a temporary guard at Alcatraz, working there for only two weeks.[21]

Finally, as I was preparing to publish this book, I had to request permission from several authors and publishers to reprint excerpts of their works. One of these authors was the pre-birth communication researcher Elisabeth Hallett, but I couldn't find an email address for her anywhere online. All I had was a snail mail address for what looked like a publishing company she might own, but I'd found that address in a book that was 24 years old, so I didn't hold a lot of hope for receiving a reply from anything I mailed there. However, as I was contemplating what to do, I suddenly remembered a coincidence that had happened to me a year previously. I had placed an online order for a used book about pre-birth memories, and when it arrived, I saw that the person who had sent it to me was actually an author whose name I recognized from my research: Elisabeth Hallett. I thought this was such a neat coincidence at the time that I actually cut out Ms. Hallett's return address label and taped it inside the cover of the book I'd received from her. I now realized with a pleasant jolt of surprise that all I had to do to find Ms. Hallett's current mailing address was to look inside that book—and there it was!

[20] Vaughan, *Incredible Coincidence*, 122-4.
[21] Vaughan, *Incredible Coincidence*, 105-6.

Chapter 15
Material Help

We've already seen many examples of coincidences' providing material help by protecting people from physical harm or by leading them to written information that they are in particular need of. In this chapter, we examine assorted other ways that coincidences have materially helped people, beginning with the unexpected return of lost items.

Return of Lost Items

Our first, and oldest, case was reported in the influential London weekly magazine *The Spectator* in 1898.[1] Mrs. Humble-Crofts of England lost a ring she'd received from her husband, who had in turn inherited it from his father. Eighteen years later, Mrs. Humble-Crofts got a letter from her half-sister in New Zealand that happened to mention the fact that, in a pair of gloves that had been purchased and sent to her by a family member in London, she had found a ring—probably accidentally left by a shop customer who had tried on the gloves and not noticed when the ring slipped off. As you will have guessed, it turned out to be the very ring Mrs. Humble-Crofts had lost 18 years before. What is more, the half-sister who found the ring had already decided to sell it and donate the proceeds to charity. The purchaser of the ring was a Mr. Frank Arkwright, the grandson of the woman who had originally given the ring to Mr. Humble-Crofts' father! Perhaps this case

[1] W. J. Humble-Crofts, "The Romance of a Ring," letter, *The Spectator* (27 August 1898).

sounds like a bunch of embroidered hearsay, but it was subsequently investigated by Alice Johnson of the Society for Psychical Research, and the testimonies of four different individuals corroborate the events just described.[2]

Another impressive case of the unexpected surfacing of a lost item comes from a collection of coincidences published by German writer Wilhelm von Scholz in 1924. During World War I, a woman took a picture of her son and dropped the film off to be developed, but subsequent events left her unable to retrieve the finished photograph. Two years later, she developed a picture she'd taken of another child—her daughter—on a roll of film purchased in a different city. The developed photograph revealed a double exposure, in which the underlying image was the lost picture of her son![3]

This next case involves a borrowed item rather than a lost one, but it's notable because the lent item was returned at such a propitious moment. Mrs. Willard Lovell had accidentally locked herself out of her house in Berkeley, California. After spending about 10 minutes searching for a way in, she saw the mailman arrive with a letter for her. It was from her brother, who had recently stayed with her. He happened to be returning the spare key he had borrowed![4]

Provision of Other Needed Items

Often, coincidences provide items that never previously belonged to the person in question but that seem clearly destined for them in one way or another. British writer and historian Peter Elstob was once standing outside a sports shop in London when an American stranger asked him some advice on buying a tennis racket. The American went on to say that he'd been asked to get a letter to someone in Britain but couldn't find his address. He showed Elstob the letter—it was addressed to Elstob himself. "I can still remember the shock, the shiver, the wild suspicion that he must have known who I was," Elstob recounts. "But that was impossible."[5]

---

[2] Alice Johnson, "Coincidences," *Proceedings of the Society for Psychical Research* 14 (1899): 158-330, pp. 227-9.

[3] Wilhelm von Scholz, *Der Zufall: Eine Vorform des Schicksals* (Stuttgart, Germany: Hädecke, 1924). As recounted in C. G. Jung, *Synchronicity: An Acausal Connecting Principle*, trans. R. F. C. Hull (Princeton, NJ: Princeton University Press, 1960, 2010), 15.

[4] Julia Green, "One in a Million," *Modern People* (October 27, 1974), 16.

[5] Brian Inglis, *Coincidence: A Matter of Chance – or Synchronicity?* (London: Hutchinson, 1990), 18-19.

American writer Stephen Diamond was passing an almost penniless stay in San Francisco with a girlfriend. They were having a great time, and he wanted to record some of his experiences but didn't have a notebook. He went to a store thinking he might just steal one, but there were too many people around for him to feel comfortable doing that. On his way back to the house, he noticed a pad of paper on the sidewalk, face down. When he turned it over, he saw that it was personalized, and at the top of each page was written his name: Stephen Diamond, M.D. He says, "I took it as a sign, a road marker which seemed to indicate that I was on the right track in that search for the essence of my former self, the spirit of the whole."[6]

The item in the following case may not have been marked with the recipient's name, but it was much more unusual than a pad of paper, and the recipient had just explicitly expressed a need for it.

> On May 20, 1972, a group of people were standing round a swimming pool in the garden of the Hon. Mark Bonham-Carter's house…in Sussex…. The pool had been emptied to be relined, but at the bottom there remained a quantity of water too low to go down the draining hole, which made it impossible to start work.
>
> Various ideas of how to proceed were discussed and rejected, till one of the guests, the local architect, said: "What we need is a builder's pump, but the problem is how to get hold of one." At that moment a loud noise was heard from the road (about 40 yards away), and a lorry rattled slowly by, carrying a builder's pump. The architect leapt into his car, caught up with the lorry, and the pool was promptly drained.[7]

Now for a story concerning an object of even greater value. Sarah and Brent Hinze had just been informed by their landlord that they and their large brood of children had two weeks to move out of their house. While resting one afternoon, Sarah had a dream of a house with a big yard surrounded by pine trees. She started awake with a message in her mind: "If you will get in your car and drive, you will be led to your new home." So she started driving around, and at each intersection, she followed the inner impression she received about which way to go. Soon she was in a beautiful area that she knew she and her husband did not have the means to move into. Nevertheless, she saw a vacant house with an overgrown yard and a for-sale sign out front. She walked around it and discovered the yard from her dream, complete with the surrounding pine trees. "The Lord is going to give you this home," she heard in her head. It turned out, when she and her husband spoke with the realtor, that the seller of the home was extremely motivated

---

[6] Stephen Diamond, *What the Trees Said* (New York: Delta, 1971), 138-9.

[7] Alister Hardy, Robert Harvie, and Arthur Koestler, *The Challenge of Chance: A Mass Experiment in Telepathy and Its Unexpected Outcome* (New York: Random House, 1973), 181-2.

and had just dropped the price by $40,000. (And this was in the 1980s.) Sarah and Brent Hinze purchased the place, and as of her writing, they had lived there with their family for over 25 years.[8]

While I'm sure from what I know of Sarah and Brett Hinze that they had prayed about the impending loss of their home, the next two cases explicitly mention that a prayer was said before the coincidental appearance of the needed object.

Like the Hinzes, Marci Vance was threatened with the loss of her home. Her adoptive father was threatening to throw her out of the house if she didn't start working right away. When she did finally locate a job, it required her to wear a white blouse and gray pants, and she only had enough money to buy the white blouse. She started crying and prayed to God to please help her. When she looked up, Vance saw that a rainbow had formed in the sky. Feeling this was a sign that things would be all right, she decided to walk over to her aunt's house. There she discovered that, just before she'd arrived, a friend of her aunt's had dropped off some clothes for a clothing drive at her church. Vance's aunt suggested that she look and see if there was anything she wanted. There were in fact two pairs of gray pants that were a perfect fit.[9]

Mary Mueller Kraus was a volunteer firefighter who arrived at a severe car accident before any of the medical personnel. She discovered that one of the car's passengers was bleeding to death from a gash in her head. Unfortunately, Kraus had nothing sterile with which to bandage the wound and slow the flow of blood, and she knew medical personnel wouldn't arrive for another 15 or 20 minutes. At a loss over what to do, she prayed for help. She looked around her, and then when she looked back at the bleeding woman, she saw that, sitting in the snow within perfect reach was "a dark red bag with black handles and a black medical emblem," very different from the bags she was used to rescue personnel using, and with no footprints to betray who'd brought it or from what direction they had come. Inside the bag were all the medical supplies Kraus needed, and arranged in efficient order. She was able to use them to staunch the flow of blood, and the injured woman was eventually helicoptered out, with Kraus's hand still pressed over her wound. Only hours later did Kraus drive back to the accident site to take a second look at the mysterious medical bag. However, although the site was being carefully surveilled and workers had collected any debris from the accident they could find, that bag was never found. Nor did the workers find

---

[8] Sarah Hinze with Laura Lofgreen, *The Memory Catcher* (Provo, UT: Spring Creek Book Company, 2012), 93-94.

[9] Joan Wester Anderson, *Where Miracles Happen: True Stories of Heavenly Encounters*, updated (Chicago: Loyola Press, 1994, 2009), 25-26.

any of the blood-soaked bandages that Kraus had discarded while saving the woman's life.[10]

Here now are a few more light-hearted examples of the mysterious provision of needed objects, showing that even our more frivolous desires can be served by coincidences and that whoever is creating them may very well have a sense of humor.

Bob Treuhaft was in London looking to purchase a copy of the game Boggle for a friend. He came to a big toy store, but the entrance was so crowded and the day was getting so hot that he decided not to go in after all. When he kept walking by, something fell from above and landed near his feet. It was a Boggle set, marked with a price tag from the store.[11]

In October of 1957, Patricia Dietsch was doing some early Christmas shopping and looking for a very special present for her aging father: a violin and piano recording of a piece called "Humoresque." To her great disappointment, her music store informed her that it was out of press and couldn't be ordered. However, a couple of months later, a few weeks before Christmas, the store called her and asked her to stop by. That morning, one of their regular deliveries from a record company had contained a recording of "Humoresque," even though they hadn't ordered it and it wasn't even produced by the company that delivered it. The store gave it to Dietsch free of charge.[12]

Maybe you'll recall a similar experience had by Matthew Manning, which I related in Chapter 6. Manning went to buy the Ringo Starr record "It Don't Come Easy" but couldn't find it in either of the two stores he visited. However, when he returned home, a brand-new copy was sitting on his desk, and he was never able to figure out where it had come from. He was certain that no one else who shared his residence owned one.[13]

Here's a case we haven't looked at yet that also happens to involve a record store. Dr. Kirby Surprise's friend Kieth went to a store looking for a particular CD but discovered upon arrival that the store had relocated, and he didn't know where. When he asked the first teenager he passed if he knew the new location, it turned out that this teenager was actually on his way to work there! Kieth walked along with him, found the CD he wanted, and even got an employee discount. In an interesting coda to this experience, when Kieth then went outside to have a smoke, he realized he was out of cigarettes. But someone else who'd been in the record store came up to him and

---

[10] Anderson, *Where Miracles Happen*, 45-50.

[11] Inglis, *Coincidence*, 40.

[12] Alan Vaughan, *Incredible Coincidence: The Baffling World of Synchronicity* (New York: J. B. Lippincott Company, 1979), 87-88.

[13] Matthew Manning, *The Link: Matthew Manning's Own Story of His Extraordinary Psychic Gifts* (New York: Holt, Rinehart and Winston, 1974, 1975), 97.

spontaneously offered him some, having recognized him as a local performer.[14]

To close out this section, I've got two more cases that may be too clearly paranormal to be called "coincidences," but I'm including them here because they fit the theme of locating sought objects and because they may illuminate some of the less blatantly paranormal cases.

The first is something that happened to Bonnie Rose Loveall when she was a penniless single mother. One day, she was completely out of food. She searched all of her cabinets and then the entire house looking for something she could possibly feed to her children. She even looked under the bed, but it was no use. She wasn't a religious person, but she prayed the simple prayer, "God, the children need food." She then felt a need to recheck the cupboards. Inside, she found a box of mac and cheese, which she knew hadn't been there previously. Of course, she prepared it. But then something even stranger happened. Though she and her ravenous children ate a great deal, the pan was still full afterward. At each meal, they would reheat the mac and cheese, eat some more, and the pan would still seem close to being as full as before. "We ate out of that pan for an entire week," says Loveall. "I knew I was having a supernatural experience. But who could I tell?"[15]

This last experience happened to Canadian archeologist Charles Garrad in the fall of 1972. He had been digging for a week in a location he believed to be a Wyandot village but had found nothing of value. Finally, he was so tired, cold, and hungry that he started yelling at the deceased Wyandots that they'd better give him something in five minutes or he was quitting. He then went to put his shovel in the dirt yet again, but it glanced off and raised some dust. "[W]hile the dust was lifted," he says, "I plainly saw in the ground several [ritual] pipes, and then the dust settled and the pipes were obscured from view." This was an utterly remarkable find, and Garrad quickly set to work trying to retrieve these pipes. Oddly, however, they were no longer covered only in a layer of dust. They were now almost 12 inches below the surface, and getting them out was no easy task. When Garrad finally had them in hand, he felt he needed to apologize for the way he'd earlier been shouting at the Wyandots. "I didn't know what to do," he says,

> but I lifted one of the pipes to the sky, and to the ground, and to the four winds, saying aloud, "Thank you." That remark was greeted by laughter. I looked over to where the sound was coming from, and there, several hundred feet away, on the other side of the field, was a cluster of Indians. There were three boys in the front, and four adults in the back. It was just a blinding flash, they weren't there for more than a maximum space

---

[14] Kirby Surprise, *Synchronicity: The Art of Coincidence, Choice, and Unlocking Your Mind* (Pompton Plains, NJ: New Page Books, 2012), 93-94.
[15] Anderson, *Where Miracles Happen*, 227-8.

> of a second. I could just see the right hand of the nearest male rested on the left shoulder of the boy in front of him. They were arranged as though posed for a photograph.

Garrad says that the Wyandots were not insulting him with their laughter. Rather, he says, "in some way I did not understand they had been helping me...they approved of what I had been doing."[16]

Broken Items

We now turn to a couple of cases involving broken items. In the first, the item is mysteriously repaired, possibly by the spirit of a deceased person. In the second, it's the *breakage* of the items that's the coincidence, happening as it does during a particularly propitious time.

A woman named Tammi woke up one night to find herself ripping from her neck the special charm necklace she always wore, which had charms containing the birthstones of each of her children, including her toddler son Colton who had drowned just two months before. She didn't know why she'd ripped it off in her sleep and was upset to see that it was now broken. This sad event worsened her grief for her little boy. The next day, Tammi's mother saw the necklace lying on Tammi's nightstand and discovered that it was broken in not just one but two places. On the day after that, the two women were preparing to go to the cemetery to see Colton's new headstone and decided that, on the way, they would stop and get a new chain for Tammi's necklace. However, when Tammi went over to the nightstand to retrieve it, she discovered that it was no longer broken. Her mother, who denied having repaired it, was the only other person to touch it since it had been damaged.[17]

An acquaintance of Drs. Allan Combs and Mark Holland told them how her recently retired father had taken up an interest in doing "handyman" work around the house, a hobby that helped compensate for his no longer having the stimulation or satisfaction of a full-time job. Strangely, when her father came to visit one week in early summer, an incredible number of things suddenly went wrong with the house, more than during the entire six years she'd owned it. Combs and Holland describe the problems thus: "Windows jammed, doors stuck, light bulbs flashed and burned out. One evening a pipe under a bathroom sink split open for no apparent reason and began to spray

---

[16] Stephan A. Schwartz, *The Secret Vaults of Time: Psychic Archaeology and the Quest for Man's Beginnings* (New York: Grosset & Dunlap, 1978), 198-202.
[17] Dianne Arcangel, *Afterlife Encounters: Ordinary People, Extraordinary Experiences* (Charlottesville, VA: Hampton Roads, 2005), 95-97.

water. The father was busy every minute fixing one thing after another."[18] The funny thing was, when the father's visit was over, the problems suddenly stopped occurring. Combs and Holland suggest that the problems were actually created by the father's need for satisfying work. But it might also be the case that problems that might have arisen sooner or later were simply delayed or hastened in order to coincide with the week when a willing handyman would be around to fix them—and draw satisfaction from them.

Transportation

We now turn to another kind of material help: the sort that helps us get where we're going. Robert Moss tells how he and a friend were walking in the New Forest in New Hampshire when, after going 15 or 20 miles over the course of the day, they discovered they were lost. Moss said to his friend, "I wish a guide would just appear out of nowhere and show us the way. Wouldn't that be fabulous?" His friend laughed at the suggestion, since they'd seen no one else in the forest all day long. However, it wasn't but a minute or two later that a runner appeared along the trail. "You two look lost," he said. "Need some help?" The runner told them that he didn't want to break his stride but that he'd leave them markers on the trail ahead. So, at each fork in the trail, they found an arrow made of sticks telling them which way to go. In two miles, they'd found their way back to the road.[19]

Other people, who are less in need of direction than of a means of transportation, will sometimes get an unexpected lift—and from a particularly fitting source! For instance, from a young age, SQuire Rushnell wanted to be a radio announcer. His hero was Dean Harris, the DJ of a station based 60 miles south of Rushnell's home. At age 15, Rushnell got an interview with a radio station 10 miles in the other direction, but he had to hitchhike to get there. Nobody was picking him up until finally a car pulled over. Behind the wheel was none other than Dean Harris himself, who carried Rushnell to the interview where he got the job.[20]

Alan Vaughan tells how he once became impatient waiting for a bus, so he stuck out his thumb to hitchhike. The very first car to pass stopped. It was a woman who had attended a lecture of his the night before (a lecture on synchronicity, as it happens), and it turned out that she was going to the San Carlos Hotel, which was his destination as well. She pointed out to Alan

---

[18] Allan Combs and Mark Holland, *Synchronicity: Through the Eyes of Science, Myth, and the Trickster*, 3rd ed. (New York: Marlowe & Company, 1996, 2001), 118.

[19] Robert Moss, *The Three "Only" Things: Tapping the Power of Dreams, Coincidence & Imagination* (Novato, CA: New World Library, 2007), 141.

[20] SQuire Rushnell, *When God Winks: How the Power of Coincidence Guides Your Life* (New York: Atria, 2001), xvi-xviii.

Vaughan the further coincidences that her own last name was Allen and that she lived on Vaughan Road.[21]

For the grand finale of this chapter, we have the experience of Peter Caddy, a founder of the famous Findhorn Community in Scotland, who once got from northwest Scotland to the southern coast of England and back—a total distance of some 1,100 miles—with nothing but a single shilling and his intuition. As was Caddy's style, he set off on this journey because of a sudden "inner prompting." He was having tea with his wife and a close friend in Oban, Scotland, when he felt the need to see a fellow in Bournemouth to whom he owed a significant amount of money. He left the others at the table and emerged from the café to see a Rover passing. He discovered that its driver was going all the way to London and happy to have him along. What was more, during the ride, they had a lot of excellent conversation on spiritual matters, and the driver even had a picnic that she gladly shared. When Caddy got to Bournemouth, he spoke to the man to whom he owed money, and the man was very understanding—though he said he might not have been had Caddy not come to see him in person.

But that's only half the story. Caddy recounts that, on his way back to Scotland, he got a ride in a truck going up the Great North Road, but at a traffic light in Grantham, he saw a lady in a sports car stopped next to them. Bidding good-bye to the truck driver, he went to ask the woman if she was going to Scotch Corner, which she was. In fact, it turned out that she was going all the way to Carlisle, and she drove at quite a clip!

Upon their arrival in Carlisle, night was falling, and Caddy contemplated how to complete the last leg of his journey. He stopped a passing fish truck, knowing that they often drove through the night. This one was indeed headed to Oban, Caddy's final destination. Caddy climbed aboard, but after a bit, he noticed that the driver looked tired, so he offered to take over the wheel. "While the driver slept," says Caddy, "I drove all through the night on the winding Scottish roads, arriving at Oban at 7.30 in the morning. The driver was so delighted that he bought me a huge Highland breakfast. By following that inner prompting to take immediate action, all my needs had been perfectly met throughout the journey; and I doubt whether the fastest public transport could have taken me there and back again in so short a time—for a shilling!"[22]

---

[21] Vaughan, *Incredible Coincidence*, 37.

[22] Peter Caddy with Jeremy Slocombe and Renata Caddy, *In Perfect Timing: Memoirs of a Man for the New Millennium* (Forres, UK: Findhorn Press, 1995, 1998), 130.

Chapter 16

Meetings & Reunions

We come now to a classic arena for coincidence stories: that of "chance" meetings. As you might guess, a lot of these involve people who end up becoming lovers, sometimes for life. However, there are many other less romantic varieties of relationship that can benefit from coincidental meetings as well. Consider, for instance, the case of a witness who was accidentally called to testify in court regarding an armed robbery about which he had no knowledge. He might have been annoyed at the inconvenience, except that it turned out he recognized the defendant. It was someone who had robbed him of $1,000 about two months prior and who, until that moment, had eluded apprehension![1]

In this chapter, we'll examine cases of serendipitous meetings pertaining to a whole variety of relationships, from the professional to the familial to the romantic. We'll even examine the fascinating phenomenon of pre-meetings, in which people coincidentally cross paths long before their lives intertwine in any significant way. And we'll end the chapter with a discussion of star-crossed lovers: couples driven apart by coincidence.

Professional Relationships

Let's start with professional relationships. These sorts of coincidental meetings are not always life-changing, but they do frequently give people a

[1] Rex G. Stanford, "Psi in Everyday Life," *American Society of Psychical Research Newsletter*, no. 16 (Winter 1973).

momentary boost in the pursuit of their professional interests, usually by helping them find someone that they were unable to contact by normal means.

For example, French journalist Pierre Jovanovic was conducting research on the subject of angels when he was told by a colleague that they had just met an artist who painted nothing *but* angels. Jovanovic wanted very much to meet this woman, but the colleague could only remember her agent's name and wasn't sure of the spelling or of exactly where in Paris the agent was located. After half a day of fruitless telephone calls, Jovanovic concluded that the search was hopeless. That evening, however, Jovanovic got a phone call from his neighbor out in Los Angeles, who was taking care of Jovanovic's sheepdog while Jovanovic was in Paris. The neighbor was also French and asked Jovanovic to pay a visit to his grandparents while he was in Paris. Jovanovic dutifully went to the grandparents' apartment the next day—only to discover that the grandmother was the angel artist he'd spent half the previous day looking for![2]

Consider, too, what happened to a woman in Québec named Lise, who was opening a *bar à chansons*—a venue for singer/songwriters. She was told that, unless she had a celebrity like singer Félix Leclerc involved, she wouldn't be able to get any press. While Lise didn't have any luck trying to contact Leclerc, she did have the optimistic feeling that life would somehow bring her what she needed. That night, despite its being cold and dark out, she had an impulse to go for a ride in the car. Suddenly, right in front of her, she saw another car veer into a snowbank. She stopped and saw the driver emerge. It was Félix Leclerc! Because of that meeting, Leclerc ended up helping Lise open her *bar à chansons* two weeks later.[3]

Car trouble was instrumental in this next case as well. Parapsychology writer Martin Ebon was in India on a reporting assignment for which he needed to interview several people in the Indian government, including a particular person on the staff of the Indian Ministry of Agriculture. He was unable to reach this person and ended up passing the time before his next important interview by accompanying a junior member of the U.S. Embassy on a brief pleasure trip to the foothills of the Himalayas. On their way, however, the car began making a "dangerous-sounding knock." So they stopped, and Ebon ended up flagging down help. The car that offered him a lift was driven by none other than the man from the Ministry of Agriculture that he'd been previously unable to contact.[4]

---

[2] Pierre Jovanovic, *Enquête sur l'existence des anges gardiens* (Paris: J'ai Lu, 1993), 18-19.
[3] Jeff Vézina, *Necessary Chances: Synchronicity in the Encounters That Transform Us*, trans. Carl Anger (Pari, Italy: Pari Publishing, 2009), 76. This story was originally published by journalist Erik Pigani in the September 1999 issue of *Psychologies*.
[4] Alan Vaughan, *Incredible Coincidence: The Baffling World of Synchronicity* (New York: J. B. Lippincott Company, 1979), 83-84.

While car trouble seems to be a common way for coincidence to get two people who are traveling on the same road to take notice of each other, when people are on foot, they can make the connection without the need for any mechanical failures. For example, a husband and wife wanted to invite the clinical neuropsychologist and acclaimed speaker Dr. Paul Pearsall to give a talk at an educational function, but he lived in Hawaii, far away from their home in the Midwest. Nevertheless, while they were vacationing in New York City, the couple went for a walk in Central Park, and, just as they were discussing how they might contact Dr. Pearsall, they happened to run into the man himself![5]

Busy places like New York City are particularly conducive to coincidences, because of the sheer number of people one is continually passing. Nevertheless, coincidental meetings can find us even when we're just sitting at home wondering what to do next. Dr. Stanislav Grof relates the story of a time when he flew to Prague with the goal of organizing an International Transpersonal Association (ITA) conference there. The communist government of Czechoslovakia had only just fallen, and though Czechoslovakia was Grof's native country, he hadn't visited it in over 20 years and was at a loss as to where to begin in his organizing efforts. On his first day in Prague, he was sitting in his mother's apartment wondering what to do when the doorbell rang. It was an old friend and colleague of his: Tomáš Dostál. Dostál said he'd been on his way out the door to visit Grof and welcome him back to the country when he'd gotten a phone call from Ivan Havel, brother to President Václav Havel and leader of a group of progressive scientists who knew nothing about Grof's visit to Prague but were interested in getting in contact with him to ask him to be a guest lecturer. Havel was of course surprised to hear from Dostál that Grof was in Prague and that Dostál was on his way to visit Grof at that very moment. This fortuitous event gave Grof the perfect entrée for organizing his conference, which the president of the newly formed Czech Republic attended as a guest of honor.[6]

While Grof was lucky to have such a momentous coincidence show up on his doorstep, at other times, coincidence calls us to go looking for it. Mary Helen Hensley was a student at Sherman College of Straight Chiropractic when a court order filed by an agency that had previously accredited the school threatened to make it impossible for Sherman's students to receive federal aid for the next two years. Hensley happened to pop into the college president's office just after the bad news arrived. She was devastated, and yet, as she was crying outside afterward, she heard a voice in her head tell her,

---

[5] Gary E. Schwartz, *Super Synchronicity: Where Science and Spirit Meet* (Vancouver, BC: Param Media, 2017), 22.

[6] Stanislav Grof, *When the Impossible Happens: Adventures in Non-Ordinary Realities* (Boulder, CO: Sounds True, 2006), 67-69.

"Get the document, get into your car, and drive through the night to Washington, DC." Hensley had no idea what document was being referenced, but she went back into the president's office and asked what was going on surrounding a "document." It turned out that Sherman College had prepared a file explaining why its shutdown was unjust, but they couldn't seem to get it into the right hands in Washington. With some trepidation, the president handed the document to Hensley.

Just as Hensley and her husband were about to hit the road for Washington, however, Hensley's mental voice spoke again. This time, it said, "Do Not Go." Although this reversal of orders was a tad annoying, Hensley listened to the voice and stayed put.

The next morning, she was in class when the voice spoke again. "GO NOW!" it told her, twice in a row. This time, Hensley and her husband actually made it onto the highway. They got all the way from Spartanburg, South Carolina, to Richmond, Virginia. There they spent the night before starting out again early the next morning. When they arrived at the Department of Education in Washington at 9:30am, Hensley signed them in as having an appointment with the director of Secondary Education, even though they did not. Hensley and her husband proceeded to take the elevator to the appropriate floor but quickly discovered that the director in question had taken a personal day. They were promptly shown out of the building.

Instead of giving up, however, Hensley and her husband decided to sneak back in and take the elevator straight to the top floor, where they ended up in the office of the chief of staff. They told the secretary they wanted to thank the chief of staff for an act of kindness to their school and were let into her office. Once inside, they described their predicament and found her highly sympathetic. Thanks to this conversation, Sherman College's federal funding was only cut for a period of six months rather than two years. Though it was still a hurdle for Sherman's students, it wasn't insurmountable, and Hensley was able to finish her degree. Hensley credits the delay urged by the voice in her head with making it all possible, since it was the absence of the director of secondary education on the particular day of her arrival in DC that prompted her to take her problem "to the top," where she ultimately got the help she needed.[7]

This next story contains another chain of coincidences leading to the achievement of a professional goal, although this time all the coincidences were packed into the space of just a few moments. After a talk that author Robert Moss gave on his book *Dreamways of the Iroquois*, a woman in the line for book signing told him that she did *her* dreaming during the day, in the form of coincidences. "I need to know if I should accept an invitation to go

---

[7] Mary Helen Hensley, *Promised by Heaven: A Doctor's Return from the Afterlife to a Destiny of Love and Healing* (New York: Atria, 2015), 87-93.

out west," she explained, "and I look up and there are three geese in flight, flying west like an arrowhead, with a hawk in front of them." Hearing this, a man waiting in line behind her came forward and displayed his business card. His business was named "Three Geese in Flight," and in addition to Iroquois books, he also happened to specialize in Celtic ones. Moss told him this was interesting to him. "Since I started dreaming in the Mohawk language, and studying Aboriginal peoples," explained Moss, "some of my fierce Scottish ancestors have started walking through my dreams, basically saying, 'Look here, laddie. We know a thing also. Don't forget to talk to *us*.' Sometimes they say things in Scots Gaelic. I really don't know how I'm going to cope with that. Mohawk was bad enough." Now it was the turn of another fellow to unexpectedly come forward. He said that, after retiring from being a professor of English, he had devoted himself to putting together "the definitive grammar of Scots Gaelic." He gave Moss his *own* card, offering to help him translate the Gaelic in his dreams![8]

Yet another story with a long coincidence chain is related by renowned spirituality author Dr. Deepak Chopra. Chopra needed an illustrator to provide some cover art for a project he was working on, and just as he was thinking about whom he might find to do it, his daughter called him from India. When he told her about the problem, she suggested an Irish artist, whom Chopra refers to by the fictitious name "Suzanne Malcolm." Neither of them knew where Malcolm lived, however. That afternoon, a publisher in London called Chopra, and Chopra asked him if he might know Suzanne Malcolm, but he unfortunately did not. Chopra recounts what happened next:

> An hour later [the publisher] found himself at a cocktail party when the person next to him got a call on his cellular phone. He put it to his ear and said, "Suzanne?"
>
> My publisher friend gave in to a sudden impulse. "Could that possibly be Suzanne Malcolm you're talking to?" he asked. Astonishingly, it was. My friend took down her telephone number and also asked her to call me. By this time—we are still on the same day—I had flown to Los Angeles for a scheduled lecture. I was early, however, so I pulled my rental car over to the curb; I had no idea exactly where I was. Checking my messages on the cell phone, I found one from Suzanne Malcolm. This was good news, and I dialed the number she had left me.
>
> "Hello?" a woman's voice answered.
>
> "Suzanne," I said, introducing myself, "I was wondering whether you could fly over from Dublin. I think I have an art assignment for you."
>
> "Well, actually, I'm not in Ireland at the moment. I'm in Los Angeles."

---

[8] Robert Moss, *The Three "Only" Things: Tapping the Power of Dreams, Coincidence & Imagination* (Novato, CA: New World Library, 2007), 115-6.

> "Really? Where are you staying?" I asked.
>
> "I'm not sure," she replied. "Oh yes, it's 3312 Dominic." I looked outside the car window and felt a shudder pass through me—I was parked directly in front of her house.[9]

If you think *that's* an amazing story, wait until you hear what happened to eminent parapsychologist Dr. Dean Radin. He and computer scientist Dr. Richard Shoup were looking for an affordable space to rent as a laboratory for the Boundary Institute, their newly founded non-profit dedicated to psi research. They finally found what they were looking for in an end-unit in an office complex in Los Altos, California. As they settled into their new digs, Radin began designing the laboratory he wanted. "I envisioned that it would consist of a large electromagnetically shielded chamber," he says, "plus a variety of devices used to test for mind-matter interactions, some psychophysiological monitoring gear, a comfortable reclining chair, and so on." Though he was worried he might be overreaching financially, he drew a sketch of this lab on the white board that hung against the wall separating their office from the one next door.

Radin was actually curious to find out who worked in the office on the other side of that wall. He had peeked in its window, but no one ever seemed to be around. After a few weeks had gone by, he noticed a sign by the office door that read "PSI Quest Labs." He thought this was a "delightful coincidence" and assumed that the "PSI" in PSI Quest must be an acronym for something completely unrelated to parapsychology, something like "Personnel Services Incorporated." After all, there were only a few labs anywhere in the world that studied psi phenomena, and they were all pretty well aware of each other.

One day, Radin finally noticed someone in the office, so he knocked on the door. The fellow who answered went immediately pale with shock. "*Dean Radin?*" he said, clearly incredulous that the famous parapsychologist was standing in his doorway. It soon came to light that this fellow, Jon, had spent the last month trying to find Radin to ask him to be on the board of his new endeavor, PSI Quest, which against all odds was indeed dedicated to psi research. Not being able to find contact information for Radin anywhere, Jon had begun using the vivid mental imagery of Tibetan dream yoga to try to "manifest" him. The fact that these two psi researchers ended up with their labs right next to each other in the same office complex seemed like startlingly clear evidence that Jon's efforts had been successful.

But Radin himself appeared to have had a hand in the creation of this "coincidence" as well. When he told Jon that he'd been focusing his own mental energy on the laboratory he soon hoped to furnish, Jon beckoned

---

[9] Deepak Chopra, *How to Know God: The Soul's Journey into the Mystery of Mysteries* (New York: Three Rivers, 2000), 118-9.

him toward the door of the lab that he had already outfitted. It contained an electromagnetically shielded chamber of precisely the kind and type Radin had been envisioning, as well as the recliner and the psychophysiological monitoring equipment. Everything that Radin had wanted was right there, in the office on the other side of his whiteboard.[10]

Friends & Acquaintances

We turn next to stories of coincidental meetings between some people who already know each other: old friends. We saw one excellent example of this in Chapter 7, with the radio coincidences that caused Kirby Surprise to go visit his old friend Bob, only to discover that he was getting on a plane in a few hours to move to Puerto Rico. The fact that Surprise's reunion with Bob happened at a particularly significant moment in one of their lives is a pattern that we'll see repeated in the majority of the meetings about to be described.

One Saturday, Dr. Judith Orloff was browsing the stores on Main Street in Santa Monica, California. Out of nowhere, her mind filled with memories of her childhood best friend Barbara, even though it had been 20 years since they'd last seen each other. Enjoying these happy thoughts, Orloff stopped into the Rose Café for a snack. Who should be there but…Barbara! As they caught each other up on their lives, Barbara told Orloff, "our timing is unbelievable…. I'm getting married tomorrow." Orloff writes, "For our paths to be crossing at such a significant moment sent a chill running through me."[11]

A man named Richard H. was going through a very difficult time in his life. One day, he passed a phone booth where a phone book lay open. In the book, he noticed two initials and a last name that reminded him of a woman he'd known years before, even though he'd known her by her married name and this was her maiden name. He decided to call the number nevertheless, and the person who answered was the woman he'd been thinking of. She started laughing, saying she had just been thinking about *him*. They spent several days talking with each other, and their conversations helped Richard through his rough patch. After a couple of years, they again lost touch, but

---

[10] Dean Radin, foreword to *Exploring the Collective Unconscious in the Age of Digital Media*, ed. Stephen Brock Schafer (Hershey, PA: Information Science Reference, 2016), xiv-xv.

[11] Judith Orloff, *Second Sight: An Intuitive Psychiatrist Tells Her Extraordinary Story and Shows You How to Tap Your Own Inner Wisdom*, rev. ed. (New York: Three Rivers Press, 2000), 250.

Richard says, "I do believe…that if I ever need her again, she'll be back."[12] With the subsequent disappearance of both phone booths and phone books, however, I guess the universe will have to find another way of connecting them next time!

This next story shows that when a first "chance" meeting gets botched, the universe is good at finding a backup plan. In this case, a friend of English police constable Peter Moscardi had been trying to call him but couldn't get through because the number of the police station had just been changed. Fortunately, the two men ran into each other on the street, and Moscardi gave his friend the station's new number. Or rather, he gave him what he *thought* was the station's new number. The next day, he realized that he had gotten a digit wrong, but he unfortunately had no way to get in touch with his friend to let him know about the error. Nevertheless, while out on patrol the following night, Moscardi and a colleague of his saw the door of a factory strangely ajar, with a light on inside. They entered to investigate, and the telephone rang in the factory office. Moscardi answered. It was his friend. The phone number of the factory Moscardi had happened into was the number he had mistakenly given his friend![13]

Interestingly, this isn't the only case I've found of people receiving calls on telephones that they just happened to be passing near. Ken Gaub was a traveling missionary who was beginning to wonder if he was in the right line of work. One day, as he was driving down the interstate in Ohio, he asked God whether he was doing any good in his ministry and whether this was what God really wanted him to be doing. He pulled off at an exit and parked his ministry bus, then walked over to a Dairy Queen to get a drink. On his walk back to the bus, he was still thinking about what to do with regard to his ministry when he heard a nearby pay phone ringing, at a service station next door to the Dairy Queen. No one seemed to want to answer it, and after 10 or 15 rings, Gaub got impatient with the noise and picked it up himself. The operator proceeded to announce that she had a long-distance call for Ken Gaub. Gaub was obviously a bit confused by this turn of events, but soon he was speaking with a woman who introduced herself as "Millie" and began to beg for his assistance. She'd apparently been on the verge of suicide when she'd started praying for God's help and thinking what a difference it might make if she were able to talk to a particular minister she'd once seen on TV: Ken Gaub. She knew of no way to reach him, but then some numbers came into her mind and she thought to herself, "Wouldn't it be wonderful if I had a miracle from God, and he has given me Ken's phone number?" She'd thought she was calling Gaub at his office, which would have been amazing

---

[12] Caroline Myss, *Invisible Acts of Power: Personal Choices That Create Miracles* (New York: Free Press, 2004), 236-7.

[13] Vaughan, *Incredible Coincidence*, 63. Originally published in Arthur Koestler, "The Mysterious Power of Chance," *The Sunday Times* (London: May 4, 1974).

enough, given that she'd seemingly pulled the number out of thin air. The fact that she'd found him at a service station pay phone right after he'd been praying about the effectiveness of his ministry was nothing short of astonishing.[14]

Here's yet another case of being next to the right telephone at the right time, this one recounted by a French musician named Maxime. He and his musician friend Sophie were having a midnight drink on the Champs-Elysées in Paris and discussing a piece Maxime was currently composing. He had the idea of adding a flute to it, which made him think of a flautist he used to know but whom he no longer had any way of contacting. It then started to rain, so Maxime and Sophie took cover in a nightclub stairwell. There were some public phones in the stairway, and suddenly one of them started ringing. Sophie decided to pick up, and the man on the line started talking to her as if she were his insurance agent. When she couldn't seem to help him understand what had actually happened, she passed the phone off to Maxime. He, too, was trying to explain that he was not an insurance agent when the guy on the other end of the line suddenly said, "Maxime?" The caller was Maxime's flautist friend, who had recognized his voice! His friend also lived in Paris, so Maxime invited him to come join them in their night on the town. And whom should he happen to bring along? Sophie's old piano teacher! As Maxime says, "It was quite a strange night."[15]

I've run across two more cases of telephone calls' being mysteriously redirected. In one, a London woman was having tea with a friend when the phone rang and the call turned out to be for her. It was her accountant. He had dialed her number but somehow been connected to her friend's house where she happened to be visiting. The numbers were apparently not similar except for being on the same exchange.[16]

In the other case, also from England, a woman answered the phone one morning to discover that, though the caller had the wrong number, it was someone she knew and had felt guilty about not being in touch with. As a result, she tried to disguise her voice and got off the phone without identifying herself. Later that day, she called an arts center in another part of England. But somehow she also got a wrong number and fell upon the same woman who had called her on a wrong number that morning![17]

---

[14] Joan Wester Anderson, *Where Miracles Happen: True Stories of Heavenly Encounters*, updated (Chicago: Loyola Press, 1994, 2009), 256-8.
[15] Joachim Soulières, *Les coïncidences* (Paris: Dervy, 2012), 23. My translation.
[16] Brian Inglis, *Coincidence: A Matter of Chance – or Synchronicity?* (London: Hutchinson, 1990), 57.
[17] Vaughan, *Incredible Coincidence*, 64.

Missional Relationships

The case just described suggests that some people are brought together to accomplish a specific goal, and if that purpose is ignored at the first meeting, coincidence will thrust them together again. Here's another example of the same phenomenon, in which the mission—an evangelical one, in this case—is made particularly clear.

Minister Dr. Larry Poland was traveling on a plane in the country of Colombia and chatting with his seat neighbor when he felt God prompting him to talk to this man about God. Poland ignored the suggestion but felt badly about it afterward. He told God that, if given the chance to speak to that man again, he would do it without fail. Poland then spent the next two weeks traveling to Peru and Bolivia. After that, he was supposed to take an 1,100-mile flight to São Paulo, Brazil, but his flight was cancelled, and the next one didn't leave for three more days. It did have the advantage of being advertised as nonstop, however, so in some ways this seemed like a positive development. Nevertheless, about halfway through the supposedly nonstop flight, the plane made an unscheduled landing to pick up two or three more passengers. Poland was amazed to discover that one of these additional passengers was the man with whom he had previously been prompted to share his faith. Poland had an empty seat next to him, so he motioned to the fellow to take it. The guy had a strange look on his face, and he eventually explained to Poland, "This is weird. When I left you at the Bogotá airport, a voice said to me, 'You will see this man again. He has a message to which you must listen.'" Poland went on to share with him his faith in Jesus.[18]

In the next chapter, we will explore in more depth coincidences that are directed toward a mission we need to accomplish or a destiny we have to fulfill.

Family

Let's now look at some coincidences that have brought together long-lost family members. The first of these uses a strategy already familiar to us: car trouble. A man whom Robert Hopcke calls "Keith" was out making a sales call one day when his car overheated near the town of Brookside, Texas. While he was waiting for a new radiator hose to be installed, he headed to a roadside diner for lunch. Behind the counter, he noticed a woman who looked very familiar—in fact, very much like the woman he'd been raised by,

---

[18] Eric Metaxas, *Miracles: What They Are, Why They Happen, and How They Can Change Your Life* (New York: Dutton, Plume, 2014, 2015), 286-9.

whom he believed to be his mother. Before leaving the diner, he asked this stranger if they'd ever met before. She shrugged and gave him a little smile, saying she was sorry if she was staring, but they didn't get many strangers here. He mentioned that he was from Austin, and she just said, "Austin, huh?" before he went on his way.

A couple of months or so later, Keith was over at his parents' house when he saw in their pile of mail a letter with a return address in Brookside. He asked who they knew there, telling them about his car breaking down in that town. His mother got a weird look on her face and said something about an old girlfriend. Then, a week later, his parents decided to tell him the truth. The woman he'd seen in Brookside was his biological mother, who gave birth to him at a very young age and chose to give him to her sister and brother-in-law to raise. The mail he'd seen on the table was his biological mother writing to his adoptive mother to say she thought she'd seen him in Brookside and asking if it was really him. When he volunteered the information that he'd been in Brookside, they knew they had to tell him. All of this, of course, was occasioned by a radiator hose that broke outside exactly the right town, at exactly the right time for Keith to go looking for lunch at his mother's diner.[19]

Another long-lost parent was discovered by "accident" when Mary Taylor suddenly decided that she needed to take her 19-year-old son to the Chinese Exhibition at the British Museum in London. They were drinking coffee at her sister's house before setting off when it hit her that they needed to go to the museum *right then*. Once they arrived, however, mother and son got separated. When Taylor's son found her again, his face was completely white. He told her that he'd just run across his father, whom he hadn't seen since the age of a year and a half. Taylor saw the man and confirmed he was in fact the father of her son. "They are actually very similar in appearance," she says, "and were even wearing identical spectacle-frames." When they all got a drink together, the father revealed that he'd had a sudden urge to leave a meeting he was attending and take a taxi to this exhibition.[20] I find this case particularly interesting because it seems that both the mother and father were suddenly taken with an unexpected urge to visit this particular exhibition, and thus it doesn't look like the urge originated with either one of them. It seems more like an outside source determined that this was where they should meet and planted the idea in both of their heads at the same time.

In this next case, there is explicit reference to an outside source. Hospice physician John Lerma relates that a dying woman wanted to locate her ex-husband so that he could care for her three young children. On what

---

[19] Robert H. Hopcke, *There Are No Accidents in Love and Relationships: Meaningful Coincidences and the Stories of Our Families* (Asheville, NC: Chiron Publications, 2018), 156-61.

[20] Inglis, *Coincidence*, 64.

turned out to be the day before her death, Jesus appeared to her and told her that her ex-husband would indeed care for her children. She was even shown the angel that had been sent to her ex-husband to nurture in him a "feeling of love and longing for his children and ex-wife." Moments after she told Dr. Lerma this, Lerma was paged to the nurse's station and informed that the woman's ex-husband had just called the nurse's station. The ex-husband explained that, two days previously, he'd had a dream where an angel informed him that his ex-wife was dying and needed him. He flew in from Michigan the following day—the day of her death—and agreed to care for all three of her children, only two of whom were biologically his.[21]

This next coincidence involves three generations of mothers. A woman named Marilyn lost her daughter when the daughter died giving birth. Marilyn also lost contact with the child who'd been born, because the father was apparently not someone she could deal with. She worried about the child for many years but had no idea what had become of her. Then *Marilyn's* mother died. The day after her mother's memorial, Marilyn received a phone call from a woman who introduced herself as Marilyn's granddaughter's adoptive mother. Apparently, Marilyn had gone to a convention that this other woman had been involved in organizing. At the convention, someone had asked this woman to staff the registration desk while they went to the bathroom. While she was sitting there, the first person to come along and register was Marilyn. The woman recognized Marilyn's name from her daughter's adoption papers, and this prompted her to save Marilyn's address. She and her husband had promised each other that they would tell their daughter about her past when she was 19 years old, so presumably she was going to save the information for that occasion. However, she explained in her phone call that "for the last few days I have just been *weighted* with a feeling that I have to call you." Marilyn was not terribly surprised. She knew that, "when my mother died, if there was one thing she would try to bring about, it would be to put us in touch with each other."[22] I'll just mention that, if this meeting was indeed the work of Marilyn's deceased mother, then the deceased appear to sometimes bring about coincidences by putting timely pressure on people's bladders! What will they think of next?

Our last coincidence in the category of family reunions also appears to have been facilitated by a deceased mother. It's recounted in the biography of Anne Gehman, a renowned spiritualist medium, and it's one of my favorite coincidence stories of all time.

---

[21] John Lerma, *Into the Light: Real Life Stories about Angelic Visits, Visions of the Afterlife, and Other Pre-Death Experiences* (Pompton Plains, NJ: New Page Books, 2007), 141-3.

[22] Sylvia Hart Wright, *When Spirits Come Calling: The Open-Minded Skeptic's Guide to After-Death Contacts* (Nevada City, CA: Blue Dolphin Publishing, 2002), 133-5.

A woman named Carolyn Miller called Gehman asking for a reading as soon as possible. Ordinarily, a last-minute appointment would not have been possible, but it happened that, only a few minutes before, someone else had cancelled their appointment for that day, so Gehman told Miller to come on. When Miller showed up, however, she had a friend in tow and asked if her friend might be able to get a reading, too. Gehman told her there was someone scheduled directly after her appointment, but if her friend could wait, she might be able to fit her in once that was over.

During Miller's reading, Gehman was able to bring through messages from Miller's mother and grandfather, but when Miller asked if Gehman saw her brother Jack, she had to say no. She did, however, get an image of a red Victorian house. When she mentioned this to Miller, Miller said, "That's the house where I was born. It's the last place I saw my brother." Unfortunately, Gehman still wasn't able to make any contact with him. When Miller's appointment was over, she went out onto the porch to wait with her friend until the next client had finished.

Gehman's next client was a fellow who had driven all the way from New York down to Gehman's home in Florida, just for his reading. But when Gehman tried to read him, she kept seeing *Miller's* mother and grandfather. She assumed they probably had something more they wanted to say to Miller, but for the time being, Gehman tried to ignore them and bring through someone for the man who'd come all the way from New York. Finally, she saw a spirit named Henry whom the client identified as his brother-in-law who had been killed in a car accident. After she delivered a message from him, however, she then saw the image of the red Victorian house from Miller's reading. Attempting to ignore these "crossed wires" once more, she told the male client that she sensed he'd be coming back to Florida soon. He told her that she was wrong about that. The only reason he'd come to Florida, he said, was because he'd been trying for years to find his sister, and he had heard that Gehman was the best. She was his last hope. With that, it finally dawned on Gehman what was going on. She jumped up and told the client to come with her. "You've come all the way from New York to try to find your sister," she said, "and she's sitting on my porch."[23] As indeed she was.

Pets

We are about to turn to the many coincidence stories that revolve around romantic relationships, but very briefly, before we do that, I want to

---

[23] Suzanne Giesemann, *The Priest and the Medium: The Amazing True Story of Psychic Medium B. Anne Gehman and Her Husband, Former Jesuit Priest Wayne Knoll, Ph.D.* (Carlsbad, CA: Hay House, 2009), 105-11.

mention that coincidences have also been known to lead people to their pets. For instance, psychologist and coincidence aficionado Dr. Gary Schwartz recounts in his recent book *Super Synchronicity* how he told his wife they should get a Cardigan Welsh Corgi and then, less than an hour later, they encountered a dog of exactly this breed on a New York City street. What was more, when they told its owner that they wanted to adopt an older Cardigan that needed a home, she started crying, saying that it must be an answer to her prayers, because she'd been worrying about finding a home for the very dog she had with her. Of course, Schwartz and his wife ended up adopting it.[24]

Strangely, just three days before I read about this experience of Schwartz's, I got a reply to an email I'd sent a friend a couple of months before, asking whether she'd ever experienced any significant coincidences. In her reply, she told me about two coincidences, one of which was how she found her new Corgi after her old one—to whom she was very attached, to the point of calling him "the dog of my heart"—passed away. It was only the month after her Corgi died that she was at a Labor Day picnic at her parents-in-law's house and her father-in-law suggested that they visit a nearby Amish family that raised Corgis and see when they might have their next litter. When they drove over there, it turned out that their current litter had turned eight weeks old that very weekend and were just old enough to take home! My friend was also happy to see that they were a different coloring than her former dog, which is exactly what she'd wanted, so as to set her new dog distinctly apart from her old one. She ended up choosing for her pet the very first puppy that had come up to her father-in-law, sniffing and untying his shoe.

Romantic Relationships

I want to introduce this section on coincidences in romantic relationships by relating an episode from Betty J. Eadie's near-death experience. Back in Chapter 5, we read her account of seeing children who were preparing to come to earth to be born. In this case, she saw a spirit who was attempting to bring his earthly parents together so that his body could be conceived. He was not having an easy time of it, as they were "unwittingly very uncooperative." His efforts to "coach" them kept failing, and finally some other spirits got on board in an effort to help him direct his future parents in the path chosen for them.[25]

---

[24] Schwartz, *Super Synchronicity*, 52-54, 70.

[25] Betty J. Eadie with Curtis Taylor, *Embraced by the Light* (Carson City, NV: Gold Leaf Press, 1992), 92.

This case gives us an idea of the elaborate unseen efforts that could very well have gone into producing the coincidences that will be described in this section—as well as many others that escape our notice. How often are we "unwittingly very uncooperative" with those who are pulling the strings?

When Christine Jones lost her husband of 41 years to a heart attack, she was devastated and convinced that, as a shy woman in her 60s, she would never find love again. Her deceased husband, Peter, had raised and shown golden retrievers, and after his death, Jones gave all of his dogs away except for his favorite, Daisy. Daisy was so perfectly trained that, when they went on walks together, she would never stray from Jones's side. That is, until one day three years after Peter's passing, when Daisy suddenly took off running and would not stop despite all of Jones's yelling. The dog only halted her gallop when she came upon a man walking in the opposite direction. He stopped to pet her and was still doing so when Jones caught up to them. Jones reprimanded the dog, and Daisy reluctantly followed her when she walked away.

A week later, Jones and Daisy were out in a field when Daisy suddenly took off again, ignoring all of her field dog training as well as Jones's shouts. Then Jones saw where the dog was headed: towards the very same man, who was again walking towards them! This time Jones talked to the man long enough to find out that he had recently lost his wife and was having a hard time of it, but her shyness kept her from chatting more than a few minutes before walking on.

It was three months later—three months during which Daisy didn't run from Jones a single time—that Jones and Daisy were walking on a city street when Daisy once again took off. And, once again, she had gone after the same man. This time, the man asked Jones to get a coffee with him. They married a year later. Jones says, "I often reflect on what made [Daisy] run. Perhaps she heard the call of her beloved master, Peter, directing me out of my loneliness."[26]

If Jones's deceased husband was behind her meeting with her new love, who might the matchmaker be in this next case? Life coach Martha Beck tells the story of one of her clients, "Ernie," who developed a sudden, intense interest in photography. Just after telling Beck about this new interest, he found an ad for a photography club. He was thoroughly excited to attend, but when he turned up for his first meeting, he was disappointed to discover that, except for himself and one other person, everyone in the club was over 80 and "spent the evening learning to make decorative cut-out borders for pictures of their grandchildren." He was leaving the meeting early when something nevertheless told him to turn around and go back. On his way

[26] Joyce Vissell and Barry Vissell, eds., *Meant to Be: Miraculous True Stories to Inspire a Lifetime of Love* (Berkeley, CA: Conari Press, 2000), 187.

back in, he ran into the one other attendee who'd been under 80. She, too, was leaving in disappointment. They ended up getting coffee together. Strangely, by the next day, Ernie's passion for photography had evaporated. Four years later, however, he and the woman he met in that photography class were still inseparable.[27]

Perhaps the matchmaker in that last case was one of the couple's future children or a guardian angel, but I like to think it was one of Ernie's deceased grandparents watching over him—perhaps one who enjoyed scrapbooking, or at least a good joke!

In this next story, the actors behind the scenes are clearly identified. Gordon Miller's wife of 10 years, Ruby, died of a placenta separation eight months into pregnancy with their only child. The child survived, and Miller named her Summer, after his wife's favorite season. In the depths of his grief, Miller had occasional dreams of his wife that were quite comforting, but then he began to have dreams that he didn't like. In them, Ruby told him that their daughter needed a mother. In fact, for two entire weeks, Ruby appeared in his dreams every night saying that Summer needed a mom.

Two years after Ruby's passing, Miller's father, who'd been helping him take care of Summer, decided it was time for him to move out. That very night, Ruby again came to Miller in a dream. "This time," he says, "there was a figure of another woman whom I could barely see. Ruby spoke in the dream, saying there was another woman for me."[28] The following night, Ruby came again. She once again pointed out Summer's need for a mother. Then she said that Miller would not be dreaming of her again for some time. Instead, a man now appeared in the dream, and Ruby said Miller should listen to him. The man introduced himself and pointed to a table full of jewelry. Miller got the impression that this man wanted him to meet the woman who had made it. When he woke up, he wrote down everything he could remember from the dream.

After all this time, Miller was finally starting to open up to the idea of a new relationship. True to her word, Ruby did not reappear in his dreams, but Miller began to have *other* dreams, featuring a table of jewelry and a woman he couldn't see. Miller began taking Summer to jewelry stores and craft fairs, hoping that he would somehow meet this woman from his dreams. But, by the time Summer was four years old, that idea had come to seem crazy. Nevertheless, Miller finally felt ready to love again, and for the first time since he was a little boy, he prayed. He prayed for help in finding another partner.

Two months after his prayer, as Christmas drew close, Summer asked to go to a craft show. She was all decked out in her four-year-old's conception of a beautiful assortment of jewelry, and as the two of them walked past a

---

[27] Martha Beck, *Finding Your Own North Star: Claiming the Life You Were Meant to Live* (New York: Three Rivers Press, 2001), 236-7.
[28] Vissell and Vissell, 172.

small jewelry display without noticing it, the woman behind the table called out to Summer, telling her how lovely she looked. She ended up giving Summer a piece of her jewelry as a gift. The next day, Miller decided to go back to the woman's stand and buy Summer a Christmas present. There weren't many people around, so he sat down to visit with the woman and discovered that her name was Melissa and her husband had died three years previously in a motorcycle accident. He ended up asking for her phone number.

One thing led to another until it was two nights before their wedding. For the first time in more than two years, Ruby came to Miller in a dream. She raised her arms as if in blessing and then pointed to a journal. The next morning, Miller dug out the dream journal where he'd written about his dreams of Ruby telling him Summer needed a mother, as well as the final dream in which Ruby had passed him off to the man who showed him the table of jewelry. Miller read the entry aloud to his bride-to-be: "The man said his name was Joseph and he had short curly dark hair with a mustache. He had a bright smile with two big dimples." His bride said slowly, "That is an accurate description of my Joseph."[29] And so it was that Miller's late wife and his bride's late husband—with perhaps a smidgen of help from God—brought them together to form a new family.

This next case demonstrates that sometimes coincidence succeeds where a living matchmaker fails. In his book *Only Love Is Real*, psychiatrist and hypnotic regressionist Dr. Brian Weiss tells the story of a man and woman who were both in therapy with him and, despite being strangers to one another, both remembered scenes from the same past life in Palestine where they had apparently been father and daughter. Weiss wanted the two of them to meet in *this* life, but of course he couldn't breach client confidentiality by telling them why. Cagily, he set their appointments up back to back—twice. However, though their eyes lingered on one another, nothing came of these brief meetings. Soon afterward, the man moved away to Mexico.

Then, one day, this man and woman both happened to be waiting for airplanes in the same airport. He was waiting for a plane to Newark and she for one to Boston. When her flight was cancelled due to mechanical issues, she had to be rerouted and was given a seat on a plane to Newark—the same one on which the man was flying. He recognized her in the waiting area outside the gate and finally decided to approach. As Weiss writes, "[t]he attraction was mutual, immediate, and very strong."[30] The couple ended up marrying and living together in Mexico.[31]

---

[29] Vissell and Vissell, 176.

[30] Brian Weiss, *Only Love Is Real: A Story of Soulmates Reunited* (New York: Warner Books, 1996), 162.

[31] Weiss, *Only Love Is Real*, 176.

Now we turn to a story involving two interconnected stories of meeting and reunion. Alice Marina despaired of ever getting married and finally asked God to pick out her husband. She also finally went to a singles' group her sister had been recommending to her. As she started to leave the gathering, she met a man sitting near the exit, and they talked for three hours. When she eventually had to go, she mentioned that the next weekend she was attending a wedding in Victoria, Texas, which was a seven-hour drive away. It turned out that this man was going to the very same wedding. In fact, it was their cousins who were marrying each other, so they decided to drive to the wedding together. But that's not all. When Marina told her uncle the name of the man she'd met, his distinctive last name rang a bell. Fifty years earlier, the uncle had made a friend with that last name on the boat coming to America, but they'd lost track of each other. Marina, however, provided the link to reconnect them, and a year and a half later, they were reunited after 50 years![32]

Old Loves

Now for a special class of romantic coincidences: the stories of old loves brought back together. Not all of these reunions are entirely comfortable, as a fellow named Ian Livingstone discovered. In Cape Cod, he met an English girl with whom he spent a week but didn't exchange contact information. Not long afterward, he was in Greece, where he met an Irish girl. A month or two after that, he decided to visit the Irish girl at her home in Manchester, England. But when he arrived at her apartment, the door was opened by none other than the English girl he'd met in Cape Cod. The two ladies were roommates![33]

Another uncomfortable reunion happened to Englishman Michael Relph, who was having an affair with a married woman. When she told her husband that she was leaving him, he threatened to commit suicide, and though she seemed ready to go ahead with her plans nonetheless, Relph decided he couldn't take that kind of responsibility and sent her back to her husband. Wanting to go someplace where he wouldn't be reminded of the whole business, Relph decided to visit a relative in a small town in Sussex. Together, they headed to a pub in the deserted town square. As they were crossing the square, Relph was basking in the knowledge that there was no chance of his running into his former love in this place, or even of his seeing anything that reminded him of her. That's when a car pulled up in front of a

---

[32] SQuire Rushnell, *When God Winks: How the Power of Coincidence Guides Your Life* (New York: Atria, 2001), 13-17.

[33] Inglis, *Coincidence*, 62-63.

nearby hotel, and out stepped Relph's ex and her husband. "We were the only people in the little square and confrontation was inevitable," he says. It turned out that the couple had only ended up in that place because of a wrong turn.[34]

Though it's not clear from Relph's account what purpose, if any, was served by this unexpected reunion, we *are* told that his relationship with this woman was "briefly rekindled" some years later. Perhaps their coincidental meeting in an obscure town square was an indication that their story together was not yet at an end. What is more, there is some indication that their coincidental meeting may have hastened the demise of the woman's marriage. Perhaps this meeting in the town square was the universe's way of confirming a bond that the couple was trying to suppress.

Consider a somewhat similar case. While on vacation 150 miles from home, Dr. Eleanor Criswell saw in a store window a metal fountain that she fantasized about buying, all the while knowing that it was too expensive for her. Then, after getting a coffee next door, she ran into her ex-husband, whom she hadn't seen in several years. He and his new wife had come 400 miles from *their* home...to buy the very fountain she'd been fantasizing over.

Alan Vaughan discussed with Criswell the significance of this coincidence, and together they concluded that, while the coincidence demonstrated that she would have been able to afford the fountain had she stayed married to her ex-husband, it also confirmed for her that such outward trappings were less important to her than her own self-confidence. It showed, too, that emotional bonds between people can cause their destinies to continue to interweave long after they've stopped intentionally seeking each other out.[35]

You'll notice a similar theme of "parallel lives" in the next story. Fortunately, the reunion between former high school sweethearts Linda and Steve was decidedly less awkward than those we've already looked at.

After they made love for the first time back in high school, Steve told Linda that he needed to be on his own for a while, and they parted. Four years later, unbeknownst to each other, they both married other people in the very same month. Five years after that, they both divorced within a week of each other, and then in the same month both returned to their hometown. Linda was in financial difficulty, so she decided to pawn a dulcimer Steve had made for her in high school. Just two hours later, Steve walked into the pawn shop and saw it. He asked how long it had been there, and when he found out it had only arrived two hours ago, he purchased it and set out to find Linda. They were married within the week.[36]

---

[34] Inglis, *Coincidence*, 63.

[35] Vaughan, *Incredible Coincidence*, 136-7.

[36] Caroline Myss, *Anatomy of the Spirit: The Seven Stages of Power and Healing* (New York: Three Rivers Press, 1996), 145-8.

Sylvia and Walter were another pair of high school sweethearts, living in upstate New York. They were torn apart by Sylvia's father, a Roman Catholic who didn't want his daughter dating the son of a Jewish father and atheist mother. Walter was left in such despair that he dropped out of school and joined the Army, serving in Europe during World War II. When he returned from the war, he tried to find Sylvia, but her family had secretly moved away, due to some illegal activities in which her father was involved. For 20 years, Walter actively searched for her, spending much time and money on the effort. On his 50th birthday, he says, he finally accepted that it was useless.

When Walter was in his late 60s, he was working in a family medical practice he'd set up in the "small western town" he'd moved to. A young couple began bringing their child to see him, and he felt a strange affinity for them, almost as though they were family. When they called and said their visiting grandmother was having chest pains, he was happy to go check her over. "When I took her hand to check her pulse," he says, "a happy feeling stirred within me." He began asking her about her life, and she told him how she'd been forced to marry at a young age, to a man who turned out to be an abusive alcoholic. He had finally died five years ago when his liver gave out, and her life had since been improving. Walter went to write her a prescription for some medication and asked her name. "My name is Sylvia," she said with a smile. It wasn't long before they were hugging and crying. After 50 years apart, it took less than a month for Sylvia to move from her home in Philadelphia to be with Walter.[37]

If you had to grab a tissue at the end of that story, you might want to keep another handy. Jennifer and Bobby didn't meet in high school. They met in day care, at the age of two. From that time, they were inseparable—that is, until Jennifer was eight years old and her mother decided to leave Jennifer's abusive father. She carried Jennifer off to California and refused to let her write to Bobby, as it might allow Jennifer's father to find them. Jennifer grew up knowing very little about her past, not even the city in which she'd spent her younger years.

At age 17, Jennifer married an older man who ended up abusing her. When she finally got up the courage to leave him, she decided she would never trust men again. One day, a customer in the restaurant where she worked showed her an ad for a workshop on relationships and urged her to go. Jennifer was so scared of getting hurt again that she ripped up the ad and threw it away. And yet, something that night prompted her to pray that she would one day be able to trust someone again. When she woke up in the morning, she says she "knew with certainty" that she had to go to the

[37] Vissell and Vissell, 77-78.

relationship workshop. Fortunately, she was able to get the contact number out of the garbage and register.

When Jennifer arrived at the workshop, she found a quiet spot in a corner to wait for things to begin. Very soon, a young man approached and sat down next to her, saying he felt a little overwhelmed and needed a friend. He was part American Indian and named Sun Bear. He and Jennifer got on wonderfully and began dating. Soon, she was taking him home with her for Thanksgiving.

Her mother was happy to meet Sun Bear, but she asked him a lot of questions, which annoyed Jennifer. Then a strange look came over her mother's face. She left the room and came back with a photo album. "Did you have a different name in childhood?" she asked Sun Bear. He seemed uncomfortable but told her, "Yes, my mother and friends called me Bobby." Jennifer's mother revealed the picture she'd found: Jennifer and Bobby/Sun Bear sitting together on a swing as children.

Jennifer and her childhood friend had been apart for 17 years before meeting again at that relationship workshop. At the time that Jennifer wrote up her story for Joyce and Barry Vissell's book *Meant to Be*, she and Sun Bear had been married for 30 years.[38]

Pre-Meetings

Our next topic is a peculiar class of coincidences in which people who are significant to each other discover that, unbeknownst to them, their paths actually crossed in some way long before they "officially" met. For instance, a few weeks before marrying actress Barbra Streisand, James Brolin remembered something that had happened to him 20 years earlier when he'd been acquiring a new apartment in New York. He was told by the broker that he was really lucky to get it, because Barbra Streisand had just been in to see it and said she loved it but needed to think it over because of the lack of air conditioning.[39]

While there's no indication in that story that Brolin had any doubts about marrying Streisand, some pre-meeting coincidences seem to serve as confirmations that the parties were indeed intended to find each other. Sixteen-year-old Allison, for example, was not sure about her mother's recent remarriage. Then, while looking at an old family album with her new stepfather, she discovered that he was in the background of one of the pictures! Eleven years previously, she and her mother had been eating at a

---

[38] Vissell and Vissell, 6-11.

[39] Rushnell, 22.

restaurant in the Bahamas, and he'd been seated at a table right behind them.[40]

In another, somewhat different case, an eight-year-old girl named Nicola Lane once found eight shillings and sixpence behind a holly bush in Holland Park, London. Thirteen years later, walking through the same park with her boyfriend, she watched him point at a holly bush and say, "I stashed eight shillings and sixpence under that bush when I was a kid, but somebody came along and dug them up." They laughed and joked about the meaning of this coincidence. "It always seemed natural to me that mind and matter influence one another," says Nicola. "We touched the coins and they brought us together like a magnet."[41]

Of course, magnetic attraction doesn't guarantee a healthy relationship. A 14-year-old girl was in Brittany, France, visiting the Mont Saint-Michel with her family when she decided to explore the vast parking lot in front of the abbey and climbed into a parked car that she for some reason found attractive. The driver of the car angrily said something in a language she didn't understand and made her get out. Years later, she was married to a Scandinavian man she'd met in Munich. While looking at a photo album of his, she found a picture of the Mont Saint-Michel that included that very car and driver. The angry driver was the man who was now her husband!

A few years after the discovery of this coincidence, this woman's husband divorced her. German parapsychologist Dr. Hans Bender, who had actually accompanied her family on their long-ago trip to the Mont Saint-Michel, suggests that her future husband's throwing her out of the car when she was 14 was an omen, portending the fact that he would one day eject her from their marriage as well.[42]

Star-Crossed Lovers

Clearly, not all romances that are accompanied by coincidences end in happily ever after. Recall the case from the Introduction in which Stanislav Grof's meeting with his first wife was filled with coincidences and yet their marriage lasted only a brief time. As with other types of coincidences, we

---

[40] Rushnell, 59-61.

[41] John Stickney, "Coincidence," *New Times* (August 1975): 36. Quoted in Vaughan, *Incredible Coincidence*, 66.

[42] Hans Bender, "Meaningful Coincidences in the Light of the Jung-Pauli Theory of Synchronicity and Parapsychology," in *The Philosophy of Parapsychology: Proceedings of an International Conference Held in Copenhagen, Denmark, August 25-27, 1976*, ed. Betty Shapin and Lisette Coly (New York: Parapsychology Foundation, 1977), 66. Quoted in Vaughan, *Incredible Coincidence*, 137-8.

must keep in mind that the purpose of those that grace our romantic meetings may not always be what we think at first glance.

Let me share an example from my own life. In my mid-20s, I was single and living in Paris. One night, I had the sudden urge to go swing dancing, even though I had only ever been dancing once or twice in my entire life. I tried to convince some friends to come along with me, but without any luck. So I headed to the Caveau de la Huchette on my own. It was the *only time* in my life that I have ever gone to a dance club or bar by myself.

I had been at this club for maybe half an hour when I saw a couple of young men walk through the door. I don't know what it was, but something about one of them made me immediately think to myself, "I would love to dance with *him*." But I didn't make eye contact. I just turned back to the band and continued listening, until a few moments later when I heard someone approach me and ask, "Would you like to dance?" It was him.

He and I ended up dancing together the entire night, and then, when the swing club closed around 3am, we stayed together until dawn. I had never in my life felt so immediately smitten by anyone, never so quickly swept up by passion. But he was Canadian and only visiting Paris for a week, and somehow I knew, in my heart of hearts, that our encounter would be brief. When we parted at morning light, I didn't ask for his email address or even his last name. I just had the feeling that this was the way it was meant to be.

Nevertheless, a few nights later, I got to missing him and regretted not having any way to get in contact. I was returning to my room at the Ecole Normale Supérieure, where he knew I lived, and I found myself wishing that I'd arrive at my room and discover he'd left me a note under my door. I specifically remember asking the universe, "Couldn't I have what I want—*just this once*?"

Lo and behold, when I opened the door to my room, I heard the scratchy sound of a piece of paper being pushed over the floor. It was indeed a note, from him, asking me to meet him again that night at the Caveau de la Huchette. Of course, I went, and we proceeded to spend another passionate night together. It was quite enough to make me forget my initial conviction that this was supposed to be a brief romance. When we parted that second time, I asked him for his email address, which he spelled out for me and I hastily wrote down as soon as he was gone. A few days later, after I knew his plane had landed back in Canada, I sent him an email thanking him for the amazing two nights we had spent together.

The email came back to me undeliverable. I tried every variation of the address I could think of, but nothing worked. I agonized, desperate that this man not think that I hadn't written to him because I didn't *want* to write. At that point, I was so head over heels for him, I would have seriously considered flying to Canada if I could just figure out a way to contact him. But I had nothing else to go on but his first name and a vague idea of his profession, so my internet searches, too, were all in vain.

At one point, I thought I had a breakthrough. I remembered he'd given his business card to the singer at the Caveau on our first night there. I found her on the web and wrote asking if she could pass along his email address. She kindly replied that she had indeed gotten a card from him but that she seemed to have lost it. Nevertheless, she was expecting him to get in touch with her, and she would let me know when he did. I never heard another word.

The whole affair struck me as incredibly bizarre. Everything had seemed so perfectly orchestrated for us to meet—not just once but twice—and to share two of the most romantic nights of my life. And then, just as perfectly, everything seemed to be arranged to prevent us from being able to contact one another ever again. I was an atheist at the time, but I remember telling a friend, "It's so absurd that it almost makes me believe in God!" In fact, I realized some years later that, just a few doors down from the Caveau de la Huchette stood the Théatre de la Huchette, a theater that had continuously produced the same two plays for decades: Eugène Ionesco's *La cantatrice chauve* and *La Leçon*—the most famous absurdist plays by France's most famous absurdist playwright. Quite the setting for the gods to stage their own absurdist drama.

But, by the time I realized that coincidence, I no longer saw my story with the Canadian swing dancer as quite so absurd. As it happened, just two months after that affair, I fell in love with another man, someone who would change the entire course of my life and open me up to some crucial lessons in love and spirituality. If I had been able to contact the swing dancer again, I might have missed out on these vital experiences. And I believe that's at least part of the reason that "fate" worked so hard to keep us from seeing each other again.

At the same time, I do believe that it was destiny that brought us together for those two nights in Paris. Those two nights were *also* vital to my development as a person. And I'm not sure that, if I hadn't experienced that brief, passionate romance, I would have had the same confidence to start a relationship with the man I loved after him.

It is tempting, especially when we are hungry for love, to assume that, if our meeting with a lover is blessed by a touch of heavenly magic, then it must mean everything in the relationship will work out flawlessly. This is far from the truth, and such an assumption belies a lack of understanding of the deeper forces at work in our lives. If coincidences make it possible for us to meet certain people, it is not necessarily in order to make the rest of our lives happy and carefree. I would say that it is in fact much more likely that the people brought to us by coincidence are in our lives for a deeper purpose. In the next two chapters, we are going to explore these deeper purposes, first by looking at the concept of destiny and life plan, and then by looking at the purpose that underlies so much of our life plan: the goal of spiritual growth.

For now, I want to leave you with a couple more of Dr. Andrew Paquette's psychic dreams. In the first of these, he relived two weeks' worth of what appeared to him to be memories of a past life as the son of a wealthy department store owner and the brother of a boy named James. As coincidence would have it, about a month after having this dream, Paquette discovered that his father in his present life (with whom he had never discussed the topic of reincarnation) had memories of having lived before as someone else, and these memories matched the circumstances of Paquette's dream. Paquette's father even remembered that, in his former life, his name had been James, the name of Paquette's younger brother in the dream.[43]

I provide this first dream and its corroborating details to help you understand why I take seriously the content of this next one. Paquette had another dream in which he and his wife were back in the year 1941, in the hospital where his father was born. For some reason, they were shown several possible scenarios for his father's future life, and in particular for his marriage to Paquette's mother. In actuality, Paquette's parents did not get along with each other, and Paquette didn't meet his father until the age of 16.[44] In this dream, he saw that there was one scenario that would have allowed his parents to be happy together, but in that scenario, they didn't have any children. Paquette says, "The funny thing is, it seems someone wants me to be born when I am and through these parents, so it is considered the best of all possible alternatives for them, despite making impossible the one variation where they remain happy together."[45]

We began this section on romantic meetings with Betty J. Eadie's account of seeing a spirit trying to get his parents together. It was a sweet, romantic image, but Paquette's dream reminds us that the interests of our children (present or future) may not always match up with our own. Our destinies are likely controlled by a vast number of interlocking interests, each of which can influence the events of our lives in both pleasant and not-so-pleasant ways.

---

[43] Andrew Paquette, *Dreamer: 20 Years of Psychic Dreams and How They Changed My Life* (Winchester, UK: O Books, 2011), 118-9.
[44] Paquette, *Dreamer*, 56.
[45] Paquette, *Dreamer*, 121.

Chapter 17
Destiny

French novelist André Malraux once said, "Coincidence is the language of destiny."[1] Many of us have had moments in our lives when things slipped so perfectly and unexpectedly into place that we couldn't escape the conclusion that they were destined to be. Or we've had moments when things were aligning so repeatedly *against* our efforts that we couldn't escape the feeling that we were destined to fail at that particular endeavor.

The idea of destiny has a long history, in the Western world as elsewhere. Thousands of years ago in ancient Israel, David wrote his psalm proclaiming to God, "All the days ordained for me were written in your book before one of them came to be."[2] In ancient Greece, Plato's *Republic* recounted the near-death experience of a man named Er, in which he observed souls choosing the lives they would live, complete with information about the level of wealth they would achieve and the amount of disease they would suffer.[3] A millennium or so later, Muhammad said that, just before an angel breathes a soul into a fetus, the angel writes God's decree about the baby's future life on a scroll, including their future profession and date of death.[4] And, to take just one example from another part of the globe, the

---

[1] In private conversation with Arthur Koestler, as quoted in Alister Hardy, Robert Harvie, and Arthur Koestler, *The Challenge of Chance: A Mass Experiment in Telepathy and Its Unexpected Outcome* (New York: Random House, 1973), 211.

[2] Psalm 139:16.

[3] Plato, *The Republic*, 617d-618b.

[4] Sahih al-Bukhari, 3036.

Indonesian Batak believe that, before a soul enters a fetus, it is informed of the experiences it will undergo in that body.[5]

Destiny is also alive and well in the present-day Western imagination. One excellent and entertaining example is the 2010 film *The Adjustment Bureau*, starring Matt Damon and Emily Blunt. Based on a short story by Philip K. Dick, the film portrays a world in which every person's life is carefully scripted and a team of "adjustment" agents works to make sure that no one deviates from their assigned plan. Of course, even in a movie about things going according to plan, things don't go according to plan. The movie explores the nature of love, will, and sacrifice and culminates in an ending that on its face seems like a victory for free will but still gives a subtle nod to the power of fate.

One might think that, in this day and age, talk of destiny would be limited to literature and cinema, with our scientific culture having "outgrown" the idea of a divine plan. But, in fact, the idea of destiny still survives beyond the realm of fiction, as this chapter will make abundantly clear. To take just one prominent example, the British statesman Winston Churchill, who on multiple occasions appeared to have been supernaturally protected from death, told an audience in 1943, "I sometimes have a feeling—in fact I have it very strongly—a feeling of interference. … I want to stress it. I have a feeling that some guiding hand has interfered."[6]

Others offer us even more explicit information on the nature of this guiding hand. Recall from Chapter 3, "Angels & Guides," some information that Dr. Mary C. Neal was given during her near-death experience:

> In preparation for our journey to earth, we are able to make a basic outline for our life. This is not to imply that we, the humans, are entirely in charge of our life's design. It is more like God creates it, then we review it and discuss it with our "personal planning" angel. Within the algorithm are written branch points in our lives at which times we may exit, returning to God, or we may be redirected to a different task and goal.
>
> We may be directed to these branch points by our own conscious choice and by our circumstances, or we may be pushed along by angelic intervention.[7]

---

[5] Holger Kalweit, *Dreamtime & Inner Space: The World of the Shaman*, trans. Werner Wünsche (Boston: Shambhala, 1984, 1988), 23. Kalweit cites Johannes Gustav Warneck, *Die Religion der Batak* (Göttingen, 1909).

[6] Brian Inglis, *Coincidence: A Matter of Chance – or Synchronicity?* (London: Hutchinson, 1990), 140.

[7] Mary C. Neal, *To Heaven and Back: A Doctor's Extraordinary Account of Her Death, Heaven, Angels, and Life Again* (Colorado Springs, CO: WaterBrook Press, 2011, 2012), 98.

Neal then specifically states that angels "are the ones orchestrating the 'coincidences' that occur so commonly in our lives."[8]

This brief description of Neal's is an excellent summary of my own conclusions after years of research into the reality of destiny, a term which I will here use as synonymous with 'life plan'. Evidence gleaned from many different quarters corroborates what Neal was told in her NDE about our lives' being planned, and I'm going to lay out much of that evidence for you in this chapter. As you will see, the sources of this evidence include:

- dreams, waking visions, and spontaneous premonitions of future events,
- voices informing people of future events or giving them instructions about such events,
- spontaneous memories had by both children and adults of a plan for their lives established before they were born, particularly with regard to the choice of parents,
- deathbed visions,
- near-death experiences,
- messages and impressions gained through mediumship, and
- spontaneous spiritual experiences.

I have been reading material from all of these sources for several years now, and it is amazing what a coherent picture emerges from them: a picture of a realm in which, before one's birth, one cooperates with spiritual advisors to lay out a plan for one's earthly life. The degree to which one participates in the creation of this plan apparently varies from person to person, with some people very involved in choosing the future course of their life and other people content to let those more spiritually "advanced" make most of the decisions. *Some* form of planning, however, seems the rule.

I should also briefly mention an additional source that accords with those listed above: pre-birth memories elicited by hypnotic regression, such as those reported by hypnotists Dr. Helen Wambach,[9] Dr. Joel Whitton,[10] and Dr. Michael Newton.[11] I haven't included in this chapter any specific

---

[8] Neal, 99.

[9] Helen Wambach, *Life Before Life* (New York: Bantam, 1979).

[10] Joel L. Whitton and Joe Fisher, *Life Between Life: Scientific Explorations into the Void Separating One Incarnation from the Next* (New York: Warner Books, 1986).

[11] Michael Newton, *Journey of Souls: Case Studies of Life Between Lives* (Woodbury, MN: Llewellyn, 1994); Michael Newton, *Destiny of Souls: New Case Studies of Life Between Lives* (Woodbury, MN: Llewellyn, 2000); Michael Newton, *Life Between Lives: Hypnotherapy for Spiritual Regression* (St. Paul, MN: Llewellyn, 2004); and Michael

examples drawn from hypnotic regression for two reasons: (1) the reliability of hypnotically retrieved memories is disputed by parapsychologists, and (2) there's quite enough non-hypnotic material on the subject to make a strong case for the existence of life planning. Nevertheless, I do want to mention that the material drawn from hypnotic regression by the three researchers listed above does line up with the various sources I'll cite here, and those who are particularly interested in the topic of life plans will likely want to investigate the detailed accounts of the planning process given by the hypnotic subjects of these three authors. They are definitely thought provoking, and I recommend Newton's books in particular.

Let's turn now to examining the non-hypnotically derived evidence for the existence of destiny, beginning in the area of parent-child relationships.

Parent-Child Relationships

Our first evidence is the testimony of a 73-year-old woman who still remembers a time before her birth when she was looking down at various couples and asked to choose one of them for her parents. "I was told that whichever couple I chose would teach me what I needed to learn in this lifetime," she says. "I pointed to my parents and replied, 'I'll take them.'" She remembers telling her parents about this memory as a three-year-old, but they didn't take her seriously.[12]

Fortunately, these days many parents are paying attention when their children report these kinds of memories and take care to record them for the benefit of others. For example, one parent recounts the following.

> We are not a religious family, but since the age of two, Jessa would tell us stories about God. She said that before she was born, she was God's daughter and she sat by God. She said before she was born, she picked us as parents because we needed someone like her in our lives![13]

Robin Lisa Haywood tells how her eight-year-old son Sean talked about missing his "mother in heaven." She gently urged him to elaborate, and he explained how his mother in heaven had given him "pure love" and how,

---

Newton, ed., *Memories of the Afterlife: Life Between Lives: Stories of Personal Transformation* (Woodbury, MN: Llewellyn, 2009).

[12] Wayne W. Dyer and Dee Garnes, *Memories of Heaven: Children's Astounding Recollections of the Time Before They Came to Earth* (Carlsbad, CA: Hay House, 2015), 69.

[13] Carol Bowman, *Return from Heaven: Beloved Relatives Reincarnated within Your Family* (New York: HarperCollins, 2001), 142.

along with God, she had told him to pick Robin to be his mother on earth.[14] A woman named Stacy reports that, when her son Catcher was almost four, he told her that he was not in her belly when she was pregnant, that he was in heaven waiting for his parents to be ready for him. He explained, "That is what we do. I chose you. And Michael chose his parents and Mitchell chose his parents. We wait for you to be ready, but we have already chosen you. That is what you guys did, whether you remember it or not."[15]

Researcher Carol Bowman alone has collected dozens of cases of children who've mentioned choosing their parents.[16] Some of them go into quite a bit of detail about the process. For instance, four-year-old Courtney says,

> When you go to heaven, you have a little time to rest, kind of like a vacation, but then you have to get to work. You have to start thinking about what you have to learn in your next life. You have to start *picking out your next family*, one that will help you learn whatever it is you need to learn next.[17]

Some children remember some of the reasons that they chose their parents, though they're not all as surprising as the following explanation given by a three-year-old girl named Amanda. She approached her mother one day and asked, "Mommy, remember a long, long time ago—before you were born?" When her mother said no, her daughter gravely informed her, "I killed you!" Here's the mother's account of what happened next.

> Without expressing surprise or disbelief, I asked, "You did? Why?"
>
> She said, "I was so mad at you." She got a really sad look on her face and moved onto the couch and cuddled up.
>
> I asked, "How did you kill me?"
>
> "With a shotgun."
>
> I wasn't expecting that! I was curious how she felt about all of this and asked, "Well, if that's what happened, what are we doing now?"
>
> Her response chilled me. "Mama, I was so sad for you. I wanted to be your friend again. I'll never do that again. I just want to be in your family now."[18]

Thinking of our children having murdered us in a past life is probably not very comforting, but in moments when we feel like we're inadequate

---

[14] Dyer and Garnes, 4-5.

[15] Elizabeth M. Carman and Neil J. Carman, *Cosmic Cradle: Spiritual Dimensions of Life Before Birth*, rev. ed. (Berkeley, CA: North Atlantic Books, 2013), 7.

[16] Bowman, *Return from Heaven*, 130.

[17] Bowman, *Return from Heaven*, 136; and Carol Bowman, *Children's Past Lives: How Past Life Memories Affect Your Child* (New York: Bantam, 1997, 1998), 341.

[18] Bowman, *Return from Heaven*, 143.

parents, the knowledge that our children most likely chose us *can* be a source of consolation. Celestia Jasper recounts in Elisabeth Hallett's book *Soul Trek* that, when one of her sons was an infant, she had trouble feeding him and keeping him happy. "I don't think I'm the right mother for Ivan," she said out loud, within hearing of the baby's four-year-old brother. "I can't do anything right for him," she continued. Her four-year-old son then piped up and said, "But Mom, you are. Ivan looked down and picked you out to be his mom."[19]

Another reassuring story comes from Wayne Dyer and Dee Garnes's book *Memories of Heaven*. Elsie Farfan had divorced from her husband when her daughter was still a baby, and when the girl was three, she told her mother that she wished her father was at home with her. At first, this made Farfan sad. Then her daughter added, "But that's okay, because I knew it would be like this." Her mom asked her to explain, and she said, "Mommy, when I was in heaven, I picked you. And I knew we were going to be alone, so that's okay. Don't worry, Mommy, I love you so much."[20]

Elisabeth Hallett does say, however, that the evidence is not univocal that children always choose their parents, or at least it is not univocal that their voice is the only one that matters. She presents from her pre-birth research at least one case in which a mother, Isadora Paymer, apparently chose for her child to be the reincarnation of her beloved grandmother.[21] Hallett also notes that,

> [a]longside memories of choosing and memories of being guided by a wise counselor, there are accounts in which the pairing seems unconscious or even random. … That said, there remains plenty of evidence that choosing, accommodating, and negotiating do go on between potential parents and unborn souls as they prepare to become a family.[22]

It may be that it seems to us as though children are the ones who choose their parents rather than the other way around because it is the children who tend to remember the event, while adults have long forgotten any pre-birth negotiations. Hallett does present the case of one woman who, as a young girl, remembered plans that had been made regarding her future children. Her memory was jogged when she was about three years old and she saw a pair of twins for the first time. There was something familiar about it that she couldn't quite put her finger on. Then it came to her. She yelled to her

[19] Elisabeth Hallett, *Soul Trek: Meeting Our Children on the Way to Birth* (Hamilton, MT: Light Hearts Publishing, 1995), 158.
[20] Dyer and Garnes, 66.
[21] Hallett, *Soul Trek*, 158.
[22] Elisabeth Hallett, *Stories of the Unborn Soul: The Mystery and Delight of Pre-Birth Communication* (San Jose: Writers Club Press, 2002), 69.

dad and grandfather, "I'm going to have twins! Me too! I'm supposed to have twins!" And indeed, many years later, she did have identical twin girls.[23]

Other children who possess knowledge of their own future children include Debbie, whose near-death experience was recounted in Chapter 5. Recall that five-year-old Debbie was told she had to return to her earthly life because she needed to raise her future children, who were shown to her during her NDE. "Messiah" brought in four beings, and she knew they were her four children. The oldest two were boys and the youngest two girls, and each had a distinctive look. They insisted they wanted her to be their mother, otherwise their plans would be frustrated. Debbie asked Messiah, "Is there no other way?" and he replied, "Not if you want to fulfill the commitments you made with your children and with others before you were born." Debbie returned to her earthly life, and many years later, she indeed had four children, about whom she says, "These children are the spirits that I met when I was five years old."[24]

Let's look at one more case regarding parent-child relationships, this one involving an adult's NDE. In this case, a soldier in Vietnam was injured during combat and found himself in an NDE in which he was given a choice about whether to return to life and raise his children. Besides this choice itself, another intriguing aspect of the case is that he was informed of some unexpected circumstances under which he would have to raise them. According to the report of Dr. John B. Alexander,

> [this soldier] had been given an option to stay on the other side, or to return to his badly injured body and continue his life. There was, however, more to the offer. He was informed that should he return to the living, he would become a single parent and would be needed to raise his boys as they reached adolescence. At the time, this information made no sense. At the time, he had been happily married for a few years, so obviously he chose to return. But three years later, without warning, his wife filed for divorce and left him to raise the children on his own.[25]

One wonders which aspects of the resulting situation had been agreed upon before the children were born. Did these children, when choosing their life, know which of their parents would be raising them to adulthood?

---

[23] Hallett, *Stories of the Unborn Soul*, 210.
[24] Sarah and Brent Hinze, "Visions of Future Children in Near-Death Experience," presentation at IANDS 2012 Conference in Scottsdale, AZ, available at https://www.youtube.com/watch?v=kdSL-HCxl4o, 29:13-33:27.
[25] John B. Alexander, *Reality Denied: Firsthand Experiences with Things that Can't Happen—But Did* (San Antonio, TX: Anomalist Books, 2017), 154.

Siblings

Though it's less common than the memory of choosing parents, some children remember also choosing their siblings. Maureen Suhadolnik reports that her daughter Caroline, who was not yet two, told one of her sisters, "I 'member picking Mommy, Daddy, Liana, and you! I could see you from up there!"[26] Trish Sullivan says her nine-year-old son Michael talked about helping God choose his sisters.[27]

Friends

Destiny apparently extends to non-biological relationships as well. Four-year-old Daniel Jones told his mother many details about the place where he lived before he was born. One thing he remembered was that he'd been good friends with lots of other children there. Authors Mary and Peter Harrison report,

> A strange thing that Daniel said was that he knows some of his friends were going to be born at the same time as he was and they all knew that they would meet up with each other while they lived on earth. When his mother asked him if he knew any of these friends Daniel told her that he hadn't met them yet, but he was sure that as soon as he did meet one of them they would know each other straightaway.[28]

Romantic Relationships

Now we turn to some cases providing evidence that romantic relationships are at least sometimes prearranged. Interestingly, none of this evidence comes from memories of the pre-birth planning process. Instead, it seems that certain people are sometimes purposely given hints later in life of the relationships that are soon to come their way.

Joel Gilbert was on his way to live for a year in Israel, but first he decided to spend a week in the Findhorn Community in Scotland and then do a little traveling around Europe. Due to his Jewish roots, he was adamant that the one place he was *not* interested in visiting was Germany. However, at Findhorn, his first two roommates were both German, and he met many

---

[26] Dyer and Garnes, 7.
[27] Dyer and Garnes, 11.
[28] Mary Harrison and Peter Harrison, *The Children That Time Forgot* (1983, 1989, 2014), 96.

other Germans who became close friends as he extended his stay long beyond the original week he'd had planned. Then, while cleaning up after a community meal one Sunday, he saw a German woman he'd never met before. "Inside," he says, "I simply heard the words, '*You will be with this woman.*'" Nevertheless, his idea of the inner spiritual path he was engaged on did not allow for romantic involvement, so he purposely avoided this woman, over and over. But when they were eventually thrust together, the power and energy that emerged between them was enough to make him change his plans entirely. He ended up following this woman to Germany and marrying her.[29]

As a teenager, Carolina Williamson dreamt about "a tall, handsome man with green eyes and dark hair." At 19, she married a man whom she says "fit the physical description but didn't have the right character." After divorcing him, she spent 14 years as a single mother of two. Then, one day, she had a dream that, "when a man on the Internet said he was from California, I should say 'hello.'" Since she sometimes visited single-parent chat rooms, this made some sense to her. She was online one night when someone asked one of the guys in the chatroom where he was from. Thinking he was from somewhere else, she was surprised to see him reply, "California." But she obeyed her dream instructions and said hello. They immediately clicked, and when she eventually met him, she discovered that he was "a tall, handsome man with green eyes and dark hair." She discovered some other interesting things about him as well, including the fact that they had lived in the same town as kids. Even more intriguingly, a few years before they met, Williamson had been planning to marry another man, and it turned out that, during this same period of time, the fellow from California used to have nightmares "that his future partner was committing to another man." When Williamson wrote her account of these events, she and this man were about to be married.[30]

Here's another story of a girl who was informed at a relatively young age about the man she was meant to be with. In fact, this is the personal experience of Joyce Vissell, one of the co-editors of the book from which the other two accounts in this section are drawn. As a child, Joyce felt incredibly lonely and sad. Her body, she says, felt like a prison, and she just wanted to find a way out of it. When she was nine years old, however, something changed. She writes,

> As usual I went to my bed and cried as a growing despair grew within me. Suddenly I felt myself enfolded by loving arms. No one was with me, yet I felt a strong loving presence speak to me in my heart, "*Someone is now*

---

[29] Joyce Vissell and Barry Vissell, eds., *Meant to Be: Miraculous True Stories to Inspire a Lifetime of Love* (Berkeley, CA: Conari Press, 2000), 64-67.
[30] Vissell and Vissell, 68-71.

> *growing up who you are meant to be with. This person will understand your feelings, will love your sensitivity, and will hold you when you cry. You will recognize him as a tall, dark-haired young man who will become a doctor.*"[31]

Instantly, Joyce's life transformed. She was no longer sad and no longer felt entirely alone. She easily weathered the sudden end of her relationship with her first boyfriend, knowing that he was "not the one." When it was time to go to college, she could have gotten into much more prestigious institutions but decided to apply to only one school: Hartwick College. "Something clicked inside me," she says, "and it was the only school I applied to."[32]

Joyce proceeded to spend her first three months on campus deliriously happy for no particular reason. And then things suddenly fell into place, when she discovered that the boy she was partnered with as a server at the college cafeteria was studying to become a doctor. At the moment she discovered this, "a shiver ran through [her] body," she says. Soon after, they went on a date, and at the time of their collaboration on the book *Meant to Be*, they had been a couple for 36 years.

But their story wouldn't be complete without the mention of an important coincidence that happened to Joyce's husband, Barry, before they met. Unlike his future wife, Barry applied to several colleges, and he was rejected by all of them, even his safety school. One day, while finishing out his last year of high school, he was "trudging in a fog of self-pity from one class to another" when he suddenly heard a voice over the school loudspeaker ask him to come to the principal's office. He was worried he'd gotten in trouble for a prank, but when he got to the office, the secretary was smiling at him. She showed him into an office where a man was waiting for him. Barry recounts,

> He shook my hand and said he was from Hartwick College in Oneonta, New York. He took probably one minute to tell me about the school, and then pointed to some papers on the table next to him.
>
> "This is an application for admission to Hartwick College. With the help of your school officials, we've filled it out with information from your school records."[33]

Barry hadn't even heard of Hartwick College, and the situation seemed very strange. He hardly had time to think before the fellow was handing him a pen and telling him, "If you'd like to join us next fall at Hartwick, sign here." Though Barry was a little nervous, he did sign the paper. Going home after school that day, he felt joyful and light. "It's funny about youth," he says. "I gave no real thought to who that man was, or how he found out about me. I

---

[31] Vissell and Vissell, 20.
[32] Vissell and Vissell, 22.
[33] Vissell and Vissell, 14.

just accepted it as a matter of course and showed up that next fall at Hartwick College in the rolling Catskill Mountains of upstate New York."[34]

When Barry arrived on campus, he noticed Joyce before she noticed him. He saw her at a soccer game and for several weeks couldn't get her out of his head. Then he applied to work at the college cafeteria and ended up being partnered with her. But you already know how this story ends.

Professional Life

In his book *Into the Light*, hospice physician Dr. John Lerma says that he dreamt at age four that a nice lady told him he was going to be a doctor when he grew up. It affected him so much he told his mother about it, and she bought him a stethoscope. Many years later, once he was a doctor, a patient's three-year-old son told him, "I'm going to be a doctor like you. The angels said that, when you were little, they told you to be a doctor, too. They told me to tell you that." The boy then added, "They told me that thing around your neck is a stet-ta-cope and that I should have one to remind me that I'm going to be a doctor someday."[35]

Our profession is arguably as influential in our life as the people who raise us and the people we marry. This area of our life is also strongly characterized by coincidences. Psychologists Dr. Deborah G. Betsworth and Dr. Jo-Ida C. Hansen conducted a survey of older adults, including many retirees, and found that nearly two-thirds of them viewed their careers as having been influenced by "serendipitous events."[36] Author Robert Moss echoes the experience of many when he writes, "When I followed my calling, doors opened in astonishing ways. When I slipped back and away from my path, doors stayed resolutely closed."[37]

In fact, "negative" coincidences can be particularly common in this area of life. When people aren't doing what they are meant to do, not only are they unhappy and continually plagued by things that won't seem to fall into place, but some people actually become physically ill. Life coach Martha Beck provides several examples. For instance, one woman who now runs a dog rescue told Beck,

---

[34] Vissell and Vissell, 15-16.

[35] John Lerma, *Into the Light: Real Life Stories about Angelic Visits, Visions of the Afterlife, and Other Pre-Death Experiences* (Pompton Plains, NJ: New Page Books, 2007), 150.

[36] Deborah G. Betsworth and Jo-Ida C. Hansen, "The Categorization of Serendipitous Career Development Events," *Journal of Career Assessment* 4, no. 1 (Winter 1996): 91-98.

[37] Robert Moss, *The Boy Who Died and Came Back: Adventures of a Dream Archaeologist in the Multiverse* (Novato, CA: New World Library, 2014), 11.

> I was almost leveled by cluster headaches and fatigue. There were some miserable years in there, while I tried to live a "normal" life. Then I realized that, for me, "normal" means being around a lot of animals, outside, almost all the time. When I started living by my passion for helping people and animals find each other, the symptoms went away.[38]

Another woman had to quit her job as a management consultant when she developed chronic fatigue syndrome. It wasn't until she began learning and practicing Reiki, a type of energy healing, that her symptoms started to go away. She has returned to doing consulting work, but she says, "If I stop doing Reiki, I get sick again."[39]

Some of Beck's clients, however, have experienced more positive coincidences. For instance, her client Kim was a nurse, but one day she told Beck that, when she was little, she'd wanted to be a marine biologist. She said it with some embarrassment in her voice, as if this were a very strange, unrealistic sort of goal. *The very next day*, Kim had a patient come into her medical clinic with a sea urchin spine stuck in his thumb—a rather unusual injury, given their location in Arizona. The patient explained that he was a marine biologist, and he was able to give Kim help in finding out about the profession.[40]

A similar coincidence helped Dr. Mary Helen Hensley take the leap into becoming a chiropractor. She already had some exposure to the profession, as she had been seeing a chiropractor to help her recover from a car accident. She had also received a visit from her deceased grandfather telling her that she would become a chiropractor. But she was still undecided as to whether she had the commitment that educating herself for this profession would require. One day, she was eating lunch in an almost empty restaurant while trying to make up her mind about the matter when she saw someone at one of the few other occupied tables playing with some sort of weird device that had an outline of a human body on it. Intrigued, she went over to ask him about it and discovered that he was a chiropractor and that his device was an educational tool he'd built for his patients. Her decision was made.[41]

But that wasn't Hensley's only occupational coincidence. Some years later, she desperately wanted to move to Ireland. While on a visit to the Emerald Isle, she had seen a chiropractic office in the little town of Athlone and daydreamed about working there. She later made another several-month

---

[38] Martha Beck, *Finding Your Way in a Wild New World: Reclaim Your True Nature to Create the Life You Want* (New York: Atria, 2012), 79.
[39] Beck, *Finding Your Way in a Wild New World*, 78-79.
[40] Martha Beck, *Finding Your Own North Star: Claiming the Life You Were Meant to Live* (New York: Three Rivers Press, 2001), 235.
[41] Mary Helen Hensley, *Promised by Heaven: A Doctor's Return from the Afterlife to a Destiny of Love and Healing* (New York: Atria, 2015), 66-67.

trip to Ireland, with hopes of finding a way to stay in the country for good. Unfortunately, months passed with nothing materializing. Then, when she was about to return to the States, she got a call from an Irish chiropractor she knew, asking if she'd cover an office where a doctor had left. It turned out to be the very practice she'd daydreamed about joining in Athlone. And she's been living in Ireland ever since.[42]

In Po Bronson's book *What Should I Do with My Life?*, we find the story of Kat James, who wanted to leave her career in public relations and become a landscape gardener but wasn't sure if she was crazy. After all, she didn't even have a garden as a hobby. But she subsequently got a tarot card reading in which she was told, "You would be really good at tending people's gardens," and it got her thinking. She talked to a neighbor about the idea, and the neighbor gave her a course catalog she happened to have for Brighton City College. Looking at it, James discovered that their two-year horticulture program started the following week, and enrollment was *that afternoon.* When Bronson talked to her a year and a half later, she was about to earn her "advanced level" in garden design and was working on her first independent garden design contract. She was sure that she had chosen the right path.[43]

Experiences like these are common when people make professional decisions based on heartfelt intuition. Could this be because, when we follow our hearts, we come into alignment with our destiny? If we are doing what we are intended to do—what our souls agreed to do before birth—then we are likely not only to feel a sense of profound rightness about our lives but also to have significant material aid from those on the other side whose job it is to make our destiny a reality.

That is not to say that we will not encounter difficulties. Challenges, too, are frequently part of the path we set ourselves. But this is only because confronting challenges is how we grow into our best, most splendid selves. And, whatever the challenges, if we are following our destiny, we can be sure that we are not walking the road alone. As Robert Moss says, speaking from his own extensive experience of this phenomenon, "When we are passionately engaged in a creative venture—love, art, or something else that is really worthwhile—we draw support from other minds and other beings, seen and unseen. The greater the challenges involved in our venture, the greater the support we draw. Great spirits love great challenges."[44]

---

[42] Hensley, 153-5.

[43] Po Bronson, *What Should I Do with My Life? The True Story of People Who Answered the Ultimate Question* (New York: Random House, 2002, 2003), 20-23.

[44] Moss, *The Boy Who*, 220.

Death, Illness, and Injury

In near-death experiences, people are frequently told to return to their life on earth because it's "not their time." This explanation implies that there *is* a time at which the people in question are intended to die, and the experiences recounted in this section confirm and elaborate on this idea. At the end of this section, we'll also encounter a few cases that imply that illness and injury, too, can serve a purpose in our life plan.

Sometimes the simplest of phrases can convey a wealth of meaning. A Congregationalist minister reports being at the deathbed of a 22-year-old man who said, just before slipping into unconsciousness, "We agreed on twenty-two years this time."[45] This man's deathbed utterance not only lends support to the idea of a pre-arranged life plan but also implies that he's been through the process of incarnation more than once.

In 1993, a man named Tony had a near-death experience in which he saw things happening at remote locations on earth (for instance, his house-sitter having sex with a girlfriend in Tony's house) and was also told the date of his eventual death—a date which he refused to share with his wife, for understandable reasons. However, over a year after he eventually died, his wife discovered a piece of paper in his desk on which were written the words, "Return date: August 29." It was in fact the date on which he had died.[46]

Shelley E. Parker had a dream of her fiancé's death the night before it happened. In the dream, God told her the death would occur the next day or the following, depending on other events. Parker told God that, because she had cancer, *she* ought to be the one to go, but God firmly told her that she had "more to do here."[47]

Many children who die young indicate prior to their deaths that they know something of what is coming. Betty Jean Gushanas' five-year-old son stated that he couldn't be ringbearer at his uncle's wedding because he wouldn't be there. Months later, he died from an introventricular hemorrhage in his brain. His mother also remembers that, when she was buying him clothes for kindergarten, he had said he would never go to school, nor would he live anywhere but their current home.[48]

Dr. Mary C. Neal reports that, when her son Willie was four or five years old, she said something to him about, "When you are eighteen…," and

---

[45] Lisa Smartt, *Words at the Threshold: What We Say as We're Nearing Death* (Novato, CA: New World Library, 2017), 170.
[46] Barbara R. Rommer, *Blessing in Disguise: Another Side of the Near-Death Experience* (St. Paul, MN: Llewellyn, 2000), 5-7.
[47] Penny Sartori, *The Wisdom of Near-Death Experiences: How Brushes with Death Teach Us to Live* (London: Watkins, 2014), 91-93.
[48] Dyer and Garnes, 143.

he responded with a startled look and said, "But I'm not going to be eighteen." When she asked him to repeat himself, he said, "You know. I'm never going to be eighteen. That's the plan. You know that."[49]

In fact, Willie did eventually turn 18, and while he was that age, Neal had a dream in which a boy she didn't know said that he had "traded places with Willie." She discovered the next day that a young man in their community had died in an accident.[50] Her son Willie went on to live past his 19th birthday. But he was then killed when he was struck by a car while roller skiing.

Interestingly, Willie had still seemed vaguely aware that his death was approaching. The day before he left home on the trip that would lead to his death, Willie asked his mother about writing a will and getting a life insurance policy.[51] On the day he died while roller skiing with a friend, he talked to this friend about death and specifically about his desire to be cremated. After they looked out over a particularly beautiful view, he said, "If we died, wouldn't this be an incredible last vision?" Less than three minutes later, he was gone.[52]

Willie's story suggests that the plans that have been made for our death may be somewhat flexible. In fact, I've encountered more than one source suggesting that some people build multiple "exit points" into their life plans. That idea seems to be borne out in this next story. Bella was somewhere between the ages of six and eight when a dream informed her that she would "have an opportunity to live or die before [she] was twenty-four years old." In fact, she was involved in a serious water-skiing accident just three months and 12 days before her 24th birthday. She had an NDE in which she was asked whether she was ready to die and was shown her grave with her two children crying next to it. Sensing she couldn't leave her children behind, she returned to life.[53]

Now, here are the stories I promised about the role of illness in life plans. The first is about a nine-year-old boy who was dying of a retinoblastoma that had caused him to have his eyes removed. Dr. John Lerma asked him how he had managed to live so long with everything he'd been through. After hesitating a moment, the boy replied that it was "a gift from God's angels." He went on to explain that he had asked his angels for "extra time to allow my mother and sisters to accept my illness and death and especially to accept God."[54] He said that he had wanted to be healed in the

---

[49] Neal, 149-150.
[50] Neal, 151.
[51] Neal, 167.
[52] Neal, 174.
[53] Jeffrey Long with Paul Perry, *God and the Afterlife: The Ground-Breaking New Evidence for God and Near-Death Experience* (New York: HarperCollins, 2016), 88.
[54] Lerma, *Into the Light*, 25.

beginning, but he later realized that, if he was healed, his mother wouldn't find God. According to the boy, the angels

> showed me the things that made me choose to be sick. They said they'd make me well if I wanted, but I'm trying to help my family, and that's more important. When people volunteer to suffer for others, it changes the lives of the people you suffer for.[55]

Another of Lerma's patients was a 42-year-old woman dying of cervical cancer who received regular visitations from angels. Sometimes, they showed her scenes of the future. Lerma describes one of her visions thus:

> She saw her daughters growing up to help other people and carrying on an incredible legacy for the family of healing through music and through witnessing. Katarina was also able to see herself communing with Jesus and agreeing to her life's direction. She saw that what she had agreed to was much greater than the suffering she would experience.[56]

Katarina also told Lerma the following, which he found "somewhat challenging" to his current beliefs.

> We choose our lives, but we don't remember that choice. When the angels show our life to us, they give back the memory of that choice, and then we know our truth. Nothing is forced on us. We are all working together. We're part of the consciousness of the whole world. … For instance, when some of us choose the dark side, others have to take on the incredible energy of that darkness and defeat it so as to restore balance. … I was shown that even the cancer cells are still of God. By choosing to take on another person's darkness, I accelerated my cell growth so fast that I got cancer.[57]

She told Lerma that she had been shown the positive effects of her cancer as well, and that mainly these were its effects on her children's paths in life.[58]

The concept of destiny and a life plan may explain a puzzle that has long bothered those who consider the possibility of a higher consciousness influencing human affairs. For each case in which a person appears to be miraculously protected from harm, there are many others where people are not so protected and they experience great suffering and/or succumb to death. In a case reported by H. C. Moolenburgh, two teenage girls were out bicycling one day when they were overcome by an inexplicable sensation of fright. Suddenly, a man in overalls with "an extraordinarily beautiful face

---

[55] Lerma, *Into the Light*, 35.
[56] Lerma, *Into the Light*, 78-79.
[57] Lerma, *Into the Light*, 87-88.
[58] Lerma, *Into the Light*, 88.

which radiated great love" was standing in front of them, his arms outstretched, saying, "It is forbidden to go any further!" They turned back and went home. The next day, they discovered that, at the time this stranger had turned them away, a girl slightly younger had been raped and murdered in the area where they were biking.[59] It's reasonable to ask why, if the two bicycling girls were miraculously protected, this same protection wasn't given to the younger girl who was raped and killed.

Christian writer Eric Metaxas contemplates a similar puzzle in the context of two coincidences that saved the life of a young woman named Joni Eareckson, when no one saw her dive into shallow water and gravely injure herself. The first coincidence was that, right after the accident, a crab bit her sister's toe, causing her sister to turn toward Eareckson in an attempt to warn her about the crabs. It was then that her sister saw Eareckson's hair waving in the water as she floated there, disabled by fractured vertebrae. The second coincidence was that her sister was only able to see her hair because, just the night before, Eareckson had dyed it peroxide blond on a whim. Metaxas asks why, if God could so obviously save Eareckson's life, he didn't also prevent the spinal damage that ended up permanently paralyzing Eareckson from the neck down.[60]

If there is some powerful protective force in the universe, why does it not save everyone all the time? I believe our life plans likely hold the answer. Not everyone's life plan is the same. Different people are here to experience and accomplish different things, and we are only rescued from events when they would not serve that purpose. Joni Eareckson Tada has had an enormously inspirational Christian ministry as a result of her quadriplegia, and it is not hard to imagine, given all the other information we've read here, that this ministry was part of her destiny.

In many cases, such as that of the young girl who was raped and killed while two other girls were miraculously protected, we don't have the knowledge necessary to understand the differences in plans between people's lives. However, countless stories of extraordinary protection—some of which we've seen in Chapters 3 and 13—offer us strong evidence that such protection is widely available and that, if something bad happens to us or to those we love, it is most likely *not* an accident. The evidence suggests that negative events are allowed to happen when they are part of a greater plan, a plan that we may have agreed to before we were born.

---

[59] H. C. Moolenburgh, *Meetings with Angels*, trans. Tony Langham and Plym Peters (Saffron Walden, UK: C. W. Daniel, 1992), 112.
[60] Eric Metaxas, *Miracles: What They Are, Why They Happen, and How They Can Change Your Life* (New York: Dutton, Plume, 2014, 2015), 58.

The Life-Planning Experience

The idea that we sometimes agree to the major events of our lives before birth may still seem implausible. Perhaps its plausibility will be increased if we take a look at the detailed memories that a few people have concerning the life-planning process.

After Philip Schultz's adult son David was murdered, Schultz remembered something David had confided in him when he was just four years old. They were walking in a redwood grove, and David said, "I've got a really, *really* big secret to tell you!" He told his dad about "before I was born, and it was up in the sky." He said that there were 12 men, which he specifically said he'd counted. "And they were in a circle," he said. "Like they were sitting around a cloud or a table, but I didn't see any table. I could see they had faces, but they didn't have bodies." The oldest-looking one "told me I had to go down there…way down there I had to go to be tested." When the four-year-old repeated this bit about having to be tested, his father asked him if he thought he would pass. "Oh, yes!" David replied. And then, a little further along the path, he added, "But I won't be here long."[61]

Another account comes from a 35-year-old woman named Summer who still remembers planning her life before birth. She recalls,

> I had an ongoing dialogue with an angel, God, an aspect of God, or Saint Peter. It is hard to say exactly who he was. I desired to achieve the maximum in terms of clearing up karma and reaching enlightenment. We discussed what I needed and how to achieve my purpose with certain people. I saw my goals as well as all the choices that I could make as if I were looking at a computer board, only the computers seemed like stars. When I saw a quality I needed to develop, like kindness or compassion, I pressed the corresponding light. Then in a millisecond, I witnessed a panoramic view of roads I could take with different people in order to fulfill those objectives.[62]

Now let's look at a much more detailed account. This one comes from one of Dr. Andrew Paquette's dreams. It may seem odd for me to be recounting a dream as though it had some relation to fact, but, as we've seen throughout this book and will continue to see in Chapter 19, "Interpreting Coincidences," Paquette has shown that many of his dreams are in fact accurate reflections of objective events. I am including his account of the life-planning process here because of how well it makes sense of and summarizes the piecemeal accounts gleaned from various other sources,

---

[61] Bowman, *Return from Heaven*, 155-7.

[62] Carman and Carman, 28-29.

including pre-birth memories and near-death experiences. What is more, it is a spontaneous experience that provides independent confirmation of many of the details of life planning apparently remembered by people who undergo life-between-lives hypnosis.

In Paquette's dream, he was taken to view his "upcoming" life—the life he was actually in the middle of living when he had this dream—in order to decide whether he wanted to choose this life as his own. The life preview took place in a space that he describes as something like "a vast theatre with many thousands of screens," though the screens were three-dimensional and multisensory. They demonstrated all of the sights, sounds, tastes, feels, and odors this life would afford. What was more, there was an immense audience, composed of the spirits of every person his life would affect to any degree, great or small, and when something in Paquette's life affected them, more screens appeared in the theater to demonstrate those effects, and then the effects of *those* effects on still other people. In the account of this dream that Paquette recorded immediately after waking from it on April 17, 1990, he wrote,

> It is exactly as if I am reliving my entire life, from my birth in 1965 to my death at some future date. …
>
> Because I experience the life from multiple perspectives simultaneously, I am able to evaluate all of my life choices. When I do something that causes harm to someone else, I not only see myself commit the act and the person's reaction on the screen, but I also see his spirit in the audience react as well.
>
> Seeing each event from this variety of perspectives is crucial to my decision about the life. The ripples my actions will cause to those around me will define the success or failure of my life more than any other measure. The life has a serious purpose, and is not designed for entertainment.[63]

Mission

Many of those who return from near-death experiences agree with Paquette that life has a "serious purpose." In fact, many of them feel that they have been given a specific mission of some kind. Interestingly, many NDErs who know they have a mission don't remember what it is. As NDE

[63] Andrew Paquette, *Dreamer: 20 Years of Psychic Dreams and How They Changed My Life* (Winchester, UK: O Books, 2011), 157-8.

researcher Debra Diamond puts it, "All they know is they're meant to do something, but darn if they can figure out what it is."[64]

For instance, when 25-year-old Leonard Spade had his NDE, God was apparently ready to accept him into the afterlife, but Spade didn't feel ready to present himself to God. He says, "I didn't feel satisfied because I had the feeling of having promised to do something with my life that I hadn't done."[65]

John Stirling, on the other hand, had an NDE in which a voice asked him three times if he was "finished," and he said yes each time. The voice then suggested they take a look at his life. Finally, he realized that he needed to go back to raise and educate his son, and when he acknowledged this, he was immediately back in his body.[66]

Betty J. Eadie's NDE provides some explanatory detail on the topic of life missions. Not only did she see that we choose our missions before we are born, but she saw that our life experiences, our social status, and even the personal relationships we will have are all designed to fulfill those missions.[67]

Researchers Ohkado Masayuki and Ikegawa Akira questioned 21 Japanese children who had memories of life between their lives on earth, and they found that 13 of the children remembered why they'd chosen to be born. According to Ohkado and Ikegawa's report, "The reasons were: to meet or help their mothers (3); to help other people (5); to become happier than they were in their previous lives (2); and to enjoy life (3). One child said he did not remember why he was born because he forgot the reason when he was born in order to find what it is in the current life."[68]

There is evidence that we don't need to know our mission in life in order to accomplish it. P. M. H. Atwater's study of thousands of NDEs has led her to the conclusion that "[o]ur mission…reveals itself as we go along. … [I]t is simply an urge of 'rightness' we follow or associate with or are open to, when we are receptive enough."[69] Paquette affirms this perspective as well. He says that his dream of choosing his current life showed him that all the little details of our lives achieve much more than we know. "[J]ust as a

---

[64] Debra Diamond, *Life After Near Death: Miraculous Stories of Healing and Transformation in the Extraordinary Lives of People with Newfound Powers* (Wayne, NJ: New Page Books, 2016), 102.

[65] Pierre Jovanovic, *Enquête sur l'existence des anges gardiens* (Paris: J'ai Lu, 1993), 94. My translation.

[66] Jovanovic, 218-9.

[67] Betty J. Eadie with Curtis Taylor, *Embraced by the Light* (Carson City, NV: Gold Leaf Press, 1992), 48-49.

[68] Ohkado Masayuki and Ikegawa Akira, "Children with Life-between-Life Memories," *Journal of Scientific Exploration* 28, no. 3 (2014): 477-490, p. 482.

[69] P. M. H. Atwater, *Beyond the Light: What Isn't Being Said About Near-Death Experience* (New York: Birch Lane Press, 1994), 188.

worm fulfills its purpose by simply living," he says, "we accomplish far more than we realize."[70]

In many cases, it seems, life will bring our mission *to* us. Caroline Myss relates the pre-birth memories of one of her clients, Paul, who remembered two "beings of light" who had helped him shape his current life. She writes,

> Paul had been presented with an array of choices and was urged to shape his life's mission based on events and influences from previous lives, obligations that he needed to fulfill to be able to help others in their spiritual development, personal debts he owed, and some new experiences that he was allowed to select. All of the events and relationships that he chose, with the help of his spiritual advisers, were woven together around one major path. The beings had been very specific about certain events he was meant to be a part of, adding that the details of getting to these events would be taken care of from their end.[71]

Here we see an explicit acknowledgment that the spiritual beings who help us plan our lives are also working "behind the scenes" to make sure we get to where we're supposed to be. Our experiences of coincidences may very well be glimpses of their backstage efforts.

Free Will

With all this evidence that important events in our lives are arranged before our birth, it's quite natural to wonder whether any space is left in our lives for free will. Perhaps you'll recall from Chapter 6 the precognitive vision of Professor Richard Szumski who, as a teenager, was raking leaves in his yard when he suddenly had the experience of being somewhere else. He was holding a brick in front of another house, accompanied by a young girl and boy whom he knew were his children. The vision was exceptionally detailed, and 20 years later, it was precisely fulfilled, except for one major discrepancy: in the vision, there was a brick wall that couldn't be seen from where he was standing when the vision came true. Szumski realized, however, that if he had lived in the house *next door*, everything would have been exactly as it had been in his vision. He remarked that a difference of only 30 feet in 20 years wasn't a particularly reassuring amount of "leeway" with regard to personal choice.[72]

---

[70] Paquette, *Dreamer*, 208.
[71] Caroline Myss, *Sacred Contracts: Awakening Your Divine Potential* (New York: Harmony Books, 2001), 60.
[72] Alan Vaughan, *Incredible Coincidence: The Baffling World of Synchronicity* (New York: J. B. Lippincott Company, 1979), 194.

Nevertheless, near-death experience researcher Dr. Barbara R. Rommer has found that most NDErs believe in free will. "A very small percentage of NDErs feel that everything in our lives is predestined," she says. But "[m]ost of the subjects feel that every moment of this lifetime involves a choice."[73] For instance, NDEr Betty J. Eadie says we can change the course of our lives at any time. "God made the promise that he wouldn't intervene in our lives *unless we asked him*," she says. "The choice would be ours through our decisions."[74]

How do we square NDErs' affirmation of free will with everything we've just read about destiny and life plans? Is it possible that *both* things could be true? In fact, I believe they are. And some other descriptions of NDEs as well as of pre-birth memories and other spiritual experiences will help to paint the picture of how this can be so.

Let's start with Toni Maguire, who was born with memories of life before her body. These memories included viewing a book whose pages displayed movies of the events of her future life. She writes in her memoir that "[i]t was understood that events within my future life could be changed if I made the decision to change them after birth, but effort would be required to do this."[75] That is, the events of her life were not set in stone, but changing them would mean swimming against the current and would not be easy. Reflection on this memory as well as her subsequent earth experiences ultimately led Maguire to the belief that our lives are actually a combination of free choices we make and other events that are destined to happen no matter what. She says she knew that "somehow my free will would always meet back up with my destiny at some point in the future."[76]

In an out-of-body experience, Robert Monroe once met a being who told him, "Because free will is such a vital part of the human learning experience, deviations from the design are frequent and predicted, as you would express it. Such adjustments are no more than...fine-tuning...."[77]

Psychic Rebecca Rosen believes our life plan is like a "loose script," and that free will is essential in determining how it plays out. When she does psychic readings, she's able to tell clients what is likely to happy given the current trend in their decision making, but this is always subject to change.[78]

---

[73] Rommer, 181.
[74] Eadie with Taylor, 49.
[75] Maguire, 7.
[76] Maguire, 192.
[77] Robert A. Monroe, *Far Journeys* (Garden City, NY: Doubleday & Company, 1985, 1987), 100.
[78] Interview with Rebecca Rosen, reported in Jenniffer Weigel, *Psychics, Healers, and Mediums: A Journalist, a Road Trip, and Voices from the Other Side* (Charlottesville, VA: Hampton Roads, 2017), 103.

Author Michael Talbot tells us that "Hawaiian kahunas, widely esteemed for their precognitive powers, also speak of the future as fluid, but in the process of 'crystallizing,' and believe that great world events are crystallized furthest in advance, as are the most important events in a person's life, such as marriage, accidents, and death."[79]

It might also be helpful to understand the interweaving of destiny and free will along the lines of a metaphor invoked by Dr. Gary Schwartz: that of an enormous jazz band. Schwartz notes that jazz is both a collective and an individual process, where the individuals have freedom to improvise based on a communally determined harmonic structure.[80] Perhaps our pre-life planning involves choosing, as a group, the basic structure that we'll all later improvise to.

In an out-of-body experience in her late 20s, Mary Helen Hensley found herself conversing with the "voices" that had been guiding her for a long time. They told her that there had been times in her life when it looked like she might not end up on the path she'd originally selected for herself, in which case other people would have had to fill the gap until she found her way back to her destiny. Interestingly, when Hensley asked if the beings behind these voices had caused the serious automobile accident in which she was involved—an accident that provoked an NDE and changed the course of her life—they told her, "No, *you did*. You reached deep into your core and rediscovered your purpose. We only obliged your request for immediate change."[81] Hensley says that this accident was an option inserted in her life plan for the event in which she made it through childhood without remembering what she was made to do. It would then help her to remember when she came of age.

So it seems that our life plan may include plans for various contingencies. Hensley says she learned in her NDE that we "play our roles in one another's lives, loosely following a script, allowing the freedom of improvisation at each actor's discretion."[82] Hensley's life actually provides an additional example of something that seems like a "change" to the original plan. While going through a difficult transition in her mid-20s, she met someone she recognized from her life before birth. In fact, *he* recalled more than she did about the plan they had made together on the other side. He told her, "It was actually going to be another fifteen years or so, before we

---

[79] Michael Talbot, *The Holographic Universe: The Revolutionary Theory of Reality* (New York: Harper Perennial, 1991, 1992, 2011), 212. Talbot references Max Freedom Long, *The Secret Science Behind Miracles* (Tarrytown, NY: Robert Collier Publications, 1948), 165.

[80] Gary E. Schwartz, *Super Synchronicity: Where Science and Spirit Meet* (Vancouver, BC: Param Media, 2017), 246-7.

[81] Hensley, 304.

[82] Hensley, 13.

had planned to meet.... [But] I was told that you were having a bit of trouble, that you have doubted whether or not the incredible things that have been going on in your life were genuine. I am here to tell you that *this is very real*."[83]

Rerouted Destinies

One final bit of evidence that our destinies are not set in stone comes from young children who report enduring rather large upsets to the lives they planned before birth. Arlene Mora says that, when her daughter Alannah was born, Mora had the strange feeling that she wasn't her mother, even though she had obviously just given birth to her. Then, when Alannah was about three years old, she approached her mother with something important to say: "Mommy, when I was looking to come here, I was looking for Nani [Mora's mother], but I couldn't find her. I searched for her and still couldn't find her. I really wanted her to be my mommy, but I found you and then I chose you. Mommy, we are supposed to be sisters, did you know?"[84]

Brett was also around three years old when he got angry at his mom and told her, "I hate you, Mommy. You weren't even my first choice for a Mommy." When she asked who had been his first choice, he said, "It was a woman from the Philippines, but she had already been taken."[85]

Nevertheless, it seems that those on the other side can find ways of making things right again. Carol Bowman recounts a story about two young cousins, Charlotte and Sarah, who were inseparable every time their families got together. Finally, the girls decided to reveal their secret to Charlotte's mother. Charlotte said, "Before Sarah and I came here to this life, we were supposed to come together. We were twins and we were supposed to be in Tricia's [Sarah's mother's] stomach. Just before we came, that person held me back. Remember him, Sarah? Do you remember what he told me?" Sarah replied, "He told you that you couldn't come. That it wasn't your time yet, but that he'd make it so we could always be near each other. He said you'd have to wait and we were so upset—but look! Here we are! He kept his promise!"[86]

---

[83] Hensley, 109.
[84] Dyer and Garnes, 66-67.
[85] Hallett, *Soul Trek*, 159.
[86] Bowman, *Return from Heaven*, 148.

Chapter 18

Spiritual Growth

We saw a great deal of evidence in the last chapter that the events of our lives are ordered according to a purpose. While the specifics of this purpose seem to differ from person to person and life to life, there is one giant, overarching theme that emerges from all of the literature I have reviewed. That theme is love.

When the Near Death Experience Research Foundation (NDERF) asked experiencers about the meaning and purpose of life, they received many responses similar to the following: "Life's meaning or purpose is love," "Life is an opportunity for us to express and experience love," and "The only thing that mattered was love."[1]

Learning to love—both ourselves and others—is often referred to as "spiritual growth." I think this is very apt terminology, as learning to love does indeed expand the reach of our spirit. In learning to love, we encompass and integrate increasingly more of ourselves and of those around us. And we develop spiritual strength as well, learning to give and receive love even in the face of the most difficult obstacles, such as fear. Fear is something that life on earth offers in abundance, and perhaps that is a major part of the reason we choose to live lives in this environment: it's a perfect testing ground. As NDEr Jean R. points out, when we're on the "other side," it's obvious to us what the right spiritual decisions are, but earth is the place where we attempt to live out those decisions under the pressures of physical existence.[2]

---

[1] Jeffrey Long with Paul Perry, *God and the Afterlife: The Ground-Breaking New Evidence for God and Near-Death Experience* (New York: HarperCollins, 2016), 97-98.
[2] Long with Perry, 101-2.

Clearly, however, we are not just sent to earth and left to our own devices. Story after story in this book has shown that, when we are in need of help, that help is close and available. But it should be understood that the purpose of this help is not primarily to meet our material needs or to give us a spouse with whom we can live happily ever after. This should be clear from the fact that *sometimes* coincidences intervene to give us these things and *sometimes* they don't. Sometimes coincidences put us in a materially *worse* situation. This can make them seem capricious, but I believe there is an important logic behind the vagaries of what appears to us as chance. The events of our lives are specifically designed to stretch our ability to give and receive love. They are designed with the goal of facilitating spiritual growth.

This underlying current in our lives has long been noted by mental health professionals, most famously by Swiss psychiatrist and depth psychologist Dr. Carl Jung. As the Jungian astrophysicist Dr. Victor Mansfield notes, "Depth psychology provides us with abundant evidence that a superior intelligence takes a particular and specific interest in our psychological and spiritual development,"[3] and Mansfield's book *Synchronicity, Science, and Soul-Making* is filled with examples that complement those given by Jung. We'll have a chance to look at some of them in this chapter.

Experience of meaningful coincidences in the practice of psychotherapy is in fact so common that it can easily turn a skeptic into a believer. One excellent example is that of psychiatrist Dr. M. Scott Peck. In *The Road Less Traveled*, he tells us that, at the time of his graduation from medical school, he firmly believed that miracles did not exist. Fifteen years in the practice of psychiatry, however, left him confidently asserting that miracles were everywhere. His change in perspective followed an abundance of experiences that he says "initially seemed quite commonplace but which, when I thought about them more deeply, seemed to indicate that my work with patients toward their growth was being remarkably assisted in ways for which I had no logical explanation."[4]

Peck recounts a time when he was talking with a patient and the word 'Pinnochio' kept coming unwantedly to mind. He ignored it and attempted to concentrate on what his patient was saying, but the word kept intruding on his thoughts. Finally, he realized that this mental intrusion could be an important prompting from his unconscious. When he took a moment to think about it, it occurred to him that his patient was indeed very much like Pinnochio—a puppet on a string. In the end, this turned out to be an extremely useful insight.

---

[3] Victor Mansfield, *Synchronicity, Science, and Soul-Making* (Chicago: Open Court, 1995), 199.

[4] M. Scott Peck, *The Road Less Traveled: A New Psychology of Love, Traditional Values and Spiritual Growth* (New York: Simon & Schuster, 1978), 229.

Peck specifically comments on the way this kind of information often comes to us unbidden and against our wishes. He says it's the conscious resistance we have to such information that originally led Freud and others to see the unconscious in an unseemly light. "It is as if they assumed," he says, "from the fact that our consciousness did not want it, that unconscious material was therefore 'bad.'"[5] Peck points out, however, that the problem is not the unconscious material itself but rather our unwillingness to acknowledge this psychological material and process it.

Indeed, coincidences can often play the role of bringing to mind feelings or thoughts that a person's conscious mind doesn't want to deal with. Remember from the chapter on meetings the story of the woman who answered the phone one morning to discover that, though the caller had the wrong number, it was someone she knew and had felt guilty about not being in touch with. She tried to disguise her voice and got off the phone without identifying herself, but later that day, she attempted to call a location in another part of England when she *herself* got a wrong number and fell upon the same woman who had accidentally called her that morning![6] It seems very likely to me that this double coincidence occurred in order to encourage this woman to confront her feelings of guilt and work to resolve them.

In fact, I believe that the need to confront trials and challenges head on is at the root of many of the seemingly negative coincidences we experience. For example, a woman whom Brian Inglis calls "Diana Finer" recounts that she once had a dream that she was walking down a train platform when she saw her husband's mistress (whom she knew from real life) standing in front of her, her suitcase at her feet to her left. Finer started to run away, but an invisible figure took her by the shoulders and told her she had to speak to this woman.

When Finer woke up from the dream, she hesitated about making a train trip to London she'd had planned for the day, but ultimately she decided to go. When she reached the train station, she looked around to see if the mistress might be there, but she wasn't. So Finer boarded the train, chose a seat in an empty car, and left a newspaper to mark her place while she went to the dining car. When she later returned to her seat, she was amazed to see that her husband's mistress was seated in the place facing hers. Finer thought about moving elsewhere, but she remembered the prompting she'd gotten in her dream to speak to this woman. She sat down.

For two and a half hours, Finer talked with her husband's mistress. She learned an enormous amount about her husband and his relationship with this woman. And she could also clearly tell that her marriage was beyond repair. When Finer finally disembarked from the train in London, she

---

[5] Peck, *The Road Less Traveled*, 247.

[6] Alan Vaughan, *Incredible Coincidence: The Baffling World of Synchronicity* (New York: J. B. Lippincott Company, 1979), 64.

transferred to the Underground. "As I went," she says, "I thought about the dream and the fact that I had seen [my husband's mistress]…standing on the platform at Exeter, whereas in reality she had been on the train. I walked onto the Underground station and, looking across at the opposite platform, saw her standing facing me with her suitcase on her left just as she had stood in the dream."[7]

In reviewing this case, I am especially impressed by the fact that, in the woman's dream foreshadowing these events, there was an invisible someone who took hold of her shoulders and bodily turned her toward her husband's mistress, telling her she had to speak to her, and that this was an instruction remembered by the woman when she was confronted with the mistress in real life. Clearly this was no ordinary dream, and this was no chance meeting. Someone was obviously looking out for this woman's welfare and telling her in no uncertain terms that she must confront this difficult situation in her life. The upshot? This woman learned some very important information about her husband and realized that their marriage was over. One can only imagine that, although this information hurt her in the short term, she was better off in the long term not waiting in vain for her marriage to improve. And perhaps she also learned something about the value of facing challenging situations.

A similar purpose may stand behind many other unwelcome coincidental meetings: for instance, that of a man who had a sudden feeling that, if he proceeded along the path he habitually walked, he would run into a friend he didn't particularly want to see. "I therefore, without hesitation, took another road," he says, "and having arrived at one of the street corners, whom should I meet but my friend."[8] In this case, the man's desire *not* to see his friend is ironically employed to bring about precisely this effect. How many times do such things happen to us and we rail at our bad luck (or the malevolence of the universe!) instead of appreciating the opportunity we've been given to confront a problem that's been silently eating at us?

Here's the case of a man who recognized the potential gift that lay in an unwelcome reminder. Four weeks after his first son was born, this man dreamt for the first time about his own father, who had been an alcoholic and abandoned him in infancy. In fact, two nights in a row this man had very similar dreams in which his father explained to him that he was a sensitive person who had been unable to live with his son's mother because of her aggressivity and stubbornness. In the day following the second of these dreams, the son got a call from his father's brother—his first contact with that side of the family in 15 years. His uncle told him that his father was in the hospital dying and he should go see him.

---

[7] Inglis, *Coincidence*, 166.

[8] Inglis, *Coincidence*, 190. This quotation originally comes from a letter written to the 19th-century parapsychologist Frederic W. H. Myers.

The son was so angry with his father for never having been part of his life that he told his uncle no, he wouldn't visit him. But later that day he began to feel torn, thinking he would like to tell his father that he was now a grandfather. Not knowing what else to do, the son decided to cast coins and consult the *I Ching*, an ancient Chinese divination method. The resulting hexagram was "Gathering," and the interpretation of it he read included the phrase, "The family gathers about the father as its head." Startled at receiving such a pointedly relevant message, he decided to visit his father in the hospital after all. Over the course of their visit, his experience of his father's suffering dissolved his bitterness, and his father died a few days later. The son credits his dreams and his *I Ching* reading with helping him pierce the emotional armor he'd built up against the hurts of his childhood and with promoting a deeper healing than he had otherwise been able to achieve.[9]

That story is one of those appearing in Mansfield's book *Synchronicity, Science, and Soul-Making*. Here is another, this one reported by a woman. When she was six or seven years old, she had a pearl ring that she decided to trade with a friend for a ring she liked better. When her parents discovered she'd traded away her valuable ring for a trinket from a bubble gum machine, they were quite shocked, and the rings were ultimately traded back under the parents' watchful eyes. Fast forward 15 or 20 years. The woman was in a serious relationship that, in her words, "had reached a stagnant point where I knew that if things didn't change, it wasn't going to last." Meanwhile, she became attracted to another man, foreign and exotic. She was thinking about leaving her serious relationship for a fling with this other guy when she reached into her pocketbook for some change and instead came out with the pearl ring from her childhood. She says, "it was instantaneously clear to me that if I were to have this affair, I was going to once again trade my pearl for the flashy imitation."

This woman goes on to say that the discernment of the true value of things has been an ongoing theme in her life. She has repeatedly had to choose between tempting, flashy appearances and things more deeply important, and she hasn't always chosen wisely. Pulling out this pearl ring caused her to realize that she was at a turning point in her life and needed to make this decision carefully. She ultimately chose to stay in her long-term relationship.[10]

Turning points in our lives seem to attract coincidences like magnets. Very often, the coincidences will build in number and in intensity, peaking just as we become conscious of a life-changing insight or just as we make a crucial choice. Philosopher and cultural historian Dr. Richard Tarnas elegantly describes this progression in his book *Cosmos and Psyche*. He writes,

---

[9] Mansfield, 41-44.

[10] Mansfield, 38-40.

> The first stage is usually marked by the experience of various ambiguously suggestive coincidences and patternings that may seem somewhat remarkable, curious, or even vaguely uncanny, but can still be regarded as perhaps merely fortuitous or subjective, and are therefore usually ignored and forgotten. Eventually, there may occur one or more especially powerful synchronicities, unambiguous in their coincidental force and precision of patterning, that have a revelatory effect on the individual and mark a decisive threshold in his or her psychological and spiritual development. Not infrequently, synchronicities of this category occur in association with births, deaths, crises, and other major turning points in life. On occasion, there may take place a sudden convergence of many such synchronicities, intricately interconnected, occurring in close proximity or in rapid succession, and having the effect of an overpowering epiphany of new meaning and purpose in the life of the individual.[11]

This is a pattern I have observed in my own life on more than one occasion. My best example to date is made up of such a long series of coincidences that describing it could fill a book of its own, but I do have a more compact example to offer. Like the case of the pearl ring recounted above, my example also pertains to a repeating life theme.

In my case, I had been dogged for some time by my inability to move on from a certain romantic relationship. Then one day it dawned on me that this was a repeating theme in my life. After each of the three strongest romantic relationships I'd had to part with over the years, I'd spent a great deal of emotional energy wishing to be reunited with the person—energy that could likely have been used much more profitably on something else. In any case, it finally dawned on me that I had established this pattern, and I knew at that moment that something needed to change. I needed to let go, not just of the past, but also of my continual thoughts of a possible future with this particular person. At the moment I realized this, I experienced the coincidence I related in the chapter "Confirmation": I saw emerge in the traffic jam in front of me a car with the license plate "LETGO."

But that was only the beginning. The day following the license plate coincidence, I was on an errand and happened to be driving past the turnoff to a bookstore when I had the thought that there might be a book there that I needed to read. So I made a last-minute turn and pulled into the parking lot. I started walking up to the store when I caught sight of a taxi in the parking lot. Taxis are uncommon where I live, but it was the phone number displayed on the taxi that really drew my attention. You may remember from the chapter "A New Perspective on the Universe" that the number 33 holds a special meaning for me. It's a number that I consider to be something like

---

[11] Richard Tarnas, *Cosmos and Psyche: Intimations of a New World View* (New York: Plume, 2006, May 2007), 55-56.

God's "signature"—the number God likes to leave as a calling card when God sends me a particularly nice coincidence. Well, in this case, the phone number of the taxi was 333-3333. I had the very strong feeling that I was on the right track in entering this bookstore.

Inside, I decided that I would attempt to follow my intuition to find the book I was supposed to have. I walked toward the spirituality section, where I normally find a lot of good reads, but that aisle was blocked by two employees of the bookstore and a cart. So, I went down the next aisle, and as I walked down it, my eyes fell on a book titled *Widow to Widow*. I immediately stopped. Since my breakup, I'd derived a lot of help from books written for those who've lost their partners to death, and this title intrigued me. Right next to *Widow to Widow*, however, I saw a book by Dr. Elizabeth Kübler-Ross called *Life Lessons*, and that was the one I picked up.

I opened the book at random, falling on page 104. The first two sentences I read were these:

> After meeting someone like Jack, you begin to understand how this moment can be robbed by your past and future. You have no idea what a better experience you would have if you let go of the past, at this moment, to focus on this moment, to fully experience it and really live your life. ...[12]

I was flabbergasted by the precision of the message, right down to the fact that the very first sentence mentioned that thoughts of the *future* can be just as deleterious to the present as can those about the past. I was constantly worried about what might happen in the future, because I had the feeling that the value of my present suffering depended on the eventual outcome of things. After reading this passage, however, I knew that I had to stop thinking this way. Ultimately, those two days in which I saw the LETGO license plate and then read this randomly chosen line in Kübler-Ross's book proved to be a crucial turning point for me. Somehow, these coincidences helped me to release my preoccupation with this other person, and after that, I never again worried with anything like the same intensity about what the future of our relationship might hold.

The twists and turns of relationships are particularly fertile ground for coincidences, probably because they offer so many opportunities for spiritual growth. In romantic relationships, the parties involved run up against all sorts of obstacles that force them to come nose to nose with their own weaknesses, and coincidences may come along to help illuminate and guide this confrontation. Brian Inglis relates a case in which a man had a fight with his girlfriend in which his behavior was gratuitously destructive. As he was

---

[12] Elisabeth Kübler-Ross and David Kessler, *Life Lessons: Two Experts on Death & Dying Teach Us About the Mysteries of Life & Living* (New York: Scribner, 2000), 104.

driving home afterward and turning onto his road, he saw someone throw a brick through the window of a house and drive off. Strangely, the license plate of the malefactor's car bore his own initials. This caused him to realize that this brick through the window was a reflection of his own needlessly hurtful behavior.[13]

I want to close this chapter by describing in detail one more coincidence that occurred at a crucial moment in a romantic relationship and resulted in profound spiritual growth for both of the parties involved: Nancy and Leo Whitmore.

The Whitmores' 30-year marriage had been strained for some time, but when their youngest child moved away from home, the true size of the gap that had grown between them became apparent. One night, they discussed divorce. Understandably, neither of them slept very well after that. The next morning, Nancy had a sudden desire to go camping. Camping had served as the context for many happy family moments through the years, and to Nancy's surprise, Leo was willing to go with her. They argued during the drive, however, which led to their taking some wrong turns and not even noticing when they passed a sign saying the road they were on was closed in winter. It was warm for November, so they hadn't been paying attention to the possibility that they might hit bad weather. But, by the time they realized they were unintentionally off-roading and had gotten themselves stuck in a patch of mud, it had started to snow. They did everything they could think of to get themselves out but eventually decided there was nothing to do but stay put for the night and hopefully be rescued in the morning.

Unfortunately, Nancy and Leo awoke the next morning to a blizzard and realized they were going to be there a lot longer than they'd thought. Still, they had food and propane enough to last several days, so they decided to make the best of things. It was while they were stuck there, snowed into their camper, that they finally began to listen to one another and discover how each of them had truly felt over the last 30 years. The next day, the snow continued to fall, and Leo and Nancy continued to grow closer. They kissed for the first time in many years. And then they made love. Leo asked Nancy afterward if, instead of getting divorced, they could get married again.

It was only another day later that they realized exactly how much physical danger they were in. Four feet of snow had fallen, and after many hours of calculations, Leo determined that they were 50 miles from the nearest plowed road. There was no way they could walk out. And, with their camper stuck under a tree, there was no way for the rescue helicopter that flew past to notice them. Nancy made a bright red HELP sign that they placed on a nearby road in case any other vehicles should fly over, but it brought no results.

---

[13] Inglis, *Coincidence*, 41.

In the end, Nancy and Leo were stranded for four weeks by the snow, and for the last three of those, they had no heat or food. It looked like Leo was not going to survive, and Nancy decided that she would stop eating snow and join him in death. "I wanted to die with Leo," she says. It was the morning after she made that decision that a helicopter finally landed nearby and flew the starving couple out on stretchers. "We are now in our seventies," says Nancy, "and not a day goes by that we don't remember our ordeal in the snow. We are grateful to have survived, but even more grateful that love guided us back into each other's arms."[14]

---

[14] Vissell and Vissell, 157.

Chapter 19
Interpreting Coincidences

The last several chapters have dealt primarily with coincidences that have an obvious purpose. However, I would venture to say that *most* of the coincidences people experience are nowhere near this clear in their significance. Some of them may resemble the coincidences described in the preceding chapters enough that it makes sense to assume their goal is similar, but the majority of coincidences are likely still to leave us scratching our heads. It's for those of you who are attempting to interpret these more ambiguous coincidences that this chapter is written.

A Second Look at Stanislav Grof's First Marriage

Let's begin by taking a closer look at one of the coincidence cases I described in the Introduction. In that case, Dr. Stanislav Grof and his first wife, Joan, took the striking coincidences they experienced during their courtship as signs that they were meant to marry and spend their lives together, and they were surprised and disappointed when things didn't turn out as expected. One can hardly blame them, given how clearly some of their coincidences pointed to their living "happily ever after." In addition to the coincidences that preceded their first meeting, which are recounted in the Introduction, their first meal together was at a Chinese restaurant, and the fortune cookies they received there bore messages that seemed particularly auspicious. His said, "Your heart was hers from the moment you met," and hers read, "After long waiting, your dream is finally coming true!"

The pair married on the spur of the moment while in Iceland for the First International Transpersonal Conference, only weeks after their first meeting. There were multiple scholars of mythology present at the conference, including the famous Joseph Campbell, and the group of them decided to reconstruct an ancient Viking ritual for the wedding. An old Icelandic dress was brought for Joan to wear, and it fit her like a glove. During the hours of festivities, a huge double rainbow arched through the sky, disappearing and reappearing twice more. It turned out as well that the name of the place where they were married, Bifrost, meant the "Rainbow Bridge of the Gods" and that, according to the Viking ritual they were recreating, the rainbow symbolized the coming together of Mother Earth and Father Sky. Campbell actually spoke about Grof's wedding in his lectures, citing it as an example of a marriage that, because of its solid mythological foundation, would endure for eternity.

Yet Grof recounts that he knew as soon as he awoke the morning after the wedding that "something was terribly wrong." He recounts,

> All the thrill and ecstatic feelings of the preceding day were gone; I felt sober and somber. The wave of excitement we had experienced the last few days suddenly felt illusory and deceptive. And what was worse, marrying Joan suddenly seemed like a serious error.

Grof and his bride soon divorced, and Grof described the lesson he learned from this experience thus: "The ecstatic feelings associated with emergence of archetypal forces do not guarantee a positive outcome. It is essential to refrain from acting out while we are under their spell and not to make any important decisions until we have again both feet on the ground."[1]

Grof implies that he made a mistake in marrying Joan. Perhaps he did, but that is not the only possible interpretation of what happened. As we will see throughout this chapter, the forces expressed by coincidences are often highly mysterious, and their purposes often don't fit the neat categories of our expectations.

It seems clear to me that Grof and Joan were meant to meet each other. Perhaps they were even meant to marry. But perhaps that was *all* they were meant to do: to participate in that one highly symbolic ceremony and then move on to separate lives. That doesn't fit our Western ideal of marriage, but should we *expect* the mysterious, complex forces of the universe to conform themselves to our human ideals? Should we not rather expect them to lead us to the experience of something *greater* than our preconceived notions of life?

---

[1] Stanislav Grof, *When the Impossible Happens: Adventures in Non-Ordinary Realities* (Boulder, CO: Sounds True, 2006), 18-26.

Grof's story reminds me of an experience related by Jonette Crowley in her 2007 book *The Eagle and the Condor.* While traveling in Peru, Crowley met a man with whom she felt an overwhelming spiritual connection. This greatly troubled her, because she was married to another man, whom she deeply loved. But she discovered over the course of that trip (as well as a second one a few months later) that, though she was intended to come to the Andes and participate in some important ceremonies with her Peruvian "twin flame," that was all. She realized, to her relief, that she did not need to break up her marriage. And, once the ceremonies were completed, she happily returned home to her American husband.[2]

Crowley's experience suggests that Grof's marriage to Joan might have been important on a level entirely different from what they expected. It could be that the purposes of the universe in bringing them together were far different from their own desires. Psychologist Jeff Vézina has written an entire book on the role of coincidences in relationships. In *Necessary Chances,* he observes that

> this type of highly symbolic encounter cannot be pursued over a long period of time without some difficulty. The people who have the greatest symbolic impact on our lives are not always those with whom we live. They open doors for us but it is rare that we cross those thresholds in their company.[3]

Vézina suggests that one purpose of these short but intense relationships is the alteration of consciousness. "Somewhat like alcohol and drugs," he says, "we feel the need to live intense experiences that are sometimes destructive, but that unconsciously aim to transform us."[4]

Vézina gives the example of a woman he calls Catherine. At her doctoral graduation in French Canada, her attention was drawn to the name of one of the graduates, called out of the normal order. It happened to match down to one letter the name of a play she'd seen two days before. That evening, she saw an attractive man in a restaurant in another section of town and discovered, after approaching him, that he was the man whose name she'd noticed. It turned out as well that he lived in the city where she was headed the next weekend to give a talk.

The two of them began seeing each other, but the man warned her that he had plans to go back to his home in Morocco and that he had no intention

---

[2] Jonette Crowley, *The Eagle and the Condor: A True Story of an Unexpected Mystical Journey* (Greenwood Village, CO: StoneTree Publishing, 2007).

[3] Jeff Vézina, *Necessary Chances: Synchronicity in the Encounters That Transform Us*, trans. Carl Anger (Pari, Italy: Pari Publishing, 2009), 48.

[4] Vézina, 48.

of marrying her. A few months later, he indeed returned to Morocco, and they broke up.

A year or so after the man left, however, he invited Catherine out to visit him for summer vacation. At just that time, she received a check from a client for the same amount as the plane ticket cost and took this as a sign that she was meant to go. She was actually still hoping to marry this man, despite his previous warning that this wouldn't happen, and she even put her house up for sale before leaving. When she arrived in Morocco, however, he repeated his assertion that he would not marry her, and she had to return home. Not long after she flew home to Canada, she found out that he had married someone else.

Vézina expresses the opinion that this encounter "was associated with transformations that this woman was undertaking in her own life."[5] For instance, Catherine had just earned her PhD and was moving into a new professional role that apparently left little room for her more artistic, intuitive side—a side that seemed to be drawn to her lover's Arab culture. Vézina suggests, "This woman, who had given up her entire life to her scientific career, was perhaps being prompted, thanks to this man from another culture, into a transformation and a questioning of her values."[6]

Intense romantic relationships indeed have the power to revolutionize our view of ourselves, our world, and our potential contributions to that world. But we can't always integrate this new understanding and develop it to its full potential while we are still under the influence of the person who provoked it. We need the catalyst of their presence, and then we need space to develop independently.

Getting back to Stanislav Grof's case, it may be that Grof and Joan met and married in order to be transformed in some way, in order to take a step forward in their personal evolution, which they would then continue separately. On the other hand, it might be the case that the dissolution of their marriage was not part of the universe's intention. Perhaps Grof and Joan *could* have been happy staying together, if they'd reacted to their marital difficulties in a different way.

Consider, too, another possibility evoked by psychic Echo Bodine. A client asked her to tell her whether a man she was seeing was "the one." Bodine says she was able to perceive this woman's guides, and they told her, "Yeah, tell her it's Mr. Right." Bodine noticed the guides seemed a bit hesitant, but she conveyed their message nevertheless. Fast forward six months and the client returned to see Bodine, saying, "That was the worst relationship of my life! Why did my guides say that?" Bodine says the guides explained the situation thus: "She had some heavy karma with him, and if we

[5] Vézina, 51.
[6] Vézina, 51.

would have told her, 'The next six months are going to be hell,' she would have bailed." Instead, she completed her mission with him and was thus spared having to deal with him again in the future. "[I]t's the guide's job to steer us down roads to complete certain relationships," says Bodine.[7]

This case suggests that certain coincidences may be given to us with the express purpose of misleading us about where a situation is headed, *if* that's the only way to get us in the position necessary for the accomplishment of our larger soul purposes. It may be unsettling to think of our spiritual guides lying to us, but there is a more comforting way to look at this story. It's one more piece of evidence that, as we saw in the chapter on destiny, we don't always have to know *why* things are happening in order for our life mission to be accomplished. If we are doing the best we can with the knowledge we've been given, we can trust that those who know even more than we do are working diligently behind the scenes to do the rest.

Clarificatory Coincidences

But what about cases when it seems like coincidences are telling us to do something that just feels *wrong*? In those cases, it's good to keep in mind that certain events of our lives can be given to us as tests.

For example, in her book *La Mort transfigurée*, Evelyne-Sarah Mercier describes a near-death experience in which a woman who, along with her husband, was about to be in a car accident suddenly found herself out of her body, watching the approaching accident in slow motion. She realized that "an immense Being, like an Angel" was there with her, and that he was waiting for something, waiting for her to figure something out. Suddenly, it came to her that her daughter would suffer terribly if she lost both of her parents at once, and so she asked if her husband might be spared. The being said to her, "Since you're not asking for anything for yourself, return, it's not time." She saw that he had been testing her, and that he was happy with her response.[8]

In another case, a woman named Mary Steffey came to psychic Laura Lynne Jackson wanting to know if she should adopt a child she was fostering, a girl named Aly. In particular, Steffey wanted to know if she would harm her biological daughter Mariah by doing so. Jackson told her, "The Other Side cannot advise you about Aly because the decision is part of your soul

---

[7] Interview with Echo Bodine, reported in Jenniffer Weigel, *Psychics, Healers, and Mediums: A Journalist, a Road Trip, and Voices from the Other Side* (Charlottesville, VA: Hampton Roads, 2017), 40.

[8] Evelyne-Sarah Mercier, *La Mort transfigurée: Recherches sur les expériences vécues aux approches de la mort* (Paris: Belfond, 1992). My translation.

test. It is yours to make. This is about you discovering your true path and purpose in life. What happens next will be decided by you."[9]

While these two stories don't deal with coincidences, I know firsthand that coincidences, too, can sometimes be tests. Several years ago, I had what at first seemed like a straightforward confirmation coincidence but was actually a test of my own inner knowledge and resolve. Back in 2010, I decided to leave my career as an academic philosopher. Since getting my PhD, I'd been teaching for two years on a postdoctoral fellowship at Brandeis University outside Boston, and even though I had all the credentials to have an excellent shot at a tenure-track position at a good university, as my time at Brandeis drew to a close, I realized I wasn't interested in applying for such a position. I agonized a fair amount over the decision, but ultimately, I knew that academia was not where I wanted to be. So, I left.

Some difficult events in the ensuing months made me wonder, however, if I had made the right choice. I had just enough doubt about it to be curious concerning what philosophy jobs were being advertised that year. It was just past the deadline for applying—tenure-track jobs only open for applications for a month or two each fall—but I figured that, if I looked at the advertisements and saw that none of the jobs would have been in locations that interested me, I would have excellent confirmation that I had made the right choice not to apply.

Well, when I looked at the ads, I discovered that there had been a position advertised in my home state of Virginia. Not only was it in the region of the state that most appealed to me, but the advertisement was for someone with precisely my area of specialization. What was more, when I looked closer, I saw that the deadline for this particular job was a month later than all the rest. Which meant that I still had time to apply. It seemed like a clear sign from the universe.

So, I updated my resume, wrote a new statement of research interests, and solicited new letters of recommendation. When I finished my application, I needed to send it to my alma mater, New York University, in order for them to insert the letters of recommendation and mail the whole packet on to the selection committee of this other institution. At this point, I realized that I had coincidentally already planned a trip to New York City the very weekend when I needed the application delivered to NYU. It seemed, again, like a clear sign from the universe.

So, I took my application materials to New York with me. But I didn't deliver them to NYU right away. I was in the city for three days, and I kept putting it off. On my last full day there, I was eating breakfast in a friend's apartment when I looked out his window to an office building that stood on

[9] Laura Lynne Jackson, *The Light Between Us: Stories from Heaven, Lessons for the Living* (New York: Spiegel & Grau, 2015), 103.

the other side of the narrow Manhattan street. I could see people sitting in their offices at computers, working away, and it made me think of the life I was signing up for in applying for this philosophy job, and not in a good way. It almost made me physically sick to think about dressing up and sitting in an office all day. And that's when I knew that I was not on the right track. Whatever the "signs" from the universe, I decided, I was *not* going to apply for this job.

When I went out on the town that morning, I left my packet of application materials safely on my friend's apartment floor. It is now eight years later, and I have not for a single moment regretted that decision.

The moral I took from this experience is that you should not trust "signs" over your gut. But here's a curious coda to the story. The evening after I made my decision not to submit my application, I went to dinner with my friend. I told him how I'd made my decision after looking at all those people in the office building across from his apartment. I told him, too, about how I'd recently been seeing a lot of the number "33," which I had started experiencing like a confirmation from the universe that I was not alone in my various life struggles. Well, my friend and I headed back to his apartment, and along the way he started pointing out to me various architectural landmarks. He pointed at a building designed by Philip Johnson, and I said, "That's the one you can see from your apartment, isn't it? That's the one I was looking at this morning."

"You're right," he said. "That's 33 Maiden Lane." Indeed, there was the number 33, written on a bronze plaque at the building's entrance. The fact that the address matched the number I had just been discussing with him as my confirmatory sign seemed like a clear confirmation that I had finally gotten the right message from all of the *previous* signs—that they had been sent, not to show me that I needed to go back to academia, but to help me see that I had no reason whatsoever to regret leaving, and that the ultimate confirmation of any decision *had to come from within myself.*

If there is one bit of wisdom I hope you will take from this book, it is that coincidences are never a good replacement for your own judgment. You should never allow a coincidence to make you think that what you feel and know in your heart is wrong. If anything, a coincidence is a catalyst for greater self-knowledge, for greater acquaintance with the contents of your own heart and mind.

I think it makes sense to refer to coincidences like the ones that almost led me to apply for another academic job as "clarificatory" coincidences. They don't in themselves clearly point the way to the right decision—in fact, they may clearly point in the opposite direction—but they set us up to be able to make the right decision on our own. They *clarify* our own ideas about the matter at hand.

As we'll see later in this chapter, there are strong parallels between the interpretation of coincidences and the interpretation of dreams, and I have a dream example that illustrates well this clarifying function. Some years after the incident related above, I was at another crossroads in my life, trying to decide if I ought to take some action or leave things as they were. One night, I had the following three dreams in a row.

> **Dream 1:** I see a missile taking off that is carrying an atom bomb to Japan at the end of World War II. I know that Japan has just surrendered, but it's too late: the bomb is going to fall anyway. I say to myself that it's terrible, that all these people are going to die for nothing. We don't need this nuclear bomb and all the destruction it will bring.
>
> **Dream 2:** A sort of military general tells me that it's up to me to decide if a nuclear bomb is necessary. It's a situation like at the end of World War II where it could save lives in the long term, but of course one can't ever be sure of the right decision. My husband is there, and I tell him that I'm surprised that this military man is letting me make this decision, since I don't have any military experience and I'm just a "kid."
>
> **Dream 3:** This dream is more straightforwardly a portrayal of my personal dilemma. I see that, if I am going to have the life I want, I will have to make a big change. If I don't make this change, my life will be colorless and boring, every day like the others. To avoid this, I will have to make the decision to leave my current situation. No one is going to do it for me. It's my decision, and it's scary.

I am in the habit of putting great trust in my dreams, but when I woke up from this last one, I had the unfamiliar feeling that my dreams had actually *lied* to me. I did not believe that, if I didn't extricate myself from my current situation, the rest of my life would be colorless and boring. That seemed like a vicious misrepresentation. But my dreams were normally so perceptive and accurate. Why would I have dreamt this thing that seemed so untrue?

It was sometime later that I realized that these dreams could only be rightly understood in connection with one another. I realized that they in fact offered me a striking mental triptych of my fears. In the first dream, unnecessary devastation was caused by the premature launching of an atomic missile. This was my fear related to doing something about my situation that unnecessarily caused great, explosive harm. In the third dream, my fear that my life would be colorless and boring if I *didn't* do anything was made very clear. In the dream in the middle, it was conveyed that the decision about whether to cause an explosion belonged to *me*, and that I felt unqualified to make the decision.

After realizing that these three dreams had to be analyzed together, I saw that none of the dreams was actually lying to me. They were all entirely accurate portraits of my own fears. I had just misunderstood their purpose. My dreams were making my fears clear to me so that I could look them square in the eye and see which of them were warranted and which were not. I came to see my feeling that the last dream was a lie as an indication that the fear it represented was unjustified. On the other hand, I felt that the fear represented by the first dream—the fear of wreaking unnecessary havoc—was much *more* justified. And, for that reason, I made the decision to stay in my situation and not make any big moves. Fortunately, I have not regretted that decision, either. And my subsequent life has proven to be far from boring!

Let's look now at a few more examples of coincidences that play a clarificatory role. Alan Vaughan tells the story of a time when the New York radio station WBAI had asked him for permission to broadcast a talk he'd given. Though he'd given them provisional permission, he debated with himself whether to call them back and tell them no, since the talk contained some information about another person that this person might not want on the airwaves. While walking down a New York street debating whether or not to call the station back, he spotted a pen on the sidewalk. When he picked it up, he discovered it had the initials WBAI printed on it. "That did it," he says. "I called the station and asked that the talk not be broadcast."[10]

But how clear was this sign, and how much did Vaughan read into it himself? What if he had taken the pen as a sign that WBAI was a *good* medium for the broadcasting of his talk and that he could trust them with it? The physical object itself didn't tell him what to do, one way or the other. The message he took from it was either created by his mind or received by his mind in some other way. In either case, the physical coincidence required interpretation. The decision remained Vaughan's. And I would say that the pen helped him to understand his own feelings on the matter: that he wanted to tell the station no.

Consider, too, what happened to Italian chef Massimo Bottura. While living in New York, he fell in love with a woman named Lara. When he was subsequently called back to work in Italy, he at first had to go alone but then, after some time apart from Lara, finally convinced her to join him there. Just a week after her arrival, however, Bottura received a call from famous French chef Alain Ducasse, offering him an amazing opportunity that would require

---

[10] Alan Vaughan, *Incredible Coincidence: The Baffling World of Synchronicity* (New York: J. B. Lippincott Company, 1979), 38.

him to *again* move away from Lara. We can hardly blame her for packing up and returning to the States when Bottura chose to accept Ducasse's offer.

It might seem as though Bottura's receiving this unbeatable job offer so soon after Lara's arrival in Italy was a sign that the couple's love was not meant to be. However, once Bottura had moved to Monaco to work with Ducasse, a further coincidence involving a broken lemon tart eventually led him to realize that leaving Lara had been a big mistake. When he realized this, he took a plane straight to Lara in New York. They subsequently married and moved back to Italy together, where they worked together to open the restaurant Osteria Francescana.[11]

Given the way things worked out, I think the coincidence in which Lara arrived in Italy and, just a week later, Bottura got the professional offer of a lifetime becomes best interpreted as a clarificatory coincidence. The job offer forced Bottura to make a difficult choice, and through the process of making this decision and then coming to the conclusion that he had made the "wrong" one, he came to a stronger understanding of his true feelings for Lara and was able to take steps to create an enduring relationship with her.

Robert H. Hopcke relates Bottura's story in his book *There Are No Accidents in Love and Relationships*, and he also includes in that volume another excellent example of a clarificatory coincidence: one that happened to Hopcke's friend Eddie. Eddie's father had walked out on his family many years ago, and Eddie, now an adult, hadn't seen him in a long time. One day, Eddie was driving past a town near where his parents grew up in West Virginia. On a whim, he decided to stop in to a general store to buy some gifts for his mother and sister, and while he was paying for them, he saw two old men playing checkers behind the counter. One of the men referred to the other as "Harless Hosey"—the name of Eddie's father.

It might seem that Eddie's running into his father was a sign that he and his father ought to reconcile. That would certainly be in keeping with some of the cases of unwelcome meetings we saw in the last chapter. But Eddie himself felt differently. "[I]t took me no more than a few moments," he says, "to conclude that, insofar as I had not thought of him, either in anger or in fear for such a long while, that no, I had no need for contact. And with that realization, I felt a deep calm come over me. I collected my change and walked out of the store."[12] In Eddie's mind, this meeting confirmed the internal peace he had already reached in relation to his father. And, as Hopcke points out, the calm Eddie felt in walking away seems a clear indication that his understanding of the situation was accurate.[13]

---

[11] Robert H. Hopcke, *There Are No Accidents in Love and Relationships: Meaningful Coincidences and the Stories of Our Families* (Asheville, NC: Chiron Publications, 2018), 71-74.

[12] Hopcke, *There Are No Accidents in Love and Relationships*, 153.

[13] Hopcke, *There Are No Accidents in Love and Relationships*, 155.

Jeff Vézina sums it up well:

> A synchronistic event is not a "sign" telling us to do something, like a traffic light that signals when we can cross the street. Synchronicity is rather a set of symbols and does not always imply a literal response to the impulse it creates. The meaning of a synchronistic symbol is...fleshed out through the experience resulting from the encounter, in conjunction with the unconscious issue in the process of resolving itself. The meaning of a symbol prompts us to act, to question ourselves and choose a direction, without, however, showing us the destination or the place where the answer can be found.[14]

Often coincidences are merely a way for our unconscious to get our attention. When we are not attentive to the messages we are receiving internally, these energies will frequently manifest themselves in the physical world as a way of making us take notice. Jung wrote that the importance of the *I Ching* divination method for the Chinese was "that the intelligent individual realizes his own thoughts,"[15] and I believe that is often the function of coincidences. In this materialistic age, it may sometimes happen that the only way for the deepest longings of our hearts to get the attention of our materially focused minds is through materializing those longings in physical phenomena. That may be the only way for our souls to get our minds to take them seriously. Of course, once the mind recognizes the spiritual power of these material events, it can be turned to interacting with the spiritual world more directly. And it appears that many coincidences, when they are genuine messages, are accompanied by supplementary telepathic information that helps the receiver to understand what's being conveyed. The goal of the coincidence is thus not to put the entire message into the physical world but to make us tune in and listen, to take seriously what our inner selves or our inner psychic senses have been trying to tell us for some time.

The role of coincidences as attention-getting devices is consistent with the experience often reported that, if we don't correctly interpret a coincidence, it will recur until we understand its message. One great example of this comes from author Sylvia Hart Wright. On the day that would have been her mother's 100th birthday, had she not died years before, Wright happened to walk outside her house to a spot on her property that she rarely visited. She discovered that, just on the other side of the property line, her neighbor had a blooming lilac bush that Wright had never noticed in her four years of living at that location. Lilacs were her mother's favorite flower, and she wondered whether this was just a coincidence or something more. Wright keeps a log of her seemingly paranormal experiences, but she is rather

[14] Vézina, 50-51.

[15] C. G. Jung, "Foreword to the 'I Ching'," in *The Collected Works*, vol. 11, *Psychology and Religion: West and East*, 2nd ed. (London: Routledge and Kegan Paul, 1969), 590.

selective about what she will write in it. Usually, before recording an experience, she writes herself a note on another piece of paper and thinks about it for a while. This case was no different. She wrote on a Post-it, "On mom's 100th birthday, discovered lilacs around back." Eventually, Wright decided it was not a very impressive event and threw the Post-it in the trash.

Exactly a year later, however, Wright remembered the lilacs, and she went to see if they were blooming again on the same date. They were not. However, something else rather incredible caught her eye. "[O]n my desk, in plain sight, was that yellow Post-it," she says. "*That yellow Post-it that I'd thrown away.*" This reappearance of the discarded note immediately reminded Wright of her mother, who had made a habit of checking her family's wastebaskets just to make sure no one had thrown away anything important. Clearly Wright's mother thought the lilac incident deserved to be entered into her log, and who was Wright to argue?[16]

My own experiences, as well as those of others I've read about, also support the idea that coincidences will recur if we don't get the message the first time. Psychic Carol Dryer reports that the same thing happens with images she receives in her psychic readings. She says, "If I haven't explained it correctly, it doesn't go away. It just stays in the energy field. But once I've told the person everything they need to know about a particular image, it begins to dissolve and disappear."[17] Dryer understands the psychic images she receives in readings as communications from her clients' unconscious minds. Paying attention to persistent coincidences in our lives can be similar to doing psychic readings for ourselves. But, again, the goal of these readings is not to give us all the "answers" to life or to tell us what we should do in a specific situation. Psychic Laura Lynne Jackson emphasizes that it's not her role to dispense advice. She says, "The Other Side sends us signs and signals that help us make the right decisions for ourselves."[18]

Television medium Theresa Caputo says she's been told by Spirit that

> the primary reason [for coincidences] is that Spirit's moving the chess pieces to create a situation that grabs your attention and will somehow improve your life, keep you safe, or make your day a little easier. … Spirit tells me there's a second reason coincidences exist, which is to teach you how to become more in tune with your intuition and better judgment. They encourage you to admit that you're connected to something much bigger than yourself. When a coincidence occurs, you might not realize

---

[16] Sylvia Hart Wright, *When Spirits Come Calling: The Open-Minded Skeptic's Guide to After-Death Contacts* (Nevada City, CA: Blue Dolphin Publishing, 2002), 209-10.
[17] Private communication with Michael Talbot, November 13, 1988, reported in Michael Talbot, *The Holographic Universe: The Revolutionary Theory of Reality* (New York: Harper Perennial, 1991, 1992, 2011), 182.
[18] Jackson, 97.

> it, but you have to respond to an instinctual nudge to think about or do something and then participate in how the coincidence comes together.[19]

The idea of *participation* in the coincidence—and particularly in the creation of its meaning—is crucial.

Consider a couple more examples of coincidences that clearly reflect the preoccupations of those who experience them but that don't appear to give any clear guidance as to the proper way forward. Joachim Soulières relates the story of Adrien, a young Frenchman living in the south of France who was romantically involved with a woman in Paris, Stéphanie. Their long-distance relationship was not going well, and Adrien suspected Stéphanie of seeing one of their mutual friends on the side. When he mentioned this to her, she wanted to break up, but when he went back home, all he could think about was being near her again. One day, he had 10 minutes to kill in his apartment and felt a sudden impulse to turn on the television, which he was not in the habit of watching. It happened that those 10 minutes were dedicated to the show *Expression directe*, and the show that day included video footage of the building where Stéphanie lived in Paris, with its highly recognizable courtyard.[20] So Adrien got his wish of being "near" Stéphanie, though not in the way he'd hoped for.

One could see how Adrien might have taken this coincidence as a sign that he was meant to be with Stéphanie, that the universe was working to bring them closer. The coincidence did in fact prompt him to call her, but over the course of time, he distanced himself from this woman and found a new, happy relationship. His experience of this coincidence thus seems to have been catalyzing, but not in any direct way. Interpreting its meaning required Adrien to use his own judgment and intuition.

Psychiatrist Dr. Judith Orloff tells a similar story from her own life. At the time of these events, her boyfriend had recently left her for someone else, but she was obsessively clinging to the hope that they would get back together again. She knew this state of mind wasn't good for her, so she eventually asked for a dream to guide her out of this impasse. In the middle of the night, she woke up with a phone number in her head. This being a rather unusual occurrence, she scribbled the number down and then, the next morning, gave it a call. "Together Again Productions. Can I help you?" said the woman on the other end of the line. Orloff found this fairly amusing and asked for details about what "Together Again Productions" did. The receptionist replied that they were television producers. "We make 'Movies of the Week.'" It was all Orloff could do not to burst out laughing right there on the phone. She says she took this coincidence as "a personal message to

---

[19] Theresa Caputo with Kristina Grish, *Good Grief: Heal Your Soul, Honor Your Loved Ones, and Learn to Live Again* (New York: Atria, 2017), 86.

[20] Joachim Soulières, *Les coïncidences* (Paris: Dervy, 2012), 9-11.

lighten up…[and] go on with my life."[21] But I hope it's clear that it took a fair amount of interpretation on Orloff's part to get from "Together Again Productions" to the message that she needed to stop taking things so seriously. This was not a message contained in the coincidence itself but a thought that was *catalyzed* by her experience of the coincidence.

At the same time, it seems to be the case that the harder a person has worked to try and resolve a question on their own, the more likely it is that a coincidence or other psychic occurrence will clearly and unambiguously point them in the right direction. As psychic Aron Abrahamsen says,

> If the need is great—a person is in deep inner turmoil over something, say, and has done everything they can before turning to the psychic—why, then, the answer is usually succinct and to the point. … If the need, however, is only to satisfy curiosity, or the motive is selfish, or they have *not* done everything they can at their end…well, if that is the case, the answer may be long or clouded.[22]

Similar statements can be found with regard to all sorts of paranormal phenomena. French journalist Philippe Ragueneau says about asking his deceased son to find lost objects for him, "In the end, it had almost become a game, but a game where cheating was not permitted. I could only call my son to the rescue after having searched hard on my own."[23] Joel Martin and Patricia Romanowski, authors of the book on after-death communication *Love Beyond Life*, write, "We do not think it is a coincidence that those who had the most realistic attitudes about what their communications could and could not help them achieve here [on earth] also had a greater number of intense experiences."[24] Dr. Roderick Main writes about the *I Ching*, "It is often stated…that when one consults the *I Ching* it should only be concerning matters that really are important to one and that have already defeated one's best efforts to deal with them by normal means."[25] And, finally, with regard to coincidences, SQuire Rushnell says, "When we carry ourselves as far as we

---

[21] Judith Orloff, *Second Sight: An Intuitive Psychiatrist Tells Her Extraordinary Story and Shows You How to Tap Your Own Inner Wisdom*, rev. ed. (New York: Three Rivers Press, 2000), 247.

[22] Stephan A. Schwartz, *The Secret Vaults of Time: Psychic Archaeology and the Quest for Man's Beginnings*, (New York: Grosset & Dunlap, 1978), 300-1.

[23] Philippe Ragueneau, *L'autre côté de la vie: Un message d'espoir et d'amour pour ceux qui ont perdu un proche* (Paris: Editions du Rocher, Pocket, 1995, 1997, 2001), 94-95. My translation.

[24] Joel Martin and Patricia Romanowski, *Love Beyond Life: The Healing Power of After-Death Communication* (New York: Harper, 1997), 18.

[25] Roderick Main, *Revelations of Chance: Synchronicity as Spiritual Experience* (Albany, NY: State University of New York Press, 2007), 148.

can and feel we can go no further, that's when we should be on the lookout for a God Wink."[26]

As you can see, a vast number of sources agree that whatever intelligence lies behind psychic phenomena, it is not there to help us avoid doing work, whether that work is physical, intellectual, emotional, or spiritual. Rather, psychic processes serve to enhance the efficacy of the work we are already doing, and the clarity of their messages is enhanced when we have already done everything we can to solve the problem ourselves. Psychic processes, including coincidences, are never an easy way out. In fact, if we attempt to avoid the hard work of reflection and struggle, it can cause us to misinterpret coincidences, or any other nudges we receive from our intuition. Our minds are the lens through which all psychic messages are filtered, and if the lens is smudged or cloudy, the message will be as well.

Dr. Richard Tarnas makes a very similar point in his discussion of synchronicity in *Cosmos and Psyche*. He writes,

> A painstaking cultivation of self-knowledge must be undertaken to avoid succumbing to mere projection. Discriminating such events requires a self-critical awareness of unconscious tendencies towards narcissistic distortion by which random or peripheral events are continually transformed into signs of an egocentric universe. No less crucial is the development and balanced interplay of multiple faculties of cognition—empirical, rational, emotional, relational, intuitive, symbolic. A capacity for acute yet balanced discernment has to be forged, founded not only on an alertness to meaningful pattern but also on a disciplined mindfulness of the larger whole within which the individual self seeks orientation.[27]

Clearly, interacting with coincidences and other psychic processes is not an escape for the lazy. Being lazy about coincidence interpretation results in being misled, because psychic phenomena tend to call us *beyond* our current capacities. They are not easier ways of doing what we could do by our own intellect. They are a way of going beyond what the intellect is capable of achieving, and thus they are not for the faint of heart. Coincidences push us to be more in touch with ourselves and the rest of the world than we currently are. That's not a comfortable process for many of us, and it requires a great deal of energy and discernment.

Because of the way coincidences so often push us beyond our current capacities, having the opinion of another person can often be helpful in the

---

[26] SQuire Rushnell, *When God Winks: How the Power of Coincidence Guides Your Life* (New York: Atria, 2001), 17.
[27] Richard Tarnas, *Cosmos and Psyche: Intimations of a New World View* (New York: Plume, 2006, May 2007), 55.

interpretation process. Dr. Victor Mansfield makes this point in drawing a parallel with dream interpretation. He writes,

> interpreting a synchronistic experience is at least as difficult as interpreting a big dream. Interpreting our own dreams is difficult because they are often expressing a major unconscious compensation and therefore the interpreter, the ego that needs the compensation, is in the worst position to make the interpretation. Even if the interpretation is simple and straightforward our lopsidedness prevents us from seeing the truth and instead we often fashion an incorrect interpretation based on our psychological problems. ... Not only can we impose meaning on events when none exists, but we are predisposed to make the wrong interpretations even when genuine meaning is manifesting in a synchronicity experience.[28]

I agree with Mansfield that a second opinion, especially when it is that of a close friend or therapist who knows us well, can help us see messages that are clearly conveyed by our coincidence experiences but that our conscious minds are blind to.

At the same time, I don't agree with Mansfield that we are in the *worst* position to interpret our own coincidences. Coincidences, like dreams, are extremely personal. It is not easy for someone else to understand their full meaning and impact, because that meaning and impact is so closely tied to the inner mental state of the person they are intended to reach. I agree with French writer Jean Prieur when he says that people have trouble appreciating the significance of a sign that comes to someone else because "[t]hey don't know the preoccupation, the questioning to which it's responding."[29] For that reason, if you have a clear-minded conviction about the meaning of a coincidence you've experienced, don't let the skepticism of others dissuade you from that conviction.

An excellent example of the importance of personal intuition in coincidence interpretation comes from the life of journalist Tom Shroder. He describes a cross-country road trip that he and a friend took after college. They drove together for weeks, during which they talked almost continually about women and related life decisions. Shroder had two different women in his life, each of whom represented a different future path for his life and each of whom he came to associate with a different song over the course of the road trip. The safe, predictable woman was associated with Bob Dylan's "Shelter from the Storm," and the riskier, more adventuresome lady with Bruce Springsteen's "She's the One."

---

[28] Victor Mansfield, *Synchronicity, Science, and Soul-Making* (Chicago: Open Court, 1995), 232.

[29] Jean Prieur, *Les morts ont donné signe de vie* (Paris: Sorlot et Lanore, 1990). My translation.

One night, Shroder and his buddy were hiking out West, about an hour by car from the Grand Canyon, when Shroder's need to choose between these women began to increasingly obsess him. In fact, it came to seem to him that his decision between these women also had implications for the more immediate choice of what he and his friend were going to do that very night. Were they going to stay in the nice empty campground they'd found, visit the Grand Canyon the next day, and then drive on to Los Angeles as they'd long been planning to do? Or should they take the riskier, more adventuresome path of driving to Mexico, with no idea what might happen or what they might do there? They discussed the question for hours until Shroder felt his head was about to explode. By this time, they were at their campsite. "I'm not doing this anymore," Shroder suddenly announced. "I'm just going to wait for a sign."

"Absolutely no more than sixty seconds later," says Shroder,

> we heard the faraway sound of a car engine moving through the night. … Finally, we could see that it was a van, coming down the dirt path. Remember, the campground was utterly deserted. But the van passed by the first circle, then the second, then it turned in to ours and came around all the way to the end, stopping at the very next site. … The side door of the van slid open…and the sound slapped us, the wailing voice, the grinding guitars, the pounding keyboard. Springsteen. "She's the One."[30]

It seemed as though Shroder had gotten exactly what he'd asked for: a sign as to what he ought to do. And it appeared to be telling him to choose the risky path. Or, at least, it seemed that way to Shroder's friend. Shroder himself had the deep conviction that the meaning of this coincidence was something completely different. Shroder explains,

> It was instantly clear to me that this inexpressibly absurd coincidence was in no way a practical guide to which set of specific decisions I should make. It was too *weird* for that, at once too immense and too trivial. I had the intense certainty that the universe was laughing at me, at my self-involvement, and the oddest thing happened: The anxiety I felt simply vanished.[31]

It took Shroder years to figure out exactly what he *did* think the significance of this coincidence was, but in the end, he concluded that its primary purpose was to let him in on the fact that there was much more to the world than he'd previously thought. As we saw in Chapter 11, coincidences often lead people to a new appreciation of the grandeur of the universe and their place within it. Shroder was asking for help in making an

---

[30] Shroder, 236.

[31] Shroder, 237.

agonizing decision, and though it looked to his friend like he'd received clear direction, Shroder realized that the message was much more profound than telling him which girl to choose or whether or not to drive to Mexico. This coincidence was letting him know that there was no need for him to fear the outcome of this decision—or any other—because his fate was bound up with much larger forces consciously directing the trajectory of the universe.

Medical intuitive Caroline Myss has some very insightful things to say about the nature of the intuitive guidance that fills our lives. She says that, when she first started teaching workshops on this topic, she discovered that most people already had access to their intuition but were confused about the purpose it served. They thought intuition had to do with seeing the future in a way that would allow them to improve their lives in a material fashion. However, Myss emphasizes that following one's intuition doesn't mean being led by the hand to the promised land. Rather, it requires having the self-confidence to make hard choices. "So long as we use comfort and security as our criteria of success," says Myss, "we will fear our own intuitive guidance because by its very nature it directs us into new cycles of learning that are sometimes uncomfortable."[32]

Everything that Myss says here about intuitive guidance is directly applicable to the guidance offered by coincidences. Coincidences offer us information that challenges and stretches us, and it is often uncomfortable to acknowledge that information. Myss points out that it's a lot easier to say we don't know what to do than to acknowledge that we *do* know, but are too scared to do anything about it.[33]

Author and veteran out-of-body experiencer Graham Nicholls writes about the difficulty—and necessity—of following one's intuition. He says,

> It's hard to imagine a spiritual life, a person who has truly gained some insight into the joys and hardships of existence who had not followed these moments of heightened insight. For many these changes come when they finally submit to an idea that through fear or egotistical pride they had resisted for years. They give themselves to what they know to be right even though it may be hard or even painful. The result can be an overwhelming sense of emotion; it may even seem negative or too much to handle when it first begins to arise. These...are the initiations, the changes of consciousness that draw you towards a life that can be truly fulfilling or even world changing.[34]

---

[32] Caroline Myss, *Anatomy of the Spirit: The Seven Stages of Power and Healing* (New York: Three Rivers Press, 1996), 181.
[33] Myss, *Anatomy of the Spirit*, 230.
[34] Graham Nicholls, *Avenues of the Human Spirit* (Winchester, UK: O-Books, 2011), 81-82.

Psychiatrist Dr. M. Scott Peck believes that most people are not equal to this enormous task. "As soon as they realize that they will ultimately be required by the process of psychotherapy to assume total responsibility for their condition and its cure," he says, "most patients, no matter how eager for therapy they initially appeared to be, will drop out. They choose rather to be sick and have the gods to blame than to be well with no one to blame ever again."[35]

This may be one reason that many people prefer to believe that they could not be the source of their own coincidences. Projecting their thoughts and feelings onto other entities may actually be helpful at first, enabling them to keep their intuitive insights at a distance until they are comfortable taking personal responsibility for them. At this stage, they can still learn from the unconscious, even if they are not yet willing to identify with it. But, ultimately, there will come a time when they can only continue their growth by acknowledging that signs can only mean for them what they *choose* for them to mean. "Those who are the closest to grace are the most aware of the mysterious character of the gift they have been given," writes Peck. "… The paradox that we both choose grace and are chosen by grace is the essence of the phenomenon of serendipity."[36] We choose our coincidences just as much as our coincidences choose us.

Often, the course of action we choose is less important than the reason we choose it. Specifically, are we choosing out of faith in the goodness and beauty of our choice, or are we choosing out of fear of what will happen to us if we do otherwise? Myss affirms that "any choice made from faith has the full power of heaven behind it."[37] Among other things, I believe this means that, when we choose what feels authentic to us, that act of choice rallies supernatural forces to aid in its fulfillment. Often these supernatural forces manifest as coincidences coming to our aid.

Near-death experiencer Anita Moorjani says, "Everything that seemingly happens externally is occurring in order to trigger something within us, to expand us and take us back to who we truly are."[38] When we find ourselves continually frustrated in our activities—perhaps at the mercy of many "negative" coincidences—it can be useful to reflect on whether those activities are in alignment with our deeper self who is trying to come forth. Moorjani writes,

---

[35] M. Scott Peck, *The Road Less Traveled: A New Psychology of Love, Traditional Values and Spiritual Growth* (New York: Simon & Schuster, 1978), 295.
[36] Peck, *The Road Less Traveled*, 307.
[37] Myss, *Anatomy of the Spirit*, 132-3.
[38] Anita Moorjani, *Dying to Be Me: My Journey from Cancer, to Near Death, to True Healing* (Carlsbad, CA: Hay House, 2012), 144.

> Sometimes, when I had a lot to do and things were stressful, I was accused of wasting time if I took a break to get centered. But if I tried to resolve things purely on the physical level, I knew it would be slow going. To this day, it still feels like walking through molasses, and dealing with issues only in this way causes me great frustration and increases my stress levels.
>
> However, I discovered that if I take time out and reclaim my center, regardless of what people around me think, many of the primary stumbling blocks disappear once I'm aware of my connection to the Whole and feeling calm and happy. I receive a lot of clarity during those sessions, and purely by staying centered, many of the remaining challenges just fall away. I've found this to be a much more effective way of dealing with my life than solely dealing with it from the external.[39]

Saying that following one's inner guidance will help rally the forces of the universe to one's cause is not to say, however, that those who follow their intuition don't encounter obstacles. Any honest self-help author will acknowledge that making big life changes in order to follow your heart is going to lead to some difficult times. One author who is particularly emphatic about this is Dr. Brené Brown. She spends the second chapter of her 2015 bestseller *Rising Strong* describing how, no matter how much people learn about the process of growing—whether creatively, spiritually, or in some other way—it never exempts them from going through a dark period before the dawn. Anytime we decide to go out on a limb and attempt something new, after a period of initial excitement and conviction that we're on the right path, we'll hit a dark night of the soul: what Brown refers to as "Day 2" of the metaphorical three-day journey. It doesn't matter who you are or how experienced you are, you will always hit a period where you feel lost, fearful, uncertain, and generally miserable—until you eventually come out on the other side and see the magnificence that your willingness to sit in the discomfort has wrought.[40]

Sometimes, seeing the benefits of listening to your intuition takes a very long time. But keep in mind that this is the scale on which your deeper self is working. Your deepest self's deepest goals go far beyond worldly considerations like getting a good job, a nice house, and a decent spouse. In fact, you may have to forgo those things in order to become what your deepest self wants you to become. And you may not see the reward for those sacrifices for quite a long time.

Consider what life coach and synchronicity aficionada Martha Beck discovered while working as a research assistant at Harvard Business School

---

[39] Moorjani, 116.

[40] Brené Brown, *Rising Strong: How the Ability to Reset Transforms the Way We Live, Love, Parent, and Lead* (New York: Random House, 2015).

in the 1980s. She analyzed a study that had followed 125 HBS graduates over time and was amazed to find that

> [t]he guys (they were all guys) who'd gotten great jobs right out of business school were struggling by the 1980s; they felt trapped and unfulfilled. The subjects who had seemed a little lost at first, who had wandered around and eventually created their own small companies, were thriving financially and psychologically.
>
> "Wow," I thought as I read the data, "this is crazy!" The train-track career boys were actually less successful than those who were driving their lives more erratically and independently, like cars.[41]

The lesson is that those who listen to their intuition risk appearing a little crazy to people who judge their actions from a short-sighted, purely exterior point of view. The map to a fulfilling life generally doesn't look like a straight line. The inner guidance that nudges us off the beaten path for frequent detours is not easy to explain or justify to others. But, in the end, we are much more likely to have lived a meaningful, fulfilling life if we've paid attention to that voice. Coincidences are often outward manifestations of that inner voice, but we shouldn't forget that they can only be adequately interpreted when we have the courage to look at ourselves and our situation with the utmost honesty and to act according to what we find.

Parallels with Dream Interpretation

As I've already mentioned more than once, coincidence interpretation has many parallels with dream interpretation. For this reason, I think it will be useful to spend some time examining what dreams can teach us about coincidences.

Evidence for an Intimate Connection Between Dreams and Coincidences

One demonstration of the intimate connection between dreams and coincidences is the fact that a dream frequently constitutes one prong of a coincidence experience. For instance, in his book *Revelations of Chance*, Dr. Roderick Main contrasts the experiences of two real-life men who each experienced a long series of meaningful coincidences. One of them, Thornton, tended to receive the symbolic content first in dreams and then saw them repeated in the physical world. The other, Plaskett, first received the content in the physical world and only later in dreams. Main writes,

---

[41] Martha Beck, *Finding Your Way in a Wild New World: Reclaim Your True Nature to Create the Life You Want* (New York: Atria, 2012), 235.

> almost all of the essential spiritual content of Thornton's experiences had already been conveyed to him by his purely inner experiences (dreams, visions, and so forth). The subsequent development of these into synchronicities served primarily to intensify them and render them more actual, gripping, and effective. With Plaskett's experiences, by contrast, it was usually within the synchronicities themselves that the spiritually relevant content first appeared.[42]

Another excellent example of the interconnection between dreams and coincidences comes from a woman I know who experienced a long series of dreams and coincidences involving babies. The series began with a dream in which this woman, who had no children in real life, was interacting with a baby that she knew was hers, a baby whose name seemed to be Olivia. Some months after having this dream, she reread the account of it that she'd recorded in her diary, and then, on that very same afternoon, she received in the mail a card advertising a touch-activated baby doll named Olivia. In large script, the advertisement read, "Olivia's Gentle Touch."

This woman's baby dreams continued for a few more months, and then she encountered another strange coincidence. She received an email from Amazon.com that said, "A gift is on its way," and displayed a picture of a crawling baby. The email said that someone had recently purchased a gift for her from her baby registry. The only thing was, she didn't have a baby registry and never had. A day or two later, she received an apology note from Amazon saying that the email had been sent in error.

About six months after that, she had another baby-related dream, about going to an obstetrician's office. Ten days later, she was leaving a restaurant when a man she didn't know suddenly asked her, "Are you Olivia's mother?" She told him no but couldn't help being struck by the strongly coincidental nature of the question and wondering if, one day, she would in fact be the mother of a little girl named Olivia.

This woman says she has not been pregnant at any point since these events occurred, but the last of these coincidences occurred only about a year before this book went to press. In any case, whether these dreams and coincidences are reflective of an actual future child this woman will have or merely of an important dynamic in this woman's psychology, her case makes it very clear that the same unconscious forces that are at work in forming our dreams are also at work shaping the coincidences of our waking life.

For this reason, waking reality may be usefully understood as a long-running collective dream. If the waking world seems to reflect our mental life less consistently than dreams do, this could be because it's being affected by the thoughts of so many different people all at once. In a "sleeping" dream,

---

[42] Main, 114.

the connection between your own thoughts and feelings and what you see and hear and feel is immediate and straightforward. In our "waking" dream, *everybody's* thoughts and feelings affect what happens, so the influence of your own personal thoughts and feelings can seem minimal to nonexistent.

Experienced lucid dreamer Robert Waggoner comments that the principles he has observed to be operative in the creation of lucid dreams also appear to have clear application to the way the waking world is created.[43] Anyone who's spent time studying Eastern philosophy is familiar with the Hindu idea that the physical world is "*maya*," that is, an illusion. Waggoner, however, cites the Sanskrit scholar Wendy Doniger O'Flaherty's assertion that the Sanskrit word *maya* "first meant making something that was not there before."[44] O'Flaherty explains, "To say that the universe is an illusion (maya) is not to say that it is unreal; it is to say, instead, that it is not what it seems to be, that it is something constantly being *made*."[45] I believe that coincidences are events in which this making—this link between the fabrication of dreams and the fabrication of reality—becomes more apparent. And, because the basic process seems to be similar in both dreams and waking life, it makes sense that the principles of dream interpretation could be helpful in interpreting coincidences—those dream-like events that happen in real life.

What is more, examples throughout this book indicate that dreams are not quite the isolated products of our own psyche that we often think they are, and that even "sleeping" dreams can be shared with other people. The evidence suggests that the involvement of others in the creation of our experiences comes in degrees and that there is an entire spectrum that includes:

- dreams that are purely our own imagination,
- dreams that involve psychic information coming from others,
- dreams in which two or more people participate in the creation and/or perception of the world they experience,
- out-of-body experiences and hypnotic experiences in which *most* elements are taken from waking life but in which some seem to be imagination,[46] and

---

[43] Robert Waggoner, *Lucid Dreaming: Gateway to the Inner Self* (Needham, MA: Moment Point Press, 2009), 124.
[44] Wendy Doniger O'Flaherty, *Dreams, Illusion, and Other Realities* (Chicago: University of Chicago Press, 1984), 118.
[45] O'Flaherty, 119.
[46] For example, Waggoner has noticed that, in his out-of-body experiences, he sometimes perceives a reality that differs in minor ways from the usual one, generally in ways that respond to a subconscious desire of his. This has led him to conceptualize his OBEs as something like "reality plus one" (Waggoner, 27-28).

- the dream of waking life in which we all participate, more or less consciously.

The principle of thought taking form is the same in all these cases, but it tends to be mostly hidden in the last one, because of the vast numbers of people whose thoughts are there combined. Only rarely do we become aware of the process underlying the creation of waking reality, when the power of our thoughts and feelings rises above the noise created by those of others and allows us to glimpse a particularly strong coincidence between our thoughts and the "external" world.

Still more evidence for the strong connection between dreaming and waking life comes from cases in which dream events spill over into "real" life. One striking example is related by minister Jeremy Taylor and happened to someone who was participating in dream work with him. This young man was having a dream that he was at a party in a penthouse in the city when suddenly he realized that it was only a dream and that his alarm clock would soon be waking him up. He explained this to a woman who was sitting in his lap, emphasizing to her that none of this was real. "You mean you think I'm not real?" the woman asked him. When he replied in the affirmative, she got very annoyed. "I'll show you who's real or not!" she said, and rubbed her lit cigarette butt into the back of his right hand. He immediately woke up. The highly curious thing was that, even after waking, he could still feel the pain from the burn. When he turned on the light, he saw that his right hand had a cigarette-sized burn on it, along with what appeared to be some cigarette ash.[47]

Recall, too, the case reported in Chapter 8 in which Dr. Jacques Emmanuel Moussounga had a dream of a snake biting his heels, only to find on waking that he had two holes in his heels and his legs were becoming progressively immobilized by what was apparently poison.

While the previous two cases could possibly be explained as psychosomatic manifestations of the dreamer's own thoughts or fears (see the discussion of stigmata in the section of Chapter 6 titled "More Exotic Examples of PK"), this next case requires a different explanation, as it involves effects on an external object. French medium Geneviève Delpech relates this event that happened to her personally:

> I had brought back from a trip to Egypt a slave bracelet, which is worn on the ankles, with little bells.
>
> One night, while deeply asleep—I had put the bracelet on my night table—I have a dream. I see a long, slender hand—that I think is the hand

---

[47] Jeremy Taylor, *Dream Work: Techniques for Discovering the Creative Power in Dreams* (Ramsey, NJ: Paulist Press, 1983), 215.

> of a being of light—catch the bracelet and crush it, seemingly forbidding me to wear it. When I woke up, the jewelry was indeed crushed....[48]

A more positive example of dream carryover into waking life comes from the book *Love Beyond Life*. A woman was staying in her father's home after he had gone into the hospital with some serious health issues. In a dream one night, she saw her father enter the room where she was sleeping. He came to her and tucked her in, then closed the door as he left. When she woke up, she found that her bed covers were just as her father had put them in her dream, not at all the way she'd left them the night before. What was more, the bedroom door—which she always left open—was now closed. She was still reflecting on all this when the call came that her father had died overnight.[49]

It's natural to ask whether this woman was really dreaming or whether she may have actually been awake when she perceived her father's apparition and just assumed, based on the unexpected nature of this perception, that it must have been a dream. Either way, the connection between the two states seems to have been so close in this case as to make them practically indistinguishable.

Another case that appears in *Love Beyond Life* is one of the most interesting I've ever encountered in all my readings on parapsychology. In this case, a woman dreamt of an event that would take place the next morning, but in her dream, she was able to perceive more of the paranormal aspects of the event than she was when she experienced it in waking life.

What happened in waking life was that this woman passed her grandmother's room and heard her grandmother calling out to several of her deceased loved ones. The grandmother appeared to be pointing to some invisible figures at the foot of her bed, and the dog "began to jump up and sniff the air as if she were greeting people." This sort of interaction with deceased loved ones is not uncommon just before a person dies, and in fact the grandmother passed away from a heart attack three days later. What was unusual in this case was that, the night before this deathbed vision, the granddaughter had had a dream in which she witnessed precisely the same scene, except that, in her dream, she was able to see and identify the people gathered around her grandmother's bed.[50]

The only other case I've encountered of a dream in which someone saw the paranormal elements of a scene that later proved to be real is in Dr. David Ryback's book *Dreams That Come True*. In that case, the dreamer dreamt of a funeral home in which a wake was taking place. The dreamer saw a man

---

[48] Geneviève Delpech, *Le don d'ailleurs: Autobiographie d'une médium* (Paris: Pygmalion, J'ai Lu, 2015), 161.
[49] Martin and Romanowski, 33.
[50] Martin and Romanowski, 120-2.

floating above the scene, trying to get the attention of the people in the room. At the time of the dream, the dreamer had no idea who this man was. However, he later learned that his friend Marjorie's father had died and that the night of the dream was the last night of her father's wake. Furthermore, Marjorie's mother confessed that, at the wake, she had seen Marjorie's father floating above the coffin.[51]

Still other accounts of dream carryover involve healing from physical ailments. Dr. Judith Orloff recounts a case in which a woman's billiard ball-sized lipoma disappeared overnight when she had a dream of a three-foot hypodermic needle sucking a white, watery liquid out of it.[52] Other cases can be found in an online abstract for a talk that E. W. Kellogg III gave at the Association for the Study of Dreams Conference in Santa Cruz in July 1999, including a case in which a woman's healing efforts in a lucid dream apparently caused her six centimeter-wide plantar warts to turn black and fall off.[53] Some cases of dream healing involving the apparent intervention of Christian saints can be found in Dr. Jacalyn Duffin's 2009 book *Medical Miracles*.[54]

Jungian analyst Robert A. Johnson has advised that the connection between dreams and waking reality can be facilitated if we respond to our dreams in some concrete, "real-world" manner. He gives the example of a woman who dreamt of a monastery. After acknowledging this dream with a specially designed ritual, she immediately encountered the monastery in real life and developed an external connection to it very like the peaceful inner connection she had had in her dream.[55] "If we learn to live this way," writes Johnson, "we find that all our dreams manifest both inwardly and outwardly. It is only our unawareness that prevents us from seeing the subtle connections."[56]

Symbolism

While the dreams so far described have been primarily literal ones and their connections to waking life have been literal as well, the frequently

---

[51] David Ryback with Letitia Sweitzer, *Dreams That Come True: Their Psychic and Transforming Powers* (New York: Doubleday, 1988), 76-77.
[52] Orloff, 238-9.
[53] E. W. Kellogg III, "Lucid Dream Healing Experiences: Firsthand Accounts," abstract, 1999 ASD Conference, Santa Cruz, CA. Accessible at: https://www.asdreams.org/documents/1999_kellogg_lucid-healing.htm.
[54] Jacalyn Duffin, *Medical Miracles: Doctors, Saints, and Healing in the Modern World* (New York: Oxford University Press, 2009), 168-73.
[55] Robert A. Johnson, *Inner Work: Using Dreams and Active Imagination for Personal Growth* (New York: HarperOne, 1989), 105-7.
[56] Johnson, 107.

symbolic nature of dreams can also find its way into waking reality. Author and dream worker Robert Moss advises that "we need to take dreams more literally and the events of waking life more symbolically."[57] Moss provides the very succinct example in which, just before a stock market crash, he almost lost his wallet down an airplane toilet—a wallet that happened to contain checks from his brokerage account. Moss says that, if this had happened to him in a dream, he would have described that dream's message as something like, "If you're not careful, your stock market investments will go down the toilet."[58]

Jeff Vézina also recounts some symbolic coincidences. For instance, he tells how, at the moment when he first saw his girlfriend Elisabeth, a flock of geese flew across the sky. In Russia, Siberia, and central Asia, the goose represents the desired, chosen woman. Geese are also associated with families with lots of children. As it turned out, disagreement over the idea of having many children was the primary source of his relationship problems with Elisabeth and the reason they eventually split up. They decided to stay friends, however, and on their first outing as "just friends," they saw a movie in which the last scene showed a huge flock of geese crossing the sky.[59]

Vézina also tells the story of a man named Louis who dreamt several times that his girlfriend was a snake biting him in the stomach. She was a very dependent person, but he had trouble putting an end to the relationship. While he was still seeing her, he had a medical exam that revealed he had a tapeworm that was causing him considerable health trouble. At the same time, he kept breaking up and getting back together with this woman. Finally, after a particularly difficult breakup with her, he passed the head of the tapeworm in his stool. And he never heard from the girlfriend again.[60]

Recall, too, the experience recounted in the chapter "Spiritual Growth" in which a woman found in her pocketbook a pearl ring from her childhood that had no business being there. As a child, she had been scolded for trading this pearl ring to a classmate for a cheap ring from a bubble gum machine, and she quickly realized that its appearance now symbolized the error of a decision she was considering making to abandon a long-term relationship for a fling. She says, "As I retrieved the ring, it was instantaneously clear to me that if I were to have this affair, I was going to once again trade my pearl for the flashy imitation."[61]

---

[57] Robert Moss, *Dreaming True: How to Dream Your Future and Change Your Life for the Better* (New York: Pocket Books, 2000), 43.
[58] Robert Moss, *The Three "Only" Things: Tapping the Power of Dreams, Coincidence & Imagination* (Novato, CA: New World Library, 2007), 115.
[59] Vézina, 55-56.
[60] Vézina, 57.
[61] Mansfield, 38-39.

The theme of "throwing pearls before swine" appears in another jewelry-related coincidence as well. Elise and Jimmy were driving and having a discussion about their troubled marriage when they pulled into the parking lot of a country store. Elise was well acquainted with mediumistic encounters but was nevertheless quite surprised when they were sitting in the Jeep and Jimmy's deceased grandfather suddenly started pinching her ear, the way he used to do to Jimmy when he was young. Apparently, this was just to get her attention, as the grandfather stopped as soon as Elise asked him to. Then Jimmy asked his grandfather what he had to say to him, and Elise found herself telling him, "This is like throwing pearls before swine." The grandfather tried to say something else to her, too, but Elise wasn't understanding it. She then felt her hand fly up in the air and her wedding ring fly off and out the Jeep window. It landed in a mud puddle outside. "Ah," said Jimmy, "he's telling me I'm throwing the marriage down the drain into the mud."[62] Even a ghost knows a picture is worth a thousand words.

Another case in which a symbolic coincidence seems to provide specific guidance is related by psychic Susan Reintjes. On an occasion on which Reintjes was feeling betrayed and exposed by some unfavorable newspaper publicity, she saw a big opossum walk brazenly across her backyard in the middle of a sunny morning. Immediately, she realized its significance. The opossum was telling her to do exactly what Jamie Sams and David Carson describe in their book *Medicine Cards* under the entry for "opossum":

> Rely upon your instincts for the best way out of a tight corner. If you have to pretend to be apathetic or unafraid, do it! Oftentimes if you refuse to struggle or show that hurtful words bother you, your taunter will see no further fun in the game.[63]

Reintjes followed the advice of this coincidence to "play dead" and did not respond to the unfair reporting. In the end, she got several new clients out of the article and discovered that its unfair portrayal of her had been motivated by the journalist's fear of the power of Reintjes' psychic abilities.[64]

In this next case, the guidance provided by a symbolic coincidence was literally life-saving. Englishman Michael Young was in New Zealand and had an open plane ticket east to Vancouver, from where he could continue home eastward to England. He'd considered taking a boat home instead—going

---

[62] Sylvia Hart Wright, *When Spirits Come Calling: The Open-Minded Skeptic's Guide to After-Death Contacts* (Nevada City, CA: Blue Dolphin Publishing, 2002), 137.
[63] Jamie Sams and David Carson, *Medicine Cards: The Discovery of Power Through the Ways of Animals* (Rochester, VT: Bear & Company, 1988). As quoted in Reintjes, 121.
[64] Susan Reintjes, *Third Eye Open: Unmasking Your True Awareness* (Third Eye Publishing, 2003), 120-1.

west the way he had when he was a boy—but instead he went to the airline terminal to book his seat on the Vancouver flight. Now, before he'd left on this trip, his mother had given him a good luck charm: a small white elephant figurine, seemingly made of ivory. He'd packed it with his toilet items. While at the airport, but before booking his seat, Young looked to make sure the elephant was still where he'd packed it. It wasn't. In its place was a bunch of white dust. The elephant appeared to have completely disintegrated. Young took the pulverization of his good luck charm as a sign that he shouldn't get a seat on the plane after all. And his interpretation appeared to be correct, since that plane subsequently disappeared over the Pacific, leaving no survivors.[65]

The following coincidence did not provide guidance, exactly, but it was clear to its recipient, Laura Lynne Jackson, that it was symbolic of something of great importance. Jackson relates that she was at Jones Beach in New York when a cloud of migrating monarch butterflies—tens of thousands of them—suddenly obscured the sun overhead. Butterflies had particular importance for Jackson because of some experiences she'd had involving her grandfather, now deceased. What was more, she had specifically asked those close to her on the Other Side to use a monarch butterfly as a sign of their presence. "Without fail," she says, "monarch butterflies would appear before a big test or an important choice, to let me know they were there for me and that I wasn't alone."[66] When she saw the enormous cloud of monarchs at Jones Beach that day, she knew that something important was going on, and that it was a celebration of some kind. On the very next day, she discovered she was pregnant.

You may have noticed that five out of the eight symbolic coincidences just related involve animals. This was not an intentional theme on my part. It just so happens that the symbolic coincidences that I've come across are filled with animals. Animals, it seems, are potent symbols—as I'm sure the writers of *Medicine Cards* would agree!

While the symbolism in the forgoing examples is quite clear, we should keep in mind that we may miss the significance of some coincidences because we are not familiar with their mode of symbolism. I believe it will be helpful to our understanding of the symbolism of coincidences if we review some of what's been written about dream symbolism.

To begin with, one oft-noted sign that a dream element is symbolic is its being associated with strong emotion, especially emotion that's more intense than what the dream situation seems to warrant. My research suggests this is also true of coincidences. When a coincidence strikes us with unusual emotional force, something important is likely being expressed by that

---

[65] Brian Inglis, *Coincidence: A Matter of Chance – or Synchronicity?* (London: Hutchinson, 1990), 93-94.
[66] Jackson, 79.

coincidence, whether it's psychically derived information or information about our own deepest thoughts and feelings. Our emotion is a reaction of recognition from our unconscious—recognition of this information's importance.

But even if one realizes from the strong emotion accompanying a dream or a coincidence that it is likely symbolic, the *meaning* of the symbolism can often be difficult to figure out. Unfortunately, symbol dictionaries are generally of little help. Though symbolism is rife in the psychic world, it is usually very personal, dependent on one's own individual set of associations. For instance, consider this telepathic experience had by Jung. He was on a train when he suddenly found his mind filled by a vision of a drowning he'd once witnessed while in the military. Upon arrival at his destination, Jung discovered that this vision had come to him at the very time that one of his grandchildren had been on the point of drowning.[67] It appears that his unconscious received a psychic message about drowning and his conscious mind represented this using the most vivid image of drowning he'd personally encountered.

Here's another example of a personal association, this one involving a dream. Near-death experiencer Cherylee Black was participating in a precognitive dream group in which members viewed four images and ranked them according to how well they reflected the dreams they'd just had. A random number generator then chose one of the four images, which became the official "target," and the precognitive ability of the dreamers was measured based on how often they were able to select the target image ahead of time based on its similarity to their dreams. On one occasion, Black dreamt of NDE researcher Dr. Bruce Greyson "holding a picture that looked something like a turtle in the water." The image selected by the random number generator turned out to be a mechanical shark from *Jaws*, which Black knew had been named "Bruce," like the Bruce Greyson who'd appeared in her dream.[68] Puns, a linguistic form of association, are not uncommon in dreams or coincidences.

Even professional psychics and mediums report receiving their messages by way of processes of association like those we've seen in the previous two examples. Dr. Gary Schwartz, who has investigated mediumship in a laboratory setting, reports a phenomenon that clearly echoes Jung's experience. He writes, "our team of mediums tell us that symbols from their own personal lives often come to them, and they learn

---

[67] C. G. Jung, *Memories, Dreams, Reflections*, ed. Aniela Jaffé, trans. Richard and Clara Winston, rev. ed. (New York: Vintage Books, 1961, 1989), 302-3.
[68] Titus Rivas, Anny Dirven, and Rudolf H. Smit, *The* Self *Does Not Die: Verified Paranormal Phenomena from Near-Death Experiences* (Durham, NC: IANDS Publications, 2016), 197.

how to interpret these symbols."[69] Psychic Alan Vaughan points out that some symbols in psychic images may be shared among mediums—for instance, a casket representing death—but notes that other symbols can be more idiosyncratic. He gives the example of Dutch psychic Gerard Croiset, for whom a half-eaten peach represented terminal cancer, due to the fact that Croiset's own mother perished from cancer after consuming half a peach.[70] Medium Traci Bray reports an idiosyncratic symbol based on one of her grandfathers. She says, "My maternal grandfather George was a prolific gardener. When he pops into a reading it is indicative of a person named George, the maternal grandfather figure, or of a dedicated gardener."[71]

It shouldn't be surprising with associations like this that the meaning of some symbols can be quite puzzling at first and only become apparent after repeated exposure. Psychic medium William Stillman says that he thinks of the spirits of the deceased as communicating with him in an "ethereal version of charades"[72] and that it took him 11 years to get a decent grip on interpreting the images that came to him.[73] Vaughan points out the further complicating factor that dream symbols may only be understandable in light of events that have not yet happened. They may in fact rely upon mental associations *that have not yet taken place*.[74]

At the same time that much psychic information is conveyed through highly personal associations, there are more universally recognizable symbols as well. Jung calls these "archetypes": patterns that continually recur in everyone's experience. Remember our discussion in Chapter 10 of the way our own personal consciousness is interconnected with a much wider-ranging intelligence. German writer Wilhelm von Scholz suggested in 1924 that coincidences might be events in the dream of this "greater and more comprehensive consciousness."[75]

Even these more universal symbols, however, are usually recognizable only with some help. Take, for instance, the precognitive dream that Robert

---

[69] Gary E. Schwartz with William L. Simon, *The Afterlife Experiments: Breakthrough Scientific Evidence of Life after Death* (New York: Atria, 2002), 220.
[70] Alan Vaughan, *Patterns of Prophecy* (New York: Hawthorn, 1973), 97.
[71] Julie Beischel, ed., *From the Mouths of Mediums: Conversations with Windbridge Certified Research Mediums*, Vol. 1: Experiencing Communication, reprinted in Beischel, *Investigating Mediums*, 217-322, p. 257.
[72] Lisa Smartt, *Words at the Threshold: What We Say as We're Nearing Death* (Novato, CA: New World Library, 2017), 128-9.
[73] William Stillman has recently written an entire book about the phenomenon of personal "spiritual iconography": *The Secret Language of Spirit: Understanding Spirit Communication in Our Everyday Lives* (Wayne, NJ: New Page Books, 2018).
[74] Vaughan, *Patterns of Prophecy*, 125, 132.
[75] Wilhelm von Scholz, *Der Zufall: Eine Vorform des Schicksals* (Stuttgart, Germany: Hädecke, 1924), as quoted in C. G. Jung, *Synchronicity: An Acausal Connecting Principle*, trans. R. F. C. Hull (Princeton, NJ: Princeton University Press, 1960, 2010), 15.

Waggoner had of the South African Soweto riots, described in Chapter 9. He saw "a moon cross the sky three times as a voice said that the event would occur in three years." "Then suddenly," he says, "I found myself in the midst of a ferocious riot with both blacks and whites. As I sought shelter, I noticed a Dutch-type windmill, similar to one in my hometown. Three years later, on June 16, 1976, the Soweto riots erupted in South Africa…."[76]

Waggoner's dream symbolizes the passage of three years by showing a moon cross the sky three times. The meaning of this is explained in the dream, which is particularly helpful since, in waking life, we see the moon cross the sky in a single day or night, and the period of time with which the moon is most frequently symbolically associated is a month. Waggoner would probably not have thought to interpret each of the moon's crossings as a year (rather than a day or a month) without this bit of explanation. The other symbol of the dream—the Dutch windmill—is somewhat clearer, since South Africa is a former Dutch colony and still has some of these windmills. Nevertheless, until the events foreshadowed by the dream came to pass, it may have been hard to tell exactly which country with Dutch associations was being indicated.

As another example, take a dream that Dr. Andrew Paquette had of a lion sleeping in Syria. Paquette writes,

> In a dream dated February 27, 2006, I first see, as if I am an independent witness, a group of men who wish to assassinate Syria's leader, Bashar Al-Assad. Before they enact their plan, a dream character comes to me and asks me to accompany him. He tells me there is a vision he wants me to see. He brings me to the Syrian desert outside the town we were in where he shows me a giant lion sleeping in the moonlight…. This is a symbol of a great danger, not yet awakened, coming from Syria and (presumably) related to the men who wanted to assassinate Al-Assad seen earlier.[77]

Paquette goes on to say, "the symbol and context of the dream appeared to describe something empirically real that I only found out about in 2014, 8 years after the dream, when I ran across a reference in the news to Ayman Al-Zawahiri who referred to ISIS members as the 'Lions of Syria' in a speech on August 20, 2011."[78] Paquette's research revealed that "the group of Islamic radicals currently known as ISIS started in Syria as a group of people described as the 'Lions of Syria' by their inspirational leaders. Their original goal was to assassinate Bashar Al-Assad and restore Islamic rule to Syria."[79] In this case, the lion in Paquette's dream accurately conveyed the sense of a

---

[76] Waggoner, 283.
[77] Andrew Paquette, "The Rarity of Unambiguous Symbols in Dreams: A Case Study," *Journal of Scientific Exploration* 30, no. 2 (2016): 199-216, p. 209.
[78] Paquette, "The Rarity," 214.
[79] Paquette, "The Rarity," 214.

"great danger, not yet awakened," and yet the more specific relevance of the lion symbol did not become clear to him until eight years later.

It is interesting to note that Paquette has found clearly symbolic content to be rare in his dreams, in which clairvoyant and precognitive elements are often very literally represented. When symbolic content does appear, he says, it seems to be intentionally employed by dream characters in order to convey a message and to make that message memorable when he wakes up. He gives the following example.

> [I]n a dream dated June 8, 1999, a dream character shows me a tree-like network structure as a metaphor for the many paths available to spirits in multiple lives. He then brings me to another character as a way to complete the message. This new character is aware that I am dreaming and explains that the first character was responsible for making the symbol I viewed but that she would explain it to me because her style of communication was more compatible with my abilities. In this dream, the following are explicitly clear: 1) my dream state, 2) that a specific dream object is a symbol, and 3) the meaning of the symbol. Not all dreams are as obvious, but can still be readily identified as communication from an independent source.[80]

Paquette has even had a dream in which it was explained to him how his dreams were created and sent to him. "When a message had to be given to me," he writes, "it was assigned to a servo spiritus [his term for a protective, watchful spirit] to deliver it. This servo spiritus chose how it would be delivered, very much as a craftsman might consider his options before deciding how best to approach a project."[81] It appears that symbolism in Paquette's dreams is not a haphazard affair of unconscious association but rather the deliberate work of a communicating intelligence.

Paquette specifies that, for him to categorize dream content as "unambiguously symbolic," it must be the case that "[c]larity of communication is improved by the use of symbolic rather than literal presentation."[82] Indeed, effective symbols convey content that would be difficult, if not impossible, to describe in words. Often, this content is deeply spiritual. As Jung puts it,

> when the idea or principle involved is inscrutable, when its intentions are obscure in origin and in aim and yet enforce themselves, then the spirit is necessarily felt as an independent being, as a kind of higher consciousness, and its inscrutable, superior nature can no longer be

---

[80] Paquette, "The Rarity," 209.

[81] Andrew Paquette, *Dreamer: 20 Years of Psychic Dreams and How They Changed My Life* (Winchester, UK: O Books, 2011), 238.

[82] Paquette, "The Rarity," 204.

> expressed in the concepts of human reason. Our powers of expression then have recourse to other means; they create a *symbol.*
>
> By a symbol I do not mean an allegory or a sign, but an image that describes in the best possible way the dimly discerned nature of the spirit.[83]

Jung's idea is that there exists a type of meaning in the world that is not formulable in words. If this type of meaning can be conveyed or described at all, it will be in the form of a symbol, whose power comes in part from the fact that it bears so many associative connections, and thus conveys a meaning that is expansive rather than reductive.

Christian writer Eric Metaxas describes a certain powerful dream of his as God speaking to him in "the secret language of my own heart."[84] That is an excellent way to describe the type of symbolism we are likely to encounter in dreams and coincidences. These experiences speak directly to our hearts because they are written in the heart's own language. Annie Mattingley says something very similar about after-death communications:

> These moments speak to us in the language of Spirit or God or the universe. They are not intended to be fully understood but rather to be savored and allowed to delight. More than anything else they resemble poetry, which, as Paul Valéry says, is defined by being indefinable.[85]

Mattingley's reference to poetry reminds us that words themselves are symbols. But although words tend to be reductive in their meanings—at least as they are generally used in this day and age, which puts little value on poeticism[86]—the types of symbols used in dreams and in spiritual contexts are the opposite of reductive. Instead of reducing meaning to something narrow and precise, they open the mind to consider multiple layers of significance. And, when these symbols are drawn from one's own personal experience, they connect one to the vast rivers of emotion that accompany those experiences. This is why it is such a great misunderstanding to ever say of an element in someone's dream, "It's just a symbol of such-and-such." The point of a symbol is that it's never *just* anything.

---

[83] C. G. Jung, "Spirit and Life," in *The Collected Works*, vol. 8, *The Structure and Dynamics of the Psyche*, 2nd ed. (London: Routledge and Kegan Paul, 1969), 335-6.
[84] Eric Metaxas, *Miracles: What They Are, Why They Happen, and How They Can Change Your Life* (New York: Dutton, Plume, 2014, 2015), 148.
[85] Annie Mattingley, *The After Death Chronicles: True Stories of Comfort, Guidance, and Wisdom from Beyond the Veil* (Charlottesville, VA: Hampton Roads, 2017), xxiii-xxxiv.
[86] Anyone interested in the symbolic potential of prose should read Stephen Harrod Buhner, *Ensouling Language: On the Art of Nonfiction and the Writer's Life* (Rochester, VT: Inner Traditions, 2010).

In fact, it's also rare for a dream element to be *just* literal. David Ryback writes, "Dreams lie on a continuum from totally literal to totally symbolic truth. Most lie somewhere in between, where psychic and symbolic meaning may not only meet but overlap."[87] This tendency of dream meanings to overlap is a crucial one to understand. Long experience has taught dream analysts that dreams rarely have a single meaning. While many dreams have some immediately apparent correspondence to waking life, a less obvious meaning—often symbolic—will generally piggy-back on the obvious one. As Rabbi Bana'ah says in the Talmud, "There were twenty-four interpreters of dreams in Jerusalem. Once I had a dream and went to every one of them and what any one interpreted, none of the others interpreted in the same way, and yet all of them were fulfilled."[88]

An excellent example of multiple dream meanings is a dream reported by Smartt in *Words at the Treshold.* She writes,

> Tom dreamed that the atmospheric dome around the earth collapsed, and he reached up his arms to prevent its fall and keep all those on earth from suffocating. That night a good friend of his, Florence, entered the hospital for the last time, gasping for breath as she died. At the time, he attributed the dream to her death that evening. Later in the year, Tom began having trouble with his own respiratory system. He recalled his dream of the collapsing dome and its precognitive quality in relation to Florence. He felt the image was also a warning to him. After convincing doctors to take his concerns seriously, they discovered that one of his arteries was completely blocked and deformed. "I know that the only reason that I am alive to share this tale," he told friends in a Facebook post, "is because I recognized the importance of the dream."[89]

In a similar case reported by Ryback, a woman assumed that a dream she had about happily undergoing a mastectomy was caused by the fact that the following day, *Happy* Rockefeller, Second Lady of the United States, announced that she'd be having a mastectomy performed. However, the dreamer later had another dream in which she was told, "You must have surgery soon or you will die," and her husband had several dreams in which he feared he was "losing" her. So she decided to go to the doctor, and she ended up having a large, malignant tumor removed from her breast. The doctor told her that, if she'd waited much longer to seek medical help, her life would have been in danger.[90]

In another case of overlapping meaning, a man named Calvin had a dream of one of his children in a casket, but he couldn't tell which of his

---

[87] Ryback with Sweitzer, 111.

[88] *Mishnah, Berakhot* 55b, as quoted in Moss, *Dreaming True*, 123.

[89] Smartt, 147.

[90] Ryback with Sweitzer, 58.

children it was. In the dream, the time was 4:44am. Much later, *two* of his children ended up dying in real life, 18 years apart from one another. Both of the calls that delivered the news of their deaths came at 4:44am.[91]

As these cases demonstrate, when one discovers that there is some immediate telepathic or precognitive content to a dream, it can be tempting to think that that is "all" that's going on. But, as these examples also show, that can be a mistake. Jeremy Taylor explains it well:

> [I]n the vast majority, if not all of the cases, the "spooky," telepathic or pre-cognitive material has great personal symbolic value to the dreamer, in and of itself. The inevitable consequence of the eerie connections with waking events is to bring the dream vividly to mind once again. I am persuaded that this calling to mind of the dream is one of the primary psychological functions of the "paranormal" element in dreams. It is as though the waking event were foreseen and "chosen" by the unconscious forces shaping the dream in order to forcibly recall the dream to mind when the event actually takes place, because that event is...particularly symbolically resonant with some important drama of the dreamer's own life.[92]

An excellent example of this is a detailed dream that came to a Belgian woman named Marie Françoise back in 1942. In the dream, she received a telephone call in which her brother-in-law told her that her father had just died and her presence was needed immediately. She caught a bus, but while she was on the bus, it began pouring rain. Knowing that, when she reached the small town where her father lived, she would have to walk some distance to his house, she got off the bus in the city of Louvain to purchase an umbrella. She wanted a black one, but there were none to be found, so she had to settle for brown. When Marie Françoise finally arrived near her father's house, the rain was still pouring, and she was confronted by some German soldiers who roughly questioned her about her presence there and demanded that she tell them what she knew about the people who had sabotaged some telephone wires that morning. She woke up while she was still trying to convince the soldiers of her innocence.

Marie Françoise intuitively understood this dream as symbolizing the central emotional conflict of her life: the cruel behavior of her father, the end of which appeared to be symbolized by his death in the dream. She interpreted her inability to find a black umbrella as an expression of her inability to truly mourn his passing—for her, it was actually a release. Marie Françoise was also struck by the parallels between the accusations of the

---

[91] Annie Mattingley, "Who Stops at a Green Light?", *Annie Mattingley* (blog) (August 13, 2018), https://anniemattingley.com/2018/08/13/who-stops-at-a-green-light/.
[92] Taylor, 123-4.

German soldiers and her father's perpetually accusatory behavior towards her, blaming her all her life for a matter in which she was entirely innocent.

In sum, Marie Françoise's dream clearly reflected her internal emotional landscape, employing an array of symbols that were almost textbook perfect. However, only hours after waking from this dream, Marie Françoise got a phone call from her brother-in-law. Her father was not dead, but he was dying and she needed to come right away. She hopped on the bus, only to find that it began to pour rain. When she stopped in Louvain for an umbrella, she couldn't find any black ones, and a clerk suggested brown, which she took. When she got off the bus near her father's house, German soldiers confronted her and demanded information about the sabotage of telephone wires.

The most marvelous thing was that, as Marie Françoise lived through the events of her dream in real life, she found herself processing her emotions in a significantly different way. She felt a mixture of peace about what was happening and anger at her father for the way he'd unjustly blamed her. Her father died a few hours after she freed herself from the German soldiers and arrived at his home. Ultimately, reliving her dream in real life led her to some important realizations about herself and her own self-image and allowed her to free herself from the shackles of her father's rejection.[93]

This is just one of several examples I've encountered of dreams that were helpful when interpreted symbolically and that nevertheless turned out to be literally true as well. Here's another. Jeremy Taylor mentions his discovery that, prior to the assassination of the publicly gay San Francisco Supervisor Harvey Milk, many dream work groups in the Bay area had been discussing dreams of his murder. In their interpretations of these dreams, the groups were concentrating primarily on what was going on in the dreamers' personal lives, particularly with regard to the theme of homosexuality. After it was discovered that these dreams precognized an actual event, many of the dreamers wanted to deny the value of the symbolic interpretations that had previously been arrived at. However, the dream group leaders were of the opinion that the symbolic interpretations of this real future event had nevertheless been accurate. This experience led Taylor to consider whether we dream psychically about real events precisely because those outer events are such good symbols for something going on inside of us.[94] If our psychic faculties are directed by our personal issues and interests, then it makes good psychological sense to ask why these people's psyches picked up on the coming assassination of a prominent gay figure, rather than precognizing some other event, for example. As with Marie Françoise's dream, the

---

[93] Ryback with Sweitzer, 104-8.

[94] Taylor, 125.

symbolic and precognitive aspects of these Harvey Milk dreams could very well reinforce, rather than exclude, each other.

My favorite example of double meaning in dreams comes from a patient seen by Swiss psychiatrist Dr. Carl Alfred Meier, an associate of Jung's. The patient was an American surgeon who had been working at a hospital in China for a couple of decades and became well integrated into Chinese culture. Nevertheless, she eventually became severely depressed and traveled all the way from China to Europe to get Meier's help. She mentioned to him a dream she'd had in which one of the wings of her hospital had been destroyed. Meier intuited that there was a symbolic connection to aspects of her personality that she'd lost in becoming so integrated into Chinese culture, and when the surgeon took Meier's advice and returned home to the US, her depression lifted right away. The most intriguing aspect of this story, however, is that the surgeon drew a picture of the destroyed hospital wing from her dream and, nine years later, when the Japanese attacked China and bombed that hospital, she saw in *Life* magazine a large photograph that precisely matched her drawing.[95]

Here again we have a case of a dream's using a precognitive image of a real event to reveal to the dreamer an issue of personal importance, the connection between the two being made at the symbolic level. The dream appears to be a mechanism to point out to the dreamer the symbolism of the real-life event. However, once we are sufficiently sensitized to the fact that real-life events can be symbolic in this way, dreaming of them may not be necessary. We can read the significance directly from the events themselves, as Laura Lynne Jackson did when she saw the cloud of migrating monarch butterflies, or Susan Reintjes did when she saw the opossum in her yard in broad daylight.

Sometimes the symbolism is so blatant that a coincidence is close to being a literal forerunner of actual events to come. For instance, the morning after Susan Bassett conceived one of her children, a deer delivered two fawns below her bedroom window,[96] foreshadowing the human birth that was to follow. Another example, also conception-related, comes from a woman named Becky, who answered the door one day to find a man with a bunch of balloons standing outside. "Are you the new mother?" he asked her. She told him she was not. "Isn't this the house with the newborn?" he asked. She told him he must have the wrong address. He realized she was right, though

---

[95] Michael Talbot, *The Holographic Universe: The Revolutionary Theory of Reality* (New York: Harper Perennial, 1991, 1992, 2011), 78-79. Talbot cites "Science and Synchronicity: A Conversation with C. A. Meier," *Psychological Perspectives* 19, no. 2 (Fall-Winter 1988): 324.

[96] Elisabeth Hallett, *Soul Trek: Meeting Our Children on the Way to Birth* (Hamilton, MT: Light Hearts Publishing, 1995), 32.

she says he still seemed a little confused. In any case, within a week, Becky had a positive pregnancy test.[97]

In another case, a woman named Sue Burton had been trying for over two years to have a baby, without success. It was March when a woman predicted to Burton that, by that time the following year, she would have a baby daughter. That Mother's Day, Burton discovered while getting into her car that there was an inexplicable pink baby bootie sitting in plain view in the backseat. Her mother and sister had been in and out of the car all the previous day and assured her they had never seen it before. What was more, the car had been locked every time they'd left it unattended. And Burton couldn't remember a baby *ever* having been in her car, so it didn't seem like something that could have been accidentally dropped by a former passenger. The bootie's appearance was truly a mystery. That is, until Burton discovered that she was pregnant, and had been pregnant already on that Mother's Day when she found the pink bootie. Her child also turned out to be a girl.[98]

Note that, even in these cases of unusually clear symbolism, the meaning of these coincidences was not entirely obvious at the moment they were experienced, no more than the entire meaning of a dream is plain to us in the moment of dreaming it. Jackson knew when she saw the monarch butterflies that something important was happening, but it was only the next day that she discovered exactly what that something was. And Susan Bassett and Becky may not have realized the significance of their coincidences, either, until they had their own positive pregnancy tests. Sue Burton seems to have had a pretty clear idea of what was going on, but even she was cautious about getting her hopes up until the coincidence was confirmed by a pregnancy test.

Specific Advice

So, is there any way to be *sure* about the right interpretation of a precognitive coincidence, before the events it alludes to have been confirmed in more concrete ways? And what if we get it wrong? Ryback points out that "[t]he appropriate response to a dream is usually the same whether or not the dream actually comes true,"[99] and I believe the same is true with regard to coincidences. When you allow a coincidence to help you refine your thoughts and feelings about an issue, the action that you take as a result will likely be a useful course of action whether or not the coincidence was "really" giving you that information.

---

[97] Hallett, *Soul Trek*, 24.
[98] Joan Wester Anderson, *Where Miracles Happen: True Stories of Heavenly Encounters*, updated (Chicago: Loyola Press, 1994, 2009), 6-9.
[99] Ryback with Sweitzer, 65.

Ryback provides his readers with a list of steps to take when they wake from a dream that makes a strong impression on them,[100] and I would advise following similar steps when dealing with a striking coincidence. In fact, I think we could summarize the four most crucial steps with four "R's":

- **R**ecord the details of the coincidence as close to the time of its occurrence as possible, so they are as accurate as possible.

- **R**eflect on any information the coincidence may be conveying, either positive or negative, either material or spiritual.

- **R**elay your experience to someone else, who can further help you to reflect on its meaning.

- **R**eact, by preparing yourself materially and mentally for the possibility that the message you take from the coincidence may prove accurate.

While it seems generally to be the case that, if the message is important enough, it will repeat itself in further coincidences or in other psychic events like dreams, if the stakes are very high, it would be wise not to count on this and to react with as much cautious efficiency as possible. Often the full significance of a coincidence is not uncovered until some action is taken in response to it. And remember that, even when a symbolic interpretation seems very compelling, it doesn't mean one shouldn't also be prepared for a literal interpretation as well. One of Robert Moss's experiences serves as an excellent cautionary tale. A Caribbean priest once told him, "There is a fire growing close to you," and Moss understood this as some new drama mounting in his life. However, as soon as Moss got home, a huge fire started in the apartment across from his window.[101]

I would also suggest using Jeremy Taylor's book *Dream Work* as a guide to interpreting coincidences (as well as dreams, of course). Taylor puts special emphasis on the "multiple levels and layers of significance"[102] of both dreams and paranormal waking events. He presents an extensive list of elements that are *always* present in dreams, pointing out that many different schools of dream interpretation have insights to offer, but that rather than only one of them being true, they are generally *all* true. You'll have to consult Taylor's

---

[100] Ryback with Sweitzer, 65-66.

[101] Robert Moss, *The Boy Who Died and Came Back: Adventures of a Dream Archaeologist in the Multiverse* (Novato, CA: New World Library, 2014), 6-7.

[102] Taylor, 134.

book for the complete list of elements he believes are always present in dreams,[103] but here are a few of them:

- libido and wish-fulfillment,
- replays of the previous day's mental residue (not in a meaningless fashion, but because something was personally significant or puzzling),
- symbolic representation of feelings, especially those pertaining to relationships with others,
- speculation about possible future scenarios,
- problem solving, and
- humor.

Given the many parallels between dreams and coincidences, I think we would be wise to consider how these various elements can illuminate the meaning of coincidences as well. If you feel that an event in your life is symbolically significant but you're not sure how, try on each of these interpretations in turn. You may be surprised at how many of them lead you to independently important insights. Remember Rabbi Bana'ah's words about the 24 different interpretations of a dream that were all fulfilled!

Common Errors in Interpreting Psychic Information

We have seen how much we can learn about the interpretation of coincidences from dream interpretation literature, but there is also much to be learned from the literature on precognition and clairvoyance. In particular, this literature tells us a lot about the pitfalls of interpreting psychic information.

For instance, scientific researchers of clairvoyance, which is also called "remote viewing" or "remote perception," have pointed out that it is generally counterproductive to try interpreting intuitive perceptions too soon.[104] An excellent example of this with regard to precognition is a couple of erroneous messages delivered by a psychic who (1) predicted that a specific client of hers would die in April 1969 and (2) "had a vivid vision of San Francisco's destruction" occurring at that same time. The client in question was a professor at Stanford University, in the Bay Area, so it seemed to make sense that these two events could be connected. However, when April 1969 arrived, the client did not die, and San Francisco was not destroyed by an

---

[103] Taylor, 138-42.

[104] Robert G. Jahn and Brenda J. Dunne, *Consciousness and the Source of Reality: The PEAR Odyssey* (Princeton, NJ: ICRL Press, 2011), 245-56.

earthquake. Instead, the psychic herself died.[105] One can see, in retrospect, that she might have received some accurate information about her impending death but misinterpreted it.

A less tragic misinterpretation was made by psychic Alan Vaughan, who predicted that terrible smog was going to engulf New York City on Thanksgiving Day 1967, just as it had done in 1966. As it turned out, all that happened on Thanksgiving in 1967 was that he himself walked through a thick cloud of smoke coming from a pile of burning leaves.[106]

Vaughan suggests that the biggest issue with interpreting psychic premonitions may be the fact that they "rarely carry an accurate sense of time."[107] He notes that a psychic will sometimes think an impression applies to the near future when the event won't actually occur until years later. Author Michael Crichton has made a similar observation with regard to the psychics he's consulted through the years. Crichton writes,

> They were likely to confuse time—they were much more likely to get the season of the year correct than the year itself. They often got the order of things and the amounts of things wrong. It seemed that you couldn't really expect psychics to be accurate about quantities and timing; they simply couldn't do it.[108]

The same issue applies to coincidences. While Laura Lynne Jackson's cloud of monarchs announced an event that she would discover the following day, I've encountered coincidences announcing events a full year in the future, if not more. This is yet another regard in which coincidences are like dreams. As Drs. Kelly Bulkeley and Patricia Bulkley note in their book *Dreaming Beyond Death*, dreams are often "far ahead of the dying person's conscious awareness in terms of preparing for what's to come."[109]

Indeed, sometimes the events about which we have premonitions never happen at all. Elisabeth Hallett tells about being pregnant and having a vivid dream of holding a baby boy with Down syndrome. Nevertheless, amniocentesis revealed that she was carrying a baby girl who did not have the syndrome. She cautions people against supposing that their imagination isn't sophisticated enough to produce "visions and voices." While seeing visions and hearing voices are not dangerous experiences in themselves, she says, automatically assuming that they are truthful reflections of an external reality can be.[110]

---

[105] Vaughan, *Incredible Coincidence*, 42-43.
[106] Vaughan, *Patterns of Prophecy*, 13.
[107] Vaughan, *Patterns of Prophecy*, 65.
[108] Michael Crichton, *Travels* (New York: Vintage Books, 1988), 198.
[109] Kelly Bulkeley and Patricia Bulkley, *Dreaming Beyond Death: A Guide to Pre-Death Dreams and Visions* (Boston: Beacon Press, 2005), 102.
[110] Hallett, *Soul Trek*, 202-3.

Let's look at some further examples of the ways in which psychic information can be misinterpreted. This next case involves receiving psychic information in a dream, but one can easily imagine a professional psychic receiving such information in a reading and being similarly confused. In this case, a woman dreamt that her husband's father died, but no one in the dream seemed to care or be sad, least of all the dead man's wife, who was actually throwing a party in the dream. The dreamer woke up worried, but her husband insisted there was no need to take any action. The evening after the dream, the father-in-law gave them a call to say that his obituary had just been erroneously sent out to publications all over the country, because the wire service had confused him with another doctor of the same name. He'd called his son and daughter-in-law to make sure they wouldn't think he was dead![111]

Robert Waggoner emphasizes that the visual images in psychic dreams are often misinterpreted as items that have a similar physical appearance. A balloon, for instance, might be mistaken for someone's bald head.[112] Waggoner suggests that words may be less open to misinterpretation, but many examples show that verbal messages are not immune to misunderstanding either. Waggoner himself mentions the fact that poet and painter Epic Dewfall had to learn to phrase his lucid dream incubation very carefully, by saying he would look "*at* art" not "*for* art," or else he would spend his whole dream looking for the art and never finding it![113]

I mentioned earlier in this chapter the prevalence of puns in dreams and coincidences, and I gave the example of Cherylee Black's dream of Bruce Greyson, which helped her identify her telepathic target as a mechanical shark named Bruce. In that case, the pun worked to her advantage, but psychic puns can also trip us up. For example, a Mr. Lovell wanted his wife, Margaret Lovell, to win a cartoon-captioning contest, so he spent a couple of hours trying to mentally send his wife's name to the judging panel. He eventually felt like he was "getting through," but when the winner was announced, it turned out not to be his wife but a different woman also named Margaret Lovell![114]

In a case gathered by sociologist Dr. James McClenon, a man dreamt that he'd robbed a bank and was running from law enforcement. "The next day, as he approached the bank," says McClenon, "police cars converged on it. Later he read in the newspaper that a bank robber, whose [unusual] name

[111] Ryback with Sweitzer, 13.
[112] Waggoner, 182.
[113] Waggoner, 140-1.
[114] Vaughan, *Incredible Coincidence*, 168-9.

was exactly the same as his, was apprehended while fleeing in the same direction as in his dream."[115]

Here's one more psychic pun. Dr. Mary C. Neal recounts being in a truck that got stuck in deep mud off a tiny road in a remote part of Mexico. She and her companions prayed for God to "put rock under [them]." Even though that road was very rarely traveled, they'd hardly finished praying when a pickup approached, its driver having apparently gotten lost. He offered them a ride, and they laughed when they climbed into the bed of his truck and found that he was carrying rocks, on which they would be sitting during their ride to get help.[116]

It appears that psychic communication happens in a language that is not quite like any of our normal modes of processing information, either visually or verbally. This would explain Michael Crichton's observation that the psychics he consulted tended "to speak as if they were translating." He says it was as though they were

> [t]rying to shift from one language, or one system of representation, to another. Sometimes this led them to speak very vaguely. A movie producer was "a person who is responsible for other people." A film editor was "a person who is given things previously made that he assembles into a new whole." A sabotaging secretary was "a person who thinks she is doing the right thing but who is angry and makes errors she is not aware she makes."[117]

These vague descriptions sound a lot like what people are reduced to when they try to describe their dreams. The dreaming/psychic mode of thought doesn't seem to use the same set of concepts as the waking mode, which makes it easy for errors to arise in translating from one to the other.

Psychic mistakes can also arise if, unbeknownst to us, we are not psychically accessing an actual future event but rather an erroneous *report* of a future event, or even our own future misperception of such a report. British engineer and philosopher J. W. Dunne relates in his book *An Experiment with Time* how, in the spring of 1902, he dreamt that an island with 4,000 inhabitants was about to blow up from a volcanic explosion. He endeavored in his dream to get French authorities to help him remove the inhabitants from the island before the explosion and kept repeating to everyone the number of people—4,000—who would die if they didn't do something. After Dunne woke from this dream, the next batch of newspapers he read

---

[115] James McClenon, *Wondrous Events: Foundations of Religious Belief* (Philadelphia: University of Pennsylvania Press, 1994), 46.

[116] Mary C. Neal, *To Heaven and Back: A Doctor's Extraordinary Account of Her Death, Heaven, Angels, and Life Again* (Colorado Springs, CO: WaterBrook Press, 2011, 2012), xvi.

[117] Crichton, 197.

contained a story about a volcanic disaster on the French island of Martinique. The headline reported, "PROBABLE LOSS OF OVER 40,000 LIVES." However, Dunne *misread* this headline and thought that it said 4,000, matching the number from his dream. He discovered his mistake later, along with the fact that the actual loss of life in the disaster turned out not to resemble either the number 4,000 or 40,000.[118]

Alan Vaughan says that Dr. Edgar Mitchell, the famous astronaut who founded the Institute of Noetic Sciences, once stated that he wouldn't run his life by psychic predictions because we don't understand enough about the way psychic processes function. Vaughan's *own* thought was that he wouldn't run his life according to psychic predictions either, but for a different reason: because he knew *too* much about it. "Not only errors of psychic perception make reliance on predictions hazardous in some cases," he says, "but the apparent pliability of the future necessarily limits prophetic accuracy."[119] That is, in addition to all the errors we've already mentioned, there's the fact that the future can be changed.

This should be hopeful news for those who have had psychic glimpses of what appear to be unpleasant future events. While many people have been known to have premonitions of events that they can do nothing to change, some premonitions do seem designed to spur action toward changing the future, and some people appear to have accomplished this goal. One particularly intriguing case comes from Andrew Paquette, who had a vivid and detailed dream of being shot and killed when two muggers forced him down an alley in an Amsterdam street. He was currently living in Amsterdam and took this dream as sufficient reason to make arrangements to move back to the States, where he was from. Two weeks later, he was returning from picking up his plane ticket from the travel agency when he realized he was walking on the street from his dream. Two muscular men proceeded to approach him, one of them grabbing him and asking him how much money he had on him. Paquette then realized that there, ahead of him, was the alley from his dream. Knowing that he was doomed if he let the men get him into the alley, he came up with a way to confuse them long enough to allow him to get away.[120]

Among the many intriguing aspects of this dream (and there are more than I've been able to describe here), there's the fact that Paquette was only on the street where the mugging occurred *because of his dream*.[121] If he'd never had the dream, he wouldn't have bought the plane ticket, and he wouldn't have been walking home from the travel agency and encountered the muggers. So it seems that the dream wasn't *only* designed to rescue him from

---

118 J. W. Dunne, *An Experiment with Time* (New York: Macmillan, 1927), 34-37.
119 Vaughan, *Patterns of Prophecy*, 197.
120 Paquette, 6-10.
121 Paquette, 15.

a perilous situation. It appears to have been designed to first *put him in* the perilous situation and *then* rescue him. Perhaps, above all, the purpose of this dream was to make him aware of the psychic power of his dreams. In any case, we see once again that the significance of psychic events is not a simple affair.

Can We Take Coincidences Too Far?

While many of us need to be encouraged to dig more deeply into the meaning of the coincidences and other psychic events in our lives, it's important to mention that the search for hidden meanings may go too far. For one thing, it is possible to see psychic events where nothing out of the ordinary is happening at all. Elisabeth Hallett provides an example from her own life of how easily we can forget the non-psychic sources of information we've encountered. She tells how she once found the name Devin in a baby name book and thought she'd never seen it before, but shortly thereafter she discovered that the name was in fact featured in a magazine advertisement she'd previously seen.[122] Such unconscious memories—which go by the technical name 'cryptomnesia'—can fool us into thinking we've procured information psychically when we haven't. That's not to say that information unconsciously retained can't be just as psychologically meaningful as that which is obtained through psychic means. It's just a warning that things are not always what they seem in the realm of the mind.

Numbers can be particularly seductive. The coincidence literature is full of accounts of people seeing significance in the numbers they encounter. Dr. Gary Schwartz's 2017 book *Super Synchronicity*, in particular, contains abundant examples.[123] I have myself experienced some number-based coincidences that later proved to be indicative of deeper meaning, so I know that numbers *can* be a vehicle for authentic psychic messages. However, we need to keep in mind that numbers are so ubiquitous in our society that it is difficult to get a good handle on just how often we should expect to encounter them by chance, and thus when we should take the appearance of a number as having some extra significance stemming from a psychic source. As Joachim Soulières puts it, "we should be suspicious because numbers bend so easily to our desires that we can quickly fall into illusion."[124] Then again, as long as one is aware that many genuinely psychic events are psychokinetic expressions of our internal states and that even psychic messages from other sources can be easily misinterpreted, seeing psychic

---

[122] Hallett, *Soul Trek*, 78.
[123] Gary E. Schwartz, *Super Synchronicity: Where Science and Spirit Meet* (Vancouver, BC: Param Media, 2017).
[124] Soulières, 37. My translation.

activity in places where it does not exist will not be such a big deal, because we are already so careful in interpreting its significance.

Soulières also points out that "[a]n excessive preoccupation with meaningful coincidences has long been recognized as a component of paranoia…which is where we get the persistent pathologizing of people inclined to coincidences."[125] However, he points out that the fact that paranoid people notice more coincidences doesn't mean that the coincidences they're noticing aren't genuinely anomalous. Recall the case related in Chapter 6 of Dr. Kirby Surprise's client who was convinced that people were watching him everywhere he went. In a counseling session, Surprise asked the client to come to a window that looked out over the street and show him the people who were watching him, expecting that the patient would see that no one was in fact doing this. At that moment, however, a car drove by, and both of the men in it were staring directly at them.[126] Surprise concluded from this that his client was actually *causing* other people to stare at him more often than chance. But instead of realizing that he was the psychic origin of this behavior, the client took it as external proof that his paranoia was justified.

Now, as I mentioned in the Introduction to this book, most people who experience coincidences are not in danger of being declared mentally ill. Recall that two-thirds of American adults say they've had psychic experiences,[127] and that they tend to be pretty ordinary people, if not a bit more educated and intelligent than average.[128] Experiencing striking coincidences is not, all by itself, an indication that a person is about to lose their marbles. Once again, I believe that what Jeremy Taylor says about dreams in this regard is equally applicable to coincidences. In his experience, he says, "dream work never causes the disintegration of personality, although dream work may indeed hasten the development of such processes once they have begun."[129] Similarly, I doubt that coincidences *cause* people to lose their grip on reality, but if they are already having trouble in this regard, an obsession with coincidences could exacerbate the problem.

Retired senior Army officer Dr. John B. Alexander has found that intense experiences of psychic phenomena do seem able to throw previously healthy minds into disarray. He writes,

---

[125] Soulières, 80. My translation. Soulières cites J. C. Coleman, *Abnormal Psychology and Modern Life* (Chicago: Scott, Foresman and Company, 1956).
[126] Kirby Surprise, *Synchronicity: The Art of Coincidence, Choice, and Unlocking Your Mind* (Pompton Plains, NJ: New Page Books, 2012), 51.
[127] Andrew Greeley, "Mysticism Goes Mainstream," *American Health* 6, no. 1 (January-February 1987): 47-49.
[128] Andrew Greeley, "The 'Impossible': It's Happening," *Noetic Sciences Review* no. 2 (Spring 1987): 8.
[129] Taylor, 77.

> During my foray into various [psychic] phenomena, I have personally witnessed several highly competent people simply "go off the deep end." By that, I refer to individuals who were very skilled and respected in their professional fields, yet after intense exposure to various phenomena began engaging in inexplicable, and often bizarre, behavior.[130]

Psychiatrist Dr. Montague Ullman has understood some aspects of psychosis as caused by perceiving a reality that is deeper than the person is capable of handling while staying grounded in everyday modes of thought. Psychosis, Ullman suggests, is like being unable to wake up from a dream, even when one is wide awake.[131] This psychotic "dream" may have verifiably psychic elements, but living perpetually inside of it makes normal, everyday life impossible.

For instance, schizophrenic people often think they can hear the critical, conspiratorial thoughts of others. It doesn't seem out of the realm of possibility that they are tuning into genuinely negative thoughts had by those around them, thoughts that most people generally hide out of politeness and that could certainly become overwhelming if one were constantly bombarded with them.[132] Being constantly bombarded by psychic perceptions—even true ones—could well make one incapable of functioning normally in society.

Dr. Alberto Villoldo relates the case of a patient who approached him on the second day of his psychology internship in a northern California hospital. "I know who you are," the patient said. "You can't hide from me." He started recounting events in Villoldo's childhood that only his closest family knew about. Villoldo explains that the patient's access to psychic information derived from a bad LSD trip years before. "He was in the psychiatric ward," says Villoldo, "because he did not know how to shut off his seeing, and he went around alarming people with frightening personal observations."[133]

Jung explicitly states that he himself, a prominent psychiatrist, experienced "the same psychic material which is the stuff of psychosis and is found in the insane."[134] He appears to have experienced what William James called "religious mysticism turned upside down." As mentioned in Chapter 8, James describes upside-down mysticism as

---

[130] John B. Alexander, *Reality Denied: Firsthand Experiences with Things that Can't Happen—But Did* (San Antonio, TX: Anomalist Books, 2017), 255.
[131] Talbot, *The Holographic Universe*, 63-5.
[132] Stillman, *The Secret Language of Spirit*, 159.
[133] Alberto Villoldo, *Shaman, Healer, Sage: How to Heal Yourself and Others with the Energy Medicine of the Americas* (New York: Harmony, 2000), 110.
[134] C. G. Jung, *Memories, Dreams, Reflections*, ed. Aniela Jaffé, trans. Richard and Clara Winston, rev. ed. (New York: Vintage Books, 1961, 1989), 188.

> [t]he same sense of ineffable importance in the smallest events, the same texts and words coming with new meanings, the same voices and visions and leadings and missions, the same controlling by extraneous powers; only this time the emotion is pessimistic: instead of consolations we have desolations; the meanings are dreadful; and the powers are enemies to life.[135]

Jung, fortunately, was ultimately able to navigate these treacherous waters. He was able to swim "where the madman drowns."

Integrating psychic experiences appropriately requires a great amount of psychological skill and energy, and it is not something that everyone is equally equipped to handle. Having the aid of a professional trained in these specific types of experiences can help, but not many psychiatrists understand these experiences, either. Psychiatrist Dr. Stanislav Grof notes that "modern psychiatry does not differentiate between mystical or spiritual states and mental diseases, [and] people experiencing these states are often labeled psychotic, hospitalized, and receive routine suppressive psychopharmacological treatment." However, Grof does offer the hopeful assertion that, "properly supported and treated, [these states] can result in emotional and psychosomatic healing, positive personality transformation, and consciousness evolution."[136] Details about such support methods can be found in two books written by Grof and his wife Christina: *Spiritual Emergency*[137] and *The Stormy Search for the Self.*[138]

I also highly recommend the writing of psychologist Dr. David Lukoff, who himself experienced what could be described as a psychotic episode. When he was in his 20s, he spent two months "firmly convinced that [he] was a reincarnation of both Buddha and Christ" and, filled with evangelical zeal, he took to the streets of Berkeley, California, distributing photocopies of his own "Holy Book."[139] Through the compassionate support of his friends, he made it through this period without hospitalization and soon

---

[135] William James, *The Varieties of Religious Experience*, in *Writings 1902-1920*, ed. Bruce Kuklick, The Library of America (New Yrk: Literary Classics of the United States, 1987), 384.
[136] Stanislav Grof, "Psychology of the Future: Lessons from Modern Consciousness Research," http://www.stanislavgrof.com/wp-content/uploads/pdf/Psychology_of_the_Future_Stan_Grof_long.pdf (accessed October 8, 2018), 7.
[137] Stanislav Grof and Christina Grof, eds., *Spiritual Emergency: When Personal Transformation Becomes a Crisis* (Los Angeles: J. P. Tarcher, 1989).
[138] Christian Grof and Stanislav Grof, *The Stormy Search for the Self: A Guide to Personal Growth through Transformational Crisis* (Los Angeles: J. P. Tarcher, 1990).
[139] David Lukoff, "Spirituality and Recovery from Serious Mental Problems," in *The Oxford Handbook of Psychology and Spirituality*, ed. Lisa J. Miller (New York: Oxford University Press, 2012), 410-22, p. 416.

returned to behaving in a more "normal" fashion. After spending many years profoundly embarrassed by his previous delusions, he began to realize that this episode was likely the manifestation of a genuine spiritual transformation that had been going on within him. Its mode of manifestation may have been socially ostracizing, but the religious awareness and concern expressed were real and deeply felt. During his "delusional" period, Lukoff dealt with these new feelings in the best way he could, and, thanks to the understanding and support of those around him, he appears to have later found a more socially acceptable manner of expressing them.

If the experience of intense coincidences can sometimes lead us to fear for our sanity, it is likely because they draw us into contact with parts of ourselves and the wider universe that we are not in the habit of dealing with. These contacts can provoke strong emotion, and even religious fervor on the order experienced by Lukoff. The best thing to do appears to be to relax and refrain from making any important life decisions until one is able to think calmly and clearly about the implications of this new level of awareness. On no account should coincidences be allowed to take over one's life to the exclusion of more mundane activities, since it is precisely these more mundane, everyday activities that will keep one grounded and sensible in interpreting coincidences.

This grounding in everyday life seems to have been the strategy that enabled Jung to stay sane through all of his tumultuous explorations of the unconscious processes of the mind. He writes in his memoir that his family and his professional life were the everyday realities that kept from being completely taken over by the world of the unconscious. Whatever was going on in his mind, he kept the perspective that it must serve and remain subordinate to his physical, earthly life.[140]

Dr. Judith Orloff stresses something her own psychiatric practice has taught her: that there is a time to encourage attention to intuitive experiences and a time not to. "Most important," she says,

> you must first start with a solid emotional base. Otherwise, exploring intuition may only make matters worse. … Just as a tree needs to have its roots firmly planted in the earth so as not to get blown away, your foundation must also be sturdy. Only then will there be no danger that you'll get overwhelmed.[141]

Ironically, paying less attention to the psychic may actually cause its messages to become clearer. Scott Peck writes that his patients learn much more from their dreams when they stop trying to remember every little thing that passes through their sleeping minds. They end up having fewer dreams

[140] Jung, *Memories, Dreams, Reflections*, 189.
[141] Orloff, 294.

to tell him about, but those dreams are much more insightful.[142] Peck himself advises that coincidences should be approached in the same way, and I would agree. When we worry less about the meaning of every little coincidence that crosses our path, the overall thrust of the universe's messages gradually becomes clearer, and may actually be a means for leading us out of our confusing mental labyrinth.

I believe this is good advice for all areas of our lives where we are trying to synthesize a large amount of information to make a decision. On more than one occasion when I've been trying to make a choice that has me particularly stymied, after days of frenetically analyzing every aspect of the situation and finding myself repeatedly going back and forth in my conviction about what I ought to do, I have finally just *stopped thinking* about the matter. Lo and behold, less than 24 hours after I cease my stormy analyses, the right decision just comes to me, with a calmness and conviction that I have no need to question any further.

This phenomenon reminds me of something that Mary Craig Kimbrough, an early pioneer in telepathic communication, said about the difference between mental delusions and authentic psychic communications. She wrote back in 1930,

> You want a message from the person who is sending you a message; you do not want a train of subconscious day dreams. The subconscious answers questions, and its answers are always false; its answers come quietly, like a thief in the night. But the "other" mind, the "deep" mind answers questions, too, and these answers come, not quietly, but as if by "inspiration," whatever that is—with a rustling of wings, with gladness and conviction. These two minds seem different from each other. One lies and rambles; the other sings, and is truthful.[143]

As we try to discern the meaning of the coincidences in our lives, it's that singing, truthful voice that we must listen for.

Mystery

Several examples in this book demonstrate that the universe is fully capable of being obvious when the situation calls for it, and we should take comfort in this fact. If the universe desires to give us clear direction, it's entirely capable of doing so. Nevertheless, I think that the character trait most vital for dealing profitably with coincidences is a tolerance for mystery.

---

[142] Peck, *The Road Less Traveled*, 308.

[143] Upton Sinclair, *Mental Radio* (London: T. Werner Laurie, 1930), 201.

Science has given mystery a bad reputation, implying that mystery is equal to superstition or an absence of careful thought. But that's not right. Mystery is the humbling and tantalizing quality of a universe that far outstrips our most assiduous attempts to reduce it to our mode of understanding. When we insist that this universe must limit itself to the mechanical laws that our science has so far described, we rob ourselves of the chance to discover this world's deeper truths. With coincidences, as with so many areas of life, we often think we know more than we do and are tempted to *explain* when we ought to *explore.*

We seem to get into the most trouble when we try to interpret coincidences in concrete, material terms, and I believe this is because coincidences are generally speaking to us on a more spiritual level. While we've seen that they do on occasion offer us material help, even there, this material help seems generally to be oriented towards advancing our spiritual understanding of the world. Coincidences are first and foremost geared toward giving us an awareness of aspects of ourselves and our world that we have heretofore ignored.

If there is one unfailing message I have gleaned thus far from my experiences of coincidences, it is this: The mysterious numinosity that we sense in our moments of deepest meaning and greatest love is not an illusion. Those moments are not just side effects of chemicals in our brains, hormones selected by evolution to cause us to mate and procreate and protect our offspring. What we *feel* in the most intense moments of our lives, those feelings are *real.* Realer than the physical world we see.

Coincidences show us that the physical world is actually built *from those feelings*, rather than the other way around. That is, our feelings are of a higher order of reality than the subatomic particles studied by physicists. They are a "wholer" form of truth. A holier form. Modern science, in focusing on the physical, has gotten things precisely backward. It has studied the physical because the physical is simpler, easier to see and pin down and dissect. But it is in fact less *real.* Coincidences, on the other hand, show us what is behind the façade of the physical world: something deeper and more intrinsically significant.

Coincidences are the holes in the reductive, mechanistic worldview that allow us to catch glimpses of the vast sea of meaning that awaits us on the other side. We should not be discouraged if we can't understand everything that comes to us in those glimpses. Let us have faith that a great and benevolent intelligence directs the current of our lives. Let us welcome the mystery of a world pregnant with meaning.

Penetrating so many secrets, we cease to believe in the unknowable.
But there it sits, nevertheless, calmly licking its chops.

– H. L. Mencken, *Minority Report: H. L. Mencken's Notebooks*

Acknowledgments

I would like to thank all of those who shared with me their coincidences and other unusual experiences, especially Anna, Katie, Katy, Cathy, Jeannette, Debbie, Melody, and my sisters Sarah and Rebecca. Thank you for the time you took to describe these experiences to me so thoughtfully. Special thanks go to Katie, not only for all the coincidence stories she's carefully reported to me but for her enthusiastic encouragement of this book project. Thank you, Katie, for being the first to volunteer to read the manuscript and to assure me that it was worth publishing. (And thank you, LJ, for all the food for thought you've given us from the other side!) Katy and Cathy have also been a great support in the years of this manuscript's preparation, not least because they were always willing to let me tell them about yet another weird coincidence that happened to me. Thank you, ladies, for always being there when things get freaky! And, of course, a big thank you to the person who first helped me see the magic of coincidences. I took some convincing, but I'm singing a much less skeptical tune now...parallel lives, indeed.

Thank you, as well, to Stephen Braude, Andrew Paquette, Sophy Burnham, Jim Matlock, Mary Helen Hensley, and Leslie Kean for their helpful correspondence as this manuscript was in its final stages. And thank you to all those authors and publishers who graciously allowed me to include excerpts from their work.

Thank you to my mother and father, who have continually supported me as I've made decisions to pursue both philosophy and writing in a professional way. You've been wonderful cheerleaders, always showing immense faith in my sometimes unconventional life choices.

Finally, my deepest debt of gratitude goes to my husband, who has endured my being holed up in my office for well-nigh half our married life.

Thanks for putting up with my obsession, as well as the avalanche of books that met you each day when you opened the mailbox. I love you.

References

Alamino, Carlos. *In the Footsteps of God's Call: A Cuban Pastor's Journey*. Trans. Osmany Espinosa Hernández. Ed. David Peck and Brian Stewart. 2008.

Alexander, John B. *Reality Denied: Firsthand Experiences with Things that Can't Happen—But Did*. San Antonio, TX: Anomalist Books, 2017.

Alvarez, Fernando. "A PK Experiment with Zebra Finches and a Virtual Predator." *Journal of Scientific Exploration* 26, No. 2 (2012): 261-71.

Anderson, Joan Wester. *Where Angels Walk: True Stories of Heavenly Visitors*. Carmel, NY: Guideposts, 1992.

Anderson, Joan Wester. *Where Miracles Happen: True Stories of Heavenly Encounters*. Updated. Chicago: Loyola Press, 1994, 2009.

Andrade, Hernani Guimarães. *Reborn for Love*. London: Roundtable, 2010.

Aquinas, Thomas. *Philosophical Texts*. Sel. and trans. Thomas Gilby. London: Oxford University Press, 1952.

Arcangel, Dianne. *Afterlife Encounters: Ordinary People, Extraordinary Experiences*. Charlottesville, VA: Hampton Roads, 2005.

Assante, Julia. *The Last Frontier: Exploring the Afterlife and Transforming Our Fear of Death*. Novato, CA: New World Library, 2012.

Attig, Sheryl, Gary E. Schwartz, Aurelio José Figueredo, W. Jake Jacobs, and K. C. Bryson. "Coincidences, Intuition, and Spirituality." *Psychiatric Annals* 41, No. 12 (2011).

Atwater, P. M. H. *Beyond the Light: What Isn't Being Said About Near-Death Experience*. New York: Birch Lane Press, 1994.

Atwater, P. M. H. "Is There a Hell? Surprising Observations About the Near-Death Experience." *Journal of Near-Death Studies* 10, No. 3 (Spring 1992): 149-60.

Auster, Paul. *The Red Notebook and Other Writings*. London: Faber and Faber, 1995.

Backster, Cleve. *Primary Perception: Biocommunication with Plants, Living Foods, and Human Cells*. Anza, CA: White Rose Millennium Press, 2003.

Backster, Cleve, and Stephen G. White. "Biocommunications Capability: Human Donors and *In Vitro* Leukocytes." *International Journal of Biosocial Research* 7, No. 2 (1985): 132-46.

Bailey, Lee W. "A 'Little Death': The Near-Death Experience and Tibetan *Delogs*." *Journal of Near-Death Studies* 19, No. 3 (Spring 2001): 139-59.

Barrett, William. *Deathbed Visions: How the Dead Talk to the Dying*. Guildford, UK: White Crow Books, 1926, 2011.

Barrow, John, and Frank Tipler. *The Anthropic Cosmological Principle*. Oxford: Oxford University Press, 1986.

Bauer, Dietrich, Max Hoffmeister, and Harmut Goerg. *Children Who Communicate Before They Are Born: Conversations with Unborn Souls*. Trans. Pauline Wehrle. Forest Row, UK: Temple Lodge, 2005.

Beck, Martha. *Finding Your Own North Star: Claiming the Life You Were Meant to Live*. New York: Three Rivers Press, 2001.

Beck, Martha. *Finding Your Way in a Wild New World: Reclaim Your True Nature to Create the Life You Want*. New York: Atria, 2012.

Beischel, Julie. *Among Mediums: A Scientist's Quest for Answers*. In *Investigating Mediums*. Pp. 59-172.

Beischel, Julie. "Certified Mediums' Experiences with the Afterlife." In *Investigating Mediums*. Pp. 27-34.

Beischel, Julie, ed. *From the Mouths of Mediums: Conversations with Windbridge Certified Research Mediums*. Vol. 1: Experiencing Communication. In *Investigating Mediums*. Pp. 217-322.

Beischel, Julie. *Investigating Mediums*. Tucson, AZ: Windbridge Institute, 2015.

Beischel, Julie. "Mental Mediumship Research at the Windbridge Institute." In *Investigating Mediums*. Pp. 7-14.

Beischel, Julie. "Survival of Consciousness: Animal Discarnates." In *Investigating Mediums*. Pp. 37-56.

Beitman, Bernard D. "Coincidence Studies." *Psychiatric Annals* 41, No. 12 (December 2011).

Beitman, Bernard D. *Connecting with Coincidence: The New Science for Using Synchronicity and Serendipity in Your Life*. Deerfield Beach, FL: HCI, 2016.

Beloff, John. "Psi Phenomena: Causal Versus Acausal Interpretation." *Journal of the Society for Psychical Research* 49 (September 1977): 573-82.

Bem, Daryl J. "Feeling the Future: Experimental Evidence for Anomalous Retroactive Influences on Cognition and Affect." *Journal of Personality and Social Psychology* 100, No. 3 (2011): 407-25.

Bender, Hans. "Meaningful Coincidences in the Light of the Jung-Pauli Theory of Synchronicity and Parapsychology." In *The Philosophy of Parapsychology: Proceedings of an International Conference Held in Copenhagen, Denmark, August 25-27, 1976*. Ed. Betty Shapin and Lisette Coly. New York: Parapsychology Foundation, 1977.

Bender, Hans. "Der Rosenheimer Spuk—ein Fall spontaner Psychokinese." *Zeitschrift fuer Parapsychologie und Grenzgebiete der Psychologie* XI, No. 2 (Bern and Munich: Francke Verlag, 1968): 113-31.

Bengston, William, with Sylvia Fraser. *The Energy Cure: Unraveling the Mystery of Hands-On Healing*. Boulder, CO: Sounds True, 2010.

Betsworth, Deborah G., and Jo-Ida C. Hansen. "The Categorization of Serendipitous Career Development Events." *Journal of Career Assessment* 4, No. 1 (Winter 1996): 91-98.

Björnsson, Hafsteinn. *Sögur ur safni Hafsteins midils*. Reykjavik, Iceland: Skuggsja, 1972.

Blake, John. "The Other Side: Where do coincidences come from?" *CNN*. 2015. http://www.cnn.com/2015/12/29/us/odd-coincidences-synchronicity-the-other-side/

Blum, Deborah. *Ghost Hunters: William James and the Search for Scientific Proof of Life After Death*. New York: Penguin, 2006.

Bohm, David. *Wholeness and the Implicate Order*. London: Routledge, 1980, 2002.

Bösch, Holger, Fiona Steinkamp, and Emil Boller. "Examining Psychokinesis: The Interaction of Human Intention with Random Number Generators—A Meta-Analysis." *Psychological Bulletin* 132, No.4 (2006): 497-523.

Bowman, Carol. *Children's Past Lives: How Past Life Memories Affect Your Child*. New York: Bantam, 1997, 1998.

Bowman, Carol. *Return from Heaven: Beloved Relatives Reincarnated within Your Family*. New York: HarperCollins, 2001.

Bozzano, Ernesto. *Le Visioni dei Morenti*. Verona: Salvatore Palminteri, 1947.

Brackman, Arnold C. *The Search for the Gold of Tutankhamen*. New York: Pocket Books, 1977.

Braud, William. "Toward the Quantitative Assessment of 'Meaningful Coincidences'." *Parapsychological Review* 14, No. 4 (July-August 1983): 5-10.

Braude, Stephen E. *Crimes of Reason: On Mind, Nature, and the Paranormal*. Lanham, MD: Rowman & Littlefield, 2014.

Braude, Stephen E. *The Gold Leaf Lady and Other Parapsychological Investigations*. Chicago: The University of Chicago Press, 2007.

Braude, Stephen E. *Immortal Remains: The Evidence for Life after Death*. Lanham, MD: Rowman & Littlefield, 2003.

Braude, Stephen E. *The Limits of Influence: Psychokinesis and the Philosophy of Science*. New York: Routledge & Kegan Paul, 1986.

Briggs, John P., and F. David Peat. *Looking Glass Universe: The Emerging Science of Wholeness*. New York: Simon & Schuster, 1984.

Bronson, Po. *What Should I Do with My Life? The True Story of People Who Answered the Ultimate Question*. New York: Random House, 2002, 2003.

Brown, Brené. *Rising Strong: How the Ability to Reset Transforms the Way We Live, Love, Parent, and Lead*. New York: Random House, 2015.

Brownell, George B. *Reincarnation*. 2nd ed. Santa Barbara, CA: Aquarian Ministry, 1949.

Buhner, Stephen Harrod. *Ensouling Language: On the Art of Nonfiction and the Writer's Life*. Rochester, VT: Inner Traditions, 2010.

Bulkeley, Kelly, and Patricia Bulkley. *Dreaming Beyond Death: A Guide to Pre-Death Dreams and Visions*. Boston: Beacon Press, 2005.

Bunzel, B., B. Schmidl-Mohl, A. Grundböck, and G. Wollenek. "Does changing the heart mean changing personality? A retrospective inquiry on 47 heart transplant patients." *Quality of Life Research* 1 (1992): 251-6.

Burnham, Sophy. *Angel Letters*. New York: Ballantine Books, 1991.

Burnham, Sophy. *The Art of Intuition: Cultivating Your Inner Wisdom*. New York: Jeremy P. Tarcher/Penguin, 2011.

Burnham, Sophy. *A Book of Angels: Reflections on Angels Past and Present and True Stories of How They Touch Our Lives*. New York: Ballantine Books, 1990.

Bush, Nancy Evans. *The Buddha in Hell and Other Alarms: Distressing Near-Death Experiences in Perspective*. 2016.

Bush, Nancy Evans. *Dancing Past the Dark: Distressing Near-Death Experiences*. 2012.

Bush, Nancy Evans. "Distressing Western Near-Death Experiences: Finding a Way through the Abyss." In *The Handbook of Near-Death Experiences: Thirty Years of Investigation*. Eds. Janice Miner Holden, Bruce Greyson, and Debbie James. Santa Barbara, CA: Praeger, 2009. Pp. 63-86.

Caddy, Peter, with Jeremy Slocombe and Renata Caddy. *In Perfect Timing: Memoirs of a Man for the New Millennium*. Forres, UK: Findhorn Press, 1995, 1998.

Cameron, Julia. *The Vein of Gold: A Journey to Your Creative Heart*. New York: Tarcher/Putnam, 1996.

Caputo, Theresa, with Kristina Grish. *Good Grief: Heal Your Soul, Honor Your Loved Ones, and Learn to Live Again*. New York: Atria, 2017.

Cardeña, Etzel. "The Experimental Evidence for Parapsychological Phenomena: A Review." *American Psychologist* 73, No. 5 (2018): 663-77.

Carman, Elizabeth B., and Neil J. Carman. *Cosmic Cradle: Spiritual Dimensions of Life Before Birth*. Rev. ed. Berkeley, CA: North Atlantic Books, 2013.

Carpenter, James C. *First Sight: ESP and Parapsychology in Everyday Life*. Lanham, MD: Rowman & Littlefield, 2012.

Chamberlain, David B. *Babies Remember Birth: and Other Extraordinary Scientific Discoveries about the Mind and Personality of Your Newborn*. Los Angeles: Tarcher, 1988.

Charbonier, Jean-Jacques. *Les 7 bonnes raisons de croire à l'au-delà*. Paris: Guy Trédaniel, J'ai Lu, 2012.

Chesnut, Andrew. *Born Again in Brazil: The Pentecostal Boom and the Pathogens of Poverty*. New Brunswick, NJ: Rutgers University Press, 1997.

Chopra, Deepak. *How to Know God: The Soul's Journey into the Mystery of Mysteries*. New York: Three Rivers, 2000.

Chopra, Deepak. *The Spontaneous Fulfillment of Desire: Harnessing the Infinite Power of Coincidence*. New York: Three Rivers Press, 2003.

Cicero. *De Divinatione*. Loeb Classical Library. Trans. W. A. Falconer. Cambridge, MA: Harvard University Press, 1938.

Clelland, Mike. *The Messengers: Owls, Synchronicity and the UFO Abductee*. Richard Dolan Press, 2015.

Coates, James. *Photographing the Invisible*. Chicago: Advanced Thought Publishing Company, 1911.

Cockell, Jenny. *Past Lives, Future Lives*. New York: Fireside, 1996.

Coffey, Maria. *Explorers of the Infinite: The Secret Spiritual Lives of Extreme Athletes—and What They Reveal about Near-Death Experiences, Psychic Communication, and Touching the Beyond*. New York: Jeremy P. Tarcher/Penguin, 2008.

Coleman, J. C. *Abnormal Psychology and Modern Life*. Chicago: Scott, Foresman and Company, 1956.

Coleman, Loren. "The Sudden Death of Joe Fisher." *The Anomalist.* https://www.anomalist.com/milestones/fisher.html (accessed August 4, 2018).

Coleman, Stephanie, Bernard D. Beitman, and Elif Celebi. "Weird Coincidences Commonly Occur." *Psychiatric Annals* 39, No. 5 (2009): 265-70.

Collins, Robin. "The Fine-Tuning Design Argument: A Scientific Argument for the Existence of God." In *Reason for the Hope Within.* Ed. Michael J. Murray. Grand Rapids, MI: Eerdmans, 1998.

Collins, Robin. "The Teleological Argument: An Exploration of the Fine-Tuning of the Universe." In *The Blackwell Companion to Natural Theology*. Eds. William Lane Craig and J. P. Moreland. Oxford, UK: Wiley-Blackwell. Pp. 202-81.

Combs, Allan, and Mark Holland. *Synchronicity: Through the Eyes of Science, Myth, and the Trickster.* 3rd ed. New York: Marlowe & Company, 1996, 2001.

Cooper, Callum E. *Telephone Calls from The Dead: A Revised Look at the Phenomenon Thirty Years On.* Portsmouth, UK: Tricorn Books, 2012.

Costin, George, Kristina Dzara, and David Scott Resch. "Synchronicity: Coincidence Detection and Meaningful Life Events." 41, No. 12 (2011): 572-5.

Crichton, Michael. *Travels.* New York: Vintage Books, 1988.

Crowley, Jonette. *The Eagle and the Condor: A True Story of an Unexpected Mystical Journey.* Greenwood Village, CO: StoneTree Publishing, 2007.

Davids, Paul, and Gary E. Schwartz with John Allison. *An Atheist in Heaven: The Ultimate Evidence for Life after Death?* Reno, NV: Yellow Hat, 2016.

Davies, Paul. *Superforce: The Search for a Grand Unified Theory of Nature.* New York: Simon & Schuster, 1984.

Davis, John Jefferson. "The Design Argument, Cosmic 'Fine-Tuning,' and the Anthropic Principle." *International Journal for Philosophy of Religion* 22, No. 3 (1987): 139-50.

Delpech, Geneviève. *Le don d'ailleurs: Autobiographie d'une médium.* Paris: Pygmalion, J'ai Lu, 2015.

Delpech, Geneviève. *Te retrouver: L'amour plus fort que la mort.* Paris: Editions First, 2017.

Diaconis, Persi, and Frederick Mosteller. "Methods for Studying Coincidences." *Journal of the American Statistical Association* 84, No. 408 (1989): 853-61.

Diamond, Debra. *Life After Near Death: Miraculous Stories of Healing and Transformation in the Extraordinary Lives of People with Newfound Powers.* Wayne, NJ: New Page Books, 2016.

Diamond, Stephen. *What the Trees Said.* New York: Delta, 1971.

Dijksterhuis, Ap, Maarten W. Bos, Loran F. Nordgren, and Rick B. van Baaren. "On Making the Right Choice: The Deliberation-Without-Attention Effect." *Science* 311 (March 2006): 1005-7.

Dillard, Sherrie. *You* Are *a Medium: Discover Your Natural Abilities to Communicate with the Other Side.* Woodbury, MN: Llewellyn Publications, 2013.

Dougherty, Ned. *Fast Lane to Heaven: Celestial Encounters That Changed My Life.* Charlottesville, VA: Hampton Roads, 2001.

Doyle, Tom, with Greg Webster. *Dreams and Visions: Is Jesus Awakening the Muslim World?* Nashville, TN: Thomas Nelson, 2012.

Duffin, Jacalyn. *Medical Miracles: Doctors, Saints, and Healing in the Modern World*. New York: Oxford University Press, 2009.

Dunne, Brenda J. "Co-Operator Experiments with an REG Device." Technical Note PEAR 91005, Princeton Engineering Anomalies Research, Princeton University, School of Engineering/Applied Science. Princeton, NJ: December 1991.

Dunne, J. W. *An Experiment with Time*. New York: Macmillan, 1927.

Durham, Janis Heaphy. *The Hand on the Mirror: A True Story of Life Beyond Death*. New York: Grand Central, 2015.

Dyer, Wayne W., and Dee Garnes. *Memories of Heaven: Children's Astounding Recollections of the Time Before They Came to Earth*. Carlsbad, CA: Hay House, 2015.

Dyson, Freeman. "One in a Million." In *The Scientist as Rebel*. New York: New York Review of Books, 2006. Pp. 321-32.

Eadie, Betty J., with Curtis Taylor. *Embraced by the Light*. Carson City, NV: Gold Leaf Press, 1992.

Eisenbeiss, Wolfgang, and Deiter Hassler. "An Assessment of Ostensible Communications with a Deceased Grandmaster as Evidence of Survival." *Journal of the Society of Psychical Research* 70, No. 2 (April 2006): 65-97.

Eisenbud, Jule. *Psi and Psychoanalysis*. New York: Grune & Stratton, 1970.

Eisenbud, Jule. "Seduction by Synchronicity." *Psychic* (October 1975).

Eisenbud, Jule. *The World of Ted Serios: "Thoughtographic" Studies of an Extraordinary Mind*. New York: William Morrow & Co., 1967.

Ertel, Suitbert, and Kenneth Irving. *The Tenacious Mars Effect*. Somerset: Urania Trust, 1996.

Falk, Ruma. "Judgment of Coincidences: Mine Versus Yours." *American Journal of Psychology* 102, No. 4 (Winter 1989): 477-93.

Ferris, G. A. J. "Planetary Influences on Sunspots." *Journal of the British Astronomical Association* 79, No. 5 (1969): 385-8.

Fiore, Edith. *The Unquiet Dead: A Psychologist Treats Spirit Possession*. New York: Ballantine Books, 1987.

Fisher, Joe. *The Siren Call of Hungry Ghosts: A Riveting Investigation into Channeling and Spirit Guides*. New York: Paraview Press, 2001.

Flammarion, Camille. *L'inconnu et les problèmes psychiques*. New York: Harper & Brothers, 1900.

Flohr, Caroline. *Heaven's Child: A Mother's Story of Tragedy and the Enduring Strength of Family*. 2012.

Fukurai, T. *Clairvoyance and Thoughtography*. London: Rider & Co., 1931.

Gauld, Alan, and A. D. Cornell. *Poltergeists*. London: Routledge & Kegan Paul, 1979.

Gauquelin, Michel. *L'influence des astres: Etude critique et expérimentale*. Paris: Le Dauphin, 1955.

Gauquelin, Michel. "Is There a Mars Effect?" *Journal of Scientific Exploration* 2 (1988): 29-51.

Giesemann, Suzanne. *The Priest and the Medium: The Amazing True Story of Psychic Medium B. Anne Gehman and Her Husband, Former Jesuit Priest Wayne Knoll, Ph.D.* Carlsbad, CA: Hay House, 2009.

Giesemann, Suzanne. *Wolf's Message*. 2014.

Gilbert, Elizabeth. *Big Magic: Creative Living Beyond Fear*. New York: Riverhead Books, 2015.

Gilbert, Elizabeth. *Eat Pray Love: One Woman's Search for Everything Across Italy, India and Indonesia*. New York: Viking, 2006.

Giovetti, P. "Visions of the dead, death-bed visions and near-death experiences in Italy." *Human Nature* 1 (1999): 38-4.

Gladstone, William. Foreword to *Super Synchronicity: Where Science and Spirit Meet*, by Gary E. Schwartz, xix-xxi. Vancouver, BC: Param Media, 2017.

Greeley, Andrew. *Death and Beyond*. Chicago: Thomas More Association, 1976.

Greeley, Andrew. "The 'Impossible': It's Happening." *Noetic Sciences Review* No. 2 (Spring 1987).

Greeley, Andrew. "Mysticism Goes Mainstream." *American Health* 6, No. 1 (January-February 1987).

Greeley, Andrew. *Sociology of the Paranormal: A Reconnaissance*. Beverly Hills, CA: Sage Publications, 1975.

Green, Julia. "One in a Million." *Modern People* (October 27, 1974).

Greenwood, Frederick. *Imagination in Dreams and Their Study*. London: John Lane, 1894.

Gregory, Anita. Introduction to *Experiments in Mental Suggestion*, by L. L. Vasiliev, rev. ed., xvii-xliii. Charlottesville, VA: Hampton Roads, 1976, 2002.

Greyson, Bruce, and Nancy Evans Bush. "Distressing Near-Death Experiences." *Psychiatry* 55, No. 1 (February 1992): 95-110.

Grof, Christina, and Stanislav Grof. *The Stormy Search for the Self: A Guide to Personal Growth through Transformational Crisis*. Los Angeles: J. P. Tarcher, 1990.

Grof, Stanislav. *When the Impossible Happens: Adventures in Non-Ordinary Realities*. Boulder, CO: Sounds True, 2006.

Grof, Stanislav, and Christina Grof, eds. *Spiritual Emergency: When Personal Transformation Becomes a Crisis*. Los Angeles: J. P. Tarcher, 1989.

Guggenheim, Bill, and Judy Guggenheim. *Hello from Heaven!: A New Field of Research—After-Death Communication—Confirms That Life and Love Are Eternal*. New York: Bantam, 1995.

Gurney, Edmund, Frederic W. H. Myers, and Frank Podmore. *Phantasms of the Living*. London: Society for Psychical Research, Trübner and Co., 1886.

Hallett, Elisabeth. *Soul Trek: Meeting Our Children on the Way to Birth*. Hamilton, MT: Light Hearts Publishing, 1995.

Hallett, Elisabeth. *Stories of the Unborn Soul: The Mystery and Delight of Pre-Birth Communication*. San Jose: Writers Club Press, 2002.

Haraldsson, Erlendur. *The Departed Among the Living: An Investigative Study of Afterlife Encounters*. Guildford, UK: White Crow Books, 2012.

Haraldsson, Erlendur. *Indridi Indridason: The Icelandic Physical Medium*. Hove, UK: White Crow Books, 2015.

Haraldsson, Erlendur. *Modern Miracles: Sathya Sai Baba: The Story of a Modern Day Prophet*. Guildford, UK: White Crow Books, 1987, 2013.

Haraldsson, Erlendur. "Possible Evidence of Survival." In Kean. Pp. 294-304.

Haraldsson, Erlendur. "A Psychological Comparison Between Ordinary Children and Those Who Claim Previous-Life Memories." *Journal of Scientific Exploration* 11, No. 3 (1997): 323-35.

Haraldsson, Erlendur. Review of *Telephone Calls from The Dead: A Revised Look at the Phenomenon Thirty Years On*, by Callum E. Cooper. *Journal of Scientific Exploration* 27, No. 2 (2013): 352-3.
Haraldsson, Erlendur, and James G. Matlock. *I Saw a Light and Came Here: Children's Experiences of Reincarnation*. Hove, UK: White Crow, 2016.
Hardy, Alister, Robert Harvie, and Arthur Koestler. *The Challenge of Chance: A Mass Experiment in Telepathy and Its Unexpected Outcome*. New York: Random House, 1973.
Harlow, S. Ralph. "The Day We Saw the Angels." *Guideposts* (1970).
Harner, Michael. *The Way of the Shaman: A Guide to Power and Healing*. New York: Bantam, 1980, 1982.
Harrison, Mary, and Peter Harrison. *The Children That Time Forgot*. 1983, 1989, 2014.
Hart, Hornell. "Six Theories about Apparitions." *Proceedings of the Society for Psychical Research* 50, Part 185 (May 1956): 153-239.
Hasan, Heba. "Author 'Predicts' *Titanic* Sinking, 14 Years Earlier." *Time* (April 14, 2012). http://newsfeed.time.com/2012/04/14/author-predicts-titanic-sinking-14-years-earlier/ (accessed November 10, 2018).
Hensley, Mary Helen. *Promised by Heaven: A Doctor's Return from the Afterlife to a Destiny of Love and Healing*. New York: Atria, 2015.
Hiebert, Paul G. *Anthropological Reflections on Missiological Issues*. Grand Rapids, MI: Baker, 1994.
Hiley, B. J., and F. David Peat. "General introduction: the development of David Bohm's ideas from the plasma to the implicate order." In *Quantum Implications: Essays in Honour of David Bohm*. Eds. B. J. Hiley and F. David Peat. London: Routledge & Kegan Paul, 1987. Pp. 1-32.
Hilgard, Ernest. *Divided Consciousness: Multiple Controls in Human Thought and Action*. New York: John Wiley & Sons, 1977.
Hinze, Sarah. *We Lived in Heaven: Spiritual Accounts of Souls Coming to Earth*. Rexburg, ID: Spring Creek Book Company, 2006.
Hinze, Sarah, with Laura Lofgreen. *The Memory Catcher*. Provo, UT: Spring Creek Book Company, 2012.
Hippocrates (ascribed to). *De alimento*. In *Hippocrates on Diet and Hygiene*. Trans. John Precope. London: 1952.
Holden, James Herschel. *A History of Horoscopic Astrology: From the Babylonian Period to the Modern Age*. 2nd ed. Tempe, AZ: American Federation of Astrologers, 1996, 2006.
Holmes, Oliver Wendell. *Over the Teacups*. Cambridge, MA: Riverside Press, 1890-91.
Honorton, Charles, and Diane Ferrari. "'Future telling': A meta-analysis of forced-choice precognition experiments, 1935-1987." *Journal of Parapsychology* 53 (1989): 281-308.
Hopcke, Robert H. *There Are No Accidents in Love and Relationships: Meaningful Coincidences and the Stories of Our Families*. Asheville, NC: Chiron Publications, 2018.
Hopcke, Robert H. *There Are No Accidents: Synchronicity and the Stories of Our Lives*. New York: Riverhead, 1997.
Hunt, Stoker. *Ouija: The Most Dangerous Game*. New York: Harper & Row, 1985.

Ichikawa Kimie. *Inochi no Musubi—Ai wo Hagukumu Yutaka na Shussan*. Tokyo: Koyo Shobo, 2014.

Inglis, Brian. *Coincidence: A Matter of Chance – or Synchronicity?* London: Hutchinson, 1990.

Introvigne, Massimo. "Embraced by the Church? Betty Eadie, Near-Death Experiences, and Mormonism." *Dialogue: A Journal of Mormon Thought* 29, No. 3 (Fall 1996): 99-119.

Jackson, Bill. *The Quest for the Radical Middle: A History of the Vineyard*. Cape Town: Vineyard International, 1999.

Jackson, Laura Lynne. *The Light Between Us: Stories from Heaven, Lessons for the Living*. New York: Spiegel & Grau, 2015.

Jahn, Robert G., and Brenda J. Dunne. *Consciousness and the Source of Reality: The PEAR Odyssey*. Princeton, NJ: ICRL Press, 2011.

Jahn, Robert G., and Brenda J. Dunne. "Sensors, Filters, and the Source of Reality." *Journal of Scientific Exploration* 18, No. 4 (2004): 547-70.

James, William. *The Varieties of Religious Experience*. In *Writings 1902-1920*. Ed. Bruce Kuklick. The Library of America. New York: Literary Classics of the United States, 1987.

Jasmin, Robert. *Le temps d'Alexandre*. Québec: Editions Papyrus, 1989.

Jeans, James. *The Mysterious Universe*. New York: The Macmillan Company, 1930, 1937.

Jenkins, Stephen. *The Undiscovered Country*. Sudbury, UK: Neville Spearman, 1976.

Johnson, Alice. "Coincidences." *Proceedings of the Society for Psychical Research* 14 (1899): 158-330.

Johnson, P. E. "A testimony." *Relief Society Magazine* 3, No. 8 (August 1920).

Johnson, Robert A. *Inner Work: Using Dreams and Active Imagination for Personal Growth*. New York: HarperOne, 1986.

Joplin, Laura. *Love, Janis*. New York: Villard, 1992.

Jovanovic, Pierre. *Enquête sur l'existence des anges gardiens*. Paris: Editions Filipacchi, J'ai Lu, 1993.

Jung, C. G. "Foreword to the 'I Ching'." In *The Collected Works*. Vol. 11. *Psychology and Religion: West and East*. 2nd ed. London: Routledge and Kegan Paul, 1969.

Jung, C. G. *Memories, Dreams, Reflections*. Ed. Aniela Jaffé. Trans. Richard and Clara Winston. Rev. ed. New York: Vintage Books, 1961, 1989.

Jung, C. G. "On Synchronicity." In Jung, *Synchronicity*.

Jung, C. G. "Spirit and Life." In *The Collected Works*. Vol. 8. *The Structure and Dynamics of the Psyche*. 2nd ed. London: Routledge and Kegan Paul, 1969.

Jung, C. G. *Synchronicity: An Acausal Connecting Principle*. Trans. R. F. C. Hull. Princeton, NJ: Princeton University Press, 1960, 2010.

Kalweit, Holger. *Dreamtime & Inner Space: The World of the Shaman*. Trans. Werner Wünsche. Boston: Shambhala, 1988.

Kammerer, Paul. *Das Gesetz der Serie*. Stuttgart-Berlin: Deutsche Verlags-Anstalt, 1919.

Kantrowitz, Barbara, and Patricia King. "In Search of the Sacred: America's Quest for Spiritual Meaning." *Newsweek* 124, No. 22 (November 28, 1994).

Kean, Leslie. *Surviving Death: A Journalist Investigates Evidence for an Afterlife*. New York: Crown Archetype, 2017.

Keener, Craig S. *Miracles: The Credibility of the New Testament Accounts*. Grand Rapids, MI: Baker Academic, 2011.

Kelleher, Jack. "Jack and the Mir-ack-ulous." In Davids and Schwartz with Allison. Pp. 156-74.

Kircher, Pamela M. *Love Is the Link: A Hospice Doctor Shares Her Experience of Near-Death and Dying*. 2nd ed. Pagosa Springs, CO: Awakenings Press, 2013.

Koestler, Arthur. "The Mysterious Power of Chance." *The Sunday Times* of London (May 4, 1974).

Koestler, Arthur. *The Roots of Coincidence: An Excursion into Parapsychology*. New York: Random House, 1972.

Kraft, Dean, with Rochelle Kraft. *A Touch of Hope: The Autobiography of a Laying-on-of-Hands Healer*. New York: G. P. Putnam's Sons, 1998.

Krippner, Stanley, Fariba Bogzaran, and André Percia de Carvalho. *Extraordinary Dreams and How to Work with Them*. Albany: State University of New York Press, 2002.

Kübler-Ross, Elisabeth, and David Kessler. *Life Lessons: Two Experts on Death & Dying Teach Us About the Mysteries of Life & Living*. New York: Scribner, 2000.

Kuld, J. J. E. *Í lífsins ólgusjó*. Reykjavik, Iceland: Ægisútgáfan, 1979.

LaGrand, Louis E. *Messages and Miracles: Extraordinary Experiences of the Bereaved*. St. Paul, MN: Llewellyn, 1999.

Laplace, Pierre-Simon. *Essai philosophique sur les probabilités*. Paris, 1814.

Laurentin, René, and P. Mahéo. *Bilocations de Mère Yvonne-Aimée de Malestroit*. Paris: Editions de Guibert, 1995.

Leibniz, Gottfried Wilhelm. *Discourse on Metaphysics*. 1686. In *Philosophical Essays*. Trans. Roger Ariew and Daniel Garber. Indianapolis: Hackett, 1989.

Leininger, Bruce, and Andrea Leininger, with Ken Gross. *Soul Survivor: The Reincarnation of a World War II Fighter Pilot*. New York: Grand Central, 2009.

Lerma, John. *Into the Light: Real Life Stories about Angelic Visits, Visions of the Afterlife, and Other Pre-Death Experiences*. Pompton Plains, NJ: New Page Books, 2007.

Lerma, John. *Learning from the Light: Pre-Death Experiences, Prophecies, and Angelic Messages of Hope*. Franklin Lakes, NJ: New Page Books, 2009.

Leslie, John. "How to Draw Conclusions from a Fine-Tuned Cosmos." In *Physics, Philosophy and Theology: A Common Quest for Understanding*. Eds. Robert Russell et al. Vatican City State: Vatican Observatory Press, 1988. Pp. 297-312.

Lilly, John C. *The Center of the Cyclone: An Autobiography of Inner Space*. New York: Bantam: 1972.

Littlewood, J. E. *Littlewood's Miscellany*. Ed. Béla Bollobás. Rev. ed. Cambridge, UK: Cambridge University Press, 1986.

Lodge, Oliver J. *Raymond, or Life and Death, with Examples of the Evidence for Survival of Memory and Affection after Death*. 2nd ed. London: Methuen & Co., 1916.

Long, Jeffrey, with Paul Perry. *God and the Afterlife: The Ground-Breaking New Evidence for God and Near-Death Experience*. New York: HarperCollins, 2016.

Long, Max Freedom. *The Secret Science Behind Miracles*. Tarrytown, NY: Robert Collier Publications, 1948.

Lorain-Berger, Sylvie. *Les messagers de l'au-delà*. Paris: Editions Exergue, 2006, 2008, 2014.

Lorimer, David. "Distant Feelings." *Network* 71 (December 1999).

Luke, David P., and Shelley Morin. "Exploration of the Validity and Utility of a Reward Contingency in a Non-Intentional, Forced-Choice Precognition Task." *Journal of the American Society for Psychical Research* 78 (January 2014): 207-18.

Luke, David P., Chris A. Roe, and Jamie Davison. "Testing for Forced-Choice Precognition Using a Hidden Task: Two Replications." *The Journal of Parapsychology* 72 (2008): 133-54.

Lukoff, David. "Spirituality and Recovery from Serious Mental Problems." In *The Oxford Handbook of Psychology and Spirituality*. Ed. Lisa J. Miller. New York: Oxford University Press, 2012. Pp. 410-22.

Lundahl, Craig R. "Angels in Near-Death Experiences." *Journal of Near-Death Studies* 11, No. 1 (Fall 1992): 49-56.

Lundahl, Craig R. "Near-Death Visions of Unborn Children: Indications of a Pre-Earth Life." *Journal of Near-Death Studies* 11, No. 2 (Winter 1992): 123-8.

MacGregor, Trish, and Rob MacGregor. *The Synchronicity Highway: Exploring Coincidence, the Paranormal, & Alien Contact*. Hertford, NC: Crossroad Press, 2013.

Maguire, Toni. *Memories of the Light: A Story of Spiritual Existence before Physical Birth*. Bloomington, IN: iUniverse, 2000, 2012.

Main, Roderick. *Revelations of Chance: Synchronicity as Spiritual Experience*. Albany, NY: State University of New York Press, 2007.

Manning, Matthew. *The Link: Matthew Manning's Own Story of His Extraordinary Psychic Gifts*. New York: Holt, Rinehart and Winston, 1974, 1975.

Mansfield, Victor. *Synchronicity, Science, and Soul-Making*. Chicago: Open Court, 1995.

Marris, Peter. *Widows and Their Families*. London: Routledge & Kegan Paul, 1958.

Martin, Joel, and Patricia Romanowski. *Love Beyond Life: The Healing Power of After-Death Communication*. New York: Harper, 1997.

Martin, Malachi. *Hostage to the Devil: The Possession and Exorcism of Five Contemporary Americans*. New York: Bantam Books, 1977.

Matlock, James, and Iris Giesler-Petersen. "Asian versus Western Intermission Memories: Universal Features and Cultural Variations." *Journal of Near-Death Studies* 35, No. 1 (2016): 3-29.

Mattiesen, Emil. *Das persönliche Überleben des Todes*. Vol. 2. Berlin: Walter de Gruyter, 1936-39.

Mattingley, Annie. *The After Death Chronicles: True Stories of Comfort, Guidance, and Wisdom from Beyond the Veil*. Charlottesville, VA: Hampton Roads, 2017.

Mattuck, Richard D., and Evan Harris Walker. "The Action of Consciousness on Matter: A Quantum Mechanical Theory of Psychokinesis." In *The Iceland Papers*. Ed. Andrea Puharich. Amherst, WI: Essentia Research Association, 1979. Pp. 111-59.

Mauthner, Oliver E., Enza De Luca, Jennifer M. Poole, Susan E. Abbey, Margrit Shildrick, Mena Gewarges, and Heather J. Ross. "Heart transplants: Identity disruption, bodily integrity and interconnectedness." *Health* (2014).

McClenon, James. "A survey of elite scientists: Their attitudes towards ESP and parapsychology." *Journal of Parapsychology* 46 (1982): 127-52.

McClenon, James. *Wondrous Events: Foundations of Religious Belief*. Philadelphia: University of Pennsylvania Press, 1994.

McCraty, Rollin, Mike Atkinson, Viktor Stolc, Adbullah A. Alabdulgader, Alfonsas Vainoras, and Minvydas Ragulskis. "Synchronization of Human Autonomous Nervous System Rhythms with Geomagnetic Activity in Human Subjects." *International Journal of Environmental Research and Public Health* 14, No. 7 (July 2017).

McGarey, Gladys T. *Born to Live.* Scottsdale, AZ: Inkwell Productions, 2008.

McGarey, Gladys Taylor with Jess Stearn. *The Physician within You: Discovering the Power of Inner Healing.* Deerfield Beach, FL: Health Communications, 1997.

Medhus, Elisa. *My Son and the Afterlife: Conversations from the Other Side*. New York: Atria, 2013.

Méheust, Bertrand. *Les miracles de l'esprit: Qu'est-ce que les voyants peuvent nous apprendre?* Paris: La Découverte, 2011.

Mercier, Evelyne-Sarah. *La Mort transfigurée: Recherches sur les expériences vécues aux approches de la mort.* Paris: Belfond, 1992.

Metaxas, Eric. *Miracles: What They Are, Why They Happen, and How They Can Change Your Life.* New York: Dutton, Plume, 2014, 2015.

Meyer, M. B. "Role of personality and cognitive variables in the reporting of experienced meaningful coincidences or 'synchronicity.'" PhD diss. Saybrook Institute, 1989.

Mills, Antonia, Erlendur Haraldsson, and H. H. Jürgen Keil. "Replication Studies of Cases Suggestive of Reincarnation by Three Independent Investigators." *Journal of the American Society for Psychical Research* 88 (1994): 207-19.

Mills, Roy. *The Soul's Remembrance: Earth Is Not Our Home.* Seattle, WA: Onjinjinkta Publishing, 1999.

Moisset, Jean. *Enigmatiques coïncidences: Loi des séries – Synchronicité.* St Vincent sur Jabron, France: Editions PRESENCE, 1993.

Monroe, Robert A. *Far Journeys.* Garden City, NY: Doubleday, 1985, 1987.

Monroe, Robert A. *Journeys Out of the Body.* Updated edition. Garden City, NY: Anchor/Doubleday, 1971, 1977.

Monroe, Robert A. *Ultimate Journey.* New York: Harmony, 1994.

Moody, Raymond A., Jr., *Elvis After Life: Unusual Psychic Experiences Surrounding the Death of a Superstar.* Atlanta, GA: Peachtree Publishers, 1987.

Moody, Raymond A., Jr., *Life After Life.* 25th anniversary edition. New York: HarperOne, 1975, 2001.

Moody, Raymond A., Jr., *Reflections on Life After Life.* New York: Bantam, 1977.

Moody, Raymond, with Paul Perry. *Glimpses of Eternity: An Investigation into Shared Death Experiences.* London: Rider Books, 2010.

Moolenburgh, H. C. *Meetings with Angels.* Trans. Tony Langham and Plym Peters. Saffron Walden, UK: C. W. Daniel, 1992.

Moorjani, Anita. *Dying to Be Me: My Journey from Cancer, to Near Death, to True Healing.* Carlsbad, CA: Hay House, 2012.

Morse, Melvin, with Paul Perry. *Parting Visions: Uses and Meanings of Pre-Death, Psychic, and Spiritual Experiences.* New York: Villard Books, 1994.

Moss, Robert. *The Boy Who Died and Came Back: Adventures of a Dream Archaeologist in the Multiverse.* Novato, CA: New World Library, 2014.

Moss, Robert. *Dreaming True: How to Dream Your Future and Change Your Life for the Better.* New York: Pocket Books, 2000.

Moss, Robert. *The Three "Only" Things: Tapping the Power of Dreams, Coincidence & Imagination*. Novato, CA: New World Library, 2007.

Mossbridge, Julia, Patrizio Tressoldi, and Jessica Utts. "Predictive physiological anticipation preceding seemingly unpredictable stimuli: a meta-analysis." *Frontiers in Psychology: Perception Science* 3 (October 2012).

Myss, Caroline. *Anatomy of the Spirit: The Seven Stages of Power and Healing*. New York: Three Rivers Press, 1996.

Myss, Caroline. *Invisible Acts of Power: Personal Choices That Create Miracles*. New York: Free Press, 2004.

Myss, Caroline. *Sacred Contracts: Awakening Your Divine Potential*. New York: Harmony Books, 2001.

Nahm, Michael. "Letter to the Editor: On Mediumistic Communications by Living Agents." *Journal of the Society for Psychical Research* 74 (2010): 53-56.

Nahm, Michael. "Reflections on the Context of Near-Death Experiences." *Journal of Scientific Exploration* 25, No. 3 (2011): 453-78.

Nakagaki, Toshiyuki, Ryo Kobayashi, Yasumasa Nishiura, and Tetsuo Ueda. "Obtaining Multiple Separate Food Sources: Behavioural Intelligence in the *Physarum* plasmodium." *Proceedings of the Royal Society B* 271, No. 1554 (November 2004).

Nakagaki, Toshiyuki, Hiroyasu Yamada, and Ágota Tóth. "Intelligence: Maze-solving by an Amoeboid Organism." *Nature* 407 (September 2000).

Nancy, Jean-Luc. *L'Intrus*. Expanded. Paris: Galilée, 2000, 2010.

Neal, Mary C. *To Heaven and Back: A Doctor's Extraordinary Account of Her Death, Heaven, Angels, and Life Again*. Colorado Springs, CO: WaterBrook Press, 2011, 2012.

Nelson, Lee. *Beyond the Veil*. Vol. 1. Orem, UT: Cedar Fort, 1988.

Nelson, Roger D. "Implicit Physical Psi: The Global Consciousness Project." In *Parapsychology: A Handbook for the 21st Century*. Eds. Etzel Cardeña, John Palmer, and David Marcusson-Clavertz. Jefferson, NC: McFarland & Co., 2015. Pp. 282-92.

Neppe, Vernon M. "A Detailed Analysis of an Important Chess Game: Revisiting 'Maróczy versus Korchnoi." *Journal of the Society for Psychical Research* 71, No. 3 (2007): 129-47.

Newton, Michael. *Destiny of Souls: New Case Studies of Life Between Lives*. Woodbury, MN: Llewellyn, 2000.

Newton, Michael. *Journey of Souls: Case Studies of Life Between Lives*. Woodbury, MN: Llewellyn, 1994.

Newton, Michael. *Life Between Lives: Hypnotherapy for Spiritual Regression*. St. Paul, MN: Llewellyn, 2004.

Newton, Michael, ed. *Memories of the Afterlife: Life Between Lives: Stories of Personal Transformation*. Woodbury, MN: Llewellyn, 2009.

Nicholls, Graham. *Avenues of the Human Spirit*. Winchester, UK: O-Books, 2011.

Noakes, Ben. *I Saw a Ghost: Eye-Witness Accounts by the Famous of Supernatural Encounters*. London: Weidenfeld and Nicolson, 1986.

Ochorowicz, Julian. *Mediumistic Phenomena*. Part I. Trans. Casimir Bernard and Zofia Weaver. Ed. Zofia Weaver. *Journal of Scientific Exploration* 32, No. 1 (Spring 2018): 79-154.

Ockeloen-Korppi, C. F., E. Damskägg, J.-M. Prikkalainen, M. Asjad, A. A. Clerk, F. Massel, M. J. Woolley, and M. A. Sillanpää. "Stabilized entanglement of massive mechanical oscillators." *Nature* 556 (2018): 478-82.

O'Flaherty, Wendy Doniger. *Dreams, Illusion, and Other Realities*. Chicago: University of Chicago Press, 1984.

Ohkado, Masayuki. "Same-Family Cases of the Reincarnation Type in Japan." *Journal of Scientific Exploration* 31, No. 4 (Winter 2017): 551-71.

Ohkado Masayuki and Ikegawa Akira. "Children with Life-between-Life Memories." *Journal of Scientific Exploration* 28, No. 3 (2014): 477-90.

Orloff, Judith. *Second Sight: An Intuitive Psychiatrist Tells Her Extraordinary Story and Shows You How to Tap Your Own Inner Wisdom*. Rev. ed. New York: Three Rivers Press, 2000.

Osis, Karlis, and Erlendur Haraldsson. *At the Hour of Death*. New York: Discus, 1977, 1979.

Palmer, John. "Covert Psi in Computer Solitaire." *Journal of Parapsychology* 64 (2000): 195-211.

Palmer, John, and Brian Millar. "Experimenter Effects in Parapsychological Research." In *Parapsychology: A Handbook for the 21st Century*. Eds. Etzel Cardeña, John Palmer, and David Marcusson-Clavertz. Jefferson, NC: McFarland & Co., 2015. Pp. 293-300.

Paquette, Andrew. "Can Death-Related Dreams Predict Future Deaths? Evidence from a Dream Journal Comprising Nearly 12,000 Dreams." *Journal of Scientific Exploration* 29, No. 3 (2015): 411-423.

Paquette, Andrew. *Dreamer: 20 Years of Psychic Dreams and How They Changed My Life*. Winchester, UK: O-Books, 2011.

Paquette, Andrew. "NDE Implications from a Group of Spontaneous Long-Distance Veridical OBEs." *Journal of Scientific Exploration* 26, No. 4 (2012): 791-824.

Paquette, Andrew. "A New Approach to Veridicality in Dream Psi Studies." *Journal of Scientific Exploration* 26, No. 3 (2012): 589-610.

Paquette, Andrew. "The Rarity of Unambiguous Symbols in Dreams: A Case Study." *Journal of Scientific Exploration* 30, No. 2 (2016): 199-216.

Pasricha, Satwant. *Claims of Reincarnation: An Empirical Study of Cases in India*. New Delhi: Harman Publishing House, 1990.

Pearsall, Paul, Gary E. R. Schwartz, and Linda G. S. Russek. "Changes in Heart Transplant Recipients that Parallel the Personalities of Their Donors." *Integrative Medicine* 2, Nos. 2/3 (1999): 65-72.

Peat, F. David. *Synchronicity: The Marriage of Matter and Psyche*. Pari, Italy: Pari Publishing, 2014.

Peck, M. Scott. *Glimpses of the Devil: A Psychiatrist's Personal Accounts of Possession, Exorcism, and Redemption*. New York: Free Press, 2009.

Peck, M. Scott. *People of the Lie: The Hope for Healing Human Evil*. New York: Touchstone, 1983.

Peck, M. Scott. *The Road Less Traveled: A New Psychology of Love, Traditional Values and Spiritual Growth*. New York: Simon & Schuster, 1978.

Pederson-Krag, Geraldine. "Telepathy and Repression." *Psychoanalytic Quarterly* 16 (January 1947): 61-68.

Pengelley, E. T., and S. J. Asmundsen. "Annual Biological Clocks." *Scientific American* 224, No. 72 (1971).

Peoc'h, René. "Chicken Imprinting and the Tychoscope: An Anpsi Experiment." *Journal of the Society for Psychical Research* 55 (1988): 1-9.

Peoc'h, René. "Psychokinetic Action of Young Chicks on the Path of an Illuminated Source." *Journal of Scientific Exploration* 9, No. 2 (1995): 223-9.

Perry, Paul. Foreword to *We Lived in Heaven: Spiritual Accounts of Souls Coming to Earth*, by Sarah Hinze, xiii-xvii. Rexburg, ID: Spring Creek Book Company, 2006.

Pico della Mirandola, Giovanni. *Opera Omnia*. Basel: 1557.

Pittendrigh, C. S., and V. G. Bruce. "Daily Rhythms as Coupled Oscillator Systems." *Photoperiodism and Related Phenomena in Plants and Animals*. Washington, DC: American Association for the Advancement of Science, 1959.

Plato. *Apology*. Trans. Tom Griffith.

Plato. *The Republic*. Trans. Desmond Lee. 2nd ed. Revised. New York: Penguin, 1987.

Playfair, Guy Lyon. *The Flying Cow: Exploring the Psychic World of Brazil*. Guildford, UK: White Crow Books, 2011.

Playfair, Guy Lyon. *Twin Telepathy*. 3rd ed. rev. and enlarged. Guildford, UK: White Crow Books, 2012.

Poincaré, Henri. *La Science et l'Hypothèse*. Paris: Flammarion, 1902.

Popper, Karl. *The Logic of Scientific Discovery*. London: Hutchinson & Co., 1959.

Pratt, J. Gaither, and William G. Roll. "The Seaford Disturbances." *Journal of Parapsychology* 22 (1958): 79-124.

Priestley, J. B. *Over the Long High Wall: Some Reflections and Speculations on Life, Death and Time*. London: William Heinemann Ltd., 1972.

Prieur, Jean. *Les morts ont donné signe de vie*. Paris: Sorlot et Lanore, 1990.

Prince, Walter Franklin. *Human Experiences, Being a Report on the Results of a Questionnaire and a Discussion of Them*. Boston, MA: Boston Society for Psychical Research, 1931.

Quispel, Gilles. "Gnosis and Psychology." In *The Gnostic Jung*. Ed. Robert A. Segal. Princeton, NJ: Princeton University Press, 1992. Pp. 239-56.

Radin, Dean. Foreword to *Exploring the Collective Unconscious in the Age of Digital Media*. Ed. Stephen Brock Schafer. Hershey, PA: Information Science Reference, 2016.

Radin, Dean. *Supernormal: Science, Yoga, and the Evidence for Extraordinary Abilities*. New York: Deepak Chopra Books, 2013.

Radin, Dean, Roger Nelson, York Dobyns, and Joop Houtkooper. "Reexamining Psychokinesis: Comment on Bösch, Steinkamp, and Boller." *Psychological Bulletin* 132, No. 4 (2006): 529-32.

Radin, Paul. *The Winnebago Tribe*. Lincoln, NE: University of Nebraska Press, 1923, 1970.

Ragueneau, Philippe. *L'autre côté de la vie: Un message d'espoir et d'amour pour ceux qui ont perdu un proche*. Paris: Editions du Rocher, Pocket, 1995, 1997, 2001.

Rawlette, Sharon Hewitt. "Coincidence or Psi? The Epistemic Import of Spontaneous Cases of Purported Psi Identified Post-Verification." *Journal of Scientific Exploration* 33, No. 1 (March 2019): 9-42.

Rees, W. Dewi. "The Hallucinations of Widowhood." *British Medical Journal* 4 (Oct 2, 1971): 37-41.

Reid, Chris R., Tanya Latty, Audrey Dussutour, and Madeleine Beekman. "Slime mold uses externalized spatial 'memory' to navigate in complex environments." *Proceedings of the National Academy of Sciences* 109, No. 43 (October 2012): 17490-4.

Reintjes, Susan. *Third Eye Open: Unmasking Your True Awareness*. Third Eye Publishing, 2003.

Rhine, J. B., and Sara R. Feather. "The study of cases of 'psi trailing' in animals." *Journal of Parapsychology* 26, No. 1 (1962): 1-22.

Rhine, Louisa E. *Hidden Channels of the Mind*. New York: William Sloane, 1961.

Richard, F. D., C. F. Bond, Jr., and J. J. Stokes-Zoota. "One Hundred Years of Social Psychology Quantitatively Described." *Review of General Psychology* 7, No. 4 (2003): 331-63.

Ring, Kenneth, and Madelaine Lawrence. "Further Evidence for Veridical Perception during Near-Death Experiences." *Journal of Near-Death Studies* 11, No. 4 (1993): 223-9.

Rivas, Titus, Anny Dirven, and Rudolf H. Smit. *The* Self *Does Not Die: Verified Paranormal Phenomena from Near-Death Experiences*. Durham, NC: IANDS Publications, 2016.

Rogo, D. Scott. *In Search of the Unknown*. New York: Taplinger, 1976.

Rogo, D. Scott. *Miracles: A Parascientific Inquiry into Wondrous Phenomena*. New York: Dial Press, 1982.

Rommer, Barbara R. *Blessing in Disguise: Another Side of the Near-Death Experience*. St. Paul, MN: Llewellyn, 2000.

Rothschild, Joel. *Signals: An Inspiring Story of Life after Life*. Novato, CA: New World Library, 2000.

Ruff, Betty Clark. "My Toddler Taught Me About Preexistence and Death." *Instructor* (February 1963).

Rushnell, SQuire. *When God Winks: How the Power of Coincidence Guides Your Life*. New York: Atria, 2001.

Ryback, David, with Letitia Sweitzer. *Dreams That Come True: Their Psychic and Transforming Powers*. New York: Doubleday, 1988.

Saigusa, Tetsu, Atsushi Tero, Toshiyuki Nakagaki, and Yoshiki Kuramoto. "Amoebae Anticipate Periodic Events." *Physical Review Letters* 100, No. 1 (January 2008), 018101.

Sams, Jamie, and David Carson. *Medicine Cards: The Discovery of Power Through the Ways of Animals*. Rochester, VT: Bear & Company, 1988.

Sartori, Penny. *The Wisdom of Near-Death Experiences: How Brushes with Death Teach Us to Live*. London: Watkins, 2014.

Schmidt, Helmut. "PK Experiments with Animals as Subjects." *Journal of Parapsychology* 34, No. 4 (1970): 255-61.

Schmied-Knittel, Ina, and Michael T. Schetsche. "Everyday Miracles: Results of a Representative Survey in Germany." *European Journal of Parapsychology* 20.1 (2005): 3-21.

Schwartz, Gary E. "Possible Causal Mechanisms in the Occurrence of Synchronicities: Testing the Spiritual Assistance Hypothesis." *Journal of Spirituality & Paranormal Studies* 34, No. 4 (October 2011): 182-209.

Schwartz, Gary E. *Super Synchronicity: Where Science and Spirit Meet.* Vancouver, BC: Param Media, 2017.

Schwartz, Gary E., with William L. Simon. *The Afterlife Experiments: Breakthrough Scientific Evidence of Life after Death.* New York: Atria, 2002.

Schwartz, Stephan A. *The Secret Vaults of Time: Psychic Archaeology and the Quest for Man's Beginnings.* New York: Grosset & Dunlap, 1978.

Schweizer, Eduard. *Jesus the Parable of God: What Do We Really Know about Jesus?* Princeton Theological Monograph Series 37. Allison Park, PA: Pickwick, 1994.

Serdahely, William J. "Loving Help from the Other Side: A Mosaic of Some Near-Death, and Near-Death-Like, Experiences." *Journal of Near Death Studies* 10, No. 3 (Spring 1992): 171-182.

Sharma, Poonam, and Jim B. Tucker. "Cases of the Reincarnation Type with Memories from the Intermission Between Lives." *Journal of Near-Death Studies* 23, No. 2 (Winter 2004): 101-17.

Sheldrake, Rupert. *Dogs That Know When Their Owners Are Coming Home: And Other Unexplained Powers of Animals.* New York: Crown, 1999.

Sheldrake, Rupert. *The Sense of Being Stared At and Other Aspects of the Extended Mind.* New York: Crown Publishers, 2003.

Shen, Dong. "Unexpected Behavior of Matter in Conjunction with Human Consciousness." *Journal of Scientific Exploration* 24, No. 1 (2010): 41-52.

Shermer, Michael. "Infrequencies." *Scientific American* (October 2014).

Shroder, Tom. *Old Souls.* New York: Simon & Schuster, 1999.

Sidgwick, E. M. "On the Evidence for Clairvoyance." *Proceedings of the Society for Psychical Research* 7 (1891): 30-99.

Sinclair, Upton. *Mental Radio.* London: T. Werner Laurie, 1930.

Smartt, Lisa. *Words at the Threshold: What We Say as We're Nearing Death.* Novato, CA: New World Library, 2017.

Sorensen, Michele R., and David R. Willmore. *The Journey Beyond Life.* Vol. 1. Orem, UT: Family Affair Books, 1988.

Soulières, Joachim. *Les coïncidences.* Paris: Dervy, 2012.

Sparrow, G. Scott. *Blessed Among Women: Encounters with Mary and Her Message.* New York: Harmony, 1996.

Sparrow, G. Scott. *I Am with You Always: True Stories of Encounters with Jesus.* London: Pan Books, 1995, 1996.

Spinelli, Ernesto. "Human Development and Paranormal Cognition." PhD diss. University of Surrey, 1983.

Spin'oza, Baruch. *Ethics Demonstrated in Geometric Order.* 1677.

Stanford, Rex G. "An experimentally testable model for spontaneous psi events: I. Extrasensory events." *Journal of the American Society for Psychical Research* 68 (1974): 34-57.

Stanford, Rex G. "Psi in Everyday Life." *American Society of Psychical Research Newsletter,* No. 16 (Winter 1973).

Stanford, Rex G. "Toward reinterpreting psi events." *Journal of the American Society for Psychical Research* 72, No. 3 (1978): 197-214.

Stanford, R. G., R. Zenhausern, A. Taylor, and M. Dwyer. "Psychokinesis as psi-mediated instrumental response." *Journal of the American Society for Psychical Research* 69 (1975): 127-33.

Stark, Rodney. *What Americans Really Believe.* Waco, TX: Baylor University Press, 2008.

Stefani, F., A. Giesecke, N. Weber, and T. Weier. "Synchronized Helicity Oscillations: A Link Between Planetary Tides and the Solar Cycle?" *Solar Physics* 291, No. 8 (October 2016): 2197-212.

Stevenson, Ian. "Are Poltergeists Living or Are They Dead?" *Journal of the American Society for Psychical Research* 66, No. 3 (July 1972): 233-52.

Stevenson, Ian. *Cases of the Reincarnation Type, Volume I: Ten Cases in India.* Charlottesville, VA: University Press of Virginia, 1975.

Stevenson, Ian. *Cases of the Reincarnation Type, Volume III: Twelve Cases in Lebanon and Turkey.* Charlottesville, VA: University Press of Virginia, 1980.

Stevenson, Ian. *Children Who Remember Previous Lives: A Question of Reincarnation.* Rev. ed. Jefferson, NC: McFarland & Company, Inc., 2001.

Stevenson, Ian. *Reincarnation and Biology: Contribution to the Etiology of Birthmarks and Birth Defects.* Vol. 1. Westport, CT/London, UK: Praeger, 1997.

Stevenson, Ian. "A Review and Analysis of Paranormal Experiences Connected with the Sinking of the *Titanic*." *Journal of the American Society for Psychical Research* 54, No. 4 (October 1960): 153-71.

Stevenson, Ian. "Seven More Paranormal Experiences Associated with the Sinking of the *Titanic*." *Journal of the American Society for Psychical Research* 59 (1965): 211-25.

Stevenson, Ian. "Some Questions Related to Cases of the Reincarnation Type." *Journal of the American Society for Psychical Research* 68 (1974): 395-416.

Stevenson, Ian. "The Substantiality of Spontaneous Cases." *Proceedings of the Parapsychological Association* 5 (1971): 91-128.

Stevenson, Ian. "Telepathic Impressions: A Review and Report of Thirty-Five New Cases." *Proceedings of the American Society for Psychical Research* 29 (1970).

Stevenson, Ian. *Twenty Cases Suggestive of Reincarnation.* 2nd ed. revised and enlarged. Charlottesville, VA: University of Virginia Press, 1980.

Stickney, John. "Coincidence." *New Times* (August 1975).

Stillman, William. *Autism and the God Connection: Redefining the Autistic Experience through Extraordinary Accounts of Spiritual Giftedness.* Naperville, IL: Sourcebooks, 2006.

Stillman, William. *The Secret Language of Spirit: Understanding Spirit Communication in Our Everyday Lives.* Wayne, NJ: New Page Books, 2018.

Stillman, William. *The Soul of Autism: Looking Beyond Labels to Unveil Spiritual Secrets of the Heart Savants.* Franklin Lakes, NJ: New Page Books, 2008.

Storer, Doug. "Good Samaritan on Motorcycle Is Himself Saved by Man He Helped." *National Tattler* (November 10, 1974).

Storm, Howard. *My Descent into Death: A Second Chance at Life.* New York: Doubleday, 2005.

Storm, Lance, Simon J. Sherwood, Chris A. Roe, Patrizio E. Tressoldi, Adam J. Rock, and Lorenzo Di Risio. "On the correspondence between dream content and target material under laboratory conditions: A meta-analysis of dream-ESP studies, 1966-2016." *International Journal of Dream Research* 10, No. 2 (2017): 120-40.

Streit-Horn, Jenny. "A systematic review of research on after-death communication (ADC)." PhD diss. University of North Texas, 2011.

Strobel, Lee. *The Case for Miracles: A Journalist Investigates Evidence for the Supernatural.* Grand Rapids, MI: Zondervan, 2018.

Surprise, Kirby. *Synchronicity: The Art of Coincidence, Choice, and Unlocking Your Mind.* Pompton Plains, NJ: New Page Books, 2012.

Sylvia, Claire, with William Novak. *A Change of Heart.* Boston: Little, Brown & Company, 1997.

Talbot, Michael. *Beyond the Quantum: How the Secrets of the New Physics Are Bridging the Chasm Between Science and Faith.* Toronto: Bantam Books, 1987, 1988.

Talbot, Michael. *The Holographic Universe: The Revolutionary Theory of Reality.* New York: Harper Perennial, 1991, 1992, 2011.

Tang, Edmond. "'Yellers' and Healers—Pentecostalism and the Study of Grassroots Christianity in China." In *Asian and Pentecostal: The Charismatic Face of Christianity in Asia.* Eds. Allan Anderson and Edmond Tang. Regnum Studies in Mission. Asian Journal of Pentecostal Studies Series 3. Oxford: Regnum. Baguio City, Philippines: APTS Press, 2005. Pp. 467-86.

Targ, Russell. *Do You See What I See?: Lasers and Love, ESP and the CIA, and the Meaning of Life.* Charlottesville, VA: Hampton Roads, 2010.

Targ, Russell. *The Reality of ESP: A Physicist's Proof of Psychic Abilities.* Wheaton, IL: Quest Books, 2012.

Tarnas, Richard. *Cosmos and Psyche: Intimations of a New World View.* New York: Plume, 2006, May 2007.

Tart, Charles T., ed. *Altered States of Consciousness.* Garden City, NY: Anchor Books, 1969, 1972.

Tart, Charles T. "Physiological Correlates of Psi Cognition." *International Journal of Neuropsychiatry* 5, No. 4 (1962).

Tart, Charles T. "Psychedelic Experiences Associated with a Novel Hypnotic Procedure, Mutual Hypnosis." In *Altered States of Consciousness.*

Tatz, Dennis. "Woman dies 21 years after heart-lung transplant that gave her a taste for beer." *The Patriot Ledger* (August 29, 2009). http://www.patriotledger.com/x866753736/Organ-transplant-recipient-dies.

Taylor, Jeremy. *Dream Work: Techniques for Discovering the Creative Power in Dreams.* Ramsey, NJ: Paulist Press, 1983.

Tenhaeff, W. H. C. *Aussergewöhnliche Heilkräfte.* Olton: Walter, 1957.

Thornton, Edward. *The Diary of a Mystic.* London: George Allen and Unwin, 1967.

Thurston, Herbert. *The Physical Phenomena of Mysticism.* Chicago: Henry Regnery Company, 1952.

Tucker, Jim B. *Life Before Life: Children's Memories of Previous Lives.* New York: St. Martin's Griffin, 2008.

Tucker, Jim B. *Return to Life: Extraordinary Cases of Children Who Remember Past Lives.* Reprint ed. New York: St. Martin's Griffin, 2015.

Tucker, Jim B., and F. Don Nidiffer. "Psychological Evaluation of American Children Who Report Memories of Previous Lives." *Journal of Scientific Exploration* 28, No. 4 (2014): 585-96.

Tyrell, G. N. M. *The Personality of Man: New Facts and Their Significance.* Melbourne: Penguin, 1947.

Ullman, Montague, and Stanley Krippner with Alan Vaughan. *Dream Telepathy: Experiments in Nocturnal ESP.* Baltimore, MD: Penguin, 1973, 1974.

Valandrey, Charlotte, with Jean Arcelin. *De coeur inconnu.* Paris: le cherche midi, 2011.

Van de Castle, Robert L. "Exogenous dream continuity: Exploring the matrix of entangled dreams." *International Journal of Dream Research* 5, No. 1 (2012): 9-16.

Vanderbilt, Gloria, and Thelma Furness. *Double Exposure: A Twin Autobiography.* London: Frederick Muller, 1959.

Van Dusen, Wilson. "The Presence of Spirits in Madness: A Confirmation of Swedenborg in Recent Empirical Findings." *New Philosophy* 70 (1961).

Van Eeden, Frederick. "A Study of Dreams." In Tart, *Altered States.* Pp. 147-60.

Van Praagh, James. *Adventures of the Soul: Journeys Through the Physical and Spiritual Dimensions.* Carlsbad, CA: Hay House, 2014.

Van Praagh, James. *Ghosts Among Us: Uncovering the Truth About the Other Side.* New York: HarperOne, 2008.

Vaughan, Alan. *Incredible Coincidence: The Baffling World of Synchronicity.* New York: J. B. Lippincott Company, 1979.

Vaughan, Alan. *Patterns of Prophecy.* New York: Hawthorn Books, 1973.

Vaughan, Alan. "Spontaneous Cognitive Dreaming." *Parapsychology Review* 4, No. 5 (1973).

Venn, John. *The Logic of Chance: An Essay on the Foundations and Province of the Theory of Probability, with Especial Reference to Its Logical Bearings and Its Application to Moral and Social Science.* 2nd ed. London: Macmillan, 1876.

Vézina, Jeff. *Necessary Chances: Synchronicity in the Encounters That Transform Us.* Trans. Carl Anger. Pari, Italy: Pari Publishing, 2009.

Villoldo, Alberto. *Shaman, Healer, Sage: How to Heal Yourself and Others with the Energy Medicine of the Americas.* New York: Harmony, 2000.

Vissell, Joyce, and Barry Vissell, eds. *Meant to Be: Miraculous True Stories to Inspire a Lifetime of Love.* Berkeley, CA: Conari Press, 2000.

Von Franz, Marie-Louise. *C. G. Jung: His Myth in Our Time.* Trans. William H. Kennedy. London: Hodder and Stoughton, 1975.

Von Franz, Marie-Louise. "Time and Synchronicity in Analytical Psychology." In *The Voices of Time.* Ed. J. T. Fraser. New York: Braziller, 1966.

Von Scholz, Wilhelm. *Der Zufall: Eine Vorform des Schicksals.* Stuttgart, Germany: Hädecke, 1924.

Wade, Jenny. *Changes of Mind: A Holonomic Theory of the Evolution of Consciousness.* Albany, NY: State University of New York Press, 1996.

Wade, Jenny. "Physically Transcendent Awareness: A Comparison of the Phenomenology of Consciousness Before Birth and After Death." *Journal of Near-Death Studies* 16, No. 4 (Summer 1998): 249-75.

Wade, Jenny. *Transcendent Sex: When Lovemaking Opens the Veil.* New York: Paraview/Pocket Books, 2004.

Wade, Jenny. "Two Voices from the Womb: Evidence for Physically Transcendent and a Cellular Source of Fetal Consciousness." *Journal of Prenatal and Perinatal Psychology and Health* 13, No. 2 (Winter 1998): 123-47.

Waggoner, Robert. *Lucid Dreaming: Gateway to the Inner Self.* Needham, MA: Moment Point Press, 2009.

Wambach, Helen. *Life Before Life.* New York: Bantam, 1979.

Warneck, Johannes Gustav. *Die Religion der Batak.* Göttingen, 1909.

Watson, Lyall. *Supernature: A Natural History of the Supernatural.* London: Coronet Books, 1973, 1974.

Watson, Peter. *Twins: An Uncanny Relationship?* Chicago: Contemporary Books, 1981.

Weaver, Warren. *Lady Luck and the Theory of Probability*. New York, 1963.

Weigel, Jenniffer. *Psychics, Healers, and Mediums: A Journalist, a Road Trip, and Voices from the Other Side.* Charlottesville, VA: Hampton Roads, 2017.

Weiss, Brian. *Only Love Is Real: A Story of Soulmates Reunited.* New York: Warner Books, 1996.

White, Roger. "Fine-Tuning and Multiple Universes." *Noûs* 34, No. 2 (2000): 260-76.

Whitton, Joel L., and Joe Fisher. *Life Between Life: Scientific Explorations into the Void Separating One Incarnation from the Next.* New York: Warner Books, 1986.

Williams, Donna. *Nobody Nowhere: The Remarkable Autobiography of an Autistic Girl.* Rev. ed. London: Jessica Kingsley, 1992, 1999.

Wright, Sylvia Hart. *When Spirits Come Calling: The Open-Minded Skeptic's Guide to After-Death Contacts.* Nevada City, CA: Blue Dolphin Publishing, 2002.

Yung, Hwa. "The Integrity of Mission in the Light of the Gospel: Bearing the Witness of the Spirit." *Mission Studies* 24 (2007): 169-88.

Zaleski, Carol. *Otherworld Journeys: Accounts of Near-Death Experience in Medieval and Modern Times.* New York: Oxford University Press, 1987.

Zumwalde, Allison, Kendall Ciriaco, and John Allison. "Strange Handprints in Strange Places." *Journal of Scientific Exploration* 30, No. 4 (2016): 509-23.

Zwebner, Yonat, Anne-Laure Sellier, Nir Rosenfeld, Jacob Goldenberg, and Ruth Mayo. "We look like our names: The manifestation of name stereotypes in facial appearance." *Journal of Personality and Social Psychology* 112, No. 4 (2017): 527-54.

Index

#

A

B

C

D

E

F

G

H

I

J

K

L

M

N

O

P

Q

R

S

T

U

V

Z

Printed in Great Britain
by Amazon